THE PRACTICAL GUIDE TO CANADIAN LEGAL RESEARCH, THIRD EDITION

Nancy McCormack, B.A., M.A., M.L.I.S., J.D., LL.M.,
John Papadopoulos, B.Sc., J.D., M.I.St.,
Catherine Cotter, B.A., LL.B., M.L.I.S.
(Chapter 5 on the *Canadian Abridgment* by
Michael Silverstein, B.A., LL.B.)

Founding Authors (First and Second Editions)

Jacqueline R. Castel, LL.B., Omeela K. Latchman, LL.B.

CARSWELL®

A cataloguing record for this publication is available from Library and Archives Canada.

ISBN 978-0-7798-2361-1 (2010 Edition)

Printed in Canada by Thomson Reuters.

THOMSON REUTERS

CARSWELL, A DIVISION OF THOMSON REUTERS CANADA LIMITED

One Corporate Plaza
2075 Kennedy Road
Toronto, Ontario
M1T 3V4

Customer Relations
Toronto 1-416-609-3800
Elsewhere in Canada/U.S. 1-800-387-5164
Fax 1-416-298-5082
www.carswell.com
E-mail www.carswell.com/email

To Eric, Rosanne, and Corey — with much love and gratitude

ACKNOWLEDGMENTS

A book is never written in a vacuum and we would like to take a moment to thank those who were most helpful during its writing. We would like to thank the librarians and staff past and present of the Lederman, Bora Laskin and Gerard V. La Forest Law Libraries. We are grateful to Emily Ng, Alexa Evans, Kate Culver, and Erica Maidment for assisting with various aspects of this book; and, the staff of Carswell, a Thomson Reuters business, particularly Michael Silverstein and O'Neil Smith, for their support and encouragement. Most of all, this book is dedicated to our spouses — Eric McCormack, Rosanne Renzetti, and Corey Redekop — who made the good times better and the bad times not so bad.

PREFACE

This Guide is intended for law students, lawyers, librarians and law clerks, as well as for students outside of law and all other researchers who might need a practical introduction to the various legal sources and the types of questions they are meant to answer. Legal research is not always easy, even for seasoned researchers; it can be intimidating, like trying to find a way through a jungle without the benefit of a map. Sources which might make research easier are sometimes not obvious to the untrained eye. The titles of some of the best legal sources, such as *Canadian Statute Citations, Ontario Citator Service* or *Corpus Juris Secundum*, do not necessarily make self-evident to the innocent researcher the type of information they contain. Without some guidance (i.e. using the right tools), finding the answer to a relatively easy question becomes an arduous task that takes much longer than it should. Indeed, after a researcher has stumbled by pure instinct through the 'jungle' and found some sort of answer, she has a lurking feeling that maybe there were more relevant sources to be checked which might have provided an even better answer and more current information.

This book attempts to counter precisely such problems. It will teach you efficient legal research skills and act as a reference source by providing some of the essential background required to research specific areas of the law. The advice offered here is meant to cut down on the 'floundering about' of students and other researchers when they have no idea where to start or how to move through their consideration of legal problems. It is also meant to help you avoid the detrimental consequences that can occur when relevant sources are not checked or when you are unaware the law has been updated.

A necessary preliminary to the consideration of research techniques and strategies is an understanding of the basic principles or mechanics of the legal system. The central question faced by the researcher is: "What is the law?" In Chapter 1, we discuss the sources of law and how they are prioritized and interpreted to answer this central question. The chapter concludes with a flow-chart that will help you assess and weigh the various steps in working through a legal problem. The flow-chart will also enable you to determine when you have done enough research to answer your research problem. When is it necessary, for example, to look at law in other Canadian jurisdictions? When is it necessary to look at American or English law?

The principal tool for thorough Canadian legal research is contained in Chapter 2. It consists of a comprehensive checklist. The great fear in all legal research is that there might still be something else out there you have neglected. Use of this checklist allows you to say: "No, I have been absolutely thorough." By learning how and when to use the various research tools on the checklist appropriately, you can become an efficient legal researcher who is both discriminating and thorough. The successful researcher develops an instinct about where to look in the law library, and acquires the technical skills to make effective use of the tools in that library.

The remaining chapters of the Guide will supply you with much more knowledge about such key secondary sources as Canadian legal encyclopedias (Chapter 4) and the *Canadian Abridgment* (Chapter 5), in addition to books and periodicals (Chapters 6 and 8). Information on searching case law is provided (Chapters 11 to 13), and legislation and the Constitution are also discussed in detail (Chapters 14 to 16). Electronic tools are, of course, now ubiquitous in legal studies. We discuss them throughout the book, with special attention in Chapter Three.

Law is an area that depends profoundly on the written word. Accordingly, when you have completed the research process of collecting the relevant law, you will probably need to express the results of your research in written form. We have included a chapter (Chapter 23) on writing legal essays, case comments, and legal research memoranda. The chapter provides guidance to help ensure that your legal writing is organized in a logical, focused way and is clearly expressed.

New to this edition of the Guide are chapters on Quebec (Chapter 18), Australia and New Zealand (Chapter 21), and International Law (Chapter 22). The chapters on English and American law (Chapter 19 and 20 respectively) have been greatly expanded to include some essential information on the legal regimes in each of these jurisdictions.

At the end of the Guide, you will find an updated Selective Topical Bibliography based on the types of resources highlighted in the checklist. Happy researching!

SUMMARY TABLE OF CONTENTS

TABLE OF CONTENTS

1

Essential Background

Introduction

The purpose of this book is to teach legal research — how and when to use the various legal research tools. However, before beginning your actual research, there are certain basics you need to know about the nature of law and the legal system in order to be able to discriminate between law that is "binding" and law that is merely "persuasive". Law that is binding *must be followed* by the courts. Law that is persuasive may influence judicial decisions, but courts are *not required to follow* these decisions. It is not enough to simply know how to locate cases, statutes, and treatises on your topic. The researcher must be able to ascertain what law is binding in his or her jurisdiction. In addition, when the case law and the wording of a statute on a given topic seem to be in conflict, the researcher must be able to determine which takes precedence.

This chapter aims to provide researchers with the background they need to assess when law is binding and when law is merely persuasive. The following topics will be examined:

1. What is the difference between primary and secondary sources of law?
2. What weight is attributed to the various types of primary sources of law?
3. How does jurisdiction impact on whether or not law is binding?
4. How does court structure impact on whether or not law is binding?

A flow-chart summarizing the concepts in this chapter and their applications to your research is provided at the end of the chapter.

For anyone who has had legal training, the information contained in this chapter may seem second nature. However, for those who are just beginning law school, or for those who are trained in other disciplines and require some legal research skills, this chapter will provide information that is essential to conducting effective legal research.

Primary and Secondary Sources of Law Defined

Primary sources of law consist of statutes, regulations and other delegated legislation, judicial decisions, and decisions of administrative tribunals. These sources of law are the products of legislatures, various government bodies, courts and administrative tribunals.[1] When asked to do research on a problem, you will ultimately want to find primary sources of law on your topic, as only primary sources have the force of law.

Secondary sources are commentaries on the law. They are usually written by legal scholars and practicing lawyers. They consist of legal encyclopedias, books, journal articles, and more recently, blogs, websites and other internet materials. These sources collect, explain, and interpret primary sources of law and are a means of accessing primary sources. For most research, starting with secondary sources is the best strategy as these will lead you to the relevant primary sources and also provide commentary and context on the development of the law.

Some secondary sources of law, such as a treatise or a journal article written by a well-respected scholar, may be persuasive in court, and often such sources are cited in appellate decisions to interpret the law.[2] Other secondary sources, such as legal encyclopedias, tend not to be regarded as persuasive and are rarely referred to in court decisions.[3] They are merely useful finding tools which provide an overview of the law on numerous topics. Secondary sources of law, irrespective of their level of persuasiveness, are never binding and are not the law *per se*. When using secondary sources, it is important to be aware of the biases of the particular author, and researchers should always ensure that they have read the cases and statutes cited in secondary sources for themselves rather than relying on the author's interpretations of the law. Wherever possible, it is a good practice to consider more than one author when consulting secondary sources.

Unlike secondary sources, primary sources of law may be binding, depending on a number of factors such as jurisdiction and court level. Before discussing jurisdiction and court level, it is important to understand the rela-

---

[1] Strictly speaking, administrative tribunal decisions are not law. See the section, later in this chapter, on "Decisions of Administrative Tribunals", where the status of such decisions is discussed.

[2] An interesting example is the Supreme Court of Canada's citation of a paper by Professor S.W. Waddams, written while professor Waddams was still a second year law student in the late 1960's. See the mention of Waddams, "Alter Ego and the Criminal Liability of Corporations" (1966), 24 Univ. of Toronto Faculty L. Rev. 145 in *R. v. Canadian Dredge & Dock Co.*, [1985] 1 S.C.R. 662 (S.C.C.).

[3] *Halsbury's Laws of England* is an exception to this general rule against the citation of legal encyclopedias. It is frequently cited.

tive weight of the various primary sources of law identified above — that is, when there are two different sources of primary law on the same topic, which takes precedence?

The Relative Weight of Primary Sources of Law

Legislation

The Constitution

The Constitution[4] is the supreme law of Canada. All other law, whether enacted by parliament or made by judges, must be consistent with the Constitution. The Constitution governs the division of powers between the federal and provincial governments and bestows fundamental rights and freedoms on individuals and groups.

Statutes

Statutes are laws that are passed by the legislature — federal or provincial/territorial. They usually deal with a specific subject. For example, the *Criminal Code*[5] is a comprehensive statute that defines criminal offences, prescribes punishments, and sets out the procedure for administering the *Code*. Assuming that a statute is consistent with the Constitution, it is the law in a given jurisdiction.[6] Statutes are, however, subject to interpretation by the judiciary and administrative tribunals.[7] Such interpretations form part of the law. Accordingly, statutory law can be altered by any of the following: (a) other acts of the legislature (amendments or repeals); (b) judicial or administrative tribunal interpretations; and (c) declarations of constitutional invalidity ("striking down").

Regulations

Statutes often empower administrative agencies to make rules (regulations) which provide detail about how the statute is to be implemented. For example, a statute might say, "It is unlawful to pollute." Regulations might specify which substances constitute pollutants and the registration, licensing, and monitoring requirements for those who handle such pollutants.

---

[4] *Constitution Act, 1867* (U.K.), 30 & 31 Vict., c. 3 and *Constitution Act, 1982*, being Schedule B to the *Canada Act 1982* (U.K.), 1982, c. 11.

[5] R.S.C. 1985, c. C-46.

[6] A statutory provision is binding and assumed to be constitutional unless a court has found it to be unconstitutional or has "struck down" the provision.

[7] See the section, later in this chapter, on "Decisions of Administrative Tribunals", where the status of such decisions is discussed.

Regulations, therefore, provide detail that is not found in the statute in the form of definitions,[8] licensing requirements, registration requirements, insurance requirements, performance specifications, exemptions, forms, etc.

Jurisprudence

Judicial Decisions

Judicial decisions or "case law" are judge-made law. In the absence of a statute on the topic area, case law on the topic will be binding. But note that not all case law is in fact binding. In order to assess whether a particular decision is binding, you must pay attention to both jurisdiction and level of court. These topics are discussed below. Law that is derived from the decisions of judges is known as the common law.

Even where statutes exist, judge-made law is necessary to interpret what the words and phrases of the statute mean in relation to the specific facts of a case.

Cases interpret a statute and form part of the law. In fact, if a court has ruled that a section of a statute is to be interpreted in a certain way, even if there are several other rational readings of the section, only the reading endorsed by the court is law.

Decisions of Administrative Tribunals

Administrative tribunals are not courts of law. Traditionally, they have been described as creatures of statute. This means that their powers to adjudicate are based strictly on the wording of the enabling statute that created the tribunal.

Decisions of administrative tribunals are only meant to be binding on the parties to the particular case. Unlike judicial decisions, they are not law — that is, they are not binding precedents. However, in practice, previous decisions of the same tribunal will be very persuasive.

Role of Concurring and Dissenting Opinions

There are situations where the majority of the court agrees to decide a case in a certain way and several judges write concurring opinions for the majority. These opinions may differ substantially in their reasoning. Such cases are challenging to interpret because the exact law is not clearly defined. When dealing with these cases, your analysis must be sensitive to the reasoning employed in all of the concurring judgments.

---

[8] While statutes also contain definitions, regulations may have a definition section necessary to the understanding of the content in that particular regulation.

Dissenting opinions are not binding. However, they can be persuasive depending on the judge and subsequent developments in the law or government policy.

Importance of Jurisdiction

Only statutes and case law within your jurisdiction are binding. A British Columbia statute, for instance, would never be binding in Nova Scotia. Similarly, a decision from the Saskatchewan Court of Appeal would never be binding in Alberta or any other province or territory. However, if the same Saskatchewan Court of Appeal decision was appealed to the Supreme Court of Canada, the decision of the Supreme Court of Canada, although dealing with a case that arose in Saskatchewan, would be binding on all of Canada.

Decisions from other jurisdictions, while not binding, may be persuasive depending on the level of court of the decision, the reputation of the judge or panel of judges who wrote the decision, and the actual jurisdiction. In Canada, for example the British Columbia and Ontario appellate courts are regarded as very persuasive throughout the country. This is not to say that decisions of these courts will necessarily be followed elsewhere. Yet it is not unusual for courts of a province or territory to at least consider decisions from appellate courts of other provinces or territories.

Foreign law, while never binding in Canada, may also be persuasive. When an area of Canadian law has not been well developed or is in a state of confusion, courts will often look to the case law of other jurisdictions, particularly Britain and the United States, to consider how other courts have approached a similar legal problem.

Statutes from other jurisdictions are generally limited in their persuasive value. However, there are some exceptions. If another jurisdiction has a similar statute, judicial interpretation of that statute may be relevant persuasive authority. For example, many provinces or territories have similar business corporations legislation. Accordingly, cases decided under one province's statute may be persuasive authority when considering the interpretation of another province's statute. An American example is the *American Law Institute's Uniform Commercial Code*, a comprehensive code dealing with commercial law, that has been adopted by many state legislatures. Treatises, articles and statute concordances will identify these similar statutory regimes for you.

Importance of Court Structure

The court structure is hierarchical. The basic rule is that given two decisions from two different levels of court, the decision from the higher court is binding. It is, therefore, essential to know the court structure of the jurisdiction for which you are doing research.

In Canada, there are two main court systems — federal and provincial. The highest court in both of these systems is the Supreme Court of Canada (and prior to that, the Privy Council). Below is a general overview of the Canadian court structure.[9]

Federal Court System

The federal court system consists of two main separate courts: the Federal Court and an appellate court called the Federal Court of Appeal. Appeals from the Federal Court of Appeal are heard in the Supreme Court of Canada. The jurisdiction of the federal courts is limited to specific subjects that are outlined in the *Federal Courts Act*[10] including copyright, trade-mark, industrial design, maritime law, immigration, federal employment law, etc. The Tax Court of Canada and the Court Martial Appeal Court of Canada are also federal courts with their jurisdiction limited to their subject area.

Provincial Court System

The provincial court system comprises a provincial "superior" court of general jurisdiction[11] and an appellate court usually called the Court of Appeal.[12] Appeals from the provincial courts of appeal are heard in the Supreme Court of Canada.

Each province also has "inferior" provincial courts, which are courts of limited jurisdiction.[13] The judges of these courts are provincially appointed,

---

[9] For a more specific description of the court structure in your province or territory, consult the chart from the *Canadian Abridgment* reproduced in Appendix I.

[10] R.S.C. 1985, c. F-7. See sections 17–28.

[11] When a court has general jurisdiction, it has the authority to hear a variety of cases. The names of the provincial superior courts vary from province to province: in Alberta, Manitoba, New Brunswick, and Saskatchewan, they are called the Court of Queen's Bench; in British Columbia, Newfoundland and Labrador, Northwest Territories, Nova Scotia, Prince Edward Island, and Yukon Territory, they are called the Supreme Court; in Ontario and Quebec, they are called the Superior Court of Justice; in Nunavut, it is the Court of Justice.

[12] The appeal court in all provinces and territories is generally named the "Court of Appeal" or "Appeal Division" with some variation as to the exact wording. See Appendix I for details.

[13] Limited jurisdiction courts either hear only specific types of cases (e.g., bankruptcy, probate) or cases less serious than those heard by courts of general jurisdiction.

in contrast to the judges of the above-mentioned courts who are federally appointed. The provincial inferior courts can have civil, criminal and, in some provinces, family and youth court divisions. The civil courts are small claims courts, which hear civil cases where the amount claimed or value of property in question does not exceed specified amounts (not every provincial Small Claims Court is recognizable as an inferior court. In Ontario, for example, the Small Claims Court is a branch of the Superior Court of Justice). The criminal courts deal with less serious criminal offences. The pathway of appeals from the inferior provincial courts is determined by the specific statutory provisions regulating the type of case or matter.

How a Case Makes Its Way Through the Court Structure

The majority of cases are the result of opposing parties resolving a conflict over:

(a) the constitutionality of a statute;

(b) the legality of an action or activity;

(c) an entitlement to compensation or to a remedial order for an action or activity;

(d) an entitlement to property; or

(e) the rights and obligations between parties.

When the parties litigate, a trial is held and a decision is rendered by a judge or by a judge and jury. The court in which the trial is held is referred to as the court of first instance. Usually this decision will be the final one. However, should one of the parties be dissatisfied with the decision and if that party has a right of appeal, he or she may choose to appeal some or all of the legal and/or factual issues in his or her case to the next level of court. The decision of the appeal court will take precedence over the decision of the trial court.

It may be possible to appeal the decision of an appeal court further. Any subsequent appeal(s) will displace those decisions preceding them in the appeal process, unless the decision is affirmed (i.e., the appeal court decides that the decision of the lower court was correct).

It should be kept in mind that the right to appeal does not exist for every case. For any given case, any one of four situations is possible:

(a) an automatic right of appeal (as explicitly provided by statute);

(b) a right to seek leave to appeal as provided by statute (where the appeal court, after hearing submissions, decides whether it will hear the appeal);

(c) no right of appeal; or

(d) no further appeal because there is no higher court.

Prioritizing the Law

The principles for determining precedence among sources of law discussed in this chapter translate into a hierarchy. Set out at the end of this chapter is a flow chart that will help you to identify what, if any, binding law there is on a given topic area and to assess the relative persuasiveness of various sources of law. A common complaint of law students is, "I don't know when to stop my research". Often, students do more research than is required to analyze the problem they have been assigned. The flow chart helps you to know when you have done enough research to answer your research question effectively. If, of course, there is no clear answer in your jurisdiction or the answer is one that is not helpful to your client, you will want to look at more of the sources identified in the flow chart.

Similarly, sometimes the objective of your research is broader than answering a legal question. For instance, if you are writing a law school research paper or journal article, you may be interested in examining the need for legal reform in a particular area of law. If this is the case, you will probably want to look at all of the sources of law identified on the flow chart. The flow chart is organized to give you a sense of what the law is. Scholarly papers and articles often focus not on what the law is but on what it should be. In considering what the law should be, your research will often encompass all sources identified on the flow chart.

Primary sources of law (statutes and case law) are at the top of the flow chart. This is because only these sources are legally binding. This does not, however, imply that you will begin your research by searching for a statute or a case. Throughout this book we argue that the most effective way to begin your research is by consulting secondary sources (books, encyclopedias, journals, etc.) that will lead you to the relevant primary sources.

Statutes are the first reference on the flow chart. When researching a legal problem, your first objective is to determine whether statutes exist on the topic. The most effective way of doing this is to consult an encyclopedia or book on your topic. If there is a statute which contains the answer, your research will be complete once you have checked for judicial consideration of the relevant statutory provision. If there is no statute on your topic, look for judicial decisions in your jurisdiction, preferably from the Supreme Court of Canada or the Court of Appeal, as these will be binding. If you cannot find decisions from an appellate court in your jurisdiction, look for lower court decisions. Decisions of lower courts may or may not be binding. Sometimes you will find two or more decisions of a lower court (*e.g.* Ontario's Superior Court of Justice) which reach different conclusions on the same legal question. Not all of these decisions can be binding, and it is unclear which decision will be authoritative in a given case. Other times, decisions of lower courts are widely followed and viewed as binding. Noting-up a lower court decision to see if it has been considered by other courts will help in the process of determining how important the decision is.

The upper portion of the flow chart, which depicts binding sources of law, is an accurate schema of the rigid hierarchy that exists at the heart of the common law system. Although the bottom portion of the flow chart also suggests a hierarchy, the hierarchy is in fact much more fluid. For example, we have classified appellate court decisions from other Canadian jurisdictions as the first item in the persuasive portion of the flow chart. However, in some instances, a treatise or article by a well-respected scholar or an English or American decision may be more persuasive.

The essence of the common law system is change through confrontation. The common law evolves because adverse parties disagree over what the law is. Use of the flow chart is meant to clarify the task of interpreting the law, but it is not intended to induce a passive attitude. You should always keep in mind that the law can be changed through the creative use of persuasive authority. Accordingly, if the law appears to be unfavourable to your client, and it is not absolutely binding, you should strive to find any credible persuasive authority that bolsters an interpretation more conducive to the needs of your client. Moreover, even if there is binding authority, you may be able to distinguish your case on the facts.

Flow Chart for Prioritizing the Law

Is there a statute?	If yes→	Check for judicial consideration (See Chapters 5 and 15)

If no
↓

Is there case law from the Supreme Court of Canada on your topic?	If yes→	Note-up this case law (See Chapter 13)

If no
↓

Is there case law from the Court of Appeal in your jurisdiction?	If yes→	Note-up this case law (See Chapter 13)

BINDING

If no
↓

Is there case law from lower courts in your jurisdiction?	If yes→	Note-up this case law (See Chapter 13)

MAY BE BINDING

If no
↓

Is there case law from appellate courts in other juris-dictions?	If yes→	Note-up this case law (See Chapter 13)

If no
↓

Are there Canadian treatises
or periodicals on your topic
by well-regarded legal
scholars?

If no
↓

Is there case law from lower courts in other Canadian jurisdictions?	If yes→	Note-up this case law (See Chapter 13)

If no
↓

Is there case law from appel-late courts in England and/or the United States?	If yes→	Note-up this case law (See Chapters 19 and 20) MAY BE PERSUASIVE

If no
↓

Are there English and/or
American treatises or
periodicals on your topic?

Appendix I — Canadian Court System

The following is a reproduction (with some revisions) of *Canadian Court System*, a booklet published by Thomson Carswell in 2005 to supplement the *Canadian Abridgment*. It is an overview of the Canadian court system, both past and present. It is provided for reference when assessing the weight to be given to any particular case, and for aid when the case law deals with procedural issues which may depend on the court structures in existence at a given time. Existing courts are set out in boldface type, their predecessors in lightface type.

Starting Point: For most jurisdictions, the starting point used is the year of the first general assembly of that jurisdiction. Courts listed as commencing in that year may in fact predate the first general assembly. The starting point used for British Columbia is the union of the colonies of Vancouver Island and British Columbia. The starting points used for the Yukon and the Northwest Territories are the dates of the enactment of the statutes establishing those territories.

Commencement Dates: Some of the commencement dates of the earlier courts may not be precise.

Magistrates' Courts: There have traditionally been many varieties of magistrates' courts (stipendiary, police, provincial, district, county and local.) These are listed simply as "Magistrates."

Alberta (1906-)

JUSTICES, MAGISTRATES, SMALL CLAIMS & PROVINCIAL COURTS	Magistrates (1906–1973) Provincial Court (Small Claims Division) (1980–1990) **Justices of the Peace (1906-)** **Provincial Court (1973-)** **Provincial Court (Criminal Division) (1980-)** **Provincial Court (Civil Division) (1990-)**
COUNTY & DISTRICT	District Court (1907–1979)

COURTS	District Court Judges' Criminal Court (1907–1979)
SURROGATE & PROBATE COURTS	**Surrogate Court (continued in the Court of Queen's Bench) (1967-)**
SUPERIOR COURTS, TRIAL DIVISIONS	Supreme Court (Trial Division) (1907–1979) **Court of Queen's Bench (Trial Division) (1979-)**
COURTS OF APPEAL	Supreme Court en banc (1907–1913) Supreme Court (Appellate Division) (1913–1979) **Court of Appeal (1979-)**
FAMILY & YOUTH COURTS	Juvenile Court (1914–1980) Family Court (1952–1980) Provincial Court (Juvenile Division) (1980–1984) **Provincial Court (Family Division) (1980-)** **Provincial Court (Youth Division) (1984-)**
ADMIRALTY COURTS	

British Columbia (1867-)

JUSTICES, MAGISTRATES, SMALL CLAIMS & PROVINCIAL COURTS	Magistrates (1867–1969) Small Debts Court (1886–1969) **Justices of the Peace (1867-)** **Provincial Court (1969-)** **Provincial Court (Small Claims Division) (1969-)**

COUNTY & DISTRICT COURTS	County Court (1867–1990) County Court Judges' Criminal Court (1888–1990)
SURROGATE & PROBATE COURTS	
SUPERIOR COURTS, TRIAL DIVISIONS	Supreme Court of Vancouver Island (1867–1870) Supreme Court of Civil Justice of British Columbia (1867–1870) Court of Assize & Nisi Prius (1872–1990) Court of Oyer & Terminer & General Gaol Delivery (1879–1990) **Supreme Court (1870-)**
COURTS OF APPEAL	Divisional Court (1885–1897) Supreme Court — Full Court (1870–1911) **Court of Appeal (1909-)**
FAMILY & YOUTH COURTS	Juvenile Court (1910–1963) Family Court (1948–1963) Family & Children's Court (1963–1969) **Provincial Court (Family Division) (1969-)** **Youth Court (1984-)**
ADMIRALTY COURTS	Vice-Admiralty Court (1867–1891)

Manitoba (1871-)

JUSTICES, MAGISTRATES, SMALL CLAIMS & PROVINCIAL COURTS	Provincial Judges Court (Criminal Division) (1973–1983) **Justices of the Peace/Juges de paix (1871-)**

	Magistrates/Magistrats (1871-) **Provincial Court (Criminal Division)/Cour provinciale (Division criminelle) (1983-)**
COUNTY & DISTRICT COURTS	Court of Petty Sessions (1871–1872) County Court (1872–1984) County Court Judges' Criminal Court (1883–1984)
SURROGATE & PROBATE COURTS	Surrogate Court (1881–1984)
SUPERIOR COURTS, TRIAL DIVISIONS	General Court (1835–1872) Supreme Court (1871–1872) Court of Assize & Nisi Prius & of Oyer & Terminer & General Gaol Delivery (1873–1987) **Court of Queen's Bench/Cour du Banc de la Reine (1872-)**
COURTS OF APPEAL	Court of Queen's Bench in banc (1872–1906) **Court of Appeal/Cour d'appel (1906-)**
FAMILY & YOUTH COURTS	Family Court (1953–1973) Juvenile Court (1940–1974) Provincial Judges Court (Family Division) (1973–1983) **Provincial Court (Family Division)/Cour provinciale (Division de la famille) (1983-)** **Court of Queen's Bench (Family Division)/ Cour du Banc de la Reine (Division de la famille) (1984-)**

ADMIRALTY COURTS	Vice-Admiralty Court (1871–1891)

New Brunswick (1786-)

JUSTICES, MAGISTRATES, SMALL CLAIMS & PROVINCIAL COURTS	Court of General Sessions of the Peace (1786-?) Inferior Court of Common Pleas (1786–1867) Parish Court (1876–1952) Magistrates (1826–1969) **Justices of the Peace/Juges de paix (1786-)** **Provincial Court/Cour provinciale (1969-)** **Small Claims Court / Cour des petites créances (1999-)**
COUNTY & DISTRICT COURTS	County Court (1867–1979)
SURROGATE & PROBATE COURTS	**Court of Probate/Cour des successions (1786-)**
SUPERIOR COURTS, TRIAL DIVISIONS	Court of Chancery (1786–1890) Supreme Court of Judicature (1786–1910) Supreme Court in Equity (1890–1910) Supreme Court • Chancery Division (1910–1966) • Queen's Bench Division (1910–1979) Court of Oyer & Terminer & General Gaol Delivery/ Cour d'oyer & terminer & de délivrance générale des prisons (1786-?)

	Court of Queen's Bench (Trial Division)/Cour du Banc de la Reine (Division de première instance) (1979-)
COURTS OF APPEAL	Supreme Court in Term (1786–1910) Supreme Court en banc (1910–1913) **Court of Appeal/Cour d'appel (1913-)**
FAMILY & YOUTH COURTS	Court of Governor & Council (1791–1860) Juvenile Court (1944–1987) Court of Divorce & Matrimonial Causes/Cour des divorces et des causes matrimoniales (1860–2008) Provincial Court (Family Division)/ Cour provinciale (Division de la famille) (1972–1991) **Provincial Court (Youth Court) (1987-)** **Court of Queen's Bench (Family Division)/Cour du Banc de la Reine (Division de la famille) (1979-)**
ADMIRALTY COURTS	Vice-Admiralty Court (1786–1891)

Newfoundland & Labrador (1729-)

JUSTICES, MAGISTRATES, SMALL CLAIMS & PROVINCIAL COURTS	Court of General and Quarter Sessions (1833–1990) Magistrates (1729–1979) **Justices of the Peace (1833-)** **Provincial Court (1974-)**
COUNTY & DISTRICT COURTS	Circuit Court (1833–1872) District Court (1833–1986)

	District Court Judges' Criminal Court (1949–1986)
SURROGATE & PROBATE COURTS	
SUPERIOR COURTS, TRIAL DIVISIONS	Court of Oyer & Terminer & General Gaol Delivery (1852–1974) Court of Labrador (1872-?) **Supreme Court (Trial Division) (1791-)**
COURTS OF APPEAL	Supreme Court en banc (1833–1975) **Court of Appeal (1975-)**
FAMILY & YOUTH COURTS	Family Court (1952–1978) Juvenile Court (1944–1984) **Unified Family Court (1978-)** **Youth Court (1984-)** **Provincial Court (Family Division) (1978-)**
ADMIRALTY COURTS	Marine Court of Enquiry (1866-?) Vice-Admiralty Court (1833–1891)

Nova Scotia (1721-)

JUSTICES, MAGISTRATES, SMALL CLAIMS & PROVINCIAL COURTS	General Court of Court of Judicature (1721–1749) Court of General or Quarter Sessions of the Peace (1758-?) Rotation Court (1792–1817) Inferior Court of Common Pleas (1752–1841) Court of Commissioners (1807–1851) Court of Escheat (1811–1859) Magistrates (1827–1985)

	Municipal Court (1888–1985) **Justices of the Peace (1758-)** **Provincial Court (1985-)** **Small Claims Court (1981-)**
COUNTY & DISTRICT COURTS	County Court (1873–1993) County Court Judges' Criminal Court (1889–1993)
SURROGATE & PROBATE COURTS	**Court of Probate (1758-)**
SUPERIOR COURTS, TRIAL DIVISIONS	Court of Nisi Prius (1794-?) Court of Assize & General Gaol Delivery (1758-?) Court of Oyer & Terminer (1758-?) Court of Chancery (1797–1856) Supreme Court (1758–1966) Supreme Court (Trial Division) (1966–1993) **Supreme Court (1993-)**
COURTS OF APPEAL	Supreme Court in banco (1758–1966) Supreme Court (Appeal Division) (1966–1993) **Court of Appeal (1993-)**
FAMILY & YOUTH COURTS	Court of Marriage & Divorce (1841–1866) Court for Divorce & Matrimonial Causes (1866–1972) Juvenile Court (1917–1986) **Family Court (1972-)** **Youth Court (1985-)** **Supreme Court (Family Division) (1972-)**

ADMIRALTY COURTS	Vice-Admiralty Court (1764–1891)

Northwest Territories (1875-)

JUSTICES, MAGISTRATES, SMALL CLAIMS & PROVINCIAL COURTS	Magistrates (1875–1978) **Justices of the Peace (1875-)** **Territorial Court (1978-)**
COUNTY & DISTRICT COURTS	
SURROGATE & PROBATE COURTS	
SUPERIOR COURTS, TRIAL DIVISIONS	Supreme Court (1886–1953) Territorial Court (1953–1972) **Supreme Court (1972-)**
COURTS OF APPEAL	Supreme Court en banc (1886–1907) **Court of Appeal (1971-)**
FAMILY & YOUTH COURTS	Juvenile Court (1967–1984) **Supreme Court (1972-)** **Youth Court (1984-)**
ADMIRALTY COURTS	

Nunavut (1999-)

JUSTICES, MAGISTRATES, SMALL CLAIMS & PROVINCIAL COURTS	(NWT) Justices of the Peace (1875–1999) **Justices of the Peace (1999-)** (NWT) Territorial Court (1978–1999)
COUNTY & DISTRICT COURTS	

SURROGATE & PROBATE COURTS	
SUPERIOR COURTS, TRIAL DIVISIONS	(NWT) Supreme Court (1978–1999) **Court of Justice (1999-)**
COURTS OF APPEAL	(NWT) Court of Appeal (1971–1999) **Court of Appeal (1999-)**
FAMILY & YOUTH COURTS	(NWT) Supreme Court (1972–1999) (NWT) Youth Court (1984–1999) **Court of Justice (1999-)** **Youth Court (1999-)**
ADMIRALTY COURTS	

Ontario (1792-)

JUSTICES, MAGISTRATES, SMALL CLAIMS & PROVINCIAL COURTS	Court of Requests (1792–1841) Court of General Quarter Sessions of the Peace (1801–1869) Recorders' Court (1857–1869) Magistrates (1859–1969) Division Court (1841–1970) Court of General Sessions of the Peace (1869–1985) Small Claims Court (1972–1985) Provincial Court (Criminal Division) (1968–1990) Provincial Court (Civil Division) [Small Claims Court] (1985–1990) **Justices of Peace (1792-)** Ontario Court (General Division) [Small Claims Court] (1990–1999) Ontario Court (Provincial Division) (1990–1999) **Small Claims Court (1999-)**

	Ontario Court of Justice (1999-)
COUNTY & DISTRICT COURTS	District Court (1794–1849) County Court (1849–1913) County Court Judges' Criminal Court (1873–1985) County/District Court (1913–1985) District Court (1985–1990)
SURROGATE & PROBATE COURTS	Court of Probate (1793–1858) Surrogate Court (1793–1990)
SUPERIOR COURTS, TRIAL DIVISIONS	Court of Impeachment (1859–1869) Practice Court (1850–1877) Court of Queen's Bench (1794–1881) Court of Chancery (1837–1881) Court of Common Pleas (1849–1881) Supreme Court of Judicature (High Court of Justice) • Queen's Bench Division (1881–1913) • Common Pleas Division (1881–1913) • Chancery Division (1881–1913) • Exchequer Division (1903–1913) Court of Assize & Nisi Prius & of Oyer & Terminer & General Gaol Delivery (1792–1914) Supreme Court of Ontario (High Court Division) (1913–1931) Ontario Court (General Division) (1990–1996) **Superior Court of Justice (1999-)**
COURTS OF APPEAL	Court of Error & Appeal (1850–1876) Court of Appeal (1876–1913)

	Supreme Court of Ontario (Appellate Division) (1913–1931) **Divisional Court (1881–1913), (1972-)** **Court of Appeal (1931-)**
FAMILY & YOUTH COURTS	Juvenile Court (1916–1960) Family Court (1937–1960) Juvenile & Family Court (1960–1968) Provincial Court (Family Division) (1968–1990) Unified Family Court (Hamilton-Wentworth) (1977–1994) Ontario Court of Justice (Provincial Division) (1990–1994) **Superior Court of Justice (Family Court) (1995-)** **Ontario Court of Justice (Youth Court and Family Matters) (1996-)**
ADMIRALTY COURTS	Vice-Admiralty Court (1792–1891) Maritime Court (1877–1911)

Prince Edward Island (1773-)

JUSTICES, MAGISTRATES, SMALL CLAIMS & PROVINCIAL COURTS	Small Debt Court (1860–1873) Magistrates (1875–1975) Supreme Court (General Division) [Small Claims Section] (1975–1987) **Justices of the Peace (1773-)** **Provincial Court (1975-)** **Supreme Court (Trial Division) [Small Claims Section] (1987-)**

COUNTY & DISTRICT COURTS	County Court (1873–1975) County Court Judges' Criminal Court (1922–1975)
SURROGATE & PROBATE COURTS	Surrogate Court (1843–1939) Court of Probate (of Wills) (1773–1960) Supreme Court (Estates Division) (1960–1987) **Supreme Court (Trial Division) [Estates Section] (1987-)**
SUPERIOR COURTS, TRIAL DIVISIONS	Court of Chancery (1773–1975) Supreme Court of Judicature (1773–1975) Supreme Court (General Division) (1975–1987) **Supreme Court (Trial Division) [General Section] (1987-)**
COURTS OF APPEAL	Court of Appeal in Equity (1869–1975) Supreme Court in banco (1773–1987) **Supreme Court (Appeal Division) (1987-)**
FAMILY & YOUTH COURTS	Court of Divorce (1833–1975) Juvenile Court (1910–1975) Supreme Court (Family Division) (1975–1987) **Supreme Court (Trial Division) [Family Section] (1987-)** **Provincial Court (Youth Court) (1988-)**
ADMIRALTY COURTS	Vice-Admiralty Court (1773–1891)

Québec (1793-)

JUSTICES, MAGISTRATES, SMALL CLAIMS & PROVINCIAL COURTS	Cour des requêtes (?–1793) Cour du recorder (1851–1953) Cour des sessions générales ou des sessions spéciales de la paix (1793–1964) Cour des commissaires (1843–1964) Magistrats (1795–1966) Tribunal du travail (1969–1988) Cour des sessions de la paix (1888–1988) Cour provinciale (1793–1845?), (1966–1988) **Tribunal des juges de paix (1770-)** **Cour municipale (1953-)** **Cour du Québec** **(Chambre criminelle et pénale) (1988-)** **(Chambre de l'expropriation) (1988–1998)** **(Chambre civile) (1988-)**
COUNTY & DISTRICT COURTS	
SURROGATE & PROBATE COURTS	
SUPERIOR COURTS, TRIAL DIVISIONS	Cour des plaids communs (?–1793) Cour du Banc de la Reine (1793–1975) Cour de circuit (1793–1953) Cour de circuit du district de Montréal (1892–1953) Cour d'oyer & terminer & de délivrance générale des prisons (1793–1964)

	Cour supérieure (1849-)
COURTS OF APPEAL	Cour d'appel provinciale (1793–1849) Cour supérieure de révision (1888–1920) Cour du Banc de la Reine (juridiction d'appel) (1849–1966) **Cour d'appel (1966-)**
FAMILY & YOUTH COURTS	Cour des jeunes délinquants de Montréal (1910–1950) Cour des jeunes délinquants de Québec (1940–1950) Cour de bien-être social (1950–1978) Tribunal de la jeunesse (1978–1988) **Cour supérieure (1849-)** **Cour du Québec (Chambre de la jeunesse) (1988-)**
ADMIRALTY COURTS	Cour de Vice-Amirauté (1793–1891)

Saskatchewan (1906-)

JUSTICES, MAGISTRATES, SMALL CLAIMS & PROVINCIAL COURTS	Magistrates (1906–1978) **Justices of the Peace (1906-)** **Provincial Court (1978-)**
COUNTY & DISTRICT COURTS	District Court (1907–1981) District Court Judges' Criminal Court (1907–1981)
SURROGATE & PROBATE COURTS	**Surrogate Court (1907-)**

SUPERIOR COURTS, TRIAL DIVISIONS	Supreme Court (1907–1918) **Court of Queen's Bench (1918-)**
COURTS OF APPEAL	Supreme Court en banc (1907–1918) **Court of Appeal (1918-)**
FAMILY & YOUTH COURTS	Family Court (1975–1978) Juvenile Court (1917–1990) **Unified Family Court (1978-)** **Youth Court (1988-)** **Court of Queen's Bench (Family Law Division) (1994-)**
ADMIRALTY COURTS	

Yukon (1898-)

JUSTICES, MAGISTRATES, SMALL CLAIMS & PROVINCIAL COURTS	Magistrates (1898–1980) Small Debts Court (1908–1980) **Justices of the Peace (1898-)** **Small Claims Court (1980-)** **Territorial Court (1980-)**
COUNTY & DISTRICT COURTS	
SURROGATE & PROBATE COURTS	
SUPERIOR COURTS, TRIAL DIVISIONS	Territorial Court (1898–1971) **Supreme Court (1971-)**
COURTS OF APPEAL	Territorial Court en banc (1898–1914) **Court of Appeal (1971-)**

FAMILY & YOUTH COURTS	Juvenile Court (1945–1987) **Supreme Court (1971-)** **Youth Court (1987-)**
ADMIRALTY COURTS	

Federal Courts (1875-)

Exchequer Court of Canada (1875–1971)
Exchequer Court of Canada (1891–1971) (Admiralty Issues)
Exchequer Court of Canada — Divorce (1968–1971)
Board of Referees (1917–1923) (Taxation Issues)
Exchequer Court (1923–1946) (Taxation Issues)
Income Tax Appeal Board (1946–1950) (Taxation Issues)
Tax Appeal Board/Exchequer Court (1950–1970) (Taxation Issues)
Tax Review Board /Federal Court (1970–1983) (Taxation Issues)
Tax Court of Canada/Federal Court (1983–1990) (Taxation Issues)
Court Martial Appeal Board (1950–1959)
Federal Court — Trial Division (1971–2003)
Federal Court (2003-)
Federal Court — Appeal Division (1971–2003)
Federal Court of Appeal (2003-)
Tax Court of Canada (1983-)
Court Martial Appeal Court (1959-)

Supreme Court of Canada (1875-)

The Supreme Court of Canada was established in 1875 as the final Canadian court of appeal for all jurisdictions. Further appeal to the Judicial Committee of the Privy Council was abolished for criminal matters in 1933 and for civil matters in 1949.

2

The Legal Research Checklist

The Legal Research Checklist is located in Appendix I to this chapter. We suggest you turn to the checklist now and scan it quickly. This will give you a better sense of the purpose of this chapter.

Function of the Checklist

Research Guide and Record of Your Research Path

Every legal research problem is different; however, a checklist outlines a logical way of approaching most legal research problems. Using a checklist will ensure that you don't overlook any of the major research tools when working on a legal query. We suggest photocopying it and using it to guide your research.

Checklists serve a dual purpose: they guide the course of research and serve as a written record of your research history. Even if you have looked at a source under a certain heading and have found nothing, you should make a note of it on the checklist.

A key research skill is keeping notes of where you have looked. It is easy to forget that you have consulted a certain source. If you forget, you might look there again duplicating your work, or worse yet, you might mistakenly think that you have looked at something when you have not. You do not need to write detailed notes, but they should not be just a list of the sources you relied on. Instead, you should enumerate the sources you discarded for irrelevance with brief reasons. This way, if you are subsequently asked why your research results did not include a certain case, you will know why.

In addition, sometimes the relevance of certain aspects of a case will only become more apparent once you have spent more time on a topic. Your notes will help you to retrieve cases you discarded earlier in your search. There will also be occasions when you will be asked to research a problem on which no information exists. In order to have confidence in the results of your research in such an event, you need to be able to prove that you have done a thorough search of the relevant sources.

For particularly thorny research problems, the use of an unusual source may be a creative solution. The checklist will direct your mind to such sources.

How is the Checklist Organized?

The checklist is the skeleton of this book. It lists, in an organized fashion, the various sources you need to access the law. While it is impossible to include all sources, we have selected the most useful legal research tools.

The checklist begins with the main secondary sources in law, as these serve as a means of accessing and interpreting primary sources of law. General or broad secondary sources, such as legal encyclopedias, are discussed first. Specific secondary sources, such as treatises and periodicals, come next. After specific secondary sources, the checklist enumerates primary sources of law — cases, statutes, and regulations — and how to update them. The order of the items on the checklist reflects what is usually the most logical and efficient sequence to approaching your research.

Keep in mind that you will not need to look at every item on the checklist for every research problem. The instructions in this book concerning the use of each item on the checklist will indicate when their use is necessary. For example, you may be referred to the leading case in the topic area. In that situation, you would begin your research by reading the case and the sources that the case cited. You would also note-up the case to see how it has been considered by subsequent courts. For other research problems, the most efficient approach may begin with a phone call to the relevant government ministry. This chapter gives a brief overview of each of the sections on the checklist. The remaining chapters flesh out the various parts of the checklist.

Description of Issue(s)

At the top of the checklist, we have left space for you to identify the issues or describe the topic that you are researching. This is important because the way you phrase the issue sets out the parameters for your research. The ability to identify the legal issues raised in a factual situation is a complex skill that is acquired through legal training at law school. However, since legal research often involves delving into areas of the law with which the researcher has never had contact, the issue may not be obvious at the outset. Accordingly, the sources listed on the checklist may be helpful in formulating the issues, particularly the *Canadian Encyclopedic Digest* or *Halsbury's Laws of Canada* and any treatises on your topic.

You should also keep in mind that you may have identified the issue but not necessarily the vocabulary used in the legal literature. For example, your issue may deal with the person responsible for paying a courier. If you try to answer this question by looking under *couriers*, you will find nothing. There is, however, a well developed body of law dealing with *carriers*. In phrasing your issue, you should be sensitive to synonyms and, before you conclude that there is nothing on an issue, consider whether the answer is under a synonym for the term that you were searching. Are you using the correct legal terminology to search? If you can't think of the terms, try using the index volume to the *Canadian Encyclopedic Digest* or the *Canadian Abridgment*. These volumes are useful in supplying synonyms and leading researchers to the appropriate area of law.

Research Tools — Secondary Sources

Secondary sources comment on the law but they are not the law itself. They take the form of legal encyclopedias, books, loose-leaf services, Continuing Legal Education materials, Law Reform Commission reports, journal articles, legal dictionaries, words and phrases publications, and non-legal materials.

1) — Legal Encyclopedias

The *Canadian Encyclopedic Digest* (*C.E.D.*) is a legal encyclopedia in loose-leaf format that contains narrative descriptions of various subject areas of the law. The descriptions are accompanied by footnotes that cite cases and legislation as authority for the content of the narrative. There are two *C.E.D.* versions, one for Ontario law (*C.E.D. (Ont.)*) and one for the law of the Western provinces (*C.E.D. (West)*). Federal law is covered in both *C.E.D.*s. The *C.E.D.* is a useful place to begin your research, particularly if you know little about the topic or area of law you have been asked to research. It will provide you with a broad overview of the topic before you delve into the subtleties.

A more recent Canadian legal encyclopedia is *Halsbury's Laws of Canada*, which at the time of writing was still being published a few volumes at a time. When complete, it will be a 70-volume, hardbound set containing black-letter statements of the law supported by references to primary sources.

2) — Books, Loose-leaf Services, Continuing Legal Education Materials, and Law Reform Commission Reports

There are a variety of books which can help with research including treatises, casebooks, textbooks, and practitioners' guides. Treatises, for example, are scholarly books written by experts in various areas of the law. They provide a more detailed interpretation and discussion of the law than can be found in legal encyclopedias. Casebooks are used primarily by law students; they provide information on primary sources in a more digestible way. Law textbooks contain a "black letter law" overview of a certain area of law. Nutshells, in contrast, are pocket-size introductions to an area of law referencing only the most important cases and legislation. Practitioners' guides are works meant to be used as guides and/or reference tools by practicing lawyers. Legal encyclopedias, treatises, consolidated versions of statutes and regulations, annotated statutes and court forms and precedents are often published in loose-leaf format.

The main advantage of loose-leaf services is that they save time updating material. Loose-leaf services, as their name suggests, are published in binders so that pages containing new developments in the law can be inserted into the binder as the publisher makes them available and pages containing information on obsolete law can be removed. Because loose-leaf services are generally up-to-date, you should always check to see if a loose-leaf service exists on your topic.

Continuing Legal Education (CLE) materials are published by a number of organizations (Law Society of Upper Canada, Ontario Bar Association, Canadian Bar Association, Insight, etc.) which offer conferences and seminars for members of the legal profession and/or industry. These conferences generally include written material that summarizes and supplements the oral presentation. CLE publications generally focus on recent developments in the law and are geared primarily towards practitioners.

Law Reform Commissions are independent legal bodies which study and publish reports on legal reform. The reports outline what the law is, demonstrate why the law should be reformed, and make concrete recommendations as to how the law can be reformed. Law Reform Commission reports can be used to obtain an overview of selected legal and procedural topics. These reports are particularly useful when your research requires you to comment on legal reform.

3) — Journal Articles

Journal articles are a useful source for interpreting the law and often provide greater detail on specialized topics than treatises. In addition, they are usually more current than many treatises due to a shorter publication schedule and a quicker turnaround time.

Thousands of legal journals, law reviews, and newsletters exist in Canada, the U.S., the U.K., Australia and New Zealand. As a result, the most efficient way to locate the titles and related information of useful articles is through a legal periodical index like the *Index to Canadian Legal Literature* (covering Canadian materials), *LegalTrac*, and *Index to Legal Periodicals* (covering the U.S., Canada, the U.K., Australia and New Zealand).

4) — Legal Dictionaries and Words and Phrases

Legal Dictionaries and Words and Phrases volumes help you research the meaning of certain legal terms and the legal interpretation of words and phrases. This can be helpful when you are trying to interpret a statute for which there is no clear case law or trying to discern the meaning of a word in a key legal document like a contract or a will. It is also useful if you are having difficulty determining which keywords should be used in a search, and whether there are frequently-used synonyms.

5) — Non-legal and Other Materials

This section of the checklist encourages the use of less obvious research tools not always found in the law library such as newspapers, government information, and social science and business research. These resources, in appropriate circumstances, allow you to shortcut your research or to access necessary information which you would not otherwise find.

Primary Sources and Related Tools

1) — The Constitution

The Constitution is the supreme law of the country. All other laws are valid only to the extent that they are consistent with the Constitution. There are two main categories of constitutional research problems: federalism and rights and freedoms.

2) — Cases and Case Law Digests

Cases may be located in a variety of ways, including: 1) secondary sources such as treatises, journal articles, and legal encyclopedias, 2) digests such as the *Canadian Abridgment* (the *Abridgment*), 3) indexes to topical law reports, and 4) keyword searches of legal databases such as Westlaw Canada and LexisNexis Quicklaw.

The *Abridgment* is a comprehensive research tool which allows the user to research 1) the case law on a topic, 2) the judicial consideration of a case (this feature of the *Abridgment* is used to determine how a case has been interpreted, applied or followed), and 3) all of the citations of a case (this is used to determine where a case has been reported). The *Abridgment* is a good place to continue the search for cases once secondary sources have been consulted.

Topical law reports are report series that contain cases dealing with a specific area of the law (e.g., *Canadian Native Law Reporter, Canadian Criminal Cases, Administrative Law Reports*). Topical law reports are primary sources of law, in that secondary sources will refer you to cases reported in them. However, topical law reports can also be viewed as an access tool because they have indexes which are organized by topic.

Fee-based databases such as Westlaw Canada and LexisNexis Quicklaw, and free databases such as CanLII are searchable by subject. They also contain unreported decisions which, as their name suggests, are decisions that have not been published in a report series. There are two types of unreported decisions: 1) decisions that have just been released by a court and may or may not be reported in the future, and 2) older decisions that have never been reported. The first type of unreported decision will usually be more useful and will ensure that your research is up-to-date.

3) — Noting-up Cases

Noting-up a case involves finding the history of a case and the subsequent cases that have considered the case you are noting-up. It is crucial to ensure that a case you are relying on has not been subsequently overturned. Even if the case has not been overturned, it is important to determine if and how your case has been considered, distinguished, applied, etc., by the courts. The *Canadian Case Citations: Cases Judicially Considered* portion of the *Abridgment* is used for this purpose. It should be supplemented with a computer database search. Noting-up services are never entirely complete; as a result, it is better to use more than one if you really need to know *all* the cases that have cited a particular case.

4) — Statutes

Our law is composed of statutory law that is brought into being by the government, and cases that are decided by the courts. Whenever there is a statute that handles an issue that you are researching, the statute, subject to any judicial interpretations, is always paramount. Statutes, like the rest of the law, are constantly changing. It is essential to find statutes relevant to your research, and to ensure that the statute you are using is up-to-date. More and more government websites offer access to current statutes. In addition, LexisNexis Quicklaw, Westlaw Canada, and CanLII contain current statute databases.

Finding case law which has interpreted the various provisions of a statute is also a key component of statute law research. Judicial consideration of the statute can be found using the *Canadian Abridgment: Canadian Statute Citations*.

5) — Regulations

Regulations are passed by specific ministries, agencies, crown corporations, local public bodies, the governing bodies of professions or occupations and others pursuant to the authority of statutes, and are similarly subject to judicial interpretation; they are, however, much less frequently interpreted by the courts than statutes. Regulations are also constantly changing. You must be able to find regulations relevant to your research and ensure that they are up-to-date. Fee-based legal databases, in addition to government websites and CanLII, are a good way to find current regulations.

English and American Legal Research

American and English law, although not binding in Canada, can be persuasive, particularly when the Canadian law on the topic has not been well developed or when the Canadian law is in a state of confusion. Research from other foreign jurisdictions may be relevant; for Canadian purposes, however, English and American research are the most prevalent.

Appendix I — Research Checklist

File/Course Name _____

Date Assigned: _____ *Date Due*: _____

Issues/Keywords:

_____

_____

_____

_____

_____

_____

_____

_____

_____

_____

_____

_____

Secondary Sources

❏ *Legal Encyclopedias*

(use the *Canadian Encyclopedic Digest* or *Halsbury's Laws of Canada* for Canadian research, *American Jurisprudence* or *Corpus Juris Secundum* for the U.S., and *Halsbury's Laws of England* for the U.K.).

❏ *Books, Loose-leaf Services, Continuing Legal Education Materials, Law Reform Commission Reports*

(to locate any of the above, look for titles with the assistance of a law library catalogue online. A number of these works can also be located through the *Index to Canadian Legal Literature* (LexisNexis Quicklaw, Westlaw Canada, and print)).

❏ **Articles**

_____

_____

_____

_____

_____

_____

_____

_____

_____

_____

_____

_____

(to find articles on your topic, look at the *Index to Canadian Legal Literature* (LexisNexis Quicklaw, Westlaw Canada and print) for Canadian materials, *LegalTrac* or *Index to Legal Periodicals* for Canadian, U.S., the U.K., Australian, New Zealand materials, and *Index to Foreign Legal Periodicals* for all jurisdictions except the United States, the U.K., Canada, and Australia).

❏ **Legal Dictionaries and Words and Phrases**

_____

_____

_____

_____

_____

_____

_____

_____

_____

_____

_____

_____

_____

(use the *Canadian Abridgment's Words & Phrases Judicially Defined in Canadian Courts and Tribunals* (in print or online), *Sanagan's Encyclopedia of Words and Phrases* (in print or online via LexisNexis Quicklaw), or *Canadian Legal Words & Phrases* (via LexisNexis Quicklaw) to find out whether specific words and phrases have been considered by the courts. Dictionaries include *The Dictionary of Canadian Law* (Dukelow), *Canadian Law Dictionary* (Yogis and Cotter), and *Black's Law Dictionary*).

❏ **Non-legal and other materials (Newspapers, Government Information, Business/Social Science/Science info, internet searches)**

_____

_____

_____

_____

_____

_____

_____

_____

_____

_____

_____

(check your nearest library for newspapers online, government information, books/articles in other fields of study, and more. Internet searches are sometimes useful for locating recent government information, legal newsletters and information bulletins, some scholarly articles, etc.).

Primary Sources and Related Tools
❏ *Constitutional Research*

_____

_____

_____

_____

_____

_____

_____

_____

_____

_____

_____

(begin with Peter Hogg, *Constitutional Law of Canada*, 5th ed., loose-leaf (Toronto: Carswell, 2007-), and John Laskin, *et. al. The Canadian Charter of Rights Annotated*, loose-leaf (Aurora: Canada Law Book, 2009-). Search a library catalogue for more titles).

❏ *Cases and Case Law Digests*

_____

_____

_____

_____

_____

_____

_____

_____

_____

_____

_____

(begin with secondary sources mentioned above, the *Canadian Abridgment* and/or indexes to topical law reports (available in print and shelved with the print reporters themselves), then a legal database such as Westlaw Canada, LexisNexis Quicklaw, or CanLII).

❏ *Cases Judicially Considered (Noting-up)*

_____

_____

_____

_____

_____

_____

_____

_____

_____

_____

_____

(use an online noting-up system such as *Keycite* on Westlaw Canada or *Quickcite* on LexisNexis Quicklaw, or use *Canadian Abridgment: Canadian Case Citations* in print to note-up your cases).

❏ *Statutes*

_____

_____

_____

_____

_____

_____

_____

_____

_____

(check LexisNexis Quicklaw, Westlaw Canada, or CanLII (which contains much of the same information as the government websites) for current legislation. To locate older statutes, consult annual statutes and revised statutes for Canada or the provinces).

❑ *Statutes Judicially Considered*

(check *Canadian Abridgment: Canadian Statutes Citations* in print and/or note-up a statute section in Westlaw Canada or LexisNexis Quicklaw to determine whether and how the courts have dealt with legislation).

❑ *Regulations*

(check LexisNexis Quicklaw, Westlaw Canada, or CanLII (which contains much of the same information as the government websites) for current or near-current regulations. To locate older regulations, consult the official *Gazettes* and revised regulations volumes in each jurisdiction. Some additional information on how the courts have treated regulations is available via *Canadian Citations: Rules Judicially Considered*).

❏ *English Legal Research*

❏ *American Legal Research*

The Legal Research Checklist

3

Electronic Legal Research

What is Electronic Legal Research?

Electronic legal research refers to conducting legal research using an electronic device such as a computer or portable media player. This has become the chief way that research is conducted. Although such research has become ubiquitous, it is important to discuss it so that the researcher will understand the pros and cons involved and can make a more informed decision when deciding how to approach a legal research query.

When talking about electronic legal research, we are referring to databases and research systems that are available on the internet. In the past, CD-Roms were a popular electronic legal research tool but are now a dying breed and will not be discussed in this chapter.[1]

Electronic Legal Research Versus Print Legal Research

Print sources are still an essential component of conducting legal research. Researchers, however, now tend to focus primarily on using electronic sources; this is a common mistake which may result in your research being incomplete.

There are nine things to keep in mind when conducting electronic legal research:

1. In most jurisdictions in Canada, the official, recognized versions of legislation and case law are print-based, which means you must use print sources. For example, in Manitoba legislation is available online

---

[1] There are still some CD-Roms of interest to researchers; although we are not discussing CD-Roms in this chapter, keep in mind that this is still a valid media storage system and you may be required to use a CD-Rom to find information on your topic.

through a government website,[2] but such electronic documents are not, at the moment, considered official. The official print sources should be used if you are going to rely on them in court.

2. Not everything is online. Resources such as municipal by-laws, older statutes, and lower court cases are not always available electronically. Although more and more publishers are publishing secondary sources electronically, most books, treatises, and loose-leaf services are not available online.

3. Electronic legal research can be expensive. Unless you use government or non-profit resources, it can cost a great deal to conduct electronic research. In practice, these costs are passed on to clients; you must be able to justify the research costs to them when you issue your bill. If you can easily or quickly find the same information using a print source, consider doing so as a way to keep costs down.

4. There is no one legal research system that has everything. This means that you will have to have access to more than one electronic legal research source in order to conduct thorough research. If you do not have access to more than one electronic legal research system, you will likely have to use print volumes to supplement your research.

5. If you must find a statute as it looked at a particular point in history, only a few electronic resources are available that have such historical information, and they only go back a few years. For example, on the Department of Justice website, you can see what statutes looked like only back to 2003.[3]

6. Oftentimes, in major legal research systems, the smaller jurisdictions[4] are not given the same attention as larger jurisdictions. For example, in LexisNexis Quicklaw, you can find British Columbia repealed statutes, but you cannot find repealed statutes for New Brunswick. If you conduct legal research in a smaller jurisdiction, some of the electronic sources may not be as helpful to you.

7. Electronic legal research is only as good as the researcher using it. If you have poor research skills, the results you find using an electronic legal research system will likely not be promising. If you do not know how to search using Boolean or proximity commands,[5] if you do not

---

[2] See online: <http://web2.gov.mb.ca/laws/index.php>.

[3] See the chapter titled 'Researching Statutes', which discusses some of the few electronic resources that provide access to older statutes.

[4] For example, Prince Edward Island, New Brunswick, and Nunavut.

[5] These are discussed in more depth later in this chapter.

understand which database within the larger research system to use, or if you do not comprehend how different components of the legal research system work together, your research will very likely be insufficient and inadequate.

8. Depending on the question, using an electronic legal research system may actually be slower than using a print source. For example, if you want to find the judicial treatment of a particular word, using a words and phrases resource in print is likely faster than using one that is housed within a large legal research system.

9. Many publishers include unreported cases in their databases and these often have little precedented value. They also complicate research as more time and money is spent sifting through a much higher number of cases.

There are of course many benefits to using electronic legal research systems, including:

1. Electronic legal research systems are constantly updated with new judgments, legislation, etc. This currency is vital to a legal researcher, as any change in the law must be found quickly and efficiently. With print volumes, the speed in updating the law is much slower.

2. With electronic legal research, you do not have to rely only on the print sources available in your library. Most libraries do not have the space or finances to purchase every law-related print source. If you have access to an electronic legal research system, you can find materials to which you would not normally have access. For example, a small law library in northern Saskatchewan may not have the space or funds to purchase the annual volumes of New Brunswick statutes, but a researcher in northern Saskatchewan has access to such laws through the New Brunswick government website,[6] CanLII, and commercial vendors.[7]

3. Depending on your research question, electronic research can speed up the research process considerably. If you need to obtain a copy of one particular case and you have the name and citation, you can find it and print it off quickly electronically.

4. Electronic research allows you to search materials in novel ways. Secondary legal materials in print, such as the *Canadian Abridgment*, al-

---

[6] http://www.gnb.ca/0062/acts/.

[7] These will be discussed later in the chapter.

low a researcher to access primary legal materials because the editors of the *Abridgment* have a team of lawyers who scan the cases for certain phrases and legal subjects. For example, to find cases on the law of parol evidence, you may look in the print version of the *Abridgment* to find them easily and quickly. However, to find all Supreme Court of Canada cases that mention 'goats', the *Abridgment* and most other print sources would be of no use. You can, however, easily and quickly perform this search electronically. The *Abridgment* is also available electronically and you can find cases dealing with the parol evidence rule and Supreme Court of Canada cases mentioning 'goats' using the online version.

5. Electronically, you can better search for cases based on a certain set of facts. It is becoming increasingly important to find cases that display particular facts, and electronic sources make this endeavour much easier.

6. Electronically, you have access to a larger number of cases because more cases are published online than in traditional print reporters. Many cases that would never be printed in a print reporter may be found in online legal research systems.

7. In some jurisdictions, electronic legislation found on a government website is considered official, which means you can use these instead of print documents as an official source of the law.[8]

8. Oftentimes, there are many value-added options in electronic legal sources that make a researcher's life easier. For example, providing all parallel citations, providing links from cases to legislation and vice versa, providing access not only to primary documents but also secondary documents, and the ability to download, print, or email the desired material.

9. If you need to use the most current consolidated version of a statute, electronic research is the best way to find it. Most jurisdictions do not keep a current consolidated version of statutes in print, which means you would have to look at several annual volumes in order to see what a statute currently looks like. But online, such consolidations are readily available.

---

[8] For example, legislation housed on the government websites for Canada, Ontario, and Quebec are all considered official copies.

Types of Electronic Legal Research Providers

There are three different kinds of electronic legal research providers: commercial vendors, government providers, and non-profit providers.

Commercial Vendors

There are several commercial vendors that gather together case law, legislation, government documents, journal articles, books, loose-leafs, and other commentary, and make it available in full-text for the user. Such vendors provide quick access to an enormous amount of information. One of their main benefits, besides having so much information, is that they also provide value-added features. For example, many of these publishers provide headnotes or quick summaries of cases so that researchers will only need to read a few lines in the headnote, as opposed to the whole case, to determine if the case is relevant for their needs.[9] They also allow researchers to print, download, or email documents, and some have monitoring services that will automatically email researchers when a new development in a particular area of law has occurred.

Although there are several commercial electronic legal research systems available, two have become the main ones used by researchers: Westlaw Canada and LexisNexis Quicklaw. These resources are similar in that they both provide access to cases, up-to-date legislation, and a variety of commentary, but there are some key differences.

Westlaw Canada

Westlaw Canada, owned by Carswell, a Thomson Reuters business, was formerly known as WestlaweCarswell.[10] A large electronic legal research system, its primary advantage over other electronic systems is that it contains most of the components of the *Canadian Abridgment*[11] and the entire *Canadian Encyclopedic Digest*. The *Canadian Abridgment* is one of the most useful resources for legal researchers. Among other things, it allows researchers to find cases under similar topics, provides a list of parallel citations, and allows you to note-up cases, statutes, regulations, and rules. In Westlaw Canada, the *Canadian Abridgment* is integrated within the entire

---

[9] This does require a word of caution, however, because headnotes are not going to give you all the important facts in the case and may even leave out some issues. They are useful, but they cannot be relied upon to give you all the information you need.

[10] This name change occurred in 2009.

[11] Currently, the only component of the *Canadian Abridgment* not available in Westlaw Canada is *Canadian Current Law: Legislation*.

system. If you conduct a search and find a case relevant to your issue and you want to see more judgments on the same topic, you can click through to the related *Canadian Abridgment* case digests and then to other cases listed under the same digest. This is an excellent way to find cases on the area of law in question. See Illustration 3.1 below.

Illustration 3.1

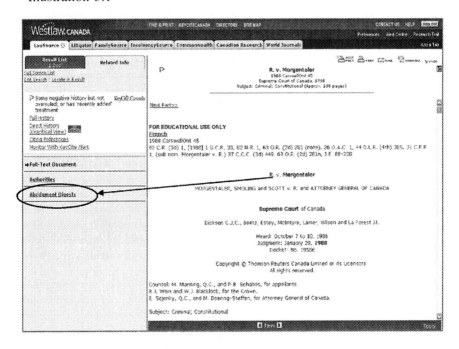

Electronic Legal Research

One of the important components of the *Canadian Abridgment* is the *Index to Canadian Legal Literature*. This journal index is the only current comprehensive journal index for Canadian legal literature, and it is available electronically through Westlaw Canada.

With the *Canadian Encyclopedic Digest*, the researcher is able to read about an area of law and is provided with references to statutes and links to cases of relevance. This allows the researcher to go directly from the secondary source to cases of interest, which is useful and may save time and money. This also reinforces the importance of starting your research using secondary sources. You must know something about the area of law you are researching before looking for cases and legislation. Using an encyclopedia such as the *Canadian Encyclopedic Digest* is an excellent starting point.

In Westlaw Canada, the researcher has access to hundreds of thousands of cases in full-text, legislation from all jurisdictions, numerous secondary sources such as textbooks, loose-leafs, and newsletters, and international materials. If you are conducting research in a particular area of law, it would be wise to utilize one of the Source subject services: LawSource, Litigator, CriminalSource, Estates&TrustsSource, FamilySource, InsolvencySource, IPSource, and SecuritiesSource. If you must conduct research in any of these areas, much of the material available in Westlaw Canada will be grouped under the same heading, making it easier to find information. LawSource is the general search page where the researcher has access to all cases and legislation, along with some secondary sources.[12] Litigator, as the name suggests, is a service for those who litigate and require access to precedents, practice guides, directories, and so forth.

With Westlaw Canada, researchers are also able to note-up cases, legislation, regulations, and rules. This is done using the *KeyCite Canada* option. There is also a *Rules Concordance* tool so that you can find concording rules from each jurisdiction in Canada.

There are many other useful tools available in Westlaw Canada; take your time to learn this resource as efficiently as possible so that you know how to research issues in an effective and cost-efficient manner. See Illustration 3.2 for sample search pages from Westlaw Canada.

---

[12] Not all secondary sources available in Westlaw Canada can be accessed through the LawSource search page. You may need to use one of the Source subject areas or search for the secondary source using the directory.

Electronic Legal Research

Illustration 3.2 — Main Search Page

The Practical Guide to Canadian Legal Research

Cases Search Page

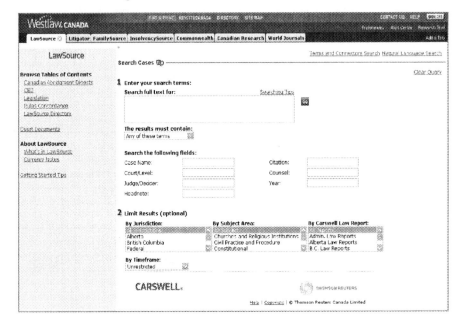

Legislation Browse Page

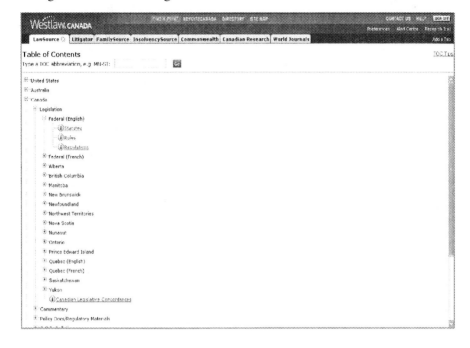

Canadian Encyclopedic Digest Results Page

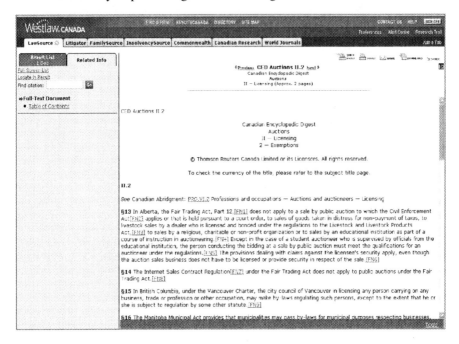

LexisNexis Quicklaw

Quicklaw was a Canadian legal publishing company based in Kingston, Ontario. It was founded in 1973 and was purchased by LexisNexis in 2002. Since then, the legal research system has been known as LexisNexis Quicklaw.

LexisNexis Quicklaw provides access to hundreds of thousands of cases in full-text, legislation from each jurisdiction, hundreds of thousands of tribunal decisions (many of which are unique to LexisNexis Quicklaw), case digests, forms and precedents, books, journals, loose-leaf services and international material. Recently, LexisNexis Quicklaw added subject-specific *Practice Areas*. Some *Practice Areas* include Criminal*Practice*, Employment*Practice*, Family*Practice*, Immigration*Practice*, IP&IT*Practice*, and Labour*Practice*. If you are researching any of these areas, many of the different resources found in LexisNexis Quicklaw are grouped under these subject areas. For example, under the Family*Practice* area, users have access to the entire loose-leaf *Wilson on Children and the Law*.[13] LexisNexis

---

[13] Jeffrey Wilson, *Wilson on Children and the Law*, loose-leaf (Toronto: Butterworths, 1994-).

Quicklaw also has an *Essentials* series aimed specifically at sole practitioners and small firms where key resources on certain topics are grouped together.[14] See Illustration 3.3 for samples of the types of resources to which you have access from the Family*Practice* section of LexisNexis Quicklaw.

Illustration 3.3

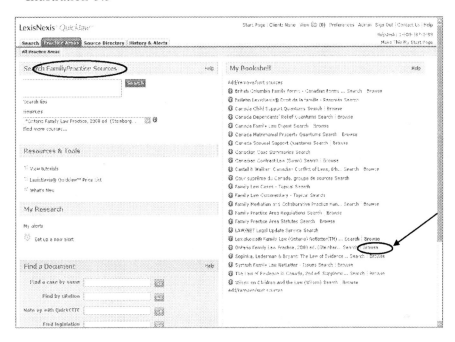

Reprinted with the permission of LexisNexis Canada Inc. LexisNexis is a registered trademark of Reed Elsevier Properties Inc., used under licence. Quicklaw is a trademark of LexisNexis Canada Inc.

---

[14] At the time of writing, there were six *Essentials* areas: *Criminal Essentials, Employment Essentials, Family & Estates Essentials, SME Business Essentials, Civil Litigation Essentials,* and *General Practice Essentials.*

The Practical Guide to Canadian Legal Research

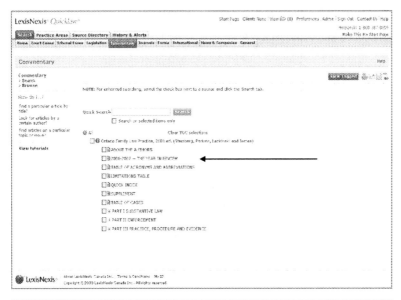

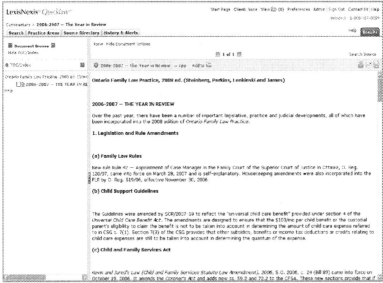

LexisNexis Quicklaw has its own case digest, similar to the *Canadian Abridgment Case Digests*, called simply *The Canada Digest*. With this source, you can search for case summaries under different topic headings, which is a useful way to start your research. The *Index to Canadian Legal Literature* is also available on LexisNexis Quicklaw, as are the *Index to Canadian Intellectual Property Literature* and the *Canadian Law Symposia Index*, which indexes papers presented at conferences and continuing legal education workshops.

LexisNexis Quicklaw also offers access to an electronic encyclopedia: *Halsbury's Laws of Canada*. This is an excellent legal encyclopedia that provides information on different areas of laws and points to key cases and pieces of legislation, many of which you can link to directly within Lexis-Nexis Quicklaw.

With LexisNexis Quicklaw, researchers are able to note-up cases and statutes, but not regulations or rules. This noting-up is done using the *QuickCite* option. One of the important features of LexisNexis Quicklaw is its *Source Directory*. In the general search pages for cases, legislation, tribunal decisions, etc., the user is searching broad databases that include cases, decisions, etc. from all jurisdictions and levels of court, as well as from all areas of law. Using the *Source Directory*, you can narrow your search by choosing a specific, narrow database. For example, using the *Source Directory* you can find a source called *British Columbia Employment Standards Tribunal Decisions*; you can use this to search just these decisions and nothing else, which will help focus your search.

There are many other useful tools available in LexisNexis Quicklaw; take your time to learn this tool as efficiently as possible so that you know how to research issues in an effective and cost-efficient manner. See Illustration 3.4 for sample search pages from LexisNexis Quicklaw.

The Practical Guide to Canadian Legal Research

Illustration 3.4 — Homepage

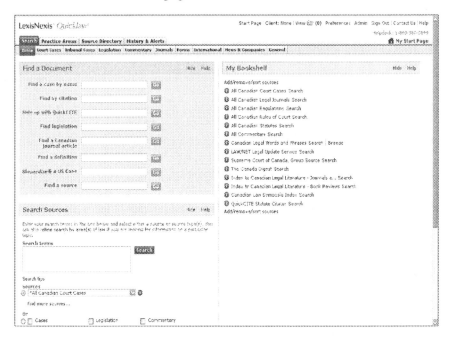

Reprinted with the permission of LexisNexis Canada Inc. LexisNexis is a registered trademark of Reed Elsevier Properties Inc., used under licence. Quicklaw is a trademark of LexisNexis Canada Inc.

Electronic Legal Research

Cases Search Page

Reprinted with the permission of LexisNexis Canada Inc. LexisNexis is a registered trademark of Reed Elsevier Properties Inc., used under licence. Quicklaw is a trademark of LexisNexis Canada Inc.

The Practical Guide to Canadian Legal Research

Legislation Browse Page

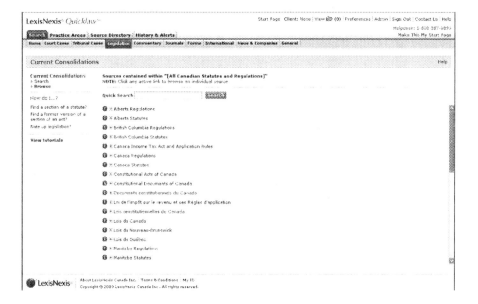

Reprinted with the permission of LexisNexis Canada Inc. LexisNexis is a registered trademark of Reed Elsevier Properties Inc., used under licence. Quicklaw is a trademark of LexisNexis Canada Inc.

Electronic Legal Research

Source Directory Page

Reprinted with the permission of LexisNexis Canada Inc. LexisNexis is a registered trademark of Reed Elsevier Properties Inc., used under licence. Quicklaw is a trademark of LexisNexis Canada Inc.

Along with Westlaw Canada and LexisNexis Quicklaw, there are other electronic legal research systems that you should know about. Some of the most frequently utilized are described below.[15]

Canada Law Book Electronic Sources

Canada Law Book (www.canadalawbook.ca) has several electronic legal sources. Some examples are *BestCase, Canada Statute Service, Labour Spectrum, Martin's Online Criminal Code, Criminal Spectrum*, and *O'Brien's Encyclopedia of Forms*. Many of these resources focus only on one area of law; if you are researching heavily in an area of law that has a dedicated Canada Law Book research service, you may wish to purchase a subscription. *BestCase* is a general search database of cases printed in case reporters published by Canada Law Book, as well as hundreds of unreported cases. *Martin's Online Criminal Code* provides access to the *Criminal Code* electronically back to the 1950s, as well as related commentary and annotations. Talk to your librarian for more information on other Canada Law Book sources. See Illustration 3.5 for a sample of the *Martin's Online Criminal Code* search page.

Illustration 3.5

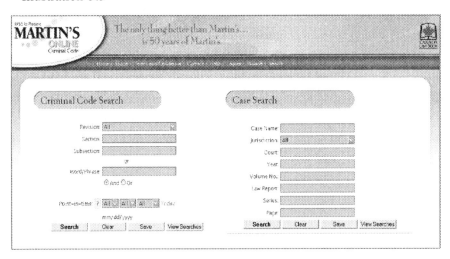

Reproduced with the permission of Canada Law Book, A Division of The Cartwright Group Ltd. (1-800-263-3269, www.canadalawbook.ca).

---

[15] A discussion of all electronic resources available is beyond the scope of this book. The sources listed here are some of the more popular resources used in Canada.

CCH Online

CCH Online (www.cch.ca) is a major electronic research tool that provides practitioner-oriented sources in areas such as law, business, finance, tax, etc. Along with subject-specific texts, loose-leafs, and newsletters, there is access to legislation and cases. Helpful documents such as forms, guides, bulletins, circulars, treaties, as well as letters from various government departments are also available. At some point in the future, CCH Online will house the *Canadian Legislative Pulse*, a bills and regulations tracker. This source is discussed in further detail in the chapters on statutes and regulations. See Illustration 3.6 for a sample of the CCH Online homepage.

Illustration 3.6

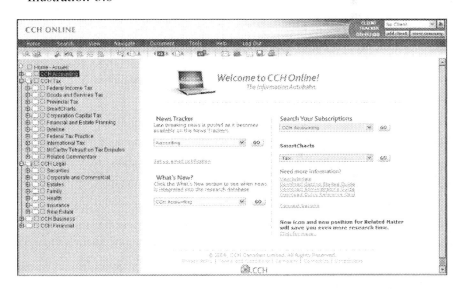

Maritime Law Book — National Reporter System

Maritime Law Book is a publishing company based in Fredericton, New Brunswick. Their online *National Reporter System* (www.mlb.nb.ca) allows the researcher to find cases that have been published in Maritime Law Book case reporters (for example, *Ontario Appeal Cases*). One of the key components of the *National Reporter System* is the Key Number System. The editors at Maritime Law Book have given different areas of law different topic headings and key numbers; cases that deal with a particular area of law are listed under the related key number and topic. If you find a case and want to find similar cases on the same topic, click on the key number and topic listed for that case and you will be taken to every other case within the *National Reporter System* that deals with that topic. It makes for a quick and efficient way to search.

Maritime Law Book has recently made many of their cases available free on their website which means that you do not have to have a subscription to find cases. With these free cases, however, you do not have access to the headnotes which help summarize the case; access to headnotes requires that you purchase a subscription. From the Maritime Law Book homepage, just click on the "Raw Law" link to access the search function for the free cases.

HeinOnline

HeinOnline (www.heinonline.org) is a large full-text journal database. At the time of publication, it had more than 1,100 journals available in full-text. This is an excellent resource for accessing journal articles in full-text. Along with journals, *HeinOnline* also has different libraries that house all types of useful material. For example, *HeinOnline* includes the English Reports, Full Reprint; numerous Legal Classics books; and the U.S. Presidential Library. It also has one of the most comprehensive collections of image-based U.S. treaties, along with other international agreements.

LegalTrac

LegalTrac (www.gale.com) is an online journal index that includes some full-text journal articles. While many of the articles indexed are from the United States, several Canadian journals are included.[16]

There are many more commercial legal research systems to assist you in finding Canadian law (as well as foreign and international law) and secondary sources. Make sure you check with your local or law firm library to find out the electronic legal resources to which you have access.

Government Providers

In every jurisdiction in Canada, the government posts legislation and other selected related documents online for public accessibility. For example, the Ontario government has established a website called e-Laws where all legislation, regulations, tables, etc. are posted.[17] The sophistication of these websites varies widely, from detailed searching (such as the federal

---

[16] For example, the *University of New Brunswick Law Journal* and the *University of Toronto Faculty of Law Review*.

[17] http://www.e-laws.gov.on.ca/index.html.

Department of Justice website)[18] to the very basic (such as the Yukon government website).[19] See Appendix I in the chapter titled *Researching Statutes* for a list of government websites that include access to legislation and related documents.

Although an excellent resource, keep in mind that, due to lack of funding and personnel, changes to legislation may not be reflected on government websites as quickly as they would be made in a commercially-provided resource.

Also, please note that in a few jurisdictions access to some related documents is only available for a fee. For example, statutes and regulations in British Columbia are available free online through the government website, but resources such as the *British Columbia Gazette* and legislative tables are only available for a fee through their QP LegalEze online system.[20]

Non-Profit Organizations

CanLII, or Canadian Legal Information Institute, is a non-profit organization created by the Federation of Law Societies of Canada. This online resource provides both lawyers and members of the public with free access to the law in an organized, functional way. Commercial legal research systems are quite costly to use, so many people cannot afford to utilize them. With CanLII, individuals have online access to case law and legislation at no cost. The CanLII search function, which you can access at www.canlii.org, is intuitive and user-friendly. See Illustration 3.7.

---

[18] http://laws.justice.gc.ca/en/.

[19] http://www.gov.yk.ca/legislation/.

[20] http://www.qplegaleze.ca/default.htm.

Illustration 3.7

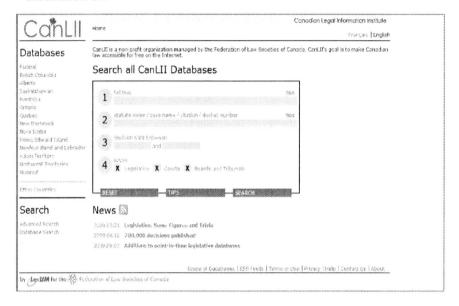

Reproduced with permission from CanLII (Canadian Legal Information Institute).

Although this is a useful online resource, it does not have the same depth and breadth as commercial legal research resources. CanLII does not have as many older cases, and there are no secondary sources available. One advantage of CanLII, however, is that it offers a point-in-time service for legislation for every jurisdiction as well as a side-by-side legislative comparison tool. The date to which you can view a statute depends on the jurisdiction and the statute itself.

There are several other legal information institutes (LIIs) around the world that provide free access to the laws of a particular jurisdiction. If you need to conduct any foreign legal research, remember that you may use one of these LIIs to find what you need. To find these other LIIs, from the CanLII website, click on the "Other Countries" link on the left-hand side of the page (see Illustration 3.7 above).

How to Conduct Electronic Legal Research

Each electronic legal research system is uniquely organized and must be used and searched differently. This is important to remember because if you use one particular electronic resource, you need to make sure your research is conducted according to how that source is organized. You must know how to phrase your questions in a form that allows you to search the given electronic legal research system, as each system has its own method of entering queries. We provide only a basic introduction to searching electronic legal systems; please consult the manuals (both in print and online) of the various electronic systems in order to better learn how to formulate your queries.

Time is money when searching electronic legal research systems. For every search you conduct a charge is incurred, which is passed on to a client. Clients will want assurances that legal research conducted on their behalf is done in a cost-efficient manner. Accordingly, you should always plan out your search before beginning. By planning your research, you will focus your search and conduct fewer unnecessary searches.

The following are general steps that will assist you in planning your search:

1. Electronic research does not replace the need to use conventional legal research materials. Before you commence any search, ensure that you understand the legal problem and know how to express the problem in the form of one or more queries. If you need to define the issues, use the conventional approaches (i.e., consult a legal encyclopedia, monograph, journal article, etc.) outlined in other chapters of this book.

2. Once you understand the legal problem, think about how to express the issues the problem raises in the form of queries. You must do this before you actually start searching so that you are focused and prepared, which will reduce the amount of time and money you expend accordingly. By specifying a number of legal terms or phrases, you can narrow your search by subject. You can also describe a fact situation in your search in order to retrieve cases analogous to the set of facts in your case. By combining factual and legal descriptions, you increase the likelihood that the retrieved cases are on point. Consider using synonyms or alternate terms to describe the law or facts. See *Tips for Conducting Research* below for more information. In addition, cases may be found by case name or citation. In some online systems, your search may be limited to a specific jurisdiction, level of court or date range. You may also be able to limit your searches to certain judges or even counsel. If your queries are too vague, you are apt to pull up a multitude of entries irrelevant to your topic. If, for example, you have to sift through two hundred cases about goats to find cases that deal with disease in goats, you are wasting time. Focus on what you are searching for and then try to exclude any irrelevant situations. Always write down your queries so you know exactly what you are doing before you begin your research.

3. Consult a list of databases or components available within the electronic research system you are using to see which ones are appropriate to your search. If you only need to look at Manitoba cases, do not use a global database that has judgments from across Canada. Your search will also be faster if you use a database that consists of summaries or headnotes as opposed to full-text.[21] However, if you are searching for an obscure phrase, a search of summaries or headnotes would not be appropriate.

4. Once you have come up with your research plan, you must then conduct the search. If the search produces no hits (i.e., no material is retrieved), make a note of this and try further searches. If a large amount of material is retrieved that will take you a very long time to scan, try a more narrow query. If the search retrieves a reasonable amount of material, scan it and eliminate those that are irrelevant. You may wish to print, download, or email the relevant information you find.

Tips for Conducting Research

Here are a few helpful tips on how to conduct effective research:

1. Write down every search you conduct and the words and phrases used when doing your search. This way you will not waste time and money redoing searches in the future.

2. Know the different Boolean and proximity connectors used in a particular legal research system. Boolean connectors are operations that will relate two different words in a particular way. For example, if you do a search for *"defamation* OR *libel* OR *slander"*, in using the Boolean connector OR, you are asking the system to find cases that include the word "defamation" or the word "libel" or the word "slander". So if in one case the judge uses the word "defamation", and in another case a different judge uses the word "libel" or the word "slander," you will be able to find both cases. Another example which highlights the importance of using synonyms: if you are searching for cases involving injuries to fans at a sporting event, you might search for *"arena* OR *stadium* OR *rink* OR *field"*, etc. Understanding these connectors and how to use them is crucial as not all judges will refer to something the same

---

[21] Keep in mind the caution mentioned in note 9.

way; by using such connectors, you will be able to find more cases on point. Common Boolean connectors are OR, AND, and NOT.

A proximity connector is an operator used to find words that are within a certain proximity to one another. For example, if you do a search for "*duty /2 care*", that means you are looking for the word "duty" within two words of the word "care". Common proximity connectors are /n (n can be any number), /p (within the same paragraph), and /s (within the same sentence). Remember that not all electronic legal research databases use the same Boolean and proximity connectors — make sure you find out the types of connectors that are used in a particular resource before you start your search.

Other connectors to be aware of include root expanders (which allow you to find words with different endings — searching for "*defam!*" in either LexisNexis Quicklaw or Westlaw Canada will allow you to find "defame", "defamed", "defamation", "defamatory", etc.); wildcards (these will search for variables in a word, e.g., *d*g* in either LexisNexis Quicklaw or Westlaw Canada will find "dog", "dig", "dug"); and phrase connectors (using quotation marks means the words will be found only as a phrase, e.g., "lecture notes").

Most electronic research systems use such tools. Make sure you consult the manual or online help page for more information about using them. If you use Boolean and proximity connectors properly, your research queries will be more successful and you will find fewer irrelevant cases.

3. Take advantage of any training opportunities. Each electronic legal research system is different, and they are all rather complicated. You cannot search them as you would a search engine. Your searches need to be deliberate and precise. By taking advantage of any training opportunities provided by your librarian or the electronic legal research publisher, you ensure that your knowledge of the system will improve, along with your searches.

4

Canadian Legal Encyclopedias

What are Legal Encyclopedias?

Legal encyclopedias provide a broad narrative of the law for a particular jurisdiction. In Canada there are two main encyclopedias: The *Canadian Encyclopedic Digest* (*C.E.D.*) and *Halsbury's Laws of Canada* (*H.L.C.*). Both of these encyclopedias provide overviews of most areas of Canadian law. These overviews briefly discuss the current state of the law and provide references to statutes and leading cases. The general format that legal encyclopedias follow is a brief paragraph discussing a specific point of law combined with footnotes that reference primary sources. Encyclopedias are usually updated on a regular basis.

When are Encyclopedias Useful?

We recommend starting your research by consulting one of the two Canadian legal encyclopedias, particularly if you are unfamiliar with the topic you have been asked to research. An encyclopedia will provide you with an overview of the law and direct you to the major cases and the relevant legislation. You will not ordinarily find detailed analysis of particular cases or statutory provisions. Encyclopedias are not exhaustive, as their focus is on the *leading* case law and current legislation. Therefore, encyclopedias are useful as a starting point to research and should not be used as a substitute for a thorough canvassing of the law.

If you are doing part of your research outside of a law library and do not have ready access to treatises, both encyclopedias are available online which allows you to get a start on your research anywhere so long as you have access to a computer. In most circumstances, you will then continue your research by consulting other resources in the library.

While it is appropriate to cite certain treatises in legal memoranda or a law school essay, citations to encyclopedias should be avoided. The encyclopedias are valuable as finding tools that lead you to the primary resources but references should be made to the primary law sources on which the encyclopedia's text is directly based.

In this chapter, we will discuss the two main encyclopedias, their key features and how to use each of them. We will discuss the print version of the encyclopedia followed by a brief description of the features of the electronic version.

The *C.E.D.* and *H.L.C.* each have a different editorial perspective. The encyclopedias are also updated on different schedules, so that at any given time one may be more current than the other on your topic. For these reasons, it is often useful to consult both encyclopedias at the outset of your research.

The Canadian Encyclopedic Digest

The *C.E.D.* is currently the only *complete* Canadian legal encyclopedia.[1] It is available as a loose-leaf multivolume print set, and online as part of the Westlaw Canada database (or as a CD-ROM). New legal developments are incorporated into the text and footnotes on a regular basis.

The *C.E.D.* is its fourth edition. There are two different versions of the *C.E.D.* available: The Ontario *C.E.D.* (*C.E.D.* (*Ont.*), focuses on Ontario and federal laws, whereas the Western *C.E.D.* (*C.E.D.* (*West*), focuses on the law in the four Western provinces and incorporates the law from the territories as well as important federal laws. Both the Ontario and Western *C.E.D.* cite decisions from other common law provinces where appropriate to the subject matter.

How is the C.E.D. Organized?

The fourth edition of the *C.E.D.*, consists of close to 200 alphabetically organized subject titles housed in approximately 50 loose-leaf binders. Each title covers a broad area of law (such as Contracts, Evidence and Family Law) or a more specific topic (such as Drainage, Fires, and Prisons). When using the *C.E.D.*, consider whether your topic has a broader or more specific aspect. For example, while the *C.E.D.* has a title for Torts, it also has separate titles for Negligence and for Nuisance.

The structure of each title is set out in its Table of Classification, which is essentially a table of contents. All paragraphs in the *C.E.D.* are numbered, which makes it easy to move from the Table of Classification to the actual text. Paragraphs contain statements of law which are supported by cases and legislation.

---

[1] As of the date of this publication, *Halsbury's Laws of Canada* was not yet published in full.

All *C.E.D.* titles also contain a Table of Cases, a Table of Statutes and individual subject indexes. These tables will refer you to the specific paragraph(s) in the text where the case, statutory provision or subject matter is to be found.

In addition to the main volumes of the *C.E.D*, the *Research Guide and Key* and *Index* volumes facilitate easy access to all of the titles of the *C.E.D.* The *Research Guide and Key* volume contains:

- A short *Research Guide* that describes the main components of the *C.E.D.*
- A *Table of Statutes* listing in alphabetical order all statutes referred to in the various subject titles with references to the volume and paragraph numbers where specific provisions of the statutes are discussed.
- A *Table of Rules and a Table of Regulations* listing in alphabetical order the rules of court and regulations referred to in the subject titles with references to volume and paragraph numbers.

The Index Volume contains:

- A *List of Titles* listing the titles in each of the main volumes of the *C.E.D.* The title number and volume in which each subject title can be found are indicated.
- An *Index Key* that combines the individual subject indexes from all the titles, together with extensive cross-references within and among titles.

You can refer directly to the subject index at the end of each title if you know what subject title to look under. However, these indexes will only refer you to the appropriate paragraph numbers within the subject title in which you are looking. In contrast, the *Index* volume has extensive cross-references and will refer you, where applicable, to volume, title and paragraph numbers in a variety of subject titles.

The major titles of the *C.E.D.* (such as Constitutional, Criminal, Labour, Torts, etc.) are updated annually. Other titles are updated at least once every three years. Each title's updated supplement pages are filed at the beginning of the title and contain updated case and statute references as well as other significant developments that have occurred since the publication of the title itself. The paragraph numbers in the supplement correspond to the paragraph numbers in the main body of the text. If the paragraph number you have been researching in the main body of the text does not appear in the supplement, this would indicate that there have been no changes in the law up to the time that title was last updated. The precise statement of currency is on the title page of the supplement (and on recently re-issued titles), and refers to specific issues of *Canadian Current Law* used in preparing the supplement (or title).

How to Use the Canadian Encyclopedic Digest

1. If you already know the subject title you require, go directly to the volume containing the title and scan the table of classification for your specific topic. If you do not know the subject title, consult the *Index Key* under your topic. The *Index Key* will often be the most useful starting point, particularly if you are unsure under which title(s) your issue falls. You will be referred to volume, title and paragraph numbers. In using the *Index*, try to be creative and persistent and make use of the cross-references provided. An area of law about which you know nothing may use unfamiliar terminology. Be sure to try several approaches to ensure that you canvass everything the *C.E.D.* has to offer on your issue.

2. Consult the index(es) at the end of the title(s) to which you have been referred for a finer breakdown of key words or phrases, or go directly to the paragraphs indicated in the *Index Key* entries.

3. Refer to the appropriate paragraph numbers under your title(s). In doing this, you are up-to-date to the date at the bottom of the page which you are reading.

4. Update further by referring to the cumulative supplement section, the pages filed at the front of the title you are using. Look for paragraph numbers in the supplement which correspond to the paragraphs you have consulted in the main body of the text. You are *now* current, at minimum, to the date on the bottom of the page in which you are researching, and up-to-date, specifically, to the *Canadian Current Law: Case Law Digests* and *Legislation* issues used in preparing the update to the title. These are identified on the first page of the supplement. If no updates to the relevant paragraph appear in the supplement, there have been no changes in the law as of the date to which that title in the *C.E.D.* was last updated.

Accessing the Canadian Encyclopedic Digest on Westlaw Canada

The *C.E.D.* is available on the Westlaw Canada service as part of LawSource. As many law firms have cancelled their print subscription to the *C.E.D.* in favour of online access, this is how many readers will use the *C.E.D.* The general principles of using the online version of the *C.E.D.* are the same as described above for the print version.

An advantage of the online version is that the updates are integrated into the text — there is no need to look for separate updates. As with the print version, there is a currency statement that tells you how up-to-date the title is.

Another advantage of the online *C.E.D.* is the ability to quickly link to cases, legislation and *Canadian Abridgment* digests from within the *C.E.D.* This allows you to take advantage of the organizational scheme of the *Canadian Abridgment*, as well as making consulting and noting-up statutes and legislation easier.

There are two entry points to the online *C.E.D.*: browsing and searching.

Browsing

The table of contents menu allows you to browse all of the titles and their tables of contents. Expanding on a title entry will reveal each of the chapters in that title as well as the currency information. As you expand each entry by clicking on the "+" symbol, you will drill down through the table of contents into the subheadings. See Illustration 4.1 for an example of an expanded table of contents.

Illustration 4.1

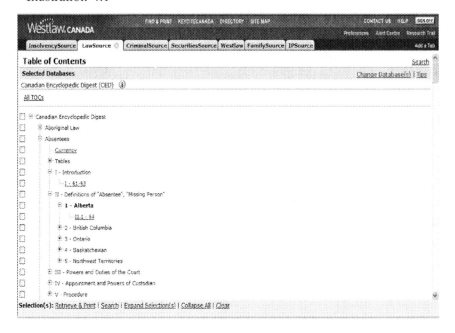

Once you have drilled down to the lowest level, you will find the actual paragraphs and footnotes of the text. The browsing approach is an excellent way to familiarize yourself with the terminology of your topic as well as related issues that you may wish to explore further.

Searching

An important feature of the online version is the ability to search across the entire contents of the *C.E.D.* or within a particular title. To search the *C.E.D.*, use Westlaw Canada's custom search template. While the Westlaw Canada version of the *C.E.D.* does include tables with each title, there are no tables for the entire *C.E.D*, nor are there any indexes. If you are using the online version, you should use the search function if you need to find references to a particular statute, regulation or case. See Illustration 4.2 for an example of the *C.E.D.* on Westlaw Canada.

Illustration 4.2

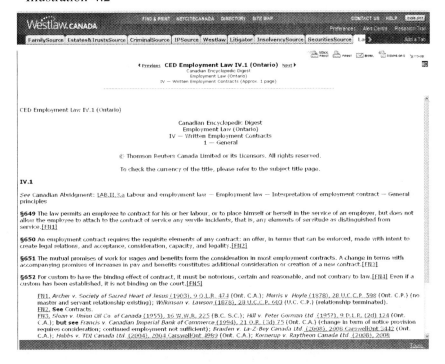

Using the Canadian Encyclopedic Digest in Conjunction with the Canadian Abridgment and Noting-up

While the *C.E.D.* selects and synthesizes the leading case law, and places it in the context of the legislative and regulatory scheme governing the subject area, the *Canadian Abridgment* provides a more *complete* body of organized case law for a particular subject area. Using the two together will allow you to quickly review the case law on your topic.

The leading cases cited in the *C.E.D.* should always be noted-up[2] using Westlaw Canada's *KeyCite Canada*, the *Canadian Case Citations* component of the *Canadian Abridgment*[3] or LexisNexis Quicklaw's *QuickCITE*. Although the *C.E.D.* will always tell you if a case has been overturned, as of the date to which the *C.E.D.* was last updated, it does not provide full judicial treatments of how the case has been subsequently applied, distinguished, or interpreted. A detailed examination of the subsequent judicial

---

2 See Chapter 13 for more information on noting-up.

3 See Chapter 5 on how to use the *Canadian Case Citations* portion of the *Canadian Abridgment*.

consideration of the cases on which you are relying can be vital to your research.

Halsbury's Laws of Canada

Halsbury's Laws of Canada (H.L.C.) is a relatively new Canadian encyclopedia. It has not yet been published in its entirety; however, a number of volumes dealing with major topics are available. It is expected that the full set will be completed in 2010. *H.L.C.* is modeled on *Halsbury's Law of England* which is the leading English encyclopedia[4]. *Halsbury's Law of England* is a highly respected tool and is used widely in the common law world (including Canada) to this day. While most major common law jurisdictions also have had their own *Halsbury's*[5], Canada's *Halsbury's* came relatively late, first published in 2006.

H.L.C. is available as a set of bound volumes or via the LexisNexis Quicklaw database. The print encyclopedia is updated by supplements to the main volumes.

Another more obscure Halsbury's publication relevant to Canadian law is the set of *Halsbury's Laws of England (3ʳᵈ) Canadian Converter* volumes. These current volumes are used to supplement the old third edition of *Halsbury's Laws of England*[6] and provide references to Canadian cases and statutes. If you can find a paragraph in *Halsbury's Law of England (3ʳᵈ)* that relates to your topic, looking up that paragraph number in the *Canadian Converter* may lead to references to Canadian cases, and most usefully sometimes a cross-Canada list of provincial statutes that deal with a specific issue.

How is Halsbury's Laws of Canada Organized?

Once complete, *H.L.C.* will consist of approximately 70 volumes covering over 100 subject areas. As with the *C.E.D.*, the service is organized alphabetically by subject. Within each subject there is a detailed table of contents. The table of contents refers the readers to the main work's numbered paragraphs which contain statements of law substantiated by cases and statutory provisions. Whereas the *C.E.D.*'s paragraphs can be pithy, *Halsbury's* often read more like treatises — each approach has its advantages.

---

[4] See Chapter 19 for more information on *Halsbury's Laws of England*.

[5] Two examples are: *Halsbury's Laws of India* and *Halsbury's Laws of Australia*.

[6] *Halsbury's Laws of England* is currently in its 5th edition.

Each subject in *H.L.C.* includes a currency statement, a discussion of the scope of the titles as well as tables of cases, statutes and statutory instruments and other tables such as conventions that are applicable to that title. Each volume also includes an index.

How to Use Halsbury's Laws of Canada

H.L.C. is accessed and employed using similar methods described above for the *C.E.D.*:

1. Locate your subject title or consult the Consolidated Index in the *Companion* volume.

2. Browse the table of contents of your subject volume or consult the index in that volume.

3. Refer to the appropriate paragraph numbers for your topic.

4. Update your research by consulting the *Cumulative Supplement* volume. *H.L.C.* plans to update each title on an annual basis following each title's publication. The *Cumulative Supplement* contains updated paragraphs for the entire encyclopedia. To use this volume, look up your subject title and then check to see if there are any updates corresponding to the paragraph numbers in the main volume. For example, if you are referring to paragraph HAP-245 in the Access to Information and Privacy volume, you would look up this same paragraph in the *Cumulative Supplement* to see if there have been any updates. Because each title is on a different updating schedule, make sure to check currency information at the beginning of each title update.

Accessing Halsbury's Laws of Canada on LexisNexis Quicklaw

H.L.C may be available online via LexisNexis Quicklaw depending on your subscription package. *H.L.C.* is accessed by clicking on the "Commentary" link in the Source Directory. One can browse the table of contents or perform a keyword search within one or more titles. The online version incorporates updates into the text of each paragraph. Make sure you check the statement of currency for each title you use. See Illustration 4.3 for a sample of *H.L.C.* on LexisNexis Quicklaw.

Illustration 4.3

Reprinted with the permission of LexisNexis Canada Inc. LexisNexis is a registered trademark of Reed Elsevier Properties Inc., used under licence. Quicklaw is a trademark of LexisNexis Canada Inc.

Comparing Halsbury's Laws of Canada and the Canadian Encyclopedic Digest

As mentioned at the start of this chapter, if you have access to both encyclopedias, and time and money permits, it is useful to consult both. Each will offer a slightly different perspective and will be updated on a different schedule. Other differences between the encyclopedias include:

1. *H.L.C.* is national in scope, whereas the *C.E.D* provides national coverage with some regional specialization.

2. *H.L.C.* tends to read more like a treatise, whereas the *C.E.D.*'s discussions are briefer.

3. If you are using the print version, the *C.E.D.*'s method for updating content is more convenient because the updates are in the same volume. *H.L.C.* requires the researcher to consult a supplement volume.

4. The online versions of each provide links to case law and legislation, but the *C.E.D.* content is also integrated with the *Canadian Abridgment.*

5

The Canadian Abridgment

The Canadian Abridgment is a collection of seven research tools with which you can perform many of the most fundamental legal research tasks. Most of these tools offer different strategies for finding case law, and have been available in print for years. Over the last 15 years, there have been several electronic versions of many of its components, both in online and CD ROM formats, the most comprehensive and most widely used of which was on Westlaw Canada's **LawSource** service. Each may be used independently or in combination to deal with different aspects of your research.

This chapter provides an overview of each component that makes up the *Canadian Abridgment*, explains where it can be useful in the research process, and provides brief instructions on how to use the component, both in its print format and on LawSource.

Illustration 5.1: Overview of Abridgment Components and When to Use Them

Use:	When:
The Canadian Abridgment Case Digests	You need to find all Canadian cases on a particular issue.
The Consolidated Table of Cases	You need to find where a particular Canadian decision has been reported or classified in the *Abridgment's* classification system.
Words & Phrases Judicially Defined	You need to find cases interpreting a particular word or phrase.

Use:	When:
Canadian Case Citations (KeyCite Canada for Cases)	You need to find out if a decision is (still) good authority for the point you wish to make.
Canadian Statute Citations; Regulations Judicially Considered; Rules Judicially Considered (KeyCite Canada for Legislation)	You need to find cases interpreting a particular section of a statute, regulation or rule.
Canadian Current Law — Legislation	You need to track the progress of a bill or find out if a section of a statute or regulation has been amended, repealed or proclaimed in force.
Index to Canadian Legal Literature	You need to find legal literature (books, articles, case comments, etc.) analyzing a legal topic or particular case or statute.

The Canadian Abridgment Case Digests: Finding Cases on a Particular Issue

The core of the *Canadian Abridgment* is a comprehensive collection of case digests, or summaries, of decisions of Canadian courts and administrative tribunals. The digests are organized by issue according to a detailed classification scheme consisting of 55 subject titles which are further broken down into as many as seven levels of headings and subheadings. There is a separate digest written for each issue discussed in a decision. By identifying the subject title for the issue you are researching and navigating its classification scheme, you can pinpoint Canadian cases on very specific issues.

When This Information is Useful

The *Canadian Abridgment Case Digests* have been available in print since the 1930s. Until recently, it was the only research tool by which you could do a single search to find all Canadian cases relevant to a particular topic. However, even after it has become possible to search comprehensive case law databases by key word, the *Canadian Abridgment Case Digests* have retained their importance as a tool for finding case law, and are available in print, CD ROM, and online as part of Westlaw Canada.

A combination of several factors makes the *Abridgment* a uniquely valuable tool for finding case law on a particular issue:

- **the breadth of its content:** with the exception of Québec civil law, it covers all major topics;
- **its historical depth:** its mandate is to cover all cases going back to the beginning of law reporting in Canada since the early 1800s;
- **the comprehensiveness and detail of its organization:** the *Abridgment* Key organizes every case into a detailed taxonomy that enables you to find the issue you are researching within the broader framework of Canadian law, and to see summaries of the cases decided under that issue;
- **its editorial compilation and maintenance:** lawyers/editors have read through every Canadian decision to determine the legal issues involved and where it fits within the classification, adding a summary of the facts and decisions reached on each issue.

It is these last two features that best characterize the difference in approach between doing a key word search across a broad case law database and consulting a tool like the *Canadian Abridgment* to find cases:

1) **Difficulties inherent in key word searching:** In key word searching of legal databases, success depends on your finding the right combination of terms to retrieve the relevant cases; your search terms need to be broad enough that the terms searched will appear in every relevant decision while at the same time sufficiently narrow to omit a flood of irrelevant decisions. How easy that will be depends on the particular topic, how skilled you are at Boolean search techniques, and your ability to guess the particular vocabulary that judges have used in writing opinions.

   With the *Canadian Abridgment*, decisions are assigned by editors to the appropriate classification by identifying the concepts discussed in them without reference to the particular words used. While this method is not infallible, it depends on the editors correctly identifying the issues, and the researcher correctly navigating the classification scheme. Using the *Abridgment* will often retrieve many relevant decisions that will be missed in a key word search because the vocabulary used in the decision to express the concepts does not match the search terms used.

2) **Putting cases in context:** Part of the appeal of searching for case law by key word is that it enables you to find cases on point by entering any terms you choose without having to characterize the legal issues

involved and see where those issues fall within the broader framework of the law. But this very characterization is a task that you need to do to build any good legal argument (whether in a court room, in an opinion letter, a legal memorandum, or on an exam).

Research using the *Abridgment* classification, on the other hand, both requires and helps guide you through this type of analysis.

The case digest approach to finding case law needs to be learned, then, either as a preferred method or as a useful supplement to key word searching, because it will often be a better way to find cases on point rather than through a keyword search, and because it helps you to identify and understand the context of the issues involved, thus giving you a better foundation for building your legal argument.

Where the Abridgment Case Digests Fit into the Research Process

The *Abridgment* is not the best tool for getting an overview of an area of law with which you are unfamiliar. For that purpose, a legal encyclopedia or treatise is a better first step, followed up by an *Abridgment* search to find the relevant cases (to help you move easily from one to another, at the beginning of each section of the latest edition of the *Canadian Encyclopedic Digest* there is a reference to the equivalent classification for that section in the *Abridgment*).

Although it is encyclopedic in scope and organization, the *Abridgment Case Digests* service does not attempt to present a unified picture reflecting the current state of the law. You will see older cases that no longer reflect the law, and divergences among different Canadian jurisdictions and among different judges and courts within the same jurisdiction. It is important, therefore, to note the decision dates, provincial jurisdictions and court levels of the decisions digested.

Also, the *Abridgment* should never be the final step in research. Its value is to help identify the decisions that are relevant to your issue prior to reading the full-text of these decisions for a fuller understanding of what they stand for and how they can be used. *Abridgment* digests should not be cited or quoted as authority in court or appear in a factum or case book.

Using the Canadian Abridgment Case Digests in Print

Components

Main Work: The 55 subject titles are set out alphabetically through approximately hardcover volumes. The date on the spine of the volume tells you how current the volume is.

Annual Supplement: There is a single soft-cover volume for each main work volume. The case digest cumulative Annual Supplement volumes contain all digests from the cut-off date on the spine of the main work to December of the previous year.

Monthly Updates: Updates appear in monthly issues of the updating service *Canadian Current Law: Case Digests.*

How to Do a Case Digest Search

1) **Determine the appropriate subject title and classification for your search by consulting the Key & Research Guide:** The starting point for case law research using the *Canadian Abridgment* is the *Key & Research Guide ("Key")*. This is a loose-leaf volume that contains the subject classification scheme by which the case law is organized. You can find all the cases relevant to your research by locating your issue within this classification scheme and then looking through the digests falling under the appropriate title, heading and subheadings in the main volume and supplement. Using the *Key* allows you to see how your specific topic fits into the broader classification scheme. The *Key* is extensively cross-referenced with *"see. . ."* and *"see also. . ."* references to guide you so that you can use the *Key* as a starting point to find the right subject title and classifications for any term you look up.

   Note: Although the subject titles appear on the spines of the *Abridgment* case digest volumes, it is always safer to consult the *Key* to find all the places where cases on your issue are located, rather than simply taking what appears to be the appropriate volume off the shelf. Topics often appear within the *Abridgment* in more than one place. For example, cases dealing with the rule in *Rylands v. Fletcher*, are digested within the 'Torts' title, but applications of this rule also appear under the 'Environmental' title, as the cross-references in the *Key* advise you.

   The entry for every subject title within the *Key* is followed by an overview of the contents of that subject title and the detailed classification. By noting the relevant classification numbers, you will be able to identify appropriate digests at a glance.

Illustration 5.2: Abridgment Key Classification

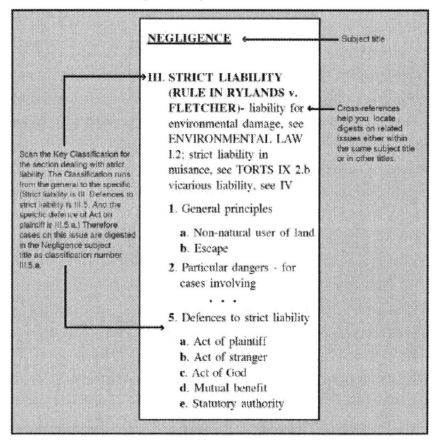

NEGLIGENCE ← Subject title

→**III. STRICT LIABILITY (RULE IN RYLANDS v. FLETCHER)**- liability for ← Cross-references help you locate digests on related issues either within the same subject title or in other titles.

environmental damage, see ENVIRONMENTAL LAW 1.2; strict liability in nuisance, see TORTS IX 2.b vicarious liability, see IV

Scan the Key Classification for the section dealing with strict liability. The Classification runs from the general to the specific. (Strict liability is III. Defences to strict liability is III.5. And the specific defence of Act on plaintiff is III.5.a.) Therefore cases on this issue are digested in the Negligence subject title as classification number III.5.a.

1. General principles

   a. Non-natural user of land
   b. Escape

2. Particular dangers - for cases involving

· · ·

5. Defences to strict liability

   a. Act of plaintiff
   b. Act of stranger
   c. Act of God
   d. Mutual benefit
   e. Statutory authority

2) **Consult the main case digest volume that contains your subject title. Scan the digests falling under the appropriate subject title and classification, noting the names and citations of important cases:** The digests are formatted so as to make it easy to scan through large numbers quickly to find cases on point.

Trial level and appeal decisions are consolidated so that there is only one digest within any classification for all levels of a case, representing the reasoning of the higher court unless that court was silent on a particular issue.

Within each classification, the digests appear in reverse chronological order, with the most recent digests appearing first.

Illustration 5.3: Abridgment Case Digest

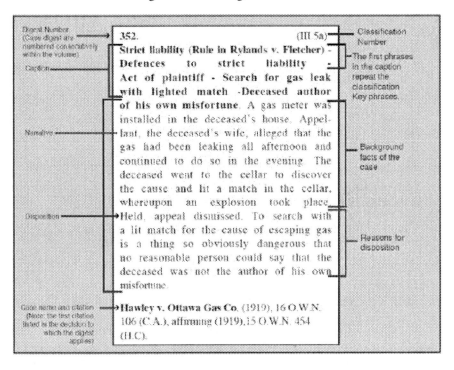

Note: A full digest is pictured here. Many digests, especially more recent ones, consist only of caption phrases, and others, published after 1998, may consist of only key classification phrases.

3) **Update your research:** To update your research past the year the main work volume was published, look up your classification in the corresponding supplement volume, which will bring you up-to-date to the end of the previous year. To complete your research, check any monthly issues of *Canadian Current Law — Case Digests* issued in the current year.

Using The Canadian Abridgment Case Digests on Westlaw Canada

The *Canadian Abridgment* case digests are available online as part of all Westlaw Canada's Source services.

How to Access the Abridgment Case Digests on Westlaw Canada

Case digests can be found in a similar way to print: by browsing the *Abridgment* Classification System and viewing all the digests under a particular classification.

But the online format makes possible new strategies for using the *Abridgment* digests in your research to find relevant cases:

- You can **first browse the *Abridgment* classification system** to locate the general area of interest and **then do a keyword search** within the identified classifications to narrow down your results
- You can do a **keyword search** of the *Abridgment* digests
- You can **link from the full-text of a decision** to the *Abridgment* digests to find other cases on the same issue
- You can **link from any section of the *Canadian Encyclopedic Digest*** to the equivalent *Abridgment* classification to canvas all relevant case law on the issue discussed

Note: whether you browse the Key Classification to scan through all digests within the classification or do a search to restrict the digests that you see, all digests in your results within the same classification are put together into a single continuous document so that you can scan through a large number of digests easily.

Strategy 1: Browse the *Abridgment* Key and scan all digests under the relevant classifications [Recommended when you want to find all Canadian cases on a particular issue].

1) **Access the *Canadian Abridgment* Key Classification** by going to the 'Browse Tables of Contents' section located in the left frame of the LawSource home page and clicking on the '*Canadian Abridgment* Digests' link.

   Initially you will see the 55 subject titles [*See Illustration 5.4 below, Box A*], set out alphabetically.

2) **Expand the various *Abridgment* subject titles** by clicking the plus signs [*See Illustration 5.4 below, Box B*], to reveal the detailed Classification.

   When you can't drill down any further, you will see the last level of classification as a blue link [*See Illustration 5.4 below, Box C*].

3) **Click on the link** to view digests of all cases on that particular issue.

Note: All digests within a particular classification appear together so that you can view or print them in a single document. [*See Illustration 5.4a below*].

Illustration 5.4: Browsing the Abridgment Key

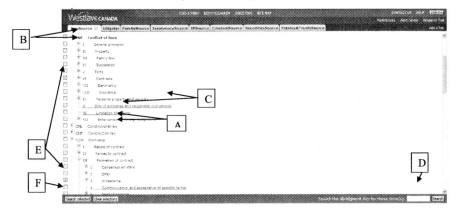

Illustration 5.4a: Case Digest Result

Tip: Help in Navigating the *Abridgment* Key — The version of the *Abridgment* Key on Westlaw Canada is not cross-referenced as the print is. It does, however, have a small search box at the lower right of the screen [*See Illustration 5.4 above, Box D*], which helps you locate where your issue appears within the *Abridgment* classification.

Strategy 2: Browse the *Abridgment* classification system to locate the general area of interest and then do a key word search within the identified classifications to narrow down your results. [Recommended where it is difficult to narrow down your search to one or two particular classifications *or* where there are many digests falling under your selected classifications and you are able to narrow your results by key word and/or jurisdiction].

1) **Access the *Abridgment* Key Classification,** as above.

2) **Choose the classifications you want to search** by selecting the appropriate checkbox(es) to the left of the classification of interest [*See Illustration 5.4 above, Box E*].

   You may check multiple boxes at any level of granularity or in any location in the classification.

3) **Click the Search selected button** [*See Illustration 5.4 above, Box F*] at the bottom of the screen.

   You will be taken to a search template, with your selected classifications listed in the **Your digest selection(s)** box [*See Illustration 5.5, below*].

4) **Type your search term(s)** in the **Add search terms and/or connectors (optional)** box, e.g. "shipping" (you can also restrict your digests to a particular jurisdiction).

Illustration 5.5: Searching Selected Classifications

Strategy 3: Do a key word search of the *Abridgment* digests [Recommended where relevant digests will contain terminology not likely to be found in the classification scheme, and where relevant digests may appear

under any number of areas, or where you have no idea of where they will be classified].

1) **Access the *Canadian Abridgment* digests custom search template** [*See Illustration 5.6, below*] by clicking on the *Canadian Abridgment* digests link in the Custom Search Templates section of the **LawSource** home page.

2) **Enter your search term(s)** in the **Search full-text for** box, e.g. "neck whiplash." [To see a list of all connector symbols and wildcards, with examples, click the **Searching Tips** link located above the **Search full-text for** box].

3) **[Optional] Limit the digests you retrieve** by entering information in specific fields (subject title, classification number or phrase, case name, citation, and year).

4) **[Optional] Limit your results by jurisdiction and/or by time frame** by using the pulldowns provided.

Illustration 5.6: The Abridgment Custom Search Template

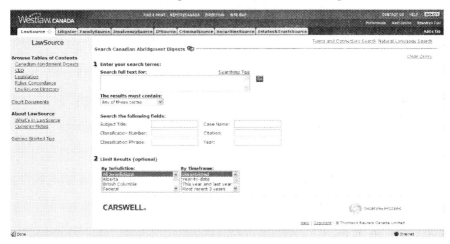

Strategy 4: Link from a decision on point to digests of other cases on the same issue: [Recommended where you already know a relevant case and want to find all other cases that deal with the same issue, or where you have begun your case research with a key word search, and want to make sure you have all cases on point].

1) **Select the *Abridgment* digests link on the Related Info tab** in the left pane of any case law document [*See Illustration 5.7 below, Box A*]. All digests for that case will appear in the right frame.

2) **Click on the Classification Number hypertext link** of any digest of interest to retrieve digests of all cases dealing with that legal issue. [*See Illustration 5.7a below, Box A*].

Illustration 5.7: Display of Full-text Decision Showing Link to Abridgment Digests

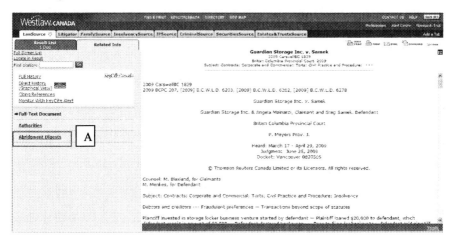

Illustration 5.7a: Link from Any Digest to All Other Digests with the Same Classification

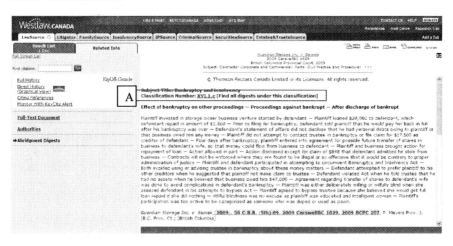

Strategy 5: Link from a section of the *Canadian Encyclopedic Digest* to the equivalent *Abridgment* classification to canvas all relevant case law on the issue discussed. [Recommended when you have begun your research by getting an overview of the law on your issue through the *Canadian Encyclopedic Digest*, and now want to follow up by canvassing the relevant case law. **Note:** Links to the equivalent *Abridgment* classification will be found on all *Canadian Encyclopedic Digest* documents by the end of 2010.]

1) **Click on the blue hypertext link to the *Canadian Abridgment*** found at the beginning of any section of the *Canadian Encyclopedic Digest*. [*See Illustration 5.8 below, Box A*].

   You are taken to the equivalent *Abridgment* classification, opened to reveal the particular classification to which you have just linked. [*See Illustration 5.9 below, Box A*]. Note that the specific classification linked to is bolded.)

Illustration 5.8: Linking from the Canadian Encyclopedic Digest to the Canadian Abridgment Case Digests

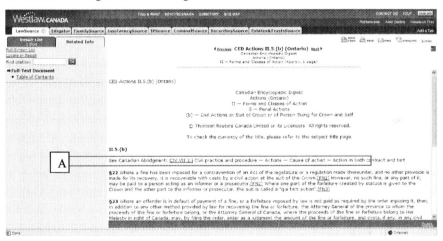

Illustration 5.9: The Abridgment Digest Classification, opened to reveal the Target of the Link from the Canadian Encyclopedic Digest

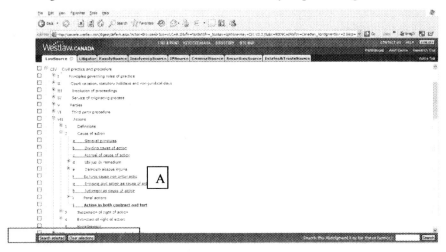

The Consolidated Table of Cases: Finding Cases by Name

The *Consolidated Table of Cases* is an alphabetical listing of all cases digested in the *Canadian Abridgment* Case Digests.

When This Information is Useful

This collection can aid your research in two ways:

1) It tells you where you can find the full-text of any Canadian decision:

Each listing in the *Consolidated Table of Cases* provides you with all reported citations (judgment date, court docket number, jurisdiction and court where unreported, and judges) of each level of case digested in the *Canadian Abridgment*. It is cross-referenced according to every significant variation in the name of the case as reported by different law report series and according to the name of the defendant.

Because the *Canadian Abridgment* digests virtually all judicial decisions published in Canada since the beginning of law reporting, the *Consolidated Table of Cases* is especially useful for locating published versions of older cases which fall outside the scope of online databases.

2) **If you know a case relevant to your research, it will lead you to other cases on the same issue:**

If you know a case on point, you can use the *Consolidated Table of Cases* to find other cases on the same issue by noting the classification under which the case is digested in the *Canadian Abridgment* and looking at the cases under that classification.

Using the Consolidated Table of Cases in Print

Components

Main Work: The fifteen hardcover volumes are arranged alphabetically.

Annual Supplement: There is a single softcover volume for each main work volume. The *Consolidated Table of Cases* cumulative Annual Supplement volumes contain all cases from the cut-off date of the main work volume to March of the current year.

Quarterly Supplement: New entries after March are gathered together in a quarterly supplement covering cases from April to June. This supplement is replaced by one covering April to September, and then by one covering April to December.

Monthly Updates: Updates after the latest quarterly supplement appear in monthly issues of *Canadian Current Law: Case Digests*.

How to Find a Case in the Consolidated Table of Cases

1) **Look at the letter ranges on the spines of the main volumes to locate the volume containing your case. Look up the case by name:** If you know that your case was decided after the cut-off date of the main volume, proceed directly to the corresponding supplement volume.

Note: Every case is cross-referenced according to the name of the defendant in the case and every known variation of the case name.

2) **Note the volume(s) and digest number(s) at the end of the entry for the case:** This reference tells you what subject area(s) the case deals with and where to find the digests of the case in the *Case Digest* component of the *Abridgment*. The three-letter code tells you the subject title of the digest, the volume and the digest number.

Illustration 5.10: Consolidated Table of Cases Entry

> **R. v. Anderson** (2003), 174 Man. R. (2d) 252, 2003
> CarswellMan 156, Wright J. (Man. Q.B.); affirming
> (2002), 169 Man R. (2d) 96, 2002 CarswellMan 477,
> Garfinkel Prov. J. (Man. Prov. Ct.) **CRM 28C45**.77

The reference **CRM 28C4.2719** tells you that the case is digested within the Criminal Law title, and can be found in volume 28C4, where it is the 577th digest in the volume.

3) **Update your research:** Check the annual supplement, quarterly supplement and monthly updates for the current year if you haven't found the decision you are looking for in the main volumes, and to see if there have been any updates to your decision — you may find that your decision has been appealed or that the *Abridgment* volume it originally appeared in has been reissued.

Finding Cases and Where They are Digested on Westlaw Canada

The *Consolidated Table of Cases* does not appear as a separate component on Westlaw Canada, but the two functions it serves can be performed by entering all or part of the case name in the "Find/KeyCite Case by Name" template found on the **LawSource** home page.

Once you have accessed the case, you can link to the digest for the case and to the digests of all other cases on the same issue as was described earlier in this section.

Tip: Although many older cases digested in the *Abridgment* are not available in full-text on Westlaw Canada, any decision that is digested in the *Abridgment* is represented in Westlaw Canada's case law database by a placeholder which will give you all available citations for the case and allow you to link to the *Canadian Abridgment* digest and classification for that case.

Words & Phrases Judicially Defined: Finding Cases Interpreting a Word or Phrase

Words & Phrases Judicially Defined in Canadian Courts and Tribunals is a specialized tool for finding case law consisting of an alphabetical list of words and phrases that have been interpreted by Canadian courts. Each entry is accompanied by excerpts from the decisions quoting the interpretations given.

The value of a words & phrases service is that it is compiled editorially. There is no reliable way to search for occurrences of a word or phrase in the context of an interpretation as opposed to another context. To compile the *Words & Phrases* service, editors read each case as it comes in and identify instances where the judge not merely uses a term, but offers an interpretation of what the word or phrase means, either generally or in a particular legal context.

Words & Phrases is available both in print and online on Westlaw Canada's LawSource.

When This Information is Useful

A words & phrases search is useful whenever you need to know how the courts will interpret a particular word or phrase, whether the terminology appears in legislation, refers to a legal principle, or is a non-legal term. It not just useful in the context of litigation research, but also when drafting agreements or advising clients on the implications of legislative provisions (legislative definitions are not included but the interpretation of legislative terminology made by the courts is included within the scope of this service).

Using Words & Phrases in Print

Components

Main Work: The entries are set out in eight hardcover volumes.

Annual Supplement: There is a single softcover supplement volume for each hardcover main work volume.

Monthly Updates: Monthly updates appear in *Canadian Current Law — Case Digests*.

How to Do a Words & Phrases Search

1) **Look up the word or phrase in the appropriate hardcover main volume:** Words and phrases that have been the subject of judicial interpretation are set out alphabetically through the main volumes. The main work contains interpretations made up to the end of 1992.

Tip: You will find a large number of *See. . .* and *See also. . .* references in this publication. These are especially important in an alphabetically organized words & phrases service because often the word or phrase you are interested in will be imbedded within a larger phrase. For example, if you are looking for interpretations of the words "probable cause," you will probably be interested in also looking at the phrase "reasonable and probable cause" and "without reasonable or probable cause."

Each entry includes an extract from each judgment in which the word or phrase was considered, as well as the citation, jurisdiction, area of law (*Abridgment* subject title), judge or adjudicator and court level.

Illustration 5.11: Words & Phrases Entry

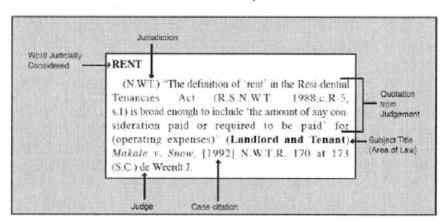

2) **Update your research:** For interpretations in decisions later than 1992, look up the word or phrase in the Annual Supplement volume corresponding to the main work volume containing your term. For updates in print in the current year, consult the *Words & Phrases* section in issues of *Canadian Current Law — Case Digests* issued after the cut-off date of the latest Annual Supplement.

Using Words & Phrases on Westlaw Canada

Words & Phrases is available on Westlaw Canada's **LawSource** service. The ability to search terms by key word does not remove the need for a words & phrases service online; a key word search for a term cannot reliably distinguish instances where the term searched for is being interpreted from those where the term is otherwise used. Indeed using *Words & Phrases* is in some ways more effective online than in print; to find relevant entries in print you must look up your term alphabetically, and the term you want defined may be embedded within a larger phrase that begins with another word. When you search for interpretations of a word or phrase through the *Words & Phrases* search template, you will retrieve *all* entries that have your word or phrase embedded in them. For example, if you searched for **reasonable cause** in print, you would see only entries adjacent to that entry:

reasonable cause of action
reasonable cause to believe
reasonable cause to terminate

But by searching online, you would also retrieve entries for:

discloses no reasonable cause of action or answer
discrimination without reasonable cause
dismissal for sufficient and reasonable cause
has reasonable cause to believe
just and reasonable cause
no reasonable cause of action
other reasonable cause
unless reasonable cause exists
without reasonable cause and to the prejudice of the corporation

How to do a Words & Phrases *Search on Westlaw Canada*

1) Access the *Words & Phrases* custom search template by clicking on the *Words & Phrases* link in the Custom Search Templates section of the **LawSource** home page.

2) Enter the word or phrase you want to find definitions for in the **Word/Phrase** box [*See Illustration 5.12 below, Box A*].

3) Use other fields to restrict your results.

Illustration 5.12: Words & Phrases Template

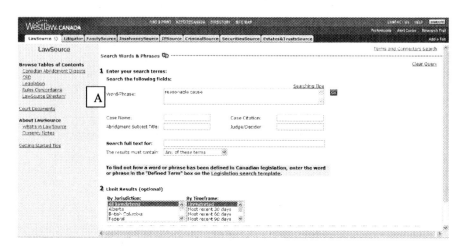

Tips for Finding Interpretations of the Words or Phrases You Want

a) Use the Word/Phrase box: Always enter the word or phrase you want to find interpretations for in this box. That way you will only retrieve documents that contain your query terms in the word or phrase being interpreted.

b) Know the effect of quotation marks ("quotes"): By putting quotation marks around a phrase, you are specifying that you are only interested in phrases where the words come in the order you entered them and without any words separating them. Entering "reasonable cause" in quotes will retrieve everything with that phrase, but will not retrieve "reasonable and probable cause." If you are interested in these variations as well, you should enter the terms as in Illustration 5.12 above, simply separated by a space without quotes. This will search for any phrase that contains **both** the words you entered.

Finding Legislative Definitions

The content set searched by this template contains judicial interpretations of what terms in legislation mean, but not the definitions that appear in the legislation itself. To find how terms are defined in Canadian legislation, follow the link to the **Legislation** template and enter your term in the **Defined Term** box.

Viewing Your Results

The entries retrieved by your search will appear in alphabetical order in your result list [*See Illustration 5.13, below*]. If you searched for **reasonable cause** as in Illustration 5.12 above, the first entry in the list (out of 20) will be **absence of reasonable and probable cause**. The entry for **reasonable cause** is number 13, under the "R"s.

Note: All interpretations of a word or phrase appear in a single document, making it easy to browse through several interpretations at one time.

Interpretations are organized within the *Words & Phrases* entry by jurisdiction. Each interpretation contains: the relevant passage from the decision; the subject area; the name, citation, court level and judge(s) who gave the decision.

Illustration 5.13: Words & Phrases Entry

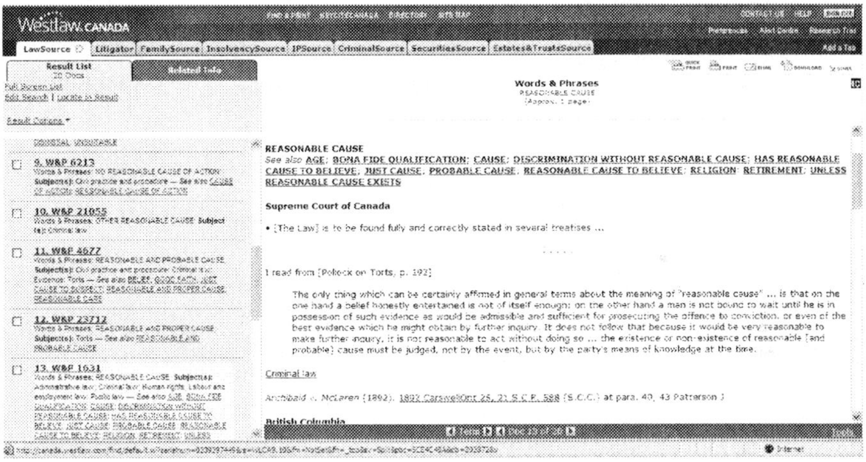

Linking to Words & Phrases Entries from a Particular Decision

Words and phrases interpreted in a decision appear within Westlaw Canada's Citator, *KeyCite Canada*, as citing references for that decision. By clicking on a *Words & Phrases* entry, you can find interpretations of those words or phrases in other cases:

Illustration 5.14: KeyCite Canada: Words & Phrases within Citing References for a Case

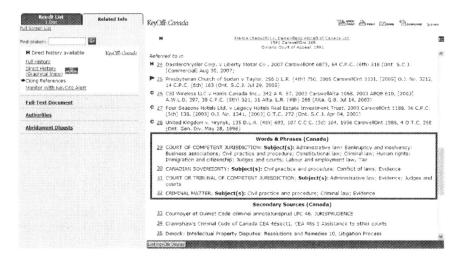

Canadian Case Citations/KeyCite Canada: Finding the History and Judicial Treatment of a Case ("Noting-up")

Canadian Case Citations provides you with the history of Canadian decisions (e.g. whether a decision has been affirmed, reversed, granted or refused leave to appeal, or had additional reasons given), plus the judicial treatment of Canadian and foreign decisions (e.g. whether a decision has been followed, distinguished, or considered in a subsequent Canadian case). *Canadian Case Citations* is drawn from analyses of reported decisions of Canadian courts and tribunals since 1867, and unreported decisions of Canadian courts since 1986.

When This Information is Useful

1) **When you need to verify** that a decision you want (or your opponent wants) to rely on is still good law, you may find that:

a. The decision, although it may once have been good authority, has since been reversed or overruled, or has not been followed in your jurisdiction.

b. The decision may be good law, but is not applicable in the circumstances you want to use it in.

c. The decision may be good law, but there is better authority you can use for the point you wish to make (e.g. more recent decisions; decisions in higher courts; decisions of courts in your own jurisdiction; decisions with more similar fact situations).

The task of verifying the continuing validity of relevant decisions is central to all case law research. Typically, you will want to note-up any decision that bears materially on your case.

2) **When you need to see if a foreign decision has been applied in a Canadian decision.** The scope of the cases that you can note-up includes any decision, no matter from what jurisdiction or what time frame, that has been referenced in a Canadian decision.

3) **When you need to find other decisions on the same issue(s) as a decision you know.** Aside from the critical role of verification, a case citator is a valuable tool for finding case law that deals with the same issue as a case you know. This method of finding cases can be especially useful when the case you note-up is a leading case from a higher level court, and you are reasonably confident that any later Canadian decision on that issue will refer to it.

4) **[Online version only] When you have found a case on point near the outset of your research and you want to find analysis in secondary sources.** Bear in mind as well that the online version of *Canadian Case Citations* on Westlaw Canada, **KeyCite Canada**, gathers together not just judicial decisions, but also analysis in the form of books, journal articles, and case comments that have discussed the case you are noting-up, which makes it a valuable source of guidance as to the legal significance of your case within the framework of Canadian law.

Using Canadian Case Citations in Print

Components

Main Work: Thirty-two hardcover volumes contain histories and judicial treatments to 2006.

Annual Supplement: There is a softcover supplement volume corresponding to each main work volume. It is replaced each year on a cumulative basis.

Quarterly Supplement: A single softcover volume, replaced every three months, provides updates after the cut-off date of the annual supplement.

Monthly Updates: appear in monthly issues of *Canadian Case Citations*.

How to Note-up a Case

1) **Begin your research by looking up your case in the appropriate main volume.** The cases are arranged alphabetically. Every case is routinely cross-referenced according to the name of the defendant, so you can look up either party. If you know that your case was decided after the cut-off date of the main volume, proceed directly to the supplement volume.

2) **View the history of the case.** When you find your case, the first thing you will see is a report of the appellate history of the case through the Courts. Each court level is listed from lowest to highest, connected by an indication of what happened at that level [*See Illustration 5.15*].

Illustration 5.15: History Dispositions Used in Canadian Case Citations

HISTORY OF CASES

Affirmed Decision affirmed on appeal or on reconsideration; or application for judicial review refused

Amended Correction of wording of decision by decision maker to conform to intended meaning

Additional reasons Additional reasons for decision

Allowed leave to appeal Leave to appeal to an appellate court allowed

Refused leave to appeal Leave to appeal to an appellate court refused

Referred for further consideration or clarification Decision referred

back by an appellate court to lower level for further consideration or clarification

Granted reconsideration or rehearing Application for reconsideration or rehearing of decision by same court granted

Refused reconsideration or rehearing Application for reconsideration or rehearing of decision by same court refused

Reversed Decision reversed on appeal or on reconsideration

Varied Decision varied or modified by either the decision maker or an appellate court without reversing the result.

3) **View the judicial treatments.** Immediately following the appellate history is a report of the later Canadian decisions that have cited your case, divided according to which court level was cited and the type of treatment given by each: did it follow, not follow, distinguish your case or simply consider it without approving or disapproving it? [**Note:** in the print version of *Canadian Case Ci-*

tations, decisions that have merely referred to your case in passing, without substantial comment are omitted].

The later treatment of a decision can be critical to evaluating its continuing validity as precedent or its applicability to your argument, especially if it is discussed by a higher court in your jurisdiction. See Illustration 5.16 for a description of the treatment symbols.

Illustration 5.16: Treatment Symbols used in Canadian Case Citations

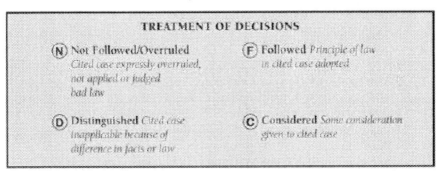

4) **Update your research.** To update your research past the cut-off date of the main volume, look up your legislative provision in the corresponding annual supplement, followed by the quarterly supplement and then the monthly updates. The dates appearing on the spines of the volumes will help you find the appropriate volumes.

Using Canadian Case Citations on Westlaw Canada: KeyCite Canada

All the information in *Canadian Case Citations* is included in the online version-KeyCite Canada-which is part of all offerings on Westlaw Canada. But in addition to the information found in the print *Canadian Case Citations*, KeyCite Canada offers additional information and capabilities that make it an even more valuable research tool.

• **Citing references to cases from commentary:** KeyCite Canada records not only subsequent case law references to the decision you are noting-up; it also records references in any document on Westlaw that has referred to the decision, including treatises, the *Canadian Encyclopedic Digest*, journal articles and case comments and annotations. The inclusion of citing references from commentary within KeyCite Canada is a powerful research tool;

they allow you to understand the legal issues in the case and its place in the larger framework of the law.

- **More judicial treatments recorded:** In identifying the nature of judicial treatment given to a case, editors distinguish between significant considerations and passing references. The latter are omitted from the print version of *Canadian Case Citations* for lack of space but are included in the electronic version. These considerations appear under the heading "Referred to."

- **Greater currency:** Between the time a decision has been released and the time editors have had a chance to record and characterize the judicial treatments found in a decision, provisional treatments are recorded on KeyCite Canada under the heading "Recently added."

- **More information on Leaves to Appeal to the Supreme Court of Canada:** Both the print and online versions of KeyCite Canada report decisions allowing or refusing leave to appeal. In addition to this information, KeyCite Canada tells you as soon as a leave application or notice of appeal has been filed, allowing you to link to a document that keeps you updated as to its status.

- **Automated updates:** Through the KeyCite Alert function, you can arrange to be notified by email of any new developments in the history or treatment of a specified case.

- **Judicial treatments of the case from other jurisdictions:** References from other countries that have KeyCite applications on Westlaw, including Australia, Hong Kong, and Singapore and U.S. commentary, are included in your results.

- **The ability to limit your results:** KeyCite Canada provides a number of strategies to help you narrow your results.

- **Graphical view of case history:** The report of a case's progress through the courts is sometimes quite complex. KeyCite Canada provides the option of viewing a graphical representation of the history of a case.

- **Status icons:** When looking at the full-text or result list entry for any decision on Westlaw Canada that has history or treatment in KeyCite Canada, you will see one of four graphical icons at the head of the entry. The presence of one of these icons tells you that there is history and/or treatments for the decision. The icons also give some indication of whether there has been a later decision that negatively affects the continuing validity of your case. In increasing order of severity, they indicate:

[No icon] — There is no history or treatment for this decision on Westlaw Canada.

Green C — There is no appellate history for the decision, but there are citing references, in case law or commentary, none of which are negative.

Blue H — There is prior or subsequent appellate history for the decision. There may also be citing references. Nothing in the history or citing references is negative.

Yellow Flag — There is either appellate history and citing references or both. Something in the subsequent history or citing reference may negatively affect the validity of the case or limit its application, but the decision has never been reversed or overruled.

Note: A yellow flag is also put on every decision that is under appeal and any case that has recent but as yet unanalyzed citing references.

Red flag — The decision has been reversed or has not been followed within its own jurisdiction or by the Supreme Court of Canada.

How to Access KeyCite Results

1. Noting-up a Case from the Home Page

You can find the history and any citing references for any Canadian decision from the home page of **LawSource** or most other Westlaw Canada services. Click on the **KeyCite** toggle [*See Illustration 5.17 below, Box A*] and

Either

[To note-up by name]: Enter all or part of the name of the decision you want to note-up in the **Case Name** box [*See Illustration 5.17 below, Box B*], and click the GO button. You can restrict your results by entering the jurisdiction of your decision; if there are still multiple decisions that match your criteria, you will see a pick list with additional information to help you choose the decision you are interested in.

Or

KeyCite by Citation: Enter the citation of the decision in the **Citation** Box [*See Illustration 5.17 below, Box C*] and click the GO button. You can ignore spacing, capitalization and punctuation (e.g. **26dlr4th200**).

Foreign and Privy Council Decisions:

Any foreign decision which has been referenced in a Canadian decision can be noted-up. To note-up a non-Canadian decision. Click on the **Global KeyCite by Name/Title** link [*See Illustration 5.17 below, Box D*].

Tip: All Privy Council decisions can be noted-up from the Global KeyCite page. However, Privy Council decisions originating in Canada can also be noted-up by name from the home page in the same way as other Canadian decisions.

Illustration 5.17: Noting-up a Decision from the Home Page

2. Noting-up a Case Directly from a Decision

A KeyCite flag or other icon appearing at the top left of a decision [*See Illustration 5.18 below, Box A*] indicates that there are KeyCite results for that decision. You can: click on the icon to view the history and citing references for the case

    – or –

Click the Full History or Citing References link on the Related Info tab on the left frame of the decision [*See Illustration 5.18 below, Box B*].

Tip: When you access the "Full History" of the decision, you will see not only the appellate history, but also any citing references that may negatively affect the decision. Note, however, that to view all citing references for a decision, you need to click on the **Citing References** link from the left frame.

Illustration 5.18: Accessing KeyCite from the Full-text of a Decision

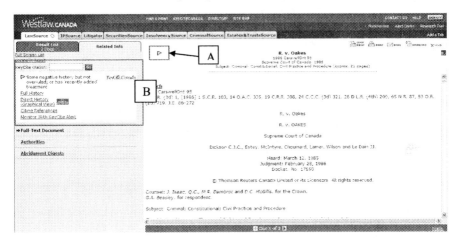

Viewing KeyCite Results

a) Viewing History

The appellate history of the decision appears under the heading "Direct History". When viewing the history of a case, you should be aware of the following:

- The decisions in the history chain are always set out from lowest to highest — with a blue arrow to the left of the level you have noted-up [*See Illustration 5.19 below, Box A*].

- When the history of a case is too complicated to follow easily, you can view a graphical version by clicking on the Direct History (Graphical View) link in the left frame [*See Illustration 5.19 below, Box B*; an example of the graphical display is shown in Illustration 5.20].

Illustration 5.19: KeyCite History Display

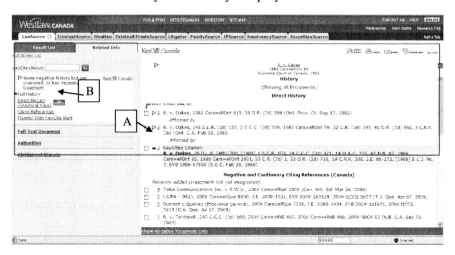

Illustration 5.20: Graphical View of Appellate History

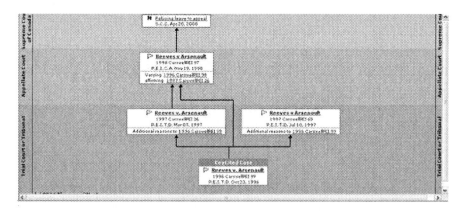

b) Viewing Citing References

Although negative citing references are displayed along with the direct history, to see *all* citing references for a decision, you need to click on the Citing References link. You will see any or all of the following:

Judicial decisions which have referenced your case, beginning with negative and cautionary references (which may undermine the authority or applicability of the decision you are noting-up), followed by positive and neutral references to your decision;

Court documents filed by the parties in support of your decision;

Quantum digests for the decision;

Words & Phrases entries that quote the decision;

Secondary sources that have referenced your decision.

Limiting Citing References: You will often find, especially when noting-up a leading case, that there are hundreds, or even thousands, of citing references. You should be aware of the different strategies available for limiting the references you are shown:

Avoid "Referred To" citing references: References gathered under this heading consist of decisions that have mentioned the case you are noting-up in passing but do not discuss it in any meaningful way.

Use the Limits function to narrow your results: When viewing Citing References, a button enabling you to limit the references you view in various ways appears at the lower left of the page [*See Illustration 5.21 below, Box A*]. KeyCite Canada provides a number of strategies to help you restrict results; used individually or in combination, you can restrict your results:

- by date (view recent references only);
- by jurisdiction (view only references from your jurisdiction);
- by court level (view only references from higher courts);
- by document type (view only references in court cases or commentary);
- by any terms found within the references: (view only documents referring to your case that contain specific terms).

Illustration 5.21: KeyCite Citing References

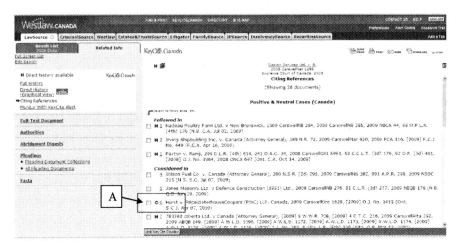

Legislative Citators: Canadian Statute Citations, Regulations Judicially Considered, Rules Judicially Considered, KeyCite Canada: Finding the Judicial Treatment of a Statute, Regulation or Rule of Practice ("Noting-up")

The *Abridgment's* suite of legislative citators enable you to find cases (and, in its online format, authored annotations) that discuss the interpretation or application of Canadian and foreign legislation and international treaties. The information in the legislative citators is drawn from analysis of reported and unreported decisions of Canadian courts and tribunals. Editors go through each decision and note every time a legislative provision is cited, and indicate the nature of the treatment. When you look up the legislation you are interested in, you will find a comprehensive list of the cases that cite it, arranged by section and the nature of treatment.

When This Information is Useful

1) **you need to see how the courts have interpreted a legislative provision** or whether the provision has been held to apply in a particular situation. The interpretations of legislation made by the courts in deciding cases are as binding or persuasive as other judicial pronouncements.

2) **you want to find other decisions on the issue dealt within particular legislation.** For example, any cases dealing with the defence of insanity to a criminal charge can be found by simply noting-up s. 16 of the *Criminal Code.*

3) **you want to see whether a provision has been declared unconstitutional by the courts.** It is important to note that the legislative citators, like the other components of the *Abridgment* discussed earlier, are tools for finding cases, not legislation. Except in the relatively rare instances where legislation has been declared unconstitutional, noting-up legislation will not tell you about the status of the legislation, e.g., whether it has come into force, been amended or repealed. For that purpose, you can consult the *Abridgment's* Legislation service, discussed below.

Using the Legislative Citators in Print

Components

Main Work:

> *Canadian Statute Citations* — multiple hardcover volumes, organized into jurisdictional sets;
>
> *Regulations Judicially Considered* — multiple hardcover volumes;
>
> *Rules Judicially Considered* — multiple hardcover volumes.

Annual Supplement:

> *Canadian Statute Citations* — there are softcover supplement volumes corresponding to each jurisdictional set of Canadian Statute Citations main work volumes;
>
> *Regulations Judicially Considered* — softcover supplement volumes;
>
> *Rules Judicially Considered* — softcover supplement volumes. The annual supplement volumes are replaced with updated supplement volumes each year.

Quarterly Supplement: Softcover volumes, replaced every three months, provide updates after the cut-off date of the annual supplement.

Monthly Updates: Updates appear in monthly issues of *Canadian Statute Citations.*

Note: there are separate main volumes and annual supplement volumes for each of the three components of this service: statutes, regulations and rules. There is, however, only a single set of quarterly and a single set of monthly issues, which updates all three components.

How to Note-up a Statute, Rule or Regulation

1) **Begin your research by looking up the legislative provision in the appropriate main volume.** Find the volumes containing the jurisdiction of your statute, regulation or rule. In *Canadian Statute Citations* and *Rules Judicially Considered*, statutes and rules are simply set out alphabetically by name. In *Regulations Judicially Considered*, regulations are organized by their enabling statute, so you must find them by looking up the statute under which the regulation was enacted.

2) **View the judicial treatments.** Within the entry for each statute, the sections, subsections and clauses that have been the subject of judicial consideration are set out in order, with the cases that have cited them listed underneath. Cases considering statutes/regulations/rules as a whole appear at the beginning of the entry under the heading "Generally."

Illustration 5.22: Canadian Statute Citations Entry

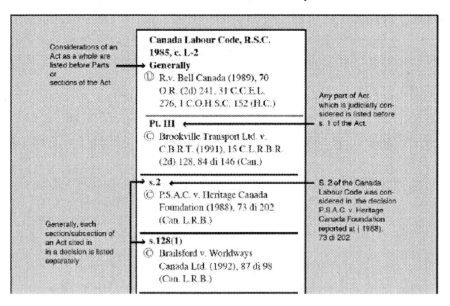

To the left of each citing case you will see a treatment symbol indicating how the case treated the legislative provision:

Illustration 5.23: Treatment Symbols for References to Legislation

Ⓤ unconstitutional	Where a section of a statute has been found by the Court considering it to be unconstitutional or invalid, the symbol Ⓤ is used.
Ⓒ considered	Where a section of a statute has been analyzed or interpreted in a particular case, the symbol Ⓒ is used.
Ⓟ pursuant to	Where a proceeding was undertaken pursuant to a section of a statute, the symbol Ⓟ is used.
Ⓡ referred to	When a section of a statute has been mentioned in passing but cannot be said to have been considered in any meaningful way by the court, the symbol Ⓡ is used.

Legislatures periodically issue new consolidated versions of the legislation for their jurisdiction. You should be aware that *Canadian Statute Citations* always has a separate entry for each consolidation of a statute. Thus in Illustration 5.24 below, there are separate entries for the 1970 and the 1985 consolidations of the *Criminal Code*.

Tip: If you are looking for judicial treatments of an equivalent section of legislation in earlier consolidations, you should be aware that the section numbers often change from one consolidation to the next.

Illustration 5.24: Separate Entries for Each Consolidation

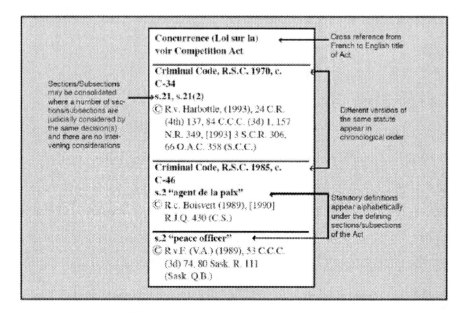

3) **Update Your Research.** To update your research past the cut-off date of the main volume, look up your legislative provision in the corresponding annual supplement, followed by the quarterly supplement and then the monthly updates. The dates appearing on the spines of the volumes will help you find the appropriate volumes.

Noting-up Legislation on Westlaw Canada: KeyCite Canada

All the information in the *Abridgment*'s legislative citators — *Canadian Statute Citations, Rules Judicially Considered and Regulations Judicially Considered* — is available through KeyCite Canada which is included as part of all Westlaw Canada services. But in addition to the information found in the print citators, KeyCite Canada offers additional information and capabilities:

- **Citing References from annotated services:** For key legislation, such as the *Criminal Code*, the *Bankruptcy Act* and the Federal Child Support guidelines, citing references include not only judicial treatments, but links to authored annotations on the provision.

- **The ability to limit your results:** KeyCite Canada provides a number of strategies to help you narrow your results.

- **Automated updates:** Through the KeyCite Alert function, you can arrange to be notified by email of any new developments in the treatment of a specified legislative provision.

How to Access KeyCite Results

1. Noting-up a Case from the Home Page

You can find citing references for any legislative provision from the home page of LawSource or most other Westlaw Canada services. See Illustration 5.25 below.

Illustration 5.25: Accessing KeyCite from the LawSource Home Page

Click on the **KeyCite** toggle [*See Illustration 5.25 above, Box A*].

Either

a) **KeyCite by title:**

Enter all or part of the Title of the statute, rule or regulation you want to note-up under the **Title** box [*See Illustration 5.25 above, Box B*] and click the GO button. For statutes and rules, enter all or part of the commonly used short title in the Title field. Also, enter the appropriate jurisdiction.

Tips:

> **General References:** To see cases that discuss a statute, rule or regulation generally, without reference to a particular section, simply leave the section box empty.
>
> **Noting-up Subsections and Clauses:** Even if you are interested only in cases considering a particular subsection or clause within a section of legislation, you should simply enter the section number. You will always see the entry for the whole section in any case, with references to particular subsections or clauses broken set out after references to the section as a whole [*See Illustration 5.27 below*].
>
> **Regulation Names:** For regulations, which often do not have descriptive names, you can enter a term from the title of the statute under which the regulation was made. For example, if you wanted to note-up a section of the *General Regulation* made under the Alberta *Cemeteries Act*, you could enter **cemeteries**.
>
> **Specifying current version:** To specify the current (or any other) version of a statute, you can enter the year of its enactment or consolidation in the Title box.

Or

b) KeyCite by Citation:

Enter the citation of the legislative provision in the Citation Box [*See Illustration 5.25 above, Box C*] and click the GO button. The Citation box is not sensitive to spacing, capitalization or punctuation used for abbreviations. However, when a form of punctuation is an essential part of a citation style, it needs to be included. For example: "rso1990ce.2s310" or "rsc1985cc-46s16".

Foreign Legislation and International Conventions:

Foreign legislation which has been referenced in a Canadian decision can be noted-up *only* by title and section number from the home page. To specify the country of origin, simply include the country in the Title box, e.g., **penal code india**.

2. Noting-up a Case Directly from a Legislative Provision

A KeyCite icon consisting of a green C appearing at the top left of a decision [*See Illustration 5.26 below, Box A*] indicates that there are citing references for that legislative provision. You can click either on the icon to view them or on the Citing References link on the Related Info tab on the left frame of the document [*See Illustration 5.26 below, Box B*].

Illustration 5.26: Accessing KeyCite from the Full-text of a Legislative Provision:

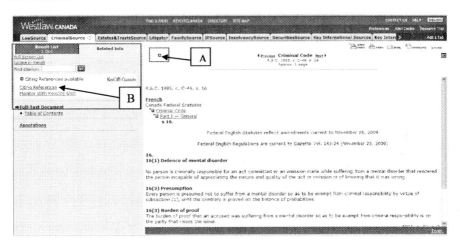

Viewing Citing References for Legislation

Citing references for legislative provisions include one or both of the following:

Citing Cases: You will see cases citing the section generally first, followed by cases citing various subsections or clauses. Citing cases are organized according to the type of treatment, which, as in the print citators, include cases:

- which have found the legislative provision **unconstitutional**,
- brought **pursuant** to the provision,
- which have **considered** the provision, and
- which **referred** to the provision without significant discussion.

Secondary Sources: For key legislation, such as the *Criminal Code*, the *Bankruptcy Act* and the Federal Child Support guidelines, citing references include not only judicial treatments but also links to authored annotations on the provision.

Limiting Citing References: As with the case citator, you will often find that there are more citing references provided for a legislative provision than you are able to look up. Similar strategies are available for limiting the references as were discussed with regard to KeyCite for cases]:

> Avoid **Referred To** citing references, and
>
> Use the **Limits** function (available from the bottom left of the KeyCite Citing References display) to narrow your results [*See Illustration 5.27 below, Box A*]:

Illustration 5.27: KeyCite Citing References

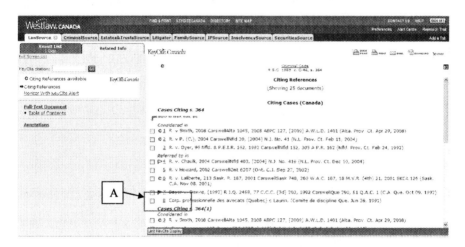

Canadian Current Law — Legislation: Tracking Developments in Legislation

A part of the *Canadian Abridgment's* updating service, which is, at present, only available in print, *Canadian Current Law — Legislation* enables you to track the progress of bills through the federal parliament and provincial and territorial legislatures, and tells you if there have been recent or pending changes to any Canadian statute or regulation.

When This Information is Useful

Legislation, like case law, changes constantly. When making any legal argument or giving legal advice, you must always be sure that any legislation you rely on in providing legal advice or preparing a legal argument is still valid-that it hasn't been repealed, or amended in any key respect-and that there is no new legislation in the works that will affect the position you are arguing.

There are three sections in each issue of *Legislation*:

1) *Progress of Bills:* tracks every federal, provincial and territorial bill from first reading through to Royal Assent and proclamation.

2) *Statutes Amended, Repealed or Proclaimed in Force*: alerts you to developments in any Canadian federal, provincial or territorial statute that has been amended, repealed or proclaimed in force, and gives you the chapter number and section number of the amending Act so that you can find and read the text of the amendment.

3) *Regulations*: lists by enabling statute, regulation name and section number the making, repeal and amendment of regulations.

Note: For several jurisdictions it is possible to find this information more easily and with greater currency through government websites. The value of *Canadian Current Law — Legislation* is that it provides a way to track developments of legislation in all Canadian jurisdictions.

Components

Eight issues of *Canadian Current Law — Legislation* are published over the course of the year.

A *Legislation Annual* is produced once per year and replaces the seven regularly issued volumes, summarizing and retaining the permanent information previously published in those issues.

How to Track the Progress of a Bill

1) **Consult the Statutes Enacted section of the *Legislation Annual* for the previous year to see if your bill has been recently enacted.** Statutes are organized by jurisdiction: federal statutes come first, followed by statutes for the provinces and territories in alphabetical order.

2) **Consult the Progress of Bills sections in the issues of *Canadian Current Law — Legislation* after the cut-off date of the most recent *Legislation Annual*.** Bills are organized as in the Statutes Enacted section. After the title of the Bill, you will find the chapter number (if available) and the Bill number, followed by any developments (e.g. First, Second or Third Reading, Royal Assent date, In Force date) that occurred during the time frame covered by that issue.

Illustration 5.28: Progress of Bills Entry

MANITOBA

Fourth session of the 36th Legislature convened November 27, 1997 and adjourned December 11, 1997, reconvened March 6, 1998 and adjourned June 29, 1998.

Victims Rights and Consequential Amendments Act, S.M. 1998, c. 44 (Bill 43, 1998)
First Reading: April 30, 1998
Second Reading: June 18, 1998
Third Reading: June 29, 1998
Royal Assent: June 29, 1998
In Force: Proclaimed in force January 4, 1999.

Note: On the inside back cover of each issue of *Legislation* you will find "Updates to the Minute", a list by jurisdiction of telephone numbers that you can call to update the status of a bill pending before Parliament or any provincial or territorial legislature.

How to Find Developments in the History of a Statute

1) **Consult the Statutes Amended, Repealed or Proclaimed in Force section in the earliest relevant *Legislation Annual*.** Statutes are organized alphabetically by jurisdiction. The entries for each statute provide the section affected, the nature of the development, and the provision that brought about the development.

2) **Consult the Statutes Amended, Repealed or Proclaimed in Force sections in the issues of *Canadian Current Law — Legislation* after the cut-off date of the most recent *Legislation Annual*.**

Illustration 5.29: Statute History Entry

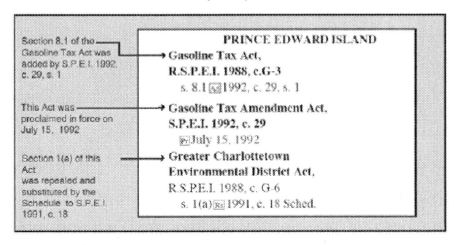

Note: Where changes are made in terminology affecting every statute in a jurisdiction, the terms affected are entered at the beginning of the entries for that jurisdiction.

How to Find Developments in the History of a Regulation

1) **Consult the Regulations section in the earliest relevant** *Legislation Annual.* Find your regulation first by jurisdiction, then alphabetically by the name of its enabling statute, and then by the name of the regulation. The entries provide the name or title of each regulation, the regulation number and the issue of the particular *Gazette* in which the regulation was published.

2) **Consult the Regulations sections in the issues of** *Canadian Current Law — Legislation* **after the cut-off date of the most recent** *Legislation Annual.*

[**Note:** the entry below tells you that the Schedule to the *Designated Provisions Regulations* (cited as SOR/90-138), was amended by a regulation cited as SOR/92-287, as reported in the June 3, 1992 issue of the *Canada Gazette*, on page 2102].

Illustration 5.30: Regulation History Entry

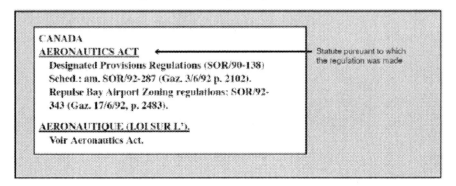

The Index to Canadian Legal Literature: Finding Legal Literature

The *Index to Canadian Legal Literature* ("ICLL") is a comprehensive bibliography of Canadian legal literature, in English or French, which is of interest to the Canadian legal community, including: books, articles, looseleaf services, electronic resources, government publications, continuing legal education material, case comments and annotations. ICLL is divided into five separate indexes, enabling you to search: by subject, by author, for case comments, for articles dealing with particular legislation, for book reviews.

When This Information is Useful

1) **As a first step in research:** Finding expert analysis on the particular issue you are researching can provide a valuable road map for research, saving time and making sure you don't miss key cases and legislation or ignore significant issues. Legal encyclopedias (covering comprehensively all topics in Canadian law) are available both in print and online, as are well-known treatises covering major areas of law; ICLL is the key to a wealth of commentary published each year on thousands of detailed topics in the form of articles published in legal periodicals.

2) **In preparing your legal argument:** ICLL can also be helpful towards the end of the research process after you have found the relevant cases and applicable legislation you wish to rely on. In both the print and online formats of ICLL, it is easy to look up a particular case or piece of legislation to find expert analysis in case comments and legislative annotations.

Using ICLL in Print

Components

Main Work: There are twelve hardcover volumes, which cover all materials indexed to the year 2000. There are five separate indexes set out through the volumes, each providing a different way to access the material. Most of the main work volumes are devoted to the Subject index, which is the largest and most comprehensive. Towards the end, you will see volumes dedicated to Author, Case, Legislation and Book Review indexes.

Annual Supplement: There is a single softcover supplement for each main work volume, current to the end of the previous year. These are replaced annually.

Update Issues: Updates to the annual supplement are published eight times per year in *Canadian Current Law — Canadian Legal Literature*.

How to Find Canadian Legal Literature

1) **Find the main work volume you need.**
2) **Update your search by consulting the annual supplement for the volume and any update issues:**

- All indexes organize their material alphabetically except for the legislation index which is organized by jurisdiction first, and then alphabetically within the jurisdiction.
- Cases are cross-referenced by the name of the defendant, enabling you to search for a case under the name of either party.
- Book reviews are entered under the title of the work reviewed, under the name of the author, and under the name of the reviewer.

Tip: If you want to find the most recent treatment of an issue, or if you are looking for a comment on a recently decided case or enacted statute, you should start with the supplement, which covers all materials indexed since 2000, rather than the main work.

Illustration 5.31: ICLL Subject Index Entry

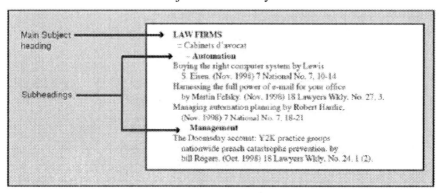

Illustration 5.32: ICLL Author Index Entry

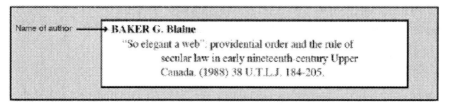

Illustration 5.33: Table of Cases Entry

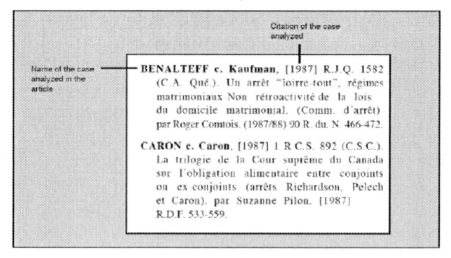

Illustration 5.34: Table of Statutes Entry

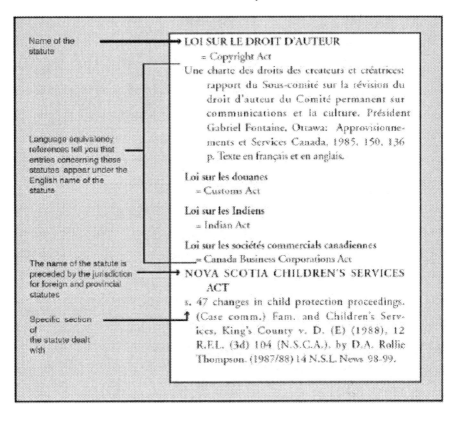

Illustration 5.35: Book Review Index Entries

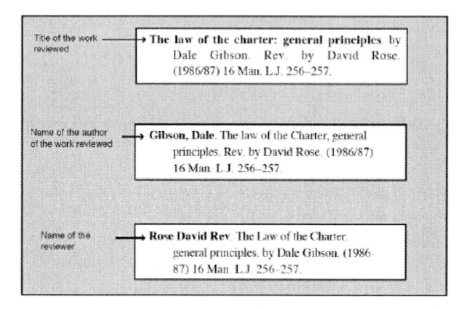

Title of the work reviewed → The law of the charter: general principles. by Dale Gibson. Rev. by David Rose. (1986/87) 16 Man. L.J. 256–257.

Name of the author of the work reviewed → Gibson, Dale. The law of the Charter, general principles. Rev. by David Rose. (1986/87) 16 Man. L.J. 256–257.

Name of the reviewer → Rose David Rev. The Law of the Charter, general principles. by Dale Gibson. (1986–87) 16 Man. L.J. 256–257.

Using ICLL on Westlaw Canada: LawSource

Accessible as part of **LawSource**, ICLL can be accessed by subject, author, case or statute, and results can be limited to exclude or include only book reviews. ICLL is also available as a database on LexisNexis Quicklaw.

Features available exclusively in Westlaw Canada's implementation include:

- **A link from the search template to a browseable and searchable Table of Subject Headings:** This is a valuable aid as ICLL does not have a Table of Contents; the Table of Subject Headings is heavily cross-referenced to help you find the headings under which the entries are organized [*See Illustration 5.36 below, Box A*].

- **A link to a Table of Periodicals Indexed:** This resource tells you what the abbreviations used in the citations to legal journals stand for [*See Illustration 5.36 below, Box A*].

- **ICLL entries that deal with a particular case appear among the KeyCite Canada citing references for the case:** This last feature is especially valuable as it means that even if you don't make an ICLL search a separate research step, the service will let you know, when you note-up any decision, if there is a case comment available that discusses it, either on the Westlaw service or in any other print or electronic resource.

How to Access Canadian Legal Literature on LawSource

Using the ICLL Custom Search Template

Access the Index to Canadian Legal Literature (ICLL) template [*See Illustration 5.36 below*] by linking from the **LawSource** home page.

Enter terms as prompted into the text and field boxes provided. The function served in print by having five separate indexes for different ways of accessing ICLL entries is served more economically online by the ability to enter terms in particular fields: [*See Illustration 5.36 below, Box B*]. Enter a name in the Case box to find case comments; enter a term in the **Legislation** box to find articles dealing with a particular act or regulation.

Use the pull-downs to restrict your results by document type and/or time frame, if desired [*See Illustration 5.36 below, Box C*].

Illustration 5.36: The ICLL Custom Search Template

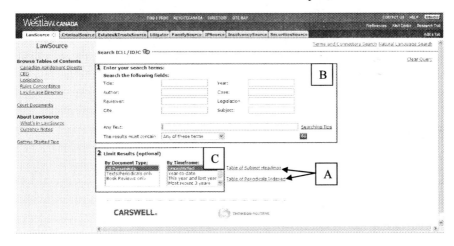

Accessing ICLL Results via KeyCite

To view a list of case comments that have been written on a particular decision:

Access the citing references for that decision [*See Illustration 5.18 above, Accessing KeyCite from the Full-text of a Decision*]. All case comments indexed in ICLL will appear among the Citing References under the **Secondary Sources (Canada)** heading [*See Illustration 5.37 below*].

Click the numbered link to the left of the ICLL result to be taken to the ICLL entry. If the full-text of a case comment is available on Westlaw, there will also be an entry among the citing references for the article itself, apart from the ICLL entry.

Illustration 5.37: Finding ICLL Entries Dealing with Your Particular Case

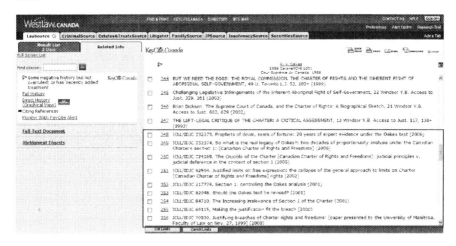

6

Books and Loose-leaf Services

The term "books" (sometimes called "texts" or "monographs") in law is an umbrella term for many different types of bound print volumes aimed at the differing needs of researchers and their various levels of sophistication. In contrast, loose-leaf services are not bound like books, but rather are binders containing "loose" sheets of paper which can be inserted or removed simply by opening the binder. These distinctions are important because books (in their bound form) are generally frozen in time[1] whereas loose-leaf services can be kept up-to-date by the publisher who (for a fee) sends new pages updating the volume(s) on a regular basis.

Books

Treatises

A treatise is an extensive, scholarly discussion of a specific area of law. Treatises provide an in-depth narrative and interpretation of the law. They are written by experts in the field (lawyers, judges, professors) and, as such, can be persuasive sources of secondary legal literature, depending on the author and the quality of the work. They are frequently cited or quoted in judicial decisions.

Treatises were traditionally available only in print; however, more and more are appearing online through fee-based subscription services such as LexisNexis Quicklaw and Westlaw Canada. In addition, more and more publishers are selling packages of electronic books to universities and colleges, and these are accessible through their library catalogues. Books that are out of copyright, or books for which the publisher has provided permission are freely available in full-text on the internet through Google Books. Limited previews (i.e., a limited number of pages to view) of newer books

---

[1] Some hardbound volumes are kept up to date with "pocket parts" — pockets are glued to the back inside cover of the book into which slim pamphlets can be kept which update the book. These pamphlets are replaced with updated versions by the publisher on a regular basis. Pocket part updates are used widely in the U.S. but are not as common in Canada.

are available in Google Books where the publisher or author have provided permission.

When is a Treatise Useful?

After you have consulted a legal encyclopedia to obtain a broad overview of your topic (assuming that you require such an overview), we recommend checking to see if there are any treatises on your subject area. Treatises will provide a more in-depth analysis of your subject than a legal encyclopedia. In addition, a treatise will direct you to many of the relevant cases and statutes on your subject and provide important commentary on these primary sources. Treatises will also alert you to any peculiarities of a certain area of law.

A treatise is, however, only a starting point. Never assume that the author of a treatise has cited all of the relevant case law on your subject. Generally, important cases will be discussed but it is highly unlikely that the author will have dealt with *all* cases dealing with the issue. Accordingly, there may be case law which is relevant to your research problem but is not cited in the treatise.

You should also always read the cases cited in a treatise. Never rely on one author's interpretation of a case without reading it yourself. Obviously, a similar caveat applies to any statutes that are mentioned.

You might begin by checking the list of treatises in the Selective Topical Bibliography provided in this book. Also, use a library catalogue to see if there is a treatise on your topic.

Casebooks

A casebook is distinguishable from a treatise in that casebooks are intended primarily for the classroom and the education of law students. They contain full cases or excerpts of cases in a given area of law. There may be some editorial commentary, but not a detailed interpretive guide to the law. As a result, they are not always adequate for legal research, but they may provide a brief overview of an area of law in the event that a treatise is not accessible. Casebooks are not considered authoritative by the courts and should not be cited as authority in documents such as Facta intended for the courts.

Introductory Texts and Textbooks

Law textbooks are generally one-volume legal works written primarily for law students and others requiring an introduction to a specific area of law. They are not as sophisticated or as in-depth as treatises; nonetheless, they contain an overview of the history of an area of law along with a good discussion of the law as it stands today. Law textbooks provide a black letter law overview (i.e., the general and accepted legal principles) of an area of law. Because they are not as sophisticated as treatises, they are not as authoritative, and are generally not cited in court decisions.

In the United States, such textbooks are referred to as "Hornbooks." Other publishers have used wording such as "Fundamentals" (Irwin Law),[2] "Black Letter" series (West), "Examples and Explanations" (Aspen), and "Understanding the Law" (LexisNexis) to signal to the reader that this is an introductory text.

Nutshells

Nutshells are shorter legal books which are intended to include only the most essential information on an area of law. They are often pocket size (i.e., smaller than regular books) and usually much shorter than a treatise. "Nutshell" usually appears in the title: *Admiralty in a Nutshell, Advanced Criminal Procedure In A Nutshell*, etc. The term "nutshell" is used primarily in the United States and England, but these types of books exist in Canada as well. Nutshells tend to avoid overly complicated language and refer to only the most important statutes and case law. The aim is to provide a speedy overview where there is no need (or perhaps no time) to consult a weighty treatise or textbook.

Practitioners' Guides

Practitioners' guides are written specifically for the practicing lawyer. These books often contain key legislation, procedural information, court forms, and other types of precedents. Many practitioners' guides come with a CD-ROM of forms and precedents.

Forms and Precedents

A large part of the practice of law has to do with the drafting of legal documents. This is discussed in greater detail below.

Loose-leaf Services

What is a Loose-leaf Service?

Loose-leaf services are published in binders so that new pages discussing up-to-date developments in the law can be inserted in appropriate locations regularly and old pages discussing obsolete law can be removed. These ser-

---

[2] It is now the case that some of the original "Fundamentals" are nearer to treatises than to introductory texts.

vices save the researcher a tremendous amount of time and effort updating the law.

There are four main types of loose-leaf services:

(a) legal encyclopedias and other works which summarize or analyze the law in a particular area (living texts);

(b) consolidated versions of statutes and regulations;

(c) annotated statutes; and

(d) court forms and precedents.

Loose-leaf services which are *living texts* may provide a broad overview of the law (e.g., the *Canadian Encyclopedic Digest*) or a detailed analysis and interpretive guide of a specific area of the law (e.g., *Environmental Regulation in Canada*). Many texts and treatises which were initially published in bound volumes are being reprinted in a loose-leaf form so that pages setting out recent developments in the law can be inserted without the necessity of waiting for another bound edition to come out.

Loose-leaf versions of statutes and regulations will save the researcher time in the updating process. Where a loose-leaf version of a statute exists, it will generally not be necessary to refer to the bound sessional volumes, nor will it be necessary to check all editions of the *Gazette*.

A loose-leaf version of a statute or regulation that is *annotated* will include commentary, citations, and/or summaries of the cases which have interpreted the provisions of the statute. Annotated statutes may save you having to check the *Canadian Statute Citations* portion of the *Canadian Abridgment*. However, the researcher should be aware that many annotated statutes do not cite all cases which have interpreted the provisions of the statute. Instead, some of the more important cases are selected under each section of the statute. Therefore, depending on the depth of your research, it may still be necessary to consult the *Canadian Statute Citations* resource.

The final category of loose-leaf service is a compilation of forms or precedents to assist in legal drafting. An example is *Williston & Rolls Court Forms* (Toronto: Butterworths) which is a four-volume set that contains the forms used at every stage of a civil action and offers detailed guidance in the preparation of these forms. The sequence and format of the material covered in this loose-leaf accords with the sequence and format of the *Rules of Civil Procedure*.

Other valuable loose-leafs exist which fall less neatly into the four categories outlined above. For instance, there are two excellent loose-leaf services on limitation periods, *Federal Limitation Periods* and *Ontario Limitation Periods* (Toronto: Butterworths), listing all limitation periods under federal and Ontario statutes, respectively. The limitation periods are listed according to both statute name and subject. These loose-leafs are time-savers, particularly when the researcher does not know under which statute the relevant limitation period falls.

How to Use a Loose-leaf Service

All loose-leaf services are different, so it is best to begin by reading the instructions in the first volume of the loose-leaf service (if there are multiple volumes) you are using at the time. When reading the instructions, there are two vital pieces of information you will want to obtain:

(a) how to access the information you need; and

(b) how to determine whether the information you have accessed is up-to-date.

Generally, you will be able to access the information you require by looking in the table of contents or index of the loose-leaf.

To determine to what extent the information you have accessed is current, check the date on the page you are reading (usually located at the bottom). The information will be accurate, at minimum, as of that date. The front page of the loose-leaf service may also indicate when the loose-leaf was last updated.

Some loose-leafs — usually those which summarize the law — have a section in the front or back entitled "Recent Developments". Often this section is denoted by pages of a different colour. Always check whether there have been any new developments in the law you are researching by checking under this section.

Generally, the titles or headings used in the main body of the loose-leaf will correspond to the titles used in the "Recent Developments" section. In this case, simply look for the title you are researching in the main body of the loose-leaf. If the title does not appear in the "Recent Developments" section, then there have been no new developments as of the date on which the loose-leaf was last updated.

Sometimes titles or headings are not used in the "Recent Developments" section. Instead, paragraph numbers which correspond to the paragraphs in the main body of the text will be used. Look for the paragraph numbers in the "Recent Developments" section which correspond with the paragraphs you are researching in the main body of the text. If the relevant paragraph numbers do not appear in the "Recent Developments" section, there have been no changes in the law as of the date on which the loose-leaf was last updated.

Forms and Precedents

In legal practice, a significant amount of work involves drafting legal documents such as contracts and court documents. By using forms and precedents, you can save time in drafting and you will be able to use information provided by a client more effectively. Some forms are legislated and have to be used in certain circumstances, for example, court forms. You need to learn how to find and use these forms; if you don't, you could jeopardize your client's case. Other forms, such as contracts, might use some "boiler plate" provisions (clauses that are used from contract to contract). Even so, where some clauses are standard, others will be a hybrid (boiler plate and original) and some clauses will be completely original in order to suit the specific needs of the client.

Remember that not all forms are connected with civil procedure *Rules* but with other legislation as well. For example, under the regulations of the *Condominium Act, 1998*, S.O. 1998, c. 19, there are forms that a practitioner is directed to use, depending on the matter.

In terms of finding forms and precedents, it's a good idea to get to know your courthouse library and academic law library. Knowing how to use their catalogues will help you find the resources you need. Also, keep in mind that where a precedent isn't available in print or online, it might be retrievable through a more informal source. Law firms, for example, often have their own in-house precedents (either in print or available through a database). Rather than re-inventing the wheel, make sure to check there.

The titles listed below are some of the resources which should be consulted for the form or precedent you require.

Print Products

O'Brien's Encyclopedia of Forms — This work is constantly updated. *O'Brien's* provides commonly used agreements, clauses, letters, memoranda, along with Ontario court forms. *O'Brien's* is available in print and electronically through Canada Law Book.

Canadian Forms & Precedents — LexisNexis provides a number of loose-leaf services in various areas of law, including information technology, intellectual property, licensing, sale and operation of a business, commercial tenancies, etc. These are also available on CD Rom (which comes with the print product) and via LexisNexis Quicklaw.

Williston and Rolls Court Forms — *Williston and Rolls* is a popular reference for court forms (they are based on Ontario court forms). A law firm, academic or courthouse library may have this resource in stock. *Williston and Rolls* is also available online from LexisNexis Quicklaw.

CLEs and Conference Material — Canadian law societies and bar associations provide continuing legal education for lawyers and students. Take advantage of these — often the documentation for a CLE or conference presentation will include a precedent which can be very helpful because the more traditional sources do not include every type of agreement. CLE and conference materials are still primarily available only in print. You will have to conduct a search in a library catalogue and on the respective Law Society or conference website in order to find these materials.

LexisNexis Quicklaw has a good finding tool for Canadian CLE and conference materials: the Canadian Law Symposia Index. You can find this source by clicking on the Source Directory tab and then searching for the Canadian Law Symposia Index. The index provides access to the titles of papers presented at various continuing legal education seminars since January of 1986.

One popular CLE resource is the *Law Society of Upper Canada: Annotated Document Series* which includes annotated forms, precedents and drafting tips. The series contains titles such as *The Annotated Retainer Agreement, Annotated Business Agreements, The Annotated Agreement of Purchase and Sale for Residential Property, The Annotated Will, The Annotated Share Purchase and Asset Purchase Agreement*, and so on. Once again, check a library catalogue to see if a law library near you has what you need in its collection or call the Law Society of Upper Canada which might have these available for sale.

Bar Examination Material — Bar examination material often has numerous precedents and these are available through bar associations in print or in electronic form (depending on the jurisdiction). Also, depending on the jurisdiction, these may be available through academic and other law libraries.

Monographs — Numerous monographs include sample forms and precedents. Make sure you look at a textbook or monograph in your particular topic area to see if it has any precedents.

Electronic Products

Online Court Forms — Most jurisdictions in Canada have their court forms online. The following is a list of websites which provide access to court forms:

The Practical Guide to Canadian Legal Research

Jurisdiction and Court	Website
Canada	
Supreme Court of Canada	\<http://www.scc-csc.gc.ca/ar-lr/for/2006/doc-eng.asp\>
Federal Court of Canada	\<http://cas-ncr-nter03.cas-satj.gc.ca/portal/page/portal/fc_cf_en/Forms\>
Alberta	\<http://www.albertacourts.ab.ca/default.aspx\>
British Columbia	\<http://www.bccls.bc.ca/cms/index.cfm?group_id=2652\>
Manitoba	\<http://web2.gov.mb.ca/laws/rules/forms_e.php\>
New Brunswick	\<http://www.gnb.ca/cour/04cqb/index-e.asp\>
Newfoundland	
Court of Appeal	\<http://www.court.nl.ca/supreme/appeal/forms.htm\>
Supreme Court — Trial Div.	\<http://www.court.nl.ca/supreme/trial/forms.htm\>
Provincial Court	\<http://www.court.nl.ca/provincial/forms.htm\>
Northwest Territories	\<http://www.justice.gov.nt.ca/legislation/legislation_Rules.shtml\>
Nova Scotia	\<http://gov.ns.ca/just/Court_Services/forms.asp\>
Nunavut	\<http://www.nucj.ca/rules.htm\>
Ontario	\<http://www.ontariocourtforms.on.ca\>
Prince Edward Island	\<http://www.gov.pe.ca/courts/supreme/index.php3\>
Supreme Court	\<http://www.gov.pe.ca/courts/provincial/index.php3\>
Provincial Court	
Quebec	\<http://www.justice.gouv.qc.ca/English/formulaires/formulaires-a.htm\>
Saskatchewan	
Court of Appeal	\<http://www.sasklawcourts.ca/default.asp?pg=ca_rules_forms\>
Queens Bench	\<http://www.qp.gov.sk.ca/documents/English/Rules/qbforms.pdf\>
Yukon	
Court of Appeal	\<http://www.yukoncourts.ca/courts/appeal/rules.html\>
Supreme Court	\<http://www.yukoncourts.ca/courts/supreme/rules.html\>

O'Brien's Encyclopedia of Forms — available online through Canada Law Book. This is one of the most used forms resources in Canada.

LexisNexis Quicklaw — LexisNexis Quicklaw has a Forms and Precedents tab for customers who purchase this resource. The material available through this tab includes many of the forms and precedents available in print products, including *Canadian Forms and Precedents* discussed above. See Illustration 6.1 for a sample of this product on LexisNexis Quicklaw.

Illustration 6.1

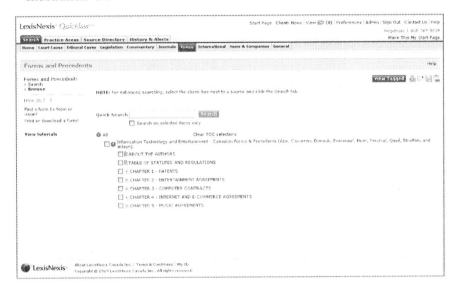

Reprinted with the permission of LexisNexis Canada Inc. LexisNexis is a registered trademark of Reed Elsevier Properties Inc., used under licence. Quicklaw is a trademark of LexisNexis Canada Inc.

Westlaw Canada (formerly Westlaw*e*Carwell) — In Westlaw Canada, there is no one source to find all forms and precedents; you will have to look under each Source tab to find it. For example, in the InsolvencySource tab, there is a link to *Houlden and Morawetz Bankruptcy and Insolvency Precedents* (left hand side of page). But in the FamilySource tab, you have to look under each commentary title to see if there are forms and precedents.

Litigator on Westlaw Canada — The *Litigator* component of Westlaw Canada provides access to thousands of court documents (motion materials, facta, pleadings, etc.). See Illustration 6.2 for an example of Litigator.

Illustration 6.2

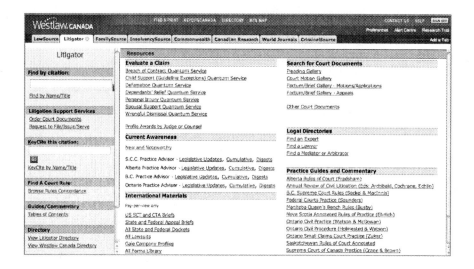

Precedents are taken from the court material filed in connection with cases reported in various Carswell reporters, including *Canadian Cases on Pensions and Benefits, Canadian Environmental Law Reports, Construction Law Reports, Dimock Stratton Intellectual Property Law Newsletter, Estates & Trusts Reports, Municipal & Planning Law Reports, Business Law Reports, Real Property Reports, Canadian Cases on the Law of Torts, Canadian Cases on the Law of Insurance, Canadian Cases on Employment Law* and *Carswell Practice Cases.*

7

Legal Dictionaries/Words and Phrases

What are Legal Dictionaries? What are Words and Phrases?

Legal dictionaries are, as their name suggests, dictionaries that define legal terminology. For the purpose of this book, we have a more expansive definition of legal dictionary. We include in the definition of dictionary various tools available for interpreting words and phrases, since they serve the same conceptual purpose. Words and Phrases resources tell you how the courts define or interpret a word or phrase and provide citations of cases that have interpreted the word or phrase in question.

Dictionaries or Words and Phrases?

Legal dictionaries and Words and Phrases are used for two main reasons:

1. when you need to know the meaning of a legal word or term; or
2. when you need to know how a specific word or phrase has been interpreted judicially.

The difference between these can best be demonstrated by examples. An example of a "legal" word is "laches". It refers to the doctrine under which a person can lose his or her legal rights if he or she delays in enforcing them. A source that actually has the label "legal dictionary" should be consulted for this definition if you don't know what it means.

An example of a word for which you might need an interpretation is "highway". The layperson's understanding of this word is fairly straightforward, but it has also been the subject of judicial and statutory consideration. A legal dictionary will be useful here, but even more important will be the various Words and Phrases tools available.

A Words and Phrases resource will provide you with references to cases that have considered the meaning and scope of the term "highway", whether it includes a parking lot, bridge, or tunnel, and whether the definition includes a road on which the public does not have the right to travel. It will also tell you if the "highway" extends beyond the paved surface to ditches and fences, and whether it also can be used to describe smaller roads, lanes, or paths. These are all matters which judges have considered when trying to work out what a highway is. Such detail will not be found in a dictionary. In addition, some of this case law could be binding and therefore crucial to your research.

Dictionaries[1]

Canadian Law Dictionary, 6th ed., John A. Yogis and Catherine Cotter (Hauppauge, NY: Barron's Educational Series, 2009).

The alphabetical list of words and phrases in this dictionary is supplemented with information drawn from relevant source materials, particularly cases and statutes. The work also provides information on the Canadian court system, legal citation, and abbreviations. Some human rights legislation appears in the Appendix, as well as a reproduction of the *Canadian Charter of Rights and Freedoms*.

The Dictionary of Canadian Law, 3rd ed., Daphne Dukelow (Toronto: Carswell, 2004).

This dictionary is compiled solely from Canadian legal sources. It contains over 30,000 legal definitions and expressions found in case law, legislation, and secondary sources. It also defines Latin terms and maxims. It is the only comprehensive Canadian legal dictionary.

Black's Law Dictionary, 9th ed., Bryan A. Garner, ed. (St. Paul, MN: Thomson Reuters, 2009). Also available on Westlaw Canada (database: BLACKS).

Black's Law Dictionary is an American law dictionary; it is, however, widely used in Canadian jurisprudence. The 9th edition contains approximately 43,000 definitions, 3,000 quotations, and synonyms or equivalent terms for over 5,000 words (serving in part as a thesaurus). It also defines over 1,000 abbreviations and acronyms. The dictionary uses West Key Numbers which allows readers to move from the dictionary to any West product to find related cases.

Words and Phrases

Canadian Abridgment (Scarborough, ON: Carswell, n.d.).

The *Abridgment* has eight Words and Phrases volumes which list various words and phrases that have been judicially considered, as well as the cases

---

[1] More titles of dictionaries are available in the chapters dealing with American, English, Australian and New Zealand legal research.

in which they were considered. These volumes are updated by eight softcover supplements which correspond to the main volumes. The set also exists online via Westlaw Canada. For more detail on how to use the *Abridgment* Words and Phrases service, see the Words and Phrases section in the *Abridgment* chapter.

Sanagan's Encyclopedia of Words and Phrases, Legal Maxims, 5th ed., loose-leaf, John D. Gardner and Karen M. Gardner, eds. (Carswell, 2008-).

Sanagan's provides an alphabetical listing of words and phrases interpreted by judges in Canadian court cases. Summaries of judicial comments and ratios of the cases in which the words and phrases have been defined are also provided along with legal maxims. This product is available in print and online as part of the Carswell eReference Library.

Carswell Topical Report Services.

The cumulative indexes, as well as the indexes to each volume of the Carswell Topical Reports Services, contain words and phrases with a listing of cases that have considered the meaning of a given word or phrase. See, for example, the *Business Law Reports* or the *Reports of Family Law*.

Stroud's Judicial Dictionary of Words and Phrases, 7th ed., loose-leaf, Daniel Greenberg (London: United Kingdom, 2006).

This is a U.K work which was first published in 1890. It not only contains definitions from the U.K. and other commonwealth sources, but also prides itself on defining and setting out the history of both common and obscure legal terms and expressions in case law and in legislation.

Canadian Legal Words and Phrases (LexisNexis Quicklaw).

This source provides over 13,000 words and phrases as interpreted by Canadian courts and tribunals since 2000.

8

Legal Periodicals

What are Periodicals?

A periodical is a publication that is produced at regular intervals. Legal journals, along with publications such as legal magazines, newspapers, and newsletters, provide timely and practical information to the reader.

Legal journals publish articles, case comments, and book reviews on various areas of the law. There are two types of legal journals: (a) general, which publish articles on all areas of law; and (b) topical, which publish articles on specific areas of the law only.

In Canada, academic institutions, commercial publishers, or associations such as the Canadian Bar Association generally publish legal journals. Articles published in academic journals tend to be written by professors or law students and often provide a deeper scholarly and theoretical analysis of legal issues. Commercial and Bar Association journals tend to be focused on more practical discussions of the law and its development. Journals can be persuasive sources of secondary legal literature depending on the thoroughness and quality of the author's analysis, and the reputation of the law journal itself.

Legal magazines and newspapers provide practical information for readers. Often, articles in such publications are not scholarly but instead aim to be short, functional, and offer useful advice for the practicing lawyer. Such articles are an excellent way for lawyers to stay current on what is happening in the legal profession and in various legal fields.

Newsletters also can be useful for researchers. Many publishers produce newsletters, as well as associations and law firms. Articles in newsletters focus primarily on practical aspects of legal practice and are not usually of an academic nature.

When are Periodicals Useful?

Periodicals are particularly useful when you are researching an area of law you have not previously studied, a new field of law, or a field that has just undergone changes or developments. Periodicals are published more frequently than treatises, and thus often provide more current information. Periodical articles also tend to be more focused than treatises. A treatise, for instance, may provide an overview of the entire law of contracts; a journal article, on the other hand, will likely focus on a discrete area of contract law. For this reason, if you are unfamiliar with the area of law, we recommend first looking at a legal encyclopedia or treatise to get an overview and then consulting periodical articles in order to narrow your focus.

Since publishing a periodical is usually less costly than publishing a treatise, topics that are narrow in scope will be more likely published in a journal. Periodicals, especially journals, often provide references to relevant primary materials, as well as to other useful secondary sources. This is an efficient way to begin your research — by reading an article on your topic in a legal journal, you could discover many other useful resources. You should not rely solely on the references made in a journal article or other periodical, especially if you are not certain where your research should go next.

Another valuable feature of periodicals is that there are more periodicals available in full-text online than there are treatises. This means periodicals are easier and quicker to access and therefore have become a preferred manner by which to obtain information.

Case comments of significant decisions are also useful as they show how a decision has affected the law and, therefore, often contain an overview of the law on the topic. It is a good idea to look for case comments once you have found the relevant case law on your topic. You will tend to find case comments on decisions that are contentious or have made a significant contribution to the law.

Never assume that an article or case comment has cited all of the relevant law on your topic and always read the case law for yourself to ensure that your interpretation corresponds with the author's. In addition, the researcher should be aware that articles are often written from a certain political or theoretical perspective such as torts through a law and economics lens or property law via a feminist perspective.

Print Versus Online

For most of their existence, periodicals were only available in print format. Since the proliferation of the internet, however, many legal periodicals have become available online, making it easier and faster to find periodicals on the topic at issue.

Online full-text legal periodicals are typically available in two ways — freely available on the internet or available within a for-fee database. Legal periodicals which are freely available online obviously do not require payment for access and anyone with an internet connection can access the documents; however, the vast majority of legal periodicals available online are housed within for-fee databases, especially law journals. Unless you are associated with a business, organization, or library that subscribes to for-fee databases, these legal periodicals may be difficult to obtain. For example, a law professor may have access to such databases as *HeinOnline* and *Legal-Trac*,[1] but it is atypical that a lawyer working at a small firm would have access to such tools.

Along with periodicals available in full-text online, many periodical indexes are also available on the internet, either freely available or in subscription-based databases.

Several factors must be kept in mind when searching for legal periodicals and in periodical indexes electronically. When searching for full-text journals, unless your search strategy is finely tuned, your search may give you too many results or hits, making it difficult to determine which articles in your results list are germane to your issue. This is when the research skills of the searcher can make a difference in the results of a search. As well, if you are using a for-fee database to search for full-text articles, it will cost money each time you conduct your searches. If they are not effective, you will incur high search fees for few results. This is not efficient or cost-effective. Finally, researchers must keep in mind that many legal periodicals available electronically do not go back very far, limiting how much information you may find.

Periodical Indexes

A periodical index is a list, often by title, subject and author, of articles in journals, newsletters and other similar sources. Periodical indexes facilitate quick access to journal articles, case comments, book reviews, newspapers, magazines, and newsletters. In the print versions, there are different volumes for different years. Materials are generally indexed as follows: articles according to subject; articles according to author; case comments according to case name; case comments according to subject; and book reviews according to author and/or title of the book.

Many periodical indexes are now available online in subscription databases and have overtaken their print versions as the most favoured way to find articles. If you have access to such indexes, they can be very helpful for your research. Experienced researchers usually begin their search for

---

[1] These databases will be discussed later in this chapter.

journal articles with a journal index. This is because indexes categorize articles by subject and allow you to quickly determine what has been written on a topic. Indexes also tend to cover a wider spectrum of periodicals than full-text sources.

When searching electronic periodical indexes, you must keep in mind some of their drawbacks. Most periodical indexes in print index articles much further back than electronic periodical indexes; for example, the *Index to Foreign Legal Periodicals* indexes journal articles back to 1960 in print, but online only back to 1985. This limits the information a researcher will find. Although many researchers want to find newer journal articles, many older articles will be relevant to the issue at hand. Indeed, missing an older article could be detrimental to your research. As well, some indexes may not search by subject headings but only author, title, and citation. This can make it difficult to find relevant materials, as some article titles are rather esoteric and not indicative of the subject matter. In print indexes, you can find articles by subject headings, which makes it easier to find several articles that deal with the same matter in law.

There are several legal periodical indexes available for use in print and electronic formats; the indexes listed below are the ones that are most commonly used in Canada:

1. *Canadian Abridgment: Index to Canadian Legal Literature*;

2. *LegalTrac*;

3. *Index to Legal Periodicals Full Text*;

4. *Index to Legal Periodicals Retrospective*;

5. *Index to Canadian Legal Periodical Literature*;

6. *Current Law Index*;

7. *AGIS Plus Text*;

8. *Index to Foreign Legal Periodicals*; and

9. *Index to Periodical Articles Related to Law*.

Each of these indexes is discussed below:

• *Canadian Abridgment: Index to Canadian Legal Literature* is a broad index in that it does not restrict itself to indexing journals. In addition to journals, the following forms of secondary legal literature are indexed: treatises, academic publications (casebooks, theses), essays from edited collections, government publications, law society and bar association publications, continuing legal education materials, audiovisual materials, and legal newspapers and newsletters. This index is

Legal Periodicals

available in print and it is also available electronically through both Westlaw Canada and LexisNexis Quicklaw. This resource indexes materials from approximately 1985 onwards.[2] See Illustration 8.1 for an example of using the *Index to Canadian Legal Literature* using Westlaw Canada.

Illustration 8.1

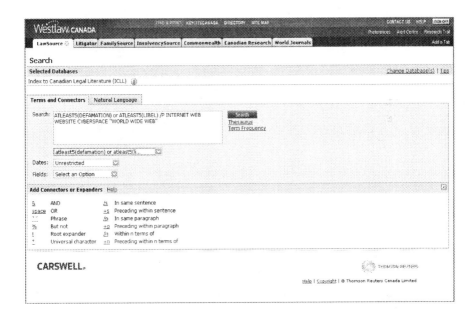

- *LegalTrac* is a comprehensive index which catalogues more than 1,500 law reviews and journals, newspapers, and specialty publications from as far back as 1980; more than 200 titles in *LegalTrac* are available in full-text. *LegalTrac* focuses mostly on American publications, but journals from Canada and other countries are indexed as well. This index is available electronically through *Gale Cengage*.

- *Index to Legal Periodicals Full Text* covers over 1,000 legal journals, reviews, yearbooks, government documents, and other specialty publications from Canada, the United States, England, Ireland, Australia, and New Zealand. Of these, over 325 publications are available in full-text, either in full or in part. Approximately 1,400 monographs are in-

---

[2] For more information on the *Index to Canadian Legal Literature*, see Chapter 5 on the *Canadian Abridgment*.

dexed every year. In some instances, coverage goes back to 1982. This index is available electronically through *H.W. Wilson.*

- *Index to Legal Periodicals Retrospective* indexes over 800 legal periodicals of all kinds from several countries, including Canada, the United States, England, Ireland, Australia, and New Zealand. This historical index allows the researcher to search for articles published between 1908 and 1981. It is available electronically through *H.W. Wilson.*

- *Index to Canadian Legal Periodical Literature*, which is no longer published, indexed Canadian legal literature from 1961 until 2005. It includes selective indexing of articles, case comments and book reviews published in Canada and considered to have legal significance. This product is only available in print. It is less comprehensive than the *Index to Canadian Legal Literature* but since it indexes materials from 1961, it is a useful resource to find historical Canadian materials.

- *Current Law Index* covers over 900 periodicals published in the Commonwealth and the United States. Specialty journals treating subjects such as criminology and accounting are also indexed. The electronic version of the *Current Law Index* is called *LegalTrac*, which is described above.

- *AGIS Plus Text* indexes over 400 periodicals from Australia, New Zealand, and other Pacific nations; a select number of Canadian, American, and British journals are also indexed. Several of the periodicals are available in full-text. Indexing begins in 1975. *AGIS Plus Text* is available electronically through *Informit.* See Illustration 8.2.

Legal Periodicals

Illustration 8.2

Reproduced with permission from RMIT Publishing/Informit.

- *Index to Foreign Legal Periodicals* covers articles dealing with international and comparative law in addition to the law of common law countries excluding Canada, the United Kingdom, the United States and Australia. Over 450 periodicals are indexed. This is available in print and electronically through *Ovid Technologies* (online, periodicals are indexed only from 1985; the *Index to Foreign Legal Periodicals* in print goes back to 1960).

- *Index to Periodical Articles Related to Law* covers articles published since 1958 throughout the English-speaking world on social science, scientific, and medical topics with legal dimensions. This index *does not* cover law journals or any periodicals that are directly law-related, with the exception of newer periodicals not yet indexed elsewhere. This index is available in print and electronically through *HeinOnline*.

While each index will catalogue several hundred periodicals, no one index covers the entire legal field. The wise researcher will always use more than one index as she will never find all the commentary on a subject using only one research tool.

Full-text Periodicals

Many journals are now available electronically in full-text. Whether in a for-fee database or on their own website, journal articles available in full-text are a favoured resource for researchers.

The following are some common full-text periodical databases:

1. *HeinOnline*;
2. Westlaw Canada;
3. LexisNexis Quicklaw;
4. *Legal Scholarship Network; and*
5. *JSTOR.*

These are discussed below.

- *HeinOnline* is a full-text database that includes over 1,100 legal and law-related periodicals from Canada, the United States, and several other countries. The articles are available for download in PDF. Most of the periodicals available on *HeinOnline* go back to the first volume in the series; this means that a researcher can find articles from as far back as the late 1800s in full-text. See Illustration 8.3.

Illustration 8.3

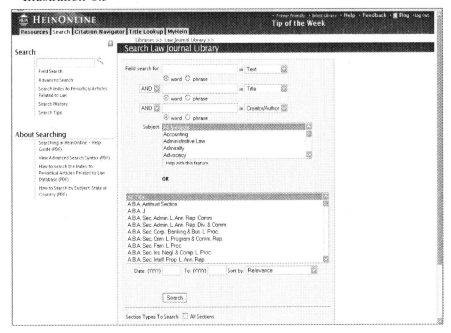

Reproduced with permission from William S. Hein & Co., Inc.

- Westlaw Canada is an enormous research database that allows researchers to find case law and legislation, as well as journals and other periodicals. There are several databases within Westlaw Canada which house full-text periodicals (only a few databases are mentioned here; see Westlaw Canada for more information on other full-text periodical databases): CANADA-JLR (full-text articles from many major Canadian journals; most only go back to the mid-to-late 1990s); WORLD-JLR (this is the most comprehensive Westlaw journal database containing journals and law reviews from many countries around the world); JLR (American law reviews, journals, and continuing legal education materials); TP-ALL (full-text accessibility to all law reviews, texts, bar journals, and continuing legal education materials); TP-CANADA (full-text accessibility to legal texts, journals, reviews, and articles in case law reporters for many legal periodicals published in Canada); CLRA-ALL (full-text access to articles and case comments which appear in numerous Carswell case law reporters). See Illustration 8.4.

Illustration 8.4

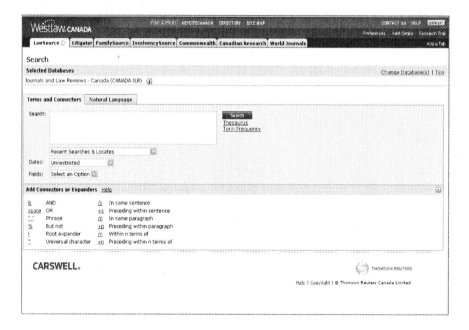

- LexisNexis Quicklaw is another large research database that allows researchers to find case law and legislation, as well as journals and other periodicals. There are several databases within LexisNexis Quicklaw which house full-text periodicals (only a few databases are mentioned here; see LexisNexis Quicklaw for more information on other full-text periodical databases): ALL CANADIAN LEGAL JOURNALS (full-text of all Canadian legal journals available in LexisNexis Quicklaw from 1980 onwards); ALL COMMENTARY (full-text of Canadian legal journals, newsletters, netletters, and treatises available within LexisNexis Quicklaw); CANADIAN LAW JOURNALS, COMBINED (full-text accessibility to Canadian university law journals); COMBINED CANADIAN LAW REVIEWS (full-text accessibility to documents of interest to academics and students); U.S. & CANADIAN LAW REVIEWS COMBINED (full-text access to several Canadian and American law reviews); U.K. LAW JOURNALS (full-text access to several U.K. legal periodicals); ABA JOURNALS COMBINED (full-text access to several American Bar Association Journals); BAR JOURNALS COMBINED (full-text access to several American bar journals); U.S. LAW REVIEWS AND JOURNALS, COMBINED (full-text access to hundreds of American law journals and reviews); AUSTRALIAN LAW JOURNALS, COMBINED (full-text access to several Australian law journals). See Illustration 8.5 for an example of the LexisNexis Quicklaw journals search screen.

Illustration 8.5

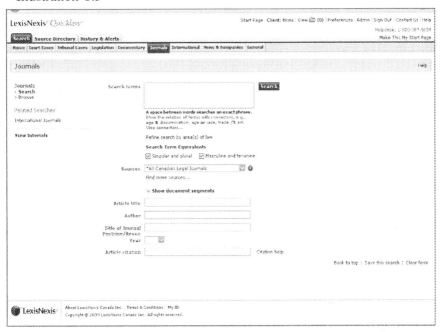

Reprinted with the permission of LexisNexis Canada Inc. LexisNexis is a registered trademark of Reed Elsevier Properties Inc., used under licence. Quicklaw is a trademark of LexisNexis Canada Inc.

- *Legal Scholarship Network* (LSN) provides full-text access to research papers written by legal and other scholars; the papers are not necessarily published in journals or reviews, but are academic papers that are of interest to legal researchers. In order to access some papers in LSN, researchers or their institutions must have a subscription with the *Social Sciences Research Network*. A subscriber has the option of having a weekly email sent with a listing of new papers released that week in particular areas of interest. The papers are searchable in a database.
- *JSTOR* is not a purely legal database. It is a database that archives full-text academic journals from many different disciplines, including law. This is a good resource to use if you need to find historical articles.

Again, keep in mind that the wise researcher will always search more than one database as you will never find all the commentary on a subject using only one journal database.

Periodical Lists and Other Tools

Along with indexes and full-text databases, you can consult a table of contents resource to assist you in finding additional legal information. This type of resource allows a researcher to see what the tables of contents are in particular journals. One popular table of contents resource is the *Tarlton Law Library Contents Pages from Law Reviews and Other Scholarly Journals* (http://tarlton.law.utexas.edu/tallons/content_search.html). With this service, you can view the table of contents from over 750 law journals over the last three months. Another table of contents service, which also acts as an index, is *Washington & Lee Law School Current Law Journal Content* (http://lawlib.wlu.edu/CLJC/index.aspx).

A current awareness service is another helpful tool. One of the most popular is the *Current Index to Legal Periodicals* (CILP). A weekly list of newly-published articles from over 570 journals is generated and indexed by topic. Subscribers can arrange for a personalized email to be sent to them periodically containing a list of articles on legal topics of interest. For more information, consult the Marion Gould Gallagher Law Library at the University of Washington School of Law: (http://lib.law.washington.edu/cilp/cilp.html). CILP is also available in Westlaw Canada.

There are many law firms that publish newsletters on different issues. These can be very informative, although not scholarly in nature. These newsletters, traditionally, have been difficult to find as they are not routinely indexed in a periodical index, but there are now new ways to search for them. The *FeeFieFoeFirm* search engine, for example, allows a researcher to search for newsletters from numerous law firms in Canada (http://www.feefiefoefirm.com/ca/). Ted Tjaden created a Google™ custom search engine to search exclusively for Canadian law firm and law journal websites along with Canadian law blogs (http://www.google.com/coop/cse?cx=013523832710591119429%3Ac59xpqf_uh8). Other search engines that will search for law firm documents are *LinexLegal* (http://www.linexlegal. com/) and *Lexology* (http://www.lexology.com/).

How to Find Periodical Articles Electronically and in Print

Electronically — Using Indexes and Full-text Journal Databases

1. Make sure the database is appropriate for what you are searching. You should determine if the index or database you want to use will provide you with the information you are looking for — if you want articles from a certain time period but the database you are using does not provide access to periodicals from that time, it is not a database you should use. Most online

indexes and databases will provide a list of which periodicals are included in their system.

2. Identify the various Boolean and proximity connectors the database employs. Each one will use different connectors, and it is important to know how they differ from one another. This is particularly important for full-text databases, as the words you use could be totally unrelated if you do not use correct connectors.

3. Before beginning your search, take a few minutes to plan your search strategy: what words will you use; what connectors will you employ; what date range do you want to use; do you want to search by title, subject heading, entire full-text of the journal, or in some other field? You should also determine the costs that will be associated with your search — if the costs will be high, you will want to ensure that your search is as efficient as possible.

4. Begin your search by using an appropriate search string in your index or database search function. When searching an index, you will be provided with a citation to the article, including the title, author, journal name, volume number, and page number for each item listed in your results. Some indexes provide a list of subject headings or an abstract, which makes it easier to determine if the article in question is relevant. If you are using a full-text database, review the list of results to determine which articles are on point.

5. After determining which articles or citations are relevant, download them and, if desired, print them off.

6. If you used a periodical index, use the citations you found to look up the articles either in a print version of the journal or an electronic version. If you do not have access to a journal in print or electronically, you will need to make an interlibrary loan request through your library.

In Print

1. Refer to the appropriate volume(s) in the print periodical index(es) to which you have access. Some indexes publish their volumes by year, others publish them by subject; if the index you are using publish by year, you will need to look at more than one year in order to find all the appropriate literature on your topic.

2. Skim through the section on subject headings, which you will find at the beginning of each volume. Review the headings carefully, as an article may not always be indexed under the heading that appears most obvious to you.

3. Refer to the appropriate subject headings where you will find a list of articles with citations. Jot down the citation information for any citations which appear relevant.

4. The citation of the journal will be an abbreviation. If you do not understand what the abbreviation means, refer to the front of the index where you will find a list of all the journals covered in the volume with their abbreviations.

5. Using the citation you can find the article either electronically or in print.

How to Find Case Comments Electronically and in Print

When You Know the Case Name — Electronically

1. Determine which index or database you wish to use to find a case comment.

2. In the title, subject heading, or keyword field, enter the name of the case. You may wish to narrow the years searched to the year of the case and the year after — most case comments are written shortly after a case is decided.

3. Review the results of your search. If searching an index, write down or download the citation information. If searching a full-text database, download the article.

4. If using an index, use the citation information to find the article in full-text either in print or electronically. If you do not have access to the article either in print or electronically, you will need to make an interlibrary loan application through your library.

When You Know the Case Name — in Print

1. Refer to the appropriate volume(s) in the periodical index(es) to which you have access. Some indexes publish their volumes by year, others publish them by subject; if the index you are using publishes by year, refer to the volume from the year in which the case was decided and the year after the case was decided. Most case comments are written shortly after a case is decided.

2. Look up the case name in the table of cases. If a case comment has been published, you will find it listed here with a citation.

3. Use the citation information to find the article in print or electronic format.

When You Know the Subject but Not the Case Name — Electronically

1. Determine which index and/or database you wish to use to find a case comment.

2. In the keyword or subject heading field, enter the subject matter of the case. You may wish to narrow the years searched to the year of the case and the year after — most case comments are written shortly after a case is decided. You may also want to include the words "case comment" in a keyword field; some indexes will indicate in the citation whether the article in question is a case comment.

3. Review the results of your search. If searching in an index, write down or download the citation information. If searching in a full-text database, download the article.

4. If using an index, use the citation information to find the article in full-text either in print or electronically. If you do not have access to the article either in print or electronically, you will need to make an interlibrary loan application through your library.

When You Know the Subject but Not the Case Name — in Print

1. Refer to the appropriate volume(s) in the periodical index(es) to which you have access. If the index(es) you use publish by year, you will likely need to review the volumes for the year of and the year after the decision (most case comments are written shortly after the case is decided).

2. Skim through the section on subject headings, which you will find at the beginning of each volume. Review the headings carefully, as a case comment may not always be indexed under the heading that appears most obvious to you.

3. Refer to the appropriate subject headings. If there has been a case comment, it will be listed after the articles on the subject.

4. Use the citation information to find the article in print or electronic format.

Commentary on Supreme Court of Canada Decisions

When your research involves a topic where there has been Supreme Court of Canada jurisprudence, it is a good idea to check if there has been a case comment or article on point. The *Supreme Court Law Review* is a particularly useful periodical. It is an annual publication of articles on developments in various areas of law as a result of recent Supreme Court of Canada jurisprudence. The areas of law covered are: administrative law; constitutional law; criminal law and procedure; contracts and torts; droit civil; evidence; employment; property; and leave to appeal applications: (i) criminal, (ii) civil, and (iii) administrative. This journal is not currently available electronically, but it is indexed in several electronic and print periodical indexes.

Determining Which Database Holds Which Periodicals in Full-text

When searching for full-text journals, one of the most frustrating experiences is going to a particular database and then realizing it does not have the journal for which you are searching. Along with looking at the content list provided by the database vendor, there are a few online resources you can use to determine where a particular journal appears in full-text. One is the *Bora Laskin Journals Database*, which is a database of law journals available electronically and at the Bora Laskin Law Library at the University of Toronto (http://www.law-lib.utoronto.ca/journals/search.asp). A similar database is available from the Sir James Dunn Law Library at Dalhousie University's Faculty of Law (http://www.library.dal.ca/Law/Journals/). Please note that these resources are not complete and may not be updated regularly; if there are changes in the holdings of legal research systems such as LexisNexis Quicklaw, Westlaw Canada, *HeinOnline*, etc., the information in the Bora Laskin Database or Dalhousie Database may be inaccurate.

9

Continuing Legal Education Materials

What are Continuing Legal Education Materials?

A number of organizations offer Continuing Legal Education (CLE) conferences and seminars for members of the legal profession and its various offshoots. These conferences generally include written material that summarize and supplement each speaker's presentations.

When are CLE Conference and Seminar Materials Useful?

Papers from CLE conferences and seminars, like journal articles, may save the researcher time by providing a summary of the law in a specific area or on a particular topic. Conference and seminar materials tend to have a very practical focus given that their purpose is to educate and update practicing lawyers. Because CLE materials tend to highlight recent developments in the law and their implications for lawyers and their clients, you will often find recent seminar materials to be more up-to-date than journal articles due to the publication lag with respect to journals.

Most Canadian law societies encourage their members to participate in CLE activities and some law societies have or are considering mandatory professional development requirements for their members.[1]

There is a wide range in the quality and usefulness of CLE materials. At one end of the spectrum, a CLE paper may provide the same quality and depth of analysis as a journal article. At the other end, the printed materials from a CLE seminar may simply be a printout of the presenter's slides which, while short on analysis, may still be useful as they could contain references to case law and legislation.

---

[1] The Law Society of Upper Canada will require 12 hours of professional development annually for all practising lawyers. This recommendation is expected to be in force in 2011. See: http://www.lsuc.on.ca/media/factsht_cpd_feb2010.pdf.

When you refer to CLE materials, the usual caveat respecting the use of secondary sources applies — you should verify and update any references to statutes or cases.

How to Find Conference and Seminar Materials

Websites

The various organizations that offer CLE seminars and conferences usually list recent and upcoming seminars on their websites. The Federation of Canadian Law Societies maintains a useful list of each law society's CLE website.[2] CLE websites typically include lists of upcoming programs as well as the option to purchase materials from previous programs. Two excellent examples of CLE materials websites that organize past CLE materials by topic are the Law Society of Upper Canada's AccessCLE website[3], and the website of the Continuing Legal Education Society of British Columbia.[4] Many provincial law society libraries and CLE organizations provide useful indexes of CLE conferences in their jurisdiction.

In addition to the provincial law societies, lawyer's associations, academic institutions and private companies also offer CLE seminars. The Great Library at the Law Society of Upper Canada provides a list of the major CLE providers at the bottom of its online CLE Calendar.[5]

Indexes

Canadian Law Symposia Index

The Canadian Law Symposia Index (CLSI) available on LexisNexis Quicklaw provides a national index to CLE materials since January 1986. The index is updated quarterly. The CLSI is a useful tool that allows the researcher to search for individual papers or presentations by author, title or subject. This index is little known outside the circle of Canadian law librarians and thanks to its use of subject headings, it is an excellent way to discover otherwise hard-to-find information about a paper from a recent seminar. Once you find a reference to a paper, you will need to consult a library[6] or the conference organizers to obtain a copy of the conference materials.

---

2 http://www.flsc.ca/en/lawSocieties/cleLinks.asp.

3 http://ecom.lsuc.on.ca/home/accesscle.jsp.

4 http://online.cle.bc.ca/CourseMaterialsDefault.aspx.

5 http://rc.lsuc.on.ca/library/services_cle_current.htm.

6 Most law firm libraries collect materials from conferences that the firm's lawyers have attended. CLE materials are also often available at law society and courthouse libraries.

On LexisNexis Quicklaw the CLSI can be accessed by going to the "Source Directory" and choosing "Legal Indices and Tables."

Index to Canadian Legal Literature

Some seminar and conference materials are also indexed under subject headings in the *Canadian Abridgment's Index to Canadian Legal Literature*.[7]

---

[7] See Chapter 5 on the *Canadian Abridgment* on how to use this research tool.

10

Law Reform Commission Reports

What are Law Reform Commission Reports?

Law reform commissions are independent legal think-tanks that study and publish reports on legal reform. The reports typically begin by outlining what the law is on a given topic (for instance, the law on drug and alcohol testing in the workplace). Next, they demonstrate why the law or procedure being studied should be reformed. Finally, they make concrete recommendations to government on how the law could be reformed. In developing these recommendations, they often examine the laws and/or procedures of other jurisdictions.

Law reform commission reports are regarded as highly persuasive secondary authorities. They are frequently quoted in judicial decisions and often form the basis of legislative reform.

The federal Law Reform Commission of Canada was discontinued in 1993 but was reinstated in 1997 as the Law Commission of Canada; it was then discontinued a second time in 2006. Many provinces in Canada have their own law reform commissions, although they have been at times discontinued and reinstated. This highlights the complex relationship law commissions have with governments — while law commissions are independent bodies, they are highly dependent on government funding and political will.

When are Law Reform Commission Reports Useful?

Law reform commission reports can be used to obtain an overview of selected legal and procedural topics, since they outline what the law is, before discussing suggested reforms. Like periodicals, law reform commission reports are particularly useful when researching new fields of law (or new areas within a well-developed field). Often when researching a new field of law, you will not find a treatise on your topic and a loose-leaf service may only have a few sentences or paragraphs on point; however, you may find an entire law reform commission report that deals exclusively with your topic. In general, law reform commission reports are thoroughly researched, in-depth examinations into specific areas of law.

Law reform commission reports are also very useful when your research requires you to analyze and comment not only on what the law is but also on what it could and should be.

A legal researcher would be remiss to overlook law commission reports, but as with other secondary legal literature, never assume that a law reform commission report has cited all of the case law on your topic and always read the case law for yourself to ensure that your interpretation corresponds with the commission's.

How to Find Law Reform Commission Reports

The availability of law reform commission reports electronically has significantly increased as a result of the internet. Many commissions post their reports on their websites. This allows the public to access their reports at any time, and has resulted in law reform commissions becoming much more accessible. Appendix I contains a listing of several Canadian and foreign law reform commission websites.

Along with law reform commissions posting material on their websites, there are a few online research tools that assist individuals who wish to find commission reports. *Manas Media's World Law Reform* database (http://www.manasmedia.com/) indexes over 7200 law reform publications from around the world from as far back as the 1930s. Some law reform commission papers published in 2000 or later are available in *Manas Media* in full-text. Only those who subscribe to *Manas Media* have access to it; check with your local law, public, or academic library to inquire whether or not they subscribe to this product.

Two other useful resources include the *WorldLII Law Reform Project* (http://www.worldlii.org/int/special/lawreform/) and the *Law Reform Database* from the *British Columbia Law Institute* (http://www.bcli.org/bclrg/law-reform). The *WorldLII Law Reform Project* allows you to search for law reform papers available within any of the Legal Information Institutes from around the world.[1] Because this search engine takes you directly to the Legal Information Institute which houses the law reform paper you are looking for, you can use this tool to find such publications in full-text (see Illustration 10.1). The *Law Reform Database* from the BCLI lists many law reform commission papers from numerous commonwealth countries. This database is purely an index with no full-text capabilities.

---

[1] Legal Information Institutes are not-for-profit institutions whose main goal is to provide free access to law. See, for example, the Canadian Legal Information Institute at www.canlii.org.

Illustration 10.1

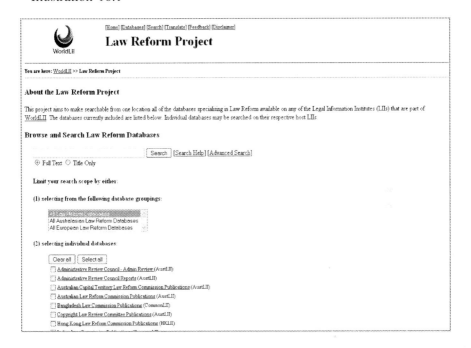

Reproduced with permission from World Legal Information Institute (WorldLII).

Because there are so many law reform commissions and so many reports published each year, no one resource will list all the reports for which you are searching. It's best to ensure you use more than one resource during your research. Also make sure you go to the website of the law reform commission in your jurisdiction of interest to peruse the materials made available on the site.

There are ways to find law reform commission reports other than online. You will find many law reform commission reports in your local public, academic, or law library, indexed by subject or author (i.e., Law Commission of Ontario). The *Canadian Abridgment: Index to Canadian Legal Literature* also indexes law reform commission reports.[2] You can also write to the law reform commission of interest for a list of commission reports and order such reports directly from the commission.

---

2 For more information on the *Canadian Abridgment: Index to Canadian Legal Literature*, consult Chapter 5 on the *Canadian Abridgment*.

Appendix I — Links to Canadian and Select Foreign Law Reform Commissions and Institutes

Canadian

Not every jurisdiction in Canada has a separate, independent law reform commission or institute; some jurisdictions' justice departments have a law reform section, and in other jurisdictions the provincial or territorial law foundation may have law reform as one of its mandates. These jurisdictions are not listed here.

Law Commission of Canada (LCC)
In 2006, the federal government removed all funding for the LCC and it was abolished. *Library and Archives Canada* has archived some LCC materials in their collection: http://epe.lac-bac.gc.ca/100/206/301/law_commission_of_canada-ef/2006-12-06/www.lcc.gc.ca/default-en.asp@lang_update=1.

British Columbia Law Institute
<http://www.bcli.org/>

Alberta Law Reform Institute
<http://www.law.ualberta.ca/alri/>

Law Reform Commission of Saskatchewan
<http://www.lawreformcommission.sk.ca/>

Manitoba Law Reform Commission
<http://www.gov.mb.ca/justice/mlrc/>

Law Commission of Ontario
<http://www.lco-cdo.org/>

Law Reform Commission of Nova Scotia
<http://www.lawreform.ns.ca/>

Foreign

Many countries throughout the world have law commissions, but only a few are listed below. Some of those listed have publications on their website free for download:

Law Reform Commission Reports

The Law Commission (U.K.)
    <http://www.lawcom.gov.uk/>

Scottish Law Commission
    <http://www.scotlawcom.gov.uk/>

The Law Reform Commission (Ireland)
    <http://www.lawreform.ie/index.htm>

The American Law Institute
    <http://www.ali.org/>

Australian Law Reform Commission
    <http://www.alrc.gov.au/>

New Zealand Law Commission
    <http://www.lawcom.govt.nz/>

Law Commission of India
    <http://lawcommissionofindia.nic.in/>

Law Reform Commission of Hong Kong
    <http://www.hkreform.gov.hk/en/index/index.htm>

South African Law Reform Commission
    <http://www.doj.gov.za/salrc/index.htm>

11

Law Reports

What are Law Reports?

Law reports are regularly issued collections of judgments that contain a court or tribunal's written reasons for judgment in a case. Law reports are available as printed volumes or online in commercial legal research databases such as Westlaw Canada or LexisNexis Quicklaw. Until the advent of online legal databases, the vast majority of cases referred to by lawyers, academics and courts were accessed from printed law reports.

With the exception of some judicial origin reports (see below), law reports are selective in their reporting of cases. Most law reports do not attempt to report all available decisions. Instead, each law reporter's editorial board selects cases that its members believe are of legal significance, i.e., those which fit within that reporter's mandate, and are of interest to its readers. For example, of the many family law cases decided by Canadian courts in a particular year, the editors of the *Reports of Family Law* will only choose to report that small percentage of decisions whose facts or interpretation and application of the law make them potentially of interest to the practicing bar. In effect, this means that only a small number of decisions issued by the courts will be "reported" in a published law report.

Law reports therefore provide a useful service to researchers, as the fact that a case has been selected for inclusion in a law report suggests that the decision might be important in some way and has some potential research value. Of the thousands of decisions issued in a given year, law reports filter out the vast majority of cases that are of interest only to the parties involved, and report only those with a broader applicability.

Leading cases that change or clarify the law are typically reported in more than one reporter. For example, *R. v. Oakes*[1] which sets out the test

---

[1] [1986] 1 S.C.R. 103, 26 D.L.R. (4th) 200, 53 O.R. (2d) 719, 65 N.R. 87, 14 O.A.C. 335, 24 C.C.C. (3d) 321, 50 C.R. (3d) 1, 19 C.R.R. 308.

for the interpretation of s.1 of the *Charter of Rights and Freedoms*[2] is reported in a number of reporters including the *Supreme Court Reports* (S.C.R.), *Dominion Law Reports* (D.L.R.) (as the case is of national significance), *Ontario Reports* (O.R.) (as the case originated in Ontario), as well as a number of criminal law reporters.

Law reports can be classified as either *official reports, semi-official reports* or *unofficial reports*. Often a case will be included in more than one type of report.

Official reports are published pursuant to a statute by an official government printer. The statute is generally one that provides for the creation of the court whose decisions the report publishes. There are only two official reporters in Canada. The Supreme Court of Canada and the Federal Courts of Canada both have an official reporter: the S.C.R. and *the Federal Courts Reports* (F.C.R.). There are no official provincial report series.

Semi-official reports are published under the authority of a statutorily created regulatory body (such as a law society or bar association). Examples of semi-official reports include the *Ontario Reports* and the *Alberta Reports*.

Unofficial reports are published by private commercial publishers. Most topical reports are unofficial reports.

The distinction between official and unofficial reports is especially relevant for cases from either the Federal Court or the Supreme Court of Canada where the official report must be cited whenever the case is reported in an official report. The *McGill Guide*[3] rule 3.2.5 goes into more detail on when to cite official reports.

Law reports can also be categorized by the type of decision they report:

> *Judicial Origin Reports*: Report cases from a particular court or courts. An example is the *Supreme Court Reports* (which reports cases only from the Supreme Court of Canada).

> *Cross-Canada Reports*: Report selected cases decided at all court levels in all Canadian jurisdictions on all legal topics. The *Dominion Law Reports* is an example of a cross-Canada reporter.

> *Regional Reports*: Report selected cases decided at all court levels on all topics in a particular region of the country. There are two regional law reports, the *Atlantic Provinces Reports* (covers New Brunswick, Newfoundland and Labrador, Nova Scotia, and Prince Edward Island)

---

[2] Part I of the *Constitution Act, 1982*, being Schedule B to the *Canada Act, 1982* (U.K.), 1982, c. 11.

[3] *The Canadian Guide to Uniform Legal Citation*, 6th ed., (Toronto: Thomson Carswell, 2006). Usually referred to as the *McGill Guide*.

and the *Western Weekly Reports* (covers Alberta, Saskatchewan, Manitoba, and British Columbia).

Provincial Reports: Report selected cases decided at all court levels within a province or territory. Examples include the *Ontario Reports* and the *Northwest Territories Reports*. Every province has its own law report series except Newfoundland and Labrador and Prince Edward Island which share a reporter.

Topical Reports: Report selected cases decided on a particular subject.[4] Examples include *Canadian Bankruptcy Reports, Canadian Environmental Law Reports*, and *Reports of Family Law*. Topical reports occasionally include case comments written by leading lawyers or academics.

Reports of Decisions of Administrative Tribunals: These reports tend to be *de facto* subject reports since administrative tribunals have jurisdiction over defined subject areas. Some of the reports of administrative tribunals, in addition to publishing the decisions of the tribunal, also publish judicial decisions arising in the subject-area. Examples include *Canadian Labour Relations Board Reports* and the *Ontario Municipal Board Reports*.

Frequently used abbreviations for Canadian law reports include the following:

Judicial Origin Reports (current and historical)

Supreme Court of Canada

S.C.R.	Canada Law Reports. Supreme Court (1923–1969)
S.C.C. Cam.	Canada Supreme Court Cases (Cameron) (1887–1890)
S.C.C. Coutl.	Canada Supreme Court Cases (Coutlée) (1875–1907)

---

[4] See the Selective Topical Bibliography at the end of this book to find reporters by topic.

S.C.C. Cam. (2d)	Canada Supreme Court Reports (Cameron) (1876–1922)
S.C.R.	Canada Supreme Court Reports (1877–1922); (1970-)

Federal Courts

F.C.	Canada Federal Court Reports (1971–2003)
Ex. C.R.	Exchequer Court of Canada Reports (1875–1922)
Ex. C.R.	Canada Law Reports: Exchequer Court (1923–1970)
F.C.A.D.	Federal Court of Appeal Decisions (1981–1991)
F.C.R.	Federal Courts Reports (2004-)
F.T.R.	Federal Trial Reports (1986-)

Cross Canada Reports (current)

D.L.R.	Dominion Law Reports
N.R.	National Reporter

Regional Reports (current)

A.P.R.	Atlantic Provinces Reports
W.A.C.	Western Appeal Cases

W.W.R.	Western Weekly Reports

Provincial Reports (current)

Alberta

Alta L.R.	Alberta Law Reports
A.R.	Alberta Reports

British Columbia

B.C.A.C.	British Columbia Appeal Cases
B.C.L.R.	British Columbia Law Reports

Manitoba

Man. R.	Manitoba Reports

New Brunswick

N.B.R.	New Brunswick Reports

Newfoundland and Labrador and Prince Edward Island

Nfld. & P.E.I.R.	Newfoundland and Prince Edward Island Reports

Nova Scotia

N.S.R.	Nova Scotia Reports

Ontario

O.A.C.	Ontario Appeal Cases

O.R.   Ontario Reports

Quebec

R.J.Q.   Recueils de Jurisprudence du Québec

R.L.   Revue Légale

Saskatchewan

Sask. R.   Saskatchewan Reports

Selected Topical Law Reports (current)

Admin. L.R.   Administrative Law Reports

B.L.R.   Business Law Reports

C.T.C.   Canada Tax Cases

C.B.R.   Canadian Bankruptcy Reports

C.C.E.L.   Canadian Cases on Employment Law

C.C.L.I.   Canadian Cases on the Law of Insurance

C.C.L.T.   Canadian Cases on the Law of Torts

C.C.P.B.   Canadian Cases on Pensions and Benefits

C.R.D.   Charter of Rights Decisions

C.C.C.   Canadian Criminal Cases

C.E.L.R.   Canadian Environmental Law Reports

C.H.R.R.   Canadian Human Rights Reporter

Law Reports

I.L.R.	Canadian Insurance Law Reporter
C.L.L.C.	Canadian Labour Law Cases
C.N.L.R.	Canadian Native Law Reporter
C.P.R.	Canadian Patent Reporter
C.R.R.	Canadian Rights Reporter
C.T.R.	Canadian Tax Reporter
C.P.C.	Carswell's Practice Cases
C.L.R.	Construction Law Reports
C.A.L.R.	Criminal Appeals Law Reporter
C.R.	Criminal Reports
D.T.C.	Dominion Tax Cases
E.T.R.	Estates and Trusts Reports
Imm. L.R.	Immigration Law Reporter
L.A.C.	Labour Arbitration Cases
L.C.R.	Land Compensation Reports
M.V.R.	Motor Vehicle Reports
M.P.L.R.	Municipal and Planning Reports
P.P.S.A.C.	Personal Property Security Act Cases

R.P.R.   Real Property Reports

R.F.L.   Reports of Family Law

S.O.L.R.   Sexual Offences Law Reporter

T.T.R.   Trade and Tariff Reports

Law Reports in an Online Environment

Most legal researchers now access reported cases via commercial online databases such as Westlaw Canada and LexisNexis Quicklaw, or via internet case law databases such as CanLII. Whereas in the pre-online era the only cases to have wide distribution were the "important" or "interesting" cases selected for reporting, online databases attempt to include *all* cases issued by the courts in their jurisdiction — not just traditionally reported cases. This means that a lawyer doing online research is now faced with a much larger set of cases to consider.

Researchers can rely on the editorial selection process for reporting cases as a guide to which cases might be legally significant. When doing online case research, you will want to pay more attention to the cases that include a citation to a print reporter. Although the line between reported cases and unreported cases has become blurred, the distinction is still relevant to experienced legal researchers as well as to judges and courts.

Anatomy of a Reported Decision

Most reported decisions (whether online or in print) will include the following elements:

> *The Style of Cause*: The name of the case, also called the title of proceedings, e.g. *R. v. Oakes*.
>
> *Court and Judges*: The name(s) of the deciding court and judges.
>
> *Dates*: The date the judgment was issued and the hearing dates.
>
> *Headnote*: A brief description of the facts and law in the decision provided by the editors of the reporter. Note the headnote is not a part of the decision and would not normally be quoted.
>
> *Authorities Used*: Lists of cases, statutes, regulations and other authorities to which the court referred.

Counsel: The names of the lawyers for each party as well as those of any interveners.

Judgment: The text of the Court's decision.

How are Law Reports Organized?

Printed law reports are organized in volumes which cover cases over a given time period. Many law reports have several series. For instance, the *Dominion Law Reports* currently has four series: the "old" first series (1912–1922); the "new" first series (1923–1955); the second series (1956–1968); the third series (1969–1984); and the fourth series (1984 to present). Other reporters are published annually in that each year the volume numbering starts over at volume one (for example, the *Supreme Court Reports*).

Each volume of a law report generally contains a table of cases and a subject index of cases reported in that particular volume or law report. A synopsis of the cases listed under each subject heading is also generally included. Use of these features saves having to look up cases which, although under your subject heading, are irrelevant to your research needs. See Illustration 11.1 for an example of a subject index with case digests (55 C.C.E.L. (3d) xi).

Illustration 11.1

DIGESTS OF CASES

Administrative law

Requirements of natural justice — Bias — Personal bias — Actual ——Employee was hired for management position pursuant to employment agreement — Employer dismissed employee after three months, and paid employee two weeks' pay in lieu of notice — Parties submitted dispute to consensual arbitration under Arbitration Act — In course of hearing, CEO of employer made comment disparaging work ethic of Newfoundlanders, and arbitrator replied that he was insulted by comment — Arbitrator ruled that employee had been wrongfully dismissed and awarded eleven and one-half months' notice, which included three months for Wallace damages — Employer brought application for judicial review — Application granted in part — Arbitrator's decision was set aside with respect to Wallace damages only — Employer's allegations of bias or reasonable apprehension of bias on arbitrator's part were totally without merit — Exchange between CEO and arbitrator did not raise reasonable apprehension of bias — Arbitrator was responding to what he considered to be objectionable comment by CEO — Reasonable person would consider arbitrator's response to be immediate reaction to extraneous comment, not indication of inability to fairly adjudicate proceeding — Further, arbitration hearing immediately continued after exchange without objection from CEO or his counsel — Further, CEO subsequently requested new hearing before same arbitrator.

Charles River Consultants Corp. v. Coombs, 2006 CarswellNfld 303 . . . .
. . . . N.L. T.D. 65

Alternative dispute resolution

Judicial review of arbitration awards — Grounds for review — General principles —— Standard of review — Employee was hired for management position pursuant to employment agreement — Employer dismissed employee after three months, and paid employee two weeks' pay in lieu of notice — Parties submitted dispute to consensual arbitration under Arbitration Act ("Act") — Arbitrator ruled that employee had been wrongfully dismissed and awarded total of eleven and one-half months' notice, which included three months for Wallace damages — Employer brought application for judicial review — Application granted in part — Arbitrator's decision was set aside with respect to Wallace damages only — Arbitrator was entitled to degree of deference on questions other than questions of law — Act and arbitration reference contained partial privative clause and limited right of review, suggesting some degree of deference — Arbitrator's expertise was not greater than that of reviewing court — Arbitrator's expertise was in labour arbitration, but case at bar involved contract of employment — Questions of law would therefore attract little deference, while findings of fact and their application would attract degree of deference — Act contemplated expeditious adjudication of private disputes, and did not involve policy considerations — These factors called for some deference, but not as much as would be awarded to labour relations board — Reviewing judge commented in further detail on standard applicable to each ruling by arbitrator.

Charles River Consultants Corp. v. Coombs, 2006 CarswellNfld 303 . . . .
. . . . N.L. T.D. 65

THOMSON

CARSWELL

Consolidated or cumulative indexes are published at intervals. They index decisions in a series of volumes so that you do not have to refer to the index in every volume of the series.

The cumulative index of topical law reports also typically index:

- cases considered
- statutes considered
- treaties considered
- rules considered
- regulations considered
- forms considered
- authorities considered
- words and phrases judicially considered
- annotations of articles by subject
- annotations of articles by author

Since topical law reports only report cases on a particular subject, the cumulative index of a topical law report series will not refer you to statutes, rules, and words and phrases etc, as they have been considered in other fields of law. Therefore, depending on the scope of your research, you will have to consult other sources as well.

When are Law Reports Useful for Research Purposes?

Law reports can be used to supplement research conducted using secondary sources. While encyclopedias, the *Canadian Abridgment*, treatises, journals and CLE materials will provide you with the best organized access to case law, you may also find it useful to refer to the index of a topical or administrative tribunal reporter as a means of quickly locating recent case law on your topic. The indexes of reports can also be used to research statutes, regulations, rules, forms, authorities, and words and phrases that have been judicially considered in a particular reporter.

The most common current use of printed reporters is for current awareness. Lawyers may refer to the newest issues of their regional or provincial reporter as a quick way to stay on top of current developments in their jurisdiction. A lawyer who receives the *Ontario Reports* on a weekly basis can easily scan the case synopses in the index of cases reported to inform herself of new developments. Topical reporters can serve the same current awareness function. For example, a litigator in any province might regularly review the case digests and case comments in new issues of *Carswell's Practice Cases* as a way to stay current on significant cases dealing with civil procedure.

12

Research Tools for Accessing Unreported Decisions

What are Unreported Decisions?

Unreported decisions are, as their name suggests, decisions that have not been published in a report series. There are two types of unreported decisions:

1. Decisions that have just been released by a court and may or may not be reported in the future; and

2. Older decisions that have never been reported.

One reason cases are not reported is because there is limited space available in case reporters and it would be financially prohibitive to print every single case that comes out of every court in Canada. As well, many cases remain unreported because the issues dealt with in them are not of significant legal importance. If a case is not going to augment judicial jurisprudence, it is unlikely that a publisher will go through the expensive and lengthy process of printing the case. That being said, unreported cases are just as valid and useful as reported cases and may certainly be used as legal authority.

When are Unreported Decisions Useful?

Usually, the first type of unreported decisions — recent decisions — will be of more use to you. Checking for recent unreported decisions will ensure that your research is absolutely up-to-date. For example, your issue may be answered by a six-month-old Ontario Court of Appeal case that has been reported. However, you will want to know if there have been any cases since that case that have considered it and whether they have treated the issue in the same manner. You may find that the Court of Appeal of another province has recently followed or declined to follow the case. You may even find that the Ontario Court of Appeal has changed its position on the issue. You may also be interested in examining how the lower courts have responded to the Court of Appeal decision. These more recent decisions will likely be unreported because they are so new.

Unreported decisions are also useful if you are researching an issue for which you can find nothing in the reported literature, or if you are looking for a case with similar facts to the one you are researching and cannot find one in the reported literature. Just because you cannot find anything on a given issue does not mean that it has not been considered. In these situations, you will be interested in both old and recent unreported decisions.

Research Tools

There are several tools you can use to find unreported cases:

1. Legal database systems and online tools:

- Westlaw Canada
- LexisNexis Quicklaw
- Maritime Law Book
- BestCase
- CanLII
- Courthouse websites

2. *All-Canada Weekly Summaries* (A.C.W.S.)
A digest, published weekly, of civil cases from across Canada. This is available in print as well as electronically through *BestCase.*

3. *Weekly Criminal Bulletin* (W.C.B.)
A digest, published weekly, of criminal cases from across Canada. This is available in print as well as electronically through *BestCase* and as an email alert through *caseAlert.*

4. *Alberta Weekly Law Digest* (A.W.L.D.)
A weekly digest of Alberta cases dealing with all areas of the law. This is available in print and as an email updating service.

5. *British Columbia Weekly Law Digest* (B.C.W.L.D.)

A weekly digest of British Columbia cases dealing with all areas of the law. This is available in print and as an email updating service.

6. *Supreme Court of Canada Reports Service* (S.C.C.R.S.)

A print digest of Supreme Court of Canada decisions by year and subject.

7. *Lawyers' Weekly*

A weekly legal newspaper that discusses recent legal developments, this is available in print and electronically through LexisNexis Quicklaw.

8. *Law Times*

A weekly newspaper published in print and electronically by Canada Law Book.

9. *Commercial Delivery Services*

In some municipalities, law firms and other establishments can hire a commercial delivery service to search for and provide all or most of the judgments delivered at a particular courthouse. Once received at the law firm or business, the judgments are then filed in the library for ease of use. This is only available in select municipalities so check with the law firm or organization at which you work or the local courthouse to determine if this service is available in your municipality.

How to Use the Research Tools

Legal Database Systems and Online Tools

Consult the chapter titled *Electronic Legal Research* for more information on legal database systems and online research tools.

A.C.W.S. and W.C.B.

A.C.W.S. and W.C.B. are softcover booklets that are published on a weekly basis. Eventually, these softcover booklets are replaced by bound volumes. Case digests are organized in alphabetical order by subject in each issue. In order to find cases, turn to the appropriate subject heading and read the cases digested under that heading. If you want a copy of a case, there are instructions about how to order it from the publisher. This of course will involve some expense depending on the number of pages in the case. You may also use this information to find the case in an electronic database.

To locate case digests in the bound volumes, you can use the table of cases and the topical indexes found in each bound volume. You should also check for the index volumes, which are published periodically and consolidate the indexes of several volumes, in order to save time.

In *BestCase*, you can conduct a search to find any digests from these resources. The W.C.B. is also available electronically through *caseAlert*, which is a service whereby you can receive either a weekly or monthly email update with the digests from your practice areas of choice attached as a PDF.

A.W.L.D. and B.C.W.L.D.

These digest booklets are published weekly. As with A.C.W.S. and W.C.B., the decisions can be ordered from the publisher using the instructions. Bound volumes and cumulative indexes are issued periodically. To locate cases, use the topical indexes.

These resources are also available as an email updating service; with this, you receive a weekly email with a PDF list of that week's digests.

S.C.C.R.S.

This digest service for Supreme Court of Canada cases does not provide a means of ordering cases. However, it may be a way to alert you to the existence of a case, which you can then locate quickly on a computer database.

Law Times

Law Times, published by Canada Law Book, is a weekly legal newspaper aimed primarily at Canadian lawyers and the legal community. In each issue, new and noteworthy cases are discussed. At the back of each issue, notable unreported civil and criminal cases are digested. For a fee, copies of the full-text of any of these decisions are available by contacting the paper.

Lawyers' Weekly

The *Lawyers' Weekly* is a newspaper dealing with issues of interest to Canadian lawyers. Many of its articles deal with recent cases. At the end of each article a citation to the case at issue is provided. The citation is usually a neutral citation or a LexisNexis Quicklaw citation. There is also a section in each issue in which various cases of interest, organized alphabetically by subject area, are digested. Each case digest is accompanied by a neutral citation or a LexisNexis Quicklaw citation. In LexisNexis Quicklaw, you can search the Lawyers' Weekly for the articles as well as digests; links to the cases as they are available are provided, making it easy to find and read the case.

13

Noting-up Case Law

It is important to "note-up" any cases that you will be referring to in your memorandum, pleadings, or research paper. Noting-up is the process by which a researcher checks whether a case is still "good" law by seeing how a case has been judicially considered by subsequent decisions. Because the common law can and does evolve to adapt to social, cultural, political and economic changes, a case that may have been good law at one point in time may have been superseded by later legal developments. Noting-up will help you place a case within the context of the developing common law. Even if you used a recent treatise or any other secondary sources discussed in this book to identify relevant case law, you will still need to note-up your cases.

In this chapter, we will discuss how to note-up a Canadian case, as well as the process for determining if a case from another jurisdiction has been judicially considered in Canada.

Why Note-up?

There are three main reasons to note-up a case:

1. *To learn the history of a case.* It is essential to know if the case you are researching has been overturned or affirmed by a higher court. If your case has been affirmed by an appeal court, the appeal decision will be binding if it is from your jurisdiction or will be more persuasive if it is from another jurisdiction. If your case has been reversed or varied by a higher court, you will need to read the appeal decision closely to determine if the appeal affects the issue that you are researching and if the appeal court's reasoning overrules the lower court. If, of course, noting-up leads you to a Supreme Court ruling, that decision will be binding on all Canadian courts. The importance of noting-up a case to see if it has been overturned or affirmed by a higher court cannot be overstated.

Knowing the history of a case may also be useful if you need to find any decisions of a lower court in the same matter. A lower court's decision often has a richer depiction of the facts of a case. If you are writing a case comment or doing academic writing, it may be a useful exercise to compare and evaluate the reasoning of the case's trial and appeal decisions.

2. *To learn how your case has been considered or applied by subsequent decisions.* Even if the case you are researching has not been appealed, or if it is a Supreme Court of Canada decision, you will want to know if and how your case has been judicially considered by other courts. If other courts consistently apply and treat the reasoning in your case favourably, then this will indicate that your case may be a good authority. If on the other hand, subsequent courts have criticized your decision, your case may not be as strong an authority as you might have hoped.

In some circumstances, a case may appear to stand for a broad general principle, but noting-up will reveal that in subsequent decisions the courts have limited the principle's applicability by applying it to a narrower set of facts or law. Finally, your case may never have been considered by another court. This could mean a number of things. Your case may be too recent to be cited; other cases with similar law or facts have not been decided, or perhaps other courts have not found the case to be persuasive enough precedent to discuss.

3. *To find other cases on your topic.* There is a good possibility that a subsequent decision that cites your decision deals with similar law or facts. While digests and secondary sources are good ways to find other similar cases, noting-up may also provide you with cases that are similar to yours.

Canadian Case Law Citators

Noting-up in Canada has become much simpler thanks to the existence of online citators (citators are tools for checking if a case has been cited) and full-text case law databases.

The three major Canadian citators are:

1) *Canadian Case Citations*: this print citator is a part of the *Canadian Abridgment*. It is discussed in Chapter 5. Before the appearance of on-line citators, this was the main tool for noting-up case law in Canada.

2) *KeyCite Canada*: this online citator is an essential component of Westlaw Canada, and is integrated with most other Westlaw Canada content. *KeyCite* provides citation information for all reported Canadian decisions and most unreported decisions. There are two main ways to note-up a case in *KeyCite*: entering your case's citation on the *KeyCite* search page or checking the "Related Info" tab when you have the full-text of a decision on your screen.

Once you have the "Related Info" tab up for your case, you can click on "Full History" to see if there any other decisions in the same matter. If a case has been reversed, affirmed or varied by a higher court, you will find that information here.

"Citing References" will produce a list of any cases or secondary materials that have cited your case. The secondary resources are very helpful in finding journal articles that have referred to your case. *KeyCite Canada* uses the following terminology to describe how a case has been treated by subsequent case law; positive and neutral treatments are: "Followed," "Considered" and "Referred To," with "Followed" being the strongest treatment. Negative and cautionary treatments are: "Not Followed" and "Distinguished." These treatment designations are applied by *KeyCite's* editors and are helpful guides to the status of a case. If you are going to refer to a citing case, you will need to read the case to confirm whether the treatment applied by the editors is correct or relevant to your use of the case. See Illustration 13.1 for a sample and/of a *KeyCite Canada* record.

Illustration 13.1

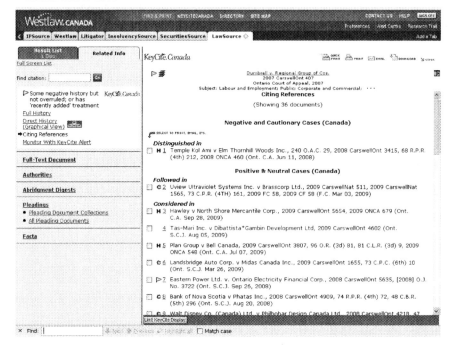

3) *QuickCITE*: this is LexisNexis Quicklaw's online citator. It covers reported Canadian decisions and most unreported decisions. To note-up using *QuickCITE*, enter your citation on the *QuickCITE* citator page or click on the "Note-up with QuickCITE" link when you are looking at the text of a decision. You will find the history of the decision along with a list of citing cases.

QuickCite's treatment designations differ slightly from those of *KeyCite*. For case history, there are a number of potential designations, the most important being: "Affirmed," "Reversed," "Varied" and "Quashed."

The major positive and neutral designations for case treatments are: "Explained," "Followed" and "Mentioned," with "Explained" being the strongest. Negative considerations include: "Not Followed," "Questioned" and "Distinguished." Again, while the treatment designations are useful, you should read citing cases for yourself to verify exactly how your case was treated. See Illustration 13.2 for a sample of a *QuickCite* record.

Illustration 13.2

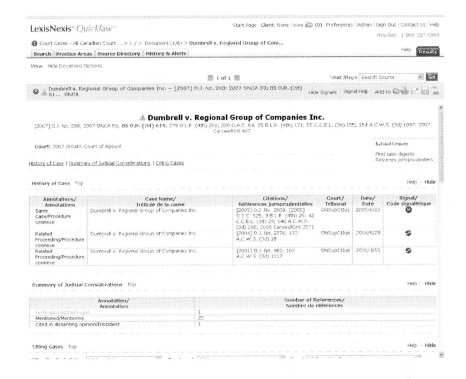

Reprinted with the permission of LexisNexis Canada Inc. LexisNexis is a registered trademark of Reed Elsevier Properties Inc., used under licence. Quicklaw is a trademark of LexisNexis Canada Inc.

How to Note-up Case Law

Noting-up English and American case law within each of those jurisdictions is covered in the chapters on English Legal Research and American Legal research. Here we will discuss how to check for *Canadian* judicial consideration of Canadian, U.S. and U.K. decisions.

Note-up Canadian Cases in Canada

Because both online citators are very current, most researchers rely on them for noting-up. If cost is an overriding concern or you do not have access to an online citator, use the print *Canadian Case Citations*.

Checking only one of the two citators is usually sufficient. You may sometimes want to check both, especially if you are dealing with a recent decision, an unreported decision, or one where your preferred citator has produced few or no results. You may also consider checking both citators if you cannot risk missing *any* cases that have cited your case.

For most cases use:

KeyCite Canada: Use the "Limit KeyCite Display" button to narrow your results by keyword, jurisdiction, date and document type.

QuickCITE: Use the "Filter By" and "Sort By" options to narrow your results by jurisdiction, treatment, court and date.

For cases not covered by the citators:

Westlaw Canada: in the "Cases" custom search template, search for: *partya /10 partyb* (e.g. donoghue /10 stevenson). This full-text search will find any cases that mention the two parties in your case within ten words of each other. You will then need to look at each citing case to determine how your case has been treated by other courts. If your style of cause contains very common names or only the initials of the parties, you may need to make your search more complex (by adding a date restriction or adding more keywords) to zero in on only the cases that are relevant to your research.

LexisNexis Quicklaw: in the "Court Cases" tab, search for partya /10 partyb.

Checking for Canadian Consideration of U.K. and U.S. Cases

If you are referring to a U.K. or U.S. case (or any foreign decision for that matter), you may want to note it up in Canada to see if Canadian courts have considered it. Depending on the topic and how well developed Canadian law is in an area, a leading English House of Lords decision, for example, may be widely cited in Canada or not cited at all. A foreign decision that has been treated favourably by Canadian appeal courts will have more persuasive value.

KeyCite Canada will allow you to see how post 1977 (and selected earlier) U.K. and U.S. decisions have been considered in Canada. If no *KeyCite* record is available you will need to do a "partya /10 partyb" search to find any citing references.

QuickCITE provides limited coverage of U.K. and U.S. decisions. If you do not find a record for your case, you will need to do a partya /10 partyb search.

All England Law Reports Canadian Annotations: this loose-leaf print source is a selective guide to how cases that have been reported in the *All England Law Reports* have been cited in Canada. This service usually only lists serious considerations of English cases in Canada.

14

Constitutional Research

What is Constitutional Research?

The Constitution is the supreme law of the country, and the validity of all other laws is determined by their consistency with the Constitution. Accordingly, an understanding of constitutional research is important to the study or practice of Canadian law. There are generally two main categories of constitutional legal research problems: (a) federalism, and (b) rights and freedoms.[1] Constitutional issues regularly arise in some areas of law (such as criminal law and Aboriginal law). Constitutional questions often loom in the background of many other public law problems.

Federalism

When you are researching a federalism question, you will need to determine whether a given law is within the scope of the powers conferred on the federal or provincial governments under the *Constitution Act, 1867*[2] (the *"Constitution Act"*). For instance, the postal service is listed under s. 91 of the *Constitution Act* as a federal power, whereas the regulation of municipalities is listed under s. 92 as a provincial power. Accordingly, the province of Ontario could not pass laws to regulate the postal service, and the federal government could not pass laws to regulate municipalities. Federalism, therefore, deals with the division of powers between the federal and provincial governments.

---

[1] "Classical" constitutional law encompasses more than the *Charter* and federalism. It also includes broader issues such as "constitutional convention" and the role of the Governor General. A good illustration is the constitutional crisis provoked by Governor General's proroguing of Parliament in late 2008. See Lorne Sossin and Peter H. Russell eds., *Parliamentary Democracy in Crisis* (Toronto: University of Toronto Press, 2009).

[2] (U.K.), 30 & 31 Vict., c. 3.

Rights and Freedoms

The second broad category of constitutional research deals with the rights of individuals and groups as against the state. This category of research involves the *Canadian Charter of Rights and Freedoms*[3] (the "*Charter*"). The *Charter* provides individuals and groups with certain substantive rights and freedoms. The rights and freedoms guaranteed in the *Charter* may, however, be infringed upon by the government if the law or government action is deemed under s. 1 of the *Charter* to be a reasonable limit that is prescribed by law and demonstrably justified in a free and democratic society.

References

Most constitutional judgments originate in a dispute between an individual or corporation and a government authority. However, s.53 of the *Supreme Court Act*[4] allows the Governor in Council (i.e. the Governor General acting by and with the advice and consent of the Cabinet[5]) to:

> refer to the Court for hearing and consideration of important questions of law or fact concerning
>
> > (a) the interpretation of the *Constitution Acts*;
> >
> > (b) the constitutionality or interpretation of any federal or provincial legislation;
> >
> > (c) the appellate jurisdiction respecting educational matters, by the *Constitution Act, 1867*, or by any other Act or law vested in the Governor in Council; or
> >
> > (d) the powers of the Parliament of Canada, or of the legislatures of the provinces, or of the respective governments thereof, whether or not the particular power in question has been or is proposed to be exercised.

The provinces also have legislation that allows the provincial Lieutenant Governor in Council to refer a question to the provincial Court of Appeal (which may then be appealed to the Supreme Court). Because references allow governments to go straight to their highest court, they will sometimes refer urgent matters of pressing national importance to the courts in this manner. Many high-profile constitutional cases are decisions in government references[6]. Although technically a reference is an advisory opinion and not

---

[3] Part I of the *Constitution Act, 1982*, being Schedule B to the *Canada Act, 1982* (U.K.), 1982, c. 11.

[4] R.S.C, 1985, c. S-26.

[5] *Interpretation Act*, R.S.C. 1985 c. I-21, s. 35.

[6] For example, *Re Same-Sex Marriage*, [2004] 3 S.C.R. 698 and *Reference Re Secession of Quebec*, [1998] 2 S.C.R. 217.

a judgment, in practice reference opinions are treated the same as judgments and are followed by subsequent decisions.[7]

Research Involving the *Constitution Act, 1867*

In both federalism and *Charter* research there are usually two main steps:

1. Determining the meaning of the relevant constitutional provision. This step involves first reading the provision and then finding the case law and commentary which has interpreted the provision.

2. Obtaining evidence to prove, based on the accepted interpretation of the constitutional provision, that the impugned law or government action is or is not in violation of the Constitution.

These steps will be described in greater detail below for the two different categories of constitutional problems.

Interpretation of a Constitutional Provision

As with all other types of research, treatises and loose-leaf services will be useful in assisting you to locate and interpret the leading cases on your topic.[8] Looking up your constitutional provision in a leading treatise such as Hogg's *Constitutional Law of Canada*[9] will lead you to discussion and commentary on the leading cases from the Supreme Court of Canada and the provincial Courts of Appeal. This will help you understand the key issues and how the law might develop.

A treatise or loose-leaf service will generally not identify all of the case law on your topic. If the leading cases do not address your issue or facts, you may wish to look for more cases that interpret your provision. To find all (or almost all) cases that interpret a provision of the *Constitution Act*, look up that section of the Constitution in the *Canadian Statute Citatations* portion of the *Canadian Abridgment*, or use the *KeyCite* service on Westlaw Canada, or the *QuickCITE Statute Citator* on LexisNexis Quicklaw to look up your section. These tools will bring you to a list of cases which have considered your provision(s).

---

[7] See Robert J. Sharpe & Kent Roach, *The Charter of Rights and Freedoms*, 4th ed. (Toronto: Irwin Law, 2009) at 115.

[8] For a list of loose-leaf services and treatises, consult the Constitutional Law section of the Selective Topical Bibliography.

[9] Peter W. Hogg, *Constitutional Law of Canada*, 5th ed., loose-leaf (Toronto: Carswell, 2007-).

Historical Element

Research under the *Constitution Act* might have a historical component. If the circumstances call for it, you might want to investigate the purpose or intent of the provision by examining the parliamentary debates around the time of Confederation. On several occasions, the Supreme Court of Canada has looked at the history of a provision of the *Constitution Act* — i.e., what the Fathers of Confederation intended for certain provisions, and/or how those provisions came to be as a result of various negotiations at the time — to gain insight into how the provision should be interpreted. For example, in *Reference re Bill 30, An Act to Amend the Education Act,*[10] the Court considered the Constitution in light of the history of schools at the time of Confederation. As Wilson, J. noted:

> The protection of minority religious rights was a major preoccupation during the negotiations leading to Confederation because of the perceived danger of leaving the religious minorities in both Canada East and Canada West at the mercy of overwhelming majorities. Given the importance of denominational educational rights at the time of Confederation, it seems unbelievable that the draftsmen of the section would not have made provision for future legislation conferring rights and privileges on religious minorities in response to new conditions.[11]

The Court also looked at debates around that time which discussed the role of minority rights and guarantees in the Constitution in this regard.

Historical inquiries can also involve an examination of the powers of the Courts and other bodies in existence at the time of Confederation. For example, in *Re Residential Tenancies Act, 1979,*[12] the Supreme Court of Canada was asked to determine whether a provincial commission could make orders evicting tenants from residential premises. Part of the inquiry involved:

> consideration, in the light of the historical conditions existing in 1867, of the particular power or jurisdiction conferred upon the tribunal. The question here is whether the power or jurisdiction conforms to the power or jurisdiction exercised by superior, district or county courts at the time of Confederation.[13]

Determination of the question would be one step in a multi-step exercise to decide whether the powers of the Commission were those properly attributable to a tribunal or, instead, those more properly exercised by a court.

---

[10] [1987] 1 S.C.R. 1148.

[11] *Ibid.* at 1173.

[12] *Reference re Residential Tenancies Act (Ontario),* [1981] 1 S.C.R. 714.

[13] *Ibid.* at 715.

Specifically, the question was whether superior, district or county courts exercised the power of eviction in 1867. The answer was yes. Even though the term at the time was "ejectment" rather than "eviction," the court determined that, in fact, they meant the same thing.[14] As a result, the Court decided that the Commission was exercising powers like those of the s. 96 courts at the time of Confederation, and continued to the next portion of its multi-step examination to determine, ultimately, whether or not this was appropriate.

Clearly, historical inquiries can play an important role in Constitutional research. At the same time, one must keep in mind Lord Sankey in *Edwards v. A.G. of Canada*[15] who stated that "(t)he *British North America Act* planted in Canada a living tree capable of growth and expansion within its natural limits." Almost a century later, the judiciary continues to use the metaphor. As Binnie and LeBel JJ only recently wrote about the provinces and the Federal government:

> . . . the powers of each of these levels of government were enumerated in ss. 91 and 92 of the *Constitution Act, 1867* or provided for elsewhere in that Act. As is true of any other part of our Constitution — this "living tree" as it is described in the famous image from *Edwards v. Canada (Attorney General)* (1929), [1930] A.C. 124 (Canada P.C.), at p. 136 — the interpretation of these powers and of how they interrelate must evolve and must be tailored to the changing political and cultural realities of Canadian society.[16]

Historical research, then, is only one part of the assignment.

Government Policy and Social Science Evidence

Evidence such as government reports, law reform commission reports, social science studies, or statistics can be useful in proving or disproving whether a particular statute is a lawful exercise of legislative authority. These types of sources can provide insight into the social purposes the legislation was intended to achieve, the context against which the legislation was enacted, and the institutional framework in which the legislation is intended to operate. All of these factors may be relevant.

In *Reference Re Anti-Inflation Act*,[17] the Supreme Court of Canada was asked to assess whether the federal government's anti-inflation legislation addressed a matter of national importance affecting the peace, order, and

---

[14] Legal dictionaries or words and phrases services are good references for historical terminology and should be consulted to ascertain the meaning of unfamiliar terms.

[15] [1930] A.C. 124 (Canada P.C.).

[16] *Canadian Western Bank v. Alberta*, 2007 SCC 22.

[17] *Reference re Anti-Inflation Act, 1975 (Canada)*, [1976] 2 S.C.R. 373.

good government of Canada. In assessing this question, the court admitted an economic study by Professor Lipsey dealing with the harm caused by inflation, the Canadian inflationary experience, the state of the economy in 1975, and various policy options.

Other evidence admitted relating to the then prevailing level of inflation included the White Paper tabled in the House by the Minister of Finance and material from Statistics Canada. Subsequent cases have also relied on evidence of this nature. In *Re Residential Tenancies Act, 1979*, for example, the Supreme Court of Canada indicated that a flexible approach should be adopted with respect to the admissibility of extrinsic materials in government references:

> Material relevant to the issues before the court, and not inherently unreliable or offending against public policy should be admissible, subject to the proviso that such extrinsic materials are not available for the purpose of aiding in statutory construction.[18]

Research Involving the *Charter of Rights and Freedoms*

Structure of the *Charter*

As with the *Constitution Act*, the *Charter* is also meant to be interpreted in a progressive way, in tune with the way in which society is changing. The "living tree" doctrine was said to apply to the *Charter* in *Reference re s. 94(2) of the Motor Vehicle Act (British Columbia)*.[19]

To conduct effective research on *Charter* issues, it is necessary to have a basic knowledge of the structure of the *Charter*. For the purposes of this discussion on research techniques, we will focus on four main parts of the *Charter*: 1) Application, 2) Substantive Rights and Freedoms, 3) Governments' Rights to Limit Substantive Rights and Freedoms, and 4) Remedies.

1) Application

Section 32 of the *Charter* indicates that the *Charter* applies to the actions of governments. For example, in *Canadian Federation of Students v. Greater Vancouver Transportation Authority*,[20] a transit authority's policies placed restrictions on political advertising, thus possibly violating the s.2(b) *Charter* protection of freedom of expression. The Supreme Court ruled that the transit authority was "government" for the purposes of s.32 and therefore subject to the *Charter*. The scope of s.32, the definition of government

---

[18] *Supra* note 12 at para. 15.

[19] [1985] 2 S.C.R. 486.

[20] [2009] 2 S.C.R. 295.

action, and the applicability of the *Charter* on non-governmental actors has been considered by the courts on a number of occasions. Consulting a treatise such as those by Hogg[21] or Sharpe and Roach[22] to understand how s.32 has been interpreted by the courts would be wise, especially if your research involves facts where it is not clear if the violation of a right or freedom involves government authority.

2) Substantive Rights and Freedoms

This part of the *Charter* (ss. 2–23) provides substantive rights and freedoms to individuals and groups. The onus is always on the party asserting that a *Charter* violation has occurred to prove such infringement on a balance of probabilities. There are two aspects to consider under this part of the *Charter*:

1. Is the person or group wishing to mount a *Charter* challenge entitled to do so (i.e., does the person or group have standing)?

2. Has a right or freedom under the *Charter* been infringed?

3) Governments' Rights to Limit Substantive Rights and Freedoms

Even if an individual's *Charter* rights have been infringed, the government is still given an opportunity under s. 1 to show that such infringement is justified because the government action is a reasonable limit demonstrably justified in a free and democratic society. Under this section, the onus is on the government to prove that the infringement is justified on a balance of probabilities.

4) Remedies Available

If the government did not succeed in establishing that the infringement of the right or freedom under s. 1 is justified, the onus reverts to the plaintiff to prove on the balance of probabilities that he or she is entitled to a particular remedy — i.e., the remedy is necessary to cure the constitutional wrong done to him or her. There are two remedial sections under the *Charter*: s. 24(1) and s. 52(1).

Section 24(1) provides:

---

[21] *Supra* note 9.

[22] *Supra* note 7.

> Anyone whose rights or freedoms, as guaranteed by this Charter, have been infringed or denied may apply to a court of competent jurisdiction to obtain such remedy as the court considers appropriate and just in the circumstances.

As the wording of this section indicates, the person must have suffered an infringement of his or her rights or freedoms in order to qualify for a remedy under s. 24(1).

Section 52(1) provides:

> The Constitution of Canada is the supreme law of Canada, and any law that is inconsistent with the provisions of the Constitution is, to the extent of the inconsistency, of no force or effect.

Under s. 52(1) declaratory relief is available. This means that the court can declare a law that has been found to be inconsistent with the *Charter* to be of no force or effect.

Stages of Research

Researching under the *Charter* can involve answering five questions:

1. Does the *Charter* apply?
2. If the answer to the first question is yes, then does the party have standing to bring a *Charter* claim?
3. If the answer to the second question is yes, then is there an infringement or denial of one of the rights or freedoms guaranteed under the *Charter*?
4. If the answer to the third question is yes, then is the denial or infringement justified under s. 1?
5. If the answer to the fourth question is no, then what is the appropriate remedy?

1) Does the Charter Apply?

To determine how government action has been judicially interpreted, the best strategy is to consult a constitutional law treatise's treatment of the question of the application of the *Charter* (s. 32). In addition to the Hogg and Sharpe texts mentioned above, a particularly useful loose-leaf service on the *Charter* is the six volume *Canadian Charter of Rights Annotated*.[23]

---

[23] John B. Laskin *et al.*, eds. *Canadian Charter of Rights Annotated*, loose-leaf (Aurora: Canada Law Book, 1982-).

This service provides short digests of cases organized by topic for every section of the *Charter*. To stay completely current you may also want to consult the *Canadian Statute Citations* portion of the *Canadian Abridgment* under s. 32 or use *KeyCite* to note-up s.32. Because new cases are being litigated under the *Charter* daily, you should also check for recent unreported decisions by using an online database.

2) Does the Party Have Standing to Bring a Charter Claim?

Standing has two aspects in that you must satisfy the requirements under the section conferring the right or freedom as well as the requirements under one of the remedial sections.

To determine whether you have standing under the substantive right or freedom, refer to the wording of that right or freedom and consult a treatise or loose-leaf service discussing the appropriate section of the *Charter*. For example, s. 15 of the *Charter* states:

> Every individual is equal before and under the law and has the right to the equal protection and equal benefit of the law without discrimination and, in particular, without discrimination based on race, national or ethnic origin, colour, religion, sex, age or mental or physical disability.

An individual who has suffered an alleged infringement of his or her rights under s. 15 could bring a claim. However, note that an "individual" likely does not include a corporation.[24] Corporations, however, *do* have standing under other sections of the *Charter*. For example, s. 8 of the *Charter*, which protects against unreasonable search and seizure, applies to both individuals and corporations. It is therefore necessary to examine the wording of the *Charter* provision under which you wish to mount your challenge, as well as any applicable case law, in order to see if you satisfy the standing requirement.

To locate jurisprudence on standing — both under the substantive right or freedom and under the remedial sections of the *Charter* — the same research process we outlined under the above section ("Does the *Charter* apply?") should be used.

3) Is There a Charter Infringement?

To assess whether a right or freedom has been infringed or denied, you must determine how the right of freedom in question has been interpreted by the courts. For instance, is there a test for assessing whether freedom of expression has been denied under s. 2(b)? Or, what is the meaning of "arbi-

---

[24] See Hogg, *supra* note 9 at para. 55.5(a).

trary detention" under s. 9? In the early years of *Charter* jurisprudence, the courts relied on a number of sources when interpreting the terms of the *Charter*, including journal articles by legal scholars,[25] the works of legal theorists and philosophers,[26] and American constitutional jurisprudence.[27] Presently, these sources are being cited less frequently, as there is now a well-developed body of Canadian jurisprudence under most sections of the *Charter*. To locate this jurisprudence, the same research process that we have outlined under the above section, ("Does the Charter Apply?") should be used.

Once you have ascertained how the right or freedom has been interpreted (i.e. how the right or freedom has been defined and the test for establishing that the right or freedom has been denied), the onus is on the plaintiff to prove on the balance of probabilities that his or her right or freedom has been denied. Sometimes it will be possible to prove that a right or freedom has been denied by relying solely on the facts of the case. For instance, to prove that someone has been arbitrarily detained in contravention of s. 9, the manner in which the person was detained would have to be described. These facts must be applied to any Supreme Court of Canada's tests for determining what constitutes a detention and what constitutes arbitrariness for the purpose of s. 9.

In other cases, social science evidence, government reports and other studies may be instrumental in establishing the existence or denial of a right or freedom. For instance, in *Irwin Toy Ltd. c. Québec (Procureur général)*,[28] which involved a challenge to the provisions of the Quebec legislation prohibiting television advertisements directed towards children under 13 years of age, numerous social science studies on the effect of advertising on the development and perceptions of young children were introduced. In *Ford c. Québec (Procureur général)*,[29] which involved a challenge to the provisions of the Quebec *Charter of the French Language*,[30] the Attorney

---

[25] For instance, in *Skapinker v. Law Society of Upper Canada*, [1984] 1 S.C.R. 357, the Supreme Court of Canada cited with approval an article by John B. Laskin entitled "Mobility Rights under the *Charter*," (1982) 4 Sup. Ct. L. Rev. 89.

[26] In *Dolphin Delivery Ltd. v. R.W.D.S.U., Local 580*, [1986] 2 S.C.R. 573 at 583, the Supreme Court of Canada quoted John Stuart Mill on freedom of expression.

[27] In *Canada (Director of Investigation & Research, Combines Investigation Branch) v. Southam Inc.*, (sub nom. *Hunter v. Southam*) [1984] 2 S.C.R. 145, the Supreme Court of Canada looked at case law decided under the Fourth Amendment of the American *Bill of Rights* to interpret s. 8 of the *Charter*, which guarantees security against unreasonable search and seizure.

[28] [1989] 1 S.C.R. 927.

[29] [1988] 2 S.C.R. 712.

[30] R.S.Q. 1977, c. C-11, ss. 58 and 69.

General of Quebec introduced studies on sociolinguistics and language planning in addition to articles, reports, and statistics describing the position of the French language in Quebec and Canada that gave rise to and justified the language planning policy reflected in the *Charter of the French Language*.

4) Is the Infringement Justified Under s. 1?

Under s. 1 of the *Charter*, the onus is on the government or the defendant to establish on the balance of probabilities that the denial of the right or freedom is "demonstrably justified in a free and democratic society." Your first step is to consider the test for interpreting s. 1. The test was first enunciated by the Supreme Court of Canada in *R. v. Oakes*.[31] Professor Hogg summarizes the test as follows:

1. Sufficiently important objective: The law must pursue an objective that is sufficiently important to justify limiting a *Charter* right.

2. Rational Connection: The law must be rationally connected to the objective.

3. Least Drastic Means: The law must impair the right no more than is necessary to accomplish the objective.

4. Proportionate effect: The law must not have a disproportionately severe effect on the persons to whom it applies.[32]

Since the *Oakes* case, much subsequent Supreme Court jurisprudence has focused on the "least drastic means" requirement. To locate case law that applies and interprets the *Oakes* test, the same research process that we have outlined above under the section, "Does the Charter Apply?" should be used.

Once you have determined the appropriate test under s. 1, proving that you have met the test may involve tracing the history of the impugned legislation and the use of research tools such as law reform commission reports and social science literature.

Tracing the History of the Impugned Legislation

The first requirement of the *Oakes* test is to establish that the purpose of the impugned legislation is of "pressing and substantial" importance in a free and democratic society. To ascertain the purpose, you may need to

---

[31] [1986] 1 S.C.R. 103.

[32] *Supra* note 9 at para. 38.8(b).

trace the history of the legislation to the time in which it was enacted.[33] This historical inquiry is vital because, as Dickson C.J.C. stated in *R. v. Big M Drug Mart Ltd.*, "Purpose is a function of the intent of those who drafted and enacted the legislation at the time, and not of any shifting variable."[34] Therefore, an objective that did not prompt the enactment of the legislation is irrelevant to the s. 1 inquiry, even if that objective might be considered pressing and substantial today. For instance in *R. v. Zundel*,[35] the history of the impugned legislation was traced back to the thirteenth century. Because the purpose of the legislation at the time of enactment in the thirteenth century is no longer of pressing and substantial importance today, the requirement of the first component of the *Oakes* test was not satisfied. This outcome was dictated by requirements of the *Oakes* test notwithstanding the fact that other arguably pressing and substantial purposes could be ascribed to the legislation today.

a) Hansard

Federal or provincial *Hansard* can be useful in determining the purpose of the legislation. Legislative debates may also indicate whether alternative legislation or wording was considered, and if so, why it was rejected. Debates which reveal why alternative legislation or wording was rejected may give insight into what the legislators were trying to achieve in enacting the impugned legislation. *Hansard* records everything that is said in the legislature or House of Commons. To find the appropriate portions of *Hansard*, you will have to trace the history of the legislation to see when it was enacted and/or amended.

When reading *Hansard*, you should be aware that all parliamentary debate about the legislation will not be of equal weight or relevance. The Minister who introduced the legislation generally summarizes the objectives of the government which is especially useful. Statements by opposition members or backbenchers about the purpose and effects of the legislation will have less weight.

b) Legislative Committee Reports and Minutes

In addition to being debated in the legislature, most legislation is also referred to a legislative committee for review after second reading in the legislature. Legislative committees will usually review a bill section by section. Committees usually include members from all parties in the legisla-

---

[33] For instructions on how to trace the history of a statutory section, consult Chapter 15 on Statutes.

[34] [1985] 1 S.C.R. 295 at 335.

[35] [1992] 2 S.C.R. 731.

ture. Committees reviewing a bill may also invite the public to submit comments.

Committee reports and minutes can be particularly useful if there was serious debate about the wording of sections of a bill. Recent legislative committee materials can be found on the federal and most provincial legislature websites as well as in law libraries. Older materials can be found in larger law libraries as well as in academic libraries.

Law Reform Commission Reports and Royal Commission Reports

Law Reform Commission Reports[36] and Royal Commission Reports can be useful in assessing the various components of the s.1 test. These reports often provide in-depth analysis of the history of specific legislation, the effects of the legislation on various groups in society, and alternative legislation. For instance, in *R. v. Videoflicks Ltd.*[37], a Law Reform Commission Report entitled *Report on Sunday Observance Legislation* (1970) was the key piece of evidence considered for the purpose of s.1.

Many Law Reform Commission Reports and Royal Commission Reports are indexed in the *Index to Canadian Legal Literature*. Recent Royal Commissions and Law Reform Commission Reports will have their own websites where the commission's materials (including their final report) can be found.

Social Science Research

As discussed above, the Supreme Court of Canada has indicated a willingness to admit social science evidence under s. 1 of the *Charter*.

Social science evidence can be obtained from a wide variety of sources, but an excellent starting place is journal articles.[38] The *Index to Periodical Articles Related to Law* indexes articles in non-legal journals that have a legal dimension. In addition to general indexes such as the *Social Sciences Index*, most major disciplines have a journal index associated with that discipline.[39] Many academic libraries have created research guides to the leading sources for journal articles in a wide variety of disciplines.[40]

---

[36] See Chapter 10 on Law Reform Commission Reports.

[37] [1986] 2 S.C.R. 713.

[38] See Chapter 17, "Other Legal Research Tools", for a discussion of how to access social science data.

[39] For example, MEDLINE for medicine and health literature and EconLit for economics articles.

[40] An excellent guide to subject specific literature is the University of Toronto Library's "Find the Best Research Resources for Your Topic", online: http://main.library.utoronto.ca/eir/articlesbytopic.cfm.

Legislation from Other Jurisdictions

With respect to item three of the *Oakes* test (minimal impairment test), as modified by subsequent case law, it can be useful to compare the impugned legislation with legislation in other jurisdictions (in Canada and abroad). Inquire whether other jurisdictions have legislation which seeks to achieve the same objective as the impugned legislation. If so, does this legislation achieve its objective in a manner that results in a less serious denial of a right or freedom than the impugned legislation, or is the impugned legislation comparable with the legislation in other jurisdictions?

For instance, in *Chaoulli v. Quebec (Attorney General)*,[41] the Supreme Court considered the constitutionality of Quebec legislation that prohibited private health insurance from providing care that was covered by public insurance. The court considered the relationship between public and private health insurance in other provinces as well as in Australia, the United Kingdom and a number of European countries.

Often, comparative legislation will be examined in Law Reform Commission Reports, Royal Commission Reports, treatises, journal articles, and other studies. You will save time by checking such sources first.

5) What is the Appropriate Remedy?

The researcher should examine what other types of remedies have been granted in similar cases and determine the legal tests which must be met to obtain particular remedies. This can be done by locating the jurisprudence under s. 24(1) or s. 52(1) of the *Charter* in a treatise or loose-leaf service. To locate this jurisprudence, the same research process that we have outlined above under "Does the Charter Apply?" should be used.

Aboriginal Constitutional Research

Many Aboriginal law questions have a constitutional component. Questions of land rights, treaties and self-determination all have fundamental constitutional implications. Section 25 of the *Charter* states that the *Charter* will not "derogate from any aboriginal, treaty or other rights or freedoms that pertain to the aboriginal peoples of Canada. . . ." Section 35 of the *Constitution Act, 1982* being Schedule B to the *Canada Act 1982* (U.K.), 1982, c. 11 recognizes and affirms "the existing aboriginal and treaty rights of the aboriginal peoples of Canada." In addition to being discussed in treatises on constitutional law, there is a growing body of secondary literature on Aboriginal law generally that analyses and discusses how the courts have ap-

---

[41] [2005] 1 S.C.R. 791.

plied ss. 25 and 35. You should consult this literature when doing research on a question that involves Aboriginal law.[42]

---

[42] For a list of loose-leaf services and treatises, consult the Aboriginal Law section of the Selective Topical Bibliography.

15

Researching Statutes

What are Statutes?

Statutes or acts are a primary source of law. They are written enactments by governments to codify, reform, and/or deal with issues not always addressed by the common law (also known as case law). Statutes are the laws made by legislatures as opposed to case law which is law as it exists in judicial decisions.

Statutes are written according to a standard format. Each statute is assigned a chapter number, which you will need to know for citation purposes. The long title, as its name suggests, is a lengthy and detailed title for the statute. Long titles usually begin with the phrase "An Act respecting . . ." Long titles are useful because they provide a description of the subject matter of the statute and can be cited in court as an interpretive aid. Statutes also usually have short titles. These are typically preceded by the phrase "This Act may be cited as . . ." The actual text of the statute is written with numbered and alphabetized section and paragraph numbers for easy citation. See Illustration 15.1 for an example of the first page of a federal act.

Illustration 15.1

CHAPTER A-2	CHAPITRE A-2
An Act to authorize the control of aeronautics	Loi autorisant le contrôle de l'aéronautique

SHORT TITLE

Short title   **1.** This Act may be cited as the *Aeronautics Act*

R.S., c. A-3, s. 1

HER MAJESTY

Binding on Her Majesty   **2.** This Act is binding on Her Majesty in right of Canada or a province

1976-77, c. 26, s. 1

INTERPRETATION

Definitions   **3.** (1) In this Act,

ANS Corporation « société »   "ANS Corporation" means NAV CANADA, a corporation incorporated on May 26, 1995 under Part II of the *Canada Corporations Act*;

aerodrome « aérodrome »   "aerodrome" means any area of land, water (including the frozen surface thereof) or other supporting surface used, designed, prepared, equipped or set apart for use either in whole or in part for the arrival, departure, movement or servicing of aircraft and includes any buildings, installations and equipment situated thereon or associated therewith;

aeronautical product « produit aéronautiques »   "aeronautical product" means any aircraft, aircraft engine, aircraft propeller or aircraft appliance or part or the component parts of any of those things, including any computer system and software;

air carrier « transporteur aérien »   "air carrier" means any person who operates a commercial air service;

aircraft « aéronef »   "aircraft" means

     (*a*) until the day on which paragraph (*b*) comes into force, any machine capable of deriving support in the atmosphere from reactions of the air, and includes a rocket, and

     (*b*) [Not in force]

TITRE ABRÉGÉ

Titre abrégé   **1.** *Loi sur l'aéronautique*

S.R., ch. A-3, art. 1

SA MAJESTÉ

Obligation de Sa Majesté   **2.** La présente loi lie Sa Majesté du chef du Canada ou d'une province

1976-77, ch. 26, art. 1

DÉFINITIONS

Définitions   **3.** (1) Les définitions qui suivent s'appliquent à la présente loi.

« aérodrome » "aerodrome"   « aérodrome » Tout terrain, plan d'eau (gelé ou non) ou autre surface d'appui servant ou conçu, aménagé, équipé ou réservé pour servir, en tout ou en partie, aux mouvements et à la mise en oeuvre des aéronefs, y compris les installations qui y sont situées ou leur sont rattachées.

« aéronef » "aircraft"   « aéronef »

     a) Jusqu'à l'entrée en vigueur de l'alinéa *b*), tout appareil qui peut se soutenir dans l'atmosphère grâce aux réactions de l'air, ainsi qu'une fusée;

     b) [Non en vigueur]

« aéronef canadien » "Canadian aircraft"   « aéronef canadien » Aéronef immatriculé au Canada.

« aéroport » "airport"   « aéroport » Aérodrome agréé comme aéroport au titre d'un document d'aviation canadien en état de validité

« arrêté d'urgence » "interim order"   « arrêté d'urgence » Arrêté pris en vertu des paragraphes 6.41(1) ou (1.1).

« Canada » [Abrogée, 1996, ch. 31, art. 56]

1

Often near the beginning of the statute, you will find a definition section that defines terminology used in the act. Application sections, which indicate the situations to which the statute is expected to apply, are also common. Brief notes usually appear in the margins that indicate the subject matter of various sections. For example, the word "Definitions" in a margin note indicates that the section contains definitions for words and phrases used in the act. Margin notes are useful tools for finding your way around a statute, but they do not constitute part of the statute and therefore cannot be used for interpretive purposes. See Illustration 15.1 above for an example of margin notes.

There are two different types of acts — substantive acts and amending/repealing acts. A substantive act sets out the laws in a particular topic or area; for example, the *Criminal Code*.[1] Amending/repealing acts do nothing but amend or repeal substantive acts. These acts do not stand alone as acts that state the law in a particular area; they amend or repeal the substantive acts that we have to follow. For example, the *Bankruptcy and Insolvency Act*[2] is a substantive act that outlines the laws regarding bankruptcy and insolvency. If a person wants to declare herself bankrupt, she has to do so according to the rules in this act. But what if a section of the *Bankruptcy and Insolvency Act*[3] needed to be changed because it was no longer appropriate for how society works? To do that, another act would have to be passed that would amend the *Bankruptcy and Insolvency Act*.[4] It could be called *An Act to Amend the Bankruptcy and Insolvency Act*. This act simply amends the act mentioned in the title (the *Bankruptcy and Insolvency Act*); it is not a new act nor has it been replaced; it has just been altered slightly. The vast majority of acts that come into force each year are amending/repealing acts.

All jurisdictions in Canada make their statutes available online through a government website. Statutes are also available within commercial or open-access electronic databases such as Westlaw Canada, LexisNexis Quicklaw, and CanLII. In some jurisdictions, the versions of the statutes available online through the government websites are considered official and can be cited in court.[5]

---

[1] R.S.C. 1985, c. C-46.

[2] R.S.C. 1985, c. B-3.

[3] *Ibid.*

[4] *Ibid.*

[5] For example, Ontario, Quebec, and Canada.

How are Statutes Made and Amended?

Statutes are created and amended by bills, which are proposed statutes that must go through a governmental approval process in order to become part of existing law. Federal bills originate from either of the two chambers of Parliament: the House of Commons or the Senate. Provincial and territorial bills originate in the provincial or territorial legislature, as the case may be.

There are two different types of bills — public and private. Public bills affect public policy and are far-reaching; for example, the *Criminal Code*[6] codifies the criminal law of the country and affects the entire Canadian population. Public bills are usually introduced only by cabinet ministers. However, a member of the Parliament or provincial or territorial legislature who is not a cabinet minister may also introduce public bills, and these are called private members bills or private members public bills.[7]

The second type of bill, private bills, only affect a particular person, corporation, or institution and not the public at large. For example, *The Mennonite Educational Society of Manitoba Incorporation Act*[8] deals with the continuation, objects, and powers of an educational society focused on instruction in the Mennonite faith in Manitoba.

In order for a federal bill to become law, it must be read and voted on three times by both the House of Commons and the Senate. Provincial and territorial bills must be read and voted on three times by the legislature.

Federally, on first reading the bill is introduced and copies of it are distributed. The bill is not debated at first reading. On second reading, after the members of the House of Commons or Senate, as the case may be, have had time to read the bill, it is fully debated and in many cases referred to a committee. The committee will study the bill and provide a report recommending the bill remain unchanged or suggest amendments.

On third reading, the House or Senate considers the report of the committee and the bill is voted on. The bill will then go through the same process in the Senate or the House, depending on where the bill originated. Bills that originate in the House of Commons are numbered C-1 to C-200; pri-

---

[6] *Supra* note 1.

[7] In Ontario, there is another type of public bill — a committee bill. Three standing committees in Ontario may study a particular area of law that relate to their mandate and propose bills in that same area. The committees are: Standing Committee on Social Policy, Standing Committee on Justice Policy, and Standing Committee on General Government. In the past, the Standing Committee on Social Policy and the Standing Committee on Justice Policy were together as one standing committee.

[8] R.S.M. 1990, c. 106.

vate members' public bills are numbered C-201 to C-1000. Those that originate in the Senate are numbered beginning with S-1.[9]

Provincially and territorially, the procedure is essentially the same, although the bill only has to move through one chamber, not two. Provincial and territorial bills are numbered in the order they are introduced.

Where to find it: Bills can be found on the fourteen government websites in Canada. In some jurisdictions, bills are removed from the government websites once they become law. Other jurisdictions have bills available electronically for the last number of years (for example, on the House of Assembly website in Newfoundland and Labrador, bills are available online back to 2000).

You can also use an online commercial database called *Canadian Legislative Pulse* by CCH Canadian Limited to find bills (http://pulse.cch.ca/). This resource provides full-text access to bills from all jurisdictions in Canada. Users are able to receive email notifications when information on a particular bill the user is interested in has been updated. The user can also find information on bills from previous sessions and proclamation dates. This flexible and powerful resource will be useful to those who need to track bills at their various stages of development. Currently, this is the only Canadian electronic bill-tracking resource. *Canadian Legislative Pulse* is hosted on its own platform, but at some point in the future the *Canadian Legislative Pulse* will be housed within CCH Online, a large online legal research system (http://www.cch.ca/). See Illustration 15.2 for an example of a page from the *Canadian Legislative Pulse*.

---

9 For more information, see the Parliament of Canada website at http://www.parl.gc.ca/.

Illustration 15.2

Canadian Legislative Pulse

Home | Recent Updates | My Bills & Regs | Search | View | Tools | Help | Log Out

Updates to the site since 10:17 AM on Wednesday, November 11, 2009 are highlighted in yellow.

	Legislation			Regulations	
	Current Session	Previous Sessions	Other Proclamations	Current Year	Previous Years
Federal		View	View	Updated!	Updated!
Commons Bills	Updated!				
Senate Bills	Updated!				
Alberta	Updated!	View	View	View	View
British Columbia	Updated!	View	Updated!	Updated!	Updated!
Manitoba	Updated!	Updated!	View	Updated!	Updated!
New Brunswick	Updated!	Updated!	View	Updated!	Updated!
Newfoundland and Labrador	Updated!	Updated!	View	Updated!	Updated!
Northwest Territories	View	View	View	View	View
Nova Scotia	Updated!	View	View	Updated!	Updated!
Nunavut	Updated!	View	View	View	View
Ontario	Updated!	View	View	Updated!	Updated!
Prince Edward Island	Updated!	View	View	Updated!	Updated!
Quebec	Updated!	Updated!	View	View	View
Saskatchewan	Updated!	View	View	Updated!	Updated!
Yukon	View	View	View	View	View

Reproduced with permission from CCH Canadian Limited, a Wolters Kluwer Business.

When is a Statute in Force?

Once a bill has made its way through the legislative process and been given approval after third reading, it must be given Royal Assent. Royal Assent signifies the approval of the bill by the head of state, Her Majesty Queen Elizabeth II. The Queen's representatives in Canada — the Governor General for federal bills, the Lieutenant Governor for provincial bills, and the Commissioner for territorial bills — give such approval. This is now considered a formality and it is rare for the Queen's representative to refuse to give Royal Assent. The date on which Royal Assent was given is shown at the beginning of the statute right after the title. Once Royal Assent is given, the bill becomes an act, is given a chapter number, and it becomes law.

Simply because an act has been given Royal Assent and becomes law does not mean the statute is in force. Finding the coming into force (CIF) date is very important. An act that is law but not in force cannot be acted upon or applied. An act may come into force in one of three ways. A statute may:

(a) specify the actual date on which the statute will come into force;

(b) state either explicitly or by its silence that the statute will come into force upon receiving Royal Assent; or

(c) state that the statute will come into force on a date fixed by proclamation. (See below for more information).

To find out which way an act will come into force, look at the last or next to last section of a statute. This is usually where the CIF information will be listed; however, if you do not find the CIF information near the end of the act, you should look through the entire act to make sure the CIF information is not located elsewhere.

Sometimes statutes do not specify when they come into force (i.e., they are "silent"). As of the date of publication, in all common-law jurisdictions in Canada a statute comes into force on the date of Royal Assent unless otherwise stated in the act.[10] However, you should always check the relevant interpretation or statute act in your jurisdiction to ensure this is in fact the case as these acts may be amended periodically.

The Governor General or Lieutenant Governor will proclaim a statute in force upon the advice of the cabinet or the legislature, respectively. This delay in having a statute come into force is often to give the government, public, and various institutions time to appropriately prepare for the law.

When an act is to come into force upon proclamation, you will have to use other resources and products to find out when the act actually came into force. When conducting this research, keep in mind that only government publications are considered official copies of the law (in some jurisdictions, electronic laws and tables published by the government are considered official);[11] commercial publications are not considered official and should not be relied upon in court.

Where to find it: Federally, CIF dates may be found using the following resources:

(a) the *Proclamations of Canada and Orders in Council Relating to the Coming Into Force of Acts* table in the latest annual statutes volume;

---

[10] For example: *Interpretation Act*, R.S.C. 1985 c. I-21, s. 5(2); *An Act Respecting the Form and Interpretation of Statutes*, R.S.N.S. 1989, c. 235, s. 3(2); *Interpretation Act*, R.S.B.C. 1996, c. 238, s. 3(2); and *Legislation Act, 2006*, S.O. 2006, c. 21, Sch. F, s. 8(1).

[11] The federal Department of Justice and the New Brunswick Attorney General Websites are two examples.

(b) *Canada Gazette, Part III*. This is available in print and online at <http://www.gazette.gc.ca/rp-pr/p3/index-eng.html>. You can also look in the *Canada Gazette, Part II* in print and online at <http://www.gazette.gc.ca/rp-pr/p2/index-eng.html>;

(c) the *Table of Public Statutes and Responsible Ministers*, which can be found in the latest annual volume. This table is also published quarterly in a separate document and is available online: <http://laws.justice.gc.ca/en/publaw/index.html>. In November 2009, it was announced that the *Table of Public Statutes and Responsible Ministers* would no longer be available in print. See Illustration 15.3 for a sample page from the *Table of Public Statutes and Responsible Ministers*.

(d) Parliament of Canada LEGISINFO website: <http://www2.parl.gc.ca/Sites/LOP/LEGISINFO/index.asp?Language=E>. LEGISINFO is the Library of Parliament electronic research tool to find information on legislation that is before Parliament; it also provides access to historical legislative information. See Illustration 15.4 for a sample from LEGISINFO.

Researching Statutes

Illustration 15.3

Table of Public Statutes and Responsible Ministers

A

s. 16, 2006, c. 3, s. 10
s. 17, 2006, c. 3, s. 10
s. 18, 2006, c. 3, s. 10
s. 19, 2006, c. 3, s. 10
s. 20, 2006, c. 3, s. 11
s. 21, 2004, c. 25, s. 183; 2006, c. 3, s. 12
s. 23, 1999, c. 26, s. 46; 2008, c. 7, s. 6
s. 24, 2006, c. 3, s. 13
s. 33.1, added, 2006, c. 3, s. 14
s. 34, 2006, c. 3, s. 15
s. 40, 1999, c. 26, s. 47; 2006, c. 3, s. 16; 2008, c. 7, s. 7
s. 42, 2006, c. 3, s. 17; 2008, c. 7, s. 8
s. 51.1, 2006, c. 3, s. 18
s. 52.1, 2006, c. 3, s. 19
Sch., added, 2006, c. 3, s. 20
Transitional, 2006, c. 3, s. 21
Transitional, 2008, c. 7, s. 9
General, 1999, c. 26, s. 48 *re* application
CIF, 1997, c. 20, except ss. 44 to 46, in force 01.01.97 *see* s. 56(1); ss. 44 to 46 come into force on a day or days to be fixed by order of the Governor in Council *see* s. 56(2) Not in force
CIF, 1998, c. 17, s. 30 in force 01.08.98 *see* SI/98-85
CIF, 1999, c. 26, ss. 42 to 48 in force on assent 17.06.99
CIF, 2000, c. 12, s. 2 in force 31.07.2000 *see* SI/2000-76
CIF, 2001, c. 27, s. 203 in force 28.06.2002 *see* SI/2002-97
CIF, 2004, c. 25, s. 183 in force on assent 15.12.2004
CIF, 2006, c. 3 in force 27.11.2006 *see* SI/2006-136
CIF, 2008, c. 7 in force on assent 28.02.2008

Agricultural Products Act, Canada
— R.S., 1985, c. 20 (4th Supp.)
(Produits agricoles au Canada, Loi sur les)

Minister of Agriculture and Agri-Food

s. 2, 1994, c. 38, s. 25(1)(*d*); 1995, c. 40, s. 27; 1997, c. 6, s. 38
s. 4, 1995, c. 40, s. 28
s. 4.1, added, 1995, c. 40, s. 29
s. 4.2, added, 1995, c. 40, s. 29; 2003, c. 22, par. 224(*i*)(E)
s. 4.3, added, 1995, c. 40, s. 29
s. 4.4, added, 1995, c. 40, s. 29
s. 5, 1995, c. 40, s. 29
s. 6, 1995, c. 40, s. 30; 2003, c. 22, par. 224(*i*)(E)
s. 7, 1995, c. 40, s. 31; 2003, c. 22, par. 224(*i*)(E)
s. 7.1, added, 1995, c. 40, s. 31
s. 8, 1995, c. 40, s. 32
s. 10, 1995, c. 40, s. 33
s. 11, 1995, c. 40, s. 35
s. 12, 1990, c. 8, s. 42; 1995, c. 40, s. 36; 2002, c. 8, par. 182(1)(*c*)
s. 12.1, added, 1995, c. 40, s. 36
s. 12.2, added, 1995, c. 40, s. 36

s. 18, 1995, c. 40, s. 37
s. 19, 1997, c. 6, s. 39; 2005, c. 38, s. 33
s. 26, 1995, c. 40, s. 38
s. 27, 1995, c. 40, s. 39
s. 28, 1993, c. 34, s. 12(F); 1995, c. 40, s. 40
s. 29, 1993, c. 34, s. 13(F); 1995, c. 40, s. 41
s. 30, 1995, c. 40, s. 42(F)
s. 31, 2001, c. 4, s. 63
s. 32, 1991, c. 24, s. 51 (Sch. III, item 2); 2001, c. 4, s. 64(E)
s. 33, 1995, c. 40, s. 43
s. 34, repealed, 1992, c. 47, s. 84 (Sch., item 1)
s. 40, 1995, c. 40, s. 44
s. 41, 1995, c. 40, s. 45
General, 1995, c. 40, s. 34
General, 1994, c. 38, s. 25(2)
CIF, R.S., c. 20 (4th Supp.) in force 07.07.88
CIF, 1990, c. 8 in force 01.02.92 *see* SI/92-6
CIF, 1991, c. 24, s. 51 (Sch. III, item 2) shall come into force on a day or days to be fixed by order of the Governor in Council *see* s. 53. Not in force
CIF, 1992, c. 47, s. 84 (Sch., item 1) shall come into force throughout Canada or in any province on a day or days to be fixed by order of the Governor in Council made throughout Canada or in respect of that province *see* s. 86(2) and *also* 1996, c. 7, s. 42. Not in force
CIF, 1993, c. 34, ss. 12(F) and 13(F) in force on assent 23.06.93
CIF, 1994, c. 38, s. 25 in force 12.01.95 *see* SI/95-9
CIF, 1995, c. 40, ss. 27 to 45 in force 30.07.97 *see* SI/97-89
CIF, 1997, c. 6, ss. 38 and 39 in force 01.04.97 *see* SI/97-37
CIF, 2001, c. 4, ss. 63 and 64 in force 01.06.2001 *see* SI/2001-71
CIF, 2002, c. 8, s. 182 in force 02.07.2003 *see* SI/2003-109
CIF, 2003, c. 22, s. 224 in force 01.04.2005 *see* SI/2005-24
CIF, 2005, c. 38, s. 33 in force 12.12.2005 *see* SI/2005-119

Agricultural Products Board Act
— R.S., 1985, c. A-4
(Office des produits agricoles, Loi sur l')

ACT REPEALED 1997, c. 20, s. 43
Transitional, 1997, c. 20, ss. 47 to 49
CIF, 1997, c. 20, s. 43 and 47 to 49 in force 01.01.97 *see* s. 56

Agricultural Products Cooperative Marketing
Act — R.S., 1985, c. A-5
(Vente coopérative des produits agricoles, Loi sur la)

Minister of Agriculture and Agri-Food

Reproduced from the Department of Justice, Government of Canada website (http://www.justice.gc.ca/).

Illustration 15.4

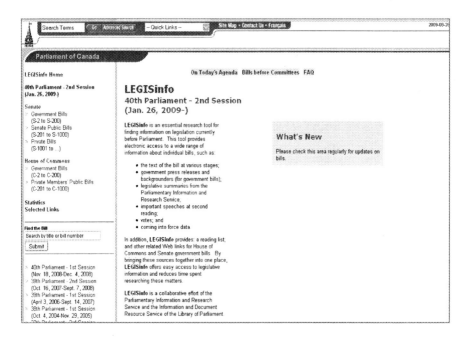

Library of Parliament / Bibliothèque du Parlement. Reproduced with permission from Library of Parliament / Bibliothèque du Parlement. Taken from the following URL: <http://www2.parl.gc.ca/Sites/LOP/LEGISINFO/index.asp?Language=E>.

(e) each issue of *Canadian Current Law — Legislation*, a component of the *Canadian Abridgment*, contains a heading entitled "Statutes Amended, Repealed, or Proclaimed in Force" which provides the CIF information for federal, provincial, and territorial statutes. See Illustration 15.5.

Researching Statutes

Illustration 15.5

Uniformed Services Pensions Act, 1991,
S.N.L. 1991, c. 19
s. 24(5) [Am] 2008, c. 23, s. 15;
s. 24.1(1) [Am] 2008, c. 23, s. 16(1);
s. 24.1(2) [Rep] 2008, c. 23, s. 16(2);
s. 24.2 [Ad] 2008, c. 23 s. 17

NORTHWEST TERRITORIES

Adoption Act,
S.N.W.T. 1998, c. 9
Preamble [Am] 2008, c. 8, s. 1(2);
s. 39 [Am] 2008, c. 8, s. 1(3)(a), (b);
s. 72(2) [Am] 2008, c. 8, s. 1(4);
s. 77 [Rep] 2008, c. 8, s. 1(5);
s. 77.1 [Am] 2008, c. 8, s. 1(6);
s. 77.2 [Am] 2008, c. 8, s. 1(7);
s. 78 (and headings preceding) [Rep] 2008, c. 8, s. 1(8);
s. 79 (and headings preceding) [Rep] 2008, c. 8, s. 1(8)
Agricultural Products Marketing Act,
R.S.N.W.T. 1988, c. 115 (Supp.)
s. 26(d) [Am] 2008 c. 8, s. 2(2);
s. 31 [Rep] 2008, c. 8, s. 2(3);
s. 32(2) [Am] 2008, c. 8, s. 2(4);
s. 35 [Rep] 2008, c. 8, s. 2(5)
Apprenticeship, Trade and Occupations Certification Act,
R.S.N.W.T. 1988, c. A-4
s. 19(k) [Am] 2007, c. 13, s. 107
Appropriation Act, 2008-2009,
S.N.W.T. 2008, c. 4
[P] April 1, 2008
Architects Act,
S.N.W.T. 2001, c. 10
s. 1(1) "professional engineer", "professional engineering" [Am] 2006, c. 16 s. 66
Archives Act,
R.S.N.W.T. 1988, c. A-6
s. 1 "government body" (a) [Am] 2007, c. 2 s. 2(a)(i);
s. 1 "government body" (b) [Am] 2007, c. 2 s. 2(a)(ii);
s. 1 "government body" (c) [Rep] 2007, c. 2, s. 2(a)(iii);
s. 1 "public record" [Am] 2007, c. 2, s. 2(b);
s. 1 "Public Records Committee" [Rep] 2007 c. 2, s. 2(c);
s. 1 "record" [Am] 2007, c. 2, s. 2(d);
s. 4(a) [Am] 2007, c. 2, s. 3(a);
s. 4(b) [Am] 2007, c. 2, s. 3(b);
s. 5(1) [Am] 2007, c. 2, s. 4(1);
s. 5(4) [Am] 2007, c. 2, s. 4(2);
s. 5(5), (6) [Rep] 2007, c. 2, s. 4(3);
s. 6 [Rep] 2007, c. 2, s. 5;
s. 9 [Rep] 2007, c. 2, s. 6;
s. 11 [Am] 2007, c. 2, s. 7
Archives Amendment Act,
S.N.W.T. 2007, c. 2
[P] May 1, 2008
Business Licence Act,
R.S.N.W.T. 1988, c. B-4
s. 4(2), (3) (both Fr.) [Am] 2007, c. 21, s. 177, Sched., item 1(2)(b);
s. 4(2), (3) [Am] 2007, c. 21, s. 177, Sched., item 1(2)(a);

s. 7(d) [Am] 2007, c. 21, s. 177, Sched., item 1(3)(a);
s. 7(d) (Fr.) [Am] 2007, c. 21, s. 177, Sched., item 1(3)(b)
Change of Name Act,
R.S.N.W.T. 1988, c. C-3
[Re] 2007, c. 12, s. 25
Change of Name Act,
S.N.W.T. 2007, c. 12
[P] April 1, 2008
Child and Family Services Act,
S.N.W.T. 1997, c. 13
Preamble [Am] 2007, c. 5, s. 2;
s. 1 "apprehension hearing", "apprehension order" [Ad] 2007, c. 5, s. 3;
s. 1.2(1) [Rep] 2007, c. 5, s. 4(1);
s. 1.2(2) [Rep] 2007, c. 5, s. 4(2);
s. 1.2(4), (5) [Rep] 2007, c. 5, s. 4(3);
s. 4 "child protection order" [Ad] 2007, c. 5, s. 5(b);
s. 4 "order" [Am] 2007, c. 5, s. 5(a);
s. 10 (heading preceding) (Fr.) [Am] 2007, c. 5, s. 6;
s. 10(1)(b) [Am] 2007, c. 5, s. 7(1);
s. 10(1)(c) [Rep] 2007, c. 5, s. 7(2);
s. 11 (heading preceding) (Fr.) [Rep] 2007, c. 5, s. 8;
s. 11(3)(b) [Rep] 2007, c. 5, s. 9(1);
s. 11(3)(c) [Am] 2007, c. 5, s. 9(2);
ss. 12.1–12.7 [Ad] 2007, c. 5, s. 10;
s. 13(2)(b) [Rep] 2007, c. 5, s. 11;
s. 14(1)(a), (b) [Am] 2007, c. 5, s. 12(1);
s. 14(2) [Rep] 2007, c. 5, s. 12(2);
s. 16(1) preceding (a) [Ad] 2007, c. 5, s. 13(1)(a);
s. 16(1)(b) [Rep] 2007, c. 5, s. 13(1)(b);
s. 16(3) [Am] 2007, c. 5, s. 13(2);
s. 16(4) preceding (a) [Am] 2007, c. 5, s. 13(3)(a);
s. 16(4)(b) [Rep] 2007, c. 5, s. 13(3)(b);
s. 17(1)(a) [Am] 2007, c. 5, s. 14;
s. 18(1) [Am] 2007, c. 5, s. 15(1);
s. 18(4) [Am] 2007, c. 5, s. 15(2);
s. 19(2) [Am] 2007, c. 5, s. 16;
s. 22(2) [Am] 2007, c. 5, s. 17(1);
s. 22(3) [Am] 2007, c. 5, s. 17(2);
s. 23(1)(a) [Rep] 2007, c. 5, s. 18(1)(a);
s. 23(1)(b) [Am] 2007, c. 5, s. 18(1)(b);
s. 23(2) [Am] 2007, c. 5, s. 18(2);
s. 23.1(1) [Am] 2007, c. 5, s. 19;
s. 24 (heading preceding) [Rep] 2007, c. 5, s. 20;
s. 24 preceding (a) [Am] 2007, c. 5, s. 21;
s. 25(1) [Rep] 2007, c. 5, s. 22(1);
s. 25(2) [Am] 2007, c. 5, s. 22(2);
s. 26 [Am] 2007, c. 5, s. 23;
s. 27(1), (2) preceding (a) [Am] 2007, c. 5, s. 24;
s. 28(1) preceding (a) [Am] 2007, c. 5, s. 25(1);
s. 28(2) [Am] 2007, c. 5, s. 25(2);
s. 28(5) preceding (a), (5.1) [Am] 2007, c. 5, s. 25(3);
s. 28(6) [Am] 2007, c. 5, s. 25(4);
s. 28(7), (8) [Am] 2007, c. 5, s. 25(5);
s. 28(9) preceding (a) [Am] 2007, c. 5, s. 25(6);
s. 29(1) preceding (a) [Am] 2007, c. 5, s. 26(1);
s. 29(2) [Am] 2007, c. 5, s. 26(2);
s. 31(1), (2) [Am] 2007, c. 5, s. 27(1);
s. 31(3) [Am] 2007, c. 5, s. 27(2);
s. 31(4) preceding (a) [Am] 2007, c. 5, s. 27(3)(a);
s. 31(4)(c) [Am] 2007, c. 5, s. 27(3)(b);
s. 31(6) [Am] 2007, c. 5, s. 27(4);
s. 31(6.1)–(6.3) [Ad] 2007, c. 5, s. 27(5);

227

(f) *Canada Statute Citator*, which provides amendment information as well as CIF information for federal statutes (statute citators are discussed in greater depth below);

(g) *Canada Legislative Index*, which includes a proclamation section for statutes; and

(h) *Canadian Legislative Pulse*. This is an online database that tracks bills and legislation. One option they provide the user is the CIF date of statutes.

Provincially and territorially, CIF dates may be found using the following resources:

(a) the provincial or territorial *Gazette*. In most jurisdictions, this is available in print and online (although in some jurisdictions there is a fee to access the *Gazette* electronically);

(b) all jurisdictions have a table of public statutes (although it may have a different name depending on the jurisdiction). For each jurisdiction, this table is available in print in each annual volume, in print in a separate volume, and/or online;

(c) many jurisdictions have a table of proclamations available in print and/or online. With these tables, the CIF date of statutes is listed;

(d) each issue of *Canadian Current Law — Legislation*, a component of the *Canadian Abridgment*, contains a heading entitled "Statutes Amended, Repealed, or Proclaimed in Force" which provides the CIF information for provincial, territorial, and federal statutes;

(e) provincial statute citators. Only the larger provinces (for example, Ontario and British Columbia) have dedicated citators (statute citators are discussed in greater depth below);

(f) some jurisdictions may have a dedicated legislative digest. These tools are only usually available for the larger provinces; and

(g) *Canadian Legislative Pulse*. This is an online database that tracks bills and legislation. One option available in the *Canadian Legislative Pulse* is finding the CIF date of statutes.

How are Statutes Published?

Sessional or Annual Volumes

Sessional volumes contain statutes passed during a session of Parliament or the legislature. Annual volumes contain statutes passed in a given year. The provisions of a statute that have been amended many times will likely be spread over a number of annual volumes.

At the federal level, prior to 1984 all statutes passed during a session of Parliament were bound in sessional volumes. Sessions can cover more than one year. As of 1984, federal statutes are published in annual volumes.

Sessional or annual volumes are published in print at the end of each session or year respectively. It can take some time for the final printed volumes to be available to the public in a library — it often takes six months or more for the hardbound volume to be printed. A person does not have to wait for this hardbound volume to find out the law in a particular jurisdiction, however. All jurisdictions in Canada post their statutes online, and some jurisdictions post their *Gazette* and the different tables that often appear in the hardbound annual or sessional volume. In print, a person can refer to the *Gazettes* that have been published in paper parts throughout the year or session.

Where to find it: In libraries that purchase the annual and sessional statutes. As well, please see Appendix I for a list of websites for each jurisdiction in Canada where the government has made legislation and various other legislative resources available electronically.

Revised Statutes

Periodically, statutes published in the sessional or annual volumes are consolidated into a bound master set of statutes;[12] these are called "revised statutes". Revised statutes replace and consolidate most of the sessional volumes or annual volumes preceding it as the official text of the statute. In the revised statutes, acts are ordered alphabetically and given consecutive chapter numbers. Note that some obscure statutes may not be included in the consolidation.

It is important to periodically revise statutes because over time there may be many amendments to a statute and it can look very different several years after being enacted. To find all amendments and see what the law looked like at a specific point in time can be very difficult. By revising or consolidating a statute, a picture can be taken of the statute as it stood on a

---

[12] For instance, the latest consolidation of federal statutes occurred as of 1985.

particular day, with all the changes that had taken place over the years. This essentially cleans up the statute and shows what it looked like at a given period of time.

Such revisions are becoming less common as electronic versions of statutes housed within electronic databases and government websites make it easier to access current consolidations of the law. In databases such as Westlaw Canada and LexisNexis Quicklaw, the acts are continually consolidated — if an act has been amended, the amendment is made in the act electronically so that the act is current, with all amendments, revisions, repeals, and so forth, to the day it is accessed by the user. In addition, this continuing consolidation occurs in the free website CanLII,[13] and on many government websites, although such changes are not made as quickly as on commercial databases due to lack of funding and personnel — with commercial databases, customers pay high fees to access them and therefore demand that the law be as up-to-date as possible.

With some resources, such as LexisNexis Quicklaw, CanLII, and the Department of Justice website,[14] you can also choose to see what an act looked like on a particular day in the past (called a point-in-time reference). This is useful because if a client is charged with an offence under an act, he or she will be subject to the act as it appeared on the day the offence took place. For example, if you have a client who is charged on February 10, 2010 with a murder that took place on June 3, 2003, your client will be charged under the *Criminal Code*[15] as it stood on June 3, 2003, not as it stood on February 10, 2010. This has important consequences for clients, so this information is very important for practitioners. See Illustration 15.6 for an example of the point-in-time search template from the Department of Justice.

---

[13] See the chapter titled "Electronic Legal Research" for more information on CanLII.

[14] Other government websites, such as the e-Laws website from Ontario, also offer point-in-time services.

[15] *Supra* note 1.

Illustration 15.6

Reproduced from the Department of Justice, Government of Canada website (http://www.justice.gc.ca/).

Due to the ability to find current consolidated statutes electronically and to see how an act appeared on a particular day in the past, it is likely that revised statutes in print will occur less and less frequently.

Loose-leaf Format

Loose-leafs are published in binders so that new amendments or other developments can be inserted on a regular basis. You should be aware that many loose-leaf services are published by commercial publishers. These commercial services, while very useful for research purposes, do not have legal effect and should not be cited in court. Loose-leaf statutes that are published by the government are official documents. When citing a statute, always cite the official version that is published by the government printers, whether in print or online.[16]

Statute Citators

Statute Citators are loose-leaf services that show the current state of the statutes since the publication of the latest revised statutes. Some cases interpreting sections of the statute are also listed. There is a Citator for federal acts (*Canada Statute Citator*), but usually only the larger provinces have a designated Citator (for example, the *Ontario Statute Citator*). These Citators are published by commercial publishers, not the government, so the statutes as they appear in the Citator are not official versions.

NOTE: Tax statutes are not covered in the Citators. There are many commercial services that deal exclusively with tax statutes.[17]

Doing Statutory Research

Statutory research involves five steps:

1. determining whether a *relevant statute exists*;
2. *locating* the statute;
3. determining if the statute is *in force*;
4. *updating* the statute; and
5. checking whether the sections of the statute you are concerned with have been *judicially considered*.

In the past, these steps were completed almost entirely using print products; however, as electronic access to statutes has increased, most of these steps can be done electronically.

Step One: How to Determine Whether a Statute Exists

If you do not already have a statute name or citation, you will need to determine whether or not a statute exists that deals with your topic.

---

[16] Some jurisdictions have made their electronic statutes official, for example Canada, Ontario, and Quebec.

[17] See the tax section in the Selective Topical Bibliography.

Secondary Sources

You should begin your research by looking for your topic in a treatise, journal article, legal encyclopedia, loose-leaf service (including a Citator), dictionary or words and phrases resource, or other secondary source. These sources may refer you to the name and citation of the relevant statute, if one exists. Many of these resources are available in print as well as electronically; while it may be tempting to use electronic sources, do not ignore the sources available in print — not all secondary sources are available online. If you disregard print resources, you will miss information that could be related to your topic. In law, missing such details can be very detrimental to your client's case.

Web-based Legal Research Databases

If you are not successful in using some of the secondary sources listed above, you can also search or browse within the various government websites that list legislation or an electronic legal research database such as CanLII, Westlaw Canada, or LexisNexis Quicklaw to find legislation on your topic. When searching online, you need to make sure you use the correct words and synonyms. The website or database will only search for the words you ask it to search and nothing more; for example, if you need to find statutes which deal with defamation and you search for "defamation" but not "libel" or "slander," you would find statutes that have the word "defamation", but not necessarily the other words. This would mean you would miss statutes. In Saskatchewan, the *Libel and Slander Act*[18] refers to libel and slander but not defamation, so this statute would have been missed in your search, yet it could have been the very statute for which you were searching.[19] See Illustration 15.7 for an example of searching using CanLII.

---

[18] R.S.S. 1978, c, L-14.

[19] See the chapter titled "Electronic Legal Research" for more tips on how you should search electronically.

Illustration 15.7

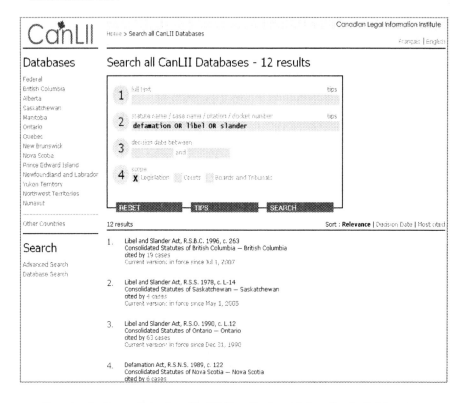

Reproduced with permission from CanLII (Canadian Legal Information Institute)

Table of Public Statutes

If you still have not had success finding a statute on your topic, you can try to find one by using the *Table of Public Statutes* in the annual statutes volume or online through the various government websites (remember, as of the end of 2009, the federal *Table of Public Statutes* will no longer be printed and will only be available online). These tables provide an alphabetical listing of those statutes included in the last revision and any new statutes that have been passed since the last revision. You can skim the list to determine if there are any statutes on your topic. The titles of statutes are generally suggestive of their subject. However, we do not recommend relying on the *Table of Public Statutes* alone. Sometimes there is a subject index that lists relevant statutes by subject; unfortunately, these do not always exist.

Step Two: How to Locate Statutes

Once you know that a statute on your subject exists and you have the title and/or citation, the next step is to go and find the statute in full-text. If you already had the name of the statute or the citation and you did not need to determine if a statute in your topic area exists, this would be your first step.

Web-based Legal Research Databases

It is easiest to find the current version of the statute by using an electronic database such as Westlaw Canada, LexisNexis Quicklaw, CanLII, or the government website in the jurisdiction of interest. To do this, choose the resource and then use its search function to find the statute by name or citation.[20] For some of the government websites, you will not be able to search for the statute but will instead have to browse from their list of annual or revised statutes.

If you need to find the statute as it appeared when it was first enacted, you will likely have to use print resources. As mentioned previously, most online databases provide access to the statute as it looks on the day it was accessed, not the day it was first enacted. If you are using one of the resources that have a point-in-time function whereby you can find previous versions, you may be able to find the statute in its original form, but only if the statute is not very old. Most of these databases only go back a few years,[21] and on LexisNexis Quicklaw this function is not active for every jurisdiction.

Currently, there are only a few resources that have digital copies of older statutes, including LLMC Digital, the Internet Archive, and the Alberta Law Collection. With LLMC Digital, the user has access to the annual and sessional federal statutes from 1867 to 1994, with some years not represented. These are available in PDF format and can be viewed one page at a time. This resource is available only by subscription.

The Internet Archive is a non-profit organization whose goal is to permanently archive digital copies of documents available online.[22] Through this endeavour, the Internet Archive has archived some digital copies of federal and provincial statutes, such as the Revised Statutes of Canada from 1906 and the Revised Statutes of Ontario from 1914. The Law Society of Upper Canada Library has created a webpage with links to Canadian and Ontario

---

[20] For more details on how to search electronically, see the chapter titled "Electronic Legal Research".

[21] For example, the Department of Justice point-in-time service goes back only to January 1, 2003. On e-Laws, the Ontario legislation websites, the point-in-time service goes back to January 1, 2004.

[22] See the internet Archive "About Us" page for more information at http://www.archive.org/about/about.php.

legislation archived in the Internet Archive and can be found at <http://rc.lsuc.on.ca/library/research_law_ca_legis.htm>.

The Alberta Law Collection is a digitization project aimed at putting as much of Alberta's legislative history online, freely available to the public. Through this site, the user has access to Alberta annual statutes from 1906 to 1990, revised statutes from 1922 to 1980, and other documents such as older debates and bills. This resource can be found at <http://www.ourfutureourpast.ca/>.

While it is useful for these documents to be available electronically, if you need to look at an act in its entirety, compare it to another act, or find a particular section, using the statutes in print is much more efficient. One of the main reasons is that you will often have to have several volumes open in front of you at the same time, and doing this electronically can be difficult.

Please keep in mind that often the online statutes are not considered official copies of the law. For example, the statutes found in Westlaw Canada, LexisNexis Quicklaw, and CanLII are not considered official copies of the law. There are some electronic statutes that are considered official — they are the electronic statutes available on some government websites, such as statutes from the Department of Justice website, the Ontario e-Laws website, the Quebec government website, and the New Brunswick Attorney General website.[23] If you must rely on statutes in court, it is advisable to use the official government versions using either electronic or print resources.

Annual or Revised Statutes

If you need to find the statute as it originally appeared and you know the name of the statute or have its citation, it is fairly straightforward to find the statute. If you have the statute name, you can go directly to the annual or revised volumes, as the case may be, from the jurisdiction in question, look in the index and find the chapter number associated with the statute. Statutes are arranged in order by chapter number. If you have a citation, you can go directly to the volume for the year of your statute and use the chapter number to find it — as mentioned above, statutes are arranged in order by chapter number. You can also use one of the electronic resources mentioned above to find historical statutes, but it is usually faster and easier to find older statutes using the print volumes. And keep in mind that the statutes housed in these databases are not considered official copies of the law.

---

[23] See Appendix 1 for the URLs for these and other government websites.

Loose-leaf Services and Office Consolidations

Always begin by checking if there is: (a) a loose-leaf version of the statute; or (b) an office consolidation.

If both a loose-leaf and office consolidation exist, we recommend using the loose-leaf.

Loose-leaf services are published in binders so that new developments in the law can be inserted regularly and obsolete law removed. These services save having to update the statute by referring to the sessional or annual volumes. The text of the statute will be up-to-date, at minimum, as of the date in which the loose-leaf was last updated. The front page of the loose-leaf service usually indicates when the loose-leaf was last updated.[24]

As noted above, many loose-leafs are printed by commercial publishers. Commercial services do not have legal effect and should not be cited. When citing a statute, always cite the official version that is published by the government printers.

Office consolidations are published by the government. Unlike loose-leaf services, office consolidations are not published in binders and cannot be updated on a regular basis. Using an office consolidation may still involve referring to other resources to ensure the information is current, depending on the date of the consolidation.

NOTE: Loose-leafs or office consolidations are rarely absolutely current. Some of the steps enumerated below for updating statutes may have to be followed, even when using a loose-leaf or office consolidation.

Step Three: Determine if the Statute is in Force

As mentioned above, an act can be in existence but not be in force. If the act is not in force, it cannot be applied or used.

See the section above entitled "When is a Statute 'In Force'?" for information on determining the CIF date of statutes. This is a crucial component and needs to be completed before moving on to the next steps.

Step Four: Updating Your Statutes

At this stage, it is very important to update your statute, which means to determine what amendments or changes have been made to the statute. You want to ensure that the version you use is the most current version of the statute. Although electronic commercial publishers purport to give you access to the most recent version of a statute, they are not perfect and you

---

[24] A more detailed discussion of loose-leaf services is found in the chapter titled "Books and Loose-Leaf Services". Also refer to the Selective Topical Bibliography for a selective list by subject of loose-leaf services.

have to be sure of all the amendments, repeals, and other changes. If you do not want to use the most current version of the statute because of the nature of the charge against your client or the topic you are researching, it is still important to update the statute to ensure the version you use is the version that reflects all amendments and changes up to the date you require.

Below, we outline how to update federal, British Columbia, Nova Scotia, and Ontario statutes. If you need to do research on statutes from provinces or territories other than the ones with which we deal in this book, the general principles given here should be helpful.[25] The basic method of finding and updating statutes in the various provinces and territories is similar. Depending on the services which your law library subscribes to, the steps may differ slightly from those outlined here but the basic approach is the same.

Please note that you can update a statute the official way or the unofficial way. The official way is to use government publications; the unofficial way is to use tools published by commercial publishers. It is best to use an official way, especially if what you are looking for is going to be relied upon in court.

Federal Statutes

Official

1. Check the most recent publication of the *Table of Public Statutes and Responsible Ministers*. The table is published in each annual statute volume; it is also published quarterly in a separate document and online.[26] Using the most recent table, look up the statute by name and examine the changes made to the statute listed under the title. The CIF information for each change is provided at the end of all the listed changes.

2. Check the individual parts of the *Canada Gazette, Part III* that were published subsequent to the *Table of Public Statutes and Responsible Ministers* to find information about any amendments to your statute that have been made and proclaimed in force.

3. Because the *Table of Public Statutes and Responsible Ministers* is published only three times per year and the *Canada Gazette, Part III*, is published less often than other parts of the *Gazette*, it is unlikely that using these two products will provide you with the most up-to-date information on your statute. You will have to look up the status of bills to see if any bills purport to change the statute at issue. Federal bills are available in print from the Queen's Printer or local law, public, or academic libraries

---

[25] See also Mary Jane T. Sinclair, *Updating Statutes and Regulations for All Canadian Jurisdictions*, 4th ed. (Toronto: Carswell, 1995).

[26] To find the Table online, see http://laws.justice.gc.ca/PDF/TOPS_E.pdf.

(libraries may not necessarily carry bills from every jurisdiction in Canada, but likely only from the federal government and the jurisdiction in which the library is located). You can access the bills online from the Parliament of Canada website.[27] It would be useful to look at the Status of House Business and Progress of Legislation webpages, which will update you as to where each bill before the House or Senate currently stands.[28] You will also have to check to see if any of these bills have been given Royal Assent and proclaimed in force. Follow the directions above for finding the CIF information for statutes.

Unofficial

1. Locate your statute in the *Canada Statute Citator*. The statute is up-to-date as of the date on the lower right-hand side of the page. Check the green pages of the *Citator* (the Monthly Bulletin) to see if there have been any more recent amendments to the statute. If the statute you are researching is not listed, there have been no amendments. The statute is now up-to-date as of the date indicated on the top of page one of the latest Monthly Bulletin.

2. Check the individual parts of the *Canada Gazette, Part III* that were published subsequent to the latest Monthly Bulletin in the *Canada Statute Citator* to find information about any amendments that have been made and proclaimed in force.

3. Check the issues of *Canadian Current Law: Legislation*, subsequent to the date of the latest Monthly Bulletin, under the name of your statute in the "Progress of Bills" section.

4. Using Westlaw Canada, LexisNexis Quicklaw, CanLII, government websites or other reliable electronic databases, search for the statute at issue. When you find it, make note of the consolidation date — that is, the date up to which the statute in the electronic resource is current. If the effective date is not the same date as you are searching, you will have to use other resources to see if there were any changes subsequent to the consolidation date. See Illustration 15.8.

---

[27] See online: http://www.parl.gc.ca.

[28] Links to both of these webpages can be found online at http://www.parl.gc.ca/common/bills.asp?Language=E.

Illustration 15.8

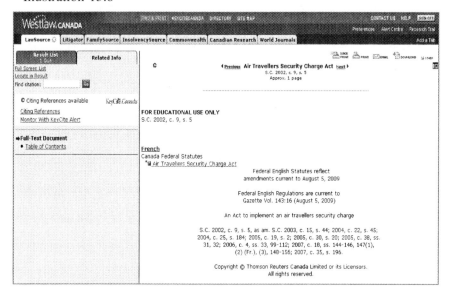

You will notice that in most electronic databases, either at the top of the statute or after a particular section within the statute, you will find a partial citation; this is the amendment information for the act or section in question. For example, in CanLII, directly after s. 5 of the *Fisheries Act*[29] is the following: 2008, c. 32, s. 28. This means that s. 5 of the *Fisheries Act*[30] was amended in 2008 by the statute that is chapter number 32 and by s. 28 of that statute. Keep in mind that these annotations are added by the publisher and not by the drafters of the legislation, so they do not form part of the act.

5. Although the resources listed above will give you information that is quite current, it may not be current to the day you are searching. You will have to check the *Canada Gazette, Part III* and the status of any bills that could affect your statute. Along with finding these bills in print and online as described above, if you have access to the *Canadian Legislative Pulse*, you can use this resource to track bills from your jurisdiction. This provides current information for the user.

---

[29] R.S.C. 1985, c. F-14.

[30] *Ibid.*

British Columbia Statutes

Official

The statutes of British Columbia are published in annual volumes; the *Revised Statutes of British Columbia* are available in both hardbound and loose-leaf formats (which are easy to update).

1. Your statute is current as of the date on the top of the user's guide found at the beginning of each volume of the loose-leaf edition. Disregard the dates printed on the pages of the actual statute.

2. Check the status sheet at the beginning of each statute in the loose-leaf resource for greater detail about the status of the statute — whether portions of the statute are in force, whether there are amendments not yet in force, or whether the particular statute has been updated beyond the date given on the user's guide at the beginning of the volume. Also look at the *Table of Legislative Changes* to determine what amendments have been made to the statute and the *Changes Not in Force* to see what amendments are on the horizon for the statute. You will then have to check the status of these changes to see if any of them have come into force since the loose-leaf was last updated.

3. Look at the *Table of Legislative Changes* in the most recent annual volume of the statutes. Look under the title of your act to see if there is any amendment information.

4. Look at the editions of the *Gazette* for information on proclamations (if necessary) subsequent to the last update in the loose-leaf resource.

5. Look at the bills for the current session to see if any of them purport to amend the statute at hand. This can be done using print version of the bills or electronic versions (please note that electronic versions might not be considered official). You will also have to conduct research to determine if any of the bills have been given Royal Assent and if they have a CIF date. See the information above about how to find CIF information.

Unofficial

1. Locate your statute in the *British Columbia Statute Citator*. The *British Columbia Statute Citator* is up-to-date as of the date on the release sheet filed at the front of the volume.

2. Refer to the "Progress of Bills" section in editions of *Canadian Current Law: Legislation* under the name of your statute.

3. Check the title index in the *B.C. Legislative Digest* for the title of your statute. This digest will tell you the title of bills introduced and acts affected. To ascertain the exact nature of the amendment, you will have to refer to a copy of the bill and read the amending legislation. Also refer to

the proclamations section of the index to determine if any new statutes that affect your statute are in force.

4. Using Westlaw Canada, LexisNexis Quicklaw, CanLII, or a government website, search for the statute at issue. When you find it, make note of the consolidation date — that is, the date up to which the statute in the electronic resource is current. If the effective date is not the same date as you are searching for the statute, you will have to use other resources to see if there were further changes.

You will notice that in most electronic databases, either at the top of the statute or after a particular section within the statute, you will find a partial citation; this is the amendment information for the act or section in question. For example, in Westlaw Canada, directly after s. 1.1 of the B.C. *Employment and Assistance Act*[31] is the following: 2006, c.22, s. 2. This means that s. 1.1 of the *Employment and Assistance Act*[32] was amended in 2006 by the statute that is chapter number 22 and by s. 2 of that statute. Keep in mind that these annotations are added by the publisher and not by the drafters of the legislation, so they do not form part of the act.

5. Check the *Table of Legislative Changes* that is available online through QP LegalEze, the British Columbia Queen's Printer website.[33] Look under the title of your act to see amendment information. Please note that to use this resource online, you will need to pay a fee.

6. Although the resources listed above will give you information that is quite current, it may not be current to the day you are searching. You will have to check the status of any bills that could affect your statute. Along with finding these bills in print and online, if you have access to the *Canadian Legislative Pulse*, you can use this resource to track bills from British Columbia. This provides current information for the user.

Nova Scotia Statutes

Official

The *Revised Statutes of Nova Scotia*, as well as the annual statutes, are published in bound volumes. The *Revised Statutes of Nova Scotia* are also published in a convenient consolidated loose-leaf format that is easy to update. The last revision in Nova Scotia took place in 1989.

1. Your statute is current as of the date on the top of the user's guide found at the beginning of each volume of the loose-leaf edition. For the

---

[31] S.B.C. 2002, c. 40.

[32] *Ibid.*

[33] http://www.qplegaleze.ca/default.htm.

purpose of currency, disregard the dates printed on the pages of the actual statute.

2. Check the *Table of Public Statutes* in the most recent annual volume of statutes for a list of changes to all current Nova Scotia statutes since the last revision.

3. Look at the editions of the *Royal Gazette, Part II* for information on proclamations (if necessary) subsequent to the last update in the loose-leaf resource.

4. Look at the bills for the current session to see if any of them purport to amend the statute at hand. This can be done using print versions of the bills or electronic versions (please note that electronic versions may not be considered official). You will also have to conduct research to determine if any of the bills have been given Royal Assent and if they have a CIF date. See the information above about how to find CIF information.

Unofficial

1. Locate your statute in the *Nova Scotia Statute Citator*. The *Nova Scotia Statute Citator* is up-to-date as of the date on the release sheet filed at the front of the volume.

2. Refer to the "Progress of Bills" section in editions of *Canadian Current Law: Legislation* under the name of your statute.

3. Using Westlaw Canada, LexisNexis Quicklaw, CanLII, or the government website, search for the statute at issue. When you find it, make note of the consolidation date — that is, the date up to which the statute in the electronic resource is current. If the effective date is not the same date as you are searching for the statute, you will have to use other resources to see if there were any other changes.

You will notice that in most electronic databases, either at the top of the statute or after a particular section within the statute, you will find a partial citation; this is the amendment information for the act or section in question. For example, in CanLII, directly after s. 16 of the Nova Scotia *Livestock Health Services Act*[34] is the following: 2007, c. 19, s. 4. This means that s. 16 of the *Livestock Health Services Act*[35] was amended in 2007 by the statute that is chapter number 19 and by s. 4 of that statute. Keep in mind that these annotations are added by the publisher and not by the drafters of the legislation, so they do not form part of the act.

4. Although the resources listed above will give you information that is quite current, it may not be current to the day you are searching. You will

---

[34] 2001, c. 8, s. 1.

[35] *Ibid.*

have to check the status of any bills that could affect your statute. Along with finding these bills in print and online, if you have access to the *Canadian Legislative Pulse*, you can use this resource to track bills from Nova Scotia. This provides current information for the user.

Ontario Statutes

The laws of Ontario are published in annual volumes. As well, all Ontario legislation and related tables and source documents are available online at <http://www.e-laws.gov.on.ca/index.html> (e-Laws). All Ontario source law online through e-Laws are considered official copies of the law and can be cited instead of the printed statutes.

Official

1. Check the most recent publication of the *Table of Current Consolidated Public Statutes — Legislative History Overview*. Since 2002, this table has only been published online, not in the annual statutes.[36] In the table, look up the statute by name and examine the changes made to the statute listed. The table is updated periodically — look at the top of the table to see when it was last modified. You can also use the *Consolidated Public Statutes — Detailed Legislative History* table, which is also available online.[37] This table, however, does not say when it was last updated, so you should supplement your search by using another resource.

2. Because the table may not have been updated recently, also look at the *Ontario Gazette* for recent changes or new bills that have been introduced that would affect your act.

3. Look at the bills for the current session to see if any of them purport to amend the statute at issue. This can be done using print version of the bills or electronic versions. You will also have to conduct research to determine if any of the bills have been given royal assent and if they have a CIF date. See the information above about how to find CIF information.

Unofficial

1. Locate your statute in the *Ontario Statute Citator*. Amendments subsequent to the Revised Statutes of Ontario, 1990 are listed here. The *Ontario Statute Citator* is up-to-date as of the date on the lower right-hand side of the page. Check the pink pages of the *Ontario Statute Citator* (the Weekly Bulletin), which are filed in the front section of the first binder, to see if

---

[36] This table can be found on the ServiceOntario e-Laws website at http://www.e-laws.gov.on.ca/index.html.

[37] *Ibid.*

there have been any more recent amendments to the statute. If the statute you are researching is not listed, there have been no amendments. The statute is now up-to-date as of the date indicated on the top of page one of the latest Weekly Bulletin.

2. Check the "Progress of Bills" sections of *Canadian Current Law: Legislation* in issues subsequent to the release date of the latest Weekly Bulletin under the name of your statute. You will then have to look up the bill to review it and determine whether it has gone on to receive Royal Assent and if it is in force.

3. Check the status of bills on the Ontario Legislative Assembly website.[38] From here you will see whether or not a bill has been given Royal Assent. If necessary, you will have to look in other resources to determine a date of proclamation (see above for information on how to find CIF information).

4. Using Westlaw Canada, LexisNexis Quicklaw, CanLII, or e-Laws, search for the statute at issue. When you find it, make note of the consolidation date — that is, the date up to which the statute in the electronic resource is current. If the consolidation date is not the same date as you are searching, you will have to use other resources to see if there were any other changes.

You will notice that in most electronic databases, either at the top of the statute or after a particular section within the statute, there is a partial citation; this is the amendment information for the act or section in question. For example, in CanLII, directly after s. 25 of the Ontario *Bees Act*,[39] is the following: 1994, c. 27, s. 12(4). This means that s. 25 of the *Bees Act*[40] was amended in 1994 by the statute that is chapter number 27 and by s. 12(4) of that statute. Keep in mind that these annotations are added by the publisher and not by the drafters of the legislation, so they do not form part of the act.

5. Although the resources listed above will give you information that is quite current, it may not be current to the day you are searching. You will have to check the status of any bills that could affect your statute. Along with finding these bills in print and online, if you have access to the *Canadian Legislative Pulse*, you can use this resource to track bills from Ontario. This provides current information for the user.

---

[38] http://www.ontla.on.ca/web/go2.jsp?Page=/bills/bills_main&menuItem=bills_header&locale=en.

[39] R.S.O. 1990, c. B.6.

[40] *Ibid.*

Step Five: Statutory Interpretation

Judicial Consideration

Cases wherein the courts have interpreted provisions of a statute are highly relevant.[41] Accordingly, you should always check for judicial consideration of the provisions of the statute you are researching (this is called noting-up). When you note-up a case, you will find out how the courts have treated a statute or particular section of a statute, and this could have a major impact on your client. This jurisprudence may be found in:

(a) a *Statute Citator* (but only since the revision was published — for example, federally since 1985 and in Ontario since 1990). These citators exist for federal legislation and legislation from the larger provinces;

(b) the *Canadian Abridgment: Canadian Statute Citations*.[42] See Illustration 15.9 for a sample page.

---

[41] In contrast, if there is case law that predates the statute that is in conflict with the statute, the statute will take precedence.

[42] See Chapter 5 on the *Canadian Abridgment* for information on how to use the *Canadian Statute Citations*.

Illustration 15.9

Statutes/Lois   **B.C. / Legitimacy Act, R.S.B.C. 1960, c. 217**

S.C. [In Chambers])

s. 3(2)(a)
Ⓒ Park v. Legal Services Society (British Columbia) (2001), 2001 BCSC 828, 2001 CarswellBC 1547 (B.C. S.C.)

s. 3(2)(d)
Ⓒ Skrdla v. Graham (2000), 2000 BCSC 1613, 2000 CarswellBC 2188, 81 B.C.L.R. (3d) 335 (B.C. S.C. [In Chambers])
Ⓒ Ainscough v. Legal Services Society (British Columbia) (1998), 1998 CarswellBC 2226, 57 B.C.L.R. (3d) 382 (B.C. S.C.)
Ⓒ Ainscough v. Legal Services Society (British Columbia) (1998), 1998 CarswellBC 2529 (B.C. S.C. [In Chambers])

s. 9
Ⓑ Griffin v. British Columbia (Ministry of Social Development & Economic Security) (2000), 2000 BCSC 1070, 2000 CarswellBC 1458, [2000] B.C.J. No. 1470 (B.C. S.C. [In Chambers])
Ⓑ Griffin v. British Columbia (Ministry of Social Development & Economic Security) (2000), 2000 BCSC 1071, 2000 CarswellBC 1457 (B.C. S.C. [In Chambers])

s. 10
Ⓒ Skrdla v. Graham (2000), 2000 BCSC 1613, 2000 CarswellBC 2188, 81 B.C.L.R. (3d) 335 (B.C. S.C. [In Chambers])
Ⓒ Ainscough v. Legal Services Society (British Columbia) (1998), 1998 CarswellBC 2226, 57 B.C.L.R. (3d) 382 (B.C. S.C.)
Ⓒ Ainscough v. Legal Services Society (British Columbia) (1998), 1998

CarswellBC 2529 (B.C. S.C. [In Chambers])

s. 12
Ⓑ Legal Services Society (British Columbia) v. British Columbia (Information & Privacy Commissioner) (2001), 2001 BCSC 203, 2001 CarswellBC 222, 84 B.C.L.R. (3d) 344, [2001] 3 W.W.R. 311, [2001] B.C.J. No. 201 (B.C. S.C. [In Chambers])

s. 19
Ⓒ Tremblay v. British Columbia (Attorney General) (2002), 2002 BCSC 602, 2002 CarswellBC 1103, [2002] B.C.J. No. 993 (B.C. S.C.)
Ⓑ Tremblay v. British Columbia (Attorney General) (2002), 2002 BCCA 285, 2002 CarswellBC 977, 175 B.C.A.C. 1, 289 W.A.C. 1, [2002] B.C.J. No. 942 (B.C. C.A.)

s. 19(1)
Ⓒ Tremblay v. British Columbia (Attorney General) (2002), 2002 BCSC 602, 2002 CarswellBC 1103, [2002] B.C.J. No. 993 (B.C. S.C.)

s. 44(4)
Ⓑ Tremblay v. British Columbia (Attorney General) (2002), 2002 BCSC 602, 2002 CarswellBC 1103, [2002] B.C.J. No. 993 (B.C. S.C.)

Legislative Assembly Allowances and Pension Act, R.S.B.C. 1996, c. 257
s. 4
Ⓑ Parker v. Blencoe (2000), 2000 BCSC 1563, 2000 CarswellBC 2204, 193 D.L.R. (4th) 752 (B.C. S.C.)

Legislative Assembly

Allowances and Superannuation Act, R.S.B.C. 1960, c. 240
s. 12, s. 12(1)(b) [am. 1979, c. 6, s. 24]
Ⓒ Loffmark v. British Columbia (Attorney General) (1980), 19 B.C.L.R. 395, 110 D.L.R. (3d) 42, 1980 CarswellBC 66 (B.C. S.C.)

Legislative Assembly Management Committee Act, R.S.B.C. 1996, c. 258
s. 3
Ⓑ Parker v. Blencoe (2000), 2000 BCSC 1563, 2000 CarswellBC 2204, 193 D.L.R. (4th) 752 (B.C. S.C.)

Legislative Assembly Privileges Act, R.S.B.C. 1960, c. 215
s. 2
Ⓒ Wallace v. British Columbia (Attorney General), [1978] 1 W.W.R. 411, 7 C.P.C. 127, 82 D.L.R. (3d) 423, 1977 CarswellBC 453 (B.C. S.C.)

Legitimacy Act, R.S.B.C. 1960, c. 217
s. 2
Ⓒ Brown v. Brown (1980), 19 B.C.L.R. 280, 1980 CarswellBC 45 (B.C. S.C.)
Ⓒ Earle v. Earle (1969), 69 W.W.R. 699, 6 D.L.R. (3d) 174, 1969 CarswellBC 136 (B.C. S.C.)

s. 2(1)
Ⓒ Bryson v. Bryson (1975), 55 D.L.R. (3d) 365, 20 R.F.L. 351, 1975 CarswellBC 42 (B.C. S.C.)

s. 5
Ⓒ Hapi v. Crary (1966), 56 W.W.R. 340, 1966 CarswellBC 72 (B.C. S.C.)
Ⓑ O'Callaghan v. Knight (1977), 2 B.C.L.R. 141, 1977 CarswellBC 23 (B.C. S.C.)

Ⓑ inconstitutionnel   Ⓒ considéré   Ⓕ conformément à   Ⓜ mentionné

347

(c) *Statutes Judicially Considered* series from Carswell. There are several resources of statutes judicially considered from a number of provinces — for example, British Columbia, Alberta, Saskatchewan, and Manitoba;

(d) annotated versions of the statutes. These annotated versions often include references to cases which have cited the act;[43] and

(e) electronically via Westlaw Canada (*KeyCite*), LexisNexis Quicklaw (*QuickCite*), and CanLII (NoteUp). See Illustration 15.10 for a sample of a *KeyCite* result in Westlaw Canada, and Illustration 15.11 for a sample of a *QuickCite* result in LexisNexis Canada.

Illustration 15.10

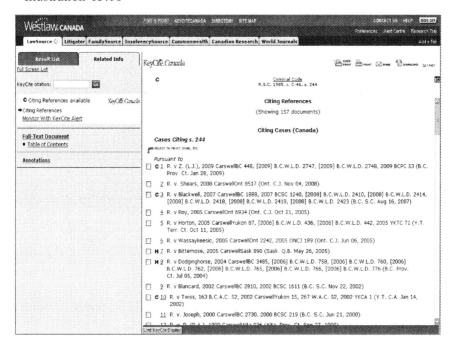

---

[43] Some annotated versions of statutes are available electronically, for example *Martin's Online Criminal Code.*

Illustration 15.11

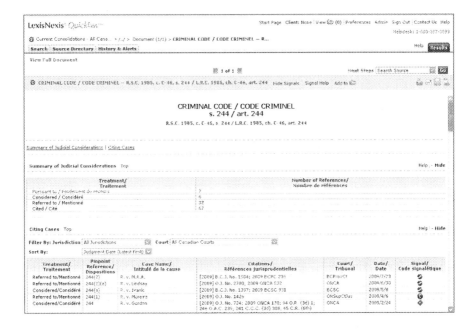

Reprinted with the permission of LexisNexis Canada Inc. LexisNexis is a registered trademark of Reed Elsevier Properties Inc., used under licence. Quicklaw is a trademark of LexisNexis Canada Inc.

Tracing the History of a Statute or Statutory Section

An understanding of the history of the statutory provision you are researching, and how it has changed over time, may help you to interpret the provision.

To obtain the history of a statute or section thereof, you must trace the versions of the statute or section as they have been published over the years. At the end of each section in a statute, there is a reference to a predecessor section in the previous revised statutes. If there is no reference, the section was passed since the last issue of revised statutes. For example, if s. 13 in an R.S.O. 1990 statute refers you to s. 12 in the R.S.O. 1980 statute, check the R.S.O. 1980 statute that will, in turn, refer you to the correct section in the R.S.O. 1970 statute. In this way, you can work your way backwards to the act that enacted the section you are tracing. Certain statutes are very old and you may find that you can trace the statute back to an English predecessor. You must continue tracing the history of the statute backwards through the English statutes in order to have absolutely complete research. Depending on the scope of your research task, this may not always be necessary or appropriate.

This historical research can be difficult to do electronically. As mentioned above, most electronic versions of statutes are currently consolidated so that they reflect the current state of the law. Only a few resources will allow you to look at previous versions of the law,[44] and even then only back a few years depending on the resource.[45] None of the past revised statutes are available in these resources. Although LLMC Digital, the Internet Archive, and the Alberta Law Collection have older Canadian, Ontario, and Alberta statutes, these are not easy resources to use. It would be faster and more efficient to use the print resources.

Since 1988, the *Canadian Abridgment* has included a service called *Canadian Current Law: Legislation* which has annual volumes and regular supplements. This service indicates the history of statutes and legislation.

Interpretation Acts

Most jurisdictions have an *Interpretation Act* that defines rules and principles of statutory interpretation and construction. In some jurisdictions, this information is found in a *Legislation Act*. Always check the application section of the act, which is normally at or near the beginning of the statute, to see if the use of the *Interpretation Act* is appropriate. Generally, the principles set out in an *Interpretation Act* will apply unless they are inconsistent with the objectives or provisions of the statute subject to interpretation.

Rules of Statutory Interpretation

There are certain maxims or "golden rules" of statutory interpretation on which courts rely when the wording of a statute is ambiguous. These rules can be found in treatises on statutory interpretation.[46] The *Canadian Encyclopedic Digest* also has a chapter on statutory interpretation (as of the date of publication, *Halsbury's Laws of Canada* does not have a volume on statutory interpretation, although there is a short paragraph discussing statutory interpretation in the *Administrative Law* volume under the heading "Judicial Review").

---

[44] For example, LexisNexis Quicklaw, CanLII, and the Department of Justice website.

[45] *Supra* note 21.

[46] See the Selective Topical Bibliography at the end of this book for a selective list of treatises on statutory interpretation.

Words and Phrases

When the provision of the statute that you are researching has not been judicially considered, there may be a word or phrase in the provision that has been interpreted in other contexts. In these circumstances, it is useful to consult one or more of the Words and Phrases tools.[47]

Hansard

Hansard, also called debates, is the verbatim record of everything said in the House of Commons or Senate or the provincial or territorial legislatures. There is a separate *Hansard* for each provincial and territorial legislature and for the House of Commons and the Senate. Before legislation is passed, the meaning, purpose, and potential impact of the legislation is debated in the legislature. Courts have indicated some willingness to consider *Hansard* as an aid for interpreting the intent of legislation where the wording is vague.[48]

When reading *Hansard*, you should be aware that all parliamentary debate about the legislation will not be of equal weight or relevance. Look in particular for the statements of the Minister when he or she introduced the legislation, as he or she will generally summarize the objectives of the government in introducing the legislation. Statements by opposition members or backbenchers about the purpose and effects of the legislation will have little or no weight. Legislative debates may also indicate whether alternative legislation or wording was considered, and if so, why it was rejected. Debates that reveal why alternative legislation or wording was rejected may give insight into what the legislators were trying to achieve in enacting the impugned legislation.

The *Hansard* is available in print as well as online in all jurisdictions in Canada except New Brunswick.

French and English Versions

The federal statutes, as well as the statutes of some of the provinces and territories, are published in French and English. Both versions are official and it may be worth examining the meaning of the provision in both languages.

---

[47] See the chapter titled "Legal Dictionaries/Words and Phrases" for more information.

[48] For instance, see *Reference re Legislative Authority of Parliament of Canada* (1979), [1980] 1 S.C.R. 54.

Appendix 1 — Links to Legislation, Bills, Hansards, and Other Legislative Materials for Each Jurisdiction in Canada[49]

Canada

Statutes

http://laws.justice.gc.ca/en/
http://laws.justice.gc.ca/en/BrowseTitle

Regulations

http://laws.justice.gc.ca/en/
http://laws.justice.gc.ca/en/BrowseRegTitle

Bills

http://www.parl.gc.ca/common/bills.asp?Language=E

Hansard

House of Commons:
http://www.parl.gc.ca

Senate:
http://www.parl.gc.ca

Tables

Table of Public Statutes and Responsible Ministers:
http://laws.justice.gc.ca/en/publaw/index.html

Table of Private Acts:
http://laws.justice.gc.ca/en/privlaw/index.html

---

[49] Please note that not all jurisdictions have their tables available electronically. The websites for tables that are listed may not provide you with the information you are seeking.

Gazette

http://www.gazette.gc.ca/index-eng.html

Parliament

http://www.parl.gc.ca

Alberta

Statutes

http://www.qp.alberta.ca/Laws_Online.cfm
http://qpsource.gov.ab.ca/ *(must pay a fee to access)*

Regulations

http://www.qp.alberta.ca/Laws_Online.cfm
http://qpsource.gov.ab.ca/ *(must pay a fee to access)*

Bills

http://www.assembly.ab.ca/net/index.aspx?p=bills_home

Hansard

http://www.assembly.ab.ca/net/index.aspx?p=adr_home

Tables

http://qpsource.gov.ab.ca/ *(must pay a fee to access)*

Gazette

http://www.qp.alberta.ca/Alberta_Gazette.cfm
http://qpsource.gov.ab.ca/ *(must pay a fee to access)*

Legislative Assembly

http://www.assembly.ab.ca/

British Columbia

Statutes

http://www.bclaws.ca

Regulations

http://www.bclaws.ca

Bills

http://www.leg.bc.ca/legislation/bills.htm

Hansard

http://www.leg.bc.ca/hansard/

Tables

http://www.qplegaleze.ca/ *(must pay a fee to access)*

Gazette

http://www.qplegaleze.ca/BCLaw_Gazette.htm *(must pay a fee to access)*

Legislative Assembly

http://www.leg.bc.ca/

Manitoba

Statutes

http://web2.gov.mb.ca/laws/index.php

Regulations

http://web2.gov.mb.ca/laws/index.php

Bills

http://www.gov.mb.ca/legislature/bills/index.html

Hansard

http://www.gov.mb.ca/legislature/hansard/index.html

Tables

http://web2.gov.mb.ca/laws/statutes/index_procs.php

Gazette

Not available online.

Legislative Assembly

http://www.gov.mb.ca/legislature/homepage.html

New Brunswick

Statutes

http://www.gnb.ca/0062/acts/index-e.asp

Regulations

http://www.gnb.ca/0062/acts/index-e.asp

Bills

http://www1.gnb.ca/legis/bill/index-e.asp?legi=56&num=3
http://www1.gnb.ca/legis/bill/print-e.asp?legi=56&num=3

Hansard

Not available online — there are links available to budget documents and speeches from the throne:

http://www.gnb.ca/legis/business/currentsession/currentsession-e.asp

http://www.gnb.ca/legis/business/pastsessions/pastsessions-e.asp

Tables

Not available online.

Gazette

http://www.gnb.ca/0062/gazette/index-e.asp

Legislative Assembly

http://www.gnb.ca/legis/index-e.asp

Newfoundland and Labrador

Statutes

http://www.assembly.nl.ca/legislation/default.htm

Regulations

http://www.assembly.nl.ca/legislation/default.htm

Bills

http://www.assembly.nl.ca/business/bills/default.htm

Hansard

http://www.assembly.nl.ca/business/hansard/default.htm

Tables

http://www.assembly.nl.ca/legislation/sr/tablestatutes/
http://www.assembly.nl.ca/legislation/sr/tableregulations/

Gazette

http://www.gs.gov.nl.ca/gs/oqp/gazette/

House of Assembly

http://www.assembly.nl.ca/default.htm

Northwest Territories

Statutes

http://www.justice.gov.nt.ca/Legislation/SearchLeg&Reg.shtml
http://www.justice.gov.nt.ca/legislation/Legislation_Acts.shtml

Regulations

http://www.justice.gov.nt.ca/Legislation/SearchLeg&Reg.shtml

Bills

http://www.justice.gov.nt.ca/legislation/legislation_certtbills16.shtml
http://www.justice.gov.nt.ca/legislation/legislation_certbills.shtml
http://www.assembly.gov.nt.ca/_live/pages/wpPages/BillsLegislation.aspx

Hansard

http://www.assembly.gov.nt.ca/_live/pages/wpPages/hansard.aspx

Tables

None available online.

Gazette

http://www.justice.gov.nt.ca/legislation/Gazette09.shtml

Legislative Assembly

http://www.assembly.gov.nt.ca

Nova Scotia

Statutes

http://www.gov.ns.ca/legislature/legc//index.htm

Regulations

http://www.gov.ns.ca/just/regulations/consregs.htm

Bills

http://www.gov.ns.ca/legislature/HOUSE_BUSINESS/bills.html
http://www.gov.ns.ca/legislature/HOUSE_BUSINESS/status.html
http://www.gov.ns.ca/legislature/legc//index.htm

Hansard

http://www.gov.ns.ca/legislature/HOUSE_BUSINESS/hansard.html

Tables

None available online.

Gazette

http://www.gov.ns.ca/just/regulations/rg1/
http://www.gov.ns.ca/just/regulations/rg2/index.htm

Legislative Assembly

http://www.gov.ns.ca/legislature/

Nunavut

Statutes

http://www.justice.gov.nu.ca

Regulations

http://www.justice.gov.nu.ca

Bills

http://www.assembly.nu.ca/english/bills/index.html

Hansard

http://www.assembly.nu.ca/english/debates/index.html

Tables

http://www.justice.gov.nu.ca

Gazette

http://www.justice.gov.nu.ca

Legislative Assembly
http://www.assembly.nu.ca/

Ontario

Statutes
http://www.e-laws.gov.on.ca

Regulations
http://www.e-laws.gov.on.ca

Bills
http://www.ontla.on.ca

Hansard
http://www.ontla.on.ca

Tables
http://www.e-laws.gov.on.ca

Gazette
http://www.ontariogazette.gov.on.ca

Legislative Assembly
http://www.ontla.on.ca

Prince Edward Island

Statutes
http://www.gov.pe.ca/law/index.php3

Regulations
http://www.gov.pe.ca/law/index.php3

Bills
http://www.assembly.pe.ca/index.php3?number=1024589&lang=E

Hansard
http://www.assembly.pe.ca/hansard/index.php

Tables
http://www.gov.pe.ca/photos/original/leg_table_acts.pdf

Gazette
http://www.gov.pe.ca/royalgazette/index.php3

Legislative Assembly
http://www.assembly.pe.ca/index.php

Québec

Statutes
http://www.publicationsduquebec.gouv.qc.ca/accueil.en.html

Regulations
http://www.publicationsduquebec.gouv.qc.ca/accueil.en.html

Bills
Public:

http://www.assnat.qc.ca

Hansard
http://www.assnat.qc.ca (French only)

Tables
None available

Gazette
http://www.publicationsduquebec.gouv.qc.ca/accueil.en.html *(must pay a fee to access)*
http://www.quebecgazette.com (access to *Gazettes* from 1764 and 1765).

National Assembly
http://www.assnat.qc.ca/eng/index.html

Saskatchewan

Statutes
http://www.qp.gov.sk.ca/

Regulations

http://www.qp.gov.sk.ca/

Bills

http://www.qp.gov.sk.ca/
http://www.legassembly.sk.ca/publications/default.htm

Hansard

http://www.legassembly.sk.ca/hansard/default.htm

Tables

http://www.publications.gov.sk.ca/deplist.cfm?d=1

Gazette

http://www.publications.gov.sk.ca/deplist.cfm?d=1

Legislative Assembly

http://www.legassembly.sk.ca/

Yukon

Statutes

http://www.gov.yk.ca/legislation/

Regulations

http://www.gov.yk.ca/legislation/

Bills

http://www.legassembly.gov.yk.ca/progressofbills.html

Hansard

http://www.hansard.gov.yk.ca/
http://www.legassembly.gov.yk.ca/handsardindex.html

Tables

http://www.gov.yk.ca/legislation/tps.html

Gazette

http://gazette.gov.yk.ca

Legislative Assembly

http://www.legassembly.gov.yk.ca/

16

Researching Regulations

What are Regulations?

Regulations are rules made pursuant to a statute and are known as subordinate legislation. Regulations always have an enabling statute; that is, a statute under which the regulations were made and operate. For example, under the *Cultural Property Export and Import Act,*[1] there are two associated regulations and one order.[2] Regulations typically provide necessary detail to broad statutory provisions and enumerate how the provisions of a statute are to be implemented. Statutes usually deal with general policies and concepts; regulations provide the fundamental and practical details that are needed for the statute to be put into operation. For example, the *Cultural Property Export and Import Act*[3] states that an individual needs an export permit in order to export certain cultural property; a regulation under that act enumerates such specific details as the number of days a permit is valid and how that permit can be amended.[4] These "nitty gritty" details are too specific to be included in statutes and are therefore included in regulations.

How are Regulations Made?

Unlike statutes, regulations do not have to go through an approval process in the Parliament of Canada or a provincial or territorial legislature. In a statute, the person, agency, department, etc., who/which can make regulations pursuant to that particular act is listed. Most often it is the Minister who is responsible for the act or the Lieutenant Governor (provincially) or

---

[1] R.S.C. 1985, c. C-51.

[2] *Canadian Cultural Property Export Control List,* C.R.C., c. 448; *Cultural Property Export Regulations,* C.R.C., c. 449; and *Order Designating the Minister of Communications as Minister for Purposes of the Act,* SI/93-228.

[3] *Supra* note 1.

[4] *Supra* note 2, *Cultural Property Export Regulations,* ss. 9-10.

Governor in Council (federally) who is authorized to make regulations under an act. For example, the *Landlord and Tenant Act* of New Brunswick states the following about who can make regulations under the statute:

> The Lieutenant-Governor in Council may make regulations
>   (a) prescribing forms required under this Act;
>   (b) prescribing a tariff of costs on distress for rent; and
>   (c) prescribing a table of fees on summary proceedings.[5]

The process for drafting regulations differs for depending on the jurisdiction. Federally,[6] there is a seven-step process in how regulations are made:

1. A draft version of a regulation is prepared;
2. The draft regulation is reviewed by the Privy Council Office or other federal department, depending on the regulation;
3. The draft regulation is published in the *Canada Gazette, Part I* for public consultation. This is published in print and online;[7]
4. The public is given an opportunity to provide feedback on the regulation. The regulation is then amended as the drafter(s) think necessary after taking the public comments into consideration;
5. The final version of the regulation is approved by the person or institution charged with drafting regulations under an act (Minister, Lieutenant Governor, Governor in Council, or named agency or federal department);
6. Once the approval has been given, the regulation is registered with the Clerk of the Privy Council; and
7. The regulation is published in the *Canada Gazette, Part II* for public distribution. This is available in print and online.[8]

The process on how regulations are made in the provinces and territories varies depending on the jurisdiction, but it is similar to the federal process

---

[5] R.S.N.B. 1973, c. L-1, s. 79.

[6] See the federal Department of Justice website for more detailed information on how federal regulations are made at http://www.pco-bcp.gc.ca/index.asp?lang=eng&page=information&sub=publications&doc=legislation/part3-eng.htm.

[7] http://www.gazette.gc.ca/index-eng.html.

[8] *Ibid.*

except that, in some provinces and territories, there is no requirement that the regulation be published first for public consultation before it is approved. In each province or territory, regulations have to be registered with the Registrar of Regulations.[9] To find out more about regulations, look at the *Regulation Act* or *Statutory Instruments Act* in your jurisdiction.

Although the process listed above can take some time, regulations are easier to draft and have approved as they do not have to go through an approval process in the Parliament of Canada or provincial or territorial legislatures. This also means they are easier to amend, which is one of the reasons very detailed provisions are often included in regulations and not in statutes — these details may need to be changed quite regularly depending on the situation, and, having to go through the approval process which a statute needs to go through, would make it difficult to amend them.

How are Regulations Published?

After federal regulations are made and approved, they must be published in the *Canada Gazette, Part II* (provincial and territorial regulations must be published in the corresponding provincial or territorial *Gazette*). The text of the regulations is found in the *Gazette* in which it was published; in most jurisdictions in Canada, *Gazettes* are available online through the individual provincial or territorial government websites.[10] Regulations are also available electronically through legal research databases such as LexisNexis Quicklaw, Westlaw Canada, and CanLII.[11]

Like statutes, regulations are consolidated periodically. For instance, federal regulations were last consolidated in 1978 in the *Consolidated Regulations of Canada* ("C.R.C."). A federal regulation that was in force before 1978 was consolidated in the C.R.C. and will have a citation to the C.R.C. For example, under the *Yukon Act*,[12] the *Oaths of Allegiance and Office Order (Yukon)* regulation has the following citation: C.R.C., c. 1611. Regulations published after the last consolidation will not have a C.R.C. citation.

When regulations are published, they are given either an SOR number or an SI number. SOR stands for *Statutory Orders and Regulations* which are regulations. SI stands for *Statutory Instrument*; these consist of statutory instruments other than regulations (i.e., orders and commissions). The SOR

---

[9] For example, see the *Regulations Act*, R.S.B.C. 1996, c. 402, s. 3.

[10] See Appendix 1 in the chapter "Researching Statutes" for a listing of provincial and territorial government websites that provide access to regulations.

[11] See the "Electronic Legal Research" chapter for more information on using electronic databases.

[12] S.C. 2002, c. 7.

or SI number appears at the top of the regulation, order, etc. in question. See Illustration 16.1 for a sample of a federal regulation as published in the *Canada Gazette, Part II.*

Illustration 16.1

2000-08-16 *Canada Gazette Part II, Vol. 134, No. 17*	*Gazette du Canada Partie II, Vol. 134, nᵒ 17* **SOR/DORS/2000-300**
Registration SOR/2000-300 27 July, 2000	Enregistrement DORS/2000-300 27 juillet 2000
DNA IDENTIFICATION ACT	LOI SUR L'IDENTIFICATION PAR LES EMPREINTES GÉNÉTIQUES
DNA Identification Regulations	**Règlement sur l'identification par les empreintes génétiques**
P.C. 2000-1109 27 July, 2000	C.P. 2000-1109 27 juillet 2000
Her Excellency the Governor General in Council, on the recommendation of the Solicitor General of Canada, pursuant to section 12 of the *DNA Identification Act*, hereby makes the annexed *DNA Identification Regulations*.	Sur recommandation du solliciteur général du Canada et en vertu de l'article 12 de la *Loi sur l'identification par les empreintes génétiques*, Son Excellence la Gouverneure générale en conseil prend le *Règlement sur l'identification par les empreintes génétiques*, ci-après.
DNA IDENTIFICATION REGULATIONS	RÈGLEMENT SUR L'IDENTIFICATION PAR LES EMPREINTES GÉNÉTIQUES
INTERPRETATION	DÉFINITIONS
1. The definitions in this section apply in these Regulations. "Act" means the *DNA Identification Act*. (*Loi*) "DNA Data Bank" means the national DNA data bank established by the Solicitor General of Canada under section 5 of the Act. (*banque de données génétiques*)	1. Les définitions qui suivent s'appliquent au présent règlement. « banque de données génétiques » La banque nationale de données génétiques établie par le solliciteur général du Canada en application de l'article 5 de la Loi. (*DNA Data Bank*) « Loi » La *Loi sur l'identification par les empreintes génétiques*. (*Act*)
SAMPLES	ÉCHANTILLONS
2. (1) In order to ensure the integrity of the convicted offenders index of the DNA Data Bank, only samples of bodily substances that were collected with a DNA Data Bank Sample Kit that meets	2. (1) Pour la préservation de l'intégrité du fichier des condamnés de la banque de données génétiques, seuls les échantillons de substances corporelles prélevés, à l'aide d'une trousse de prélè

Canada Gazette, Part II vol. 134, no. 17, page 1915, http://www.gazette.gc.ca/archives/p2/2000/2000-08-16/pdf/g2-13417.pdf (Minister of Public Works and Government Services, Government of Canada, 2000). Reproduced with the permission of the Minister of Public Works and Government Services Canada, 2009.

As you will see, this regulation's SOR number is SOR/2000-300. This means this regulation was approved in 2000 and it was the 300th regulation approved that year.

When is a Regulation in Force?

Unless stated otherwise in the regulation, federal regulations come into force on the day they are registered with the Clerk of the Privy Council.[13] If a regulation is exempt from registration, it comes into force on the day on which it was made or on a date specified in the regulations.[14] For the example shown in Illustration 16.1 above, the date of registration was July 27, 2000, which is listed at the top of the regulation.

To determine when a provincial or territorial regulation comes into force, you should check the *Regulation Act* or *Statutory Instruments Act* of your province or territory. Regulations in British Columbia, Nova Scotia and Ontario come into force on the day they are filed or registered with the Registrar of Regulations, unless otherwise specified in the regulation.[15] The registration or filing date of a regulation can usually be found just before the text of the regulation or under the title of the regulation. In order for a regulation to come into force before the regulation is filed, the act under which the regulation was made must authorize it to come into force on an earlier date.[16] This retroactive coming-into-force provision is not authorized in each jurisdiction.[17]

Doing Regulatory Research

Regulatory research involves three steps:

1. determining whether a *relevant regulation exists* and *locating* it;
2. *updating* the regulation; and
3. *interpreting* the regulation.

In the past, these steps were completed almost entirely using print products; however, as electronic access to statutes has increased, most of these steps can be done electronically.

---

[13] *Statutory Instruments Act*, R.S.C. 1985, c. S-22, s. 9.

[14] *Ibid.*

[15] *Regulations Act*, R.S.B.C. 1996, c. 402, s. 4; *Regulations Act*, R.S.N.S. 1989, c. 393, s. 3(6); and *Legislation Act, 2006*, S.O. 2006, c. 21, Sch. F, s. 22(2).

[16] For example, *Regulations Act*, S.N.B. 1991, c. R-7.1, s. 12(2).

[17] For example, *Legislation Act, 2006*, S.O. 2006, c. 21, Sch. F, s. 22(3).

Step One: How to Determine Whether a Regulation Exists and Locate It

If you do not already have a regulation name or citation, you will need to determine whether or not a regulation exists that deals with your topic.

Secondary Sources

You can begin your research by looking for your topic in a treatise, journal article, legal encyclopedia, loose-leaf service, dictionary or words and phrases resource, or other secondary source. These sources may refer you to the name and citation of the relevant regulation, if one exists. More often, however, you will be pointed to a relevant statute; look up the statute and see what regulations are associated with it that may be on your topic. Many of these resources are available in print as well as electronically; while it may be tempting to use electronic sources, do not ignore the sources available in print — not all secondary sources are available online. If you disregard print resources, you may miss information that could be related to your topic. Missing such details can be detrimental to your client's case.

You could also peruse a resource such as the *Canadian Abridgment's Canadian Current Law: Legislation* service. Among other things, this resource lists the regulations that were made, amended, or repealed in the previous year (this is published annually in September and covers from September 1 to August 31; there are also supplemental updates published every few months). See Illustration 16.2 for a sample page from *Canadian Current Law: Legislation*.

Researching Regulations

Illustration 16.2

REGULATIONS   **YUKON**

TRAFFIC SAFETY ACT.
Driver Licensing and Suspension Regulations, 2006 (R.R.S., c. T-18.1, Reg. 2) ss. 2(1)(p.1) (new), 3–7.9: am. Reg. 78/2007 (Sask. Gaz. 7/9/07, p. 520)
Traffic Safety Act Fees Regulations (R.R.S., c. T-18.1, Reg. 3) ss. 14.1, 14.2 (both new): am. Reg. 26/2008 (Sask. Gaz. 18/4/08, p. 451)

VICTIMS OF CRIME ACT, 1995.
Victims of Crime Regulations, 1997 (R.R.S., c. V-6.011, Reg. 1) s. 3; App. Table 1: am. Reg. 54/2008 (Sask. Gaz. 27/6/08, p. 524).

VITAL STATISTICS ACT, 1995.
Vital Statistics Regulations (R.R.S., c. V-7.1, Reg. 1) s. 21(1): am. Reg. 90/2007 (Sask. Gaz. 21/9/07, p. 546); s. 30(1)(c) (new): am Reg. 64/2008 (Sask. Gaz. 8/8/08, p. 596)

WILDLIFE ACT, 1998.
Captive Wildlife Regulations (R.R.S., c. W-13.1, Reg. 13) ss. 4, 25: am. Reg. 35/2008 (Sask. Gaz. 30/5/08, p. 470).
Open Seasons Game Regulations, 2004 (R.R.S., c. W-13.12, Reg. 1) ss. 12(2)(a), (b), 13(2)(a), (c), 14(2)(a)–(d), 16(2), 19(3), 29(3)(a), (b), 30(2)(a). (b) 34(2). 37, 57(2) preceding (a), (3) preceding (a): am Reg. 29/2008 (Sask. Gaz. 2/5/08. p. 457).

WILDLIFE HABITAT PROTECTION ACT.
Wildlife Habitat Lands Designation Regulations (R.R.S., c. W-13.2. Reg. 3) App. item 50(a): am. S.S. 2008, c. 28, s. 3.

YUKON

AREA DEVELOPMENT ACT.
Agricultural Development Areas Amendment Regulation (O.I.C. 2007/203) (Yuk. Gaz. 15/1/08, p. 21) registration number; date of notice: corrected (Yuk. Gaz. 15/2/08, p. 30)
Agricultural Development Areas Regulation: am. O.I.C. 2008/203 (Yuk. Gaz. 15/1/08, p. 21)
Ibex Valley Development Area Regulation Sched. B: am. O.I.C. 2008/37 (Yuk. Gaz. 15/4/08, p. 16)
Interim Whitehorse Periphery Development Area Regulations: am. O.I.C. 2008/22 (Yuk. Gaz. 15/3/08, p. 18)
Mayo Road Development Area Regulation: am. O.I.C. 2008/21 (Yuk. Gaz. 15/3/08, p. 18)

ASSESSMENT AND TAXATION ACT.
Rural Electrification and Telecommunications Local Improvement and Rural Domestic Water Well Program Tax Regulation, 2008: O.I.C. 2008/63 (Yuk. Gaz. 15/6/08, p. 18)
Yukon O.I.C. (O.I.C. 2007/204) (Yuk. Gaz. 15/1/08, p. 22) registration number; date of notice: corrected (Yuk. Gaz. 15/2/08, p. 31)
Yukon O.I.C. (O.I.C. 2007/205) (Yuk. Gaz. 15/1/08, p. 23) registration number; date of notice: corrected (Yuk. Gaz. 15/2/08, p. 32)
Yukon O.I.C. (O.I.C. 2007/206) (Yuk. Gaz. 15/1/08, p. 24) registration number; date of notice: corrected (Yuk. Gaz. 15/2/08. p. 33)
Yukon O.I.C. (O.I.C. 2007/207) (Yuk. Gaz. 15/1/08, p. 25) registration number; date of notice: corrected (Yuk. Gaz. 15/2/08, p. 34)
Yukon O.I.C. (O.I.C. 2007/208) (Yuk. Gaz. 15/1/08, p. 26) registration number; date of notice: corrected (Yuk. Gaz. 15/2/08, p. 35).
Yukon O.I.C.: O.I.C. 2008/07 (Yuk. Gaz. 15/2/08, p. 39)
Yukon O.I.C. 2007/56: repealed O.I.C. 2008/52 (Yuk. Gaz. 15/5/08, p. 52)
Yukon O.I.C.: O.I.C. 2008/52 (Yuk. Gaz. 15/5/08, p. 52)
Yukon O.I.C.: O.I.C. 2008/204 (Yuk. Gaz. 15/1/08, p. 22)
Yukon O.I.C.: O.I.C. 2008/205 (Yuk. Gaz. 15/1/08, p. 23)
Yukon O.I.C.: O.I.C. 2008/206 (Yuk. Gaz. 15/1/08, p. 24)
Yukon O.I.C.: O.I.C. 2008/207 (Yuk. Gaz. 15/1/08, p. 25)
Yukon O.I.C.: O.I.C. 2008/208 (Yuk. Gaz. 15/1/08, p. 26)

Web-based Legal Research Databases

If you are not successful in using some of the secondary sources listed above, you may also search or browse within the various government websites that list regulations or in an electronic legal research database such as CanLII, Westlaw Canada, LexisNexis Quicklaw, or *Canadian Legislative Pulse* to find regulations on your topic. When searching online, you need to make sure you use the correct words and synonyms. The website or database will only search for the words you ask it to search and nothing more; for example, if you conduct a title search for "railway" but not "train," you would find regulations that have the word "railway" in the title, but not necessarily the word "train". This would mean you would miss regulations. For example, by using the word "railway" in a title search, you would miss the *On Board Trains Occupational Safety and Health Regulations*[18] under the *Canada Labour Code*,[19] yet it might have been the very regulation for which you were searching.[20] See Illustration 16.3 for an example of searching using CanLII.

---

[18] SOR/87-184.

[19] R.S.C. 1985, c. L-2.

[20] See the "Electronic Legal Research" chapter for more tips on how you should search electronically.

Illustration 16.3

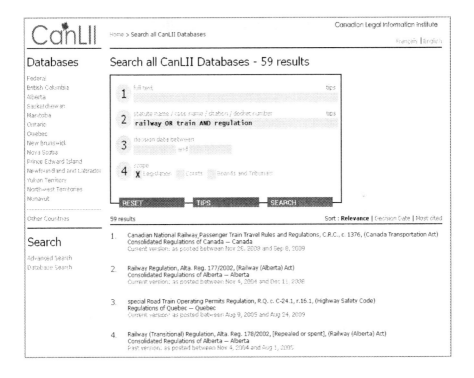

Reproduced with permission from CanLII (Canadian Legal Information Institute)

Canadian Legislative Pulse is a bills tracking service that also allows the user to track regulations from each jurisdiction in Canada. *Canadian Legislative Pulse* is currently hosted on its own platform (http://pulse.cch.ca/), but at some point in the future it will be housed within CCH Online, a large legal research database (http://www.cch.ca/). See Illustrations 16.4 and 16.5 for examples from the *Canadian Legislative Pulse*.

The Practical Guide to Canadian Legal Research

Illustration 16.4

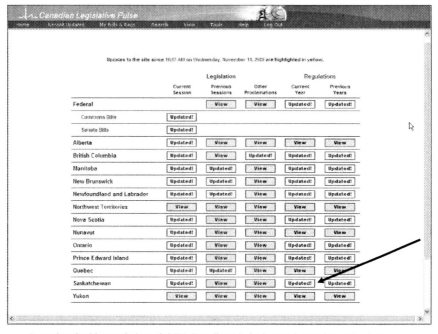

Reproduced with permission of CCH Canadian Limited, a Wolters Kluwer Business.

Illustration 16.5

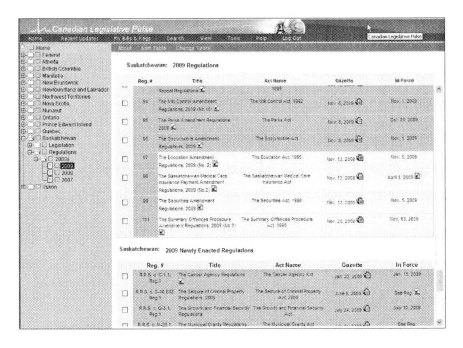

Reproduced with permission of CCH Canadian Limited, a Wolters Kluwer Business.

Loose-leaf Version of Regulations

If you have access to a loose-leaf version of regulations from a particular jurisdiction, you can look through it to see if there are any regulations that deal with the issue at hand. Loose-leaf services are books published in binders so that changes in the regulations can be inserted regularly and obsolete regulations removed. Be aware, however, that loose-leafs are only current as of the date on which they were last updated (usually indicated at the front of the loose-leaf).[21] Some loose-leafs are published by commercial publishers — these resources are helpful but are not official copies of the law.

Using the Canada Gazette, Part II and Consolidated Index to Statutory Instruments

Four times a year the government of Canada publishes the *Consolidated Index to Statutory Instruments*, which lists all the regulations and other statutory instruments that are currently in force. There are two parts to this

---

[21] See the chapter "Books and Loose-leaf Services" on how to use and update loose-leaf services.

document: *Table I* allows you to find the regulation or other statutory instrument by its title. When you look up the title, the name of the enabling act is provided; you can then find the act on the Department of Justice website or other resource and locate the regulation you are interested in. *Table II* lists regulations and other statutory instruments by the name of their enabling act. Instead of looking up the title of the regulation, you look up the title of the act and the regulations associated with that act are listed. Under *Table II*, you are also provided with the citation to the regulation (or other statutory instrument) and a list of the amendments the regulation has had (the citations to these amendments are also provided). You can then use this information to find the regulation by citation.

The process for finding regulations in the provinces and territories is slightly different. Some provinces will publish a "Table of Regulations" or something similar, which provides a listing of all the different regulations in the province. Not all jurisdictions have such a table, but most jurisdictions have a listing of regulations published in their *Gazette*. Often you can look up a regulation by the title of the statute or the title of the regulation itself.

With statutes, another step you have to take is to find the coming into force date; this, however, is not required for regulations. Generally, regulations are in force on the date they are filed; if they do not need to be filed, the date they come into force is usually listed in the regulation.

Step Two: How to Update Regulations

At this stage, it is very important to update your regulation, determining what amendments or changes have been made to it. You want to ensure that the version you use is the most current version of the regulation. Although electronic commercial publishers purport to give you access to the most recent version of a regulation, they are not perfect and you have to be sure of all the amendments, repeals, and other changes.

We outline below how to update federal, British Columbia, Nova Scotia, and Ontario regulations. The basic method of finding and updating regulations in the various provinces and territories is similar. If you need to do research on regulations from provinces other than those with which we deal in this book, the instructions given here should be helpful.[22]

Please note that you can update a regulation the official way or the unofficial way. The official way is to use government publications; the unofficial way is to use tools published by commercial publishers. It is best to use

---

[22] See also Mary Jane T. Sinclair, *Updating Statutes and Regulations for All Canadian Jurisdictions*, 4th ed. (Toronto: Carswell, 1995).

an official way, especially if what you are looking for is going to be relied upon in court.

Federal Regulations

Official

1. Look in the most recent edition of the *Consolidated Index of Statutory Instruments*, which is available in print and online,[23] for the changes that have been made to regulations up to the date of the Table.

2. Look in each issue of the *Canada Gazette, Part II* that has been published since the most recent edition of the *Consolidated Index of Statutory Instruments*. The *Canada Gazette, Part II* is available online and in print and is published bi-weekly.[24]

Unofficial

1. Consult the most recent edition of Carswell's *Canada Regulations Index*. This service lists statutes from all jurisdictions alphabetically. Below each statute you will find listed the names and citations of the regulations prescribed under that statute. You are current as of the date at the bottom of the first page of the Index.

2. Update by consulting the added pages (identifiable by the grey stripe down the side of the page) at the front of Binder I of the *Canada Regulations Index*. These added pages are a cumulative update of regulations published on a monthly basis.

3. Consult the "Regulations" section in *Canadian Current Law: Legislation*, which is a component of the *Canadian Abridgment*. New regulations that have been passed in the year, as well as regulations that were amended, repealed, etc. will be listed.

4. Using Westlaw Canada, LexisNexis Quicklaw, CanLII, government websites or other reliable electronic databases, search for the regulation at issue. When you find it, make note of the consolidation date — that is, the date up to which the regulation in the electronic resource is current. If the effective date is not the same date as the date you are searching, you will have to use other resources to see if there were any changes subsequent to the consolidation date. See Illustration 16.6.

---

[23] http://laws.justice.gc.ca.

[24] http://www.gazette.gc.ca/index-eng.html.

Illustration 16.6

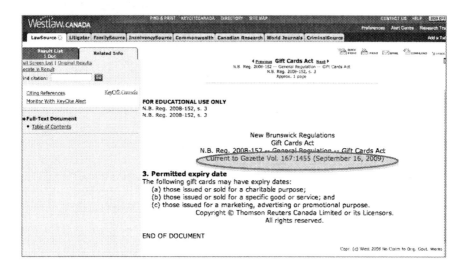

In most electronic databases, either at the top of the regulation or after a particular section within it, you will find a partial citation; this is the amendment information for the regulation or section in question. For example, in CanLII, directly after s. 11 of the federal *Marine Transportation Security Regulations*[25] is the following: SOR/2006-269, s. 2, effective November 2, 2006 (Can. Gaz. Pt. II, Vol. 140, No. 23, p. 1729). This means that s. 11 of the *Marine Transportation Security Regulations*[26] was amended in 2002 by the 269th regulation that was filed that year and by s. 2 of that regulation. That amendment was effective as of November 2, 2006 and can be found in the *Canada Gazette, Part II* in volume 140, number 23, on page 1729. Keep in mind that these annotations are added by the publisher and not by the drafters of the legislation, so they do not form part of the act. See Illustration 16.7.

---

[25] SOR/2004-144.

[26] *Ibid.*

Illustration 16.7

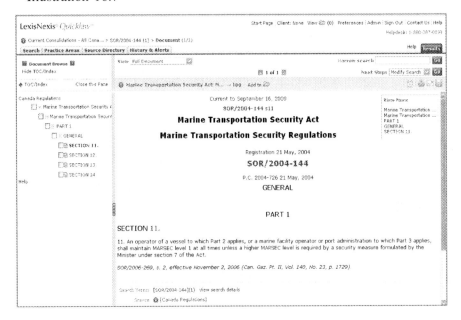

Reprinted with the permission of LexisNexis Canada Inc. LexisNexis is a registered trademark of Reed Elsevier Properties Inc., used under licence. Quicklaw is a trademark of LexisNexis Canada Inc.

5. Update by consulting the bi-weekly editions of the *Canada Gazette, Part II* which were published after the other resources listed above were last updated.

British Columbia Regulations

Official

1. Consult the Table of Contents in the *Consolidated Regulations of British Columbia* loose-leaf. Regulations that are in force can be found under the titles of their respective enabling statutes which are organized alphabetically.

2. Consult the *Index of Current B.C. Regulations*, which lists all regulations from British Columbia from 1958 to current, including all amendments.

3. Update the *Consolidated Regulations of British Columbia* and the *Index of Current B.C. Regulations* by looking through the relevant issues of the *British Columbia Gazette* published after the Consolidation and Index were last updated.

Unofficial

1. Consult the "Regulations" section in *Canadian Current Law: Legislation*, which is a component of the *Canadian Abridgment*. New regulations that have been passed in the year, as well as regulations that were amended, repealed, etc. will be listed.

2. Using Westlaw Canada, LexisNexis Quicklaw, CanLII, government websites or other reliable electronic databases, search for the regulation at issue. When you find it, make note of the consolidation date — that is, the date up to which the regulation in the electronic resource is current. If the effective date is not the same as the date you are searching, you will have to use other resources to see if there were any changes subsequent to the consolidation date.

In most electronic databases, either at the top of the regulation or after a particular section within it, you will find a partial citation; this is the amendment information for the regulation or section in question. For example, in CanLII, directly after s. 20 of the B.C. *Meat Inspection Regulation*[27] is the following: [am. B.C. Reg. 299/2007, Sch. B, s. 13.]. This means that s. 20 of the *Meat Inspection Regulation*[28] was amended in 2007 by the 299th regulation that was filed that year and by s. 13 in Schedule B of that regulation. Keep in mind that these annotations are added by the publisher and not by the drafters of the legislation, so they do not form part of the act.

3. Update by consulting the bi-weekly editions of the *Gazette* which were published after the other resources listed above were last updated.

Nova Scotia Regulations

Official

1. Consult the latest annual index of the *Royal Gazette, Part II*. Regulations that were passed in that year, as well as any amendments to regulations from that year, will be listed, along with their citations. This index is actually printed several times a year, with a final version printed at the end of the year to reflect all the changes that took place within the last twelve months. Depending on your research question, you may have to look back through several annual indexes to see what changes occurred to the regulation in question.

2. Check the editions of the *Royal Gazette, Part II* that have been published since the last time the annual index was updated. The *Gazette* is published every two weeks.

---

[27] B.C. Reg. 349/2004.
[28] *Ibid.*

Unofficial

1. Consult the latest edition of the *Sectional Index to the Royal Gazette, Part II* under the name of the enabling statute. Here you will find a list of all the amendments to the regulations currently in force in Nova Scotia. This is available exclusively online[29] and is published every three months. Although this is published by the government of Nova Scotia, it is not currently an official document.

2. Consult the "Regulations" section in *Canadian Current Law: Legislation*, which is a component of the *Canadian Abridgment*. New regulations that have been passed in the year, and regulations that were amended, repealed, etc. will be listed.

3. Using Westlaw Canada, LexisNexis Quicklaw, CanLII, government websites or other reliable electronic databases, search for the regulation at issue. When you find it, make note of the consolidation date — that is, the date up to which the regulation in the electronic resource is current. If the effective date is not the same as the date you are searching, you will have to use other resources to see if there were any changes subsequent to the consolidation date.

In most electronic databases, either at the top of the regulation or after a particular section within it, you will find a partial citation; this is the amendment information for the regulation or section in question. For example, in CanLII, directly after s. 11 of the Nova Scotia *Hunter Education, Safety and Training Regulations*[30] is the following: Section 11 amended: O.I.C. 2006-365, N.S. Reg. 152/2006. This means that s. 11 of the *Hunter Education, Safety and Training Regulations*[31] was amended in 2006 by Order in Council 2006-365 which brought a number of regulations into effect[32] including the 152nd regulation that was filed that year. Keep in mind that these annotations are added by the publisher and not by the drafters of the legislation, so they do not form part of the act.

4. Update by consulting the bi-weekly editions of the *Royal Gazette, Part II* that were published after the other resources listed above were last updated.

---

[29] http://www.gov.ns.ca/just/regulations/secindx/.

[30] R.S.N.S. 1989, c. 504.

[31] *Ibid.*

[32] 152/2006 to 162/2006.

Ontario Regulations

Official

1. Consult the "Table of Current Consolidated Regulations" available on the Ontario e-Laws website.[33] This table has been published exclusively online since 2002; before 2002, it was printed in the back of each annual volume. With this table, you are provided with information on amendments that have been made to regulations.

2. Update your search by looking at the most recent edition of the *Gazette*. The "Table of Current Consolidated Regulations" may not be updated to the current date and you will need to review the *Gazette* to ensure that your search is as up-to-date as possible.

Unofficial

1. Consult the most recent edition of Carswell's *Ontario Regulation Service*. This service lists all Ontario statutes alphabetically. Below each statute you will find listed the names and citations of the regulations prescribed under that statute. You are current as of the date at the bottom of the first page of the Index. Locate more recent regulations by consulting the yellow supplementary pages of the *Ontario Regulation Service*. This will provide you with a listing of regulations current as of the date on the first yellow page.

2. Consult the "Regulations" section in *Canadian Current Law: Legislation*, which is a component of the *Canadian Abridgment*. New regulations that have been passed in the year, and regulations that were amended, repealed, etc. will be listed.

3. Using Westlaw Canada, LexisNexis Quicklaw, CanLII, government websites or other reliable electronic databases, search for the regulation at issue. When you find it, make note of the consolidation date — that is, the date up to which the regulation in the electronic resource is current. If the effective date is not the same as the date you are searching, you will have to use other resources to see if there were any changes subsequent to the consolidation date.

In most electronic databases, either at the top of the regulation or after a particular section within it, you will find a partial citation; this is the amendment information for the regulation or section in question. For example, in CanLII, directly after s. 6 of the Ontario *General Regulation*[34] under

---

[33] http://www.e-laws.gov.on.ca/index.html.

[34] O. Reg. 442/95.

the *Business Regulation Reform Act*,[35] is the following: O. Reg. 25/03, s. 5. This means that s. 6 of the *General Regulation*[36] was amended in 2003 by the 25th regulation that was filed that year and by s. 5 of that regulation. Keep in mind that these annotations are added by the publisher and not by the drafters of the legislation, so they do not form part of the act.

4. Update by checking those issues of the *Ontario Gazette* that have been published after the other resources listed above were last updated.

Step Three: Interpreting Regulations

Regulations are not judicially considered as often as statutes; however, there are a few tools available to you that list the cases that have considered regulations. One is *Regulations Judicially Considered*, which is a component of the *Canadian Abridgment*. It lists regulations that have been judicially considered from each jurisdiction in Canada from 1997 to the present. See Illustration 16.8 for a sample page from *Regulations Judicially Considered*.

---

[35] S.O. 1994, c. 32.

[36] *Supra* note 34.

Illustration 16.8

Regulations/Règlements   **Ont. / Family Benefits Act**

Evidence Act

Certification of Recordings and Transcripts, O. Reg 158/03

Generally
- R v Singh (2004), 2004 CarswellOnt 1040, [2004] O.J. No. 1053 (Ont. S.C.J.)
- R. v. Dearaujo (2003), 2003 CarswellOnt 1935 (Ont. S.C.J.)

s. 3
- R. v. Dearaujo (2003), 2003 CarswellOnt 1935 (Ont. S.C.J.)

Form 2
- R. v. B. (E.R.) (2003), 2003 CarswellOnt 3652 (Ont. C.J.)
- R. v. Tausendfrende (2003), 2003 CarswellOnt 3648, [2003] O.J. No. 3739 (Ont. C.J.)

Exécution réciproque d'ordonnances alimentaires, Loi sur l' — see/voir Reciprocal Enforcement of Support Orders Act

Expropriation, Loi sur l' — see/voir Expropriations Act

Expropriations Act

Rules to be Applied for the Purposes of Subsection 32 (1) of the Act, R.R.O 1990, Reg. 364

Generally
- Billman Investments Ltd. v. Toronto (City) (2005), 2005 CarswellOnt 3204 (Ont. S.C.J.)

s. 1(2)
- Bernard Homes Ltd. v. York Catholic District

School Board (2004), 2004 CarswellOnt 3008, 188 O.A.C. 115, 83 L.C.R. 176, 26 R.P.R. (4th) 240 (Ont. Div. Ct.)

Family Benefits Act

General, R.R.O. 1990, Reg. 366

Generally
- Falkiner v. Ontario (Director of Income Maintenance, Ministry of Community & Social Services) (2002), 1 Admin. L.R. (4th) 235, 101 C.R.R. (2d) 188 (note), 94 C.R.R. (2d) 22, 59 O.R. (3d) 481, 159 O.A.C. 135, 212 D.L.R. (4th) 633, [2002] O.J. No. 1771, 2002 CarswellOnt 1558 (Ont. C.A.)
- Yusuf v. Ontario (Director of Income Maintenance, Ministry of Community & Social Services) (2002), 2002 CarswellOnt 1525 (Ont. Div. Ct.)
- Guy v. Northumberland (County) Department of Social Services (2001), 147 O.A.C. 261, 201 D.L.R. (4th) 752, 2001 CarswellOnt 1856 (Ont. Div. Ct.)
- Falkiner v. Ontario (Director of Income Maintenance, Ministry of Community & Social Services) (2000), [2000] O.J. No. 2433, 134 O.A.C. 324, 75 C.R.R. (2d) 1, 188 D.L.R. (4th) 52, 2000 CarswellOnt 2260 (Ont. Div. Ct.)

s. 1(1)
- Falkiner v. Ontario (Director of Income Maintenance, Ministry of Community & Social Services) (2000), [2000] O.J. No. 2433, 134 O.A.C. 324, 75 C.R.R. (2d) 1, 188 D.L.R. (4th) 52, 2000 CarswellOnt 2260 (Ont. Div. Ct.)

s. 1(1) "same-sex partner" *[en. O. Reg. 36/00]*
- Falkiner v. Ontario (Director of Income Maintenance, Ministry of Community & Social Services) (2002), 1 Admin. L.R. (4th) 235, 101 C.R.R. (2d) 188 (note), 94 C.R.R. (2d) 22, 59 O.R. (3d) 481, 159 O.A.C. 135, 212 D.L.R. (4th) 633, [2002] O.J. No. 1771, 2002 CarswellOnt 1558 (Ont. C.A.)

s. 1(1) "single person"
- Yusuf v. Ontario (Director of Income Maintenance, Ministry of Community & Social Services) (2002), 2002 CarswellOnt 1525 (Ont. Div. Ct.)

s. 1(1) "spouse"
- Yusuf v. Ontario (Director of Income Maintenance, Ministry of Community & Social Services) (2002), 2002 CarswellOnt 1525 (Ont. Div. Ct.)

s. 1(1) "spouse" *[am. O. Reg 409/95]*
- R. v. Banks (2001), 205 D.L.R. (4th) 340, 86 C.R.R. (2d) 104, 55 O.R. (3d) 374, 45 C.R. (5th)

This resource has been included in Westlaw Canada; you can note-up a regulation just like noting-up a statute or a case by using the KeyCite Canada feature.

While using *Regulations Judicially Considered* in print or online is likely the easiest way to find cases that have considered a regulation, you can also conduct a full-text search in an electronic database, such as CanLII, Westlaw Canada, LexisNexis Quicklaw, BestCase, Maritime Law Book, etc., to find more cases, especially ones from before 1997.

If you would like to obtain guidance on the interpretation and administration of regulations, you should contact the appropriate government ministry. Sometimes there are policy manuals or guidelines on the administration of regulations which you may be able to obtain.

17

Other Legal Research Tools

While most legal research you do will rely on the resources described in the previous chapters, many research problems will require you to use less traditional resources. Some of the resources described in this chapter are not published in a traditional way (e.g. government websites, knowledge management databases and blogs); others are tools that, while not legal in focus, can nonetheless be useful to a legal researcher.

Government Websites

A quick internet search will provide you with neither thorough primary source research nor in-depth analysis, but it is often a useful supplement to the traditional research tools. Most notably, a vast array of government materials including press releases, backgrounders on new legislation, policy manuals, studies and reports are easily accessed online. These types of materials can clarify how a piece of legislation is meant to work in practice or how, in the absence of any judicial consideration, the Ministry responsible for the legislation interprets a piece of legislation. In addition to federal, provincial and territorial government information, almost every government agency, board, tribunal and commission will have a website outlining that body's mandate and work.

Government Telephone Directories

It is unlikely that you can complete your research by making one phone call; however, a phone call to a knowledgeable person can reduce your research time dramatically by clarifying the existence or absence of a government policy in a particular area. There are some research problems for which there is no answer in published sources because they fall within the purview of administrative practice rather than law. For such problems, an email, letter or phone call to the responsible government body may be the only way of obtaining the information that you need.

Government legal services branches act as counsel to the government and do not provide legal advice to the public. In some circumstances, government lawyers may be willing to provide practical information on how a specific statute or regulation is interpreted or administered. Many statutes and regulations have not been judicially considered but the government body which administers the legislation may have its own interpretation. Policy guidelines or manuals may exist that contain the Ministry's interpretation of legislation and set out how the legislation is to be administered. Even when there are no written guidelines, the government body will often have informal guidelines or practices. Knowledge of these guidelines or practices can be vital to satisfying your clients' needs.

The federal and provincial governments publish government telephone directories and also make their phone directory accessible via the main page of the government's website. These directories are usually organized first by ministry and then further subdivided by ministerial department. The title, telephone number and usually e-mail address for each civil servant is listed. As government telephone directories are very detailed, it is more time efficient to use them than a regular telephone book.

Organizational Knowledge Management Databases

If you are employed by a law firm, the legal department of a government ministry or company, or a legal aid clinic, there may be an organized collection of precedents, past research memoranda (that have been completed on various issues to satisfy the research demands of previous files), or a database of experts by subject area. These internal collections are usually only accessible by members of the organization and are usually collected, organized and maintained by lawyers or librarians responsible for the organization's "knowledge management" (KM). KM resources allow members of an organization to take advantage of the firm's previous research or work and adapt or reuse it on new matters.

These KM tools can be invaluable to the researcher. A memoranda database may lead you to an earlier memorandum on exactly the same issue or on a related issue. While you will still need to update and verify the information in the memo, you will have a large head start in your research. A precedents database can lead you to previous documents or agreements that your firm has completed, which you may then be able to adapt to your present needs. Similarly, a KM system may lead you to the firm's expert on a particular topic, who may be able to speak to and clarify the issues you are researching, thus saving you hours of research time.

An example of a general memoranda database is Legal Aid Ontario's collection of over 650 standard legal memoranda.[1] This is provided by Legal Aid Ontario's LAO LAW online services. The focus is on criminal law and procedure, family law and other public law topics. These memoranda are available to Ontario lawyers who are representing a client on a legal aid certificate.

Legal Publisher Mailing Lists, Websites and RSS Feeds

An inexpensive way to increase your awareness of the ever-multiplying legal resources available is to check the major Canadian legal publishers' websites or to have your name placed on their mailing lists to receive notices of the publication of new materials as they become available. The LegalPubs.ca website[2] provides an aggregation of RSS feeds of each of the major Canadian publishers' new items and is a useful way to monitor new publications.

Legal Blogs

One of the major developments in legal research in the last five years is the proliferation of law-related blogs. A legal blog is a website that provides commentary or updates on legal issues. While many personal blogs are of little value to the researcher and can be dismissed as vanity presses, recently a number of lawyers, academics and librarians have started up or begun contributing to serious blogs on legal topics. Because of the blog format's ease of publishing and its generally informal tone, blogs can be very useful tools for finding quick analysis and reporting on current issues as they unfold. They can also be excellent tools for staying current with new research tools. Blogs may be used as finding tools that refer you to primary and other secondary sources. A blog would not be cited as an authority on a particular topic.

Some blogs that Canadian legal researchers should be aware of include:

- SLAW (http://www.slaw.ca/): SLAW covers legal research and technology and many current legal issues. Slaw's numerous contributors include lawyers, academics and librarians.

---

[1] https://www.research.legalaid.on.ca/login.html (login required).

[2] http://www.legalpubs.ca/.

- The Court — Osgoode Hall Law School's Supreme Court Blog (http://www.thecourt.ca/): The Court provides very current academic commentary on Supreme Court decisions. Comments are very timely, often within a few days of the release of a judgment.
- Canadian Law Blogs List (http://www.lawblogs.ca/): This is an excellent source for finding Canadian law related blogs.

Research and Resources from Other Disciplines

Research from other disciplines, including social science and scientific literature, may be a very useful supplement to your research, particularly when the law in the area has not been clearly defined or requires reform. Law does not operate in a vacuum. It is part of the social fabric and must change to reflect changes in society and to achieve the ultimate goal of justice. The social sciences of economics, psychology, sociology, and criminology are used and referred to frequently by courts, especially in *Charter* litigation. As noted in the chapter on Constitutional Research, the *Charter* is meant to be interpreted in a progressive way that adapts to cultural, political and social change.

Other areas of law, however, will also use non-legal resources. For example, in *Society of Composers, Authors & Music Publishers of Canada v. Canadian Assn. of Internet Providers*[3] the Supreme Court referred to an article in *The Economist* as part of their discussion of the effects of file sharing on the recording industry. Refugee decisions regularly rely on research that describes the conditions that a refugee may face in his or her home country.

There are a number of useful periodical indexes for accessing literature from other disciplines. These include:

- *Index to Periodicals Related to Law*. This index covers articles published in non-law journals that have a legal aspect to them.
- *Social Sciences Index*: indexes international English language articles in the social sciences.
- *General Science Abstracts*: a searchable database of abstracts from over 280 English language publications.

---

[3] [2004] 2 S.C.R. 427.

There are also hundreds of subject-specific periodical indexes. The catalogues and websites of university libraries are excellent tools for identifying the existence of a subject-specific periodical index.[4]

Newspapers

There are two national legal newspapers aimed at lawyers: the *Lawyer's Weekly* and the *Law Times*. These are useful tools for staying current on developments in Canadian law and the legal profession.

For legal research where the subject matter is of some notoriety, or of local or national importance, general newspapers may also be a useful research tool. You may, for example, wish to monitor a case that is of interest in your area of law or follow the coverage of a client through the press.

Knowing how a similar issue to yours has been covered before in the press may suggest avenues for research in more traditional sources. For example, press coverage of a controversial refugee decision might lead you to information on the conditions in another country that might have an impact on a refugee claim. Similarly, an article's reference to a government official or academic might open up other research avenues to explore, such as searching for other articles written by that academic or contacting the office of the official.

Newspaper coverage can also be a useful tool to determine if a high-profile matter has been settled out of court. For example, in *Scott v. TD Waterhouse Investor Services (Canada) Inc.*,[5] the B.C. Supreme Court certified a class action against an investment company that charged its clients a US dollar exchange rate that was not tied to the actual exchange rate. There are no reported decisions available after this 2001 certification leading one to suspect that there was some kind of settlement. As the traditional legal research tools usually only cover actual judgments and reasoning, searching a newspaper is sometimes a quick way to confirm the outcome of a case. Indeed, a search in the Westlaw Canada or LexisNexis Quicklaw news databases turns up a one-paragraph article in the April 30, 2003 *Globe and Mail* (p. B9) that reports that a settlement was approved by the courts.

Newspapers can also be used to help with older case research. For example, the older decisions of the Ontario Municipal Board are not indexed in a published systematic way. If you needed to track down an OMB decision from the 1960s, one option would be to search a historical newspaper

---

[4] See for example: the University of Toronto Library's "Find the Best Research Resources for Your Topic", online: http://main.library.utoronto.ca/eir/articlesbytopic.cfm.

[5] (2001), 94 B.C.L.R. (3d) 320 (S.C.).

database for the name of one of the parties. If the newspaper reported on the OMB's decision, you would then know the approximate date of the decision which would make finding the actual decision much easier.

There are a number of databases that provide access to newspapers. These include:

- Westlaw Canada: ALLNEWS database has broad international coverage of newspapers and magazines. The CANADANEWS database covers major and local papers as well as some news transcripts.

- LexisNexis Quicklaw: the "News and Companies" tab provides access to a very large collection of news sources from around the world.

- Dow Jones Factiva: another large online collection of Canadian and international news sources.

- Canadian Newsstand: a large collection of Canadian newspapers. Especially good for smaller local papers.

- Google News: While poor for historical coverage, Google News is very useful for finding broad coverage of current issues.

- *The Globe and Mail — Canada's Heritage from 1844*: An excellent research tool for questions with a historical aspect. This database contains scans of the actual pages of the newspaper.

18

Québec Law

Approaching Québec Legal Research

Our approach to Québec legal research is the same as our approach to Canadian legal research. We recommend that you begin by consulting secondary sources such as legal encyclopedias, treatises, periodicals, and loose-leaf services. These sources will refer you to the leading cases, relevant statutes, and appropriate book in the *Civil Code of Quebec*[1] (*"Code"*) on your topic, and provide an overall guide to the law. We then recommend a more detailed analysis of your topic through your own search of the law using online or print sources.

History

The law in Québec is a unique amalgam of civil and common law. This relates to how the province of Québec was governed over the last number of centuries. The French took possession of what is currently known as Québec in 1534.[2] As French settlers colonized the new territory, they brought with them the laws and customs of their region. In France, it was the norm to follow the custom of law in one's particular region, resulting in many different customs and laws throughout the country.[3] Recognizing this patchwork of laws as problematic, King Louis XIV declared in 1664 that the colony of New France would follow "Paris Custom" as a way to ensure all the people of the new colony would be subject to the same laws.[4]

---

[1] S.Q. 1991, c. 64.

[2] *Important Dates in the History of the Civil Law of Quebec*, online: Department of Justice Canada <http://www.justice.gc.ca/eng/pi/icg-gci/hist/index.html>.

[3] John E.C. Brierley & Roderick A. MacDonald, *Quebec Civil Law: An Introduction to Quebec Private Law* (Toronto: Emond Montgomery, 1993) at 7.

[4] *Ibid.* at 7-8.

This system stayed in place until 1759-1760 when England conquered New France.[5] In 1763-1764, it was decided that British law only would apply to all legal matters, both criminal and civil.[6] In 1774, after years of political struggle between the French majority and the British minority, the British Parliament passed the *Québec Act, 1774*,[7] restoring the former French civil law while maintaining British criminal law and a British court structure.[8] This compromise stayed in place until the separation of the colony into two distinct jurisdictions in 1791: Upper Canada (Ontario) and Lower Canada (Québec).[9] Lower Canada was allowed to keep its civil law tradition, while English law was applied in Upper Canada.[10]

The *Civil Code of Lower Canada*[11] came into force in 1866 and the *Code of Civil Procedure*[12] came into force in 1867. These were based on the *Code civil des Français* in France,[13] but reflected the law and customs as they stood in Lower Canada. The *Civil Code of Lower Canada* replaced most of the laws inherited from the Paris Custom and incorporated some English law as it had been applied in Lower Canada; the "completed Code thereby achieved a synthesis of the many elements of its *ancient droit* including commercial law and superimposed English elements in a rational form."[14] In the *Civil Code of Lower Canada* there were four books, all governing a different entity: Persons; Property, of Ownership and its Different Modifications; Acquisition and Exercise of Rights of Property; and Commercial Law.[15]

The *Civil Code of Lower Canada* stayed relatively the same until a major revision began in 1955;[16] many committees were struck and consultations made, but it was not until 1994 that the new *Code* came into force.[17] The

---

[5] *Supra* note 2.

[6] *Ibid.*

[7] 14 George III, c. 83.

[8] *Supra* note 2 and note 3 at 16.

[9] Jean-Gabriel Castel, *The Civil Law System of the Province of Quebec: Notes, Cases, and Materials* (Toronto: Butterworths, 1962) at 22-23.

[10] *Ibid.*

[11] S. Prov. C. 1865, c. 41.

[12] S.Q. 1867, c. 25.

[13] *Supra* note 3 at 25.

[14] *Ibid.* at 26.

[15] *Supra* note 9 at 553–561.

[16] *A Short History of the Civil Code Reform*, online: Justice Québec <http://www.justice.gouv.qc.ca/english/ministere/dossiers/code/code-a.htm>.

[17] *Ibid.*

new *Code* expanded to include 10 books, each focusing on a specific sphere: persons, the family, successions, property, obligations, prior claims and hypothecs, evidence, prescription, publication of rights; and private international law.

While the *Code* codifies much of the private law in Québec, there are also separate statutes in Québec that make up parts of the law. Québec statutes stand on their own as law in and of themselves, but they must always be referenced against the *Code* as the *Code* itself states that it is the basis of all laws in the province.[18] The *Code* deals only with private law, or the law as between individuals.

The *Civil Code of Québec* and Legislation

The *Civil Code of Québec*

"The civil law system begins with an accepted set of principles. These principles are set out in the civil code. Individual cases are then decided in accordance with these basic tenets. In contrast, the common law approach is to scrutinize the judgments of previous cases and extract general principles to be applied to particular problems at hand."[19] In a civil law system, cases are not relied upon as precedent to nearly the same extent as in a common law system. Court decisions are "primarily exemplifications of, and justifications for, the application of a rule rather than fact-specific reformulations of the general law."[20] However, there are times when cases that have interpreted the *Code* can be relied upon akin to precedent: "Where . . . the judicial decision interprets a legislative or codal text, its normative force is substantially reduced. In theory, only where there is a sufficient number of decisions that they may be understood as a consistently applied sub-rule does the judicial decision acquire pre-emptory normative force."[21]

Criminal, constitutional, and administrative law cases in Québec are based on the common law so the *Code* holds no influence in these areas. Because criminal, constitutional, and administrative cases are dealt with in the common law system, judges in those cases in Québec look to the case law for guidance.[22]

---

[18] *Supra* note 1, Preliminary Provision: "the Code is the foundation of all other laws, although other laws may complement the Code or make exceptions to it."

[19] Gerald Gall, *The Canadian Legal System* (Toronto: Carswell, 1977) at 39.

[20] *Supra* note 3 at 123.

[21] *Ibid.*

[22] Gerald Gall, *The Canadian Legal System*, 5th ed. (Toronto: Thomson Carswell, 2004) at 265.

Although case law itself is not the primary source of law in Québec for civil matters, cases are necessary in order to understand the legal atmosphere. As well, legislation sits alongside the *Code* as another source of Québec law.

Finding the *Civil Code of Québec*

The *Code* was printed in the 1991 annual statute volume, although it did not come into force until 1994. There are several commercial print copies of the *Code*[23] and it is also available online through several platforms. The entire *Code* is available within CanLII, LexisNexis Quicklaw, and Westlaw Canada.[24] These are three legal research databases commonly used in the common law jurisdictions in Canada. SOQUIJ (Société québécoise d'information juridique) was founded by the Government of Québec as a way to provide access to the laws of Québec. Through its online database, AZIMUT, an annotated copy of the *Code* is available.[25] You do, however, need to purchase a subscription in order to access AZIMUT. The *Code* is available free from the Publications Québec website.[26]

Statutes and Regulations

The current revision of Québec legislation is the Revised Statutes of Québec, 1977. Unlike most other Canadian jurisdictions, the government of Québec publishes a permanent loose-leaf revision of the law. This loose-leaf consolidation makes it much easier to keep current as to the changes in law. Annual statute volumes are also printed each year.[27]

As with the *Code*, the statutes and regulations of Québec are available from CanLII, LexisNexis Quicklaw, and Westlaw Canada.[28] They are also available on the Publications Québec website;[29] the statutes are printed in the original revised statute volumes from 1977, the annual volumes, and are kept up-to-date in the loose-leaf consolidation.

---

[23] For example: Jean-Maurice Brisson & Nicholas Kasirer, *Civil Code of Québec: A Critical Edition*, 11th ed. (Cowansville, Que.: Editions Yvon Blais, 2003); Denis Le May, *The Civil Code of Québec in Chart Form* (Toronto: Irwin Law, 2006); Jean Louis Baudouin & Yvon Renaud, eds., *Code Civil Quebec Civil Code*, loose-leaf (Montreal: Wilson & LaFleur, 1993-).

[24] www.canlii.org; http://www.lexisnexis.com/ca/legal/; http://canada.westlaw.com/.

[25] https://www.azimut.soquij.qc.ca/identification/azimut/.

[26] http://www2.publicationsduquebec.gouv.qc.ca/dynamicSearch/telecharge.php?type=2&file=/CCQ/CCQ_A.html.

[27] See Chapter 15, "Researching Statutes," for more information.

[28] Please note, however, at the time of this printing, Westlaw Canada does not include all statutes and regulations of Québec, only a small number of them.

[29] http://www.publicationsduquebec.gouv.qc.ca/accueil.html.

Regulations in Québec are akin to regulations in other jurisdictions in Canada, and go through a similar stage of development.[30] Regulations are available in print from the 1981 revision volumes (the current revision is from 1981),[31] and recent regulations are available in the Québec *Gazette*. The *Gazette* is also available online through Publications Québec, but a paid subscription is necessary in order to access the *Gazette* in full-text. AZIMUT does not include statutes or regulations.

Bills

As in other Canadian jurisdictions, members of the National Assembly may table a bill, although only a minister may table a bill that involves financial issues.[32] The stages the bill goes through on its way to becoming law are similar to other Canadian jurisdictions:

1. Introduction. This is similar to a first reading in other Canadian jurisdictions. The bill is tabled and a motion is voted on to introduce the bill.

2. Public Hearings or Special Consultations. This is an optional step, but if undertaken, the bill is sent to a standing committee for public hearing. This step is usually taken if the proposed bill would drastically change an area of law.

3. Passage in Principle. This is similar to a second reading in other Canadian jurisdictions. It is when debate on the bill begins in earnest. After the debate, the members and ministers vote on whether or not to pass the bill in principle.

4. Detailed Consideration in Committee. After being passed in principle, consideration of the bill is undertaken by a standing committee. The committee will study the bill closely and, if deemed necessary, make amendments to the bill.

5. Consideration on Report from Committee. The standing committee's report on the bill is submitted, and the National Assembly must adopt it before the bill can be passed.

6. Passage. This is similar to a third reading in other Canadian jurisdictions. After further debate, a vote is taken and the bill will ei-

---

[30] See Chapter 16, "Researching Regulations," for more information.

[31] Revised Regulations of Québec, 1981.

[32] *Stages in the Passage of Bills*, online: <http://www.assnat.qc.ca/eng/Assemblee/cheminement.html>.

ther pass or not. If it passes, it will go on for assent and become law; if it fails, the bill dies on the floor of the National Assembly.

7. Assent. After being passed by the National Assembly, the Lieutenant Governor signs off on the bill and it becomes law.[33]

Bills may be found online through the *Gazette* on the Publications Québec website, but in order to access them in full-text, you need to pay a subscription fee. They are also available through the National Assembly website.[34]

Parliament

There are two parts to the Parliament of Québec: the Lieutenant-Governor and the National Assembly.[35] The Lieutenant-Governor is the Queen's representative in the province. The role of the National Assembly and the Lieutenant-Governor in Québec is very similar as in other jurisdictions — to pass laws and oversee the government's actions.[36]

Case Law

As with legislation, case law in Québec is similar to case law in other Canadian jurisdictions. It can be difficult, however, to find Québec cases in English since there is no methodical translation of cases by the courts. Although some publishers do translate cases, these are few and far between. Unofficial translations of select cases into English can be found on the Québec Judgements website at <http://www.jugements.qc.ca/traductions/index.php>.

Digests of Québec cases are available in the *Canadian Abridgment*, as well as *Annuaire de jurisprudence et de doctrine du Québec*. This is a digest service published out of Québec, so it will digest many more Québec cases than the *Canadian Abridgment*. Cases in full-text are available in numerous places, such as AZIMUT, LexisNexis Quicklaw, Westlaw Canada,

---

[33] *Ibid.*

[34] To look at public bills in the current session, go to http://www.assnat.qc.ca/eng/39legislature1/Projets-loi/Publics/index.htm. To access private bills in the current session, go to http://www.assnat.qc.ca/eng/39legislature1/Projets-loi/Prives/index.htm. To find older bills online, go to http://www.assnat.qc.ca/eng/travaux/SessionsAnterieures.html.

[35] *Parliament and Government*, online: National Assembly <http://www.assnat.qc.ca/eng/Assemblee/parl_gouv.html>.

[36] *Ibid.*

CanLII, and others. You must always be cognizant of the translation issue, however, when you are searching.

There are several Québec-specific case law reporters. The list below represents only a few that are currently published. For more information on case reporting in Québec, see Guy Tanguay and Daniel Boyer, "Annals of Québec Case Law Reporting."[37]

1. Annuaire de jurisprudence et de doctrine du Québec
2. Droit de travail Express
3. Jurisprudence Express
4. La Revue Légale
5. Recueil de jurisprudence du Québec

Secondary Sources

As with other jurisdictions in Canada, there are several secondary sources that comment on or help you find Québec law. The basic strategies you should employ when trying to find secondary sources are described in other chapters in this book. There are several texts and monographs written on the laws of Québec; conduct a search of your local library online catalogue to find the different resources available. There are also legal dictionaries, forms and precedent materials, and loose-leaf services available that focus on Québec law. It may sometimes be difficult to find such resources, however, as many are only available in French; if your library does not normally purchase French materials, you will likely have to use other resources or obtain them through interlibrary loan. Below are listed some examples of Québec-specific books and journals. There are also some dictionaries, forms and precedents, and abbreviation materials available for Quebec; please see your local library or check online for such materials.

Books

Brierley, John E.C. & Roderick A. MacDonald. *Quebec Civil Law: An Introduction to Quebec Private Law* (Toronto: Emond Montgomery, 1993).

---

[37] In Martha Foote, ed., *Law Reporting and Legal Publishing in Canada: A History* (Kingston, Ont.: Canadian Association of Law Libraries/Association Canadienne des Bibliotheques de Droit, 1997) 92.

Lafond, Pierre-Claude. *Techniques de Repérage des Sources Documentaires du Droit : Guide Pratique*. 3e ed. (Cowansville, Que. : Editions Y. Blais, 2004).

Le May, Denis & Dominique Goubau. *La Recherche Documentaire en Droit*. 5th ed. (Montréal : Wilson & Lafleur, 2002).

Le May, Denis & Judith Mercier. *Les Références Essentielles en Droit Québecois*. (Montréal : Wilson & Lafleur, 1996).

Journals

McGill Law Journal
Revue de Barreau
Revue de droit de l'Université de Sherbrooke
Revue des étudiants en droit de l'UQÀM
Revue juridique des étudiants et étudiantes de l'Université Laval
La Revue Juridique Thémis

19

English Law

Introduction

This chapter is not a comprehensive examination of English legal research; it does, however, show you how to use the basic English legal research tools because conducting Canadian legal research often requires an examination of English legal resources.

English law[1] is especially important to Canadian legal research because it forms the basis of our own law. In its earliest days, the colony received (or had imposed upon it) English law as of a particular date, and England's courts continued to play a large role in Canadian law until the mid 20th century. Until 1949, the Judicial Committee of the Privy Council was the final court of appeal for civil appeals from the Supreme Court of Canada; criminal appeals ended in 1933. Accordingly, many older English cases are law in Canada, while more recent developments in English jurisprudence can be influential, particularly when there is no Canadian law on the topic or the Canadian law is in a state of confusion. Well-respected English treatises are also cited with approval in Canadian courts.

Approaching English Legal Research

The basic approach to English legal research is the same as the approach to Canadian legal research. You should commence by consulting secondary sources such as legal encyclopedias, treatises, periodicals, and loose-leaf services. These sources will outline the basic principles of the area of the law you are researching and direct you to the leading cases and relevant statutes. You should then consult the primary sources themselves and search for additional case law or legislation which might be applicable. Finally, don't forget to note-up.

---

[1] Scots law, Northern Ireland law and English law (England and Wales) make up the U.K.'s three legal systems.

There are four sources for law in the United Kingdom: 1) Common Law, 2) Legislation, 3) European Court of Human Rights cases (since the *Human Rights Act 1998* came into effect), and 4) European Community law (since the *European Communities Act 1972* came into effect).

Constitution

The United Kingdom has no one source as its Constitution; instead, the Constitution is the product of a variety of sources, written and unwritten. These sources include legislation (one of the written sources) extending as far back as the Magna Carta in 1215 and forward to current-day Acts like those granting powers to the devolved governments of Ireland, Scotland and Wales.[2] Other recent Acts include the incorporation of a Charter/Bill of Rights (the *European Convention on Human Rights*) into U.K. law (via the U.K.'s *Human Rights Act 1998*), and the *Constitutional Reform Act 2005* which brought to an end one of Britain's highest Courts[3] to ensure the separation of judicial and legislative functions in the country.

Court cases, ancient and new, also serve to make up part of the Constitution in that they have defined the scope of authority across varying spheres of government and have determined their limits. Over the years, for example, certain cases have specifically limited the powers of the Monarch[4] and the Executive.[5]

The Constitution is also made up of unwritten and written customs, traditions and parliamentary conventions which govern the conduct of the Monarch, the Prime Minister, the Ministers, and other government officials. The standing orders, for example, set out the rules and procedures which govern the operation of Parliament (e.g., how debates are to be carried out, the roles of the leaders of the government and opposition and so on). These types of rules are important in terms of regulating the day-to-day functions of government, yet they may be changed by Members of Parliament and Peers whenever the need arises. Constitutional conventions such as the Salisbury Convention are another example. The Salisbury Convention sets out that the Lords will not seriously challenge any government Bill which was promised in the government's election manifesto and which is in its second

---

[2] *Northern Ireland Act 1998* (U.K.), 1998, c.47; *Scotland Act 1998* (U.K.), 1998, c. 46; *Government of Wales Act 1998* (U.K.), 1998, c.38.

[3] The House of Lords judicial function was taken over by the Supreme Court of the United Kingdom in October 2009.

[4] *Case of Proclamations* (1611), 77 E.R. 1352, 12 Co. Rep. 74 (Eng. K.B.).

[5] *Entick v. Carrington* (1765), 19 State Tr. 1029 (Eng. K.B.); *M. v. Home Office* (1993), [1994] 1 A.C. 377 (U.K.H.L.).

or third reading (where that government does not have a majority in the Lords).[6] These conventions, customs, and traditions make up part of the Constitution yet they are not legislation or part of the common law, and they are not enforceable by the courts.[7]

The Royal Prerogative also makes up part of the Constitution. The Royal Prerogative is the name given to the powers, privileges and immunity of the Monarch which have come about as the result of custom and tradition rather than statute. These powers (generally exercisable by the government) include declaring war and making peace; giving Royal Assent to Bills; summoning/proroguing/dissolving parliament; the commissioning of armed forces officers; the granting of honours; the recognizing of foreign states; the ratifying of treaties; the issuing/withdrawing of passports; the regulating of the civil service and the appointment of ministers, peers and other senior officials; the granting of royal pardons; the creation of corporations by Charter; the creation of legislation by the use of Letters Patent and Orders-in-Council, etc. Courts do have the ability to determine if prerogative powers exist along with the limits on those powers.

Certain treaties may also make up part of the U.K.'s Constitution. Notable examples are the treaties entered into by the United Kingdom upon joining the European Community (now European Union), which made European law the paramount authority in certain matters in the U.K., thereby changing some of the practices of the judiciary, the parliament and the executive.

Where to find it: There are a number of books dealing in detail with the Constitution; some of the more recent among them include Peter Leyland, *The Constitution of the United Kingdom: A Contextual Analysis* (Portland, OR: Hart, 2007); Neil Parpworth, *Constitutional and Administrative Law* (Oxford: Oxford UP, 2008); and Colin Turpin and Adam Tomkins, *British Government and the Constitution*, 6th ed. (Cambridge: Cambridge UP, 2007).

The English Court Structure[8]

The judicial system of the United Kingdom is unusual in that there was no single highest national court but, rather, two courts: the House of Lords and the Judicial Committee of the Privy Council, each of which dealt with

---

6 Reasonable amendments not designed to sink the Bill are permitted.

7 *Attorney General v. Jonathan Cape Ltd.* (1975), [1976] Q.B. 752 (Eng. Q.B.).

8 Routes of appeal are too complicated for any single chart to map out. For more information on appeals, consult Terence Ingman, *The English Legal Process*, 12th ed. (Oxford: Oxford UP, 2006).

specific matters. In October 2009, however, the judicial functions of the Appellate Committee of the House of Lords were abolished and a new Supreme Court of the United Kingdom took over the work of the House of Lords in its entirety, in addition to some of the areas currently overseen by the Privy Council. Nonetheless, the Judicial Committee of the Privy Council remains the highest Court for appeals from overseas. Below is a brief description of each court.

English Courts Chart

European Court of Human Rights (Strasbourg)	European Court of Justice (Luxembourg)
Matters dealing with Human and Political Rights	References from lower courts on European law (European law enacted into English law by virtue of the *European Communities Act, 1972*)

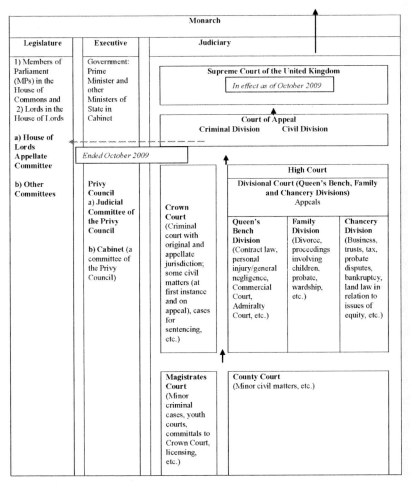

Monarch		
Legislature	**Executive**	**Judiciary**
1) Members of Parliament (MPs) in the House of Commons and 2) Lords in the House of Lords	Government: Prime Minister and other Ministers of State in Cabinet	**Supreme Court of the United Kingdom** *In effect as of October 2009*

a) House of Lords Appellate Committee

Ended October 2009

b) Other Committees

Privy Council a) Judicial Committee of the Privy Council

b) Cabinet (a committee of the Privy Council)

Court of Appeal — Criminal Division / Civil Division

High Court

Divisional Court (Queen's Bench, Family and Chancery Divisions) Appeals

Crown Court (Criminal court with original and appellate jurisdiction; some civil matters (at first instance and on appeal), cases for sentencing, etc.)

Queen's Bench Division (Contract law, personal injury/general negligence, Commercial Court, Admiralty Court, etc.)	**Family Division** (Divorce, proceedings involving children, probate, wardship, etc.)	**Chancery Division** (Business, trusts, tax, probate disputes, bankruptcy, land law in relation to issues of equity, etc.)

Magistrates Court (Minor criminal cases, youth courts, committals to Crown Court, licensing, etc.)

County Court (Minor civil matters, etc.)

Judicial Committee of the Privy Council

The Privy Council is made up of members and former members of Cabinet along with other distinguished persons appointed by the Queen. The role of the Council is to act as a body of advisors to the Queen, particularly on the matter of Royal Prerogative.[9] Membership is for life, but only members of the Government (including the devolved governments) play a real role in policy work.

The Privy Council contains several important committees. One of these is the Cabinet; another is the Judicial Committee. The latter is one of the two highest Courts in the United Kingdom.

The Judicial Committee of the Privy Council hears the following types of cases:

- Appeals from several independent Commonwealth countries,[10] overseas territories[11] and British Crown dependencies;[12]

- Appeals from the Disciplinary Committee of the Royal College of Veterinary Surgeons as well as from certain Church of England ecclesiastical courts, the Court of Admiralty for the Cinque Ports,[13] and Prize Courts;[14]

- Disputes involving the *House of Commons Disqualification Act 1975.*

The House of Lords

The House of Lords (or "the Lords") is the upper house or chamber of Parliament and, until recently, had both a legislative and a judicial function. The Appellate Committee of the House of Lords was Britain's other high

---

[9] See the section on the Constitution, above, for examples of Royal Prerogative powers.

[10] Antigua and Barbuda, the Bahamas, Barbados, Belize, Brunei, Cook Islands and Niue, Dominica, Gambia, Grenada, Jamaica, Kiribati, Mauritius, St. Christopher (also known as St. Kitts) and Nevis, St. Lucia, St. Vincent and the Grenadines, Trinidad and Tobago, Tuvalu. The right of appeal came to an end in Australia in 1986; in Canada criminal appeals to the Privy Council ceased in 1933 (civil appeals ended in 1949). Hong Kong's appeals came to an end in 1997 and New Zealand ended that route of appeal in 2003.

[11] Anguilla, Bermuda, British Antarctic Territory, British Indian Ocean Territory, British Virgin Islands, Cayman Islands, Falkland Islands, Gibraltar, Montserrat, Pitcairn Islands, Saint Helena (including Ascension Island and Tristan da Cunha), South Georgia and the South Sandwich Islands, Sovereign Base Areas of Akrotiri and Dhekelia, Turks and Caicos Islands.

[12] Crown dependencies are possessions of the British Crown, as opposed to overseas territories or colonies of the United Kingdom. They include the Channel Island bailiwicks of Jersey and Guernsey and the Isle of Man in the Irish Sea. None form a part of the United Kingdom, being separate jurisdictions, nor do they form part of the European Union.

[13] The High Court of England and Wales has jurisdiction over most admiralty law; one exception, a holdover from the days when England had a number of admiralty courts, is the Court of Admiralty for the Cinque Ports.

[14] Prize courts determine whether ships have been legitimately seized or captured during wartime or when authorized by the government. They also determine whether ships are to be saved or destroyed along with the fate of their cargo and/or its proceeds. The Prize Court is part of the Admiralty Court which in turn is part of the Queen's Bench Division.

Court. The twelve Law Lords (also known as the Lords of Appeal in Ordinary[15]) were also members of the House of Lords, and, as such, they had the same right to debate and vote as other members of the House of Lords (though, given the overlap between their judicial and parliamentary functions and the potential for conflicts of interest, they generally refrained from doing so).

Unlike the Supreme Court in Canada and the United States, individuals outside of the twelve Law Lords were allowed to sit to determine appeals, although this was rarely done. Those permitted to hear cases included former Law Lords, former Lord Chancellors, former Privy Councillors and others who had held a significant judicial office. The Appellate Committee usually heard cases in panels of five members, although on some cases as few as three members as well as more than five members were allowed depending on the importance of the case.

The House of Lords was, until October 2009, the highest appeal Court for civil and criminal cases in England, Wales and Northern Ireland. Only civil appeals were heard from Scotland where the High Court of Justiciary has the final say on criminal matters. The House of Lords had original jurisdiction only in breaches of privilege and peerage cases.

Supreme Court of the United Kingdom

The passing of the *Constitutional Reform Act 2005*[16] led to the creation of a Supreme Court of the United Kingdom which, in October 2009, took over the judicial function of the House of Lords (bringing an end to the appellate committee of the House of Lords), along with some of the judicial functions of the Judicial Committee of the Privy Council. The Judicial Committee continues to act as the final court of appeal for commonwealth countries and overseas territories.

The new Supreme Court has twelve judges (the same twelve judges from the House of Lords) and serves as the final court of appeal in all matters in England, Wales, Northern Ireland, and Scotland (for civil cases only). From the Privy Council, it took over disputes having to do with devolution issues (issues involving powers belonging to the central government which have been parcelled out to regional governments).[17]

---

[15] The name "Lords of Appeal in Ordinary" means that the twelve Lords are paid from the ordinary consolidated fund — the exchequer account at the Bank of England into which all revenues are paid. They are not paid by the House of Lords itself.

[16] *Constitutional Reform Act 2005* (U.K.), 2005, c. 4.

[17] The Scottish Parliament, National Assembly for Wales, and Northern Ireland Assembly were established in 1999. The Northern Ireland Assembly was suspended at midnight on 14 October 2002 (as a

The motivation for creating a new court had to do with the overlapping of legislative, judicial, and executive roles and power. The absence of a strict separation of powers (i.e., that the highest appeal court was situated in a Chamber of Parliament) was thought to be contrary to the requirements of the *European Convention on Human Rights* signed by the U.K. in 1953 and incorporated domestically (as the *Human Rights Act*) in 1998.

Court of Appeal

The Court of Appeal is one court which sits in two divisions — civil and criminal. Judges of the Court regularly hear both types of matters. The Civil Division deals with appeals from the High Court, the County Courts and from a number of tribunals and other bodies. The Court of Appeal (Criminal Division) hears appeals from the Crown Court.

High Court of Justice and the Crown Court

The High Court of Justice and the Crown Court both have appellate and original jurisdiction, and both hear cases for the first time where those cases are considered too serious to be heard by the lower courts (the Magistrates' Courts and the County Courts). The High Court of Justice deals primarily with civil matters while the Crown Court handles mostly criminal cases.

The Crown Court is a trial court equal in stature to the High Court. It hears cases of a more serious nature (indictable offences) such as murder, rape or robbery. It also deals with appeals from the Magistrates' courts along with cases which have been transferred or sent for sentence from those courts.

The structure of the High Court of Justice is much more complicated. It has a division focusing on trials which is divided into three sections:

1) the Queen's Bench Division which hears primarily tort, debt, contract and personal injury cases, but also has a specially constituted Admiralty court;

2) the Chancery Division which deals with partnerships, the administration of estates, trusts, insolvency, income tax, land law, and various issues in equity. In addition it has specialist courts within it which deal with intellectual property and company law;

3) the Family Division which deals with matters such as divorce, children, adoption, wardship, probate and medical treatment.

---

result of the breakdown in the Northern Ireland peace process). The Northern Ireland Assembly resumed business on 8 May 2007.

It also has an appellate division called the Divisional Court. In Divisional Court, judges (not less than two) sit and hear cases which are directed their way either via the rules of court or via statute. Appeals come from lower courts or inferior tribunals; their appeal is allowed or not allowed based on specific criteria.

The three divisions are:

1) the Divisional Court of the Queen's Bench Division, which hears appeals from county courts that have dealt with bankruptcy matters. It provides judicial review, and hears certain appeals from Crown Courts and Magistrates' courts;

2) the Divisional Court of the Chancery Division, which hears County Court bankruptcy appeals as well as appeals involving land registration;

3) the Divisional Court of the Family Division, which hears matrimonial matter appeals from Magistrates Courts in certain family matters.

Magistrates' Court

The Magistrates' Court is England's lowest court handling approximately 95% of all criminal cases from traffic offences to bail and minor trials. It also hears a small number of civil cases. Most magistrates are members of the public and have no formal legal training. They sit in panels (usually of three) and they are given legal advice in open court by a clerk to the court who is also a professional lawyer. In addition to lay magistrates, a smaller number of Magistrates' Courts employ a District judge who is qualified as a lawyer.[18] District judges are found primarily in Inner London, whereas lay magistrates sit in courts in Outer London and beyond.

In terms of criminal matters, only summary offences and either-way offences (those offences which may be tried either in Magistrates' Court or the Crown Court) may be heard in Magistrates' Court. These are minor offences for which the magistrates may generally impose a fine of no more than £5,000 or a custodial sentence of no more than six months. Indictment-only offences must be heard in the Crown Court. Where magistrates feel that a greater sentence is warranted in a particular case, they are permitted to send offenders to higher courts for sentencing.

---

[18] A Court of Petty Sessions is said to exist where two or more magistrates or one stipendiary magistrate are sitting for the purpose of trying summary offences and dealing with related matters under certain Acts of Parliament.

County Court

The County Courts deal with minor civil matters (debt repayment, personal injury, contract disputes), trusts and mortgages, landlord and tenant, as well as some family (divorce, adoption, etc.) and bankruptcy matters. The judges (Circuit judges) must be lawyers. Generally cases involving claims for less than £50,000 (approx $90,000.00 Canadian) or under are dealt with here along with small claims cases for matters involving sums of less than £5,000 (approx. $9,000 Canadian).

The European Union and the European Court of Justice

England passed the *European Communities Act 1972* and became a member of the European Communities (now the European Union or "EU") on January 1, 1973. Until the Act entered into force, no other law was higher in the United Kingdom than its own statutes. The effect of the Act was that European Community law became the highest form of law overriding any conflicting U.K. legislation, and allowing judges the power to refuse to apply conflicting laws.

There are four key European institutions: 1) the Council (the body which creates laws), 2) the Commission (the body which ensures member states obey the laws; it is also the executive of the EU, running the day-to-day operations, and allocating funds to the EU's common programmes), 3) the European Parliament (made up of 600 elected members and acting as a forum for discussion), and 4) the European Court of Justice ("ECJ" — the EU's judicial branch which has the power to overrule national courts on matters of European law).

The primary source of law binding on EU member states is the treaty. In addition to treaties, however, there are three types of secondary legislation:

1) *Regulations* which are the statutes of the European Community or EU and have immediate legal effect amongst member states, i.e., they do not need to be implemented at the national level in any way to have the force of law. Regulations override any inconsistent national legislation.

2) *Directives* which help to coordinate EU measures amongst states. Each member state, in order to further various EU objectives, must implement them but states generally have the freedom to choose how the implementation will take place.

3) *Decisions* which are of an executive or administrative nature and apply to specific parties, whether individuals, companies or member states. They create individual rights and obligations.

Where to find it: Treaties[19] are available online through EUR-Lex at http://eur-lex.europa.eu/en/treaties/index.htm. Regulations, directives and decisions are all available in the *Official Journal of the European Communities* which is the *Gazette* of the European Union. The last ten years (approximately) are available online through EUR-Lex at http://europa.eu.int/eur-lex/. The legal encyclopedia, *Halsbury's Laws of England*, contains information on European Law as applied in the U.K.

European Court of Justice: The ECJ hears cases involving European law and treaties. It decides whether infringements of the law have occurred and whether EU institutions have acted appropriately. It also provides advisory rulings on European law where national courts have requested them. Individuals are generally unable to bring questions themselves; however, any level of court is able to send a question to the ECJ if it would have difficulty making a decision without that advice. Once the ECJ has made its decision, the national court is expected to apply that decision to the facts before it.

Where to find it: You can find decisions of the European Court of Justice via Westlaw or LexisNexis, or free online at the Court of Justice of the European Communities website at http://curia.europa.eu. In print, the official versions of case law are published in multiple volumes: *Reports of Cases before the Court of Justice and the Court of First Instance*, *Reports of European Community Staff Cases* and *Official Journal of the European Union*. Before the creation of the Court of First Instance, *European Court Reports* contained all case law in a single-volume, official-report series.

Unofficial reports include *European Community Cases* (CCH) and *European Union Law Reporter* (CCH). Judgments of the ECJ as well as British

---

[19] The Treaty establishing the European Coal and Steel Community (ECSC), signed 18 April 1951 in Paris and entered into force on 23 July 1952, was the predecessor to the European Union. The Treaty of Rome, signed in Rome on 25 March 1957, and entered into force on 1 January 1958, created the European Economic Community (EEC). A second treaty, establishing the European Atomic Energy Community (Euratom), was signed at the same time; together both are jointly called the Treaties of Rome. The Merger Treaty, signed in Brussels on 8 April 1965 and in force since 1 July 1967, merged the then three European Communities into a single union. The Single European Act (SEA), signed in Luxembourg and the Hague and entered into force on 1 July 1987, had as its goal the establishment of a common market by 1992. The Treaty on European Union, signed in Maastricht on 7 February 1992 and entered into force on 1 November 1993, changed the name of the EEC to "the European Community" ("EC") and introduced joint political and legal cooperation in addition to economic (the three "pillars" of the European Union (EU)). The Treaty of Amsterdam, signed on 2 October 1997, entered into force on 1 May 1999, amended and renumbered the treaties already in existence. The Treaty of Nice, signed 26 February 2001 and entered into force on 1 February 2003, provided for the enlargement of the organization and merged the EU and EC's treaties into one version. The Treaty of Lisbon, intended to bring about certain institutional reform, was signed on 13 December 2007 and, as of the date of this publication, was not yet ratified by all member states.

courts dealing with EU (and former European Economic Community) law are published in *Common Market Law Reports* (Sweet & Maxwell).

The Council of Europe and the European Court of Human Rights

The United Kingdom was one of the ten founding members of the Council of Europe, an international organization which today has a membership of 47 countries situated in and around Europe. State members are parties to the Council's *Convention for the Protection of Human Rights and Fundamental Freedoms*, 4 November 1950, 213 U.N.T.S. 221 (the "*European Convention on Human Rights*"); the United Kingdom has been a party since its entry into force on 3 September 1953.

The *European Convention on Human Rights* is, more or less, the equivalent of a *Charter of Rights and Freedoms*[20] for Europe and the United Kingdom. All parties to the convention promise to protect the rights set out in the Convention and additional Protocols.[21] The rights protected in the Convention have been incorporated by most member states into national law; the United Kingdom did just that with the *Human Rights Act 1998* which came into force October 2000. Until 1998, individuals had to bring cases to the European Court of Human Rights rather than domestic courts in order to resolve disputes. Nonetheless, the House of Lords had held that since the United Kingdom was a party to the Convention, it was logical to

---

[20] It differs from Canada's *Charter of Rights and Freedoms* in that it is an Act, not part of a Constitution, and therefore can be repealed by a future Act of Parliament.

[21] The following are part of the Convention: right to life (Article 2); freedom from torture, inhuman and degrading treatment (Article 3); freedom from slavery or forced labour (Article 4); the right to liberty and security of the person (Article 5); the right to a fair trial (Article 6); the prohibition of retrospective criminal laws (Article 7); the right to respect for a person's private and family life, home and correspondence (Article 8); freedom of thought, conscience and religion (Article 9); freedom of expression (Article 10); freedom of peaceful assembly and association including the right to join a trade union (Article 11); the right to marry and have a family (Article 12); the right to an effective remedy (Article 13); the protection against discrimination (Article 14); the ability for member states to derogate from the rights guaranteed by the Convention where there are serious threats to the state (Article 15); the ability for states to restrict the political activity of foreigners (Article 16); the inability to restrict one right in the name of another right (Article 17); and restrictions on rights may only be used for the narrow purposes permitted (Article 18). The following are the rights and prohibitions set out in the various Convention Protocols: the right to the peaceful enjoyment of possessions (Protocol 1, Article 1); the right to an education (Protocol 1, Article 2); the right to fair and regular elections (Protocol 1, Article 3); the prohibition of imprisonment for contract breaches, the right to move within and exit a country freely, and the prohibition against expulsion of citizens of a country or denying entry into a country of a citizen of that country (Protocol 4 — Articles 1, 2, and 3); restriction of the use of the death penalty except in war (Protocol 6); the right to procedural fairness, appeals, compensation for crimes, and spousal equality (Protocol 7); the prohibition against discrimination (expanded) (Protocol 12); complete restriction on death penalty (Protocol 13). The text of these treaties is available online at the European Union website: http://europa.eu/.

assume that the government would not pass legislation or act in such a way as to contravene the Convention.

With the passing of the *Human Rights Act 1998*, U.K. citizens had the opportunity to ask domestic courts to enforce Convention rights. Today, while not having the power to overturn domestic legislation, judges at the High Court, Court of Appeal, and Supreme Court of the United Kingdom (and before that, the House of Lords), along with the Judicial Committee of the Privy Council and the Courts-Martial Appeal Court may all declare that a law is incompatible with the Convention. In these cases, Parliament is asked to reconsider the impugned legislation and either repeal or amend it.

Individuals may bring a case to the European Court of Human Rights in Strasbourg within a certain amount of time if they have exhausted every other domestic avenue. The Court hears cases brought by individuals against the State in addition to cases brought by one State against another. The Court may award damages and ask a State to pay the court costs of the applicant but it has no power to amend or repeal a member State's laws.

Where to find it: Case law can be found at the European Court of Human Rights website at http://www.echr.coe.int/echr/. It can also be located through Justis, a fee-based database, which contains reports of all cases back to 1960. LexisNexis and Westlaw also have decisions available online.

Case Law

English case reporting can be divided into two main periods: before and after 1865. Until 1865 there was no systematic reporting of English cases; instead, a variety of commercial reporters published a number of series which varied tremendously in terms of length and quality.

Beginning in the 16th century, private reporters published their own report series known as the *Nominate Reports* (named after the various private reporters who published them). There were more than one hundred of these private report series which varied in accuracy and quality. Some cases are reported in more than one Nominate report series.

Locating Pre-1865 Cases

1) Year Books

The earliest reports were written in Law French, not English, and these are found in the Year Books which contain fragmentary accounts ranging from the end of the 12th century to the beginning of the 16th century (Edward II to Henry VIII). While these cases often provide an interesting sociological view of the times, they are less informative in a legal sense in that they are often missing key information including facts, reasons and outcome.

2) Nominate Reports

The Nominate Reports span hundreds of years, starting in the early 16th century and ending in the 1860s. During this time, hundreds of reporters, under their own names, published accounts of the decisions in specific courts. These are reprinted in the *English Reports (Full Reprint)* (1220–1865) which, contrary to its name, contains not a full but rather a selected number of the early cases from the Nominate Reports. Although the English Reports is a reprint only of the original, information regarding the original pagination is provided. The two index volumes for the 176-volume reporter set is particularly useful for locating a case by style of cause.

Two other sources for Nominate Reports are the *Revised Reports* and the *All England Law Reports Reprint*. The *Revised Reports* contains a selected number of early cases from the *Nominate Reports*. As with the *Full Reprint*, the pagination of the original *Nominate Reports* is provided. In addition, the *All England Law Reports Reprint* contains a selection of cases covering the period from 1558 to 1935.

Making sense of a Nominate Report citation and, further, locating this type of case in the *English Reports* requires a guide. See Appendix I in this chapter for assistance with abbreviations and *English Reports* locations.

Law Reports since 1865

In 1865, the Incorporated Council of Law Reporting was founded in order to prepare and publish the decisions of the superior and appellate courts in England. Originally, there were eleven reports from 1865 to 1875 and cases cited in this series have an "L.R." in the citation.

The eleven series are:

Reporter	Example
Admiralty & Ecclesiastical (cited L.R. [vol. no.] A.& E.)	*The Mary Anne* (1865), L.R. 1 A. & E. 8
Chancery Appeal Cases (cited L.R. [vol. no.] Ch. or Ch. App.)	*Vyse v. Foster* (1872), L.R. 8 Ch. App. 309
Common Pleas Cases (cited L.R. [vol. no.] C.P.)	*Button v. Thompson* (1869), L.R. 4 C.P. 330
Crown Cases Reserved (cited L.R. [vol. no.] C.C. or C.C.R.)	*R. v. Ardley (John)* (1865–72), L.R. 1 C.C.R. 301
Equity Cases (cited L.R. [vol. no.] Eq.)	*Booth v. Hutchinson* (1872), L.R. 15 Eq. 30

Reporter	Example
Exchequer Cases (cited L.R. [vol. no.] Ex.)	*Rylands v. Fletcher* (1865-66), L.R. 1 Ex. 265
Probate & Divorce Cases (cited L.R. [vol. no.] P. & D.)	*In the Goods of Daniel Saunders* (1865), L.R. 1 P. & D. 16
Queen's Bench Cases (cited L.R. [vol. no.] Q.B.)	*The Aerated Bread Company Ltd v. Gregg* (1873), 8 L.R. Q.B. 355
English & Irish Appeals (cited L.R. [vol. no.] H.L.)	*English Credit Co. v. Arduin* (1871), 5 L.R. H.L. 64
Scotch & Divorce Appeals (cited L.R. [vol. no.] Sc. *or* Sc. & Div.)	*Bell v. Kennedy* (1868), L.R. 1 Sc. & Div. 307
Privy Council Appeals (cited L.R. [vol. no.] P.C.).	*McLean v. McKay* (1873), L.R. 5 P.C. 327

In 1876, the eleven reporters were reduced to six as a result of reorganization of the courts (brought about as a result of the *Supreme Court of Judicature Act 1873* (36 & 37 Vict. c.66) which did not come into force until 1874/75). The citations for the reporters changed somewhat in that the "L.R." no longer appeared (e.g., *London & South Western Railway Co.* (1886), 12 App. Cas. 41). The six reporters are:

Reporter	Example
Appeals Cases (cited App. Cas.)	*The Heinrich Björn* (1886), 11 App. Cas. 270
Chancery Division (cited Ch.D.)	*Button v. Thompson* (1883), 23 Ch. D. 278
Common Pleas Division (cited C.P.D.)	*Hunt v. Wimbledon Local Bd.* (1878), 3 C.P.D. 208
Exchequer Division (cited Ex.D.)	*Swinton v. Bailey* (1876), 1 Ex.D. 11
Probate Division (cited P.D.)	*The Bywell Castle* (1879), 4 P.D. 219
Queen's Bench Division (cited Q.B.D.)	*R v. Dudley* (1884), 14 Q.B.D. 273

In 1891, the reporters were reorganized again into four series that exist more or less in this form today. A volume number was no longer used in the citation; instead, the year of publication preceded the citation for the reporter (e.g., *Harbour Assurance Co. (U.K.) v. Kansa General Insurance Co. Ltd.*, [1993] Q.B. 701 (Eng. C.A.)). The four reporters are:

Reporter	Example
Appeal Cases (cited [year] A.C.) Includes the reports from the House of Lords, the Privy Council and Peerage Cases.	*Smith v. Eric S Bush (A Firm)*, [1990] 1 A.C. 831 (H.L.)
Queen's (King's) Bench Division (cited [year] Q.B. or K.B.) Includes cases heard in the Queen's Bench division of the High Court of Justice, related appeals to the Court of Appeal, and cases in the criminal division of the Court of Appeal.	*Rantzen v. Mirror Group Newspapers Ltd.*, [1994] Q.B. 670 (C.A.)
Chancery Division (cited [year] Ch.) Includes cases dealing with business law, trusts law, probate law, land law, etc.	*BHP Petroleum Great Britain Ltd v. Chesterfield Properties Ltd.*, [2002] Ch. 194 (C.A.)
Probate Division (cited [year] P.) which in 1972 became Family Division (cited [year] Fam). Includes family law and probate cases.	*Rampal v. Rampal*, [2002] Fam. 85 (C.A.)

In Scotland, the Scottish Council of Law Reporting, a not-for-profit organization, publishes the *Session Cases* — the official source for cases from the Court of Session and High Court of Justiciary. U.K. practice directions state that cases published in either the *Law Reports* or the *Session Cases* must be cited before cases published in other reports.

Other Reporters

The *Weekly Law Reports* (1953-), cited "W.L.R.," are published (weekly) by the Incorporated Council of Law Reporting. Cases reported are generally those cases which will be reported in other print reporters at a later date. Their appeal is that they appear quickly, unlike the *Law Reports* themselves which take much longer to be published. *All England Law Reports* (1936-) are perhaps the most widely known of the commercial reporters in the United Kingdom. In order to access cases, you can use the *Consolidated Tables and Index* which covers from 1936 up to (relatively close to) the present time. This can be supplemented further by use of the annual *Cumulative Tables and Index* and the bimonthly *Current Cumulative Tables and Index*. Cases are listed by name and by subject matter.

In addition, the *Canadian Supplement* lists cases reported in the *All England Law Reports* that have been cited in reported Canadian cases. The All E.R.s (as they are called) also contain many cases not found in the Law Reports.

Topical law reports are available for some English case law and are an excellent means for locating relevant case law in a specific subject area. Examples include *Criminal Appeal Reports, Lloyd's Law Reports, Simon's Tax Cases*, and *Ryde's Ratings Cases*.

United Kingdom — Case Law Online

A full search of cases generally requires a subscription (fee-based) database such as Justis (published by Justis Publishing Ltd.) which contains U.K. case law as far back as 1163 (and legislation from 1235). Westlaw, LexisNexis, or *HeinOnline* (the latter for the English Reports Full Reprint) also are good sources. Some court sites (e.g., Privy Council) provide access to their own decisions going back a limited number of years. The best overall source for free online case law is BAILII, the British and Irish Legal Information Institute (http://www.bailii.org/). The English Reports are available on CommonLII (http://www.commonlii.org/int/cases/EngR/).

Citation and Neutral Citation

British sources cited in Canadian publications or research are governed by the rules in the *Canadian Guide to Uniform Legal Citation* (Thomson Carswell). Citation style in the United Kingdom, in contrast, has been governed by convention rather than a specific set of rules; nonetheless, the *Oxford Standard Citation of Legal Authorities* (http://denning.law.ox.ac.uk/published/oscola_2006.pdf) is a guide often consulted in the United Kingdom.

Several sources exist to help researchers decode the abbreviations in a citation including Donald Raistrick's *Index to Legal Citations and Abbreviations* (London: Sweet & Maxwell, 2008) and Derek French's *How To Cite Legal Authorities* (Oxford: Oxford UP, 2003). Frequently used abbreviations for law reports (outside of those discussed above) include the following:

Abbreviation	Law Report	Abbreviation	Law Report
B.C.L.C.	Butterworths Company Law Cases	I.P. & T.	Butterworths Intellectual Property and Technology Cases
B.H.R.C.	Butterworths Human Rights Cases	J.P.	Justice of the Peace Law Reports
B.M.L.R.	Butterworths Medico-Legal Reports	I.T.L.R.	International Tax Law Reports
Con. L.R.	Construction Law Reports	L.G.R.	Butterworths Local Government Reports
Cr. App. Rep.	Criminal Appeal Reports	L.R.C.	Law Reports of the Commonwealth
E.C.H.R.	European Court of Human Rights Cases	O.P.L.R.	Occupational Pensions Law Reports
E.G.L.R.	Estates Gazette Law Reports	P.L.R.	Estates Gazette Planning Law Reports
F.C.R.	Family Court Reports	R.P.C.	Reports of Patent Cases
G.C.C.R.	Goode Consumer Credit Reports	S.T.C.	Simon's Tax Cases
I.R.L.R.	Industrial Relations Law Reports	T.C.	Official Tax Case Reports

Since 2001, the courts have used neutral citations. This type of citation does not refer to any print citation, but one which the courts themselves apply to cases. The goal is to provide greater ease of searching and more uniformity in identifying courts and cases. Citations are made up of the following parts:

Court of Appeal	R. v. Downer,	[2009]	EWCA	Crim	1361
	Style of Cause,	year	court	division	case number
High Court	JP Morgan Chase Bank & Ors v. Springwell Navigation Corporation,	[2008]	EWHC	1186	(Comm)
	Style of Cause,	year	court	case number	division

Cases are not cited to page numbers but, rather, paragraph numbers which are given in square brackets: e.g. *Douglas & Ors v. Hello Ltd. & Ors*, [2005] EWCA Civ 595 at [224].

Because this same case is also cited in a number of print reporters, it has the following additional citations: *Douglas & Ors v. Hello Ltd. & Ors*, [2005] 2 FCR 487, [2005] 3 WLR 881, [2005] 4 All ER 128. The first reference "FCR" is to the *Family Court Reports*, the second ("WLR") to the *Weekly Law Reports*, and the third ("ALL ER") to the *All England Reports*.

The chart below provides typical neutral citation abbreviations used in the United Kingdom:

Abbreviation	Court
Note: "UK" is used for courts hearing cases from the whole of the United Kingdom; "EW" is used for courts hearing cases from England and Wales.	
UKHL	House of Lords
UKPC	Privy Council
EWCA Civ	Court of Appeal Civil Division
EWCA Crim	Court of Appeal Criminal Division
EWHC (Admin)	High Court (Administrative Court)
EWHC (Ch)	High Court (Chancery Division)

Abbreviation	Court
EWHC (QB)	High Court (Queen's Bench Division)
EWHC (Comm)	High Court (Commercial Court)
EWHC (Admlty)	High Court (Admiralty)
EWHC (Fam)	High Court (Family Division)
EWHC (Pat)	High Court (Patents Court)
EWHC (TCC)	High Court (Technology & Construction Court)
HCJT	Scotland High Court of Justiciary
HCJAC	Scotland Court of Criminal Appeal
CSOH	Scotland Court of Session, Outer House
CSIH	Scotland Court of Session, Inner House

Citators (Noting-up)

There is no real print equivalent to the *Canadian Abridgment: Canadian Case Citations* (Canada) or *Shepard's Citations Service* (U.S.) for English cases or statutes. The most comprehensive English citator is JustCite, an online service. JustCite, published by Justis, provides access to lists of subsequent cases that have considered a particular case. JustCite also provides a list of parallel citations, judicial history, as well as citations to journal articles that have mentioned a case. Westlaw's online citator for English law is the United Kingdom Case Law Locator (UK-CASELOC) which provides access to brief note-up records for reported and unreported U.K. and EU cases.

In print, a variety of different tools provide somewhat less than comprehensive information on subsequent history and treatment of a case.

To trace a case since 1947, for example, you can use the *Current Law Case Citator*. The subject indexes for the *Law Reports* have, since 1951, included a table entitled "Cases Judicially Considered," and the Noter-Up volume for the *All England Law Reports* does something similar for cases since 1936.

Cases can also be noted-up using the *Digest*. Find the paragraph number of the digest of the case that you are updating. Under the digest in the main volume, you should find a listing of cases that have considered your case. Update this list by checking the *Cumulative Supplement* which will give you a further listing of cases. Digests for the cases listed in this further listing can be found in the *Cumulative Supplement* or in one of the *Continuation Volumes*.

Legislation

Bills

Public Bills[22] may be introduced in either the House of Commons or the House of Lords; the Bill number will indicate which by containing HC or HL. Bills having to do with raising revenue and public expenditures must start in the House of Commons. Bills which deal exclusively with these matters may not be initiated or amended by the Lords. In contrast, convention dictates that Bills having to do with the judicial system generally begin in the House of Lords.

In the House of Commons, at first reading, a Bill is brought by a Member of Parliament to the Clerk who reads out the short title. A date is set for second reading, and the Bill is ordered to be printed and distributed to members.

Second reading generally occurs a few weeks after first reading and this is where the Bill is debated in earnest for the first time. Once the debates have concluded, the Minster responsible for the legislation brings a motion for the second reading of the Bill and all members vote. If the Bill is defeated, it can go no further; however, those that are successful are sent to a Committee in the House of Commons (or in the House of Lords, to the Floor of the House ("Committee of the Whole House") or to a Committee Room ("Grand Committee")). The Bill is considered clause-by-clause and amendments are made. At the report stage, the amendments are considered on the Floor of the House, and at third Reading, the final text of the Bill is debated and voted on.

If the vote is successful, the Bill then goes to the House of Lords if it was introduced in the House of Commons (or vice versa) in order to go through much the same procedure. The House of Commons may reject a Bill from the Lords outright, but if the Lords do the same, there is a procedure by which the House can force the Bill through in the following Session of Par-

---

[22] Public Bills affect the rights of all citizens within a certain area, whereas Private Bills affect only a particular individual or group, charity, institution, railway, corporate body, local authority, etc. Public Bills take two forms: Government Bills which are the initiative of the government as a whole and Private Member's Bills which are usually the project of a particular member. There are also Law Reform Bills which come into being as the result of recommendations of a particular law reform body, as well as Consolidation Bills which attempt to take legislative provisions scattered across many Acts and put them into one Act in order to organize and make more sense of an area of law.

liament. Bills which have been amended in the second Chamber head back to the first Chamber until agreement regarding the text is reached.

Bills must be passed within the Session in which they are introduced, otherwise they fail. Those that do pass are given Royal Assent and come into effect either on that day or at sometime in the future as decided by the relevant Minister. A Commencement Order, which is a form of statutory instrument, is the means by which an Act (in whole or in part) comes into force.

Where to find it: The progress of bills can be tracked using the *Weekly Information Bulletin*. An online version is available at http://www.publications.parliament.uk/pa/cm/cmwib.htm. Paper copies of current and recent Bills may be found online at the United Kingdom Parliament website (http://www.parliament.uk/business/bills_and_ legislation.cfm) or may be purchased through the Stationery Office's website at http://www.tsoshop.co.uk.

Statutes

Statutes of the United Kingdom are available in a variety of print sources as well as online in a more limited way.

1) Current Statutes

The most usable and authoritative print source for current statutes from England and Wales is *Halsbury's Statutes of England*, published by Lexis-Nexis Butterworths. The work is annotated with case decisions and includes references to *Halsbury's Laws of England*.

The current set is in its fourth edition with 75 volumes and a dizzying array of accompanying volumes including the following: *Tables and Index, Annual Cumulative Supplement* (updates the bound volumes annually with legislation passed since those volumes), *Noter-up Service* (updates the information in the set every few months), *Current Statutes Service* (contains very recent legislation), and *Destinations Tables* (a guide to the consolidation of previous legislation into new legislation). All of these are explained in the "How To Use" guide which appears at the beginning of the first *Current Statutes Service* binder.

Halsbury's Statutes Citator contains repeal and amendment information on statutes from 1236 to the present, organized alphabetically. *Is it in Force?* (also published by LexisNexis Butterworths) provides the dates on which the various Acts and Measures in England, Wales and Scotland (back to 1960) came into force.

Public General Acts and General Synod Measures (1831 to present; called *The Public General Statutes* from 1831–1870) contains legislation compiled by Her Majesty's Stationery Office ("H.M.S.O.") into official *yearly* volumes printed in chronological order without annotations. Prior to 1939, volumes contained all statutes passed in a *session* of parliament (rather than in a particular year). Each volume contains a subject index and alphabetical and chronological tables of short titles. More importantly, there is a table of Acts repealed, amended or otherwise affected that can be used to see what has happened to an Act since its passage. In order to use this table, you will need to know the date the Act was first passed. The *Index to the Statutes in Force* (H.M.S.O. — 1235 to 1990 when publication ceased), and the *Chronological Table of the Statutes* (H.M.S.O. — 1235-present) serve as finding tools for the set, listing all Public General Acts from 1235 and providing information on what has been repealed and amended.

Acts are then reprinted by the Incorporated Council of Law Reporting for England and Wales (by arrangement with the H.M.S.O.) under the title *Law Reports Statutes and Public General Acts* as a companion series to the Law Reports. The Justis database provides online access to statutes published by the H.M.S.O from 1866 to the present.

2) Historical Statutes

Statutes of the Realm (1235–1713) is a 12-volume set published by the Record Commission in chronological order with both alphabetical and chronological indexes. The years 1642–1660 are not included; instead, they are published in *Acts and Ordinances of the Interregnum* which contains the laws, in chronological order, of the Civil War period (1642–49) and the Protectorate under Cromwell (1649–1660).

The Statutes at Large (1215–c1800) is a title attached to a number of sets of statutes published in the 1700s, usually edited either by Owen Ruffhead, or by Owen Ruffhead with a revision by Charles Runnington, or by Danby Pickering. It differs from *Statutes of the Realm* in that it covers approximately 80 additional years in the period (from the Magna Carta to Geo III). Justis provides online PDF access to U.K. statutes from the Ruffhead edition of *The Statues at Large.*

Legislation and Related Information Online

The following legislation and related information can be found at these sites:

- *Acts of the U.K. Parliament and Explanatory Notes* (http://www. opsi.gov.uk/acts.htm). Organized by year, then alphabetically by Act name or numerically by Act number. A keyword search is also available. It includes Public Acts from 1988 to present and a small number from 1801–1987.

- *The Statute Law Database* (http://www.statutelaw.gov.uk/). Provides an online "official revised edition of the primary legislation" in the U.K. through the Ministry of Justice Statute Law Database.
- *U.K. Parliament Hansard* (http://www.publications.parliament.uk/pa/pahansard.htm). Contains House of Commons proceedings back to Session 1988/89, House of Lords debates back to 2000 and Standing Committee debates on Bills from 1997/98.
- *Parliamentary Publications* (http://www.parliament.uk/publications/index.cfm). Includes links to Hansards, Research Papers, Parliamentary Archives, Select Committee Publications, and Standard Notes.
- *British and Irish Legal Information Institute (BAILII)* (http://www.bailii.org/form/search_legis.html). Contains statutes of England, Ireland, Northern Ireland, Scotland and Wales from varying dates along with a selection of much older statutes.

Citation

Since 1963, statutes have been cited by their title, date and chapter number, e.g., *Corporate Manslaughter and Corporate Homicide Act 2007*, c.19. Statutes prior to 1963 are cited by their regnal year rather than the calendar year. A regnal year is calculated from the Monarch's date of accession to the throne. For example, 14 Geo. VI c.26, is the twenty-sixth act passed during the fourteenth year of George the VI's reign. Some sessions of parliament overlap with regnal years and result in a citation which looks like this: 6 & 7 Geo. VI c.8.[23] In contrast, sometimes two Monarchs will overlap with one session of Parliament resulting in a statute citation which looks like this: 7 Will. 4 & 1 Vict. c.83. Because the regnal years are vital for researchers dealing with older statutes, a complete chart is provided as follows:

Regnal Years Chart

Ruler	Birth	Start of Reign	Regnal Years The numbers preceding the dates in this chart are the regnal year; the dates that follow are the calendar years. Regnal years in Latin: primo = 1st, secundo = 2nd, tertio = 3rd, quarto = 4th, quinto = 5th, sexto = 6th, septimo = 7th, octavo = 8th, nono = 9th, decimo = 10th, undecimo = 11th, vicesimo = 20th, tricesimo = 30th, quadragesimo = 40th				End of Reign	Death
William I Regnal years begin Oct 14 and end Oct 13. The final year ends on Sept. 9	1027	1066	1: 1066-1067 2: 1067-1068 3: 1068-1069 4: 1069-1070 5: 1070-1071	6: 1071-1072 7: 1072-1073 8: 1073-1074 9: 1074-1075 10: 1075-1076	11: 1076-1077 12: 1077-1078 13: 1078-1079 14: 1079-1080 15: 1080-1081	16: 1081-1082 17: 1082-1083 18: 1083-1084 19: 1084-1085 20: 1085-1086 21: 1086-1087	1087	1087
William II Regnal years begin Sept 26 and end Sept 25. The final year ends Aug 2.	1056	1087	1: 1087-1088 2: 1088-1089 3: 1089-1090	4: 1090-1091 5: 1091-1092 6: 1092-1093	7: 1093-1094 8: 1094-1095 9: 1095-1096	10: 1096-1097 11: 1097-1098 12: 1098-1099 13: 1099-1100	1100	1100

---

[23] The year in which an Act is deemed to have come into force depends on whether it was passed before the *Acts of Parliament (Commencement) Act 1793* or after. Those passed before this Act were treated as though they had come into force on the first day of the session in which they were passed even though they might have been, in reality, passed the year after the session began.

Ruler	Birth	Start of Reign	Regnal Years The numbers preceding the dates in this chart are the regnal year; the dates that follow are the calendar years. Regnal years in Latin: primo = 1st, secundo = 2nd, tertio = 3rd, quarto = 4th, quinto = 5th, sexto = 6th, septimo = 7th, octavo = 8th, nono = 9th, decimo = 10th, undecimo = 11th, vicesimo = 20th, tricesimo = 30th, quadragesimo = 40th				End of Reign	Death
Henry I Regnal years begin Aug 5 and end Aug 4. The final year ends Dec. 1.	1068	1100	1: 1100-1101 2: 1101-1102 3: 1102-1103 4: 1103-1104 5: 1104-1105 6: 1105-1106 7: 1106-1107 8: 1107-1108 9: 1108-1109	10: 1109-1110 11: 1110 -1111 12: 1111-1112 13: 1112-1113 14: 1113-1114 15: 1114-1115 16: 1115-1116 17: 1116-1117 18: 1117-1118	19: 1118-1119 20: 1119-1120 21: 1120-1121 22: 1121-1122 23: 1122-1123 24: 1123-1124 25: 1124-1125 26: 1125-1126 27: 1126-1127	28: 1127-1128 29: 1128-1129 30: 1129-1130 31: 1130-1131 32: 1131-1132 33: 1132-1133 34: 1133-1134 35: 1134-1135 36: 1135	1135	1135
Stephen Regnal years begin Dec 26 and end Dec 25. The final year ends Oct 25.	1105	1135	1: 1135-1136 2: 1136-1137 3: 1137-1138 4: 1138-1139 5: 1139-1140	6: 1140-1141 7: 1141-1142 8: 1142-1143 9: 1143-1144 10: 1144-1145	11: 1145-1146 12: 1146-1147 13: 1147-1148 14: 1148-1149 15: 1149-1150	16: 1150-1151 17: 1151-1152 18: 1152-1153 19: 1153-1154	1154	1154
Henry II Regnal years begin Dec 19 and end Dec 18. The final year ends July 6.	1133	1154	1: 1154-1155 2: 1155-1156 3: 1156-1157 4: 1157-1158 5: 1158-1159 6: 1159-1160 7: 1160-1161 8: 1161-1162 9: 1162-1163	10: 1163-1164 11: 1164-1165 12: 1165-1166 13: 1166-1167 14: 1167-1168 15: 1168-1169 16: 1169-1170 17: 1170-1171 18: 1171-1172	19: 1172-1173 20: 1173-1174 21: 1174-1175 22: 1175-1176 23: 1176-1177 24: 1177-1178 25: 1178-1179 26: 1179-1180 27: 1180-1181	28: 1181-1182 29: 1182-1183 30: 1183-1184 31: 1184-1185 32: 1185-1186 33: 1186-1187 34: 1187-1188 35: 1188-1189	1189	1189
Richard I the Lion-hearted Regnal years begin Sept 3 and end Sept 2. The final year ends Apr 6.	1157	1189	1: 1189-1190 2: 1190-1191 3: 1191-1192	4: 1192-1193 5: 1193-1194 6: 1194-1195	7: 1195-1196 8: 1196-1197 9: 1197-1198	10: 1198-1199	1199	1199
John Regnal years begin and end during varying days in May (& June in 1204). The final year ends Oct 19.	1166	1199	1: 1199-1200 2: 1200-1201 3: 1201-1202 4: 1202-1203	5: 1203-1204 6: 1204 -1205 7: 1205-1206 8: 1206-1207	9: 1207-1208 10: 1208-1209 11: 1209-1210 12: 1210 -1211 13: 1211-1212	14: 1212-1213 15: 1213-1214 16: 1214-1215 17: 1215-1216 18: 1216	1216	1216

Ruler	Birth	Start of Reign	Regnal Years The numbers preceding the dates in this chart are the regnal year; the dates that follow are the calendar years. Regnal years in Latin: primo = 1st, secundo = 2nd, tertio = 3rd, quarto = 4th, quinto = 5th, sexto = 6th, septimo = 7th, octavo = 8th, nono = 9th, decimo = 10th, undecimo = 11th, vicesimo = 20th, tricesimo = 30th, quadragesimo = 40th				End of Reign	Death
Henry III Regnal years begin Oct 28 and end Oct 27. The final year ends Nov 16.	1207	1216	1: 1216-1217 2: 1217-1218 3: 1218-1219 4: 1219-1220 5: 1220-1221 6: 1221-1222 7: 1222-1223 8: 1223-1224 9: 1224-1225 10: 1225-1226 11: 1226-1227 12: 1227-1228 13: 1228-1229 14: 1229-1230	15: 1230-1231 16: 1231-1232 17: 1232-1233 18: 1233-1234 19: 1234-1235 20: 1235-1236 21: 1236-1237 22: 1237-1238 23: 1238-1239 24: 1239-1240 25: 1240-1241 26: 1241-1242 27: 1242-1243 28: 1243-1244	29: 1244-1245 30: 1245-1246 31: 1246-1247 32: 1247-1248 33: 1248-1249 34: 1249-1250 35: 1250-1251 36: 1251-1252 37: 1252-1253 38: 1253-1254 39: 1254-1255 40: 1255-1256 41: 1256-1257 42: 1257-1258	43: 1258-1259 44: 1259-1260 45: 1260-1261 46: 1261-1262 47: 1262-1263 48: 1263-1264 49: 1264-1265 50: 1265-1266 51: 1266-1267 52: 1267-1268 53: 1268-1269 54: 1269-1270 55: 1270-1271 56: 1271-1272 57: 1272	1272	1272
Edward I Regnal years begin and end Nov 20. The final year ends July 7.	1239	1272	1: 1272-1273 2: 1273-1274 3: 1274-1275 4: 1275-1276 5: 1276-1277 6: 1277-1278 7: 1278-1279 8: 1279-1280 9: 1280-1281	10: 1281-1282 11: 1282-1283 12: 1283-1284 13: 1284-1285 14: 1285-1286 15: 1286-1287 16: 1287-1288 17: 1288-1289 18: 1289-1290	19: 1290-1291 20: 1291-1292 21: 1292-1293 22: 1293-1294 23: 1294-1295 24: 1295-1296 25: 1296-1297 26: 1297-1298 27: 1298-1299	28: 1299-1300 29: 1300-1301 30: 1301-1302 31: 1302-1303 32: 1303-1304 33: 1304-1305 34: 1305-1306 35: 1306-1307	1307	1307
Edward II Regnal years begin July 8 and end July 7. The final year ends Jan 20.	1284	1307	1: 1307-1308 2: 1308-1309 3: 1309-1310 4: 1310-1311 5: 1311-1312	6: 1312-1313 7: 1313-1314 8: 1314-1315 9: 1315-1316 10: 1316-1317	11: 1317-1318 12: 1318-1319 13: 1319-1320 14: 1320-1321 15: 1321-1322	16: 1322-1323 17: 1323-1324 18: 1324-1325 19: 1325-1326 20: 1326-1327	1327	1327

Ruler	Birth	Start of Reign	Regnal Years — The numbers preceding the dates in this chart are the regnal year; the dates that follow are the calendar years. Regnal years in Latin: primo = 1st, secundo = 2nd, tertio = 3rd, quarto = 4th, quinto = 5th, sexto = 6th, septimo = 7th, octavo = 8th, nono = 9th, decimo = 10th, undecimo = 11th, vicesimo = 20th, tricesimo = 30th, quadragesimo = 40th				End of Reign	Death
Edward III	1312	1327	1: 1327-1328	13: 1339-1340	25: 1351-1352	38: 1364-1365	1377	1377
			2: 1328-1329	14: 1340-1341	26: 1352-1353	39: 1365-1366		
			3: 1329-1330	15: 1341-1342	27: 1353-1354	40: 1366-1367		
			4: 1330-1331	16: 1342-1343	28: 1354-1355	41: 1367-1368		
Regnal years begin Jan 25			5: 1331-1332	17: 1343-1344	29: 1355-1356	42: 1368-1369		
and end Jan 24. The final			6: 1332-1333	18: 1344-1345	30: 1356-1357	43: 1369-1370		
year ends June 21.			7: 1333-1334	19: 1345-1346	31: 1357-1358	44: 1370-1371		
			8: 1334-1335	20: 1346-1347	32: 1358-1359	45: 1371-1372		
			9: 1335-1336	21: 1347-1348	33: 1359-1360	46: 1372-1373		
			10: 1336-1337	22: 1348-1349	34: 1360	47: 1373-1374		
			11: 1337-1338	23: 1349-1350	35: 1361-1362	48: 1374-1375		
			12: 1338-1339	24: 1350-1351	36: 1362-1363	49: 1375-1376		
					37: 1363-1364	50: 1376-1377		
						51: 1377		
Richard II	1366	1377	1: 1377-1378	7: 1383-1384	13: 1389-1390	19: 1395-1396	1399	1400
			2: 1378-1379	8: 1384-1385	14: 1390-1391	20: 1396-1397		
			3: 1379-1380	9: 1385-1386	15: 1391-1392	21: 1397-1398		
Regnal years begin June 22			4: 1380-1381	10: 1386-1387	16: 1392-1393	22: 1398-1399		
and end June 21. The final			5: 1381-1382	11: 1387-1388	17: 1393-1394	23: 1399		
year ends Sept 29.			6: 1382-1383	12: 1388-1389	18: 1394-1395			
Henry IV	1367	1399	1: 1399-1400	5: 1403-1404	9: 1407-1408	13: 1411-1412	1413	1413
Regnal years begin Sept 30			2: 1400-1401	6: 1404-1405	10: 1408-1409	14: 1412-1413		
and end Sept 29. The final			3: 1401-1402	7: 1405-1406	11: 1409-1410			
year ends Mar 20.			4: 1402-1403	8: 1406-1407	12: 1410-1411			
Henry V	1387	1413	1: 1413-1414	3: 1415-1416	5: 1417-1418	8: 1420-1421	1422	1422
Regnal years begin Mar 21			2: 1414-1415	4: 1416-1417	6: 1418-1419	9: 1421-1422		
and end Mar 20. The final					7: 1419-1420	10: 1422		
year ends Aug 31.								
Henry VI	1421	1422	1: 1422-1423	13: 1434-1435	25: 1446-1447	35: 1456-1457	1461	1471
			2: 1423-1424	14: 1435-1436	26: 1447-1448	36: 1457-1458		
			3: 1424-1425	15: 1436-1437	27: 1448-1449	37: 1458-1459		
			4: 1425-1426	16: 1437-1438	28: 1449-1450	38: 1459-1460		
			5: 1426-1427	17: 1438-1439	29: 1450-1451	39: 1460-1461		
Regnal years begin Sept 1			6: 1427-1428	18: 1439-1440	30: 1451-1452	(Deposed)		
and end Aug 31. The year he			7: 1428-1429	19: 1440-1441	31: 1452-1453			
was deposed ends Mar 4.			8: 1429-1430	20: 1441-1442	32: 1453-1454	49: 1470-1471		
			9: 1430-1431	21: 1442-1443	33: 1454-1455	Regained		
			10: 1431-1432	22: 1443-1444	34: 1455-1456	Throne		
			11: 1432-1433	23: 1444-1445		(Oct–April)		
			12: 1433-1434	24: 1445-1446				

326

English Law

Ruler	Birth	Start of Reign	Regnal Years — The numbers preceding the dates in this chart are the regnal year; the dates that follow are the calendar years. Regnal years in Latin: primo = 1st, secundo = 2nd, tertio = 3rd, quarto = 4th, quinto = 5th, sexto = 6th, septimo = 7th, octavo = 8th, nono = 9th, decimo = 10th, undecimo = 11th, vicesimo = 20th, tricesimo = 30th, quadragesimo = 40th				End of Reign	Death
Edward IV — Regnal years begin Mar 4 and end Mar 3. The final year ends April 9.	1441	1461	1: 1461-1462 2: 1462-1463 3: 1463-1464 4: 1464-1465 5: 1465-1466	6: 1466-1467 7: 1467-1468 8: 1468-1469 9: 1469-1470 10: 1470-1471 11: 1471-1472	12: 1472-1473 13: 1473-1474 14: 1474-1475 15: 1475-1476 16: 1476-1477 17: 1477-1478	18: 1478-1479 19: 1479-1480 20: 1480-1481 21: 1481-1482 22: 1482-1483 23: 1483	1483	1483
Edward V — April 9 to June 25	1470	1483	1: 1483				1483	1483
Richard III — Regnal years begin June 26 and end June 25. The final year ends Aug 22.	1452	1483	1: 1483-1484	2: 1484-1485	3: 1485		1485	1485
Henry VII — Regnal years begin Aug 22 and end Aug 21. The final year ends April 21.	1457	1485	1: 1485-1486 2: 1486-1487 3: 1487-1488 4: 1488-1489 5: 1489-1490 6: 1490-1491	7: 1491-1492 8: 1492-1493 9: 1493-1494 10: 1494-1495 11: 1495-1496 12: 1496-1497	13: 1497-1498 14: 1498-1499 15: 1499-1500 16: 1500-1501 17: 1501-1502 18: 1502-1503	19: 1503-1504 20: 1504-1505 21: 1505-1506 22: 1506-1507 23: 1507-1508 24: 1508-1509	1509	1509
Henry VIII — Regnal years begin April 22 and end April 21. The final year ends Jan 28.	1491	1509	1: 1509-1510 2: 1510-1511 3: 1511-1512 4: 1512-1513 5: 1513-1514 6: 1514-1515 7: 1515-1516 8: 1516-1517 9: 1517-1518	10: 1518-1519 11: 1519-1520 12: 1520-1521 13: 1521-1522 14: 1522-1523 15: 1523-1524 16: 1524-1525 17: 1525-1526 18: 1526-1527	19: 1527-1528 20: 1528-1529 21: 1529-1530 22: 1530-1531 23: 1531-1532 24: 1532-1533 25: 1533-1534 26: 1534-1535 27: 1535-1536 28: 1536-1537	29: 1537-1538 30: 1538-1539 31: 1539-1540 32: 1540-1541 33: 1541-1542 34: 1542-1543 35: 1543-1544 36: 1544-1545 37: 1545-1546 38: 1546-1547	1547	1547
Edward VI — Regnal years begin Jan 28 and end Jan 27. The final year ends July 6.	1537	1547	1: 1547-1548 2: 1548-1549	3: 1549-1550 4: 1550-1551	5: 1551-1552 6: 1552-1553	7: 1553	1553	1553

Ruler	Birth	Start of Reign	Regnal Years The numbers preceding the dates in this chart are the regnal year; the dates that follow are the calendar years. Regnal years in Latin: primo = 1st, secundo = 2nd, tertio = 3rd, quarto = 4th, quinto = 5th, sexto = 6th, septimo = 7th, octavo = 8th, nono = 9th, decimo = 10th, undecimo = 11th, vicesimo = 20th, tricesimo = 30th, quadragesimo = 40th				End of Reign	Death
Mary Regnal years: July 6 to July 5 and July 6 to July 24.	1516	1553	1: 1553-1554	2: 1554			1558	1558
Philip & Mary Regnal years begin July 25 and end July 24. The final year ends Nov 17.			1 & 2: 1554-1555 2 & 3: 1555-1556		3 & 4: 1556-1557 4 & 5: 1557-1558 5 & 6: 1558			
Elizabeth I Regnal years begin Nov 17 and end Nov 16. The final year ends Mar 24.	1533	1558	1: 1558-1559 2: 1559-1560 3: 1560-1561 4: 1561-1562 5: 1562-1563 6: 1563-1564 7: 1564-1565 8: 1565-1566 9: 1566-1567 10: 1567-1568 11: 1568-1569	12: 1569-1570 13: 1570-1571 14: 1571-1572 15: 1572-1573 16: 1573-1574 17: 1574-1575 18: 1575-1576 19: 1576-1577 20: 1577-1578 21: 1578-1579 22: 1579-1580	23: 1580-1581 24: 1581-1582 25: 1582-1583 26: 1583-1584 27: 1584-1585 28: 1585-1586 29: 1586-1587 30: 1587-1588 31: 1588-1589 32: 1589-1590 33: 1590-1591	34: 1591-1592 35: 1592-1593 36: 1593-1594 37: 1594-1595 38: 1595-1596 39: 1596-1597 40: 1597-1598 41: 1598-1599 42: 1599-1600 43: 1600-1601 44: 1601-1602 45: 1602-1603	1603	1603
James I Regnal years begin Mar 24 and end Mar 23. The final year ends Mar 27.	1566	1603	1: 1603-1604 2: 1604-1605 3: 1605-1606 4: 1606-1607 5: 1607-1608 6: 1608-1609	7: 1609-1610 8: 1610-1611 9: 1611-1612 10: 1612-1613 11: 1613-1614 12: 1614-1615	13: 1615-1616 14: 1616-1617 15: 1617-1618 16: 1618-1619 17: 1619-1620 18: 1620-1621	19: 1621-1622 20: 1622-1623 21: 1623-1624 22: 1624-1625 23: 1625	1625	1625
Charles I Regnal years begin Mar 27 and end Mar 26. The final year ends Jan 30.	1600	1625	1: 1625-1626 2: 1626-1627 3: 1627-1628 4: 1628-1629 5: 1629-1630 6: 1630-1631	7: 1631-1632 8: 1632-1633 9: 1633-1634 10: 1634-1635 11: 1635-1636 12: 1636-1637	13: 1637-1638 14: 1638-1639 15: 1639-1640 16: 1640-1641 17: 1641-1642 18: 1642-1643	19: 1643-1644 20: 1644-1645 21: 1645-1646 22: 1646-1647 23: 1647-1648 24: 1648-1649	1649	1649
Interreg-num (1649-1660)			Dates used (not regnal years).					

Ruler	Birth	Start of Reign	Regnal Years The numbers preceding the dates in this chart are the regnal year; the dates that follow are the calendar years. Regnal years in Latin: primo = 1st, secundo = 2nd, tertio = 3rd, quarto = 4th, quinto = 5th, sexto = 6th, septimo = 7th, octavo = 8th, nono = 9th, decimo = 10th, undecimo = 11th, vicesimo = 20th, tricesimo = 30th, quadragesimo = 40th				End of Reign	Death
Charles II (Date of reign said to begin with the death of Charles I (1649)) Regnal years begin Jan 30 and end Jan 29 (except May 29 1660 - Jan 30 1661). The final year ends Feb 6.	1630	1660	12: 1660-1661 13: 1661-1662 14: 1662-1663 15: 1663-1664 16: 1664-1665 17: 1665-1666 18: 1666-1667	19: 1667-1668 20: 1668-1669 21: 1669-1670 22: 1670-1671 23: 1671-1672 24: 1672-1673	25: 1673-1674 26: 1674-1675 27: 1675-1676 28: 1676-1677 29: 1677-1678 30: 1678-1679	31: 1679-1680 32: 1680-1681 33: 1681-1682 34: 1682-1683 35: 1683-1684 36: 1684-1685 37: 1685	1685	1685
James II Regnal years begin Feb 6 and end Feb 5. The final year ends Dec 11.	1633	1685	1: 1685-1686	2: 1686-1687	3: 1687-1688	4: 1688	1688/89	1701
William III *& Mary II* Regnal years 1-5 begin Feb 13 and end 12 Feb. Year 6 ends Dec 27. Years 7-13 begin Dec 28 and end Dec 27. Year 14 ends Mar 8.	1650 1662	1689 1689	1: 1689-1690 2: 1690-1691 3: 1691-1692	4: 1692-1693 5: 1693-1694 6: 1694 7: 1694-1695	8: 1695-1696 9: 1696-1697 10: 1697-1698	11: 1698-1699 12: 1699-1700 13: 1700-1701 14: 1702	1702 1694	1702 1694
Anne Regnal years begin Mar 8 and end Mar 7. The final year ends Aug 1.	1665	1702	1: 1702-1703 2: 1703-1704 3: 1704-1705	4: 1705-1706 5: 1706-1707 6: 1707-1708	7: 1708-1709 8: 1709-1710 9: 1710-1711	10: 1711-1712 11: 1712-1713 12: 1713-1714 13: 1714	1714	1714
George I Regnal years begin Aug 1 and end July 31. The final year ends June 11.	1660	1714	1: 1714-1715 2: 1715-1716 3: 1716-1717	4: 1717-1718 5: 1718-1719 6: 1719-1720	7: 1720-1721 8: 1721-1722 9: 1722-1723	10: 1723-1724 11: 1724-1725 12: 1725-1726 13: 1726-1727	1727	1727

Ruler	Birth	Start of Reign	Regnal Years The numbers preceding the dates in this chart are the regnal year; the dates that follow are the calendar years. Regnal years in Latin: primo = 1st, secundo = 2nd, tertio = 3rd, quarto = 4th, quinto = 5th, sexto = 6th, septimo = 7th, octavo = 8th, nono = 9th, decimo = 10th, undecimo = 11th, vicesimo = 20th, tricesimo = 30th, quadragesimo = 40th				End of Reign	Death
George II Regnal years begin June 11 and end June 10. The final year ends Oct 25.	1683	1727	1: 1727-1728 2: 1728-1729 3: 1729-1730 4: 1730-1731 5: 1731-1732 6: 1732-1733 7: 1733-1734 8: 1734-1735	9: 1735-1736 10: 1736-1737 11: 1737-1738 12: 1738-1739 13: 1739-1740 14: 1740-1741 15: 1741-1742 16: 1742-1743	17: 1743-1744 18: 1744-1745 19: 1745-1746 20: 1746-1747 21: 1747-1748 22: 1748-1749 23: 1749-1750 24: 1750-1751 25: 1751-1752	26: 1752-1753 27: 1753-1754 28: 1754-1755 29: 1755-1756 30: 1756-1757 31: 1757-1758 32: 1758-1759 33: 1759-1760 34: 1760	1760	1760
George III Regnal years begin Oct 25 and end Oct 24. The final year ends Jan 29.	1738	1760	1: 1760-1761 2: 1761-1762 3: 1762-1763 4: 1763-1764 5: 1764-1765 6: 1765-1766 7: 1766-1767 8: 1767-1768 9: 1768-1769 10: 1769-1770 11: 1770-1771 12: 1771-1772 13: 1772-1773 14: 1773-1774 15: 1774-1775	16: 1775-1776 17: 1776-1777 18: 1777-1778 19: 1778-1779 20: 1779-1780 21: 1780-1781 22: 1781-1782 23: 1782-1783 24: 1783-1784 25: 1784-1785 26: 1785-1786 27: 1786-1787 28: 1787-1788 29: 1788-1789 30: 1789-1790	31: 1790-1791 32: 1791-1792 33: 1792-1793 34: 1793-1794 35: 1794-1795 36: 1795-1796 37: 1796-1797 38: 1797-1798 39: 1798-1799 40: 1799-1800 41: 1800-1801 42: 1801-1802 43: 1802-1803 44: 1803-1804 45: 1804-1805	46: 1805-1806 47: 1806-1807 48: 1807-1808 49: 1808-1809 50: 1809-1810 51: 1810-1811 52: 1811-1812 53: 1812-1813 54: 1813-1814 55: 1814-1815 56: 1815-1816 57: 1816-1817 58: 1817-1818 59: 1818-1819 60: 1819-1820	1820	1820
George IV Regnal years begin Jan 29 and end Jan 28. The final year ends June 26.	1762	1820	1: 1820-1821 2: 1821-1822 3: 1822-1823 4: 1823-1824 5: 1824-1825 6: 1825-1826 7: 1826-1827	8: 1827-1828 9: 1828-1829 10: 1829-1830 11: 1830			1830	1830
William IV Regnal years begin June 26 and end June 25. The final year ends June 20.	1765	1830	1: 1830-1831 2: 1831-1832	3: 1832-1833 4: 1833-1834	5: 1834-1835 6: 1835-1836	7: 1836-1837	1837	1837

330

English Law

Ruler	Birth	Start of Reign	Regnal Years The numbers preceding the dates in this chart are the regnal year; the dates that follow are the calendar years. Regnal years in Latin: primo = 1st, secundo = 2nd, tertio = 3rd, quarto = 4th, quinto = 5th, sexto = 6th, septimo = 7th, octavo = 8th, nono = 9th, decimo = 10th, undecimo = 11th, vicesimo = 20th, tricesimo = 30th, quadragesimo = 40th				End of Reign	Death
Victoria Regnal years begin June 20 and end June 19. The final year ends Jan 22.	1819	1837	1: 1837-1838 2: 1838-1839 3: 1839-1840 4: 1840-1841 5: 1841-1842 6: 1842-1843 7: 1843-1844 8: 1844-1845 9: 1845-1846 10: 1846-1847 11: 1847-1848 12: 1848-1849 13: 1849-1850 14: 1850-1851 15: 1851-1852 16: 1852-1853	17: 1853-1854 18: 1854-1855 19: 1855-1856 20: 1856-1857 21: 1857-1858 22: 1858-1859 23: 1859-1860 24: 1860-1861 25: 1861-1862 26: 1862-1863 27: 1863-1864 28: 1864-1865 29: 1865-1866 30: 1866-1867 31: 1867-1868 32: 1868-1869	33: 1869-1970 34: 1870-1871 35: 1871-1872 36: 1872-1873 37: 1873-1874 38: 1874-1875 39: 1875-1876 40: 1876-1877 41: 1877-1878 42: 1878-1879 43: 1879-1880 44: 1880-1881 45: 1881-1882 46: 1882-1883 47: 1883-1884 48: 1884-1885	49: 1885-1886 50: 1886-1887 51: 1887-1888 52: 1888-1889 53: 1889-1890 54: 1890-1891 55: 1891-1892 56: 1892-1893 57: 1893-1894 58: 1894-1895 59: 1895-1896 60: 1896-1897 61: 1897-1898 62: 1898-1899 63: 1899-1900 64: 1900-1901	1901	1901
Edward VII Regnal years begin Jan 22 and end Jan 21. The final year ends May 6.	1841	1901	1: 1901-1902 2: 1902-1903	3: 1903-1904 4: 1904-1905	5: 1905-1906 6: 1906-1907 7: 1907-1908	8: 1908-1909 9: 1909-1910 10: 1910	1910	1910
George V Regnal years begin May 6 and end May 5. The final year ends Jan 20.	1865	1910	1: 1910-1911 2: 1911-1912 3: 1912-1913 4: 1913-1914 5: 1914-1915 6: 1915-1916 7: 1916-1917	8: 1917-1918 9: 1918-1919 10: 1919-1920 11: 1920-1921 12: 1921-1922 13: 1922-1923 14: 1923-1924	15: 1924-1925 16: 1925-1926 17: 1926-1927 18: 1927-1928 19: 1928-1929 20: 1929-1930	21: 1930-1931 22: 1931-1932 23: 1932-1933 24: 1933-1934 25: 1934-1935 26: 1935-1936	1936	1936
Edward VIII Jan 20 - Dec 11.	1894	1936	1: 1936				1936	1972
George VI Regnal years begin Dec 11 and end Dec 10. The final year ends Feb 5.	1895	1936	1: 1936-1937 2: 1937-1938 3: 1938-1939 4: 1939-1940	5: 1940-1941 6: 1941-1942 7: 1942-1943 8: 1943-1944	9: 1944-1945 10: 1945-1946 11: 1946-1947 12: 1947-1948	13: 1948-1949 14: 1949-1950 15: 1950-1951 16: 1951-1952	1952	1952
Elizabeth II Regnal years begin Feb 6 and end Feb 5.	1926	1952	1: 1952-1953 2: 1953-1954 3: 1954-1955	4: 1955-1956 5: 1956-1957 6: 1957-1958	7: 1958-1959 8: 1959-1960 9: 1960-1961	10: 1961-1962	?	?

Delegated Legislation

Parliament has the power to authorize (via statute) someone or something other than itself (usually a Ministry, Board or local authority) to create legislation (orders, rules and regulations) by means of a Statutory Instrument ("S.I."). This delegated legislation has the same legal force as the statute which authorized its creation.

Orders in Council may be primary or delegated legislation depending on whether they are made as the result of Royal Prerogative or authorized by Statute. Monarchs have reserved unto themselves various powers which have come about as the result of history, custom and tradition. These powers (the "Royal Prerogative") allow the Privy Council to create legislation in the name of the Queen (Queen-in-Council) in the form of Orders in Council. This form of delegated legislation does not depend on any statute in order to come into being. On the other hand, many Orders in Council are made as the result of a parent Act which authorizes their creation.

There is a significant distinction between Orders *in* Council and Orders *of* Council. Orders *in* Council are made with the Queen's approval at a meeting of the Privy Council; Orders *of* Council may be made by Privy Council without the approval of the Sovereign. Orders of Council, like Orders in Council, are made pursuant to legislation or prerogative, but their subject matter is much more circumscribed, generally involving the regulation of the medical profession, the veterinary profession and the universities.

By-laws are another form of delegated legislation. This power is granted to local authorities and public bodies to make rules having the force of law in a specific area.

Where to find it: Information on Orders in Council and Orders of Council since 2000 is posted on the Privy Council site at http://www.pco.gov.uk/output/Page473.asp. Both types of Orders are available online at http://www.opsi.gov.uk/ stat as well as on BAILII at http://www.bailii.org/ for more recent years.

The published version of British administrative regulations is *Statutory Instruments* (H.M.S.O.,1949-current), published annually, and *Statutory Rules and Orders* (1891–1948). *Statutory Instruments* is published in chronological order (S.I.s earlier than 1962 are arranged by subject) and also contains orders, Royal Proclamations and Letters Patent (executive documents).

The *Table of Government Orders* published by the Stationery Office provides information on whether a statutory instrument is in force, as well as chronological and numerical lists of all general rules, orders, and statutory instruments since 1671. It also contains information on what is in force, along with any amendments or repeals since 1948.

The Index to Government Orders is published every two years by the Stationery Office and allows S.I.s to be located by subject.

Halsbury's Statutory Instruments (1951-present) is an annotated series, arranged alphabetically by title, which provides some full-text content for certain statutory instruments and summaries for others. It is updated with a loose-leaf volume. The regulations can be accessed by subject in the *Consolidated Index*. To update the main volumes, consult the *Annual Supplement* and the *Monthly Survey Summaries* in the *Service Binder*.

You can also find useful summaries of the changes to Statutory Instruments that occurred within a given year by consulting the Halsbury's *Annual Abridgment* volume for the year in which you are interested.

Delegated Legislation Online

One place to find Statutory Instruments is online at the Office of Public Sector Information at http://www.legislation.hmso.gov.uk/stat.htm. U.K. Statutory Instruments and Explanatory Memorandum are available from 1987 to present. BAILII also contains Statutory Instruments for the United Kingdom (1987-), Ireland (1922-) and Northern Ireland (2001-), in addition to those made by the National Assembly for Wales (1998-), and the Scottish Parliament (1999-) at http://www.bailii.org/.

Treaties

"Command Papers"[24] are government documents published by the Foreign and Commonwealth Office. They contain State Papers (British treaties (ratified and unratified) and other international agreements), White Papers (policy and legislative proposals), Green Papers (discussion or consultation documents), reports of Royal Commissions and Committees of Inquiry, some government statistics and annual reports, and some responses to select committee Reports. They are published as a numbered series along with Explanatory Memoranda. Command Papers are produced in series (the first appeared in 1833) and the prefix (e.g., Cm or CM 1) changes each time a new series begins.

Where to find it: Ratified treaties and most of the agreements and exchanges of notes are published in the *Treaty Series* (London: H.M.S.O., 1892). Another series entitled *British and Foreign State Papers* (London: H.M.S.O., 1812) is a good source for historical treaties. Online, treaties are available through the Foreign and Commonwealth Office ("FCO") from

---

[24] The name "Command" has to do with how the papers are presented to Parliament: the documents are "presented to Parliament by command of Her/His Majesty."

1997 to present at http://www.fco.gov.uk/en/about-the-fco/publications/treaty-command-papers-ems/treaty-command-papers-by-date.

Secondary Sources

Monographs

Many of the classic treatises in the United Kingdom are published by a handful of publishers including Sweet & Maxwell, Butterworths, Hart and Oxford University Press. In addition to the classics, new books are published all the time. Keeping abreast of new titles is best done by consulting what the larger academic law libraries have been purchasing, or what is available through specialty bookstores.

One of the best ways to locate the titles of current texts on any subject in law is to consult an online library catalogue such as the Oxford Libraries Information System (OLIS) at http://www.lib.ox.ac.uk/olis/ or the University of Cambridge Newton Library catalogue at http://ul-newton.lib.cam.ac.uk/. Another way to locate titles of current legal texts is through the U.K.'s largest legal bookstore, Hammicks Legal Information Services at http://www.hammickslegal.co.uk.

Legal Periodicals

Journal articles and case comments on English law can be accessed through the *Legal Journals Index (LJI)* which indexes several hundred English and European (English language) journals. It is not available in print but is accessible electronically via Westlaw and Legal Information Services, an online service offered by Sweet & Maxwell. References to U.K. periodicals can be located in several other sources: *Current Law Index* is available in print and online (through *LegalTrac*). It is published by Gale and coverage includes approximately 1,000 journals from the U.S., Canada, Great Britain, Australia, and New Zealand.

European Legal Journals Index is available in print and online via Westlaw. It contains English language articles having to do with the European Community and its member States.

Halsbury's Laws of England, Table of Articles contains references to articles. Two more sources for U.K. law journals are the *Index to Legal Periodicals* published by H.W. Wilson, and the journals databases on LexisNexis.

Legal Dictionaries and Words and Phrases Encyclopedias

Some of the more recent or better-known legal dictionaries and words and phrases encyclopedias are:

- Ned Beale, *Dictionary of Law*, 5th ed. (London: A. & C. Black, 2007);

- Daniel Greenberg, *Jowitt's Dictionary of English Law*, 3d ed. (London: Sweet & Maxwell, 2010);

- Mick Woodley, ed., *Osborne's Concise Law Dictionary*, 11th ed. (London: Sweet & Maxwell/Thomson Reuters, 2009);

- John S. James, ed., *Stroud's Judicial Dictionary of Words and Phrases*, 7th ed. (London: Sweet & Maxwell, 2007);

- David Hay, ed., *Words and Phrases Legally Defined*, 4th ed. (London: LexisNexis Butterworths, 2007).

In addition, information on words and phrases exists in *The Law Reports*, the *All England Law Reports* and the *Weekly Law Reports*, as well as *Current Law Monthly* which lists its words and phrases under "W" in the subject headings.

Legal Encyclopedias

1) Halsbury's Laws of England (3rd Edition)

Halsbury's is a multi-volume encyclopedia of English law which also acts as part dictionary, digest and treatise. The law, including both English and European (as it applies to England) is organized alphabetically by subject. Relevant cases and statutes appear in footnotes. In order to access the relevant volume, you can use the *General Index* which will in turn refer you to the correct volume. You can also select the correct volume by making use of the titles on the spines of the volumes and the subject index within each volume. At the beginning of each subject, there is a detailed subject index. One useful feature of the third edition is the *Canadian Converters*. These volumes footnote the text with Canadian cases. While the fourth edition does not have this feature, the *Canadian Converter* volumes to the 3rd Edition continue to be published.

2) Halsbury's Laws of England (4th Edition)

The fourth edition of *Halsbury's* is the latest edition of the legal encyclopedia.[25] As with the third edition, access to the subject volumes are by way of the *General Index* or by reference to the spines of the volumes themselves. There are more detailed indexes at the beginning of each subject title. To update a given subject, you should begin by consulting the *Cumulative Supplement* which updates the main work with reference to volume

---

[25] At the time of writing, *Halsbury's Laws of England* began publication of its Fifth Edition. Pending completion of the 5th edition, the current set of *Halsbury's* is made up of both 4th and 5th edition volumes.

and paragraph numbers. There are also *Annual Abridgment* volumes issued each year that outline the development of the law — statutory and case law — and give a listing of periodical articles by subject for the year. Words and phrases can be found using the *General Indexes*. Finally, there is a loose-leaf service, *Current Service*, which has monthly reviews of the law. The current version of *Halsbury's* is available online from LexisNexis Quicklaw.

Legal material with respect to the European communities (basic treaties, along with European decisions, directives and regulations) are also found in these volumes, along with information on all legislation, rules and orders in the United Kingdom which have been implemented or are otherwise affected by European law. *Halsbury's* is very well respected and unlike Canada's *C.E.D.*, it is often cited by courts.

The Digest: Annotated British, Commonwealth, and European Cases (Formerly the English and Empire Digest)

The *Digest* performs the same function for English legal research as the *Canadian Abridgment* in the Canadian legal research setting, and contains case digests for English, Scottish, Irish, Commonwealth, European Court of Justice, and European Court of Human Rights cases.

Case digests are arranged under topics and subtopics and each digest has a paragraph number. The *Digest* also allows you to see the subsequent judicial consideration of the case, since later cases citing the digested case are listed below each digest. The digests are cross-referenced with *Halsbury's Laws of England*. The *Digest* itself has main volumes supplemented and updated by *Continuation Volumes* and a *Cumulative Supplement*.

To access cases in the *Digest*, you should consult the *Consolidated Index* by searching for a key word or phrase. If you know the name of the case in which you are interested, you may consult the *Consolidated Table of Cases*. To update a given paragraph, you should consult the *Cumulative Supplement* which will indicate any later cases that have considered the case digested in a given paragraph or will list later cases in that subject area. Those later cases can either be found in the *Cumulative Supplement* or in one of the *Continuation Volumes*.

Current Law

Current Law is a monthly digest of cases, legislation, and secondary sources. At the end of the year, the *Current Law Year Book* is published containing all the information published in the monthly volumes over the year. In addition to the year books and monthly soft cover volumes for the current year, bound index volumes assist in locating information in the appropriate year books and the *Case Citator* contains information on new cases as well as older cases cited in recent decisions.

Recommended Reading

Cane, Peter & Mark Tushnet, eds. *The Oxford Handbook of Legal Studies* (Oxford: Oxford University Press, 2005).

Charman, Mary, Bobby Vanstone & Liz Sherratt. *As Law*, 4th ed. (Devon, UK: Willan, 2006).

Clinch, Peter. *Legal Information: What It Is and Where to Find It*, 2d ed. (London: Aslib, c2000).

Cownie, Fiona et al. *English Legal System in Context*, 4th ed. (Oxford: Oxford UP, 2007).

Darbyshire, Penny. *English Legal System in a Nutshell* (London: Sweet & Maxwell, 2004).

Doherty, Michael. *English and European Legal Systems*, 4th ed. (London: Old Bailey Press, 2005).

Elliott, Catherine & Frances Quinn. *English Legal System*, 10th ed. (London: Routledge Cavendish, 2009).

Finch, Emily & Stefan Fafinski. *Legal Skills*, 2d ed. (Oxford: Oxford University Press, 2009).

Holborn, Guy. *Butterworths Legal Research Guide*, 2d ed. (London: Butterworths, 2001).

Mcconville, Mike & Wing Hong Chui, eds. *Research Methods for Law* (Edinburgh: Edinburgh University Press, 2007).

Slapper, Gary & David Kelly. *English Legal System*, 10th ed. (London: Routledge Cavendish, 2009).

Stott, D. *Legal Research*, 2d ed. (London: Cavendish, 1999).

Thomas, Philip & John Knowles. *Effective Legal Research* (London: Thomson Sweet & Maxwell, 2006).

Williams, Glanville. *Learning the Law*, 13th ed. (London: Sweet & Maxwell, 2006).

Appendix I — Nominate Reports, Abbreviations and Locations in the English Reports

Nominate reports	Abbreviations	Volume in E.R.'s	Period Covered (Approx.)	Example
Acton's Prize Cases	Act.; Acton	12	1809–1811	*Lempriere v. Le Brun* (1809) 1 Act. 7
Addam's Ecclesiastical Reports	Add.; Add. Ecc.; Add. Eccl.; Addams	162	1822–1826	*Usticke v. Bawden* (1824) 2 Add. 116
Adolphus & Ellis' Queen's Bench Reports	Ad. & E.; Ad. & El.; Adolphus & Ellis	110–113	1834–1840	*Boodle v. Davies* (1835) 3 Ad. & E. 200
Aleyn's Reports, King's Bench	Al.; Aleyn	82	1646–1649	*Combs v. Cheny* (1648) Aleyn 92
Ambler's Chancery Reports	Amb.; Ambler	27	1737–1784	*Hardcastle v. Slater* (1745) Amb. 41
Anderson's Common Pleas Reports	And.; Anders; Anderson	123	1534–1605	*Lovelace v. Lovelace* (1565) 1 Anderson 132
Andrews' King's Bench Reports	Andr.; Andrews	95	1737–1739	*Beer v. Alleyn* (1738) Andrews 247
Anstruther's Exchequer Reports	Anst.; Anstr.; Anstruther	145	1792–1797	*Corbett v. Barker* (1793) 1 Anst. 138
Atkyns' Chancery Reports	Atk.; Atkyns	26	1736–1755	*Blandford (Marchioness of) v. Marlborough (Duchess of)* (1743) 2 Atk. 542
Barnardiston's Chancery Reports	Barn. C.; Barnardiston Ch.	27	1740-1741	*Metcalf v. Royal Exchange Assurance Co.* (1740) Barn. C. 343
Barnardiston's King's Bench Reports	Barn. K.B.; Barnard.; Barnardiston K.B.	94	1726–1734	*Denail v. Brickland* (1733) 2 Barn. K.B. 292
Barnes' Notes of Cases of Practice in Common Pleas	Bar. N.; Barnes; Barnes N.C.	94	1732–1756	*Lacy v. Lock* (1742) Barnes 349
Barnewall & Adolphus' King's Bench Reports	B. & Ad.; Barn. & Ad.; Barnewall & Adolphus	109-110	1830–1834	*Hill v. Manchester and Salford Water Works* (1831) 2 B. & Ad. 544
Barnewall & Alderson's King's Bench Reports	B. & A.; B. & Ald.; Barnewall & Alderson	106	1817–1822	*Murray v. East India Co.* (1821) 5 B. & Ald. 204
Barnewall & Cresswell's King's Bench Reports	B. & C.; Barn. & Cress.; Barnewall & Cresswell	107–109	1822–1830	*Smith v. Wattleworth* (1825) 4 B. & C. 364
Beavan's Rolls Court Reports	Beav.; Beavan	48–55	1838–1866	*Arundel (Corp. of) v. Holmes* (1841) 4 Beav. 325
Bell's Crown Cases Reserved	Bell; Bell C.C.; Bell Cr. Ca.; Bell Cr. Cas.	169	1858–1860	*Regina v. Webster* (1859) Bell 154

English Law

Nominate reports	Abbreviations	Volume in E.R.'s	Period Covered (Approx.)	Example
Bellewe's King's Bench Reports	Bel.; Bellewe	72	1378–1400	*Re Generall bre, et speciall declaration, ou pleint* Bellewe 206
Belt's Supplement to Vesey Senior's Chancery Reports	Ves. Sen. Supp.; Vesey Senior Supplement	28	1746–1756	*Swynfen v. Scawen* (1748) Ves. Sen. Supp. 68
Benloe's King's Bench Reports	Benl.; Benl. K.B.; Benloe; Benloe King(')s Bench	73	1530–1628	*Hutton v. Bourman* (1626) Benloe 170
Benloe & Dalison's Common Pleas Reports	Ben. & D.; Benl. & Dal.; Benloe; Dalison; Benloe & Dalison	123	1486–1580	*Nichols v. Nichols* (1573) Benloe 245
Best & Smith's Queen's Bench Reports	B. & S.; Best & S.; Best & Smith	121-122	1861–1865	*R. v. Darlington Local Board of Health* (1864) 5 B. & S. 515
Bingham's Common Pleas Reports	Bing.; Bingham	130-131	1822–1834	*Hill v. Featherstonhaugh* (1831) 7 Bing. 569
Bingham's New Cases, English Common Pleas	Bing. N.C.; Bing. (N.C.); Bing. N. Cas.; Bingham New Cases	131–133	1834–1840	*Hodges v. Litchfield (Earl of)* (1835) 1 Bing. (N.C.) 492
Bligh's House of Lords Reports	Bli.; Bli. P.C.; Bligh; Bligh P.C.; Bligh Parliament Cases	4	1819–1821	*Eyre v. Bank of England* (1819) 1 Bligh P.C. 582
Bligh's House of Lords Reports, New Series	Bli. N.S.; Bli. N.S.P.C.; Bligh N.S.; Bligh N.S.P.C.; Bligh New Series	4–6	1827–1837	*Spain (King of) v. Hullett* (1833) 7 Bligh N.S. 359
Bosanquet & Puller's Common Pleas Reports	Bos. & P.; Bos. & Pul.; Bosanquet & Puller	126-127	1796–1804	*Constantine v. Pugh* (1802) 3 Bos. & Pul. 184
Bosanquet & Puller's New Reports, Common Pleas	Bos. & Pul. (N.R.); Bos. & Pul. N.R.	127	1804–1807	*Marshall v. Birkenshaw* (1805) 1 Bos. & Pul. (N.R.) 172
Sir J Bridgman's Common Pleas Reports	Bridg. J.; Bridgman J.; Bridgman, J.; Bridgman Sir J.; J. Bridg.	123	1613–1621	*Crawley v. Marrow* (1616) Bridgman, J. 64
Sir O Bridgman's Common Pleas Reports	Bridg. O.; Bridgman O.; Bridgman, O.; Bridgman Sir O.; O. Bridg.	124	1660–1667	*Beckman v. Maplesden* (1662) Bridgman, O. 60
Broderip & Bingham's Common Pleas Reports	Br. & B.; Brod. & B.; Brod. & Bing.; Broderip & Bingham	129	1819–1822	*Warmsley v. Macey* (1820) 2 Brod. & B. 338
Brook's New Cases King's Bench	B.N.C.; Brook; Brook's New Cases	73	1515–1558	*Re Priviledge* Brook's New Cases 153
Brown's Chancery Cases	Bro. C.C.; Brown's Chancery Cases	28-29	1778–1794	*Hanington v. Du Chastel* (1781) 1 Bro. C.C. 124

Nominate reports	Abbreviations	Volume in E.R.'s	Period Covered (Approx.)	Example
J. Brown's Cases in Parliament	Bro. P.C.; Bro. Parl. Cas.; Brown's Parliament Cases	1–3	1702–1800	*De Ghettoff v. London Assurance Co.* (1730) 4 Bro. P.C. 436
Browning & Lushington's Admiralty Reports	Br. & L.; Br. & Lush.; Brown. & Lush.; Browning & Lushington	167	1863–1865	*The "Norway"* (1864) Br. & L. 377
Brownlow & Goldesborough's Common Pleas Reports	Br. & Gold.; Brownl.; Brownl. & Golds.; Brownlow & Goldesborough	123	1569–1624	*Chapman v. Pendleton* (1609) 2 Brownl. & Golds 293
Bulstrode's King's Bench Reports	Bulst.; Bulstr.; Bulstrode	80-81	1610–1625	*Shury v. Brown* (1688) 3 Bulstrode 328
Bunbury's Exchequer Reports	Bunb.; Bunbury	145	1713–1741	*Bury (Corp. of) v. Evans* (1739) Bunbury 345
Burrell's Admiralty Cases	Burr. Adm.; Burrell	167	1584–1837	*The "Grace"* (1796) Burrell 333
Burrow's King's Bench Reports tempore Mansfield	Burr.; Burrow	97-98	1756–1772	*R. v. College of Physicians* (1771) 5 Burr. 2740
Calthrop's City of London Cases, King's Bench	Calth.; Calthr.; Calthrop	80	1609–1618	*Re An Act of Parliament for the Preservation of the River Thames* (1535) Calthrop
Campbell's Nisi Prius Cases	Camp.; Camp. N.P.; Campb.; Campbell	170-171	1807–1816	*Underwood v. Robertson* (1815) 4 Camp. 138
Carrington & Kirwan's Nisi Prius Reports	C. & K.; Car. & K.; Car. & Kir.; Carr. & K.; Carrington & Kirwan	174-175	1843–1853	*Bremner v. Chamberlayne* (1848) 2 Car. & K. 560
Carrington & Marshman's Nisi Prius Reports	C. & Mar.; C. & Marsh.; Car. & M.; Car. & Mar.; Carr. & M.; Carrington & Marshman	174	1841-1842	*Rapson v. Cubitt* (1841) Car. & M. 64
Carrington & Payne's Nisi Prius Reports	C. & P.; Car. & P.; Carrington & Payne	171–173	1823–1841	*Prendergast v. Compton* (1837) 8 Car. & P. 454
Carter's Common Pleas Reports	Cart.; Carter	124	1664–1676	*Vintner v. Allen* (1670) Carter, 212
Carthew's King's Bench Reports	Carth.; Carthew	90	1686–1701	*Starke v. Cheesman* (1699) Carthew 509
Cary's Chancery Reports	Cary	21	1557–1604	*Swayne v. Rogers* (1604) Cary, 26
Cases Determined in the Courts of Equity	Cox; Cox Chancery Cases	29-30	1783–1796	*Estcourt v. Estcourt* (1760) 1 Cox, 20
Cases in Chancery	Ch. Ca.; Chan. Cas.; Chancery Cases	22	1660–1698	*Clayton v. Newcastle (Duke of)* (1682) 2 Chan. Cas. 112
Cases temp. Hardwicke	Cas. t. H.; Cas. t. Hard.	95	1733–1738	*Sabbarton v. Sabbarton* (1738) Cas. t. Hard. 413

English Law

Nominate reports	Abbreviations	Volume in E.R.'s	Period Covered (Approx.)	Example
Cases temp. Talbot	Cas. t. Talbot; Cases T. Talbot	25	1733–1738	*Hebblethwaite v. Cartwright* (1734) Cases T. Talbot 31
Choyce Cases in Chancery	Ch. Cas.; Ch. Cas. Ch.; Choyce Cases; Choyce Cases Chancery	21	1557–1606	*Duckett v. Beswick* (1577) Choyce Cases, 116
Christopher Robinson's Admiralty Reports	C. Rob.; C. Rob. Adm.; C. Robinson; Ch. Rob.	165	1798–1808	*Robinett v. The Ship "Exeter"* (1799) 2 C. Rob. 261
Clark & Finnelly's House of Lords Cases	Cl. & Fin.; Cl. and Fin.; Clark & Finnelly; Clark and Finnelly	6–8	1831–1846	*Auchterarder v. Kinnoull (Earl of)* (1839) 6 Cl. and Fin. 646
Clark & Finnelly's House of Lords Reports New Series	H.L.C.; House of Lords Cases	9–11	1847–1866	*Ranger v. Great Western Railway Co.* (1854) 5 H.L.C. 72
Coke's King's Bench Reports	Co. Rep.; Coke; Coke Rep.; Coke Reports	76-77	1572–1616	*Heydon's Case* (1584) 3 Co. Rep. 7a
Colles' Cases in Parliament	Colles	1	1697–1713	*A.G. v. Bishop of London* (1707) Colles 399
Collyer's Chancery Cases tempore Bruce V.C.	Coll.; Coll. C.C.; Collyer; Collyer Chancery Cases	63	1844–1846	*Farquharson v. Cave* (1846) 2 Coll. 356
Comberbach's King's Bench Reports	Comb.; Comberbach	90	1685–1699	*Lovel v. Gill* (1695) Comberbach, 368
Common Bench Reports	C.B.; Common Bench	135–139	1845–1856	*Land Improvement Co. v. Richmond* (1855) 17 C.B. 145
Common Bench Reports, New Series	C.B. N.S.; C.B. (N.S.); Common Bench N.S.; Common Bench (N.S.); Common Bench New Series	140–144	1856–1862	*Morisse v. Royal British Bank* (1856) 1 C.B. (N.S.) 67
Comyn's King's Bench Reports	Com.; Comyns	92	1695–1741	*More v. Manning* (1714) 1 Comyns 311
Cooke's Practice Cases, Common Pleas	Cooke; Cooke C. P.; Cooke, C.P.; Cooke Pr. Cas.	125	1706–1747	*Littlehales v. Smith* (1732) Cooke C.P. 73
Cooper's Chancery Practice Cases	C.P. Coop.; C.P. Cooper; Coop. Pr. Ca.	47	1837-1838	*A.G. v. Newbury Corp.* (1838) C.P. Cooper 72
Cooper's Chancery Reports tempore Brougham	Coop. t. Br.; Coop. t. Brough.; Cooper temp. Brougham	47	1833-1834	*Casamajor v. Strode* (1834) Coop. t. Brough 510
Cooper's Chancery Reports tempore Cottenham	Coop. t. Cott.; Cooper temp. Cottenham	47	1846–1848	*Dietrichsen v. Cabburn* (1846) 1 Coop. t. Cott. 72

Nominate reports	Abbreviations	Volume in E.R.'s	Period Covered (Approx.)	Example
Cooper's Chancery Reports tempore Eldon	G. Coop.; G. Cooper	35	1815	*Agar v. Regent's Canal Co.* (1815) G. Coop. 221
Cowper's King's Bench Reports	Cow.; Cowp.; Cowper	98	1774–1778	*R. v. Tauton St. James (Churchwardens of)* (1776) 1 Cowp. 413
Craig & Phillips' Chancery Reports	Cr. & Ph.; Cr. and Ph.; Craig & Phillips; Craig and Phillips	41	1840-1841	*Caldecott v. Caldecott* (1841) Cr. & Ph. 183
Croke's King's Bench Reports tempore Charles I	Cro. Car.; Croke Car.	79	1625–1649	*Fish v. Wagstaff* (1633) Cro. Car. 318
Croke's King's Bench Reports tempore Elizabeth	Cro. Eliz.; Croke Eliz.; Croke Elizabeth	78	1582–1603	*Browne v. Daukes* (1583) Cro. Eliz. 11
Croke's King's Bench Reports tempore James I	Cro. Jac.; Croke Jac.	79	1603–1625	*Heliot v. Sanders* (1625) Cro. Jac. 700
Crompton & Jervis' Exchequer Reports	C. & J.; Cr. & J.; Cromp. & Jer.; Cromp. & Jerv.; Crompton & Jervis	148-149	830–1832	*Crompton v. Stewart* (1832) 2 C. & J. 473
Crompton & Meeson's Exchequer Reports	C. & M.; Cr. & M.; Cromp. & M.; Cromp. & Mees.; Crompton & Meeson	149	1832–1834	*Goubot v. De Crouy* (1833) 1 C.& M. 772
Crompton, Meeson & Roscoe's Exchequer Reports	C. M. & R.; Cr. M. & R.; Cromp. M. & R.; Crompton, Meeson & Roscoe	149-150	1834–1835	*Nowlan v. Ablett* (1835) 2 C. M. & R. 54
Cunningham's King's Bench Reports	Cun.; Cunn.; Cunningham	94	1734–1736	*Scot v. Ellary* (1734) Cun. 113
Curteis' Ecclesiastical Reports	Curt.; Curt. Ecc.; Curt. Eccl.; Curteis	163	1834–1844	*Warner v. Gater* (1839) 2 Curt. 315
Daniell's Exchequer in Equity Reports	Dan.; Daniell	159	1817–1820	*Hales v. Pomfret* (1818) Dan. 141
Davies' Irish King's Bench Reports	Dav.; Davis; Davis (Ireland)	80	1604–1612	*Case de Commenda* (1792) Davis 68
De Gex, Fisher & Jones' Chancery Reports	De G. F. & J.; De G. F. and J.; De Gex Fisher & Jones	45	1859–1862	*Simpson v. Westminster Palace Hotel Co.* (1860) 2 De. G. F. & J. 141
De Gex & Jones' Chancery Reports	De G. & J.; De G. and J.; De Gex & Jones; De Gex and Jones	44-45	1857–1859	*Scott v. Liverpool (Corp. of)* (1858) 3 De. G. & J. 334
De Gex, Jones & Smith's Chancery Reports	De G. J. & S.; De G. J. and S.; De Gex Jones & Smith; De Gex Jones and Smith	46	1862–1866	*Galloway v. London (Corp. of)* (1865) 3 De. G. J. & S. 59

Nominate reports	Abbreviations	Volume in E.R.'s	Period Covered (Approx.)	Example
De Gex, MacNaghten & Gordon's Chancery Reports	De G. M. & G.; De G. M. and G.; De Gex M'Naghten & Gordon; De Gex M'Naghten and Gordon	42–44	1851–1857	Kerr v. Middlesex Hospital (1852) 2 De. G. M. & G. 576
De Gex & Smale's Chancery Reports	De G. & S.; De G. & Sm.; De Gex & Smale	63-64	1846–1852	Great Western Railway Co. v. Rushout (1852) 5 De. G & Sm. 290
Deane & Swabey's Ecclesiatical	Reports Dea. & Sw.; Deane; Deane Ecc. Rep.; Deane & S. Eccl.; Deane & Sw.; Deane & Swabey	164	1855–1857	Foot v. Stanton (1856) Deane 19
Dearsley & Bell's Crown Cases Reserved	D. & B.; Dears. & B.; Dears. & B. C.C.; Dears. & B. Crown Cas.; Dears. & Bell; Dearsley & Bell	169	1856–1858	R. v. Gate Fulford (Township of) (1856) Dears. & Bell 74
Dearsley's Crown Cases Reserved	Dears.; Dears. C.C.; Dearsley; Dearsly; Dearsy C.C.	169	1852–1857	R. v. Hewgill (1854) Dears. 315
Denison & Pearce's Crown Cases Reserved	Den.; Den. C.C.; Denison	169	1844–1852	R. v. Bidwell (1847) 1 Den. 222
Dicken's Chancery Reports	Dick.; Dickens	21	1559–1798	A.G. v. Panther (1791) Dick. 748
Dodson's Admiralty Reports	Dod.; Dod. Adm.; Dods.; Dodson	165	1811–1822	The "Rose in Bloom" (1811) 1 Dods. 57
Donnelly's Chancery Reports	Donn. Eq.; Donnelly; Donnelly Eq.	47	1836–1837	Skinners' Co. v. Irish Society (1837) Donnelly 168
Douglas' King's Bench Reports	Doug.; Doug. K.B.; Dougl.; Dougl. K.B.; Douglas; Douglas K.B.	99	1778–1785	Le Caux v. Eden (1781) 2 Dougl. 594
Dow's House of Lords Cases	Dow; Dow P.C.; Dow Parliament Cases	3	1812–1818	Ritchie v. Canongate (Magistrates of) (1817) 5 Dow P.C. 87
Dow & Clark's House of Lords Cases	Dow & Cl.; Dow and Cl.; Dow &/and Clarke	6	1827–1832	Amicable Society v. Bolland (1830) 2 Dow and Cl. 1
Dowling & Ryland's Nisi Prius Cases	Dowl. & Ry. N.P.; Dowl. & Ryl. N.P.	171	1822-1823	Beauchamp v. Cash (1822) Dowl. & Ry. N. P. 3
Drewry's Vice Chancellor's Reports tempore Kindersley	Drew.; Drewry	61-62	1852–1859	Brandling v. Plummer (1854) 2 Drewry 427

Nominate reports	Abbreviations	Volume in E.R.'s	Period Covered (Approx.)	Example
Drewry & Smale's Chancery Reports tempore Kindersley	D. & S.; Dr. & Sm.; Drew. & S.; Drew. & Sm.; Drewry & Smale	62	1859–1865	Alliance Bank Ltd. v. Broom (1864) 2 Dr. & Sm. 289
Durnford & East's Term Reports, King's Bench	T.R.; Term Reports	99–101	1785–1800	Topping v. Ryan (1786) 1 T.R. 227
Dyer's King's Bench Reports	Dy.; Dyer	73	1513–1582	Dawson v. Alford (1572) 3 Dyer 312a
East's Term Reports, King's Bench	East	102–104	1800–1812	Hall v. Cazenove (1804) 4 East, 477
Eden's Chancery Reports tempore Northington	Eden	28	1757–1766	Cholmondeley v. Meyrick (1758) 1 Eden 77
Edward's Admiralty Reports	Edw.; Edw. Adm.; Edw. P.C.; Edw. Pr. Cas.; Edwards	165	1808–1812	"Lord Nelson" (1809) Edw. 79
Ellis, Blackburn & Ellis' Queen's Bench Reports	E. B. & E.; El. Bl. & El.; Ellis Blackburn & Ellis	120	1857-1858	Sheridan v. Phoenix Life Assurance (1858) El. Bl. & El. 156
Ellis & Blackburn's Queen's Bench Reports	E. & B.; El. & Bl.; Ellis & Blackburn	118–120	1852–1858	R. v. Shewsbury (Recorder of) (1853) 1 El. & Bl. 711
Ellis & Ellis' Queen's Bench Reports	E. & E.; El. & El.; Ellis & Ellis	120-121	1858–1861	Greaves v. Eastern Counties Railway Co. (1859) 1 El. & El. 961
Equity Cases Abridged	Eq. Ca. Abr.	21-22	1667–1744	Trott v. Vernon (1715) 2 Eq. Ca. Abr. 291
Espinasse's Nisi Prius Reports	Esp.; Esp. N.P.; Espinasse	170	1793–1810	R. v. Great Canfield (1810) 6 Esp. 136
Exchequer Reports Welsby, Hurlstone & Gordon	Ex.; Exch.; Exch. Rep.; Exchequer	154–156	1847–1856	Vauxhall Bridge Co. v. Sawyer (1851) 6 Ex. 504
Finch's Precedents in Chancery	Prec. Ch.; Pree. Ch.; Fin. T.; Precedents in Chancery	24	1689–1722	Yate v. Fettyplace (1700) Prec. Ch. 140
Finch's Reports, Chancery	Fin. H.; Rep. Temp. Finch; Rep. t. Finch; Reports Temp. Finch	23	1673–1681	Shipton v. Hampson (1674) Rep. Temp. Finch, 145
Fitzgibbon's King's Bench Reports	Fitz-G.; Fitzg.; Fitzgibbon	94	1727–1732	Law v. Davys (1729) Fitz-G. 112
Forrest's Exchequer Reports	For.; Forr.; Forrest	145	1800-1801	Withal v. Liley (1801) Forrest 94
Fortescue's King's Bench Reports	Fort.; Fortes.; Fortes. Rep.; Fortescue	92	1695–1738	Stoughton v. Reynolds (1748) Fortescue 168
Foster's Crown Cases	Fost.; Fost. Cr. Law; Fost. Crown Law; Foster	168	1743–1761	Re Mr. Deacon's Case (1746) Fost. 9
Foster & Finlayson's Nisi Prius Reports	F. & F.; Fost. & F.; Fost. & Fin.; Foster & Finlayson	175-176	1858–1867	Britton v. Royal Insurance Co. (1866) 4 F. & F. 905

English Law

Nominate reports	Abbreviations	Volume in E.R.'s	Period Covered (Approx.)	Example
Freeman's Chancery Reports	Freem.; Freem. Chy.; Freeman; Freeman Chancery	22	1660–1706	*Thexton v. Betts* (1683) 2 Freeman 87
Freeman's King's Bench and Common Pleas Reports	Free. K.B.; Freem. K.B.; Freeman; Freeman King's Bench	89	1670–1704	*Tufton v. Temple* (1672) 1 Freeman 34
Giffard's Chancery Reports	Giff.; Giffard	65-66	1857–1865	*Tinkler v. Board of Works for the Wandsworth District* (1857) 1 Giff. 412
Gilbert's Cases in Law and Equity	Gilb. Cas.; Gilb. K.B.	93	1713–1715	*Abrathut v. Brandon* (1760) Gilb. Cas. 118
Gilbert's Chancery Reports	Gilb. Rep.	25	1705–1727	*Coventry (Countess of) v. Coventry (Earl of)* (1721) Gilb. Rep. 160
Godbolt's King's Bench Reports	Godb.; Godbolt	78	1575–1638	*Blagrove and Wood's Case* (1589) Godbolt 142
Gouldsborough's King's Bench Reports	Gould.; Gouldsb.; Gouldsborough	75	1586–1602	*Wildgoose v. Wayland* (1601) Gouldsborough 147
Gow's Nisi Prius Cases	Gow; Gow N.P.	171	1818–1820	*Hardwick v. Blanchard* (1819) Gow 113
Haggard's Admiralty Reports	Hag. Adm.; Hagg. Adm.; Haggard; Haggard Admiralty	166	1822–1838	*H.M.S. "Thetis"* (1833) 3 Hagg. 14
Haggard's Consistorial Reports	Hag. Con.; Hagg. Con.; Hagg. Cons.; Hagg. Consist.; Haggard Consistory	161	1752–1821	*Pritchard v. Dalby* (1792) 1 Hag. Con. 186
Haggard's Ecclesiastical Reports	Hagg. Ecc.; Hagg. Eccl.; Haggard Ecclesiastical	162	1827–1833	*Colvin v. Fraser* (1827) 1 Hagg. Ecc. 107
Haggard's Ecclesiastical Reports Appendix	Hag. Ecc. App.; Hagg. Ecc. App.; Hagg. Ecc. (App.); Hagg. Eccl. App.; Haggard Ecclesiastical Appendix	162	1684–1796	*Savage v. Blythe* (1796) 2 Hagg. Ecc. (App.) 150
Hall & Twell's Chancery Reports	H. & Tw.; H. and Tw.; Hall & Twells; Hall and Twells	47	1849-1850	*Adams v. London and Blackwall Railway Co.* (1850) 2 H. & Tw. 285
Hardres' Exchequer Reports	Hard.; Hardr.; Hardres	145	1655–1669	*Jones v. Williams* (1655) Hardres 3
Hare's Chancery Reports	Hare	66–68	1841–1853	*Meux v. Bell* (1841) 1 Hare 73
Hare's Chancery Reports Appendix	Hare. App.; Hare, App.; Hare (App.)	67-68	1841–1853	*Crofts v. Middleton* (1853) 9 Hare App. II ixxv
Hay & Marriott's Admiralty Decisions Reports	Hay & M.; Hay & Mar.; Hay & Marriott	165	1776–1779	*The "Drie Gebroeders"* (1779) Hay & M. 270

Nominate reports	Abbreviations	Volume in E.R.'s	Period Covered (Approx.)	Example
Hemming & Miller's Chancery Reports	H. & M.; Hem. & M.; Hemming & Miller	71	1862–1865	*Taunton v. Royal Insurance Co.* (1864) 2 H. & M. 135
Henry Blackstone's Common Pleas Reports	Bl. H.; H. Bl.	126	1788–1796	*Calland v. Troward* (1794) 2 H. Bl. 324
Hetley's Common Pleas Reports	Het.; Hetl.; Hetley	124	1627–1632	*Norris v. Isham* (1628) Hetley 81
Hobart's King's Bench Reports	Hob.; Hobart	80	1603–1625	*Earl of Ormond's Case* (1792) Hobart 348
Holt's Equity Reports	Holt Eq.; Holt Equity; Holt Equity Reports	71	1845	*Short v. Emperingham* (1845) 1 Holt. Eq. 61
Holt's King's Bench Reports	Holt K.B.	90	1688–1711	*Trial of Charles Cranborne* (1696) Holt K.B. 686
Holt's Nisi Prius Reports	Holt; Holt N.P.	171	1815–1817	*Ogle v. Paleski* (1816). Holt 485
Hovenden's Supplement to Vesey Junior's Chancery Reports	Ves. Jun. Supp.; Vesey Junior Supplement	34	1789–1817	*Montesquieu v. Sandys* (1811) 2 Ves. Jun. Supp. 525
Hurlstone & Coltman's Exchequer Reports	H. & C.; Hurl. & C.; Hurl. Colt.; Hurlst. & C.; Hurlstone & Coltman	158-159	1862–1866	*Read v. Victoria Station and Pimlico Railway Co.* (1863) 1 H. & C. 826
Hurlstone & Norman's Exchequer Reports	H. & N.; Hurl. & N.; Hurl. & Nor.; Hurlst. & N.; Hurlstone & Norman	156–158	1856–1862	*Great Western Railway Co. v. Blake* (1862) 7 H. & N. 987
Hutton's Common Pleas Reports	Hut.; Hutt.; Hutton	123	1612–1639	*Beverley v. Power* (1626) Hutton 79
Jacob's Chancery Reports	Jac.; Jacob	37	1821-1822	*Colpoys v. Colpoys* (1822) Jacob 451
Jacob & Walker's Chancery Reports	Jac. & W.; Jac. and W.; Jacob & /and Walker	37	1819–1821	*Weale v West-Middlesex Waterworks Co.* (1820) 1 Jac. & W. 358
Jenkins' Exchequer Reports	Jenk.; Jenkins	145	1220–1623	*Sprint v. Hicks* (1613) Jenk. 326
Johnson's Chancery Reports	John.; Johns.; Johnson	70	1858–1860	*Patent Type-Founding Co. v. Richard* (1859) Johns. 381
Johnson & Hemming's Chancery Reports	J. & H.; John. & H.; Johns. & H.; Johns. & Hem.	70	1860–1862	*Oriental Inland Steam Co. Ltd. v. Briggs* (1861) 2 J. & H. 625
T Jones' King's Bench and Common Pleas Reports	Jones, T.; T. Jones; T. Jones' Rep.	84	1667–1685	*Gilmore v. Shuter* (1678) Jones T. 108
W Jones' King's Bench and Common Pleas Reports	Jones, W.	82	1620–1641	*Day v. Spoone* (1675) Jones W. 375

English Law

Nominate reports	Abbreviations	Volume in E.R.'s	Period Covered (Approx.)	Example
Kay & Johnson's Vice Chancellor's Reports	K. & J.; Kay & J.; Kay & John.; Kay & Johns.	69-70	1854–1858	Gresley v. Mousley (1856) 2 K. & J. 288
Kay's Vice Chancellors' Reports	Kay	69	1853-1854	Kavanagh v. Morland (1853) Kay 16
Kay's Vice Chancellors' Reports Appendix	Kay App.	69	1853-1854	Paynter v. Carew (1854) Kay App. xxxvi
Keble's King's Bench Reports	Keb.; Keble	83-84	1661–1679	Oliver v. Yeames (1662) 1 Keble 333
Keen's Rolls Court Reports	Keen	48	1836–1838	Behrens v. Pauli (1837) 1 Keen 456
Keilwey's King's Bench Reports	Keil.; Keilw.; Keilwey	72	1496–1531	(1510) Keilway 160
Kelyng's Crown Cases	Kel.; Kel. J.; Kelyng	84	1662–1669	Sir Charles Stanley's Case (1663) Kelyng J. 86
Kelynge's Chancery Reports	Kel. W.; Kelynge, W.; W. Kel.	25	1730–1735	Bank of England v. Morice (1734) W. Kel. 165
Kenyon's Notes of Cases, King's Bench	Keny.; Kenyon	96	1753–1759	Walker v. Flamstead (1754) 3 Keny. 57
Knapp's Privy Council Appeal Cases	Kn., Knapp	12	1829–1836	Bank of Bengal v. East India Co. (1834) 2 Kn. 245
Lane's Exchequer Reports	La.; Lane	145	1605–1611	Bret v. Johnson (1605) Lane, 1
Latch's King's Bench Reports	Lat.; Latch	82	1625–1628	Walden v. Vessey (1626) Latch 17
Leach's Crown Cases	Leach; Leach C.C.; Leach C.L.	168	1730–1815	R. v. Hickman (1784) 1 Leach 318
Lee's Ecclesiastical Judgments	Lee; Lee Eccl.	161	1752–1758	Bond v. Faikney (1757) 2 Lee 371
Leigh & Cave's Crown Cases Reserved	L. & C.; L. & C. C.C.; Le. & Ca.; Leigh & C.; Leigh & C. C.C.; Leigh & Cave	169	1861–1865	R. v. Isaacs (1862) Le. & Ca. 220
Leonard's Reports	Leo.; Leon.; Leonard	74	1540–1613	Forman v. Bohan (1584) 1 Leonard 13
Levinz's King's Bench and Common Pleas Reports	Lev.; Levinz	83	1660–1697	Hamond v. Jones (1667) 1 Lev. 227
Lewin's Crown Cases on the Northern Circuit	Lewin; Lewin C.C.; Lewin Cr. Cas.	168	1822–1838	Re Mead's and Belt's Case (1823) 1 Lewin 184
Ley's King's Bench Reports	Ley	80	1608–1629	Sir John Bingleys Case (1619) Ley 67
Lilly's Assize Reports	Lil.; Lilly; Lilly Ass.; Lilly Assise	170	1688–1693	Crake v. Northfolke Lilly Assise 41
Littleton's Common Pleas Reports	Lit.; Litt.; Litt. Rep.; Littleton	124	1626–1632	Howard v. Approbert (1627) Littleton 85

Nominate reports	Abbreviations	Volume in E.R.'s	Period Covered (Approx.)	Example
Lofft's King's Bench Reports	Lofft	98	1772–1774	*Somerset v. Stewart* (1772) Lofft 1
Lushington's Admiralty Reports	Lush.; Lush. Adm.; Lushington	167	1859–1862	*The "Ironsides"* (1862) Lush. 458
Lutwyche's Entries and Reports, Common Pleas	Lut.; Lut. App.; Lut. Ent.; Lutw.; Lutwyche	125	1682–1704	*Slaughter v. Pierpoint* (1688) 1 Lutwyche 451
Macnaghten & Gordon's Chancery Reports	Mac. & G.; Mac. and G.; M'Naghten & Gordon; M'Naghten and Gordon	41-42	1849–1851	*Carlisle v. South-Eastern Railway Co.* (1850) 1 Mac. & G. 689
Maclean & Robinson's Appeal Cases	Macl. & R.; Macl. and R.; Maclean &/and Robinson	9	1839	*Halkett v. Nisbet's Trustees* (1839) Macl. and R. 53
Maddock's Chancery Reports	Madd.; Maddock	56	1815–1822	*Thellusson v. Woodford* (1819) 4 Madd. 420
Manning & Granger's Common Pleas Reports	Man. & G.; Manning & Granger	133–135	1840–1844	*Christ's Hospital (Governors of) v. Harrild* (1841) 2 Man. & G. 707
March's New Cases, King's Bench	March N.C.; March N.R.; March, N.R.; March New Cases	82	1639–1642	*Re Rickebies Case* (1642) March, N.R. 213
Maule & Selwyn's King's Bench Reports	M. & S.; Maul. & Sel.; Maule & S.; Maule & Selwyn	105	1813–1817	*Metcalfe v. Rycroft* (1817) 6 M. & S. 75
M'Cleland's Exchequer Reports	McCl.; M'Cl.; M'Cle.; M'Clel.; M'Cleland	148	1824	*Ibbetson v. Ruchardson* (1824) M'Cle. 581
M'Cleland & Younge's Exchequer Reports	McCl. & Y.; McCle. & Yo.; M'Cl. & Y.; M'Cle. & Yo.; M'Cleland & Younge	148	1824-1825	*Watkins v. Phillpotts* (1825) M'Cle. & Yo. 393
Meeson & Welsby's Exchequer Reports	M. & W.; Mees. & W.; Mees. & Wels.; Meeson & Welsby	150–153	1836–1847	*Chilton v. London and Croydon Railway Co.* (1847) 16 M. & W. 212
Merivale's Chancery Reports	Mer.; Merivale	35-36	1815–1817	*Hannam v. South London Waterworks Co.* (1816) 2 Mer. 61
Modern Reports	Mod.; Mod. Cas.; Mod. Rep.	86–88	1669–1732	*Horn v. Chandler* (1670) 1 Mod. 271
Moody's Crown Cases Reserved	Mood.; Mood. C.C.; Moody; Moody C.C.	168-169	1824–1844	*R. v. Jones* (1840) 2 Mood. 171
Moody & Malkin's Nisi Prius Reports	M. & M.; Mood. M.; Moody & Malkin	173	1826–1830	*Wright v. Trezevant* (1828) M. & M. 231

English Law

Nominate reports	Abbreviations	Volume in E.R.'s	Period Covered (Approx.)	Example
Moody & Robinson's Nisi Prius Reports	M. & Rob.; Mood. & R.; Moody & Robinson	174	1830–1844	*R. v. Bishop Auckland* (1833) 1 M. & Rob. 286
Moore's Indian Appeal Cases	Moo. Ind. App.; Moore Ind. App.; Moore Indian Appeals; Moore's Indian Appeals	18–20	1836–1872	*East India Co. v. Oditchurn Paul* (1849) 5 Moo. Ind. App. 43
Sir F Moore's King's Bench Cases	Moo. K.B.; Moore K.B.; Moore (K.B.); Moore Kings Bench; Moore Kings Bench Cases	72	1519–1621	*Le Seignior Greyes Case* (1652) Moore (K.B.), 788
Moore's Privy Council Cases	Moo.; Moo. P.C.; Moore; Moore P.C.; Moore Privy Council	12–15	1836–1862	*Smith v. Sierra Leone (Justices of)* (1848) 7 Moo. 174
Moore's Privy Council Cases, New Series	Moo.; Moo. P.C. N.S.; Moore P.C. N.S.; Moore Privy Council New Series	15–17	1862–1873	*Chapman v. Oriental Bank Corp.* (1864) 2 Moo. N.S. 463
Moseley's Chancery Reports	Mos.; Mosely	25	1726–1731	*Dhegetoft v. London Assurance* (1728) Mosely 83
Mylne & Craig's Chancery Reports	My. & Cr.; My. and Cr; Mylne & Craig; Mylne and Craig	40–41	1835–1840	*Dubless v. Flint* (1839) 4 My. & Cr. 502
Mylne & Keen's Chancery Reports	My. & K.; My. and K.; Mylne & Keen; Mylne and Keen	39–40	1832–1835	*St. George v. Wake* (1833) 1 My. & K. 610
Nelson's Chancery Reports	Nels.; Nelson	21	1625–1693	*Norgate v. Ponder* (1627) Nels. 6
Noy's King's Bench Reports	Noy	74	1559–1649	*Darcy v. Allin* (1600) Noy 173
Owen's King's Bench and Common Pleas Reports	Ow.; Owen	74	1556–1615	*Kayre v. Deurat* (1583) Owen 91
Palmer's King's Bench Reports	Palm.; Palmer	81	1619–1629	*Ward and Kedgwin's Case* (1671) Palmer 407
Parker's Exchequer Reports	Park.; Park. Exch.; Parker	145	1743–1767	*Malden v. Bartlett* (1750) Parker 105
Peake's Nisi Prius Reports	Peake; Peake N.P.; Peake N.P. Cas.	170	1790–1794	*Youl v. Harbottle* (1791) Peake 68
Peake's Additional Cases at Nisi Prius	Peake Add. Cas.; Peake N.P. Add. Cas.	170	1795–1812	*Allesbrook v. Roach* (1795) Peake Add. Cas. 27
Peere-Williams' Chancery & King's Bench Cases	P. Wms.; Peere Williams	24	1695–1735	*Carteret (Lord) v. Paschal* (1733) 3 P. Wms. 197

Nominate reports	Abbreviations	Volume in E.R.'s	Period Covered (Approx.)	Example
Philimore's Ecclesiastical Reports	Phil.; Phill.; Phill. Ecc.; Phill. Ecc. R.; Phillim.; Phillim. Eccl.; Phillimore	161	1809–1821	*Musto v. Sutcliffe* (1818) 3 Phill. Ecc. 104
Phillips' Chancery Reports	Ph.; Phillips	41	1841–1849	*Gloucester (Corp. of) v. Wood* (1844) 1 Ph. 493
Plowden's Commentaries or Reports	Plow.; Plowden	75		*Platt v. Lock* (1550) 1 Plowden 35
Pollexfen's King's Bench Reports	Pollex.; Pollexf.; Pollexfen	86	1669–1685	*Weale v. Lower* (1672) Pollex. 54
Popham's King's Bench Reports	Pop.; Poph.; Popham	79	1592–1627	*Thompson v. Trafford* (1593) Popham 8
Price's Exchequer Reports	Pr. Exch.; Price	145–147	1814–1824	*Monday v. Sear* (1822) 11 Price 122
Queen's Bench	Q.B.; Queens Bench	113–118	1841–1852	*Apothecaries' Co. v. Greenough* (1841) 1 Q.B. 799
Lord Raymond's King's Bench and Common Pleas Reports	Ld. Raym.; Lord Raymond; Raym. Ld.; Raymond, Lord	91-92	1694–1732	*Booth v. Lindsey (Marquis of)* (1709) 2 Ld. Raym. 1293
Sir Thomas Raymond's King's Bench and Common Pleas Reports	Raym. T.; Raym. Sir T.; Raymond, Sir T.; T. Raym.	83	1660–1684	*Cutforthay v. Taylor* (1680) Raym. Sir T. 395
Reports in Chancery	Rep. Ch.	21	1615–1710	*Bovey v. Skipwith* (1671) 3 Rep. Ch. 67
Ridgeway's Reports in King's Bench and Chancery tempore Hardwicke	Ridg.; Ridg. t. H.; Ridgeway temp. Hardwicke	27	1733–1745	*Devenish v. Meretins* (1734) Ridg. t. H. 70
Robertson's Ecclesiastical Reports	Rob. Ecc.; Robertson	163	1844–1853	*Stockwell v. Ritherdon* (1848) 1 Rob. Ecc. 661
Rolle's King's Bench Reports	Roll. Rep.; Rolle; Rolle Rep.; Rolle Reports	81	1614–1625	*Roy v. Tollin* (1614) 1 Rolle 10
Russell's Chancery Reports tempore Eldon	Russ.; Russell	38	1823–1829	*Blackmore v. Glamorganshire Canal Co.* (1828) 5 Russ. 151
Russell & Mylne's Chancery Reports	Russ. & M.; Russ. & My.; Russell & Mylne	39	1829–1831	*Churchman v. Irland* (1831) 1 Russ. & M. 250
Russell & Ryan's Crown Cases Reserved	R. & R.; R. & Ry. C.C.; Rus. & Ry.; Russ. & R.; Russ. & Ry.	168	1799–1823	*R. v. Pooley* (1800) Russ. & Ry. 12
Ryan & Moody's Nisi Prius Reports	Ry. & Mood.; Ryan & Moody	171	1823–1826	*Poplett v. Stockdale* (1825) Ry. & Mood. 337
Salkeld's King's Bench Reports	Salk.; Salkeld	91	1689–1712	*Davy v. Smith* (1693) 3 Salkeld 395

Nominate reports	Abbreviations	Volume in E.R.'s	Period Covered (Approx.)	Example
Saunders' King's Bench Reports	Saund.; Williams' Saunders; Wms. Saund.	85	1666–1673	*Jeffreson v. Morton* (1669) 2 Wms. Saund. 6
Savile's Common Pleas Reports	Sav.; Savile; Saville	123	1689–1712	*Wakefield v. Costard* (1586) Savile 81
Sayer's King's Bench Reports	Say.; Sayer	96	1751–1756	*Bush v. Ralling* (1756) Sayer 289
Select Cases in Chancery tempore King	Ca. t. King; Sel. Cas. t. King; Sel. Cas. t. King Ch.; Select Cases tem. King; Select Cases temp. King	25	1724–1733	*Snape v. Furdon* (1724) Sel. Cas. T. King, 6
Session Cases	S.C.; Sess. Cas.	93	1710–1748	*Goring Parish v. Molesworth (Parish of)* (1760) Sess. Cas. 119
Shower's Parliamentary Cases	Show. P.C.; Shower; Shower P.C.; Shower, H.L.	1	1692–1699	*Radnor (Countess of) v. Vandebendy* (1697) Shower P.C. 69
Shower's King's Bench Reports	Show. K.B.; Shower K.B.	89	1678–1695	*Hitchins v. Basset* (1688) 1 Show. K.B. 537
Siderfin's King's Bench Reports	Sid.; Siderfin; Siderfin Reports	82	1659–1670	*Lassels v. Catterton* (1670) 1 Sid. 467
Simons' Vice Chancellor's Reports	Sim.; Simons	57–60	1826–1852	*Tooth v. Canterbury (Dean and Chapter of)* (1829) 3 Sim. 49
Simons' Vice Chancellor's Reports, New Series	Sim. N.S.; Sim. (N.S.); Simons New Series	61	1850–1852	*Rochdale Canal Co. v. King* (1851) 2 Sim. (N.S.) 78
Simons & Stuart's Vice Chancellor's Reports	S. & S.; Sim. & S.; Sim. & St; Sim. & Stu.; Simon & Stuart	57	1822–1826	*Aspinall v. Petvin* (1824) 1 Sim. & St. 544
Skinner's King's Bench Reports	Skin.; Skinner	90	1681–1698	*University of Cambridge v. Price* (1896) Skinner 665
Smale & Giffard's Chancery Reports	S. & G.; Sm. & G.; Sm. & Giff.; Smale & G.; Smale & Giffard	65	1852–1857	*Bryson v. Warwick and Birmingham Canal Co.* (1853) 1 Sm. & Giff. 447
Smale & Giffard's Chancery Reports Appendix	Sm. & G. App.	65	1852–1857	*Goodall v. Skerratt* (1853) 1 Sm. & G. App. vii
Spinks' Ecclesiastical & Admiralty Reports	Sp.; Sp. Ecc. & Ad.; Spinks	164	1853–1855	*The "Steen Bille"* (1855) 2 Sp. Ecc. & Ad. 159
Spinks' Prize Cases	Sp. P.C.; Sp. Pr. Cas.; Spinks P.C.; Spinks Prize Cas.	164	1854–1856	*The "Rapid"* (1854) Sp. P.C. 80
Starkie's Nisi Prius Reports	Star.; Stark.; Stark. N.P.; Starkie; Starkie's	171	1814–1823	*Ingledew v. Douglas* (1817) 2 Stark. 36

Nominate reports	Abbreviations	Volume in E.R.'s	Period Covered (Approx.)	Example
Strange's King's Bench Reports	Str.; Stran.; Strange	93	1716–1749	*Keilway v. Keilway* (1726) 2 Strange 710
Style's King's Bench Reports	Sty.; Style	82	1646–1655	*The Protector v. Buckner* (1655) Style 467
Swabey's Admiralty Reports	Sw.; Swab.; Swabey; Swabey Adm.	166	1855–1859	*The "Linda"* (1857) Swab. 306
Swabey & Tristram's Probate & Divorce Reports	S. & T.; Sw. & Tr.; Swab. & T.; Swab. & Tr.; Swabey & T.; Swabey & Tristram	164	1858–1865	*Callwell v. Callwell* (1860) 3 Sw. & Tr. 259
Swanston's Chancery Reports	Swans.; Swanston	36	1818-1819	*Curzon v. De La Zouch* (1818) 1 Swans. 185
Talbot's Cases in Equity	Cas. t. Talbot; Cases T. Talbot	25	1734–1738	*Law v. Law* (1735) Cases T. Talbot 140
Tamlyn's Rolls Court Reports	Taml.; Tamlyn	48	1829-1830	*Beastall v. Swan* (1829) Tamlyn 288
Taunton's Common Pleas Reports	Taun.; Taunt.; Taunton	127–129	1807–1819	*Hill v. Middlesex (Sheriff of)* (1816) 7 Taunt. 8
Tothill's Transactions in Chancery	Toth.; Tothill	21	1559–1646	*Becket v. Waller* (1597) Tothill 8
Turner & Russell's Chancery Reports	Turn. & R.; Turn. and R.; Turner &/and Russell	37	1822–1824	*Angerstein v. Martin* (1823) Turn. & R. 232
Vaughan's Common Pleas Reports	Vaugh.; Vaughan	124	1665–1674	*Stiles v. Coxe* (1667) Vaughn 111
Ventris, King's Bench Reports	Vent.; Ventr.; Ventris	86	1668–1688	*Turner v. Sterling* (1671) 2 Ventris 25
Vernon's Chancery Reports	Vern.; Vernon	23	1681–1719	*Curson v. African Co.* (1871) 1 Vern. 121
Vesey & Beames' Chancery Reports	V. & B.; Ves. & Bea.; Ves. and Bea.; Vesey &/and Beames	35	1812–1814	*Howe v. Duppa* (1813) 1 V. & B. 511
Vesey Junior's Chancery Reports	Ves. Jun.; Vesey Junior	30–34	1789–1817	*Nabob of the Carnatic v. East India Co.* (1791) 1 Ves. Jun. 371
Vesey Senior's Chancery Reports	Ves. Sen.; Vesey Senior	27-28	1746–1756	*London (City of) v. Nash* (1747) 1 Ves. Sen. 12
West's Reports, House of Lords	West	9	1839–1841	*Portugal (Queen of) v. Glyn* (1840) West 258
West's Chancery Reports tempore Hardwicke	West t. Hard.; West t. Hardwicke	25	1736–1739	*London Assurance Co. v. Johnson* (1737) West. t. Hard. 266
Wightwick's Exchequer Reports	Wight.; Wightw.; Wightwick	145	1810-1811	*Darley v Singleton* (1810) Wight 25
Willes' Common Pleas Reports	Willes	125	1737–1758	*Lloyd v. Morris* (1743) Willes 443

English Law

Nominate reports	Abbreviations	Volume in E.R.'s	Period Covered (Approx.)	Example
William Blackstone's King's Bench Reports	Bl. W.; Black. W.; Blackstone W.	96	1746–1780	*Hankey v. Trotman* (1746) 1 Black. W. 1
William Robinson's Admiralty Reports	W. Rob.; W. Rob. Adm.; W. Robinson; Wm. Rob.	166	1838–1850	*The "Gazelle"* (1844) 2 W. Rob. 279
Wilmot's Notes and Opinions	Wilm.; Wilm. Judg.; Wilm. Op.; Wilmot	97	1767–1770	*Drinkwater v. Royal Exchange Assurance Co.* (1767) Wilm. 282
Wilson's Chancery Reports	Wils. Ch.; Wilson Chancery	37	1817–1819	*Battersbee v. Farington* (1818) 1 Wils. Ch. 88
Wilson's Exchequer Reports	Wils. Ex.; Wilson Ex.	159	1805–1817	*Cockshutt v. Pollard* (1817) Wils. Ex. 132
Wilson's King's Bench and Common Pleas Reports	Wils. K.B.; Wilson K.B.	95	1742–1774	*Thrale v. Vaughan* (1742) 1 Wils. K.B. 5
Winch's Common Pleas Reports	Win.; Winch	124	1621–1625	*White v. Williams* (1621) Winch 5
Yelverton's King's Bench Reports	Yel.; Yelv.; Yelverton	80	1602–1613	*Cromwell (Lord) v. Andrews* (1602) Yelverton 3
Younge's Exchequer in Equity Reports	You.; Younge	159	1830–1832	*Pope v. Farthing* (1831) You. 263
Younge & Collyer's Chancery Reports	Y. & C. C.C.; Y. & C. Ch. Cas.; Younge & Collyer C.C.; Younge & Collyer Ch. Cas.; Younge & Collyer Chancery Cases	62-63	1841–1843	*Armytage v. Armytage* (1842) 1 Y. & C. C. C. 461
Younge & Collyer's Exchequer in Equity Reports	Y. & C. Ex.; Y. & C. Exch.; Y. & Coll.; You. & Coll. Ex.; Younge & C. Exch.; Younge & Coll. Ex.; Younge & Collyer Exchequer; Younge Exch.	160	1834–1842	*Thorpe v. Gartside* (1837) 2 Y. & C. Ex. 730
Younge & Collyer's Exchequer in Equity Reports Appendix	Y. & C. Ex. App.	160	1834–1842	*Cator v. Croydon Canal Co.* (1843) 4. Y. & C. Ex. App. 593
Younge & Jervis's Exchequer Reports	Y. & J.; You. & Jerv.; Younge & J.; Younge & Jervis	148	1826–1830	*Lennox v. Munnings* (1828) 2 Y. & J. 483

353

20

American Legal Research

Introduction

This chapter will provide a brief outline of the American legal system and will explain the key American legal research tools. The chapter will be of use to those doing American legal research for the purpose of a Canadian research problem. American law is never binding in Canada. Canadian researchers will, however, find American legal research helpful when the law on the area they are researching has not been well developed in Canada or is in a state of confusion. In such circumstances, the analysis and rationale underlying American case law may be persuasive in Canada.

Approaching American Legal Research

Our approach to American legal research is the same as our approach to Canadian legal research. We recommend that you begin by consulting secondary sources such as legal encyclopedias, treatises, periodicals, and loose-leaf services. These sources will refer you to the leading cases and relevant statutes on your topic and provide an overall guide to the law. We then recommend a more detailed analysis of your topic through the use of case law and legislation located using online or print sources. Your final step is to note-up the case and statutory law you have found.

Constitutions

Federal

The U.S. Constitution sets out the framework for the organization and governing of the country, along with fundamental rights[1] and liberties.[2] The first seven articles of the Constitution establish the Congress,[3] the Executive branch (including the powers and term of the president), and the Judiciary. They set out the relationship between States and the Federal government along with the process for amending the Constitution. These articles also establish the Constitution, the laws passed by Congress and the treaties of the U.S. as the "supreme Law of the Land," and set out the requirements for the ratification of the Constitution.

The original Constitution has been amended twenty-seven times. The first ten amendments are known as the Bill of Rights, and the rights enumerated include, among others, freedom of speech, freedom of the press, freedom of religion, and the right to trial by jury. The remaining seventeen amendments cover a variety of topics including limiting the time a President may serve in office, abolishing slavery, and allowing women to vote.

Where to find it: Both the *United States Code Annotated* ("U.S.C.A.") published by West Publishing and the *United States Code Service* ("U.S.C.S.") published by LexisNexis contain annotated versions of the U.S. Constitution. Another extensive annotated Constitution is the "Analysis and Interpretation of the Constitution: Annotations of Cases Decided by the Supreme Court of the United States," prepared by the Congressional Research Service, Library of Congress and published by the U.S. Government Printing Office (GPO). This is available online through the GPO at http://www.gpoaccess.gov/constitution/ or Onecle.com at http://law.onecle.com/constitution/.

Online, the Constitution is available through a variety of sources including the GPO at http://www.gpoaccess.gov/constitution/index.html, as well as the Legal Information Institute at Cornell Law School ("LII") at http://www.law.cornell.edu/anncon/.

---

[1] The term "civil rights" in the United States is used to refer to those rights set out in the 13th and 14th Amendments to the Constitution. These include the right to due process, as well as equality rights such as the right to equal treatment under the law, the right to vote, equal and fair treatment by police, the courts, etc.

[2] The term "civil liberties" in the United States is used to refer to First Amendment rights and freedoms including freedom of speech, assembly, religion, etc. These are freedoms which are said to be protected from interference from government.

[3] The Senate and the House of Representatives make up the bicameral legislature (Congress) which is charged with the task of making and passing laws.

State

In addition to the U.S. Constitution, each state has its own Constitution setting out the framework for government and the judiciary as well as enumerating fundamental rights. State constitutions are generally more detailed than the Federal Constitution, and have also been amended more frequently. They do not have the power to curtail the rights and protections set out in the Federal Constitution, but they can add to them. State courts are the final arbiters of their own constitutions, and state constitutions are paramount in terms of that state's other laws.

Where to find it: Annotated constitutions are generally included in the annotated Code for a particular state. Online, state constitutions are available through LII at http://www.law.cornell.edu/statutes.html.

The American Court Structure

When doing American legal research, it is essential that you have an understanding of the American court structure. The persuasiveness of legal principles derived from American decisions will depend, in part, on the level of court.

Federal and State Court Systems

The United States has a dual court system: federal and state. Federal courts have limited jurisdiction and can only hear certain types of cases. These are:

- cases which consider whether a law is constitutional;[4]
- cases involving U.S. federal laws and treaties (a "federal question");
- cases involving ambassadors and public ministers;
- disputes between two or more states;
- disputes in which the United States is a party;
- disputes between people from different states (a "diversity question;" the plaintiffs and defendants must be from different states and must meet specific criteria regarding the amount of money in dispute);
- disputes in areas over which the federal courts have clear jurisdiction including admiralty law, bankruptcy, patents law, copyright, interstate commerce, antitrust law, customs, and federal crimes.

---

[4] This refers to the federal Constitution only.

Federal courts can review and overturn judgments from the state courts which have heard and made decisions on matters involving federal law, but there is no comparable avenue of appeal from federal courts to a state court on matters of state law. Also, the U.S. Supreme Court will not decide matters involving state law, regardless of whether the matter arose in a state or federal court.

U.S. Court Organizational Chart[5]

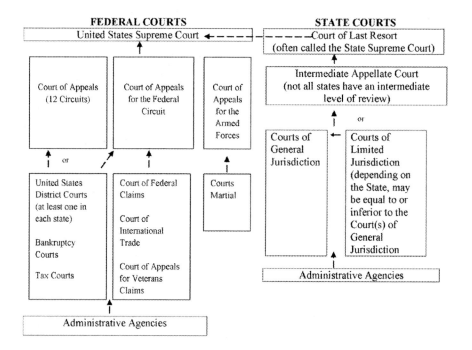

---

5 This simplified chart does not show the complexities regarding avenues of appeal. For example, the U.S. Court of Appeals for the Federal Circuit hears appeals from all U.S. District Courts, the U.S. Court of Federal Claims, the U.S. Court of International Trade, the U.S. Court of Appeals for Veterans Claims (as indicated in the chart) in addition to the U.S. International Trade Commission, the Boards of Contract Appeals, the Board of Patent Appeals and Interferences, the Trademark Trial and Appeals Board, the U.S. Merit Systems Protection Board, the decisions of the Office of Compliance of the U.S. Congress, and the Government Accountability Office Personnel Appeals Board.

Federal Courts

In the federal system, there are three court levels: (1) U.S. District Courts; (2) U.S. Courts of Appeals; and (3) the U.S. Supreme Court.

The U.S. District Courts are trial courts which deal with matters falling under the federal government's jurisdiction. There are 94 federal judicial districts — 89 spread throughout the 50 states, the District of Columbia and Puerto Rico, 3 in the U.S. territories[6] and 2 special trial courts.[7] Each district's courts also deal with bankruptcy matters.

The U.S. Courts of Appeals are the courts of first appeal from the federal district courts. The 94 districts are reorganized at this level into 13 Courts of Appeal, 11 of which serve specific geographic areas. The other two courts are the District of Columbia (which hears a number of appeals from administrative agencies) and the Federal Circuit (which deals with specific matters such as customs, government contracts, international trade, patents, appeals of certain administrative agencies, etc.).

The U.S. Supreme Court is the highest court of appeal at the federal level, and the highest court in the United States. It hears appeals from the U.S. Courts of Appeals and State Supreme Courts when federal law is involved. It decides cases which have constitutional and socially significant implications, and it can declare laws unconstitutional. The U.S. Supreme Court also is a court of original jurisdiction (i.e., a trial court) in matters involving disputes between different states (e.g., territorial/boundary disputes).

Only a small number of cases are entitled to review by the Supreme Court; most parties must file a petition for a writ of *certiorari* (Latin for "to be made certain regarding") with the Court requesting a review of the case. The court turns down the majority of these ("denied cert.").

Administrative Agencies

An administrative agency is a body created by a statute in order to supervise a particular type of commerce, trade or set of practices in which specific expertise and supervision is required. Agencies are often able to act in a quasi-judicial manner in that they have the power to prosecute, hold hear-

---

[6] The Virgin Islands, Guam, and the Northern Mariana Islands all have district courts that hear Federal cases, including bankruptcy cases. These courts also hear cases dealing with local laws made by Congress as part of its governance of its non-state territories.

[7] Two special trial courts in the United States hear specific types of cases regardless of where they originated in the country. The Court of International Trade deals with cases which involve international trade and customs matters. The United States Court of Federal Claims hears cases involving most claims for money against the United States government which might arise as the result of a federal statute, regulation, contract or the taking of private property (known as "eminent domain" in the United States or "expropriation" in Canada).

ings, consider evidence, determine guilt and make orders which affect private parties. They may also have the power to create rules and regulations.

Agencies go by a variety of different names and may be called "agency," "board," "commission," "authority," "corporation," "department" or "administration." Some examples of federal agencies include: the Environmental Protection Agency, the Federal Reserve Board, the Commodity Futures Trading Commission, the Tennessee Valley Authority, the Federal Deposit Insurance Corporation, the Department of Transportation, Social Security Administration, and so on.

State Courts

Unlike the federal sphere, state courts have much wider and broader subject-matter jurisdiction, and they may hear any cases not specifically prohibited to them by federal law. In terms of subject matter, State courts have the final say on their own laws and constitutions although any decisions involving the U.S. Constitution or federal laws may be appealed to the U.S. Supreme Court.

When using American cases for the purpose of a Canadian legal research problem, you should focus primarily on decisions from the Supreme Court or the U.S. Court of Appeals. However, there are some instances when state law can be persuasive. For example, the corporate/commercial law of Delaware is highly influential in Canada, as is the insurance law of California and New York State.

The state court system is much more complex than the federal system and can consist of multiple levels with a variety of specialty courts, depending on the state.[8] Nonetheless, states generally have four specific levels of court:

1. *Courts of Limited Jurisdiction*: These are minor or specialized trial courts which hear a limited range of cases. There are a number of these types of courts including small claims courts, justice of the peace ("JP") courts, probate courts, family courts, night courts, police courts, etc.

2. *Courts of General Jurisdiction*: These are civil and criminal trial courts which can hear and decide almost any type of case falling within the judicial purview of the state. They go by a variety of names including Circuit Court, District Court and Superior Court, and are organized according to judicial districts determined by the state legislature.

---

[8] The National Center for State Courts (http://www.ncsconline.org/) is a website which sets out the structure of the courts in "Court Structure Charts" for all 50 States.

3. *Intermediate Appellate Court*: This is the court of first appeals, which is usually called the [State] Court of Appeal. Some states provide parties with only one chance to appeal, while others offer two. Those states without an intermediate appellate court have a route of appeal directly from the trial court to a state supreme court. In those states with intermediate appellate courts, the route of appeal is from trial to state court of appeal and then to the state supreme court.

4. *Court of Last Resort*: This is the final court of appeal and it is usually called the [State] Supreme Court. The organization, along with the number of justices differs from state to state.

States use a variety of names to refer to the levels of state courts. For instance, in New York, the trial court is called the Supreme Court, the court of first appeal is called the Supreme Court Appellate Division, and the court of final appeal is called the Court of Appeal. In contrast, in Delaware, the trial court is called the Superior Court, the court of first appeal is called the Court of Chancery, and the court of final appeal is called the Supreme Court.

Below is a chart setting out all the states and the names of the various levels of court. Courts of limited jurisdiction have not been included.

State Courts Chart

State	State Supreme Court	Intermediate Appellate Court	Court of First Instance (General Jurisdiction)
Alabama	Supreme Court (9 justices — chief justice and 8 associate justices — sit in panels of 5 or *en banc*)	Court of Civil Appeals (5 judges sit in panels) Court of Criminal Appeals (5 judges sit *en banc*). Pre-1969: single Court of Appeals.	Circuit Court (41 circuits)
Alaska	Supreme Court (5 justices — chief justice and 4 associate justices — sit *en banc*)	Court of Appeals (3 judges — chief judge and 2 associate judges — sit *en banc*)	Superior Court (40 judges, 12 cities in 4 districts)

State	State Supreme Court	Intermediate Appellate Court	Court of First Instance (General Jurisdiction)
Arizona	Supreme Court (5 justices — a chief justice, a vice chief justice, and 3 associate justices — sit *en banc*)	Court of Appeals (2 divisions each with a chief judge and vice-chief judge: 16 judges in Division 1 and 6 judges in Division 2. Cases are decided in panels of 3 judges, called "departments.")	Superior Court (15 counties)
Arkansas	Supreme Court (7 justices — 1 chief, 6 associate — sit *en banc*)	Court of Appeals (12 judges — 1 chief, 11 judges — sit in panels and *en banc*)	Circuit Court (28 circuits)
California	Supreme Court (7 justices — 1 chief and 6 associate — sit *en banc*)	Court of Appeal (6 appellate districts; 105 justices sit in panels)	Superior Court (58 counties)
Colorado	Supreme Court (7 justices — chief justice and 6 associate justices — sit *en banc*)	Court of Appeals (19 judges sit in 3-judge panels)	District Court (22 districts)
Connecticut	Supreme Court (7 justices — 1 chief justice and 6 associate justices — sit in rotating panels of 5; may sit *en banc* upon order)	Appellate Court (10 judges sit in rotating panels of 3, may sit *en banc*)	Superior Court (13 districts)
Delaware	Supreme Court (5 justices — sit in panels and *en banc*)	*(none)*	Superior Court (19 judges, 3 counties)

State	State Supreme Court	Intermediate Appellate Court	Court of First Instance (General Jurisdiction)
			Court of Chancery (1 chancellor and 4 vice-chancellors, 3 counties)
District of Columbia	Court of Appeals (9 judges — sit in panels and *en banc*)	*(none)*	Superior Court (1 chief judge, 58 judges, 23 magistrates)
Florida	Supreme Court (7 justices — chief justice and 6 justices — sit *en banc*)	District Courts of Appeal (5 courts each covering specific districts; 62 judges sit in 3-judge panels)	Circuit Court (20 circuits)
Georgia	Supreme Court (7 justices — sit *en banc*)	Court of Appeals (4 divisions; 12 judges sit in panels and *en banc*)	Superior Court (49 circuits)
Hawaii	Supreme Court (5 justices — sit *en banc*)	Intermediate Court of Appeals (6 judges sit in panels of 3)	Circuit Court and Family Court (4 circuits)
Idaho	Supreme Court (5 justices — chief justice and 4 associate justices — sit *en banc*)	Court of Appeals (4 judges, chief justice and 3 associate judges, sit in panels of 3)	District Court (7 districts)
Illinois	Supreme Court (7 justices — chief justice and 6 justices — sit *en banc*)	Appellate Court (54 judges serving 5 districts)	Circuit Court (22 circuits)

State	State Supreme Court	Intermediate Appellate Court	Court of First Instance (General Jurisdiction)
Indiana	Supreme Court (5 justices — chief justice) and 4 associate justices — sit *en banc*	Court of Appeals (15 judges in 5 districts). Successor to the Indiana Appellate Court. Separate appellate Tax Court with one judge.	Superior Court (201 divisions)
Iowa	Supreme Court (7 justices — chief justice and 6 justices — sit *en banc*)	Court of Appeals (9 judges sit in panels and *en banc*)	District Court (8 districts in 99 counties)
Kansas	Supreme Court (7 justices — chief justice and 6 justices — sit *en banc*)	Court of Appeals (12 judges sit in panels)	District Court (31 districts)
Kentucky	Supreme Court (7 justices — 1 chief justice, 1 deputy chief justice and 5 justices — sit *en banc*). Pre-1976: Court of Appeals	Court of Appeals (14 judges from 7 districts usually in panels but *en banc* for policy-making)	Circuit Court (57 judicial circuits)
Louisiana	Supreme Court (7 justices — chief justice and 6 justices — sit *en banc*)	Court of Appeals (5 circuits; 53 judges sit in panels)	District Courts (42 Districts)
Maine	Supreme Judicial Court (known as the Law Court when sitting as an appellate court; 7 justices — chief justice and 6 justices — it *en banc*)	*(none)*	Superior Court (17 justices) District Court (36 judges, 13 districts)

State	State Supreme Court	Intermediate Appellate Court	Court of First Instance (General Jurisdiction)
Maryland	Court of Appeals (7 judges — chief judge and 6 judges — sit *en banc*)	Court of Special Appeals (13 judges sit in panels and *en banc*, 7 districts and 6 judges at large)	Circuit Court (8 circuits in 24 counties)
Massachusetts	Supreme Judicial Court (7 justices — chief justice and 6 associate justices — sit on the court, all justices — sit *en banc*)	Appeals Court (25 justices sit in panels of 3)	Superior Court (14 counties)
Michigan	Supreme Court (7 justices — chief justice and 6 justices — sit *en banc*)	Court of Appeals (4 districts; 28 judges sit in panels of 3)	Circuit Court (57 courts) Court of Claims (administrative agency appeals involving claims against the state)
Minnesota	Supreme Court (7 justices — chief justice and 6 justices — sit *en banc*)	Court of Appeals (19 judges sit *en banc* and in panels of 3)	District Court (10 districts)
Mississippi	Supreme Court (9 justices — one chief, 2 presiding, and 6 associate justices — sit in panels of 3 and *en banc*)	Court of Appeals (5 districts; 10 judges sit in panels and *en banc*)	Circuit Court (22 districts)

State	State Supreme Court	Intermediate Appellate Court	Court of First Instance (General Jurisdiction)
Missouri	Supreme Court (7 justices — chief justice and 6 justices — sit *en banc*)	Court of Appeals (3 districts; 32 judges sit in panels)	Circuit Court (45 circuits)
Montana	Supreme Court (7 justices — chief justice and 6 justices — sit in panels of 5 and *en banc*)	*(none)*	District Court (56 counties)
Nebraska	Supreme Court (7 justices — chief justice and 6 associate justices — sit in panels and *en banc*)	Court of Appeals (6 judges sit in panels of 3)	District Court (12 districts)
Nevada	Supreme Court (7 justices — chief justice and 6 justices — sit in panels and *en banc*)	*(none)*	District Court (9 districts)
New Hampshire	Supreme Court (1 chief justice, 4 associate justices — sit *en banc*)	*(none)*	Superior Court (10 counties, 11 courts)

State	State Supreme Court	Intermediate Appellate Court	Court of First Instance (General Jurisdiction)
New Jersey	Supreme Court (7 justices — chief justice and 6 justices — sit *en banc*). Pre-1947: New Jersey Court of Errors and Appeals	Superior Court, Appellate Division (35 judges who sit in 2- and 3-judge panels). Successor to Court of Chancery, Supreme Court, and Prerogative Court.	Superior Court — has separate law and chancery divisions, the latter consisting of General Equity, Probate and Family Parts (15 vicinages in 21 counties)
New Mexico	Supreme Court (5 justices — chief justice and 4 justices — sit *en banc*)	Court of Appeals (10 judges sit in panels of 3)	District Court (13 districts)
New York	Court of Appeals (7 judges — chief judge and 6 associate judges — sit *en banc*)	— Supreme Court, Appellate Term (14 justices sit in panels in 3 terms). Appeals from criminal cases made to Court of Appeals; civil cases: appeals made to Appellate Divisions of the Supreme Court. — Supreme Court, Appellate Division (66 justices sit in panels in 4 departments)	Supreme Court (12 districts) County Court (57 counties outside NYC)

State	State Supreme Court	Intermediate Appellate Court	Court of First Instance (General Jurisdiction)
North Carolina	Supreme Court (7 justices — chief justice and 6 associate justices — sit *en banc*)	Court of Appeals (15 judges sit in panels of 3)	Superior Court (46 administrative districts & 8 divisions)
North Dakota	Supreme Court (5 justices — chief justice and 4 justices — sit *en banc*)	Court of Appeals (composed of three temporary judges assigned by the Supreme Court for up to 1 year)	District Court (7 judicial districts in 53 counties)
Ohio	Supreme Court (7 justices — chief justice and 6 associate justices — sit *en banc*)	Court of Appeals (12 courts; 68 judges sit in panels of 3 members each)	Court of Common Pleas (88 counties)
Oklahoma	Supreme Court (9 justices sit *en banc*), Court of Criminal Appeals (5 justices — a presiding judge and vice-presiding judge and 3 other judges — sit *en banc*)	Court of Civil Appeals (12 judges sit in 4 permanent divisions of 3 members each)	District Court (77 courts)
Oregon	Supreme Court (7 justices — chief justice and 6 justices — sit *en banc*)	Court of Appeals (10 judges sit in 3 panels of 3, the Chief Judge substituting for unavailable judges)	Circuit Court (27 judicial districts in 36 counties — 36 courts)

State	State Supreme Court	Intermediate Appellate Court	Court of First Instance (General Jurisdiction)
Pennsylvania	Supreme Court (7 justices — chief justice and 6 justices — sit *en banc*)	Superior Court (15 judges sit in panels of 3), Commonwealth Court (9 judges sit generally in 3-member panels and *en banc*)	Court of Common Pleas (60 districts in 67 counties)
Rhode Island	Supreme Court (5 justices — chief justice and 4 associate justices — sit *en banc*)	*(none)*	Superior Court (4 counties, 26 justices)
South Carolina	Supreme Court (5 justices — chief justice and 4 associate justices — sit *en banc*)	Court of Appeals (9 judges sit in panels and *en banc*)	Circuit Court (16 circuits, 46 counties)
South Dakota	Supreme Court (5 justices — chief justice and 4 associate justices — sit *en banc*)	*(none)*	Circuit Court (7 circuits, 38 judges)
Tennessee	Supreme Court (5 justices — chief justice and 4 justices — sit *en banc*)	Court of Appeals (3 divisions, 12 judges sit in panels), Court of Criminal Appeals (3 divisions, 12 judges sit in panels)	Circuit, Criminal, Chancery and Probate Court (31 judicial districts, 120 judges, 34 chancellors each)

State	State Supreme Court	Intermediate Appellate Court	Court of First Instance (General Jurisdiction)
Texas	Supreme Court (9 justices — chief justice and 8 justices — sit *en banc*) Court of Criminal Appeals (9 judges — a presiding judge and 8 judges — sit *en banc*)	Court of Appeals (14 courts; 80 justices sit in panels occasionally *en banc*)	District Court and Criminal District Court (448 courts)
Utah	Supreme Court (5 justices — chief justice, associate chief justice, and 3 justices — sit *en banc*)	Court of Appeals (7 judges sit in panels of 3 — prohibited by statute from sitting *en banc* (all 7 members at once)	District Court (39 courts; 8 districts in 29 counties)
Vermont	Supreme Court (5 justices — chief justice and 4 associate justices — sit *en banc*)	*(none)*	Superior Court (14 counties) — exclusive jurisdiction over most civil cases, District Court (14 counties) — almost all criminal cases and a few civil cases.

State	State Supreme Court	Intermediate Appellate Court	Court of First Instance (General Jurisdiction)
Virginia	Supreme Court (7 justices — chief justice and 6 justices — sit in panels and en banc). Pre-1970: Supreme Court of Appeals	Court of Appeals (11 judges sit in panels)	Circuit Court (31 circuits, 120 courts)
Washington	Supreme Court (9 justices — chief justice, associate chief justice, and 7 justices — sit en banc)	Court of Appeals (3 courts/divisions; 24 judges sit in panels)	Superior Court (31 districts in 29 counties)
West Virginia	Supreme Court of Appeals (5 justices — chief justice and 4 justices — sit en banc)	(none)	Circuit Court (66 judges, 31circuits)
Wisconsin	Supreme Court (7 justices — chief justice and 6 justices — sit en banc)	Court of Appeals (16 judges sit in panels of 3 in 4 districts)	Circuit Court (72 counties)
Wyoming	Supreme Court (5 justices — chief justice and 4 justices sit en banc)	(none)	District Court (9 districts, 23 counties)

State Administrative Agencies

As with the Federal government, states have a variety of administrative agencies which produce rules, regulations, and decisions. How these decisions are published, along with where to find the related rules and regulations produced by these agencies, differs from state to state. Where one or both are needed from a particular agency, the best advice is to contact the agency itself for information.

Case Law

Law Reports (print)

Both Federal and State law reports exist, in addition to law reports which digest decisions, based on the level of court in which the case was decided, the region of the country, and the subject area. The chart below sets out some of the more widely-known print reporters.

Federal and State Reporters Chart

Federal Reporters	Examples
United States Reports Official reports of the United States Supreme Court (published by the U.S. government)	*Brown v. Board of Education*, 347 U.S. 483 (1954).
Supreme Court Reporter Published by West — contains opinions of the U.S. Supreme Court since 1882.	*Washington v. Glucksberg*, 117 S. Ct. 2258 (1997).
United States Supreme Court Reports, Lawyers' Edition LexisNexis (and previously Lawyer's Cooperative Publishing) publishes the Lawyers' Edition. *United States Supreme Court Reports, Lawyers' Edition 2d* has been published since 1956 and continued the first series. The first series dates back to the beginning of the Court.	*Kansas v. Hendricks*, 138 L.Ed. 2d 501 (1997).
Federal Reporter Covers the dates 1880–1924 along with the following courts: Commerce Court of the United States (1911–1913, abolished), Court of Appeals of the District of Columbia (established 1893), Court of Claims, United States circuit courts (abolished 1912), United States courts of appeals (established 1891), United States district courts. Published by West.	*Frick v. Webb*, 281 F. 407 (D.C. Cal. 1922).

Federal Reporters	Examples
Federal Reporter, 2d The second series ("2d") covers the dates 1924–1993 along with the following courts: Court of Appeals of the District of Columbia (until 1932), Court of Claims (abolished 1982), United States Claims Court (established 1982), United States Court of Customs and Patent Appeals (1929–1982), United States courts of appeals, United States district courts (until 1932), United States Emergency Court of Appeals (1942–1961). Published by West.	*Occidental Petroleum Corp. v. Buttes Gas & Oil Co.*, 461 F. 2d 1261 (9th Cir. 1972).
Federal Reporter, 3d The third series ("3d") covers 1993-present and publishes cases from the U.S. Courts of Appeals and the United States Court of Federal Claims.	*A&M Records, Inc. v. Napster, Inc.*, 239 F.3d 1004 (9th Cir. 2001).
Federal Supplement Covers the dates 1933–1998 along with the following courts: U.S. district courts, United States Customs Court (and the United States Court of International Trade from 1980); and the Judicial Panel on Multidistrict Litigation. Published by West.	*Time Inc. v. Bernard Geis Assocs.*, 293 F. Supp. 130 (S.D.N.Y. 1968).
Federal Supplement, 2d The second series ("2d") covers opinions from 1998 to present along with the following courts: U.S. district courts, United States Court of Federal Claims, United States Court of International Trade, and the Judicial Panel on Multidistrict Litigation. Published by West.	*United States v. Berks County*, 250 F. Supp 2d 525 (E.D. Pa. 2003).

Federal Reporters	Examples
Federal Rules Decisions Published by West and containing opinions of Federal District Courts from 1941 forward that pertain to the Rules of Civil (or Criminal) Procedure, and which have not been published in the *Federal Supplement.*	*United States ex rel. Gerald Mayo v. Satan and his Staff,* 54 F.R.D. 282 (1971).
Bankruptcy Reporter Contains cases of the United States Bankruptcy Courts (trial level) and other federal district court cases dealing with bankruptcy matters. Published by West.	*Southwest Holdings, L.L.C. v. Kohlberg & Co. (In re Southwest Supermarkets, L.L.C.),* 315 B.R. 565 (Bankr. D. Ariz. 2004).
Federal Claims Reporter Contains decisions of the United States Court of Federal Claims, a trial level federal court that handles specialized federal cases against the United States government (such as disputes over government contracts). Published by West.	*Campbell v. Sec'y of Health and Human Servs.,* 69 Fed. Cl. 775 (Fed. Cl. 2006).
Military Justice Reporter — U.S. Armed Forces Contains cases of the United States Court of Military Appeals, and Courts of Military Review of the Navy-Marine Corps, Air Force, and Coast Guard. Published by West.	*United States v. Napoleon,* 46 M.J. 279 (1997).
Veterans Appeals Reporter Contains decisions issued by the United States Court of Veterans Appeals. Published by West.	*Manio v. Derwinski,* 1 Vet. App. 140 (1991).

Seven regional reporters (published by West):

State Reporters	Examples
Atlantic: Pennsylvania, New Jersey, Maryland, Connecticut, Delaware, Rhode Island, Vermont, New Hampshire, Maine.	*Department of Transportation v. Manor Mines*, 565 A. 2d 428 (Pa. 1989).
North Eastern: New York, Massachusetts, Illinois, Ohio, Indiana.	*Palsgraf v. Long Island Railroad Co.*, 162 N.E. 99 (N.Y. 1928).
North Western: Michigan, Wisconsin, Minnesota, North and South Dakota, Nebraska, Iowa.	*Continental Cas. Co. v. Kinsey*, 499 N. W. 2d 574 (N.D. 1993).
Pacific: Kansas, Oklahoma, Arizona, Nevada, Idaho, Montana, Washington, Oregon, California, Wyoming, Colorado, and New Mexico, Alaska, Hawaii, Utah.	*Ybarra v. Spangard*, 154 P.2d 687 (Cal. 1944).
South Eastern: Georgia, North and South Carolina, Virginia, West Virginia.	*Mulberry-Fairplains Water Association v. Town of North Wilkesboro*, 412 S.E. 2d 910 (N.C. App. 1992).
Southern: Florida, Alabama, Mississippi, Louisiana.	*Western Sling & Cable Co. v. Hamilton*, 545 So. 2d 29 (Ala. 1989).
South Western: Texas, Missouri, Kentucky, Tennessee, Arkansas.	*Royal Banks of Mo. v. Fridkin*, 819 S.W. 2d 359 (Mo. 1991).

Citation

Citation styles follow the format provided in the chart above. In the U.S., *The Bluebook: A Uniform System of Citation* (18th ed.) by Harvard Law Review (2005) is the authoritative source for citation.

Neutral citation has been slower to catch on. At present, these States use neutral citation: Colorado, Florida, Louisianna, Maine, Mississippi, Montana, New Mexico, North Dakota, Oklahoma, Ohio, South Dakota, Pennsylvania, Utah, Wisconsin and Wyoming. The U.S. Court of Appeals and South Dakota District Court are the federal courts using neutral citation. Example: *State v. Ralph D. Armstrong*, 2005 WI 119, ¶158 which breaks down as the following:

State v. Ralph D. Armstrong,	2005	WI	119,	¶158
Style of Cause,	Year	Jurisdic-tion/Court	Case Number,	Paragraph Number

Finding Case Law Online

Fee-based subscription services such as Westlaw and LexisNexis are the most comprehensive sources for American case law. The most useful free online source is LII available through Cornell Law School (http://www.law.cornell.edu/), although its content can be thin for various jurisdictions.

The best way to find administrative agency decisions is to start by contacting the agency. Agency decisions are available in government and commercial print publications in addition to online through a variety of sources. The *United States Government Manual* is published yearly by the U.S. government and contains information on a variety of agencies, boards, commissions, etc. An online version is available through the GPO at http://www.gpoaccess.gov/gmanual/. The Library of Congress also maintains a useful list at http://www.loc.gov/rr/news/fedgov.html.

Noting-up American Case Law

Once you have found a case on your topic, you must always note it up. This will ensure that the case is still good law — i.e., it has not been overturned. It will also let you know how the case has been considered, distinguished, applied, etc.

Online, both LexisNexis and Westlaw provide users with the tools to note-up cases. In most circumstances you will use LexisNexis' *Shepard's Citations* or Westlaw's *KeyCite* to note-up a case. Both these services provide a list of cases and secondary sources that have cited your case. Search results can be sorted by legal issue, jurisdiction, court level, treatment level and document type.

In print, *Shepard's Citation Service* allows you to follow the history of your case and to determine the judicial treatment of the case. *Shepard's* lists cases by case citations (i.e., reporter, volume and page number; the name of the case is not included) along with articles and case comments which have considered the case.

The term "to shepardize" a case in the U.S. means to note-up the case. When the case you are shepardizing has been cited in more than one law report, alternative citations are provided. Below each citation of the case, you will find listed the citations of all cases which have considered it and an abbreviation representing the way in which the case was considered. For example, "a" means the same case was affirmed on appeal, "r" means the same case was reversed on appeal, and "d" means the case at bar is different or distinguished, either in law or fact, from the case cited for reasons provided. Check the front of the volume of the citator you are using for an up-to-date and thorough list of abbreviations and their meanings.

There are different volumes of *Shepard's* for different law reports. To shepardize a case, you must begin by finding the *Shepard's* volume which covers cases in the law reporter where your case is digested. Bound volumes of *Shepard's* cover decisions reported in a given law report over a specified number of years. For instance, one *Shephard's* volume may cover volumes 1 through 60 of a given law reporter, whereas another may cover volumes 61 through 120. Bound volumes of *Shepard's* are kept up-to-date by means of periodically published hard and soft cover supplements.

Legislation

Federal

Bills

At the Federal level, a member of the House or a member of the Senate[9] introduces a Bill at which point it is given a number (e.g. H.R. 676 or S. 612. The H.R. and S. indicate whether the Bill originated in the House of Representatives or in the Senate). Once the number is assigned, the Bill is sent to the GPO to produce additional copies.

Bills are then sent to the appropriate committee. Committees may do a number of things including assign the Bill to a subcommittee, hold hearings, and make changes to the text. The Committee has tremendous significance in that many Bills do not make it beyond this stage. Bills are studied; expert views are solicited and public hearings may be held. If the Bill is voted on favourably by Committee members, it will be reported back to the House or Senate with or without amendments. The report contains information on why there is a need for the Bill, what the proposed legislation will achieve, what it will cost, and any relevant history. It will also contain the written dissents from discontented Committee members.

Before the Bill reaches the Floor, a Rules Committee will set the rules by which the Bill will be considered and how the debate will proceed. Debates follow, and once the debates have concluded, a vote is called. If the Bill passes (a simple majority vote is required for most legislation), it is sent from the House to Senate or from Senate to the House, depending on where it originated and where it must go next. Both Chambers must pass an identi-

---

[9] Members of the House of Representatives alone can introduce Bills to raise revenue.

cal Bill for it to become law. Where significant differences in the Bill have emerged while it worked its way through both Chambers, a Conference Committee will work to reach an agreement on the text of the Bill with the final approval going back to both the House and the Senate.

At this point, the Bill is presented to the President for signing. Once the President signs it, the Bill becomes law. If the President does nothing for 10 days, the Bill also becomes law so long as the Congress is in session (in those cases where the Congress adjourns before the end of the 10 days, the Bill does not become law). Where the President vetoes the Bill, the Chambers can override the veto with a two-thirds majority vote of those present.

Where to find it: Bills are available in print as well as online. Thomas, the Library of Congress site (http://thomas.loc.gov/), is the best online source for information on Federal Bills.

Publication Of Enacted Laws

Once a Bill becomes law, it is published as a slip law, a session law and as part of the U.S. *Code*.

Slip Laws

When a Bill becomes law, it is given a public law number (e.g., Pub. L. No. 103-416, which indicates that this is the 416th law enacted by the 103 Congress) and printed as an individual pamphlet (called a "Slip law").

Where to find it: Slip laws may be obtained from the U.S. GPO at http://www.gpoaccess.gov/plaws/index.html.

Session Laws

Once a congressional session has reached its end, slip laws are compiled chronologically in the order in which they first were passed in an official, multi-volume work called the *United States Statutes at Large* (referred to as the *Statutes at Large*).[10] The statutes in these volumes are referred to as "session laws," and are published by the Office of the Federal Register, National Archives and Records Administration.

In addition to its long title, short title and text, each session law contains, either in the heading or in the margin at the beginning of the statute, its public law number, its Bill number (e.g., H.R. 1388 or S. 3487), the date on which it went from Bill to Act, its *Statutes at Large* citation (e.g., 108. Stat.

---

[10] Session laws are also published in a West publication called *The United States Code Congressional and Administrative News* (U.S.C.C.A.N.) which contains selected Congressional and administrative materials and which is published with every session of Congress.

4305), and the *United States Code* citation. Slip laws contain this same information.

Statutes at Large volumes also contain the wording of constitutional amendments (proposed and ratified) along with Presidential proclamations and concurrent resolutions. These volumes have been in existence since 1789. While they contain U.S. statutes as passed, they do not provide the researcher with an easy way to determine what the current law is. As a result, consulting the *United States Code* is necessary to find the law as it currently exists.

Where to find it: The *Statutes at Large* are available in print and online through the GPO at http://www.gpoaccess.gov/plaws/search.html. They are also available through fee-based subscription services such as *HeinOnline* and LexisNexis.

Publication as a Bill, a Slip Law, a Session Law, and as part of the *United States Code* provides several unique citations for a would-be Act and then as an Act. For example, the *Serve America Act* (short title) Bill, or *The Edward M. Kennedy Serve America Act, an Act to reauthorize and reform the national service laws* (long title) is cited as: *Serve America Act* (H.R. 1388).

Slip Laws →	Session Laws →	*United States Code*
Legislation is enacted and published as a separate document — an individual pamphlet known as a slip law.	Public laws for a session of Congress are compiled chronologically at the end of each session in the *Statutes at Large* and are known as Session Laws. The *Statutes at Large* volumes are the official source for laws and resolutions passed by Congress.	Session laws are reorganized by subject and placed within the *Code* which contains only laws in effect.

Slip Laws →	Session Laws →	*United States Code*
Example: *Serve America Act*, Pub. L. No. 111-013, 2009 U.S.C.C.A.N. (123 Stat.) 1460 (2009).	Example: *Serve America Act*, Pub. L. No. 111-013, 123 Stat. 1460 (2009). (Stat. = *Statutes at Large* citation indicating that the Act is in volume 123 at page 1460).	Example: *Serve America Act*, 42 USC §12501 note (2009).
(Pub. L. No. = Public Law number citation indicating that this is the 13th law passed by the 111th Congress. U.S.C.C.A.N = the citation to the U.S. *Code* Congressional and Administrative News).		(U.S. *Code* citation indicating that the Act's location in the *Code* is explained at Title 42, section 12501 of the *Code* in the note provided).
Available at GPO Access: http://www.gpoaccess.gov/plaws/index.html.	Available in print through the Government Printing Office and online (1789–1875) via the Library of Congress American Memory Project at http://memory.loc.gov/ammem/amlaw/lwsl.html.	Available at the Legal Information Institute (LII), Cornell University Law School: http://www.law.cornell.edu/uscode/ or at the Office of the Law Revision Counsel at http://uscode.house.gov/.

Codified Law

The *United States Code* (the "*Code*") came into being in the 1920s, and is currently maintained by the Office of the Law Revision Counsel (LRC) of the House of Representatives. The *Code* is a consolidation of all American

Federal statutes currently in effect. It is published every six years with cumulative supplements available annually to keep it current.

The *Code* takes all legislation passed by Congress and fits it into one of fifty Titles organized by topic:

Title 1 General Provisions
Title 2 The Congress
Title 3 The President
Title 4 Flag and Seal, Seat Of Government, and the States
Title 5 Government Organization and Employees
Title 6 Domestic Security
Title 7 Agriculture
Title 8 Aliens and Nationality
Title 9 Arbitration
Title 10 Armed Forces
Title 11 Bankruptcy
Title 12 Banks and Banking
Title 13 Census
Title 14 Coast Guard
Title 15 Commerce and Trade
Title 16 Conservation
Title 17 Copyrights
Title 18 Crimes and Criminal Procedure
Title 19 Customs Duties
Title 20 Education
Title 21 Food and Drugs
Title 22 Foreign Relations and Intercourse
Title 23 Highways
Title 24 Hospitals and Asylums
Title 25 Indians
Title 26 Internal Revenue Code
Title 27 Intoxicating Liquors
Title 28 Judiciary and Judicial Procedure

Title 29 Labor
Title 30 Mineral Lands and Mining
Title 31 Money and Finance
Title 32 National Guard
Title 33 Navigation and Navigable Waters
Title 34 Navy (repealed)
Title 35 Patents
Title 36 Patriotic Societies and Observances
Title 37 Pay and Allowances Of the Uniformed Services
Title 38 Veterans' Benefits
Title 39 Postal Service
Title 40 Public Buildings, Property, and Works
Title 41 Public Contracts
Title 42 The Public Health and Welfare
Title 43 Public Lands
Title 44 Public Printing and Documents
Title 45 Railroads
Title 46 Shipping
Title 47 Telegraphs, Telephones, and Radiotelegraphs
Title 48 Territories and Insular Possessions
Title 49 Transportation
Title 50 War and National Defense

Each of these Titles is then further subdivided into any number of sub-topics (e.g., subtitles, parts, subparts, chapters, and subchapters). Citations generally refer to Titles and sections (often represented by a §), for example: 21 USC §343; however, sections may be further subdivided into subsections, paragraphs, subparagraphs, clauses, subclauses, items, and sub-items.

The difficulty with codification of any new piece of legislation is that although statutes can be about one topic exclusively, they can also be about many topics that will not all logically fit under one specific heading. For example, a statute dealing with hospitals (Title 24) might also have to do with taxation (Title 26) and drugs (Title 21). Each of these topics, of course, belongs in a separate place in the *Code*. As a result, most statutes are not found, in whole, in one place in the *Code*, and it is often difficult to find out where all the parts of a statute have been scattered. However, information on how the new statute has been slotted into the *Code* is typically found in a note which provides information on how it has been classified.

Where to find it: The LRC prepares, in print, the official subject compilation of all general and permanent laws in a publication known as the *United States Code*. Two annotated versions (available in print and online through the fee-based subscription services offered by these publishers) of the *Code* are used widely: the U.S.C.A. — *United States Code Annotated* (West Publishing) and U.S.C.S. — *United States Code Service* (LexisNexis) which both provide additional information on court decisions considering the various sections, statutory history and cross-references. Each is updated with pocket parts, supplements, and reissued volumes. Citations to the *Code* are always made to the unannotated official version published by the LRC. Other unannotated (and unofficial) versions can be found online in numerous places including LII: http://www.law.cornell.edu/uscode/ and the Office of the Law Revision Counsel, House of Representatives website: http://uscode.house.gov/search/criteria.shtml.

How to Search the Code

The annotated versions provide general indexes which are the best way to search if you want to search by keywords. Also, if you know the popular name of the statute (see the next section), almost every version of the *Code* will contain a Popular Name table. Codes also contain conversion tables if you know only the *Public Law* or *Statutes at Large* citation.

Popular Names

Some statutes have what are known as "popular names" which is the legislation as it is referred to informally. Popular names can have something to do with the subject matter of the Act (*Pacific Yew Act*), the sponsors/creator of the Act (the *Sheppard-Towner Act* of 1921 sponsored by senators Morris Sheppard and Horace Mann Towner), or the desired effect of the Act (the *Take Pride in America Act* which designates certain public lands as wilderness in the State of Arizona and, clearly, sees taking pride in America as the desired effect).

Where to find it: To find out where the Act appears in the U.S. *Code* if you only have the popular name, you will have to locate a Popular Name table. This is available online at the Office of the Law Revision Counsel at http://uscode.house.gov/, Findlaw at http://caselaw.lp.findlaw.com/ casecode/uscodes/popularnames/ or through LII at http://www.law. cornell.edu/uscode/topn/.

Federal Regulations

United States administrative rulings and regulations are locatable in the *Federal Register* which is published daily each weekday. Regulations may be proposed or final. Proposed regulations are there for public comment whereas final regulations respond to comments and contain the date on which they are to come into effect. Most regulations come into force after 30 days, although some might be in force after 60 days or may even be effective immediately.

Where to find it: The Table of Contents to the *Federal Register* is organized by agency, and the publication is difficult to use for some research because it is organized chronologically. It is available in print or online through the GPO at http://www.gpoaccess.gov/fr/Index.html. Some regulations are also available via agency websites.

Most regulations are subsequently published in the *Code of Federal Regulations* ("CFR"), which rearranges the regulations published in the Federal Register by subject.[11] The CFR is available in print (through the National Archives, West, or LexisNexis) or online through the National Archives at http://www.archives.gov/federal-register/cfr/ or the GPO at http://www. gpoaccess.gov/cfr/index.html.

Regulations can be updated by checking the "List of CFR Sections Affected" ("LSA") which may be located at the GPO website at http://www.gpoaccess.gov/lsa/index.html. These are cumulative and updated monthly so only the most recent CFR pamphlet needs to be consulted. They contain the latest information on proposed, new, and amended regulations published in the *Federal Register* since the last revision date of a CFR title. As a second step, check the "Current List of CFR Parts Affected" which lists the CFR parts affected by change(s) since the LSA was last published.

---

[11] The titles in the CFR do not necessarily correspond with the titles in the *Code*. For example "Education" is at Title 20 in the *Code*, and Title 34 in the CFR.

State Bills and Statutes

State governments resemble the federal government in that all of them have two chambers (i.e., they are bicameral, with a House and Senate) with the exception of Nebraska which is unicameral. The state version of the Congress is generally called the Legislature or General Assembly.

State laws are subject to valid federal laws and to the Constitution of that particular state. Nonetheless, residual legislative power was reserved to the States via the Tenth Amendment of the Constitution which reads, "The powers not delegated to the United States by the Constitution, nor prohibited by it to the States, are reserved to the States respectively, or to the people." As a result, even where the federal government has legislative power, states are sometimes permitted to legislate concurrently.

Bills are introduced and passed in a method similar to that at the federal level. State government websites contain the text of current and recent Bills and are relatively easy to locate online.

Bills which become law are published as slip laws (pamphlet format) in many states, and all states publish session laws at the end of their legislative sessions. The names of the statute consolidations (which, like the U.S. *Code*, incorporate current statutes by subject under a fixed number of titles, chapters, sections, etc.) differ from state to state. Often, the titles of consolidations of state statutes will use the words "code", "consolidated", "compiled", or "revised".

Where to find it: In print, states have annotated *Code* services similar to those described above for federal statutes. Online, state statutes and codes are available on Westlaw, LexisNexis or on the website for that particular state. Findlaw provides links to all the states through this webpage: http://www.findlaw.com/11stategov/index.html.

Treaties

According to Article II of the Constitution, the President has the authority "by and with the Advice and Consent of the Senate, to make Treaties, 23 May 1969, 1155 U.N.T.S. 331, provided two-thirds of the Senators present concur." However, the advice and consent of Senators are not necessary for the Executive branch to negotiate and enter into an "executive agreement." Treaties are known by a variety of names such as conventions, agreements, covenants, final acts, charters, protocols, pacts, and accords. The *Vienna Convention on the Law of Treaties*, 23 May 1969, 1155 U.N.T.S. 331, treats documents with a range of synonyms of this sort as treaties. By contrast, the United States does not call any document a "treaty" which has not received the approval of two-thirds of the Senate. Given the additional work involved in securing the consent of two-thirds of the Senators, most international agreements entered into by the United States are executive agreements, not treaties.

Where to find it: Treaties to which the United States is a party may be located through a variety of sources. Useful indexes and finding aids include:

- *United States Treaty Index 1776–2000 Consolidation*. This service indexes U.S. treaties, ratified and unratified, from 1776–2000 and is kept up-to-date by the *Current Treaty Index*, a companion service published twice yearly by Hein. It provides information on treaties and agreements published in the *Treaties and Other International Acts Series* (TIAS) pamphlets along with those completed but not yet published.

- *Kavass's Guide to the United States Treaties in Force*. This service, published by Hein, provides information on whether treaties are in force.

- *Treaties in Force* (TIF). Another service providing information on whether treaties are in force is published yearly by the U.S. State Department. TIF contains information on all bilateral and multilateral U.S. treaties and agreements in force as of January 1 of each year. It is available in print and online at http://www.state.gov/s/l/treaty/index.htm.

The following chart contains some of the better-known sources for treaties and executive agreements.

Treaties/Executive Agreements Sources Chart

Date	Title (and abbreviation)	Contents	Availability
1776–1836	*Treaties and Other International Acts of the United States of America* (Miller), Hunter Miller, ed., Washington, D.C.: U.S.G.P.O., 1931–1948.	Treaties are in chronological order and in all of the official languages. Includes citations to the *United States Statutes At Large (Stat.)* and the *Treaty Series (TS)*.	In print and online via HeinOnline
1776–1937	*Treaties, Conventions, International Acts, Protocols, and Agreements Between the U.S.A. and Other Powers* (Malloy), W.M. Malloy, ed., Washington, D.C.: U.S.G.P.O. 1910–1937. (Malloy ed., v.1-2 covering 1776–1909, Redmond & Trenwith eds., v.3-4 covering 1910–1937).	Contains treaties in English. Annotated and provides citations to treaties in the *United States Statutes At Large (Stat.)* and the *Treaty Series (TS)*.	In print and online via *HeinOnline*.

Date	Title (and abbreviation)	Contents	Availability
1776–1950	*United States Statutes at Large* (Stat.) Washington, D.C.: U.S.G.P.O. Predecessor to UST (*United States Treaties and Other International Agreements*).	Official publication. Volume 8 contains all treaties from 1776 to 1845 and sessional volumes after this date contain treaties and executive agreements.	In print and online via Westlaw and *HeinOnline* Also free online (1789–1875): http://lcweb2.loc.gov/ ammem/amlaw/lwsl. html.
1776–1949	*Treaties and Other International Agreements of the United States of America 1776–1949* (Bevans), Charles I. Bevans, ed., Washington, D.C.: Dept. of State, 1968–1976. Predecessor to UST (*United States Treaties and Other International Agreements*); Supersedes Miller and Malloy.	Contains multilateral and bilateral agreements to which the United States is a party. Treaties are arranged in chronological order and are published only in English only.	In print and online via LexisNexis and *HeinOnline*.
1908–1945	*Treaty Series (TS or USTS)* Washington, D.C.: Government Printing Office, 1908–1948. Merged in 1945 with *Executive Agreement Series to form Treaties and Other International Acts Series* (TIAS). The earlier unnumbered pamphlets are published in Bevans.	This series was published in pamphlet (slip) form and contains both treaties and international agreements. It is unnumbered until 1908. After 1929, only treaties are included.	In print.
1929–1945	*Executive Agreement Series* (EAS) (Washington, DC: U.S.G.P.O, 1929–1945). Prior to 1929, this was part of the *Treaty Series*. After 1945 it became part of *Treaties and Other International Acts Series* (TIAS).	Contains international executive agreements published in pamphlet (slip) form.	In print.
1946 +	*Treaties and Other International Acts Series* (TIAS) Washington, D.C.: GPO, 1946-. Continued the TS (*Treaty Series*) and EAS (*Executive Agreement Series*).	This is an official publication. Treaties are published in pamphlet (slip) form and consecutively numbered. They are eventually bound into the UST volumes. They appear in English along with all other official languages in which the treaty is published.	Available in print and online via Westlaw, Lexis-Nexis, and *HeinOnline*.

Date	Title (and abbreviation)	Contents	Availability
1950+	*United States Treaties and Other International Agreements* (UST) Washington, D.C.: U.S. Dept. of State, 1950-.	Once treaties and agreements have appeared in the TIAS, they are bound in chronological order. They appear in English along with all other official languages in which the treaty is published.	Available in print and online via Westlaw, Lexis-Nexis, and *HeinOnline*.
1962+	*International Legal Materials.* Washington, D.C.: American Society of International Law, 1962-.	Provides the full-text of treaties, agreements and other important international documents.	Available in print and online via Westlaw, Lexis-Nexis and *HeinOnline*.
Recent Treaties Online	• *Library of Congress — Thomas — Treaties.* • *GPO Access — Senate, House, and Treaty Documents.*	• Complete coverage begins with the 94th Congress (1975) • Full-text searches available for treaties sent to the Senate beginning with the 104th Congress (1995).	http://thomas.loc.gov/home/treaties/treaties.htm http://www.access.gpo.gov/congress/cong006.html
Recent or Pending Treaties	• *U.S. State Department Treaties Pending.* • *United States Senate.*	• Contains information on treaties submitted to the Senate but not approved • Contains information on treaties received by Senate from the President along with those approved by the Senate during the current Congress.	http://www.state.gov/s/l/treaty/pending/ http://www.senate.gov/pagelayout/legislative/d_three_sections_with_teasers/treaties.htm

Secondary Sources

Monographs

There are many different types of monographs (i.e., books) available to the researcher. The treatise is the most in-depth amongst these, ranging from single-volume to multi-volume scholarly works on various areas of law (e.g., *Wigmore on Evidence, Corbin on Contracts*). Treatises are written by experts, and they provide thorough coverage of a particular subject. Harvard Law School provides a useful list of some of the seminal treatises at: http://www.law.harvard.edu/library/research/guides/united_states/legal_treatises_subject.html.

Scholarly monographs on a variety of relatively narrow topics are most often published by university presses but sometimes by more broadly-based commercial publishers (e.g. *Free Culture: The Nature and Future of Creativity* by Lawrence Lessig). These provide information on the cultural, historical or policy aspects of a particular subject and are often as authoritative as legal treatises.

Hornbooks serve the law school community in that they are written for students; however, a wider audience will find them useful in that they provide an overview of an area of law. Hornbooks and "nutshells" (e.g., *Torts in a Nutshell, Legal Research in a Nutshell*) provide an entry point into an area of law without overwhelming the reader.

Practitioners' handbooks and manuals (books intended to be useful to practising lawyers) are published by a number of commercial publishers. Continuing Legal Education materials (aimed largely at practising lawyers) are also published by professional organizations including the American Law Institute, the American Bar Association, and the various State Bar Associations. These educational publications address topics in specific areas of legal practice in addition to discussing emerging, changing, or confusing areas of the law.

Legal Periodicals

Periodicals (i.e., journals, law reviews, newsletters) are valuable in that they contain articles on a variety of subjects written by law professors, practitioners, judges and students. Analyses of various subjects are more up-to-date in periodicals given that it generally takes far less time to go from the writing to publishing stage than is the case with a book. Journal articles often provide a succinct overview of an area of law and contain citations to many primary and secondary sources.

Because thousands of articles are published in hundreds of different periodicals each year, and the periodicals themselves are produced by many diverse publishers, it is hardly possible to browse the table of contents of each periodical individually. As a result, an index which pulls all of the contents of these sources together is required so that the researcher can locate in a timely way what has been published.

Indexes to legal periodicals do allow a researcher to search for journal articles and case comments by, at the very least, subject, title, and author. If you need to find almost every article available on a subject, you will want to start with an index which will tell you what exists but not necessarily provide full-text access. The coverage in these databases continues to grow all the time, but in the meantime, each of these sources needs to be consulted by the researcher for titles and issues available.

Where to find it: Indexes like *Current Law Index* published by Gale and *Index to Legal Periodicals (ILP)* published by H.W. Wilson still exist in print but are rapidly being eclipsed by the online (and, now, often full-text) journals indexes. Since online indexes rarely have more than a few decades of coverage, however, the print indexes may still be necessary when a researcher requires access to older journal articles.[12] *LegalTrac* (the electronic version of *Current Law Index*), *ILP* and *Index to Foreign Legal Periodicals* are online sources covering a vast number of law titles. Legal database subscription services such as LexisNexis and Westlaw also contain full-text legal periodical databases as does a source like *HeinOnline*. Their coverage, however, while full-text, may not be as varied as the indexes mentioned above which will cite more articles (but not necessarily provide full-text access).

Legal Dictionaries and Words and Phrases

Legal dictionaries are useful in that legal terms often differ in meaning from the same or similar terms in a non-legal context. Dictionaries can also help provide synonyms and other additional research terms.

The most widely used American legal dictionary is *Black's Law Dictionary*, 9th ed. (West Publishing Co., 2009). Other dictionaries include:

- Ballentine, James A. *Ballentine's Law Dictionary, with Pronunciations*, 3d ed., William S. Anderson, ed. (Rochester, N.Y.: Lawyers Cooperative Pub. Co., 1969).

- Beyer, Gerry W. and Kenneth R. Redden. *Modern Dictionary for the Legal Profession*, 3d ed. (Buffalo, N.Y.: Hein, 2001 and Supplement, 2006).

- Gifis, Steven H. *Law Dictionary*, 3d ed. (New York: Barron's, c1991).

- Oran, Daniel. *Oran's Dictionary of the Law*, 4th ed. (Clifton Park, N.Y.: Thomson Delmar Learning, c2008).

Online, legal dictionaries are available through a variety of websites including Law.com at http://dictionary.law.com/.

Words and Phrases (West Publishing Co.) is the most comprehensive words and phrases encyclopedia. The multi-volume set is organized alphabetically and updated annually with pocket supplements found at the back of each volume. *Words and Phrases* purports to list all cases that have offered judicial consideration of a word or phrase. It is available in print and online.

Legal Encyclopedias

Legal encyclopedias are a good way to begin research. They provide useful information on primary as well as secondary sources of law and are very

---

[12] An exception is H.W. Wilson's online *Index to Legal Periodicals Retrospective* whose coverage begins at 1908.

easy to use. Encyclopedias exist for individual states (California, New York, Maryland, Ohio, etc.) as well as the federal sphere. The major encyclopedias worthy of note are: *Corpus Juris Secundum* and *American Jurisprudence*.

1) Corpus Juris Secundum

Corpus Juris Secundum ("*C.J.S.*") is an encyclopedia of American law consisting of more than 160 volumes organized alphabetically by subject. Every chapter or subject title contains a detailed table of contents and a scope note. The scope note, which precedes the discussion of the law on the topic, outlines what is covered in the chapter and where related topics can be found. A five-volume General Index facilitates access to the subject titles.

The General Index and subject volumes are updated with cumulative pocket supplements. The *C.J.S.* covers federal and state law and attempts to cite all relevant reported cases in footnotes. The work is also available on-line via Westlaw.

2) American Jurisprudence 2d

American Jurisprudence 2d ("*American Jurisprudence*" or "*Am. Jur.*") is an encyclopedia of American law consisting of roughly eighty volumes organized alphabetically by subject. A multi-volume index also facilitates access to the subject or title volumes. Each chapter or subject title contains a detailed table of contents. All chapters begin with a scope paragraph, which defines what is covered in the chapter, and cross references to other chapters dealing with additional aspects of the subject. The index and title volumes are kept up-to-date by pocket supplements and by a loose-leaf binder entitled *Am. Jur. 2d New Topic Service*.

American Jurisprudence covers federal and state law. Unlike the *C.J.S.*, *American Jurisprudence* does not attempt to cite all reported cases in footnotes. Citations are to *American Law Reports* (discussed below) annotations and selected court decisions. *American Jurisprudence* is also available on-line via Westlaw.

3) American Jurisprudence Proof of Facts 2d

American Jurisprudence Proof of Facts 2d ("*Proof of Facts*") is a multi-volume encyclopedia for lawyers on how to go about proving facts at civil and selected criminal defence trials. This publication was designed to assist in preparing for examination-in-chief and cross-examination. However, it is also meant to assist in preparing for discoveries and interviews with clients and witnesses.

Each subject covered is divided into three main parts. The first part ("prefatory material") includes a concise statement of the fact-in-issue. The second part ("background text") sets out the law applicable to the fact situation. Substantive law is discussed to the extent that it is necessary for a proper understanding of the proofs, which is the third part. However, there is a table at the beginning of each chapter which cross-references the treatment of substantive law in *American Jurisprudence* to the proofs in *Proof of Facts*. The third part ("proofs") involves question-and-answer interchanges between lawyers and witnesses. Where not readily apparent, the purpose of particular questions or lines of questioning are explained. Suggested answers are given to alert lawyers to the type of information that must be obtained from the witness. Textual notes containing evidentiary rules and practical suggestions for questioning witnesses are included.

Proof of Facts is organized alphabetically by subject, and a multi-volume index facilitates access to the various subject or title volumes. The index is kept up-to-date with periodic pocket supplements. It is available in print and online via Westlaw.

American Law Reports ("A.L.R.")

The *A.L.R.*, published by West, is a several-hundred-volume series of encyclopedia-like books which contain articles called "annotations." The annotations use a selected number of cases to provide a thorough discussion of the law on a particular topic along with an examination of how courts have decided these types of cases across all U.S. jurisdictions. The reported case or a summary thereof (few cases are reported in full) precedes the annotation. Next, the subject of the annotation is defined (e.g., directors' liability). While the case may deal with several legal issues, the annotation may only cover one of them. Often there is a table of contents, a table of jurisprudence cross-references, and a paragraph defining the scope of the annotation. The actual annotations summarize the case law on the subject, attempt to reconcile conflicting decisions, and assess which cases are binding and why.

The *A.L.R. Federal* covers federal law, practice, procedure, and treaties. In addition to the discussion of federal cases, an analysis of selected international cases from countries such as the United Kingdom, Canada, Australia, and New Zealand is included. In contrast, *A.L.R. 3rd* covers mainly state law. The Quick Index permits access to the *A.L.R.* and *A.L.R. Federal*. Bound Quick Index volumes are updated with pocket supplements. It is available online via Westlaw and LexisNexis.

Restatements of the Law

Restatements of the Law ("Restatements"), published by the American Law Institute, provide concise statements of the common law rules on various topics. The fundamental principles and propositions from cases are distilled into "black letter" statements of law, and these sections are followed by commentary and explanatory notes. The Restatements will also summarize areas in which the law is changing and new rules are emerging along with presenting proposed rules where the authors believe change is necessary.

There are Restatements on a number of subject areas governed largely or entirely by the common law. These areas are Agency, Conflict of Laws, Contracts, Foreign Relations Law of the United States, Judgments, the Law Governing Lawyers, Property (including volumes on Landlord & Tenant, Donative Transfers, Wills and Other Donative Transfers, Mortgages, and Servitudes), Restitution, Suretyship and Guaranty, Torts (including volumes on Apportionment of Liability, and Products Liability), Trusts, and Unfair Competition.

Restatements are highly authoritative secondary literature and are often cited in American court decisions to summarize the law in an area. *Restatements in the Courts* annotates the court decisions which have applied or interpreted the various sections of the Restatements.

Restatements are limited to common law rules; they provide commentary on the proper interpretations of rules, illustrations on how rules should apply in certain circumstances, and summaries of cases applying and interpreting the restatements.

Where to find it: Restatements are available in print, and online through Westlaw or LexisNexis.

Digests

Digests, as we have seen with the *Canadian Abridgment*, enable you to find cases under your subject. West Publishing Company's *American Digest System* is the most comprehensive American digest and facilitates access to almost all reported American case law. The system consists of a series of digests which divides all American fields of law into hundreds of topics. Each topic is further divided into numerous subtopics. Subtopics are identified by: (a) the name of the topic under which they fall, and (b) a key number that designates their specific subdivision within the topic.

West writes a very brief headnote or squib for each point of law in every case it receives. Each headnote is numbered, and the same number will appear in the reported decision where the point of law is discussed. A topic name and key number is given to each headnote to identify its substance. The digests bring together all headnotes with the same topic name and key number.[13] If you are using Westlaw online, you can follow the same key numbers provided at the beginning of cases to lead you to other similar cases. West publishes a number of digests which gather headnotes from different regions or jurisdictions. *The American Digest System* is considered a master index to all U.S. case law. What follows here is guidance on how to use the source in print.

1) American Digest System

Volumes of the *American Digest System* are issued monthly in a series called the General Digest. Each volume gathers under topic and key number all of the squibs written in any of the reporters since the last volume. Since 1976, the *General Digest* has been consolidated and republished every five years; prior to 1976, consolidations were done every ten years (these consolidations are called "Decennial" digests).[14] A multi-volume index facilitates access to the subject volumes.

There is no overall cumulative publication. This means that a researcher, when the research required involves a span of several decades, must consult these various consolidations and then update the research with the most recent volumes of the *General Digest*.

There are three main ways of locating case law on your topic using the *General Digest*:

a) Descriptive Word Approach

- The Descriptive-Word Index is arranged alphabetically. It includes all topics of the digest classification, descriptive words relating to the parties to the action, the names of places and physical objects, questions of law, legal principles, and constitutional and legislative provisions.

- Once you have located an appropriate descriptive word or phrase, you will be referred to a corresponding digest topic and key number.

---

[13] You should note that there are no explanatory notes and that the headnotes do not attempt to reconcile conflicting decisions.

[14] *General Digest*, 11th Series (2005-present), *Eleventh Decennial Digest*, Part 2 (2001–2004), *Eleventh Decennial Digest*, Part 1 (1996–2001), *Tenth Decennial Digest*, Part 2 (1991–1996), *Tenth Decennial Digest*, Part 1 (1986–1991), *Ninth Decennial Digest*, Part 2 (1981–1986), *Ninth Decennial Digest*, Part 1 (1976–1981), *Eighth Decennial Digest* (1966–1976), *Seventh Decennial Digest* (1956–1966), *Sixth Decennial Digest* (1946–1956), *Fifth Decennial Digest* (1936–1946), *Fourth Decennial Digest* (1926–1936), *Third Decennial Digest* (1916–1926), *Second Decennial Digest* (1907–1916), *First Decennial Digest* (1897–1906), *Century Digest* (1658–1896).

- Locate the volume containing your topic in the General Digest and consolidations. You will find paragraph case summaries under the digest topics and citations for the cases.

b) Topic Approach

- Only use this approach if you have a strong knowledge of the law on your topic, as it is very easy to miss important aspects of your topic by selecting incorrect topic and key numbers.
- Scan the list of topics which you will find in each Digest volume for the appropriate topic name.
- Locate the volume containing your topic in the *General Digest* and consolidations. You will find a scope note under the topic name in the General Digest. This note outlines what is included in the topic and provides the various sub-topics and key numbers. Since the same key numbers are used throughout the West system, every case on the topic can be located.

c) Case Name Approach

- If you know the name and citation of a case on your topic, you can locate the case in the *West Reporter* and obtain the relevant key number from the headnote. Alternatively, you can locate the case in the Table of Cases in the *General Digest*. Cases are listed alphabetically, along with their citations and the topic and key number for each point of law drawn from the case.
- Locate the volume containing your topic in the *General Digest* and consolidations.

Using the *American Digest System* can be time-consuming owing to the number of decisions digested. The researcher will find it necessary to read many irrelevant entries before locating the citations required. In addition, changes in statutory or case law, unless mentioned in the headnote, are not indicated.

2) Other Digests

While the *American Digest System* is a master digest for the entire country, there are more specialized digests for particular regions of the country,[15] for individual states,[16] and for particular courts.[17] These digests are useful when you know that you only need to find case law from a particular state or region or from a particular court. As these digests are not as comprehensive as the *American Digest System*, they are less time-consuming to use.

Uniform Laws and Model Acts

Uniform laws and model acts are not real laws but, rather, secondary sources, that is, generic statutes, which are intended to be adopted by any state or used as a template by that state to create new or amend existing legislation.[18] The purpose is to minimize the confusion created by unnecessarily different laws across states, particularly in the area of trade and commerce and criminal law. The *Uniform Commercial Code* and the *Model Penal Code* are perhaps the best known of these. Each state is legislatively autonomous, so before a uniform law or model act will apply, it must be enacted by that state's legislature. Unless adopted by a specific state, these generic statutes remain secondary sources without the force of law.

The American Law Institute ("ALI"), founded in 1923, is a society composed of judges, lawyers, law professors and other distinguished individuals. The ALI is the author of both the *Model Penal Code* and the Restatements. Print copies of uniform laws and model acts often also contain commentary, explanatory notes and case law summaries. These laws and acts are different from Restatements in that they cover matters which are generally governed by legislation rather than the common law.

---

[15] The Regional Digests are: *Atlantic* (CT, DC, DE, ME, MD, NH, NJ, PA, RI, VT), *North Eastern* (ceased publication in 1971) (IL, IN, MA, NY, OH), *North Western* (IA, MI, MN, NE, ND, SD, WI), *Pacific* (AK, AZ, CA, CO, HI, ID, KS, MT, NV, NM, OK, OR, UT, WA, WY), *South Eastern* (GA, NC, SC, VA, WV), *South Western* (ceased publication in 1958) (AR, KY, MO, TN, TX), *Southern* (ceased publication in 1988) (AL, FL, LA, MS). For those publications which ceased, look for a digest published for the specific state (e.g., *Florida Digest, California Digest*).

[16] State digests are published for almost all states. Those States without a digest are Delaware, Nevada and Utah.

[17] Federal Court digests have undergone a number of name changes: *Federal Digest* (covers years up to 1939), *Modern Federal Practice Digest* (1939–1961), *Federal Practice Digest 2nd* (1961–1975), *Federal Practice Digest 3rd* (1975–1988), *Federal Practice Digest 4th* (covers 1989 through the present). Other digests include *Federal Circuit Patent Case Digests, West's Veterans Appeals Digest, West's United States Supreme Court Digest, West's Military Justice Digest, West's Bankruptcy Digest*, etc.

[18] *The Model Penal Code*, for example, was completed in 1962, and was responsible for new codes which were enacted in states such as Illinois (1962), Minnesota and New Mexico (1963), New York (1967), Georgia (1969), Kansas (1970), Connecticut (1971), Colorado and Oregon (1972), Delaware, Hawaii, New Hampshire, Pennsylvania and Utah (1973), Montana, Ohio and Texas (1974), Florida, Kentucky, North Dakota and Virginia (1975), Arkansas, Maine and Washington (1976), South Dakota and Indiana (1977), Arizona and Iowa (1978), and so on.

Where to find it: West publishes uniform laws in its *Uniform Laws Annotated*. This publication includes information on those states that have adopted the various laws and what form those laws ultimately took.

Recommended Reading

Armstrong, J.D.S. *Where the Law is: An Introduction to Advanced Legal Research*, 3d ed. (St. Paul, MN: Thomson/West, c2009).

Barkan, Steven M., Roy M. Mersky, and Donald J. Dunn. *Fundamentals of Legal Research*, 9th ed. (New York: Foundation Press, 2009).

Bast, Carol M. and Margie Hawkins. *Foundations of Legal Research and Writing*, 3d ed. (New York: Thomson/Delmar Learning, c2006).

Berring, Robert C. and Elizabeth A. Edinger. *Finding The Law*, 12th ed. (St. Paul, MN: Thomson/West, c2005).

Burnham, William. *Introduction to the Law and Legal System of the United States*, 4th ed. (St. Paul, MN: Thomson West, 2006).

Cohen, Morris L. and Kent Olson. *Legal Research in a Nutshell (Nutshell Series)* (St. Paul, Minn.: West Publishing Co., 2007).

Elias, Stephen. *Legal Research: How to Find & Understand the Law*, 15th ed. (Berkeley, CA: Nolo, 2009).

Nemeth, Charles P. and Hope I. Haywood. *Learning Legal Research: A How-to Manual* (Upper Saddle River, N.J.: Prentice Hall, 2004).

Putman, William H. *Legal Research, Analysis and Writing* (Florence, KY: Delmar Cengage Learning, 2009).

Roberts, Bonita K. and Linda L. Schlueter. *Legal Research Guide: Patterns and Practice*, 5th ed. (Newark, NJ: LexisNexis Matthew Bender, c2006).

Sloan, Amy. *Basic Legal Research: Tools And Strategies*, 4th ed. (Austin, TX: Wolters Kluwer Law & Business, 2009).

21

Australia and New Zealand

Introduction

This chapter will provide you with a brief outline of the Australian and New Zealand legal systems and will explain the key legal research tools in both countries. The chapter will be of use if you need to conduct this type of legal research for the purposes of a Canadian research problem. Both Australia and New Zealand are considered together in one chapter since they share a similar legal tradition, and legal resources for one will often include information for the other. Nevertheless, both have their own individual traditions, government, and legal sources. So, while they are similar, remember they are 1200 miles apart.

Approaching Legal Research for Australia and New Zealand

Australia and New Zealand are like Canada in that the laws of both countries are derived from their constitutions, legislation (statutes and subsidiary legislation), and case law. Unlike Canada, however, where it was left to the courts to determine the date of reception of English law in the colony,[1] Australia and New Zealand both had specific dates on which English law was imported as a whole, as set out in Acts passed by the British Parliament. *An Act to Provide for the Administration of Justice in New South Wales and Van Dieman's Land*, 1828, 9 Geo. IV, c. 83, specified 25 July 1828 as the date for the reception of English law in New South Wales and in what is now known as Tasmania, Queensland and Victoria. Western Australia and South Australia followed suit on 1 June 1829 and 28 December

---

[1] *Young v. Blaikie* (1822), [1817–28] 1 Nfld L.R. 277 (S.C.) at 283 set out the date of reception of English law in Canada as the "date of the institution of a local legislature in a colony;" see Neil Craik, et. al. *Public Law: Cases, Materials and Commentary* (Toronto: Emond Montgomery, 2006) at 56-57.

1836 respectively. On 1 January 1911, the Northern Territory received the English law in effect in South Australia as of that date, while the Australia Capital Territory, in that same year, received the English law in effect in New South Wales. As for New Zealand, the date specified was 14 January 1840.

A firm date of reception was important; all common law, along with all Acts passed up to that time, were to apply to this new jurisdiction. Even if those same Acts were later repealed in Britain, they continued to apply in the colonies unless specifically intended to be repealed there as well. Conversely, legislation passed after the received date would not apply to the colonies unless clearly intended to do so.

Just as the date of reception of English law in Australia and New Zealand has played a more significant role than it did in Canada, the Judicial Committee of the Privy Council played a key role in the legal life of the two countries much longer than it did in Canada. Canada ended criminal appeals to the Privy Council in 1933 and civil appeals in 1949, whereas appeals did not end for Australia until 1986 and until 2003 for New Zealand. As a result, works on legal research in the two countries often have a much greater focus on English law than Canadian works on the same subject.

Constitutions

Australia

The Commonwealth of Australia is a federal parliamentary democracy in which power is shared between a federal government and a number of states and territories. Australia is an independent country with a shared monarch (Australia is one of several countries which recognizes the same sovereign as its head of state) represented by a Governor-General (federally) and by a Governor in each of the six states (New South Wales, Victoria, Tasmania, South Australia, Western Australia, and Queensland). Each state has its own constitution,[2] as does the federal government. The states of Australia were constituted first, then were brought together under a British Act, the *Commonwealth of Australia Constitution Act*, 1900 (U.K.), 63 & 64 Vict., c. 12. (the Australian Constitution), thereby creating one country.

The Commonwealth Parliament has two chambers: a House of Representatives and a Senate. Most of the States and Territories also have a two-chamber Legislative Assembly.

---

[2] New South Wales, *Constitution Act 1902*; Queensland, *Constitution Act 1867*; South Australia, *Constitution Act 1934*; Tasmania, *Constitution Act 1934*; Victoria, *Constitution Act 1975*; Western Australia, *Constitution Act 1889*.

Three of the territories — the Australian Capital Territory, the Northern Territory and Norfolk Island — have self-government[3] of one form or another. The Northern Territory achieved self-government on 1 July 1978 by way of the *Northern Territory (Self-Government) Act 1978*. Norfolk Island achieved limited self-government in 1979 with the passing of the *Norfolk Island Act 1979*; the Australian Capital Territory followed suit with the *Australian Capital Territory (Self-Government) Act 1988*. All of these are Commonwealth Acts which serve, effectively, as the Territories' constitutions. The Commonwealth looks after the administration of the remaining seven territories: Ashmore and Cartier Islands, Australian Antarctic Territory, Christmas Island, Cocos (Keeling) Islands, Coral Sea Islands, Jervis Bay Territory, and Heard Island and McDonald Islands.

The federal government's constitution, the *Commonwealth of Australia Constitution Act 1900* (a U.K. Act) sets out the division of powers between the state and federal levels of government. Section 51, specifically, provides an enumerated list of "powers of the Parliament" which include taxation, the census, banking, copyright, marriage, divorce, naval and military defence, external affairs, trade, and immigration. In addition to the Constitution, two other Acts — the *Statute of Westminster Adoption Act 1942*, and the *Australia Act 1986* (both Australian Acts) — changed the constitutional landscape by changing the relationship of Australia to the United Kingdom, specifically, severing former legislative and judicial ties.

Any matter not specifically spelled out as belonging to the federal government in Section 51 falls within the domains of the states so long as those laws do not conflict with a federal law. According to s. 109 of the Constitution, "When a law of a State is inconsistent with a law of the Commonwealth, the latter shall prevail, and the former shall, to the extent of the inconsistency, be invalid." States typically make laws on areas such as education, health, roads, and criminal law.

At present, there is no national Bill/Charter of Rights, although rights legislation does exist in some of the states/territories including the Australian Capital Territory (the *Human Rights Act 2004* (ACT)) and Victoria (*Victorian Charter of Human Rights and Responsibilities 2006*). There has been much discussion, however, on passing a national equivalent.

Where to find it: You will find the full-text of constitutions for the states and federal government in a variety of formats; however, the most convenient way to obtain these is through the Australasian Legal Information Institution ("AustLII" at http://www.austlii.edu.au/databases.html). Constitutions can be located under the heading "Consolidated Acts," for the desired

---

[3] Self-government means that a range of government matters (including the making of laws) is handled by a locally-elected parliament.

jurisdiction and then under "C" in the alphabetical list for the desired Constitution Act.

New Zealand

New Zealand is an independent country with a shared monarch (New Zealand is one of several countries which recognize the same sovereign as its head of state) represented by a governor-general. In striking contrast to Australia, New Zealand is not a federal system, and has one house only, a House of Representatives. There is no Upper House.

The *Constitution Act 1986* is one of the chief documents making up the constitution of New Zealand, but it is by no means the only one. Other important Acts include the *Judicature Act 1908* which sets out the role of the judiciary; the *Statute of Westminster Adoption Act 1947*, bringing about New Zealand's independence from Great Britain; the *Constitution (Request and Consent) Act 1947* which amended the 1852 *Constitution Act*; the *Legislative Council Abolition Act 1950* which abolished the Upper House of the New Zealand parliament in 1951; the *New Zealand Bill of Rights Act 1990* which set out the rights and fundamental freedoms of citizens; the *Electoral Act 1993* which established an electoral commission and entrenched rules for the elections of Members of Parliament; the *Imperial Laws Application Act 1988* which incorporated into New Zealand law specific British constitutional documents including the Magna Carta, Bill of Rights (1689); and *Act of Settlement 1701*, and the *Supreme Court Act 2003*, which created a Supreme Court for New Zealand thereby ending appeals to the Judicial Committee of the Privy Council. There is also an assortment of unwritten conventions along with treaties, orders in council and letters patent which make up New Zealand's constitution.

Where to find it: You can find the *New Zealand Constitution, 1986* along with some of the other Acts mentioned above at the New Zealand Legal Information Institution (NZLII) website under "New Zealand Acts" (http://www.nzlii.org/nz/legis/consol_act/).

Courts

Australia

States, territories and the federal government all have appellate courts, trial courts, courts of limited jurisdiction, and specialized tribunals and boards.

Federal Courts

The High Court, with a Chief Justice and six other judges, is the highest Court in Australia. It can decide cases dealing not only with federal law and the Constitution but also with state matters. Section 75 of the Constitution sets out areas in which the Court has original rather than appellate jurisdiction. This includes matters involving treaties, consuls or other foreign representatives; litigation involving the Commonwealth or a representative on behalf of the Commonwealth; disputes between states, or a state and a resident of another state, or matters involving a writ of *mandamus* or prohibition or an injunction involving an officer of the Commonwealth or judge. Section 76 sets out that the Court may, when authorized by Parliament, have original jurisdiction under any variety of federal and state laws as well as the Constitution.

The Federal Court of Australia, established by statute (*Federal Court of Australia Act 1976* (Cth)) has limited appellate and first instance jurisdiction over specific matters authorized by legislation. This includes most civil matters covered by Australian federal law, as well as restrictive trade practices, consumer protection, administrative law, taxation appeals, native title, admiralty matters, bankruptcy and so on. Cases are heard by one judge, while appeals are heard by panels of three (the "Full Court"). The court also hears some appeals from state/territory Supreme Courts.

Other federal courts include the Industrial Relations Court of Australia, which deals with labour matters, and the Family Court of Australia, which deals with Commonwealth family law matters (under the *Family Law Act 1975*, the *Family Law Regulations 1984* and the *Marriage Act 1961*) in all states and territories except Western Australia (which has its own Family Court of Western Australia). It hears divorce cases, spousal and child support issues, property and other family law related matters.

The Federal Magistrates Court of Australia shares jurisdiction with the Family Court of Australia and the Federal Court, but deals with similar but less complex matters such as administrative law, bankruptcy, family law, copyright, migration, trade practices and so on.

State and Territory Courts

State and territory courts hear criminal and civil matters involving their own laws, along with any additional matters authorized under federal statutes. The court systems in these jurisdictions generally include a Court of Appeal (the highest court in the state or territory), a Supreme Court for the most serious criminal and civil matters, a District or County court for only slightly less serious criminal and civil matters, and a Magistrates court for the least serious of these.

The chart below summarizes the main function of each of these courts. It does not list the courts of limited jurisdiction, courts dedicated to one particular area of law (e.g., Drug Courts, Land and Environment Court, Aboriginal Courts, Children's Courts), or the host of boards and tribunals in each of these states and territories.

Australia Courts Chart

State/Territory and Abbreviation	Highest State Court	Supreme Courts	District/County Courts	Court of Summary Jurisdiction
Australian Capital Territory (ACT)	Supreme Court of the Australian Capital Territory — Court of Appeal	Supreme Court of the Australian Capital Territory		Magistrates Court
	Hears criminal and civil appeals from the decisions of single Supreme Court judges.	Hears the most serious criminal matters and civil cases for claims of more than $50,000 (although it has unlimited civil jurisdiction).		Hears summary criminal cases and civil cases for claims of not more than $50,000. Magistrates may also constitute the small claims Tribunal to determine civil claims up to the value of $10,000.
New South Wales (NSW)	Supreme Court of New South Wales — Court of Appeal and Court of Criminal Appeal	Supreme Court of New South Wales	District Court	Local Court
	Hears appeals from lower courts and some administrative tribunals.	Hears the most serious criminal cases and civil cases involving more than $750,000 (although it has unlimited civil jurisdiction). Also hears cases involving wills, admiralty and injunctions. Consists of two divisions: Common Law Division in which civil, criminal and administrative law cases are heard, and the Equity Division in which judges decide on cases involving equity, probate, commercial, admiralty and related matters.	Hears most indictable offences (except murder and treason), and civil disputes involving civil claims up to $750,000. Acts as an appeal court for criminal decisions from the local court.	Hears summary and some indictable offences, in addition to civil disputes involving amounts of up to $60,000.
Northern Territory (NT)	Supreme Court of the Northern Territory —	Supreme Court of the Northern Territory		1) Court of Summary Jurisdiction

Australia and New Zealand

State/Territory and Abbreviation	Highest State Court	Supreme Courts	District/County Courts	Court of Summary Jurisdiction
	Court of Appeal and Court of Criminal Appeal			*2) Local Court*
	Appeals from single judge decisions are heard by three judges sitting as a Court of Appeal or the Court of Criminal Appeal (depending on the matter).	Has exclusive jurisdiction over indictable criminal matters and unlimited jurisdiction in civil matters. Also hears appeals from lower courts.		The Court of Summary Jurisdiction deals with the less serious criminal cases. The Local Court hears civil matters where the amount claimed is less than $100,000. The court also deals with adoptions and some appeals from certain statutory office holders or bodies.
Queensland (Qld)	*Supreme Court of Queensland — Court of Appeal*	*Supreme Court of Queensland — Trial Division*	*Queensland District Court*	*Magistrates Court*
	The Court of Appeal is a division of the Supreme Court and hears all appeals from the Supreme and District Courts, as well as many tribunals.	Hears the most serious criminal cases such as murder, manslaughter and serious drug offences, in addition to civil matters where the claims are for more than $250,000.	Hears more serious criminal cases (rape, armed robbery, etc.), Magistrate Court appeals, and civil cases for claims between $50,000 and $250,000.	The Magistrates Court deals with summary criminal offences (traffic offences, shoplifting, etc.) in addition to civil actions for claims less than $50,000. It also hears minor family law and taxation matters, child protection cases, social security cases, and cases dealing with domestic violence.
South Australia (SA)	*Supreme Court of South Australia*		*District Court of South Australia*	*Magistrates Court*
	This court is not only a trial court for the most important civil and criminal cases but is also an appellate court hearing appeals from lower courts.		Hears most civil matters and all indictable criminal matters except very serious matters such as treason and murder. Hears appeals from certain tribunals, boards and other agencies.	Deals with summary offences and civil matters for claims up to $40,000 (or $80,000 where the claim arises as a result of a motor vehicle accident).

405

State/Territory and Abbreviation	Highest State Court	Supreme Courts	District/County Courts	Court of Summary Jurisdiction
Tasmania (Tas)	Supreme Court of Tasmania — Court of Criminal Appeal and Full Court of the Supreme Court	Supreme Court of Tasmania		Magistrates Court
	Appeals from a single Supreme Court judge (and jury) are heard by three or more Supreme Court judges. In criminal matters, this is called the Court of Criminal Appeal. In Civil matters, it is called the Full Court of the Supreme Court.	Jurisdiction over indictable offences, and all civil matters (although only claims for more than $50,000 are heard here). Hears appeals from Magistrates Courts and most tribunals.	Deals with summary offences and civil law matters for claims of up to $50,000.	
Victoria (Vic)	Supreme Court of Victoria — Court of Appeal	Supreme Court of Victoria — Trial Division	County Court	Magistrates Court
	Hears appeals from Supreme and County Court trials and appeals of proceedings from certain administrative tribunals.	Hears major criminal matters, civil cases with claims over $200,000, certain appeals from inferior courts and tribunals, and other assorted matters including bail applications and winding up of corporations	Hears appeals from Magistrates Court, as well as all indictable criminal cases except very serious matters such as treason and murder. Hears civil cases involving personal injuries and other personal actions. Also hears probate, adoptions, and property matters.	Hears all summary offences and certain indictable offences (e.g., theft). Also hears civil matters involving claims up to $100,000.
Western Australia (WA)	Supreme Court of Western Australia — Court of Appeal	Supreme Court of Western Australia — General Division	District Courts	Magistrates Court
	Appellate jurisdiction over decisions made by one judge in the Supreme Court, as well as jurisdiction over other lower courts and certain tribunals.	Hears major criminal matters, civil cases with claims over $750,000, probate and wills disputes, corporate matters, admiralty, etc.	Serious criminal offences (with a max. sentence of 20 years' imprisonment), civil law cases with claims up to $750,000 (and an unlimited amount for personal injuries), and motor vehicle injury cases.	Deals with minor criminal offences and civil matters involving claims up to $75,000.

New Zealand

The Supreme Court of New Zealand is the final court of appeal, and the highest court in the country. Prior to its establishment in 2004, it was still possible to appeal cases to the Privy Council in London. The Court of Appeal is New Zealand's intermediate appellate court, while the High Court is a trial court which deals with the more serious criminal and civil matters and hears appeals from lower courts and tribunals. District courts deal with minor civil and criminal cases. In addition, New Zealand has specialized courts dealing with specific matters (e.g., Environment Court, Employment Court, Maori Court) and a variety of tribunals.

Case Law — Print and Online

AustLII is a free and surprisingly large database for Australian and New Zealand cases (http://www.austlii.edu.au/) which may or may not have been reported. If you are looking for specific court websites, the National Library of Australia, located at http://www.nla.gov.au/oz/law.html, also has a useful and quite comprehensive list of sites.

Better search results will require a subscription (fee-based) database such as Westlaw (which has as its primary focus in the U.S. but contains full-text legislation, case law and journal articles from several other jurisdictions including Australia, and New Zealand) or LexisNexis along with their local incarnations: Australia's Legal Online (Thomson Reuters) and LexisNexis AU (Australia), and New Zealand's LexisNexis NZ and Brookers Online (Thomson Reuters). Linxplus is put together by the Law Society libraries of NZ, and is available via LexisNexis NZ. It provides access to several decades of case law, unreported and reported, and a journal index. CCH Online contains a number of loose-leaf services available through CCH in addition to case law, commentary and legislation.

Law Reports Chart

Law Report (Abbreviation) ** = Authorized/Official Law Reports	Law Report (Abbreviation)
Administrative Appeals Reports (AAR)	Federal Law Reports (FLR)
Administrative Law Decisions (ALD) **	Industrial Arbitration Reports NSW AR (NSW)
Australian Bankruptcy Cases,1928–1964 (ABC)	Industrial Reports (IR)
Australian Capital Territory Law Reports 2008- (ACTLR) **	Intellectual Property Reports (IPR)
Australian Capital Territory Reports (ACTR)	Local Government and Environmental Reports of Australia (LGERA)
Australian Company Law Cases (ACLC)	Motor Vehicle Reports (MVR)
Australian Company Law Reports (ACLR)	New South Wales Conveyancing Cases (NSW ConvR)
Australian Consumer Credit Reports (ACCR)	New South Wales Law Reports 1825–1900 (NSWLR) **
Australian Contract Reports (Aust Contract Reports)	New Zealand Administrative Reports (NZAR)
Australian Corporations and Securities Reports (ACSR)	New Zealand District Court Reports (NZDCR)
Australian Criminal Reports (A Crim R)	New Zealand Family Law Reports (NZFLR)
Australian Income Tax Reports: Australian & New Zealand Income Tax Reports (AITR)	New Zealand Law Reports (NZLR) ** (Court of Appeal & High Court Cases)
Australian Industrial Law Reports (AILR)	New Zealand Resource Management Appeals (NZRMA)
Australian Intellectual Property Cases (AIPC)	New Zealand Tax Cases (NZTC)
Australian Law Journal Reports (ALJR)	Northern Territory Law Reports (NTLR) **
Australian Law Reports (ALRZ)	Queensland Conveyancing Cases (Q ConvR)
Australian Planning Appeal Decisions (APA)	Queensland Reports (Qd R) **
Australian Securities Law Reporter (ASR)	South Australian Law Reports 1865–1920 (SALR) **

Law Report (Abbreviation) ** = Authorized/Official Law Reports	Law Report (Abbreviation)
Australian Tax Cases (ATC) Australian Tax Reports (ATR) Australian Torts Reports (Aust Torts Reports) Australian Trade Practices Reports (ATPR) Butterworths Property Reports (BPR) Commonwealth Law Reports (CLR) ** (High Court of Australia) District Court Law Reports (NSW) (DCLR (NSW)) Equal Opportunity Cases (EOC) Family Law Cases (FLC) Family Law Reports (Fam LR) Federal Court Reports (FCR) ** (Federal Court of Australia)	South Australian State Reports (SASR) ** State Reports NSW 1901–1970 (SR NSW) ** State Reports. Queensland 1902–57 (St R Qd) ** State Reports. South Australia 1921–71 ** (SRSA) Tasmanian Reports (Tas R) ** Tasmanian Law Reports 1897–1940 (TLR) ** Victorian Conveyancing Cases (V ConvR) Victorian Law Reports 1875–1956 (VLR) ** Victorian Reports (VR) ** Western Australian Law Reports 1899–1959 (WALR) ** Western Australian Reports (WAR) ** Northern Territory Law Reports (NTLR) **

Citation

Citation styles for cases are very much like those in Canada where the style of cause appears first (*Mabo v Queensland (No.2)*), followed by the date (1992), a volume number (175), an abbreviation to a print reporter (CLR) and a page number (1):

Mabo v. Queensland (No.2) (1992), 175 C.L.R. 1 (Australia H.C.)

The Australian Guide to Legal Citation is available online through the Melbourne University Law Review Association at http://mulr.law.unimelb.edu.au/files/aglcdl.pdf.

Since 1998, Australian courts have used medium neutral case citations in which the reference is to the court itself rather than to a print reporter,

e.g., *Murray v. R*, [2002] HCA 26

where HCA stands for High Court of Australia and 26 is the 26th case decided in the year 2002. The frequently used abbreviations are:

Federal Courts	States and Territory Supreme Courts
HCA High Court of Australia	*ACTSC* Supreme Court of Australian Capital Territory
FCA Federal Court of Australia	
FamCA Family Court of Australia	*NSWSC* Supreme Court of New South Wales
IRComnA Australian Industrial Relations Commission	
	NTSC Supreme Court of the Northern Territory
IRCA Industrial Relations Court of Australia	
	QLDSC Supreme Court of Queensland
RRTA Refugee Review Tribunal of Australia	
	SASC Supreme Court of South Australia
IRTA Immigration Review Tribunal (of Australia)	
	TASSC Supreme Court of Tasmania
AATA Administrative Appeals Tribunal (of Australia)	
	VICSC Supreme Court of Victoria
NNTTA National Native Title Tribunal (of Australia)	*WASC* Supreme Court of Western Australia

Legislation

Bills

In the Australian federal parliament, Bills may be introduced either in the House of Representatives or in the Senate; however, spending and taxation Bills must originate in the House of Representatives. In the House, a Bill begins with the Member giving written notice that the Bill will be introduced. At its introduction, the Minister responsible for the Bill formally presents it, then the Clerk of the House reads its long title which is the first reading. At this point, copies of the Bill are distributed to members, and the Member makes a motion that the Bill be read a second time.

Several days to several weeks later, the Bill is debated. Debates can be short or long; however, once the debate is concluded, the Member's motion that the Bill be read a second time is voted on. If the vote is successful, the Clerk of the House once again reads out the long title of the Bill.

The Bill is then sent either to the Committee of the Whole House or to the Main Committee (an alternative to consideration by the entire House generally where the Bill's subject matter is not as controversial) for consideration in detail, although Members may agree to omit this stage if they feel it is not necessary. In certain circumstances, Members may also send the Bill to an advisory committee. If the Bill does go to the Committee stage, the Committee studies the Bill in detail and makes recommendations regarding potential changes to the Bill. Bills which go to the Main Committee or an advisory Committee must be reported back to the House at which point the House will consider and debate the contents of the report.

The final stage involves the Member making a motion that the Bill be read a third time. If the motion is successful, the Clerk reads the long title of the Bill once again. It is then sent to the Senate where it must also go through three readings.

Bills must be agreed to in identical form by both Houses of Parliament in order to become law. Where disagreements exist, both Houses must work to resolve them. The final stage then is the Governor General's assent to the Bill. Bills often come into effect at this point, but not necessarily. The Bill might contain a certain date on which it will come into effect or a statement that it will come into effect on proclamation (a date announced by the Government and proclaimed by the Governor General). Where no date is specified, the Act will come into effect 28 days after assent.

The federal government along with New South Wales, Victoria, Tasmania, South Australia and Western Australia all have two Houses of Parliament. Queensland, the Australian Capital Territory, the Northern Territory, and Norfolk Island (which has a legislative assembly made up of nine members) all have unicameral legislative assemblies which do not require a Bill to go through two sets of Readings. In total, nine Australian jurisdictions have the power to enact legislation.

In New Zealand, Bills are introduced in the New Zealand House of Representatives (there is no second chamber). First Reading offers the first chance for debate after which there is a vote. If the Bill is successful at this stage (i.e., if members decide it should be read a first time), it is sent to a select committee which will study the Bill and suggest changes.

A report by the Committee on completion of its work is sent to the House of Representatives at which time members may once again debate the Bill and the report's recommendations. Members must agree to second reading in order to send the Bill to a Committee of the Whole House where debate takes place once again. Once debate has concluded, Members must vote on the Bill one final time (Third Reading). The final stage involves Royal Assent which requires the assent of the Monarch or New Zealand's Governor-General.

Where to find it: For access to Bills, see the "Internet Sources" chart below.

Statutes

Legislation for both Australia and New Zealand is published in pamphlet form when it is enacted and is then assembled annually in volumes that are organized chronologically according to the date of assent for each Act. The print version for the Commonwealth of Australia is entitled *Acts of the Par-*

411

liament of the Commonwealth of Australia and, in New Zealand, *New Zealand Statutes*. The multi-volume *Acts of the Australian Parliament, 1901–1973* (published from1972–77) is another Australian official publication in print.

A commercial source for print legislation in Australia is *Australian Current Law — Legislation* published by LexisNexis Butterworths. In addition, commercial publishers offer a variety of versions of legislation both in print (loose-leaf or hardbound, annotated or not) and online.

Commonwealth Statutes Annotations published by Lawbook Co. (Thomson Reuters) provides information on principal Commonwealth Acts including amendments and updates on statutes judicially considered. *Federal Statutes Annotations* published by LexisNexis Butterworths provides information on Acts and subordinate legislation including amendments, "in force" information, information on statutes judicially considered and more.

In terms of keeping current, *Australian Current Law* (LexisNexis Butterworths) contains information on changes to statutes, regulations and other statutory instruments in all jurisdictions. Legislation is updated each month, and each year, the *Yearbooks* consolidate all the information on legislation from the previous year. *Australian Legal Monthly Digest* (Thomson Reuters) is published every two weeks and also contains information on recent legislative developments. Both sources are available in print and online.

Online, AustLII provides access to legislation for the Commonwealth and the states/territories. In addition, the Commonwealth has its own database for legislation, ComLaw (see chart below) which provides access to Commonwealth Acts, subordinate legislation, and more.

Legislation: Internet Sources Chart

Jurisdiction	Website	
General	AUSTLII	http://www.austlii.edu.au/
Databases	National Library of Australia	http://www.nla.gov.au/oz/law.html
(or lists of links)	ComLaw	http://www.comlaw.gov.au/
Federal	Bills	http://www.aph.gov.au/bills/index.htm (From 1996/97 to present)
	Acts	http://www.comlaw.gov.au/ComLaw/ legislation/act1.nsf/sh/browse& CATEGORY=act (as originally passed from 1973 to present)

Jurisdiction	Website	
	Regulations, etc.	http://www.comlaw.gov.au/ (FRLI section of ComLaw)
	Gazette	http://www.publications.gov.au/gazettes.html
Australian Capital Territory (ACT)	Bills	http://www.legislation.act.gov.au/
	Legislation	http://www.legislation.act.gov.au/
	Regulations, etc.	http://www.legislation.act.gov.au/
	Gazette	http://www.gazettes.act.gov.au/
New South Wales (NSW)	Bills	http://www.parliament.nsw.gov.au/prod/ parlment/nswbills.nsf/V3BillsHome
	Legislation	http://www.legislation.nsw.gov.au/
	Regulations, etc.	http://www.legislation.nsw.gov.au/
	Gazette	http://www.advertising.nswp.commerce. nsw.gov.au/Gazette/Gazette.htm
Norfolk Island (NF)	Bills	http://www.info.gov.nf/
	Legislation	http://www.info.gov.nf/
	Regulations, etc.	http://www.info.gov.nf/
Northern Territory (NT)	Bills	http://www.dcm.nt.gov.au/strong_service _delivery/ supporting_government/ register_of_legislation
	Legislation	http://www.nt.gov.au/lant/hansard/hansard. shtml
	Regulations, etc.	http://www.austlii.edu.au/databases.html
Queensland (Qld)	Bills	http://www.legislation.qld.gov.au/Bill_ Pages/bills_home.htm
	Legislation	http://www.legislation.qld.gov.au/ OQPChome.htm
	Regulations, etc.	http://www.austlii.edu.au/databases.html
	Gazette	http://www.goprint.qld.gov.au/web/web/ index.asp?Pg=31
South Australia (SA)	Bills	http://www.parliament.sa.gov.au/ BillsMotions/
	Legislation	http://www.legislation.sa.gov.au/index.aspx

Jurisdiction	Website	
	Regulations	http://www.legislation.sa.gov.au/index.aspx
	Gazette	http://www.governmentgazette.sa.gov.au
Tasmania	Bills	http://www.parliament.tas.gov.au/
(Tas)	Legislation	http://www.thelaw.tas.gov.au/index.w3p
	Gazette	http://www.publicinfo.tas.gov.au/
Victoria	Bills	http://www.legislation.vic.gov.au/
(Vic)	Legislation	http://www.legislation.vic.gov.au/
	Gazette	http://www.gazette.vic.gov.au/
Western	Bills	http://www.slp.wa.gov.au/index.html
Australia	Acts	http://www.slp.wa.gov.au/index.html
(WA)	Regulations, etc.	http://www.slp.wa.gov.au/index.html
	Gazette	http://www.slp.wa.gov.au/gazette/gazette.nsf
New	Bills	http://www.legislation.govt.nz/
Zealand	Legislation	http://www.legislation.govt.nz/
	Regulations, etc.	http://www.legislation.govt.nz/

Delegated or Subordinate Legislation

Delegated or subordinate legislation is known by a variety of names including regulations, orders, rules, notices, determinations, proclamations, and warrants. These terms are used to describe the laws written by ministries, agencies, crown corporations, local public bodies, the governing bodies of professions or occupations and others for the rules and detailed procedures needed to administer the statutes enacted by parliaments. In Australia, both national and state governments can, via statute, assign the power to make delegated or subordinate legislation (the rules, regulations, ordinances, by-laws, etc. mentioned above which are also called "legislative instruments") to the types of individuals, groups or bodies described above. A number of Acts also allow the Governor General to make regulations on the advice of Ministers in order to give effect to the statute. Delegated legislation can also come into existence via letters patent.[4] Some delegated legislation (but not all) is published in an annual numbered series entitled the

---

[4] Letters Patent are a type of law which comes into being under the Royal Prerogative (the residual powers of the Monarch which are left over from ancient times). The government, pursuant to s. 61 of the Constitutions, may make Letters Patent and ask the Monarch to sign them. Most of these appear, after signing, in the *Commonwealth of Australia Gazette*.

Statutory Rules Series. It is also available online via AustLII and through government websites (see chart above).

In New Zealand, the government delegates the creation of statutory regulations to individuals, groups or bodies. They may also be made by the Governor General in Council. The official publication in print is the annual *Statutory Regulations Series.* They are also available online through the New Zealand Legislation website (see chart above).

Treaties

Australian treaties, which are negotiated by the Commonwealth government, are located in the *Australian Treaties Series* published by the Australian Department of Foreign Affairs and Trade. In electronic form, treaties to which Australia is a signatory or on which Australia has taken some other action are available through the Department of Foreign Affairs and Trade (DFAT) Australian Treaties Database (ATD) at http://www.dfat. gov.au/treaties/index.html. Otherwise, treaties are available through AustLII at http://www.austlii.edu.au/au/other/dfat/.

The *New Zealand Treaty Series* is published in print; however, treaties are also published as part of the *Appendix to the Journal of the House of Representatives.* Several decades of the *Treaty Series* is also available online through NZLII at http://www.nzlii.org/nz/other/mfat/NZTS/.

Secondary Sources

Monographs

Until quite recently, Australians and New Zealanders relied largely on English legal texts, but legal publishing in Australia and New Zealand is on the rise. Perhaps the best place to look for books on a particular topic is the National Library of Australia catalogue located at http://catalogue.nla.gov.au/. The catalogues of the legal publishers (LexisNexis Australia: http://www.lexisnexis.com.au/; Thomson Reuters Australia: www.thomsonreuters.com.au/; and the Federation Press: http://www.federationpress.com.au/) are also worth searching for newer publications.

Legal Periodicals

Law journals from both Australia and New Zealand, in addition to being available in print, are available electronically through a variety of sources. Indexing services which in the past contained citations only now generally offer at least some full-text articles. Below are a number of the most useful databases; all are fee-based and require a subscription:

- *AGIS (Attorney-General's Information Service) and AGISPlusText (1975+)* — indexes Australian and New Zealand journals, government documents, documents authored by some not-for-profit organizations and law reform commissions. It provides some full-text access and also contains additional material from overseas;
- *APAIS (Australian Public Affairs Information Service) Plus Text* — indexes scholarly articles, books and conference proceedings in the social sciences, humanities and law;
- *HeinOnline* — although primarily American in focus, some full-text Australian and New Zealand journals are available;
- *Index to Legal Periodicals* — covers approximately 1,000 legal journals, law reviews, yearbooks, bar association materials and institute and government publications from a variety of countries including Australia and New Zealand. It is available in print for the years 1926–1987, and available electronically pre and post-1981;
- *Legal Online* (Thomson Reuters — formerly known as LawBook Online) — in addition to containing case law, the case citator Firstpoint and the legal encyclopedia, *Laws of Australia*. Legal Online also provides access to a select number of Australian journals available as full-text in addition to loose-leaf titles;
- *LegalTrac and Current Law Index* — *LegalTrac* indexes approximately 1,000 titles covering legal journals and law reviews, case comments, legal newspapers, bar association journals and more, from a variety of countries including Australia and New Zealand. *Current Law Index* (1980-present) is a monthly print publication which covers most of the same content as *LegalTrac*;
- *LexisNexis AU — CaseBase — CaseBase* contains case citations, digests and journal articles with links to full-text where available;
- *Westlaw & LexisNexis* — contains databases with full-text legal articles and other commentary from a number of jurisdictions including Australia and New Zealand.

Some full-text access to journal articles is also available in the databases section of AustLII at http://www.austlii.edu.au/databases.html.

Legal Encyclopedias

Two legal encyclopedias cover Australian law: *Halsbury's Laws of Australia* (LexisNexis) and *The Laws of Australia* (Thomson Reuters). Both are available in print and online, and both are arranged using broad subject areas subdivided into more discrete categories. The titles (which are chapter-like sections) in each volume of these encyclopedias contain a table of contents, a table of cases and a table of legislation/statutes. Titles consist of discrete paragraphs numbered with square brackets.

The Laws of Australia consists of 36 titles in over 50 loose-leaf binders summarizing most areas of Australian Law. A consolidated index organized alphabetically by subject also contains a section on words and phrases legally defined. The Consolidated Table of Cases and the Consolidated Table of Legislation list all cases and legislation (including subordinate legislation and international conventions) referred to in the work. Blue supplement sheets update each title.

Halsbury's Laws of Australia organizes statements of legal principle using broad subject headings ("titles") organized alphabetically and subdivided into more discrete categories. The index volume is the best place to start when searching by subject. The volume will point to the desired title (if not immediately obvious, the "Title Locator" will help). The Table of Cases can also be used to find relevant information in the main volumes. All of this information is updated by *Australian Current Law — Reporter* which uses identical titles.

To find legislation, the Table of Statutes will point to the appropriate volume. Updating this information will require looking in later issues of *Australian Current Law — Legislation* which uses the same title and numbering scheme found in *Halsbury's Laws of Australia*.

In New Zealand, *The Laws of New Zealand* (LexisNexis), a loose-leaf encyclopedia consisting of approximately 40 volumes containing 150 subject titles, covers all aspects of the law. The set also contains cross references to *Halsbury's Laws of England* and *Halsbury's Laws of Australia*.

Legal Dictionaries and Words and Phrases

Australia has several legal dictionaries while New Zealand has a proportionately smaller selection. Below are some of the titles you are likely to encounter:

- *Australian Law Dictionary* (Melbourne, Vic: Oxford University Press, 2009);
- *Australian Legal Words and Phrases* (North Ryde: Butterworths, 1993-). This service is updated annually by cumulative supplements and is also available online through LexisNexis AU;
- *Blackstone's Australian Legal Words & Phrases Simplified* (Bondi Junction, N.S.W.: Blackstone Press, 1993);
- *Butterworths Australian Legal Dictionary* (Sydney: LexisNexis, 1998);
- *Butterworths Concise Australian Legal Dictionary*, 3d ed. (Chatswood, N.S.W.: LexisNexis Butterworths, 2004);

- *Butterworths Encyclopaedic Australian Legal Dictionary* (available through LexisNexis AU);
- *CCH Macquarie Dictionary of Law*, rev. ed. (North Ryde: CCH Australia, 2001);
- *Legal Dictionary For Australians*, 2d ed. (Sydney: McGraw-Hill, 2005);
- *New Zealand Law Dictionary* (Wellington: LexisNexis, 2005);
- *New Zealand Legal Words and Phrases* (Wellington: Butterworths, 1995) and 2001 update (also available via LexisNexis AU);
- *Words and Phrases Legally Defined*, 3d ed. (Sydney: Butterworths, 1988-).

Law Reform

Australia has set up a permanent body to investigate and report on areas of potential law reform. The Australian Law Reform Commission is an independent federal statutory corporation which has changed the shape of Australia's federal laws and legal processes in a number of ways since it first came into existence in 1975. The Commission's website at http://www.alrc.gov.au/ offers full-text access to a number of its publications including final and annual reports, consultation papers, etc. To find information about older law reform publications, *The Law Reform Digest: A Digest Of The Reports Of Law Reform Agencies In Australia, New Zealand And Papua New Guinea 1910–1980* published by the Australian Government Publishing Service in 1983, and Volume 2, *The Law Reform Digest: A Supplementary Digest Of The Reports Of Law Reform Agencies In Australia, Fiji, New Zealand And Papua New Guinea, 1980–85* published in 1985 are both useful.

Digests

The *Australian Digest*, 3d ed. is a loose-leaf service organized by broad subject headings, summarizing cases as far back as 1825. It also provides information on related proceedings and references to articles which discuss the cases. It is updated by the *Australian Legal Monthly Digest*. Each title has yellow "Supplement" pages which update that particular subject. The service also contains a list of words and phrases judicially considered in cases summarized. The *Australian Digest* is available online (Thomson Reuters).

Australian Current Law — Reporter (LexisNexis) provides digests for cases recently decided by the high court, federal court and state supreme courts before they are reported. The parts are published monthly, and at the end of the year are consolidated into the *Current Law Yearbook* for that year.

In New Zealand, the *Abridgment* summarizes all reported cases from the official series, *New Zealand Law Reports* (1861–1994) in 18 volumes and a number of permanent supplements. It includes an alphabetical list of words and phrases judicially considered in New Zealand from 1861–1973. The work has limited use because it digests cases from only one reporter.

Case Citators

The *Australian Case Citator* contains all reported cases from 1825 to present along with information on whether subsequent courts and secondary sources (i.e., journal articles) have considered/discussed a given case. The service also provides information on whether the case has been applied, approved, followed, considered, overturned, disapproved, not followed, or distinguished in subsequent cases. The *Australian Case Citator* is available in print and online through FirstPoint (Thomson Reuters).

CaseBase, an electronic service available through LexisNexis AU, provides information on how a case has subsequently been considered by the courts and which secondary sources have discussed that case.

The *Australian and New Zealand Citator to the UK Reports* is useful for finding how English cases have been considered in the courts of Australia and New Zealand. It indicates whether cases have been affirmed, applied, distinguished, etc.

Australian Current Law ("ACL")

This publication consists of two parts: *Reporter* and *Legislation*, which provide up-to-date information on cases and statutes, as well as references to journal articles. The parts are published monthly and are then consolidated into a yearbook. *Australian Current Law, Reporter* contains summaries of cases from Australian (state/territory and federal) superior courts, while *Australian Current Law, Legislation* contains information about legislation for all jurisdictions organized by year, subject and jurisdiction. *Australian Current Law, Reporter* also contains a section on statutes judicially considered, words and phrases judicially considered, and references to secondary sources such as books and articles.

Australian Current Law subject headings mirror those in *Halsbury's Laws of England* up to 1990 after which they follow the subject headings in *Halsbury's Laws of Australia*, which ACL now updates.

Recommended Reading

Bott B., J.Cowley, and L.Falconer. *Nemes & Coss Effective Legal research*, 3d ed. (Sydney: LexisNexis Butterworths, 2007).

Campbell, E., Lee Poh-York, and J.Tooher. *Legal Research, Materials and Methods* (Sydney: Lawbook, 1996).

Carvan, J. *Understanding the Australian Legal System*, 5th ed. (Sydney: Thomson Reuters, 2005).

Cook, C. et al. *Laying Down the Law*, 7th ed. (Sydney: Butterworths, 2009).

Greville, M., J.S. Davidson and R. Scragg. *Legal Research and Writing in New Zealand* (Wellington: Butterworths, 2000).

Hutchinson, Terry. *Researching and Writing in Law*, 2d ed. (Pyrmond, NSW: Thomson, 2006).

McDowell, Morag and Duncan Webb. *The New Zealand Legal System: Structures, Process and Legal Theory*, 2d ed. (Wellington: Butterworths (NZ), 1998).

Meek, M. *The Australian Legal System*, 3d ed. (Pyrmont, NSW: LBC Information Services, 1999).

Milne, S. and K. Tucker. *A Practical Guide To Legal Research* (Pyrmont, NSW: Lawbook, 2008).

Morris, G. *et al. Laying Down The Law*, 7th ed. (Sydney: LexisNexis Butterworths, 2009).

Stuhmcke, A. *Legal Referencing*, 3d ed. (Sydney: Butterworths, 2005).

Vines, Prue. *Law & Justice in Australia* (Melbourne: Oxford UP, 2005).

Watt, R. *Concise Legal Research*, 6th ed. (Sydney: Federation Press, 2009).

22

International and Foreign Legal Research

As more and more legal problems now have an international component, the ability of Canadian researchers to find and make sense of the law of an international body or foreign jurisdiction has become essential. Purely domestic litigation can also benefit from research that takes a comparative law approach. Canadian courts will sometimes consider international law as a guideline for determining fundamental legal principles. Courts may also refer to the law of other jurisdictions where Canadian law is unclear or underdeveloped.[1]

Fortunately for Canadian researchers, the proliferation of international resources from official sources on the internet has made international legal research much easier and more accessible. In this chapter, we will discuss resources that are freely available via the internet as well as published resources which may be found in a larger law library. This chapter does not attempt to provide a comprehensive introduction to international law and institutions; instead, wherever possible, we will emphasize the practical resources that a Canadian researcher might typically use. For secondary sources on international law generally and its use in Canada, consult the Selective Topical Bibliography under "International Law".

One important distinction in this chapter is between "foreign" and "international" law. Foreign law is the domestic law of foreign jurisdictions. For example, searching for legislation from Italy would be considered foreign legal research. International law, by comparison, is the law between nations or between individuals and nations. We will first discuss international law research, and then consider foreign research.

---

[1] See Gibran van Ert, *Using International Law in Canadian Courts*, 2d ed. (Toronto: Irwin Law, 2008).

International Law

International law is a very broad and complex research topic. Because no single body creates international law, there is not always consensus on what "international law" is for a given subject or how it can be enforced. International law also raises issues about national sovereignty and how international institutions and agreements affect it. Despite (or perhaps because of) the fact that the basis for the legitimacy of international law is not as straightforward as the law of a sovereign nation, there is a large body of literature that addresses international law, its institutions and the effectiveness of international legal cooperation.

There are two main branches of international law: public international law and private international law.

Defining Public International Law

Public International Law (PIL) is concerned with the law between and among nations and the rights and duties of nation-states. It is sometimes referred to as the "Law of Nations." PIL is separate from domestic law although it can sometimes affect it, for example when a treaty commitment results in changes to domestic legislation.

PIL originates in the need for international cooperation on matters that affect more than one country. An early example is the signing of the *International Telegraph Convention*, 17 May 1865, 130 Consol. T.S. 198, by 20 European nations.[2] More contemporary examples include international treaties on refugees and world trade.

An important legitimacy consideration arises when one considers which bodies are competent to create and interpret international law. As there is no world government that can make public laws to govern relationships between nations, nations have to agree generally on what it is that makes up international law.

The most obvious source for this discussion is the United Nations (UN). As the world's largest international organization, the UN and its committees, councils, panels, etc. create a voluminous amount of official documentation, ranging from minutes of meetings to reports to treaties and decisions. Generally, most UN documents can be found on an official website via an internet search for the name of the document and/or its document number.[3]

---

[2] *ITU's History*, from the website of the International Telegraph Union: http://www.itu.int/net/about/history.aspx.

[3] UN documents are available through various UN sites; however, not everything exists in one location. It is possible, for example, that the UN document you require could be available through any of the following: Official Document System (ODS) of the United Nations (http://www.ods.un.org), the

If you are researching official sources for UN documents, you should consult an online or print research guide to the UN, its bodies and documentation.[4]

The International Court of Justice (ICJ) is the judicial organ of the United Nations. The *Statute of the International Court of Justice*[5] (which is annexed to the *Charter of the United Nations*, 24 October 1945, 1 U.N.T.S. XVI) comes closest to mapping out the sources of international law. Article 38 lists the following sources that it will apply when dealing with disputes:

> a. international conventions, whether general or particular, establishing rules expressly recognized by the contesting states;
>
> b. international custom, as evidence of a general practice accepted as law;
>
> c. the general principles of law recognized by civilized nations;
>
> d. subject to the provisions of Article 59, judicial decisions and the teachings of the most highly qualified publicists of the various nations, as subsidiary means for the determination of rules of law.

The first item in this list, international conventions, refers to treaties, agreements, conventions, charters and codes which are all recognized as "treaties" by the *Vienna Convention on the Law of Treaties*.[6] The second item, international custom, refers to evidence, provided by various primary (legislation, case law) and secondary sources (diplomatic interaction, government policy/decisions/practices, official manuals, press releases, etc.) that a certain practice or activity is accepted widely by nations. The third item, general principles of law, involves those principles common to major legal systems including rules of procedural fairness and *res judicata*. Finally, the "teachings of the most highly qualified publicists" refers to the writings and opinions of international groups (e.g., human rights groups) and internationally renowned lawyers, judges, and scholars.

This chapter will focus on the first and last items in this list: treaties and judicial decisions and scholarly writings.

Dag Hammarskjöld Library (http://www.un.org/Depts/dhl/), the UN Documentation Centre (http://www.un.org/documents), the Security Council (http://www.un.org/Docs/sc/), the General Assembly (http://www.un.org/ga/), or the UN High Commissioner for Human Rights (http://www.ohchr.org.).

4 See for example: *United Nations Documentation: Research Guide* (http://www.un.org/depts/dhl/resguide/) produced by the Dag Hammarskjöld Library.

5 6 L.N.T.S. 389.

6 *Vienna Convention on the Law of Treaties*, 23 May 1969, 1155 U.N.T.S., art 18 (entered into force 27 January 1980).

Treaties

Treaties and similar types of agreements are a major source of international law and can be between two (bilateral) or more (multilateral) nations. They can set out certain obligations that nations agree to, and/or set out aspirations including statements about ideals and hopes for the future.

The Vienna Convention on the Law of Treaties,[7] drafted by the International Commission of the United Nations, codifies what was formerly customary international law on how treaties are concluded, ratified and entered into force. It also contains rules on how a treaty may be amended, how signatories may choose to interpret or be bound by portions of a treaty (through the use of reservations,[8] declarations,[9] and derogations[10]), and how treaties can be terminated.

Generally, treaty research involves: a) locating treaties and information relating to treaties (e.g., history of negotiations and any reservations, declarations or derogations filed by states, and the status of treaties including number of parties, ratification and signatories, etc.), and b) determining whether and how national governments are required to implement those treaty provisions.

a) Locating Treaties and Determining Status

There are several tools, both print and online, which assist in locating treaties and determining their status. The *Multilateral Treaty Calendar* (The Hague: Martinus Nijhoff Publishers, 1998), available in print, for example, covers the years 1648–1995, and lists the names of treaties along with parties, signatures, dates, amendments, duration, termination, and status, along with citations indicating where the full-text of the treaty itself might be found. Treaties are listed chronologically.

The *Consolidated Treaty Series With Index 1648–1919* (New York: Oxford University Press, 1969) is the only collection of bilateral and multilateral treaties predating the United Nations by several hundred years. The

---

[7] *Ibid.*

[8] A reservation allows a State to declare that there might be a minor portion of the treaty with which it will not comply. The reservation allows a State to sign a treaty with which it does not fully agree; however, the reservation must be made at the time the treaty is signed, ratified, accepted, approved or acceded to, and it may not be contrary to its object or purpose. Certain treaties will prohibit the making of any reservations.

[9] Declarations drawn up by States and appended to treaties allow States to register their particular understanding or interpretation of a provision of the treaty, and what this might mean in terms of their compliance.

[10] Derogations allow a State to suspend the functioning of a portion of the treaty for a particular period of time, usually during times of national emergency.

League of Nations Treaty Series takes up where this series leaves off, covering the years 1920 to 1944. It is succeeded by the *United Nations Treaty Series* (1944 to present), published by the largest international treaty-creating body — the UN. Article 102 of the *Charter of the United Nations*[11] requires that "Every treaty and every international agreement entered into by any Member of the United Nations . . . shall as soon as possible be registered with the Secretariat and published by it." Not only are UN treaties available in print; the UN's Treaty Collection website is an excellent online source for treaties registered with the United Nations.[12]

Multilateral Treaties Deposited with the Secretary-General is published on an ongoing basis by the United Nations. It consolidates all information on multilateral treaties deposited with the Secretary-General including signatories, ratifications, accessions, reservations, declarations objections, etc. It is available in print and also online via the United Nations Treaty website.

In Canada, the major official source for treaties to which Canada is a party is the *Canada Treaty Series* (1928-) available in most academic law libraries. The Canada Treaty Information website[13] provides access to treaty information by country, subject and keyword. Treaties are also viewable according to whether they are bilateral, multilateral or plurilateral (i.e., more than two parties but less than many which would make it multilateral).

A noteworthy source for information on the application of treaties domestically is the *Canadian Statute Citations* component of the *Canadian Abridgment*. This service lists international documents including treaties, that have been considered by Canadian courts. For information on locating treaties in the United States, the United Kingdom, Australia and New Zealand, please see the sections on treaties located in the chapters on those jurisdictions.

There is a vast amount of secondary source material available on multilateral treaties. Books and journal articles can provide important information that may not be found in the official sources, including the political and legal context of a treaty, commentary and interpretation by leading scholars, and assessments of how effective a treaty has been in practice. Secondary sources will also discuss any jurisprudence arising from treaty enforcement as well as other related primary sources. Finding a book or journal that discusses your treaty can save you hours of research time and provide you with the citations that will make locating material in the official sources easier.

---

[11] http://www.un.org/en/documents/charter/.

[12] http://treaties.un.org/.

[13] http://www.treaty-accord.gc.ca/.

Almost all current multilateral treaties have their own website. These sites will usually include the full-text of the treaty, any related instruments, a description of the purpose of the treaty and a list of signatories. They might also include the *travaux preparatoires* — preparatory work used in drafting the treaty which may be used as a supplementary means of interpretation. It is important to note that information on the preparatory work leading up to a bilateral treaty is generally more difficult to find than it is for multilateral treaties.

b) Implementation

In order to fulfill treaty obligations, states often have to enact domestic law which implements treaty provisions. In Canada, the United Kingdom, Australia and New Zealand, Parliament must pass legislation in order to implement the treaty.

The U.S. Constitution, in contrast, allows treaties to become law (i.e., the treaty is "self-executing"[14]), without requiring additional domestic legislation, once the President has agreed to the treaty and the Senate has given its "Advice and Consent" on the matter. On occasion, however, the requisite number of two-thirds of the Senate has declined to give its advice and consent. As a result, in order to conclude international agreements without the possibility of the delays, the President is more likely to enter into "executive agreements" (which do not go to the Senate) with other countries, rather than treaties. There is a great deal of confusion regarding whether both treaties and executive agreements are self-executing and, in the absence of any obvious method with which to decide, courts have had to make decisions on a case-by-case basis. Treaties which specifically have a provision providing for domestic legislation, however, are not self-executing, and a search must be done for relevant legislation to determine if those provisions have been implemented.

In contrast, research involving countries with a parliamentary system will always require a search of domestic law to discover if treaty provisions have been implemented.

Guides to Treaty Research

Print:

- Anthony Aust, *Modern Treaty Law and Practice*, 2d ed. (Cambridge; New York: Cambridge University Press, 2007).

---

[14] An exception to this is that a treaty cannot enact a criminal law provision.

- Peter Calvert, *et. al. Treaties and Alliances of the World*, 8th ed. (London: John Harper, 2007).
- Scott Davidson, ed. *The Law of Treaties* (Aldershot, Hants, England; Burlington, Vt.: Ashgate/Dartmouth, 2004).
- Duncan B. Hollis, Merritt R. Blakeslee & L. Benjamin Ederington, eds. *National Treaty Law and Practice* (Leiden; Boston: Martinus Nijhoff Publishers, 2005).

Online:

- American Society of International Law (http://www.asil.org/resource/treaty1.htm)
- Columbia Law Library Guide to Treaty Research (www.law.columbia.edu/library/Research_Guides/internat_law/treaty_research)
- Harvard Law School Library — Finding Treaties: (http://www.law.harvard.edu/library/research/guides/int_foreign/finding-treaties-no-citation — ils.html)

Judicial Decisions / International Jurisprudence

A large number of international tribunals, arbitration panels, and treaty enforcement bodies exist to decide on disputes between states and to enforce the provisions of a treaty. Selected international law jurisprudence can be found in *International Legal Materials* and in the *International Law Reports*.

The most significant general tribunal is the International Court of Justice. The ICJ was established in 1945 and it is the principal judicial body of the United Nations. Its role is to apply international law to settle legal disputes that have been submitted to it by states and to give advisory opinions on legal questions referred to it by the United Nations and its agencies. Participation by states in a proceeding is voluntary, but if a state agrees to participate, it is obligated to comply with the Court's decision. The ICJ's website[15] is an excellent resource on the ICJ, its composition, basic documents and its decisions.

Other major tribunals include the International Criminal Court,[16] European Court of Justice,[17] European Court of Human Rights[18] and the Inter-

---

[15] http://www.icj-cij.org/.

[16] http://www.icc-cpi.int/.

[17] http://curia.europa.eu/.

[18] http://www.echr.coe.int.

American Court of Human Rights.[19] In addition to general tribunals, the UN has also set up tribunals to deal with specific issues such as the International Criminal Tribunal for the Former Yugoslavia[20] and the International Criminal Tribunal for Rwanda.[21]

Online, Westlaw and LexisNexis carry the decisions of a number of these courts. In addition, most bodies that issue decisions have websites that provide access to primary source material. Because international tribunals are not as prolific in issuing decisions as a domestic court, most tribunal websites will provide access to all of that tribunal's decisions and will also frequently include related materials such as evidence and transcripts of proceedings. As such, if your research involves an international judicial decision it is always wise to visit the website of the body issuing the decision.

An excellent online source that provides information about international courts, tribunals and arbitral panels is the Project on International Courts and Tribunals.[22]

Researching Public International Law

Books

Public international law research is in many ways no different than any of the other research areas discussed in this book. It is always wise to consult the wide array of secondary sources available (books, journals and encyclopedias, etc.) to help you understand the topic and to lead you to the primary sources. In addition to the titles listed in the Selective Topical Bibliography, there are highly regarded treatises on most international legal topics. The catalogue of an academic law library or a published or online research guide are the best places to search for subject-specific treatises.

Periodicals

The major periodical that publishes primary international law materials is *International Legal Materials* (I.L.M.) published by the American Society of International Law. It is available at most academic law libraries and via Westlaw Canada, LexisNexis Quicklaw and *HeinOnline.* I.L.M. publishes significant international legal materials, including important new treaties, judicial decisions, and other documents.

---

[19] http://www.corteidh.or.cr/.

[20] http://www.icty.org/.

[21] http://www.ictr.org/.

[22] http://www.pict-pcti.org/.

In addition to books, journal articles can be helpful resources for understanding international law, especially if you are researching an emerging or controversial topic. The principles discussed in Chapter 8 (Legal Periodicals) apply to journal research in international law as well.

International law literature is covered in the following indexes, all of which are discussed in the Legal Periodicals chapter:

- *Index to Foreign Legal Periodicals*;
- *LegalTrac*;
- *Index to Legal Periodicals*;
- *Index to Legal Periodicals Retrospective.*

Research Guides

When researching public international law, it is almost always safe to assume that someone (often a librarian) has tried to organize materials on a specific topic into a research guide. Research guides provide access to both easy-to-find and hidden resources on the internet as well as primary and secondary sources in print and leading commercial online resources. Some major research guides include:

Print:

- George Washington University International Law Review, *Guide to International Legal Research* (Newark, NJ: LexisNexis, 2008). This is an annual publication that covers primary and secondary sources.

Online:

- American Society of International Law (http://www.asil.org/ resource/Home.htm): An excellent guide to electronic resources in international law.
- Globalex — International Law Guides (http://www.nyulawglobal. com/globalex/index.html): The "International Law Research" section of this site provides updated research guides for a number of international law subjects.
- LLRX International Law Guides (http://www.llrx.com/ international_law.html): While guides on this site are not always updated in a timely fashion, the range of subjects covered here makes this site worth consulting.

Researching Private International Law

Private international law is the law that applies to private transactions that cross borders, and deals with the application of domestic law in an international context. Each country has its own rules for how to proceed when a private legal dispute may involve the law of more than one country — in other words, where there may be a conflict of laws between two legal systems. The body of law that considers which country's laws will prevail in a particular transaction or dispute is generally called "conflict of laws".

Conflict of laws situations can arise in a number of contexts. For example: someone from Toronto marries someone from Alberta in Bermuda and they move to France and adopt a child from the United States. If they later separate, it would be a potential conflict of laws issue to determine which laws will govern divorce, division of marital property, custody and access.

Attempts to resolve conflicts have resulted in bilateral and multilateral treaties and conventions. The main international treaty is the *Hague Conference on Private International Law*.[23]

The best starting point for conflict of laws research is to consult one of the leading treatises listed in the Selective Topical Bibliography under "Conflict of Laws".

Foreign Law

Foreign law research requires you to find and interpret the domestic law of a foreign country. A transaction or dispute that crosses borders may involve research into the law of another jurisdiction. Foreign law may also be valuable as a comparator. Canadian courts will sometimes consider foreign laws when Canadian law is silent or uncertain.[24]

Prior to the internet, only large law libraries such as Harvard or Yale held extensive print collections of primary sources of foreign law. The internet has changed everything as countries around the world now post legislation and sometimes case law on their official websites.

Despite the ubiquitous nature of the internet, however, most foreign law continues to be available in the language of that country only. A researcher interested in Swedish family law, for example, will likely have to know how to read Swedish. As a result, the major fee-based legal databases have focused their efforts primarily on providing material from jurisdictions with materials in English and with a legal system of more immediate interest to our own: i.e., the United States, United Kingdom, Australia and New Zealand.

---

[23] http://www.hcch.net/index_en.php.

[24] For example, in *Society of Composers, Authors & Music Publishers of Canada v. Canadian Association of Internet Providers*, [2004] 2 S.C.R. 427 the Court considered a number of international treaties as well as foreign legislation in determining whether music servers located outside of Canada are subject to a royalty.

One major development in access to foreign law is the rise of the Legal Information Institute (LII) movement. Legal Information Institutes aim to provide free access to primary materials from around the world. In Canada, CanLII (www.canlii.org) provides free access to current legislation and case law. The major jurisdictions covered in this book all have a Legal Information Institute. If you are researching the law of a foreign jurisdiction, you will want to check if a LII website is available. While most LII sites do not provide analysis they are good sources for primary materials. The WorldLII website[25] provides links to other LII sites as well as to basic materials from around the world.

Despite the fact that much foreign law is online, if you are required to determine what the law on a topic is in another jurisdiction, your first step should be to consult a secondary source or a research guide. If you are researching the law of a non-English speaking country, finding a book in English that deals with your topic is a great start. This will lead you to the appropriate primary sources and also provide analysis of the relevant law. There is a great deal published on the foreign treatment of some legal topics. If you cannot find a treatise, a research guide will lead you to the official sources and provide background on the nation's legal system.

Some key secondary sources on foreign law include:

- Reynolds, Thomas H. and Arturo A. Flores. *Foreign Law: Current Sources of Codes and Basic Legislation in Jurisdictions of the World*, loose-leaf (Littleton, CO: F.B. Rothman, 1989-).

  .... *Foreign Law Guide* (online database: http://www.foreignlawguide.com/).

  Reynolds and Flores is the best starting point for researching the law of another country. Both the print and online versions provide descriptions of the legal systems of over 170 jurisdictions and offer subject-based access to primary and secondary sources of law. If a foreign law is available online whether in the country's official language or in English, Reynolds and Flores will provide a link.

- *Wolters Kluwer — International Encyclopaedia of Laws* — This work consists of country-by-country descriptions on how those national legal systems govern various areas of law including labour law, intellectual property, constitutional law, environmental law, social security law, energy law, civil procedure law, family and succession law, contracts, intergovernmental organizations, medical law and so on.

---

[25] http://www.worldlii.org/.

- Germain, Claire, *Germain's Transnational Law Research*, loose-leaf (Ardsley-on-Hudson, NY: Transnational Juris Publications, 1991-).
- *Martindale-Hubbell International Law Digest*. This digest is in many law firm library collections and contains short summaries by topic for 80 countries. Each summary has references to primary sources.
- Redden, Kenneth Robert ed., *Modern Legal Systems Cyclopedia* (Buffalo: W.S. Hein, 1984-). A multi-volume set of introductions to the legal systems of over 120 jurisdictions.

There are many online research guides to foreign law including:

- Globalex (http://www.nyulawglobal.org/globalex/). The "Foreign Law Research" section of this website provides research guides to the laws of over 120 countries.
- NYU Foreign Law Guide: (http://www.law.nyu.edu/library/research/foreign_intl/index.htm).
- Cornell University Law School Legal Information Institute — Law by Source — Global. (http://www.law.cornell.edu/world/).

If you are researching the law of a foreign jurisdiction, you may also find it necessary to refer to that nation's constitution to better understand its legal system and values. Most countries make their constitution available on their website. If you cannot find an English translation on the internet, *Constitutions of the Countries of the World*[26] is an excellent guide that provides English translations and amendment histories for many countries.

---

[26] Albert P. Blaustein & Gisbert H. Flanz, eds., loose-leaf (Dobbs Ferry, N.Y.: Oceana Publications, 1971-).

23

Guidelines for Writing: Legal Essays, Case Comments, and Legal Memoranda

This chapter offers guidelines on writing legal essays, case comments, and legal memoranda. The major focus of the chapter, however, is on legal memoranda (Appendix I contains a sample legal memorandum). We have chosen legal memoranda as our focus because it is almost certain that articling students and associates will be required to write numerous memoranda, and many never will have seen or written one before. Also, since legal memoranda are not published, it can be difficult to find useful examples.[1] In contrast, examples of essays and case comments are readily available in law journals.

General Comments

Writing Style

A discussion of grammar and writing style is beyond the scope of this chapter. Suffice it to say that poor grammar and a weak writing style will confuse the reader. Complex sentence structures and a verbose writing style should be avoided. A simple, easy-to-read style is infinitely more effective.[2] Legal documents must be persuasive, concise, and clear. Writing legal documents, especially those to be filed in court, differs from writing other types of documents in that the former are meant to persuade and advocate for a particular issue or client. Literary devices may be appropriate for a novel, but not for a factum that is being filed in court or for a legal memorandum you have written for a partner.

---

[1] Many law firms and legal departments in larger organizations will have a legal memoranda database.

[2] See e.g., Margaret E. McCallum, Deborah A. Schmedemann, & Christina L. Kunz, *Synthesis: Legal Reading, Reasoning and Writing in Canada* (Toronto: CCH Canadian, 2008) and Thomas A. Cromwell, *Effective Written Advocacy* (Aurora, Ont: Canada Law Book, 2008).

Organization

An effective piece of legal writing will be organized in a logical manner that is easy to follow and understand. Inappropriate organization can mislead the reader and obscure legal argument and analysis.

Two things should drive the organization scheme you choose for your written work: the subject matter and audience. Each subject tends to have its own logic. An understanding of this logic will assist you in finding the most rational places to put headings and subheadings. The use of headings and subheadings makes your document more user-friendly and allows you to move logically from one topic to the other.

In organizing your document, you should keep in mind your audience's interests and level of understanding. A paper on recent amendments to the *Criminal Code*[3] written for a non-legal private sector audience, for example, would be different from a paper written for a strictly legal audience. Those not trained in law may not be familiar with legal terminology, court structure, or legislative history. The complexity and depth of your document should depend on the audience for which it is written.

Use of Gender-Neutral Language

Historically, the masculine gender has been assumed to be the norm. This is evidenced by terms such as "mankind", "manpower", "layman", and the use of "he" as a generic pronoun. The inherent gender bias in our language is inconsistent with the goal of achieving equality between the sexes in the workplace and in society. Accordingly, we recommend using gender-neutral language. If you find it awkward or clumsy to constantly repeat the pronouns "he or she," you may use plurals or alternate in a consistent way between using the masculine and feminine pronoun.

Legal Essays

There are many types of legal essays. For instance, an essay may:

- analyze and report on trends in an area of law and speculate on future developments;
- suggest reforms to the existing law;
- apply a theoretical framework to an area of law;
- examine the law from a historical perspective; or
- compare the law in different jurisdictions.

---

[3] R.S.C. 1985, c. C-46.

The parameters of a legal essay are generally left to the author's discretion. The introduction to your paper should clearly define these for the reader. You should consider the parameters in terms of subject matter, jurisdiction, and time frame. Other parameters, depending on your topic, may be relevant. Sometimes it will also be necessary to justify the parameters chosen. If you define them and provide adequate justification, you will insulate yourself from criticism. Furthermore, your introduction should identify the purpose and thesis of the paper.

An important principle of essay writing is never to assume your readers possess an in-depth knowledge of the topic. Whether your essay is understandable or not should not be dependent on the expertise of your readers. A number of implications follow from this principle.

You should define and/or describe any terms, concepts, or theories that are not common knowledge. For instance, if your analysis is based on economic theory, state the basic principles of this theory and any assumptions the theory makes. If your paper is about the regulation of a certain industry or market (e.g., the construction industry or securities market), you may also have to describe the special conditions which give rise to such regulation. This will enable the reader to understand and evaluate your analysis.

After your introduction, you should outline the existing law on your topic.[4] All of your subsequent comments about trends in the law, reforms, or theories will only make sense in relation to your presentation of the existing law. For instance, you cannot write a logical and effective essay proposing reforms to the law on polygamy before you first set out what the law is on the subject. The rationale underlying your proposed reforms will not be clear. Failure to outline your understanding and assumptions as to the current state of the law will also confuse readers not familiar with the law. Even readers who are familiar with the law will not have the benefit of seeing how you understand the existing law, and consequently they may misconstrue your analysis.

It is important to present the précis of the law in a separate section. Do not try to describe the existing law intermingled with your analytic comments as this will confuse the reader. Other sections of the essay may describe, for instance, the problems with the current law prompting the need for reform, the nature of the proposed reform, and the implications of such reform or how a legal theory applies.

When discussing the law on your topic, be balanced and thorough in your treatment. Do not gloss over or neglect to mention cases that do not support your thesis. Tackle any discrepancies directly. Further, you should be criti-

---

[4] You may find that the general principles outlined in the "Essential Background" chapter are helpful for gaining an understanding of the existing law in a subject area.

cal of your own position and attempt to anticipate and neutralize counter-arguments.

The conclusion of your essay should reiterate your purpose and thesis, and indicate how the paper has satisfied these by summarizing your analysis and arguments. Often you will want to suggest questions for further research in your conclusion.

Case Comments

A case comment describes and critically analyzes a judicial decision. When selecting a case on which to comment, you should choose a case which has a controversial aspect and which signals and/or clarifies the direction of the law.

The introduction of a case comment should describe in general terms the subject matter of the case. As with a legal essay, you should define the parameters of your comment. For instance, if the case covers several areas of law and you only wish to focus your comment on one area, make this explicit. The judicial history of the case (i.e., how the case was decided in lower courts) may also be something you wish to outline in your introduction. However, sometimes the judicial history will be so important that you will wish to discuss it in greater detail in the body of the comment. In addition, you may wish to briefly outline your assessment of the case, or what you intend to argue with respect to the case, in the introduction. What are the implications of the decision? Does the case represent a beneficial or potentially harmful development in the law?

When writing a case comment, you should begin by outlining the facts and the reasoning of the case. Next, your comment should attempt to answer one or more of the following questions:

1. How does this case affect the existing law on the topic?
2. What are the implications of this case for the future?
3. Does this case typify a trend that can or cannot be traced in other jurisdictions?

When analyzing the case and the law in the area, you should always be balanced and thorough, despite any interpretation you may favour. Do not gloss over or neglect to mention arguments or law that are inconsistent with your interpretation. Be critical of your own arguments.

Your conclusion should summarize your analysis of the case and comment on future implications.

Legal Memoranda

The purpose of a legal memorandum is to answer one or more legal questions in the context of a specific set of facts. The parameters of a legal memorandum are generally narrower than those of an essay. In essays, it may be desirable and interesting to discuss issues of policy, legal reform, legal theory, and so forth. In fact, a discussion of these matters sets high quality papers apart from papers of lessor quality. In contrast, legal theory, legal reform, and policy are generally outside the scope of a legal memorandum. A legal memorandum should only contain information necessary to answer the questions it has set out to assess. You are not concerned with what the law *should be*, unless you have been specifically asked to address law reform issues. Your mandate is to outline what the law is and to discuss its impact on your client's case. Ultimately, the lawyer assigning the memorandum will have to advise the client about a particular course of action. That advice may be based, in part, on what you recommend in your memorandum. An effective memorandum should, therefore, contain a thorough analysis of the relevant law and provide a well-reasoned answer to the questions posed.

Organization

We have outlined a structure which will help to ensure that your memorandum is focused and organized. This is a structure which is commonly used throughout the legal profession, and contains seven main sections:

1. Heading;
2. Introduction;
3. Facts;
4. Issues;
5. Conclusion;
6. Analysis; and
7. List of Authorities / Bibliography.

The purpose and contents of each of these sections are described below.

While we feel that this structure will serve in the vast majority of situations, the composition of your memorandum should ultimately be dictated by the logic of your subject matter and the needs of your audience. As well, the law firm or department where you work may have its own memorandum template that you must use, and it may look very different than the one described here. Furthermore, not every question will lend itself to the typical memorandum structure.

Heading

At the top of your memorandum, you need to list whom the memorandum was written for, your own name as writer, date, client involved, and subject matter. This information is especially vital because a client file can remain open for years. If you've written a memorandum and someone refers to it three years later, they will need to know this information. As well, everything in a client's file must be properly identified and the authors noted.

Introduction

It is often useful to provide an introduction to the memorandum. Further information on who the client is, why the questions were asked, and how the answers will be applied are all useful components. If, however, in the context of the questions you are answering you determine that this part of the memorandum is unnecessary, it is perfectly acceptable not to include it.

The Facts

This section will set out the factual context in which you have been asked to assess a legal issue. It is important that you provide a detailed description of the *relevant* facts so that the assigning lawyer can see from what facts you are drawing your conclusions. Facts that are not relevant to the issues you are assessing need not be cited. Facts should be presented in a clear, logical manner, which will make sense to the reader.

If you have been given insufficient facts to analyze and answer the question properly, be sure to ask for additional information or review the file yourself. Often, once you have begun your research, you will realize that further facts are needed to analyze the problem properly. It is preferable to ask for additional information before submitting the memorandum than to be asked to supplement the memorandum at a later date.

Issues

This section of the memorandum should outline the issues you have been asked to analyze. The issues should be framed in terms of questions that you will ultimately answer. The questions should be as precise and descriptive as possible. It is crucial to consider the issues within the context of the facts of the case, as this will influence how and what you research and, in turn, your analysis.

The assigning lawyer may frame the legal issues for you. Alternatively, she or he may simply outline the factual context and problems confronting the clients, leaving you to determine the relevant legal issues. In either case, it is imperative that you understand clearly the questions you have been asked to answer, otherwise your research will be unfocused and you will waste your time and your client's money. If you are unsure, confirm the instructions with the assigning lawyer. You are well advised to do this before beginning your research as the questions will rarely become more obvious after many hours spent researching.

After you have begun your research, you will often identify sub-issues that are critical to an analysis of the central issues you have been asked to investigate. These sub-issues must also be investigated. While it is crucial that you comprehend what the central issues or questions are when you begin your research, you should keep in mind that defining the issues and particularly sub-issues is an ongoing process. They will grow and evolve as you dig deeper into the literature, cases, and legislation.

The sequence of issues can also be important. It is usually preferable to deal with the central issues first. Always ensure that there is a logical connection between the central issues and sub-issues.

Once you identify the issues and have framed them in terms of questions, you then must begin the research needed to answer those questions.

Conclusions

This section should summarize your analysis and answer the questions set out in the *Issues* section of the memorandum.

Your answer to the questions should be as categorical as possible — either "yes" or "no." The assigning lawyer is relying on your advice. An inconclusive answer will be of little assistance. If the nature of the question precludes you from giving a final "yes" or "no" answer, provide a conclusion that gives the reader some details so that he/she understands what you have found; the reader will then have to read the *Analysis* section to get more information. Your answer should be supported by reasons written in general terms. Provide enough information in the conclusion so that the presiding lawyer can understand why you have come to your conclusion, but do not give so much detail that the lawyer will gloss over it. The detailed information can come in the *Analysis* section of the memorandum.

It may seem counterintuitive to have the conclusion to your memorandum at the beginning, before you even discuss the issues in depth. This, however, is how a legal memorandum should be structured. Oftentimes your supervising lawyer may not even read the *Analysis* section — lawyers are very busy and will only read the conclusion and skim the rest of the memorandum. Because they need to be able to find the conclusion quickly, it should be at the beginning of the memorandum. Later on, when the lawyer has more time, s/he may read the analysis in more depth.

Analysis

In this section, the facts are applied to the law to answer the questions posed. Your analysis should follow the sequence set out in the *Issues* section of the memorandum.

In order to analyze the law and answer the questions asked, you need to outline what the law is. Start by outlining the *relevant* legislation and case law on the questions you have been asked to analyze. Any primary sources that do not help to answer the questions are irrelevant and should not be listed. Before including law in your memorandum, always ask yourself how this law helps you to answer the questions.

The length of this section of the memorandum will depend on the complexity of the legal issue(s) you have been asked to assess. It will also depend on the number of statutes, cases, and secondary literature you need to review.

Where there is no case law on point in your jurisdiction, you will want to research case law on your topic in other jurisdictions in Canada, preferably decisions from appellate courts. While these decisions would not be binding in your jurisdiction, the rationale underlying them may prove persuasive.[5] Finally, where there is no Canadian law on your research problem, or where the Canadian law is in a state of flux, it may be useful to draw on British or American law (or both). Decisions from these countries may also prove persuasive in your jurisdiction.

Your description of the law must be thorough and balanced. Be sure to include any cases that go against the answer you or the assigning lawyer hope to reach. If the law is in a state of confusion, say so and try to summarize, as clearly as possible, where the confusion or conflict exists.

It may be helpful to quote from cases in your memorandum. The assigning lawyer will often want to know precisely how the court frames or defines legal propositions. As a general rule, avoid long quotations and only quote what is necessary to make your point.[6]

If you have been asked to analyze more than one legal issue, use separate headings for each. Separate headings make the memorandum easier to follow and promote an organized style. If each legal issue can be further broken down into subtopics, separate these with the use of subheadings. The

---

[5] Refer to the flow chart in the "Essential Background" chapter on distinguishing between binding and persuasive law and prioritizing the various sources of law.

[6] When you cite your sources, ensure you follow the legal citation rules in the *Canadian Guide to Uniform Legal Citation*, 6th ed. (Toronto: Thomson Carswell, 2006). Understand that you do not limit your citations only to direct quotations; you cite any idea, theory, analysis, etc. that you did not come up with on your own (i.e., anything that you found by reading other people's work), whether you quote it directly or paraphrase it.

layout of the legal issues in this section should parallel the way they are set out in the first section of the memorandum.

You will rarely find a case that is identical to the one you are researching. Most legal problems that you will be asked to analyze will fall into gaps between decided cases. Your task is to form legal arguments that interpolate or extrapolate from the principles of decided cases. The following are some of the questions you should address in this section of the memorandum:

1. Based on the law, does your client have a case?

2. What are the strengths and weaknesses of the case?

3. Is the law that supports or goes against your client's case binding or persuasive?

4. Can the facts of your case be distinguished from those in the case law? If so, how?

5. Will a court be likely to accept these distinctions as valid? Why or why not?

List of Authorities / Bibliography

This section includes a listing of all secondary sources that you consulted. The list will let the assigning lawyer know that you have been thorough in your research. You may also wish to include a section that lists all the case law and legislation referenced or relied upon. While these primary sources are discussed in the body of your memorandum, it may be useful to list them in one place for easy reference.

Appendix I — A Sample Legal Memorandum

Memorandum

DATE: February 13, 2009
TO: Jane Q. Smith, Q.C.
FROM: Fatima Venkatarangam
CLIENT: TrueNorth Pools Inc., File No. 2009-0310A
RE: Regulation of Patron Behaviour in Shared, Water-Based Recreational and Therapeutic Facilities: A Country Comparison

I. — Introduction

Our client, TrueNorth Pools Inc., has come to us to ensure that all its shared, water-based recreational and therapeutic facilities are in compliance with the law. As per your request, I have prepared the following memo setting out the legislation in Canada on what the various jurisdictions (federal/provincial/territorial) require in terms of the regulation of patron behaviour in these sorts of facilities. I have researched the applicable legislation (statutes and regulations) and relevant case law in this area.

II. — Facts

TrueNorth Pools Inc. is a company which builds, and sometimes operates, shared water-based recreational and therapeutic facilities such as public and semi-public pools, saunas, wading pools, hot tubs, steam baths, water parks, whirlpools, spray pools, etc. Recently, TrueNorth has received a number of complaints regarding some of its facilities, and the company would like to ensure that all facilities are in compliance with the law should a legal problem arise.

III. — The Issues

1. Which jurisdictions have, or do not have, legislation regulating patron behaviour in shared, water-based recreational and therapeutic facilities?

2. For those jurisdictions which have governing legislation, in what ways are the jurisdictions alike or different?

IV. — Conclusion

A survey of Canadian legislation and jurisprudence suggests that there are several requirements in terms of regulation of patron behaviour in shared, water-based recreational and therapeutic facilities. Most jurisdictions, excepting New Brunswick and Nova Scotia, have enacted legislation regulating patron behaviour in shared, water-based recreational and therapeutic facilities for the purposes of protecting the health and safety of their users. For those jurisdictions which have governing legislation, there are common threads among the jurisdictions in terms of construction and operating requirements affecting patron behaviour, pool admission and supervision requirements, public health and safety measures, nuisance or safety hazard strategies, regulation of use of diving boards and platforms, specific prohibited acts, regulation of spectators and signage requirements. Where the jurisdictions vary the most are with respect to whether they have special requirements for other types of pools such as therapeutic pools, wading pools, waterfun parks, wave action pools, spa pools, and whirlpools.

V. — Analysis

Issue 1: — Which jurisdictions have, or do not have, legislation regulating patron behaviour in shared, water-based recreational and therapeutic facilities?

In nearly all jurisdictions across Canada, there are regulations in effect regulating the construction, maintenance, inspection, and patron use of swimming pools. The primary purpose of the various regulations is to set out the operating and maintenance requirements for swimming pools and other water facilities in order to provide a safe and sanitary swimming environment for users.

The enabling statute in most instances is the province or territory's public health act. The only exception is in Quebec, where it is the *Environment Quality Act*, R.S.Q., c. Q-2, that enables regulations to be made with respect to public pools. In general, each jurisdiction's enabling statute allows the Lieutenant Governor in Council (or the Commissioner in the case of the Northwest Territories, Yukon and Nunavut) to make regulations in respect of public or semi-public swimming pools, whirlpools, bathing places and other recreational water facilities. In Quebec and the Yukon, the enabling statute does not explicitly state that the government may make regulations with respect to public pools, but provisions respecting sanitary and hygienic standards of public premises have been interpreted as doing so.

While most jurisdictions have enacted regulations respecting pools and other recreational water facilities, it appears that New Brunswick and Nova Scotia have not, even though there are provisions in their respective health acts allowing regulations to be enacted. The only apparent governing legislation in New Brunswick is s. 16 of the *Community Planning Act Provincial Building Regulation*, N.B. Reg. 81-126, which requires enclosures for swimming pools. In Nova Scotia, s. 5 of the *Smoke-free Places Act*, S.N.S. 2002, c. 12, prohibits smoking in recreational facilities such as pools.

Finally, in Nunavut, the applicable legislation regulating the operation and maintenance of their public pools for the protection of the health and safety of bathers was duplicated from the Northwest Territories at the time Nunavut came into being on April 1, 1999. As such, the applicable legislation is the *Public Health Act*, R.S.N.W.T. 1988, c. P-12, and the *Public Pool Regulations*, R.R.N.W.T. 1990, c. P-21, as duplicated for Nunavut by s. 29 of the *Nunavut Act*, S.C. 1993, c. 28.

Issue 2: — For those jurisdictions which have governing legislation, in what ways are the jurisdictions alike or different?

1. — Applicable water facilities

Many jurisdictions that have set out regulations with respect to the operation of public water facilities contain definition and application sections setting out which types of facilities are governed by the province's regulations. In British Columbia (B.C.), the regulations apply to all public pools such as swimming pools, wading pools, spray pools, and therapeutic pools.[1]

In Alberta, the regulations and accompanying *Pool Standards, 2006*[2] apply to swimming pools, wading pools, water spray parks and whirlpools. In Saskatchewan, the regulations apply to all public pools including designated mineral spas, paddling pools, swimming pools and whirlpools.[3] In Manitoba, the regulations apply to swimming pools and other recreational water facilities such as modified pools, public non-conforming pools, wading pools, semi-public swimming pools, wading pools and whirlpools.[4] In Ontario, the public pools regulation applies to "Class A" and "Class B" public pools as defined, including modified pools and wave action pools.[5] Ontario has separate regulations for the operation of public spas, with similar application and exclusion requirements as their public pools regulations.[6] In Quebec, there is a regulation applying to safety in public swim-

---

[1] *Swimming Pool, Spray Pool and Wading Pool Regulations*, B.C. Reg. 289/72, ss. 2–3 [*B.C. Pool Regulations*].

[2] *Swimming Pool, Wading Pool and Water Spray Park Regulation*, Alta. Reg. 293/2006, s. 1 and accompanying *Pool Standards, 2006* [*Alberta Pool Regulations*; Alberta *Pool Standards, 2006*].

[3] *Swimming Pool Regulations, 1999*, R.R.S., c. P-37.1, Reg. 7, ss. 2–3 [*Saskatchewan Pool Regulations*].

[4] *Swimming Pools and Other Water Recreational Facilities Regulation*, Man. Reg. 132/97, ss. 1–2 [*Manitoba Pool Regulations*].

[5] *Public Pools*, R.R.O. 1990, Reg. 565, ss. 1–3 [*Ontario Pool Regulations*].

[6] *Public Spas*, O. Reg. 428/05, ss. 1–2 [*Ontario Spa Regulations*].

ming pools and wading pools,[7] and a regulation as to the water quality of swimming pools and other artificial pools.[8] In Newfoundland and Labrador, the regulations apply to "Class A" and "Class B" public pools, wading pools, whirlpools and waterfun parks.[9] In Prince Edward Island (P.E.I.), the regulations similarly apply to "Class A" and "Class B" public pools, wading pools, whirlpools and waterfun parks.[10] In the Northwest Territories (NWT) and Nunavut, the public pool regulations apply to "Class A" and "Class B" pools, semi-private pools and spa pools.[11] The Yukon regulations apply to public swimming pools, wading pools, whirlpools and special purpose pools.[12]

2. — *Construction and operating requirements affecting patron behaviour*

In Newfoundland and Labrador and P.E.I., there are general operating provisions requiring public pools to be operated in a manner that is not dangerous to the health or safety of the users or the general public.[13] In B.C., Saskatchewan, Manitoba and the Yukon, there are also broad provisions allowing the local public health authority to impose such terms and conditions on operating permits or licenses that it deems appropriate.[14] In most jurisdictions there are also provisions specifying the maximum number of bathers in order to prevent overcrowding.[15] These general provisions could be interpreted as requiring owners and operators to regulate patron beha-

---

[7] *Regulation Respecting Safety in Public Baths*, R.R.Q. 1981, c. S-3, r. 3, ss. 1–2 [*Quebec Public Baths Regulations*].

[8] *Regulation Respecting Water Quality in Swimming Pools and Other Artificial Pools*, R.S.Q., c. Q-2, r. 18.1.02, ss. 1–3 [*Quebec Water Quality Regulations*].

[9] *Public Pools Regulations*, C.N.L.R. 1023/96, ss. 2–4 [*Newfoundland and Labrador Pool Regulations*].

[10] *Swimming Pool and Waterslide Regulations*, P.E.I. Reg. EC93/01, ss. 1–3 [*P.E.I. Pool Regulations*].

[11] *Public Pool Regulations*, R.R.N.W.T. 1990 c. P-21; *Public Pool Regulations*, R.R.N.W.T. 1990 c. P-21, as duplicated for Nunavut by s. 29 of the Nunavut Act, S.C. 1993, c. 28 [collectively referred to the *NWT and Nunavut Pool Regulations*].

[12] *Public Pool Regulations*, Y.O.I.C. 1989/130, ss. 1–2 [*Yukon Pool Regulations*].

[13] *Newfoundland and Labrador Regulations*, *supra* note 9, s. 7(1); *P.E.I. Pool Regulations*, *supra* note 10, s. 5.

[14] *B.C. Pool Regulations*, *supra* note 1, s. 4; *Saskatchewan Pool Regulations*, *supra* note 3, ss. 6(2) and 9(1); *Manitoba Pool Regulations*, *supra* note 4, s. 5(7); *Yukon Pool Regulations*, *supra* note 12, s. 5(2).

[15] *B.C. Pool Regulations*, *ibid.*, s. 80; *Alberta Pool Standards, 2006*, *supra* note 2 at Section III, para. 6; *Manitoba Pool Regulations*, *ibid.*, s. 14; *Ontario Pool Regulations*, *supra* note 5, s. 10; *Building Code*, O. Reg. 350/06, s. 3.1.17.3; *Quebec Public Baths Regulations*, *supra* note 7, ss. 26 and 37; *Newfoundland and Labrador Pool Regulations*, *supra* note 9, ss. 14 and 16(14)(d); *P.E.I. Pool Regu-*

viour in such a manner that they consider necessary to maintain a safe and sanitary environment for its users.

Similarly, certain construction requirements in B.C., P.E.I., the NWT and Nunavut can be interpreted as regulating patron behaviour to the extent that they require patrons to use separate washrooms/change rooms.[16] There are also general construction requirements requiring bathers to pass through a shower area before entering the pool area in B.C., Ontario, the NWT and Nunavut.[17] In Ontario, building code requirements regulate patron sanitation behaviour by requiring a foot spray to run free where access to the pool is not subject to regular cleaning and sanitizing.[18] In the NWT and Nunavut, regulations restrict the walking distance required for patrons to travel from the bathhouse to the pool.[19]

3. — Pool admission and supervision requirements

Some jurisdictions not only require patrons to *pass* through a shower area, but explicitly make it mandatory that patrons *take* a "cleansing" shower prior to entering the pool water.[20] From the case law, owners of public pools who provide soap for this purpose may also be held to owe patrons a duty of reasonable care to prevent patrons from slipping on soap residue and injuring themselves.[21] B.C. also requires patrons to be in clean bathing attire before being allowed to enter the pool area.[22] It has been held that the intent of this section is to prevent any health risk resulting from dirty bathing attire and the words "clean bathing attire" should not be interpreted to mean that bathing attire must be worn and thus prevent the use of a public pool by a nudist group with a valid rental permit.[23] It is unclear

---

lations, *supra* note 10, ss. 18 and 20(3); *NWT and Nunavut Pool Regulations, supra* note 11, s. 5; *Yukon Pool Regulations, ibid.*, s. 15.

[16] *B.C. Pool Regulations, ibid.*, s. 22(b); *P.E.I. Pool Regulations, ibid.*, s. 15; *NWT and Nunavut Pool Regulations, ibid.*, ss. 20(1) and 76(1).

[17] *B.C. Pool Regulations, ibid.*, s. 22(c); *Ontario Pool Regulations, supra* note 5, s. 6(4)(c); *Building Code,* O. Reg. 350/06, s. 3.11.9.1(6); *NWT and Nunavut Pool Regulations, ibid.*, s. 17.

[18] *Building Code, ibid.*, s. 3.11.3.1(17).

[19] *NWT and Nunavut Pool Regulations, supra* note 11, ss. 3.2 and 3.3.

[20] *B.C. Pool Regulations, supra* note 1, s. 73(f); *Alberta Pool Standards, 2006* at Section IV, para 2(1)(a); *Ontario Pool Regulations, supra* note 5, s. 15; *Newfoundland and Labrador Pool Regulations, supra* note 9, s. 16(15)(a); *P.E.I. Pool Regulations, supra* note 10, s. 20(3)(e); *NWT and Nunavut Pool Regulations, ibid.*, s. 38; *Yukon Pool Regulations, supra* note 12, s. 16(2)(b).

[21] *Callow v. British Columbia Distillers Co.*, [1972] 4 W.W.R. 614, 1972 CarswellBC 128 (S.C.).

[22] *B.C. Pool Regulations, supra* note 1, s. 73(l).

[23] *Skinnydipper Services Inc. v. Surrey (City of)*, 2007 BCSC 1625, 287 D.L.R. (4th) 514.

what interpretation would be given to the requirement in P.E.I. that "proper swim attire" be worn.[24]

Some jurisdictions also have supervision requirements, requiring children up to a certain age to be accompanied by a supervising adult or that patrons shall not swim alone when no lifeguard is present.[25] In Manitoba, unless there is a lifeguard on duty, the operator of a semi-public swimming pool is required to restrict access to the pool to members, tenants, residents or their guests. In other jurisdictions, owners must take reasonable measures to ensure the pool is not accessible for swimming, wading or diving outside of operating hours.[26]

4. — Public health and safety measures

There are also public health and safety requirements prohibiting persons infected with a communicable disease, or having open sores or rashes, or experiencing nausea, vomiting or diarrhea, or having been so instructed by a regional health authority or physician, from entering the water.[27] In Alberta, young children and incontinent persons are required to wear protective, water-resistant swimwear in order to minimize the introduction of contamination.[28] In the NWT and Nunavut, an operator may ask a person to produce a medical certificate stating that a disease, infection or health condition is not transmissible in a pool or bathhouse.[29] Alberta also requires pools to be operated so that all activities are conducted so as to minimize contamination of the pool water and provide for the safety of patrons.[30] In Alberta and Quebec, should fecal matter or vomitus be found in the pool, swimmers must leave the contaminated pool and are required to take a

---

[24] P.E.I. Pool Regulations, supra note 10, s. 20(3)(c).

[25] Alberta Pool Standards, 2006 at Section IV, para 2(2); Saskatchewan Pool Regulations, supra note 3 at s. 29; Ontario Pool Regulations, supra note 5, s. 17(19)(a); Quebec Public Baths Regulations, supra note 7, s. 26.1(d); Newfoundland and Labrador Pool Regulations, supra note 9, s. 18; NWT and Nunavut Pool Regulations, supra note 11, ss. 43, 46(1).

[26] Manitoba Pool Regulations, supra note 4, ss. 29, 34 and 40; Ontario Pool Regulations, ibid., s. 6(2); Quebec Public Baths Regulations, ibid., s. 22; Newfoundland and Labrador Pool Regulations, ibid., s. 7(2); NWT and Nunavut Pool Regulations, ibid., s. 34(1); Yukon Pool Regulations, supra note 12, s. 14.

[27] Alberta Pool Regulations, supra note 2, s. 21(a); Manitoba Pool Regulations, ibid., s. 6(2)(a); Newfoundland and Labrador Pool Regulations, ibid., s. 16(14)(a); P.E.I. Pool Regulations, supra note 10, s. 19; NWT and Nunavut Pool Regulations, ibid., s. 39(1); Yukon Pool Regulations, ibid., s. 16(2)(c).

[28] Alberta Pool Standards, 2006 at Section IV, para 3(b).

[29] NWT and Nunavut Pool Regulations, supra note 11, s. 39(2).

[30] Alberta Pool Regulations, supra note 2, s. 22(c).

shower prior to re-entering any pool.[31] In the NWT and Nunavut, pools must be closed to bathers while chlorine is added to the pool water.[32]

5. — Nuisance or safety hazard strategies

In Alberta, if a nuisance is present in a pool, all patrons must be directed to leave the pool and any adjacent area until the nuisance is removed.[33] In Manitoba, Ontario and Quebec, if there is a safety hazard or potentially hazardous situation, all persons must immediately leave the pool and remain out of the pool as long as is required.[34] From the case law, as long as the pool layout, signage and supervision procedures all meet the standard of care to be expected in the circumstances, an operator will not be held to be in breach of their duty of care if they fail to observe a swimmer swimming lengths the wrong way who ends up colliding with another patron.[35]

In some jurisdictions, patrons are required to leave the pool where safety is compromised because the clarity of water in the pool decreases below legislative visibility requirements.[36] In Ontario, if visibility requirements are not met, case law has established that a public health inspector can order the pool closed if the evidence shows that there are reasonable and probable grounds that a health hazard exists and the terms of the Order are necessary to decrease or eliminate the effect of the health hazard.[37]

6. — Regulation of use of diving boards and platforms

In B.C., Alberta, Manitoba, Ontario and Quebec, there are regulations allowing operators to use their discretion to restrict the use of diving boards and platforms in the interest of the safety of swimmers.[38] Case law in B.C. and Saskatchewan has shown that while owners have a duty to warn divers

---

[31] Alberta *Pool Standards, 2006, supra* note 2 at Schedule A; *Quebec Water Quality Regulations, supra* note 8, s. 17.

[32] *NWT and Nunavut Regulations, supra* note 11, s. 64(3).

[33] *Alberta Pool Regulations, supra* note 2, s. 18.

[34] *Manitoba Pool Regulations, supra* note 4, s. 23.2(2); *Ontario Pool Regulations, supra* note 5, s. 18(1); *Quebec Public Baths Regulations, supra* note 7, s. 31.

[35] *Geraghty v. Port Coquitlam (City of)*, 2005 BCCA 624, 361 W.A.C. 260, 2005 CarswellBC 3081 (C.A.); affirming 2005 BCSC 326, 2005 CarswellBC 535 ([In Chambers]).

[36] *Alberta Pool Regulations, supra* note 2, s. 17(2); *Ontario Pool Regulations, supra* note 5, s. 18(2); *Yukon Pool Regulations, supra* note 12, s. 13(3).

[37] *Southlake Regional Health Centre v. York (Regional Municipality)*, 2007 CarswellOnt 4677 (H.S.A.R.B.); *Southlake Regional Health Centre v. Sturgeon*, 2007 CarswellOnt 5581 (H.S.A.R.B.).

[38] *B.C. Pools Regulations, supra* note 1, s. 74; Alberta *Pool Standards, 2006, supra* note 2 at Section IV, para 2(1)(e); *Manitoba Pool Regulations, supra* note 4, s. 7(4)(a); *Ontario Pool Regulations, supra* note 5, s. 14; *Quebec Public Baths Regulation, supra* note 7, ss. 17 and 41.

of unusual dangers (such as a projecting bulkhead),[39] no duty is owed to swimmers who dive into shallow ends of swimming pools as shallow ends do not constitute concealed dangers.[40]

7. — Specific Prohibited Acts

There are also regulations in nearly all jurisdictions prohibiting certain specific acts or items. Examples include: no urination, defecation, pets, glass, breakable materials, running, fighting, hazardous or boisterous play, pushing or shoving, alcohol, drugs, street shoes, food consumption on pool deck, spitting, spouting of water, blowing nose in pool, or causing an obstruction.[41] In Newfoundland and Labrador, Nova Scotia, P.E.I. and the Yukon, there are specific provisions in their respective "Smoke-free" statutes prohibiting smoking in public pools.[42] The NWT and Nunavut are the only jurisdictions with a smoking prohibition directly in their pool regulations.[43]

8. — Regulation of spectators

In B.C., officials and spectators who may be dressed in street clothes are allowed to enter the pool area only for special functions.[44] In Manitoba, operators are required to ensure that the sanitary facilities provided for bathers are not accessible to spectators and that separate sanitary facilities for spectators are provided in addition to those provided for bathers.[45] In Ontario and Quebec, benches or seats provided to spectators for temporary use during aquatic displays or competitive events must be separated from the

---

[39] *Dominelli v. Saanich (District)*, 2005 BCSC 1455, 15 M.P.L.R. (4th) 263, 2005 CarswellBC 2676; affirmed 2007 BCCA 38, 31 M.P.L.R. (4th) 226, 2007 CarswellBC 299.

[40] *Long v. Condominium Plan No. 74R40206* (1979), 2 Sask. R. 212, 1979 CarswellSask 218.

[41] *B.C. Pool Regulations*, supra note 1, ss. 73(e) and 73(n); Alberta *Pool Standards, 2006*, supra note 2 at Section IV, paras. 2(1)(b), (d), (h) and (i); *Manitoba Pool Regulations*, supra note 4, ss. 6(2)(b) and (c); *Ontario Pool Regulations*, supra note 5, ss. 10(5) and 19; *Quebec Public Baths Regulations*, supra note 7, ss. 32(1) and (2); *Newfoundland and Labrador Pool Regulations*, supra note 9, ss. 16(14)(b) and (c); *P.E.I. Pool Regulations*, supra note 10, ss. 20(3)(a) and (b); *NWT and Nunavut Pool Regulations*, supra note 11, ss. 34(4), 36, 40–42; *Yukon Pool Regulations*, supra note 12, ss. 16(1)(d) and 17(b).

[42] *Smoke-free Environment Act, 2005*, S.N.L. 2005, c. S-16.2, s. 4; *Smoke-Free Places Act*, S.N.S. 2002, c. 12, s. 5; *Smoke-Free Places Act*, R.S.P.E.I. 1988, c. S-4.2, s. 9; *Smoke-Free Places Act*, S.Y. 2008, c. 8, s. 4.

[43] *NWT and Nunavut Pool Regulations*, supra note 11, s. 36(4).

[44] *B.C. Pool Regulations*, supra note 1, s. 73(m).

[45] *Manitoba Pool Regulations*, supra note 4, s. 25(3).

deck by a barrier[46] and where there is a permanent spectator gallery adjacent to the pool deck, spectators are forbidden access to the deck at a distance of less than 1.80 metres to the edge of the pool.[47] In Newfoundland and Labrador and P.E.I., spectators have separate entrances from the pool area and are forbidden from entering the pool or deck surrounding the pool.[48] In the NWT and Nunavut, spectators are restricted to specifically designated spectator areas.[49]

9. — *Signage requirements*

In all the jurisdictions that have enacted regulations regulating patron behaviour, there are specific provisions requiring that the rules governing the use of the pool be posted in a prominent position, easily and clearly seen by all users.[50] The rule of thumb is that those directions necessary for the health and safety of patrons must be posted. In general, an owner or operator must post signs stating: restrictions on who can and cannot enter the pool area, whether showers are mandatory, prohibited behaviour and conduct, lifeguard or supervision/children accompaniment requirements, bather load, pet restrictions, emergency procedures and telephone numbers, diving restrictions and restrictions on spectators. In B.C. and New Brunswick, the courts have held liable operators who have failed to post signs warning divers of the possible risk of injury.[51]

---

[46] *Ontario Pool Regulations, supra* note 5, s. 10(3); *Quebec Public Baths Regulations, supra* note 7, s. 38.

[47] *Ontario Pool Regulations, ibid.,* s. 19(4); *Quebec Public Baths Regulations, ibid.,* s. 32(3).

[48] *Newfoundland and Labrador Pool Regulations, supra* note 9, s. 8(1); *P.E.I. Pool Regulations, supra* note 10, s. 8(1)(g).

[49] *NWT and Nunavut Pool Regulations, supra* note 11 at s. 34(2).

[50] *B.C. Pool Regulations, supra* note 1, ss. 73(n) and 92; Alberta *Pool Standards, 2006, supra* note 2 at Section IV, para. 2; *Saskatchewan Pool Regulations, supra* note 3, ss. 20 and 29; *Manitoba Pool Regulations, supra* note 4, ss. 6(1), 7(4) and 26; *Ontario Pool Regulations, supra* note 5, ss. 17 and 19; *Building Code,* O. Reg. 350/06, ss. 3.11.3.1(25) and 3.11.4.1(8); *Quebec Public Baths Regulations, supra* note 7, ss. 26(1) and 33; *Newfoundland and Labrador Pool Regulations, supra* note 9, ss. 16(15)(a), (c) and 18; *P.E.I. Pool Regulations, supra* note 10, ss. 20(3); *NWT and Nunavut Pool Regulations, ibid.,* s. 44; *Yukon Pool Regulations, supra* note 12, ss. 16.

[51] *Parker (Guardian ad litem of) v. Courtenay (City of),* 1991 CarswellBC 1893 (C.A.); leave to appeal to SCC refused, 139 N.R. 236 (note); rev'g 1989 CarswellBC 1098 (S.C.); *Arseneau v. Fredericton Motor Inn Ltd.* (1984), 59 N.B.R. (2d) 60, 1984 CarswellNB 424 (Q.B.).

10. — *Regulations of other water-based facilities: therapeutic pools, wading pools, waterfun parks, wave action pools, spa pools, and whirlpools*

Finally, in addition to public swimming pools, some jurisdictions have enacted regulations dealing with other types of water-based facilities.

In B.C., there are provisions requiring that separate toilets and showers for each sex be provided for therapeutic, wading and spray pools.[52] Signs necessary for the safety of patrons must be posted at all entrances to therapeutic pools.[53] Wading pools and spray pools must be free of obstructions hazardous to children, and barriers must be erected to prevent the easy access of non-users.[54]

Alberta requires the body temperature of children under 2 years to be closely monitored and pregnant women, persons with heart disease, hypertension, seizures, diabetes and obesity or those greater than 65 years of age to consult with their physician prior to using a whirlpool.[55] In Manitoba, operators of whirlpools are required to post a notice requiring users to: restrain or tie up long hair in order to minimize the risk of being caught in the equipment, keep their heads above water at all times, not remain in the whirlpool longer than 10 minutes and be accompanied by an adult if they are under the age of 12.[56]

In Manitoba, where lifeguards are not provided, operators of semi-public swimming pools are required to post signs that children under the age of 12 must be accompanied by an adult and restrict access to the pool to members, tenants, residents and their guests.[57] Operators of modified pools, public non-conforming pools and wading pools are required to provide water closets for each gender.[58]

In Ontario, P.E.I., the NWT and Nunavut, every operator of a wave action pool must sound a warning using the public address system sufficiently in advance of the commencement of wave activation to give bathers the option of leaving the pool.[59] In Ontario, operators of wave action pools

---

[52] *B.C. Pool Regulations, supra* note 1, ss. 90 and 103.

[53] *Ibid.* s. 92.

[54] *Ibid.* s. 98(1).

[55] Alberta *Pool Standards, 2006, supra* note 2 at Section IV, para. 3(1)(c).

[56] *Manitoba Pool Regulations, supra* note 4, s. 6(3).

[57] *Ibid.* ss. 26(1) and 29(2).

[58] *Ibid.* ss. 35, 41 and 44.

[59] *Ontario Pool Regulations, supra* note 5, ss. 16(4); *P.E.I. Pool Regulations, supra* note 10, s. 14; *NWT and Nunavut Pool Regulations, supra* note 11, s. 78.

must also post notices that jumping or diving into the wave action pool is not permitted on portions where the depth is 2.30 metres or less.[60]

Ontario also has a separate regulation for public spas. Similar to the pool regulations, dressing rooms are to be made available for bathers prior to entering the spa deck and there is a maximum bather load.[61] In the NWT and Nunavut, spa pools must be equipped with a timing device that starts and stops the jet pump that is located so that bathers must exit the pool to start it.[62] Operators of spa pools in Ontario, the NWT and Nunavut must post similar notices with varying health and safety warnings (e.g. children under 12 must be supervised; users with open sores or rashes or experiencing nausea, vomiting or diarrhea cannot use the spa; users should cool down periodically if nausea or dizziness occurs; users should enter and exit the spa slowly; users should avoid playing or swimming near drains or suction devices and exit a spa if a drain cover or suction fitting is loose, broken or missing; and pregnant women and persons with known health or medical conditions should consult with a physician before using a spa).[63]

In Newfoundland and Labrador, a waterslide receiving pool in waterfun parks must be of sufficient length, width and depth so as to prevent each person splashing down from a flume extension into the receiving pool from contacting the walls or bottom of the receiving pool, adjacent flume extensions or other persons exiting into the receiving pool.[64] From the case law, the B.C. court has held that a city is not liable for the actions of a third person using a city waterslide who knowingly disobeys the rules concerning safe use of a waterslide and collides with another patron.[65]

---

[60] *Ontario Pool Regulations, ibid.*, s. 19(7).

[61] *Ontario Spa Regulations, supra* note 6, ss. 5(1)(f) and 17.

[62] *NWT and Nunavut Pool Regulations, supra* note 11, s. 89.

[63] *Ontario Spa Regulations, supra* note 6, s. 18(1); *NWT and Nunavut Pool Regulations, ibid.*, s. 92 and Schedule D.

[64] *Newfoundland and Labrador Pool Regulations, supra* note 9, s. 10(7).

[65] *Bengtson v. Burnaby (City of)*, 2000 BCSC 1928, 2000 CarswellBC 3044.

Bibliography

Legislation

Alberta

Public Health Act, R.S.A. 2000, c. P-37.
Swimming Pool, Wading Pool and Water Spray Park Regulation, Alta. Reg. 293/2006.

British Columbia

Health Act, R.S.B.C. 1996, c. 179.
Swimming Pool, Spray Pool and Wading Pool Regulations, B.C. Reg. 289/72.

Manitoba

The Public Health Act, S.M. 2006, c. 14.
Swimming Pools and Other Water Recreational Facilities Regulation, Man. Reg. 132/97.

New Brunswick

Community Planning Act Provincial Building Regulation, N.B. Reg. 81-126.
Health Act, R.S.N.B. 1973, c. H-2.

Newfoundland and Labrador

Health and Community Services Act, S.N.L. 1995, c. P-37.1.
Public Pools Regulations, C.N.L.R. 1023/96.
Smoke-free Environment Act, 2005, S.N.L. 2005, c. S-16.2.

Northwest Territories

Public Health Act, R.S.N.W.T. 1988, c. P-12.
Public Pool Regulations, R.R.N.W.T. 1990, c. P-21.

Nova Scotia

Health Protection Act, S.N.S. 2004, c. 4.
Smoke-free Places Act, S.N.S. 2002, c. 12.

Nunavut

Nunavut Act, S.C. 1993, c. 28.

Public Health Act, R.S.N.W.T. 1988, c. P-12, as duplicated for Nunavut by s. 29 of the *Nunavut Act*, S.C. 1993, c. 28.
Public Pool Regulations, R.R.N.W.T. 1990, c. P-21, as duplicated for Nunavut by s. 29 of the *Nunavut Act*, S.C. 1993, c. 28.

Ontario

Building Code, O. Reg. 350/06.
Building Code Act, 1992, S.O. 1992, c. 23.
Health Protection and Promotion Act, R.S.O. 1990, c. H.7.
Public Pools, R.R.O. 1990, Reg. 565.
Public Spas, O. Reg. 428/05.

Prince Edward Island

Public Health Act, R.S.P.E.I. 1988, c. P-30.
Smoke-Free Places Act, R.S.P.E.I. 1988, c. S-4.2.
Swimming Pool and Waterslide Regulations, P.E.I. Reg. EC93/01.

Quebec

Environment Quality Act, R.S.Q., c. Q-2.
Public Buildings Safety Act, R.S.Q., c. S-3.
Regulation Respecting Safety in Public Baths, R.R.Q. 1981, c. S-3.
Regulation Respecting Water Quality in Swimming Pools and Other Artificial Pools, R.S.Q., c. Q-2.

Saskatchewan

The Public Health Act, S.S. 1994, c. P-37.1.
Swimming Pool Regulations, 1999, R.R.S., c. P-37.1.

Yukon

Public Health and Safety Act, R.S.Y. 2002, c. 176.
Public Pool Regulations, Y.O.I.C. 1989/130.
Smoke-Free Places Act, S.Y. 2008, c. 8.

Jurisprudence

Arseneau v. Fredericton Motor Inn Ltd. (1984), 59 N.B.R. (2d) 60, 1984 CarswellNB 424 (Q.B.).

Bengtson v. Burnaby (City of), 2000 BCSC 1928, 2000 CarswellBC 3044.

Callow v. British Columbia Distillers Co., [1972] 4 W.W.R. 614, 1972 CarswellBC 128 (S.C.).

Dominelli v. Saanich (District), 2005 BCSC 1455, 15 M.P.L.R. (4th) 263, 2005 CarswellBC 2676; affirmed 2007 BCCA 38, 31 M.P.L.R. (4th) 226, 2007 CarswellBC 299.

Geraghty v. Port Coquitlam (City of), 2005 BCCA 624, 361 W.A.C. 260, 2005 CarswellBC 3081; affirming 2005 BCSC 326, 2005 CarswellBC 535 ([In Chambers]).

Long v. Condominium Plan No. 74R40206 (1979), 2 Sask. R. 212, 1979 CarswellSask 218 (Q.B.).

Parker (Guardian ad litem of) v. Courtenay (City of), 1991 CarswellBC 1893 (C.A.); leave to appeal to SCC refused, 139 N.R. 236 (note); rev'g 1989 CarswellBC 1098 (S.C.).

Skinnydipper Services Inc. v. Surrey (City of), 2007 BCSC 1625, 287 D.L.R. (4th) 514.

Southlake Regional Health Centre v. Sturgeon (2007), 2007 CarswellOnt 5581 (H.S.A.R.B.).

Southlake Regional Health Centre v. York (Regional Municipality), 2007 CarswellOnt 4677 (H.S.A.R.B.).

SELECTIVE TOPICAL BIBLIOGRAPHY

This Selective Topical Bibliography, on key substantive areas of Canadian law, is intended to save the researcher time by outlining some of the key topical law reports, loose-leafs, treatises, and periodicals.

The reader should be cautioned that the bibliography does not purport to be exhaustive. In addition, casebooks and non-Canadian materials have been excluded unless there was virtually nothing Canadian in the area. You should always check your law library to determine if there are any other sources relevant to your specific research problem.

Contents

1) — Aboriginal Law

Texts and loose-leaf Services

Bell, Catherine & Val Napoleon, eds. *First Nations Cultural Heritage and Law: Case Studies, Voices, and Perspectives* (Vancouver: UBC Press, 2008).

Crane, Brian, Robert Mainville & Martin W. Mason. *First Nations Governance Law* (Markham, Ont.: LexisNexis, 2008).

Dorey, Dwight A. & Joseph Eliot Magnet. *Aboriginal Rights Litigation* (Markham, Ont.: LexisNexis Butterworths, 2003).

Flatters, Michael J. *The Taxation and Financing of Aboriginal Businesses in Canada*, loose-leaf (Scarborough, Ont.: Carwell, 1998-).

Gibson, Gordon. *A New Look at Canadian Indian Policy: Respect the Collective, Promote the Individual* (Vancouver: Fraser Institute, 2008).

Halvorson, Ken. *Indian Residential School Abuse Claims: A Lawyer's Guide to the Adjudicative Process* (Scarborough, Ont.: Carswell, 2005).

Henderson, James Youngblood. *Treaty Rights in the Constitution of Canada* (Scarborough, Ont.: Carswell, 2007).

Henderson, James Youngblood, Marjorie Benson & Isobel Findlay. *Aboriginal Tenure in the Constitution of Canada* (Scarborough, Ont.: Carswell, 2000).

Isaac, Thomas F. *Aboriginal Title* (Saskatoon: Native Law Centre, University of Saskatchewan, 2006).

Leonardy, Matthias. *First Nations Criminal Jurisdiction in Canada* (Scarborough, Ont.: Carswell, 1998).

Macaulay, Mary Locke. *Aboriginal & Treaty Rights Practice*, loose-leaf (Toronto: Carswell, 2000-).

Magnet, Joseph & Dwight Dorey. *Legal Aspects of Aboriginal Business Development* (Markham, Ont.: LexisNexis, 2005).

Mainville, Robert. *An Overview of Aboriginal and Treaty Rights and Compensation for Their Breach* (Saskatoon: Purich Pub., 2001).

McCabe, J. Timothy S. *The Honour of the Crown and its Fiduciary Duties to Aboriginal Peoples* (Markham, Ont.: LexisNexis Canada, 2008).

Morellato, Maria. *Aboriginal Law Since Delgamuukw* (Aurora, Ont.: Canada Law Book, 2009).

Olthuis, John, Nancy Kleer & Roger Townshend. *Aboriginal Law Handbook*, 3d ed. (Scarborough, Ont.: Carswell, 2008).

Reynolds, James I. *A Breach Of Duty: Fiduciary Obligations and Aboriginal Peoples* (Saskatoon: Purich Pub., 2005).

Ross, Michael Lee. *First Nations Sacred Sites in Canada's Courts* (Vancouver: UBC Press, 2005).

Woodward, Jack. *Native Law*, loose-leaf (Toronto: Carswell, 1989-).

Annotated Statutes

Imai, Shin. *The Annotated Indian Act and Related Aboriginal Constitutional Provisions* (Toronto: Carswell, published annually).

Salembier, J. Paul *et al. Modern Annotated First Nations Legislation* (Markham, Ont.: LexisNexis Butterworths, published annually).

Topical Journals/Newsletters

Canadian Journal of Native Studies
Canadian Native Law Bulletin

Justice as Healing Newsletter
Native Studies Review

Topical Law Reports

Canadian Native Law Cases
Canadian Native Law Reporter

2) — Administrative Law

Texts and loose-leaf Services

Anisman, Philip & Reid Robert, eds. *Administrative Law: Issues and Practice* (Toronto: Carswell, 1995).

Arrowsmith, Sue. *Government Procurement and Judicial Review* (Toronto: Carswell, 1988).

Blais, Marie-Hélène *et al. Standards of Review of Federal Administrative Tribunals* (Markham, Ont.: LexisNexis, 2006).

Blake, Sara. *Administrative Law in Canada*, 4th ed. (Markham, Ont.: LexisNexis Butterworths, 2006).

Braverman, Lisa. *Administrative Tribunals: A Legal Handbook* (Aurora, Ont.: Canada Law Book, 2001).

Brown, Donald J.M. & John M. Evans. *Judicial Review of Administrative Action in Canada*, 2d ed., loose-leaf (Toronto: Canvasback, 2009).

Bryant, Michael & Lorne Sossin. *Public Law* (Scarborough, Ont.: Carswell, 2002).

Elliott, David W., ed. *Administrative Law and Process*, rev. 3d ed. (Concord, Ont.: Captus Press, 2003).

Finkelstein, Neil R. & Brian MacLeod Rogers, eds. *Administrative Tribunals and the Charter* (Toronto: Carswell, 1990).

Holland, Denys C. & John P. McGowan. *Delegated Legislation in Canada* (Toronto: Carswell, 1989).

Jones, David P. *Principles of Administrative Law*, 5th ed. (Toronto: Thomson Carswell, 2009).

Kligman, Robert. *Bias* (Markham, Ont.: LexisNexis, 1998).

Macaulay, Robert & James L.H. Sprague. *Hearings Before Administrative Tribunals*, 2d ed. (Toronto: Carswell, 2002).

Macaulay, Robert & James L.H. Sprague. *Practice and Procedure Before Administrative Tribunals*, loose-leaf (Toronto: Carswell, 2009-).

Manuel, William J. & Christina Donszelmann. *Law of Administrative Investigations and Prosecutions* (Aurora, Ont.: Canada Law Book, 1999).

Mullan, David J. *Administrative Law* (Toronto: Irwin Law, 2001).

Régimbald, Guy. *Canadian Administrative Law* (Markham, Ont.: LexisNexis, 2008).

.... *Halsbury's Laws of Canada: Administrative Law* (Markham, Ont.: LexisNexis Canada, 2008).

Salembier, J. Paul. *Regulatory Law and Practice in Canada* (Markham, Ont.: LexisNexis Butterworths, 2004).

Swaigen, John. *Administrative Law: Principles and Advocacy* (Toronto: Emond Montgomery, 2005).

Tardi, Greg. *The Legal Framework of Government: A Canadian Guide* (Aurora, Ont.: Canada Law Book, 1992).

Topical Journals

Administrative Agency Practice
Administrative Law Journal
Canadian Journal of Administrative Law and Practice

Topical Law Reports

Administrative Law Reports

3) — Advocacy Law

Texts and loose-leaf Services

Adair, Geoffrey. *On Trial: Advocacy Skills Law and Practice*, 2d ed. (Markham, Ont.: LexisNexis, 2004).

Cromwell, Thomas A. *Effective Written Advocacy* (Aurora, Ont.: Canada Law Book, 2008).

Fradsham, Allan. *Chambers Advocacy* (Scarborough, Ont.: Carswell, 1997).

Huberman, Marvin & Alvin Rosenberg. *Appellate Advocacy* (Scarborough, Ont.: Carswell, 1996).

Lubet, Steven. *Modern Trial Advocacy: Canada*, 2d ed., adapted for Canada by Sheila Block & Cynthia Tape (Notre Dame, Ind.: National Institute for Trial Advocacy, 2000).

Morton, James C. & Michael E. Freeman. *Written Advocacy* (Markham, Ont.: LexisNexis, 2000).

Olah, John A. *The Art and Science of Advocacy*, loose-leaf (Toronto: Carswell, 1990-).

Renaud, Gilles. *Advocacy: A Lawyer's Playbook* (Toronto: Thomson Carswell, 2006).

Salhany, Roger. *Cross-Examination: The Art of the Advocate*, 3d ed. (Markham, Ont.: LexisNexis, 2006).

Stuesser, Lee. *An Advocacy Primer*, 3d ed. (Toronto: Carswell, 2005).

Topical Journals

Advocate's Quarterly

4) — Agency

Fridman, G.H.L. *Canadian Agency Law* (Markham, Ont.: LexisNexis, 2009).

Harvey, Cameron. *Agency Law Primer*, 4th ed. (Scarborough, Ont.: Carswell, 2009).

5) — Alternate Dispute Resolution, Mediation, and Arbitration

Texts and loose-leaf Services

Adams, George W. *Mediating Justice: Legal Dispute Negotiations* (Toronto: CCH Canadian, 2003).

Barin, Babak. *Carswell's Handbook of International Dispute Resolution Rules* (Scarborough, Ont.: Carswell, 1999).

Boulle, Laurence & Kathleen Kelly. *Mediation: Principles, Process, Practice* (Markham, Ont.: LexisNexis, 1998).

Chornenki, Genevieve A. *Bypass Court: A Dispute Resolution Handbook*, 3d ed. (Markam, Ont.: LexisNexis Butterworths, 2005).

.... *The Corporate Counsel Guide to Dispute Resolution* (Aurora, Ont.: Canada Law Book, 1999).

Corry, David J. *Negotiation: The Art of Mutual Gains Bargaining*, 2d ed. (Aurora, Ont.: Canada Law Book, 2010).

Earle, Wendy. *Drafting Arbitration and ADR Clauses for Commercial Contracts: A Solicitor's Manual*, loose-leaf (Scarborough, Ont.: Carswell, 2009-).

Easterbrook, Susan A. & Francine A. Herlehy. *Mediating Estate Disputes* (Aurora, Ont.: Canada Law Book, 2003).

Hanycz, Colleen M., Trevor C.W. Farrow & Frederick H. Zemans. *The Theory and Practice of Representative Negotiation* (Toronto: Emond Montgomery, 2008).

McEwan, J. Kenneth & Ludmila Barbara Herbst. *Commercial Arbitration in Canada: A Guide to Domestic and International Arbitrations*, loose-leaf (Aurora, Ont.: Canada Law Book, 2004-).

Nelson, Robert. *Nelson on ADR* (Scarborough, Ont.: Carswell, 2002).

Pirie, A.J. *Alternative Dispute Resolution: Skills, Science, and the Law* (Toronto: Irwin Law, 2000).

Poitras, Jean & Pierre Renaud. *Mediation and Reconciliation of Interests in Public Disputes* (Scarborough, Ont.: Carswell, 1997).

Sanderson, John P. & Richard H. McLaren. *Innovative Dispute Resolution: The Alternative*, loose-leaf (Scarborough, Ont.: Carswell, 1995-).

Silver, Michael. *Mediation and Negotiation: Representing Your Clients* (Markham, Ont.: LexisNexis, 2001).

Stitt, Allan J. & Richard Jackman. *Alternative Dispute Resolution Practice Manual*, loose-leaf (North York, Ont.: CCH Canadian Limited, 1995-).

Watson, Garry *et al.*, eds. *Dispute Resolution and the Civil Litigation Process* (Toronto: Emond Montgomery, 1991).

Topical Journals

ADR Forum: The Canadian Journal of Dispute Resolution.

6) — Animal Law

Texts and loose-leaf Services

Dolan, Kevin. *Laboratory Animal Law: Legal Control of the Use of Animals in Research*, 2d ed. (Oxford: Blackwell Pub., 2007).

Jasper, Margaret C. *Animal Rights Law*, 2d ed. (Dobbs Ferry, N.Y.: Oceana Publications, 2002).

Radford, Mike. *Animal Welfare Law in Britain: Regulation and Responsibility* (New York: Oxford University Press, 2001).

Rollin, Bernard E. *Animal Rights and Human Morality*, 3d ed. (Amherst, N.Y.: Prometheus Books, 2006).

Rothschild, Max and Scott Newman, eds. *Intellectual Property Rights in Animal Breeding and Genetics* (New York: CABI Pub., 2002).

Sunstein, Cass R. & Martha C. Nussbaum, ed. *Animal Rights: Current Debates and New Directions* (Oxford: Oxford University Press, 2004).

Waisman, Sonia, Bruce A. Wagman, & Pamela D. Frasch. *Animal Law: Cases and Materials*, 2d ed. (Durham, N.C.: Carolina Academic Press, 2002).

Topical Journals

Animal Law
Journal of Animal Law and Ethics

7) — Banking Law

Texts and loose-leaf Services

a) — General

Crawford, Bradley. *The Law of Banking and Payment in Canada*, loose-leaf (Aurora, Ont.: Canada Law Book, 2008-).

.... *Crawford and Falconbridge Banking and Bills of Exchange*, 8th ed. (Aurora, Ont.: Canada Law Book, 1988).

Glavota, Dom & Tina Woodside. *Canadian Forms and Precedents: Banking and Finance*, loose-leaf (Markham, Ont.: LexisNexis, 1991).

Hatch, James & Larry Wynant. *Canadian Commercial Lending: A Guide to Credit Decision Making*, 2d ed. (Toronto: Carswell, 1995).

Manzer, Alison R. & Jordan S. Bernamoff. *The Corporate Counsel Guide to Banking and Credit Relationships* (Aurora, Ont.: Canada Law Book, 1999).

Nicholls, Christopher C. *Corporate Finance and Canadian Law* (Scarborough, Ont.: Carswell, 2000).

.... *Financial Institutions: The Regulatory Framework* (Markham, Ont.: LexisNexis, 2008).

Ogilvie, M.H. *Bank and Customer Law in Canada* (Toronto: Irwin Law, 2007).

.... *Canadian Banking Law*, 2d ed. (Toronto: Carswell, 1998).

Sarna, Lazar. *Letters of Credit: The Law and Current Practice*, 3d ed., loose-leaf (Toronto: Carswell, 1989-).

Sherman, Jeffrey. *Canadian Treasury Management*, 3d ed. (Scarborough, Ont.: Carswell, 2006).

b) — International Finance

Broome, John. *Anti-Money Laundering: International Practice and Policies* (London: Sweet and Maxwell, 2005).

Hal, Scott. *International Finance*, 2d ed. (London: Sweet and Maxwell, 2007).

Kwaw, Edmund M.A. *The Law and Practice of Offshore Banking and Finance* (Westport, Conn.: Quorum Books, 1996).

Panourgias, Lazaros. *Banking Regulation and World Trade Law: GATS, EU and "Prudential" Institution Building* (Oxford: Hart, 2006).

Reynolds, Barney. *International Financial Markets Guide* (Markham, Ont.: LexisNexis, 2004).

Wood, Philip R. *Conflict of Laws and International Finance* (London: Sweet & Maxwell, 2007).

.... *Law and Practice of International Finance: Comparative Law of Security Interest and Title Finance* (London: Sweet & Maxwell, 2007).

.... *Law and Practice of International Finance: International Loans, Bonds, Guarantees and Legal Opinions* (London: Sweet & Maxwell, 2007).

.... *Law and Practice of International Finance: Principles of International Insolvency* (London: Sweet & Maxwell, 2007).

.... *Law and Practice of International Finance: Set-off and Netting, Derivatives and Clearing Systems* (London: Sweet & Maxwell, 2007).

c) — Law of Guarantee

McGuinness, Kevin Patrick. *The Law of Guarantee: A Treatise on Guarantee, Indemnity and the Standby Letter of Credit*, 2d ed. (Toronto: Carswell, 1996).

Annotated Statutes

Sarna, Lazar & Leora Aster. *Annotated Bills of Exchange Act*, loose-leaf (Markham, Ont.: LexisNexis, 1999).

Teolis, John W. and Dawn Jetten. *Bank Act: Legislation and Commentary*, loose-leaf (Markham, Ont.: Butterworths Canada, 1998-).

Topical Journals

Banking & Finance Law Review
Canadian Banker
Journal of International Banking Law
Journal of International Banking Law and Regulation
Journal of International Banking Regulation
National Banking Law Review
National Creditor/Debtor Review: A Journal on Creditor/Debtor Relations

Topical Law Reports

Business Law Reports

8) — Bankruptcy, Insolvency, and Debtor-Creditor Law

Texts and loose-leaf Services

Ben-Ishai, Stephanie. *Bankruptcy Reforms* (Toronto: Thomson Carswell, 2008).

Bennett, Frank. *Bennett's A-Z Guide to Bankruptcy: A Professional's Handbook* (North York, Ont.: CCH Canadian, 2001).

.... *Bennett on Bankruptcy*, 12th ed. (Toronto: CCH Canadian, 2009).

.... *Bennett on Bankruptcy Precedents*, 2d ed. (Toronto: CCH Canadian, 2008).

.... *Bennett on Collections*, 5th ed. (Toronto: Carswell, 2003).

.... *Bennett on Creditors' and Debtors' Rights and Remedies*, 5th ed. (Toronto: Carswell, 2006).

.... *Bennett on Going Broke: A Practical Guide to Bankruptcy for Individuals and Small Businesses*, 4th ed. (Toronto: CCH Canadian, 1995).

.... *Bennett on Power of Sale*, 4th ed. (Markham, Ont.: LexisNexis/Butterworths, 1996).

.... *Bennett on Receiverships*, 2d ed. (Toronto: Carswell, 1999).

.... *Bennett on the Commercial List* (Markham, Ont.: LexisNexis, 2006).

.... *Bennett on the PPSA (Ontario)*, 3d ed. (Markham, Ont.: Lexis-Nexis/Butterworths, 2006.).

Dunlop, C.R.B. *Creditor-Debtor Law in Canada*, 2d ed. (Toronto: Carswell, 1995).

Franklin, David. *International Commerical Debt Collection* (Scarborough, Ont.: Carswell, 2007).

Fraser, Marcia. *Debt Collection: A Step-by-Step Legal Guide*, loose-leaf (Aurora, Ont.: Canada Law Book, 1989-).

Gaertner, Jerrard B. *Identifying and Advising Businesses in Trouble* (Scarborough, Ont.: Carswell, 2004).

Honsberger, John D. *Debt Restructuring Principles and Practice*, loose-leaf (Aurora, Ont.: Canada Law Book, 1990-).

Houlden, L.H. & C.H Morawetz. *Bankruptcy and Insolvency Law of Canada*, 4th ed., loose-leaf (Toronto: Carswell, 2009-).

Lamer, Francis L. *Priority of Crown Claims in Insolvency*, loose-leaf (Scarborough, Ont.: Carswell, 1996-).

McElcheran, Kevin. *Commercial Insolvency in Canada* (Markham, Ont.: LexisNexis, 2005).

Meehan, Eugene. *Creditors' Remedies in Ontario*, 2d ed. (Markham, Ont.: LexisNexis, 2009).

Olivo, Laurence M. *Debtor-Creditor Law and Procedure*, 3d ed. (Toronto: Emond Montgomery, 2008).

Robinson, Lyman R. *British Columbia Debtor-Creditor Law and Precedents*, loose-leaf (Scarborough, Ont.: Carswell, 1993-).

Sarna, Lazar. *Bankruptcy of Corporations*, rev. ed., loose-leaf (Markham, Ont.: LexisNexis, 2005-).

.... *The Law of Bankruptcy and Insolvency in Canada*, rev. ed., loose-leaf (Markham, Ont.: LexisNexis Butterworths, 2004-).

.... *Rank of Creditors' Rights in Canada*, loose-leaf (Markham, Ont.: LexisNexis, n.d.).

Sarra, Janis Pearl. *Rescue! The Companies' Creditors Arrangement Act* (Toronto: Thomson Carswell, 2007).

Sarra, Janis Pearl & Ronald B. Davis. *Director and Officer Liability in Corporate Insolvency: A Comprehensive Guide to Rights and Obligations*, 2d ed. (Markham, Ont.: Butterworths, 2010).

Van Kessel, Robert. *Interim Receivers and Monitors* (Markham, Ont.: LexisNexis, 2006).

Wood, Roderick J. *Bankruptcy and Insolvency Law* (Toronto: Irwin Law, 2009).

Annotated Statutes

Houlden, Lloyd W. *Annotated Bankruptcy and Insolvency Act* (Toronto: Carswell, published annually).

McLaren, Richard H. *The 2008 Annotated Alberta Personal Property Security Act* (Toronto: Carswell, 2008).

Petraglia, Philip & Lazar Sarna. *Annotated Creditors and Debtors Laws of Ontario*, loose-leaf (Montreal: Condor Books, 2002-).

Shea, E. Patrick. *Consolidated Bankruptcy and Insolvency Act and Companies' Creditors Arrangement Act with Bill C-55 & Commentary* (Markham, Ont.: LexisNexis Butterworths, 2006).

Stikeman, Elliott. *Ontario PPSA and Commentary* (Markham, Ont.: Butterworths, 2006).

Topical Journals /Newsletters

Class Action Defence Quarterly
Commercial Insolvency Reporter
National Insolvency Review
The Canadian Class Action Review
National Insolvency Review
Annual Review of Insolvency Law

Topical Law Reports

Canadian Bankruptcy Reports
Commercial Insolvency Reporter
Personal Property Security Act Cases

9) — Civil Procedure

Texts and loose-leaf Services

a) — General

Abrams, Linda S. & Kevin P. McGuinness. *Canadian Civil Procedure Law*, 2d ed. (Toronto: LexisNexis, 2010).

Abrams, Linda S. *et al. Halsbury's Laws of Canada: Civil Procedure I & Civil Procedure II* (Toronto: LexisNexis Canada, 2008).

Fradsham, Allan A. & Heather Lamoureux. *Presenting Expert Witnesses* (Toronto: Carswell, 1995).

Guide to Civil Litigation: British Columbia Edition, loose-leaf (Scarborough, Ont.: Carswell, 2008-).

Huberman, Marvin Joel & Karen E.H. Foti. *Civil Actions* (Toronto: Carswell, 1995).

Kenkel, Joseph F. & William S. Chalmers. *Small Claims and Simplified Procedure Litigation*, 4th ed. (Toronto: Butterworths, 2002).

Miller, Jeffrey. *Law of Contempt in Canada* (Scarborough, Ont.: Carswell, 1997).

Morton, James, Michael J. Iacovelli & Corey D. Steinberg. *Procedural Strategies for Litigators*, 2d ed. (Markham, Ont,: LexisNexis, 2007).

Roccammo, Giovanna *et al. Medicine in the Litigation Process* (Toronto: Carswell, 1999).

.... *et al. Personal Injury Actions* (Toronto: Carswell, 1995).

Salhany, Roger E. *The Preparation and Presentation of a Civil Action* (Markham, Ont.: Butterworths, 2000).

Sarna, Lazar. *The Law of Declaratory Judgments*, 3d ed. (Toronto: Carswell, 2007).

Stockwood, David. *Civil Litigation: A Practical Handbook*, 5th ed. (Toronto: Carswell, 2004).

Upenieks, Ed & Robert van Kessel. *Enforcing Judgments and Orders* (Markham, Ont.: LexisNexis, 2001).

Van Kessel, Robert J. *Dispositions Without Trial*, 2d ed. (Markham, Ont.: LexisNexis, 2007).

White, Robert B. *Art of Trial* (Aurora, Ont.: Canada Law Book, 1993).

b) — Appellate

Brown, Donald J.M. *Civil Appeals*, loose-leaf (Toronto: Canvasback, 2009-).

Bryant, Marian E. *Conducting a Civil Appeal* (Toronto: Carswell, 1995).

Sopinka, John & Mark A. Gelowitz. *The Conduct of an Appeal* (Toronto: Butterworths, 2000).

c) — Class Actions

Branch, Ward K. *Class Actions in Canada*, loose-leaf (Vancouver: Western Legal Publications, 1996-).

Cassels, Jamie. *The Law of Large-Scale Claim: Product Liabilty, Mass Torts, and Complex Litigation in Canada* (Toronto: Irwin Law, 2005).

Eizenga, Michael A. *et al. Class Actions Law and Practice*, 2d ed. (Markham, Ont.: LexisNexis Canada, 2008-).

Jones, Craig E. *Theory of Class Actions* (Toronto: Irwin Law, 2003).

McCarthy Tétrault LLP. *Defending Class Actions in Canada* (Toronto: CCH Canadian, 2002).

d) — Costs

Orkin, Mark M. *The Law of Costs*, loose-leaf (Aurora, Ont.: Canada Law Book, 1987-).

e) — Discovery

Archibald, Todd L. *Discovery: Principles in Practice* (Toronto: CCH Canadian, 2004).

Burke, Todd *et al. E-Discovery in Canada* (Markham, Ont.: LexisNexis, 2008).

Cudmore, Gordon D. *Choate on Discovery*, 2d ed., loose-leaf (Toronto: Carswell, 2009-).

Ross, Stuart. *Conducting an Examination for Discovery* (Toronto: Carswell, 1995).

f) — Evidence

Corbin, Dr. Ruth M. & A. Kelly Gill. *Survey Evidence and the Law Worldwide* (Markham, Ont.: LexisNexis, 2008).

Hubbard, Robert W., Susan Magotiaux & Suzanne M. Duncan. *The Law of Privilege in Canada* (Toronto, Ont.: Canada Law Book, 2005).

g) — Forms

O'Brien's Encyclopedia of Forms, 11th ed. (Aurora, Ont.: Canada Law Book, 1987-).

Rolls, R.J. *Williston & Rolls Court Forms*, 2d ed., loose-leaf (Toronto: Butterworths, 1986-).

h) — Legislation and Practice

Archibald, Todd, Gordon Killeen & James C. Morton. *Ontario Superior Court Practice* (Toronto: LexisNexis Canada, published annually).

Bouck, John C., Gordon Turriff & Janice R. Dillon. *The British Columbia Annual Practice* (Vancouver: Western Legal Publications, published annually).

Busby, Karen. *Manitoba Queen's Bench Rules Annotated*, loose-leaf (Toronto: Carswell, 1992-).

Crane, Brian A. & Henry S. Brown. *Supreme Court of Canada Practice* (Toronto: Carswell, updated annually).

Ehrlich, David S. *Nova Scotia Annotated Rules of Practice*, loose-leaf (Toronto: Carswell, 1987-).

Ferguson, Dan. *Ontario Courtroom Procedure* (Markham, Ont.: LexisNexis, published annually).

Fradsham, Allan A. *Alberta Rules of Court Annotated* (Toronto: Carswell, published annually).

Fraser, G. Peter, John W. Horn & Susan A. Griffin. *Conduct of Civil Litigation in British Columbia*, loose-leaf (Toronto: Butterworths, 2007-).

Holder, William D & John C. Fiddick. *Annotated British Columbia Court Order Enforcement Act*, loose-leaf (Aurora, Ont.: Canada Law Book, n.d.).

Hughes, Roger T., Arthur B. Renaud & L.E. Trent Horne. *Canadian Federal Courts Practice*, (Toronto: LexisNexis, published annually).

.... *Federal Courts of Canada Service*, 2d ed., loose-leaf (Toronto: LexisNexis, n.d.).

Irvine, Frederick M. *British Columbia Practice*, loose-leaf (Markham, Ont.: LexisNexis Canada, 2006-).

McMechan, Robert & Gordon Bourgard. *Tax Court Practice* (Toronto: Carswell, published annually).

Polster, Phillip & Lisa Mendlowicz. *Ontario Litigation Procedures*, 4th ed. (Scarborough, Ont.: Carswell, 2005).

Saunders, Brian J. *et al. Federal Courts Practice* (Scarborough, Ont.: Carswell, published annually).

Seckel, Allan & James C. MacInnis. *British Columbia Supreme Court Rules Annotated* (Scarborough, Ont.: Carswell, published annually).

Sgayias, David *et al. Federal Court Practice*, loose-leaf (Toronto: Carswell, 1987-).

Sprague, James & Michele Rene de Cotret. *The Annotated Ontario Legislation Act* (Scarborough, Ont.: Carswell, published annually).

The Ontario Annual Practice (Agincourt, Ont.: Canada Law Book, published annually).

Thompson, D.A. Rollie. *Nova Scotia Civil Procedure Rules*, 2d ed., loose-leaf (Toronto: LexisNexis, 2008-).

Watson, Garry D. & Michael McGowan. *Ontario Civil Practice* (Toronto: Carswell, published annually).

Watson, Garry D. & Craig Perkins. *Holmested and Watson, Ontario Civil Procedure*, loose-leaf (Toronto: Carswell, 1984-).

Wineberg, Harris S. *The Annotated British Columbia Limitation Act*, loose-leaf (Toronto: Carswell, 1999-).

Zuker, Marvin. *Ontario Small Claims Court Practice* (Toronto: Carswell, published annually).

i) — Limitation Periods

Alberta Limitations Manual (Markham, Ont.: LexisNexis Canada, 2007-).

British Columbia Limitations Manual (Markham, Ont.: LexisNexis Canada, n.d.).

Busby, Karen. *Manitoba Queen's Bench Act and Rules Annotated*, loose-leaf (Scarborough, Ont.: Carswell, 1992-).

Dukelow, Daphne A. *Guide to Ontario and Federal Limitation Periods* (Scarborough, Ont.: Carswell, 1998).

Federal Limitations Manual, 2d ed. (Markham, Ont.: LexisNexis, n.d.).

Mew, Graeme. *The Law of Limitations*, 2d ed. (Toronto: Butterworths, 2004).
Ontario Limitations Manual, loose-leaf (Markham, Ont.: LexisNexis Canada, 2006-).

j) — Motions

Hendriks, Mary Ross. *Court Motions Handbook* (Toronto: Carswell, 1996).

k) — Tax

Aron, Bernie. ed. *Tax Aspects of Litigation* (Toronto: Carswell, 1990-).

Topical Law Reports

Carswell's Practice Cases

Topical Journals/Newsletters

Advocate's Quarterly
Annual Review of Civil Litigation
Class Action Defence Quarterly

Digest Services

Nemet-Brown, Sheila, ed. *Canada Quantum Digest: The Civil Litigator's Companion* (Markham, Ont.: LexisNexis, 2008).
The Weekly Digest of Civil Procedure
Western Practice Digest 1981–1993

10) — Communications Law

Texts and loose-leaf Services

Brecher, Jay. *Halsbury's Laws of Canada: Media and Postal Communications: Medicine & Health* (Markham, Ont.: LexisNexis Canada, 2007).

Crawford, Michael G. *The Journalist's Legal Guide*, 4th ed. (Scarborough, Ont.: Carswell, 2002).

Handa, Sunny *et al. Halsbury's Laws of Canada: Communications* (Markham, Ont.: LexisNexis Canada, 2007).

Johnston, David *et al. Communications Law in Canada*, loose-leaf (Markham, Ont.: LexisNexis, n.d.).

Ryan, Michael. *Canadian Telecommunications Law and Regulation*, loose-leaf (Scarborough, Ont.: Carswell, 2009).

Salter, Liora & Felix Odarty Wellington. *The CRTC and Broadcasting Regulation in Canada* (Scarborough, Ont.: Carswell, 2008).

11) — Competition Law

Texts and loose-leaf Services

Addy, George N. & William L. Vanveen. *Competition Law Service*, loose-leaf (Aurora, Ont.: Canada Law Book, 1989-).

Affleck, Don & Wayne McCracken. *Canadian Competition Law*, loose-leaf (Toronto: Carswell, 1990-).

Facey, Brian A. & Dany H. Assaf. *Competition and Antitrust Law: Canada and the United States*, 3d ed. (Markham, Ont.: LexisNexis Butterworths, 2006).

Flavell, C.J., Michael & Christopher J. Kent. *The Canadian Competition Law Handbook* (Scarborough, Ont.: Carswell, 1997).

Gourley, Albert C. *Merger Notification and Clearance In Canada*, loose-leaf (Toronto: CCH Canadian, 2003-).

Kaiser, Gordon. *Competition Law in Canada*, loose-leaf (Toronto: Mathew Bender & Co. Inc., 1988-).

Musgrove, James, ed. *Fundamentals of Canadian Competition Law* (Scarborough, Ont.: Thomson Carswell, 2007).

Annotated Statutes

Stikeman, Elliott. *Competition Act and Commentary* (Toronto: Butterworths, published annually).

Wakil, Omar. *The Annotated Competition Act* (Toronto: Carswell, published annually).

Topical Law Reports

Business Law Reports

12) — Computer Law

Texts and loose-leaf Services

Abe, Lisa K. *Internet and E-commerce Agreements: Drafting and Negotiating Tips* (Toronto: Butterworths, 2001).

Geist, Michael A. *Internet Law in Canada*, 3d ed. (Concord, Ont.: Captus Press, 2002).

Hutchison, Scott & Robert Davis. *Computer Crime in Canada* (Scarborough, Ont.: Carswell, 1997).

Kyer, Clifford Ian & Mark J. Fecenko. *Kyer and Fecenko on Computer-Related Agreements: A Practical Guide*, 2d ed. (Toronto: Butterworths, 1997).

Limpert, Brad. *Technology Contracting: Law, Precedents and Materials* (Toronto: Carswell, 2005-).

Schelling, Jeffrey M. *Cyberlaw Canada*, 2d ed. (North Vancouver: International Self-Counsel Press, 1999).

Sookman, Barry B. *Computer, Internet and Electronic Commerce Law*, loose-leaf (Toronto: Carswell, 1989-).

.... *Computer, Internet and Electronic Commerce Terms: Judicial, Legislative and Technical Definitions* (Toronto: Carswell, 2009).

Takach, George S. *Computer Law*, 2d ed. (Toronto: Irwin Law, 2003).

Topical Journals

Computer Law

Topical Law Reports

Canadian Computer Law Reporter

13) — Conflict of Laws (Private International Law)

Texts and loose-leaf Services

Van Ert, Gibran. *Using International Law in Canadian Courts*, 2d ed. (Toronto: Irwin Law 2008).

Walker, Janet. *Castel & Walker: Canadian Conflict of Laws*, 6th ed., loose-leaf (Markham, Ont.: LexisNexis Canada, n.d.).

.... *Halsbury's Laws of Canada: Conflict of Laws* (Markham, Ont.: LexisNexis, 2006).

Topical Journals

Canadian Yearbook of International Law

14) — Constitutional Law

Texts and loose-leaf Services

Bakan, Joel *et al.*, eds. *Canadian Constitutional Law*, 4th ed. (Toronto: Emond Montgomery, 2009).

Bastarache, Michel. *Language Rights in Canada*, 2d ed. (Scarborough, Ont.: Carswell, 2004).

Beaulac, Stéphane. *Handbook on Statutory Interpretation: General Methodology, Canadian Charter and International Law* (Markham, Ont.: LexisNexis, 2008).

Cameron, Jamie. *The Charter and Criminal Justice: Twenty-Five Years Later* (Markham, Ont.: LexisNexis, 2008).

Faraday, Fay, Margaret Denike & M. Kate Stephenson, eds. *Making Equality Rights Real: Securing Substantive Equality Under the Charter* (Toronto: Irwin Law, 2006).

Funston, Bernard & Eugene Meehan. *Canada's Constitutional Law in a Nutshell* (Toronto: Carswell, 2003).

.... *Consolidated Canadian Constitutional Documents*, 2d ed. (Toronto: Carswell, 2007).

Gilbert, Taylor & Douglas Jung. *Franchising in Canada*, 3d ed. (Don Mills, Ont.: CCH Canadian Limited, 1995).

Henderson, James Youngblood. *Treaty Rights in the Constitution of Canada* (Toronto: Thomson Carswell, 2007).

Hogg, Peter. *Constitutional Law of Canada*, 5th ed., loose-leaf (Toronto: Carswell, 2007-).

Kelly, James B. *Governing with the Charter: Legislative and Judicial Activism and Framers' Intent* (Vancouver: UBC Press, 2005).

Laskin, John B. *et al.*, eds. *Canadian Charter of Rights Annotated*, looseleaf (Aurora: Canada Law Book, 1982-).

Lokan, Andrew & Christopher M. Dassios. *Constitutional Litigation in Canada*, loose-leaf (Scarborough, Ont: Carswell, 2006-).

MacIvor, Heather. *Canadian Politics and Government in the Charter Era* (Toronto: Thomson Nelson, 2006).

Macklem, P. *et al. Canadian Constitutional Law*, 2d ed. (Toronto: Emond Montgomery Publications, 1997).

Magnet, Joseph Eliot. *The Canadian Charter of Rights and Freedoms: Reflections on the Charter After Twenty Years* (Markham, Ont: LexisNexis Butterworths, 2003).

Manfredi, Christopher P. *Contested Constitutionalism: Reflections on the Canadian Charter of Rights and Freedoms* (Vancouver: UBC Press, 2009).

McAllister, Debra M. *Taking the Charter to Court: A Practitioner's Analysis* (Toronto: Carswell, 1998).

McIntyre, Sheila & Sanda Rodgers, eds. *Diminishing Returns: Inequality and the Canadian Charter of Rights and Freedoms* (Markham, Ont.: LexisNexis Butterworths, 2006).

McLeod, Roderick *et al. The Canadian Charter of Rights: The Prosecution and Defence of Criminal and Other Statutory Offences*, loose-leaf (Toronto: Carswell, 1983-).

Ribeiro, Marc. *Limiting Arbitrary Power: The Vagueness Doctrine in Canadian Constitutional Law* (Vancouver: UBC Press, 2004).

Roach, Kent. *Constitutional Remedies in Canada*, loose-leaf (Aurora, Ont.: Canada Law Book, 1994-).

Schabas, William & Stéphane Beaulac. *International Human Rights and Canadian Law: Legal Commitment, Implementation and the Charter*, 3d ed. (Toronto: Thomson Carswell, 2006).

Sharpe, Robert J. & Kent Roach. *The Charter of Rights and Freedoms*, 4th ed. (Toronto: Irwin Law, 2009).

Sossin, Lorne. *Boundaries of Judicial Review: The Law of Justiciability in Canada* (Scarborough, Ont.: Carswell, 1999).

Stratas, David. *The Charter of Rights in Litigation*, loose-leaf (Toronto: Canada Law Book, 1990-).

Stuart, Don. *Charter Justice in Canadian Criminal Law*, 4th ed. (Toronto: Thomson Carswell, 2005).

Tarnopolsky, Walter. *Discrimination and the Law Including Equality Rights Under the Charter*, loose-leaf (Scarborough, Ont.: Carswell, 1986-).

Topical Journals/Newsletters

Charter of Rights Newsletter
Constitutional Forum
National Journal of Constitutional Law

Topical Law Reports

Canadian Rights Reporter
Charter of Rights Decisions

15) — Contract Law

Texts and loose-leaf Services

Abe, Lisa K. *Internet and E-Commerce Agreements: Drafting and Negotiating Tips* (Toronto: Butterworths, 2001).

Card, Duncan Cornell. *Information Technology Transactions: Business, Management and Legal Strategies*, 2d ed. (Toronto: Carswell, 2007).

CCH Candian. *Canadian Commercial Law Guide*, loose-leaf (Don Mills, Ont.: CCH Canadian, 1980-).

Elderkin, Cynthia L. & Julia S. Shin Doi. *Behind and Beyond Boilerplate: Drafting Commercial Agreements* (Toronto: Thomson Carswell, 2005).

Fridman, G.H.L. *The Law of Contract in Canada*, 5th ed. (Toronto: Carswell, 2006).

Giliker, Paula. *Re-Examining Contract and Unjust Enrichment: Anglo-Canadian Perspectives* (Leiden, Netherlands: Martinus Nijhoff Publishers, 2007).

Goldsmith, Immanuel. *Goldsmith on Canadian Building Contracts*, 4th ed., loose-leaf (Toronto: Carswell, 1988-).

Hall, Geoff. *Canadian Contractual Interpretation Law* (Markham, Ont.: LexisNexis, 2007).

Kyer, Clifford Ian & Mark J. Fecenko. *Kyer and Fecenko on Computer-Related Agreements: A Practical Guide*, 2d ed. (Toronto: Butterworths, 1997).

MacDougall, Bruce. *Introduction to Contracts* (Markham, Ont.: Lexis-Nexis Canada, 2007).

Marcone, Martin. *Eligible Financial Contracts* (Markham, Ont.: Lexis-Nexis, 2009).

McCamus, John D. *Law of Contracts* (Toronto: Irwin Law, 2005).

Pitch, Harvin & Ronald M. Snyder. *Damages for Breach of Contract*, 2d ed., loose-leaf (Toronto: Carswell, 1989-).

Swan, Angela. *Canadian Contract Law*, 2d ed. (Markham, Ont.: Lexis-Nexis Butterworths, 2009).

Swan, Angela & Jakub Adamski. *Halsbury's Laws of Canada: Contracts* (Markham, Ont.: LexisNexis Canada, 2008).

Swan, John. *Canadian Contract Law* (Markham, Ont.: LexisNexis Butterworths, 2006).

Waddams, S.M. *The Law of Contracts*, 6th ed. (Toronto: Canada Law Book, 2010).

16) — Construction Law

Texts and loose-leaf Services

Bristow, David I. *Construction Builders' and Mechanics' Liens in Canada*, 7th ed. (Toronto: Thomson Carswell, 2005).

Coulson, David. *Guide to Builders' Liens in British Columbia*, loose-leaf (Scarborough, Ont.: Carswell, n.d.).

Davenport, Philip. *Construction Claims* (Toronto: Irwin Law, 2006).

Glaholt, Duncan. *Conduct of a Lien Action* (Scarborough, Ont.: Carswell, published annually).

.... *Construction Trusts* (Scarborough, Ont.: Carswell, 1999).

Glaholt, Duncan & Markus Rotterdam. *Halsbury's Laws of Canada: Construction* (Markham, Ont.: LexisNexis Canada, 2008).

Kirsh, Harvey J. & Lori A. Roth. *The Annotated Construction Contract* (Aurora, Ont.: Canada Law Book, 1997).

Kirsh, Harvey J. & Paul A. Ivanoff. *The Canadian Construction Law Dictionary (Judicially Considered)* (Markham, Ont.: LexisNexis Butterworths, 2006).

Macklem, Douglas & David Bristow. *Construction, Builders' and Mechanics' Liens in Canada*, 6th ed. (Toronto: Carswell, 1990-).

McGuinness, Kevin Patrick. *Construction Lien Remedies in Ontario*, 2d ed. (Toronto: Carswell Publications, 1997).

Sandori, Paul. *Bidding and Tendering: What Is The Law?*, 4th ed. (Markham, Ont.: LexisNexis Butterworths, 2009).

Scott, Kenneth & Bruce Reynolds. *Scott and Reyolds on Surety Bonds*, loose-leaf (Scarborough, Ont.: Carswell, n.d.).

Silver, Robert. *Construction Dispute Resolution Handbook* (Markham, Ont.: LexisNexis, 2004).

Wise, Howard. *Manual of Construction Law*, loose-leaf (Scarborough, Ont.: Carswell, n.d.).

Annotated Statutes

Glaholt, Duncan & David Keeshan. *The Annotated Ontario Construction Lien Act* (Scarborough, Ont.: Carswell, published annually).

Mascarin, John & Jeffrey L. Levitt. *Annotated Ontario Building Code Act* (Markham, Ont.: LexisNexis, published annually).

Topical Reports

Construction Law Reports

Topical Newsletters

Construction Law Letter

17) — Corporate Law

Texts and loose-leaf Services

a) — General

Baker, Ash V.H. *Extra-Provincial Corporate Registrations in Canada* (Markham, Ont.: LexisNexis Canada, published annually).

Bollefer, Stuart F. & David Malach. *The Business in Transition: Making the Succession Plan Work* (Markham, Ont.: LexisNexis, 2008).

Campbell, Neil. *Merger Law and Practice: The Regulation of Mergers Under the Competition Act* (Scarborough, Ont.: Carswell, 1997).

Campbell, R.L., ed. *The Legal Framework of Business Enterprises*, 4th ed. (Concord, Ont.: Captus Press, 2007).

Dorval, Thierry. *Governance of Publicly Listed Corporations* (Markham, Ont.: LexisNexis Butterworths, 2005).

DuPlessis, Dorothy *et al. Canadian Business and the Law*, 3d ed. (Toronto: Thomson Nelson, 2008).

Ellis, Mark Vincent. *Fiduciary Duties in Canada*, loose-leaf (Toronto: Carswell, 1988-).

Ellis, Mark Vincent, Keith G. Fairbairn & Michael P.J. McKendry. *Corporate and Commercial Fiduciary Duties* (Toronto: Carswell, 1995).

.... *Professional Fiduciary Duties* (Toronto: Carswell, 1995).

Estey, Wilfrid M. *Legal Opinions in Commercial Transactions*, 2d ed. (Toronto: Butterworths, 1997).

Grover, Warren. *Canada Corporation Manual*, loose-leaf (Toronto: Carswell, n.d.).

Hepburn, Lyle R. *Limited Partnerships*, loose-leaf (Toronto: Carswell, 1983-).

Kerr, Michael. *Corporate Social Responsibility: A Legal Analysis* (Markham, Ont.: LexisNexis, 2009).

Kerr, M. Kaye. *Procedures for Meetings and Organizations*, 3d ed. (Scarborough, Ont.: Carswell, 1996).

Koehnen, Markus. *Oppression and Related Remedies* (Toronto: Thomson Carswell, 2004).

Kosar, William E. *International Business and Trade Law* (Toronto: Carswell, 2005).

Lipson, Barry. *The Art of the Deal* (Scarborough, Ont.: Carswell, 2000).

Mahaffy, A. Paul. *Business Succession Guide* (Scarborough, Ont.: Carswell, 2008).

Manzer, Alison R. *Canada-U.S. Commercial Law Guide*, loose-leaf (Toronto: Thomson/Carswell, 2003-).

Martel, Paul. *Business Corporations in Canada: Legal and Practical Aspects*, loose-leaf (Scarborough, Ont.: Carswell, 2004-).

McGuinness, Kevin Patrick. *Canadian Business Corporations Law*, 2d ed. (Markham, Ont.: LexisNexis Canada, 2007).

.... *Halsbury's Laws of Canada: Business Corporations I and II* (Markham, Ont.: LexisNexis Canada, 2008).

Morritt, David S., Sonia L. Bjorkquist & Allan D. Coleman. *The Oppression Remedy*, loose-leaf (Aurora, Ont.: Canada Law Book, 2004-).

Nathan, Hartley R. *Corporate Meetings: Law and Practice* (Scarborough, Ont.: Carswell, 1995).

Nicholls, Christopher C. *Mergers, Acquisitions, and Other Changes of Corporate Control* (Toronto: Irwin Law, 2007).

O'Shea, Michael. *Records Retention: Law and Practice*, loose-leaf (Scarborough, Ont.: Carswell, 2008-).

Peterson, Dennis. *Shareholder Remedies in Canada*, loose-leaf (Toronto: Butterworths, 1989-).

Puri, Poonam. *Canadian Companies' Guide to the Sarbanes-Oxley Act* (Markham, Ont.: LexisNexis Butterworths, 2004).

.... *Corporate Governance and Securities Regulation in the 21st Century* (Markham, Ont.: LexisNexis Butterworths, 2004).

Rossiter, Gary S. *Business Legal Adviser*, loose-leaf (Toronto: Carswell, 1985-).

Sarna, Lazar. *Corporate Structure, Finance and Operations* (Scarborough, Ont.: Carswell, 1998).

.... *Mergers and Acquisitions: A Canadian Legal Manual*, rev. ed., loose-leaf (Montreal: Jewel, 2005-).

Smyth, J.E., D.A. Soberman & A.J. Easson. *The Law and Business Administration in Canada*, 10th ed. (Toronto: Prentice Hall, 2004).

Van Duzer, J. Anthony. *Law of Partnerships and Corporations*, 3d ed. (Concord, Ont.: Irwin Law, 2009).

Weir, Jan D., Karen J. Reschke & Shane A. Ellis. *Critical Concepts of Canadian Business Law*, 2d ed. (Toronto: Addison-Wesley Longman, 2001).

Welling, Bruce. *Corporate Law in Canada: The Governing Principles*, 3d ed. (Queensland: Scribblers Pub., 2006).

White, Jerry & Frank Zaid, eds. *Canadian Franchise Guide*, loose-leaf (Toronto: Carswell, 1983-).

Ziegel, Jacob. *Commercial and Consumer Transactions* (Toronto: Emond Montgomery, 1995).

b) — Alberta

MacLeod, Dixon. *Alberta Corporation Manual*, loose-leaf (Scarborough, Ont.: Carswell, n.d.).

c) — British Columbia

Owen, Robert. *British Columbia Corporation Manual*, loose-leaf (Scarborough, Ont.: Carswell, 2004-).

d) — Charities and Not-for-Profit

Bourgeois, Donald J. *Charities and Not-for-Profit Administration and Governance Handbook* (Markham, Ont.: Butterworths, 2001).

Burke-Robertson, R. Jane & Arthur Drache. *Non-Share Capital Corporations*, loose-leaf (Toronto: Carswell, 1992-).

Nemet-Brown, Sheila & Donald J. Bourgeois. *Halsbury's Laws of Canada: Cemeteries and Interment; Charities, Associations and Not-for-Profit Organizations* (Markham, Ont.: LexisNexis Canada, 2008).

e) — Directors and Officers

Davis, Ronald. *Directors' Liability in Canada*, loose-leaf (North Vancouver: STP Specialty Technical Publishers, 2006-).

Debenham, David. *Executive Liability and the Law* (Scarborough, Ont.: Thomson/Carswell, 2006).

Hansell, Carol. *Directors and Officers in Canada: Law and Practice* (Scarborough, Ont.: Carswell, 1999).

Nathan, Hartley R. *et al. Directors Manual*, loose-leaf (North York, Ont.: CCH Canadian, 1994-).

Priest, Margot & Hartley R. Nathan. *Directors' Duties in Canada*, 2d ed. (Toronto: CCH Canadian, 2002).

Reiter, Barry J. *Directors' Duties in Canada*, 3d ed. (Toronto: CCH Canadian, 2006).

Sarna, Lazar. *Directors and Officers: A Canadian Legal Manual*, rev. ed., loose-leaf (Markham, Ont.: LexisNexis 2005).

f) — Forms

Davies, Ward & Beck. *Canadian Securities Law Precedents*, loose-leaf (Toronto: Carswell, 1989-).

Emerson. H. Garfield, ed. *Canadian Corporation Precedents*, loose-leaf (Toronto: Carswell, 1987-).

Ewasiuk, Ricky. *Guide to Drafting Shareholder's Agreements* (Scarborough, Ont.: Carswell, 1998).

Harris, Gregory Harrington & Paul Richard LeBreux, *Annotated Business Agreements*, loose-leaf (Toronto: Carswell, 1993-).

O'Brien's Encyclopedia of Forms: Commercial and General Division, looseleaf (Aurora, Ont.: Canada Law Book, 1987-).

g) — Ontario

Day, Midge. *Ontario Corporate Procedures*, 4th ed. by Bernie Aron (Scarborough, Ont.: Carswell, 2001).

Kingston, Robert A. *et al. Ontario Corporation Manual*, loose-leaf (Toronto: Carswell, 1984-).

h) — Quebec

Quebec Corporation Manual, loose-leaf (Scarborough, Ont.: Carswell, n.d.).

Annotated Statutes

Adams, Stephen N. *Annotated Ontario Business Corporations Act*, loose-leaf (Aurora, Ont.: Canada Law Book, 1990-).

Cumberford, Deborah. *Annotated British Columbia Corporations Act*, 3d ed. (Scarborough, Ont.: Carswell, published yearly).

Currie, Brenda-Jean. *Annotated Business Corporations Act of Alberta*, loose-leaf (Scarborough, Ont.: Carswell, n.d.).

Fasken Martineau DuMoulin LLP. *The Annotated British Columbia Company Act*, loose-leaf (Aurora, Ont.: Canada Law Book, 2005-).

.... *Canada Business Corporations Act and Commentary* (Markham, Ont.: LexisNexis, published annually).

Gray, Wayne. *The Annotated Ontario Business Corporations Act*, loose-leaf (Toronto: Carswell, 1996-).

McLeod, Andrew & Ian N. MacIntosh. *British Columbia Business Corporations Act and Commentary* (Markham, Ont.: LexisNexis, published annually).

Records Retention: Statutes and Regulations (Federal edition), loose-leaf (Scarborough, Ont.: Carswell, 1993-).

Records Retention: Statutes and Regulations (Ontario edition), loose-leaf (Scarborough, Ont.: Carswell, 1993-).

Topical Journals

Asper Review of International Business and Trade Law
Business and the Law
Business Quarterly
Canada-U.S. Business Law Review
Canadian Business Law Journal
Corporate Governance Report
Journal of Business Valuation

Topical Law Reports

Business Law Reports
Canada Corporations Law Reporter
Personal Property Security Act Cases

18) — Criminal Law

Texts and loose-leaf Services

a) — General

Abell, Jennie, Elizabeth Sheehy & Natasha Bakht. *Criminal Law and Procedure: Proof, Defences and Beyond*, 4th ed. (Concord, Ont.: Captus Press, 2009).

Altrens, Jerome, Peter T. Burns & James P. Taylor. *Criminal Procedure: Canadian Law and Practice*, loose-leaf (Toronto: Butterworths, 1981-).

Bentley, Christopher. *Criminal Practice Manual: A Practical Guide to Handling Criminal Cases*, loose-leaf (Scarborough, Ont.: Carswell, 2000-).

Campbell, Gordon Scott. *The Investigator's Legal Handbook* (Scarborough, Ont.: Carswell, 2006).

Colvin, Eric & Sanjeev Anand. *Principles of Criminal Law*, 3d ed. (Toronto: Thomson Carswell, 2007).

Delisle, R.J., Don Stuart & Gary Trotter. *Learning Canadian Criminal Procedure*, 9th ed. (Toronto: Thomson Carswell, 2008).

Fiszauf, Alec. *The Law of Investigative Detention* (Markham, Ont.: LexisNexis, 2008).

German, Peter. *Proceeds of Crime*, loose-leaf (Scarborough, Ont.: Carswell, n.d.).

Gibson, John. *Canadian Criminal Code Offences*, loose-leaf (Toronto: Carswell, 1986-).

Gold, Alan D. *The Practitioner's Criminal Precedents*, 2d ed. (Markham, Ont.: LexisNexis, 2008).

Gold, Alan D. & Andrew James. *Halsbury's Laws of Canada: Criminal Offences and Defences* (Markham, Ont.: LexisNexis Canada, 2007).

.... *Halsbury's Laws of Canada: Criminal Procedure* (Markham, Ont.: LexisNexis Canada, 2007).

Henderson, Michael. *Commercial Crime in Canada*, loose-leaf (Toronto: Carswell, 1990).

Kenkel, Joseph F. *Criminal Lawyer's Trial Book*, loose-leaf (Markham, Ont.: LexisNexis, n.d.).

Knoll, Patrick J. *Criminal Law Defences*, 3d ed. (Scarborough, Ont.: Carswell, 2005).

Manning, Morris & Peter Sankoff. *Manning, Mewett & Sankoff: Criminal Law*, 4th ed. (Markham, Ont.: LexisNexis, 2009).

Meehan, Eugene. *The Law of Criminal Attempt*, 2d ed. (Scarborough, Ont.: Carswell, 2000).

Mewett, Alan W. *An Introduction to the Criminal Process in Canada*, 4th ed. (Scarborough, Ont.: Carswell, 2001).

Nightingale, Brenda. *The Law of Fraud and Related Offences*, loose-leaf (Scarborough, Ont.: Carswell, n.d.).

Pickard, Toni *et al. Dimensions of Criminal Law*, 3d ed. (Toronto: Emond Montgomery Publications, 2002).

Pink, Joel E. & David C. Perrier, eds. *From Crime to Punishment: An Introduction to the Criminal Law System*, 5th ed. (Toronto: Carswell, 2003).

Proulx, Michel & David Layton. *Ethics and Canadian Criminal Law* (Toronto: Irwin Law, 2001).

Quigley, Tim. *Procedure in Canadian Criminal Law*, 2d ed. (Toronto: Thomson Carswell, 2005).

Roach, Kent. *Criminal Law*, 4th ed. (Toronto: Irwin Law, 2009).

Rose, David & Lisa Goos. *DNA: A Practical Guide*, loose-leaf (Scarborough, Ont.: Carswell, 2004-).

Rossiter, James. *Law of Publication Bans, Private Hearings and Sealing Orders*, loose-leaf (Scarborough, Ont.: Carswell, 2006-).

Salhany, Roger. *Criminal Trial Handbook*, loose-leaf (Toronto: Carswell, 1992-).

.... *Cross-examination: The Art of the Advocate*, 3d ed. (Markham, Ont.: LexisNexis Canada, 2006).

Segal, Murray. *Disclosure and Production in Criminal Cases*, loose-leaf (Scarborough, Ont.: Carswell, n.d.).

Sinclair-Prowse, Janet. *Working Manual of Criminal Law*, loose-leaf (Toronto: Carswell, 1984-).

Stuart, Don. *Canadian Criminal Law: A Treatise*, 5th ed. (Scarborough, Ont.: Thomson Carswell, 2007).

.... *Learning Canadian Criminal Law*, 11th ed. (Scarborough, Ont.: Carswell, 2009).

Watt, David. *Criminal Law Precedents*, 2d ed., loose-leaf (Toronto: Carswell, 2007-).

.... *Carswell's Form and Precedent Collection: Criminal Law Precedents*, 2d ed., loose-leaf (Toronto: Thomson Carswell, 2007-).

b) — Appeals

McKinnon, Gil. *The Criminal Lawyers' Guide to Appellate Court Practice* (Aurora, Ont.: Canada Law Book, 1997).

Sopinka, John and Mark A. Gelowitz. *The Conduct of an Appeal*, 2d ed. (Toronto: Butterworths, 2000).

White, Robert B. & J.J. Stratton. *The Appeal Book* (Aurora, Ont.: Canada Law Book, 1999).

c) — Bail

Hamilton, Keith R. *Judicial Interim Release (Bail Manual)*, 4th ed., loose-leaf (Vancouver: Butterworths, 1983-).

Katz, Joel Ian. *The Art of Bail: Strategy and Practice* (Markham, Ont.: Butterworths, 1999).

Trotter, Gary T. *The Law of Bail in Canada*, 2d ed. (Scarborough, Ont.: Carswell, 1998).

d) — Charter

Barrett, Joan. *Balancing Charter Interests: Victims' Rights and Third Party Remedies*, loose-leaf (Scarborough, Ont.: Carswell, 2000).

Fontana, James A. & David Keeshan. *The Law of Search and Seizure in Canada*, 7th ed. (Toronto: LexisNexis/Butterworths, 2007).

Hutchison, Scott C. *Hutchison's Canadian Search Warrant Manual, 2005: A Guide to Legal and Practical Issues Associated with Judicial Pre-Authorization of Investigative Techniques*, 2d ed. (Toronto: Carswell, 2004).

Hutchison, Scott & James C. Morton. *Search and Seizure Law in Canada*, loose-leaf (Toronto: Carswell, 1990-).

Keeshan, David & James A. Fontana. *Police Guide to Search and Seizure* (Markham, Ont.: Butterworths, 2003).

McLeod, Roderick *et al. The Canadian Charter of Rights*, loose-leaf (Toronto: Carswell, 1983-).

Salhany, Roger E. *The Police Manual of Arrest, Seizure and Interrogation*, 8th ed. (Toronto: Carswell, 2002).

Stuart, Don. *Charter Justice in Canadian Criminal Law*, 4th ed. (Toronto: Thomson Carswell, 2005).

e) — Children

Harvey, Wendy. *Sexual Offences Against Children*, 2d ed. (Toronto: Butterworths, 2001).

Maleszyk, Anna M. *Crimes Against Children: Prosecution and Defence*, loose-leaf (Aurora, Ont.: Canada Law Book, 2001-).

f) — Commercial Crime

Henderson, Michael. *Commercial Crime in Canada*, loose-leaf (Toronto: Carswell, 1990).

g) — Driving Offences

Gold, Alan. *Defending Drinking and Driving Cases* (Scarborough, Ont.: Carswell, published annually).

Hamilton, Keith. *Impaired Driving and Breathalyzer Law*, loose-leaf (Toronto: Butterworths, 1980-).

Hutchison, Scott, David S. Rose & Philip Downes. *The Law of Traffic Offences*, 3d ed. (Toronto: Carswell, 2009).

Kenkel, Joseph F. *Impaired Driving in Canada*, 2009 ed. (Toronto: LexisNexis, 2008).

Manraj, A. Shakoor and Paul D. Haines. *The Law of Speeding and Speed Detection*, 3d ed. (Markham, Ont.: LexisNexis, 2007).

McLeod Roderick *et al., Breathalyzer Law in Canada: The Prosecution and Defence of Drinking and Driving Offences*, 4th ed., loose-leaf (Toronto: Carswell, 2009-).

McLeod Roderick *et al., Criminal Code Driving Offences: A Companion Text for Breathalyzer Law in Canada*, loose-leaf (Toronto: Carswell, 1987-).

Segal, Murray. *Manual of Motor Vehicle Law*, loose-leaf (Toronto: Carswell, 1982-).

.... *Annotated Ontario Highway Traffic Act* (Toronto: Carswell, published annually).

h) — Drug Offences

Bolton, P. Michael. *Defending Drug Cases*, 3d ed. (Toronto: Thomson Carswell, 2006).

Brauti, Peter M. & Brian G. Puddington. *Prosecuting and Defending Drug Offences* (Aurora, Ont.: Canada Law Book, 2003).

Brucker, Theresa. *The Practical Guide to the Controlled Drugs and Substances Act*, 4th ed. (Toronto: Thomson Carswell, 2008).

MacFarlane, Bruce A. *Drug Offences in Canada*, 3d ed., loose-leaf (Aurora, Ont.: Canada Law Book, 1997-).

Rockerbie, R.A. *Alcohol and Drug Intoxication* (Victoria, B.C.: Trafford, 1999).

i) — Evidence

Anderson, Glenn R., *Expert Evidence*, 2d ed. (Markham, Ont.: Butterworths Canada, 2009).

Atkinson, Paul. *Proof: Canadian Rules of Evidence* (Markham, Ont.: LexisNexis, 2007).

Bryant, Alan W. *et al. The Law of Evidence in Canada*, 3d ed. (Toronto: LexisNexis, 2009).

Chayko, G.M. *et al., Forensic Evidence in Canada*, 2d ed. (Aurora, Ont.: Canada Law Book, 1999).

Cox, Harold. *Criminal Evidence Handbook* (Aurora, Ont.: Canada Law Book, 1988-).

Delisle, R.J. *Canadian Evidence Law in a Nutshell*, 2d ed. (Scarborough, Ont.: Carswell, 2002).

Doherty, Michael P. *The Portable Guide to Evidence*, 2d ed. (Toronto: Carswell, 2006).

Ewaschuk, E.G. *Criminal Pleadings and Practice in Canada*, loose-leaf (Aurora, Ont.: Canada Law Book, 1987-).

Gibson, John. *Criminal Law Evidence, Practice and Procedure*, loose-leaf (Toronto: Carswell, 1988-).

Gold, Alan D. *Expert Evidence in Criminal Law: The Scientific Approach*, 2d ed. (Toronto: Irwin Law, 2009).

Hubbard, Robert W., Susan Magotiaux & Suzanne M. Duncan. *The Law of Privilege In Canada* (Toronto: Canada Law Book, 2005).

Kenkel, Joseph. *Defence Lawyers Trial Book*, loose-leaf (Toronto: Butterworths, 2000-).

Levy, Earl J., *Examination of Witnesses in Criminal Cases*, 5th ed. (Scarborough, Ont.: Thomson-Carswell, 2004).

Marin, René J. *Admissibility of Statements*, 9th ed. (Aurora, Ont.: Canada Law Book Inc., 1996).

McWilliams, Peter. *Canadian Criminal Evidence*, 3d ed. (Aurora, Ont.: Canada Law Book, 1988-).

Mewett, Alan & Shaun Nakatsuru. *An Introduction to the Criminal Process in Canada*, 4th ed. (Toronto: Carswell, 2000).

Paciocco, David M. & Lee Stuesser. *The Law of Evidence*, 5th ed. (Toronto: Irwin Law, 2008).

Salhany, Roger. *Canadian Criminal Procedure*, 6th ed., loose-leaf (Aurora, Ont.: Canada Law Book, 1994-).

.... *The Practical Guide to Evidence in Criminal Cases*, 6th ed. (Scarborough, Ont.: Carswell, 2002).

Sopinka, John, Sidney N. Lederman, & Alan W. Bryant. *The Law of Evidence in Canada*, 2d ed. (Toronto: Butterworths, 1999).

j) — Extradition Law

Botting, Gary. *Canadian Extradition Law Practice* (Markham, Ont.: LexisNexis Butterworths, 2009).

.... *Extradition between Canada and the United States* (Ardsley, N.Y.: Transnational Publishers, 2005).

Krivel, Elaine & Thomas Beveridge. *A Practical Guide to Canadian Extradition* (Toronto: Carswell, 2002).

La Forest, Anne W. *La Forest's Extradition to and from Canada*, 3d ed. (Aurora, Ont: Canada Law Book, 1991).

k) — Inquests

Marshall, T. David. *Canadian Law Of Inquests: A Handbook For Coroners, Medical Examiners, Counsel and Police*, 3d ed. (Toronto: Carswell, 2008).

l) — Jury Trials

Der, Balfour. *The Jury: A Handbook of Law and Procedure*, loose-leaf (Toronto: Butterworths, 1989-).

Granger, Christopher. *Canadian Criminal Jury Trials*, 2d ed. (Toronto: Carswell, 1996-).

Tanovich, David M., David M. Paciocco & Steven Skurka. *Jury Selection in Criminal Trials: Skills, Science, and the Law* (Concord, Ont.: Irwin Law, 1997).

Watt, David. *Helping Jurors Understand* (Scarborough, Ont.: Carswell, 2007).

.... *Ontario Specimen Jury Instructions (Criminal)* (Scarborough, Ont.: Carswell, 2002).

.... *Watt's Manual of Criminal Jury Instructions* (Scarborough, Ont.: Carswell, 2005).

m) — Mental Disorder

Barrett, Joan M. & Riun Shandler. *Mental Disorders in Canadian Criminal Law*, loose-leaf (Toronto: Thomson Carswell, 2006-).

Bloom, Hy & Richard D. Schneider. *Mental Disorder and the Law: A Primer for Legal and Mental Health Professionals* (Toronto: Irwin Law, 2006).

n) — Money Laundering

Beare, Margaret E. & Stephen Schneider. *Money Laundering in Canada: Chasing Dirty and Dangerous Dollars* (Toronto: University of Toronto Press, 2007).

Hall, Terry. *A Guide to Canadian Money Laundering Legislation*, 2009 ed.(Markham, Ont.: LexisNexis Butterworths, 2008).

Hubbard, Robert W. *et al. Money Laundering and Proceeds of Crime* (Toronto, Ont.: Irwin Law, 2004).

Manzer, Alison R. *A Guide to Canadian Money Laundering Legislation* (Markham, Ont.: Butterworths, 2002).

Munshani, Kalyani. *The Impact of Global International Informal Banking on Canada* (Toronto: Nathanson Centre for the Study of Organized Crime and Corruption, 2005).

o) — Police

Fiszauf, Alec. *The Law of Investigative Detention* (Markham, Ont.: LexisNexis, 2008).

Jakob, Karen. *A Guide to Police Writing*, 3d ed. (Toronto: Carswell, 2002).

Keeshan, David and James A. Fontana. *Police Guide to Search and Seizure* (Markham, Ont.: Butterworths, 2003).

Rodrigues, Gary. *The Police Officers Manual of Criminal Offences and Criminal Law*, 16th ed. (Toronto: Carswell, 1999).

Salhany, Roger E. *The Police Manual of Arrest, Seizure and Interrogation*, 9th ed. (Toronto: Carswell, 2009).

p) — Provincial Offences

Allen, John. *Defending Provincial Offences Cases in Ontario* (Toronto: Carswell, 1995).

Allen, John Pearson & Rick Libman. *Handling Provincial Offence Cases in Ontario* (Toronto: Carswell, published annually).

Capy, Ugo & Erin MacCarthy. *Provincial Offences* (Toronto: Emond Montgomery, 2000).

Gilbert, Dan & Peter Maher. *Provincial Offences: Essential Tools for Law Enforcement*, 2d ed. (Toronto: Emond Montgomery, 2008).

Libman, Rick. *Criminal Trial Rules in Provincial Courts in Canada, Fully Annotated* (Salt Spring Island, B.C.: Earlscourt Legal Press, published annually).

Stewart, Sheilagh. *Stewart on Provincial Offences Procedure in Ontario*, 2d ed. (Toronto: Earlscourt Legal Press, 2005).

q) — Robbery

Holland, Winifred H. *The Law of Theft and Related Offences* (Toronto: Carswell, 1998).

Libman, Rick. *The Law of Robbery* (Toronto: Carswell, 1990).

r) — Search and Seizure

Boucher, Susanne & Kenneth Landa. *Understanding Section 8: Search, Seizure, And The Canadian Constitution* (Toronto: Irwin Law, 2004).

Fontana, James A. & David Keeshan. *The Law of Search and Seizure in Canada*, 7th ed. (Toronto: Butterworths, 2007).

Hutchison, Scott C. *Hutchison's Canadian Search Warrant Manual, 2005: A Guide to Legal and Practical Issues Associated with Judicial Pre-Authorization of Investigative Techniques*, 2d ed. (Toronto: Carswell, 2004).

s) — Sentencing

Armstrong, Simon, *et al. Sentencing Drug Offenders* (Aurora, Ont.: Canada Law Book, 2004-).

Clewley, Gary R. & Paul G. McDermott. *Sentencing: The Practitioner's Guide*, loose-leaf (Aurora, Ont.: Canada Law Book, 1999-).

Ferris, T. W. *Sentencing: Practical Approaches* (Markham, Ont.: Lexis-Nexis Butterworths, 2005).

Manson, Allan. *The Law of Sentencing* (Toronto: Irwin Law, 2001).

Nadin-Davis, R. Paul. *Canadian Sentencing Digest Quantum Service*, loose-leaf (Toronto: Carswell, 1988-).

Nadin-Davis, R. Paul & Clarey B. S. *Canadian Sentencing Digest* (Toronto: Carswell, published annually).

Nemet-Brown, Sheila ed. *Canada Criminal Sentencing Digest*, 2d ed. (Markham, Ont.: LexisNexis Canada, 2007-).

Renaud, Gilles. *Speaking to Sentence: A Practical Guide* (Scarborough, Ont.: Carswell, 2004-).

.... *The Sentencing Code of Canada: Principles and Objectives* (Markham, Ont.: LexisNexis, 2009).

Ruby, Clayton *et al. Sentencing,* 7th ed. (Toronto: LexisNexis Canada, 2008).

t) — Sexual Offences

Daylen, Judith Lynne, Wendy van Tongeren Harvey & Dennis O'Toole. *Trauma, Trials, and Transformation: Guiding Sexual Assualt Victims Through the Legal System and Beyond* (Toronto: Irwin Law, 2006).

Fuerst, Michelle. *Defending Sexual Offence Cases,* 2d ed. (Toronto: Carswell, 2000).

Stewart, Hamish. *Sexual Offences in Canadian Law,* loose-leaf (Aurora, Ont.: Canada Law Book, 2004-).

u) — Weapons Offences

Harris, Peter J. *Weapons Offences Manual,* loose-leaf (Aurora, Ont.: Canada Law Book, 1990-).

v) — Youth Criminal Justice

Bala, Nicholas C. *Youth Criminal Justice Law,* 2d ed. (Toronto: Irwin Law, 2009).

Harris, Peter J. *Young Offenders Act Manual* (Aurora, Ont.: Canada Law Book, 1984).

.... *Youth Criminal Justice Act Manual,* loose-leaf (Aurora, Ont.: Canada Law Book, 2003-).

Tustin, Lee and Robert E. Lutes. *A Guide to the Youth Criminal Justice Act* (Markham, Ont.: LexisNexis, published annually).

Annotated Statutes

Annotated Ontario Rules of Criminal Practice (Toronto: Carswell, published annually).

Brunet, Jonathan & Pamela Goode. *Annotated Firearms and Related Legislation* (Markham, Ont.: LexisNexis, 2006).

Falconer, Julian N. & Peter J. Pliszka. *Annotated Ontario Coroners Act, 2008/2009* (Markham, Ont.: LexisNexis, 2008).

Greene, Mara et al. *Annotated Youth Criminal Justice Act Service,* loose-leaf (Markham, Ont.: LexisNexis, n.d.).

Heather, D.R.H. *Snow's Annotated Criminal Code,* loose-leaf (Toronto: Carswell, 1979-).

Libman, Rick. *The Annotated Contraventions Act* (Scarborough, Ont.: Carswell, published annually).

Martins' Criminal Code (Aurora, Ont.: Canada Law Book, published annually).

Muir, Douglas B. & Michael Libby. *Annotated British Columbia Motor Vehicle Act*, loose-leaf (Aurora, Ont.: Canada Law Book, n.d.).

Nadeau, Alain-Robert & John F. Reid. *Annotated Royal Canadian Mounted Police Act and Regulations* (Scarborough, Ont.: Carswell, 2006).

Rose, David. *Snow's Annotated Criminal Code*, loose-leaf (Scarborough, Ont.: Carswell, n.d.).

Rodrigues, Gary ed., *Crankshaw's Criminal Code of Canada*, loose-leaf (Toronto: Carswell, 1993-).

Schneider, Richard D. *The Annotated Ontario Mental Health Statutes* (Toronto: Irwin Law, 2007).

Segal, Murry D. *The Annotated Ontario Highway Traffic Act* (Scarborough, Ont.: Carswell, published annually).

.... *The Annotated Ontario Rules of Criminal Practice* (Scarborough, Ont.: Carswell, published annually).

Watt, David. *The Annotated Tremeear's Criminal Code* (Toronto: Carswell, published annually).

Topical Journals/Newsletters

Annual Review of Criminal Law
Journal of Motor Vehicle Law
Criminal Law Journal
Criminal Law Quarterly
Canadian Criminal Law Review
Canadian Journal of Criminology and Criminal Justice

Topical Law Reports

Canadian Criminal Cases
Canadian Criminal Injuries Compensation Board Decisions
Criminal Reports
Motor Vehicle Reports
Weekly Criminal Bulletin

19) — Crown

Texts and loose-leaf Services

Hogg, Peter W. & Patrick J. Monahan. *Liability of The Crown*, 3d ed. (Scarborough, Ont.: Carswell, 2000).

Horsman, Karen & J. Gareth Morley. *Government Liability: Law and Practice*, loose-leaf (Aurora, Ont.: Canada Law Book, 2006-).

20) — Damages/Remedies

Texts and loose-leaf Services

Barrett, Joan. *Balancing Charter Interests: Victims' Rights and Third Party Remedies* (Scarborough, Ont.: Carswell, 2000).

Berenblut, Mark L. & Howard N. Rosen. *Proving Economic Loss*, loose-leaf (Scarborough, Ont.: Carswell, 2000-).

Brown, Cara. *Damages: Estimating Pecuniary Loss*, loose-leaf (Aurora, Ont.: Canada Law Book, 2001-).

Bruce, Christopher J. *Assessment of Personal Injury Damages*, 4th ed. (Toronto: LexisNexis Butterworths, 2004).

Cassels, Jamie and Elizabeth Adjin-Tettey. *Remedies: The Law of Damages*, 2d ed. (Toronto: Irwin Law, 2008).

Certosimo, Matthew L.O. *The Regulation of Picketing: An Employer's Primer to Labour*, 2d ed. (Toronto: Thomson Carswell, 2004).

Cooper-Stephenson, Kenneth. *Personal Injury Damages in Canada*, 2d ed. (Scarborough, Ont.: Carswell, 1996).

Feldthusen, Bruce. *Economic Negligence: The Recovery of Pure Economic Loss*, 5th ed. (Toronto: Butterworths, 2008).

Field Atkinson Perraton LLP. *Remedies In Labour, Employment and Human Rights Law*, loose-leaf (Scarborough, Ont.: Carswell, 1999-).

Fridman, G.H.L. *Restitution*, 2d ed. (Toronto: Carswell, 1992).

Giliker, Paula, ed. *Re-Examining Contract and Unjust Enrichment: Anglo-Canadian Perspectives* (Leiden, Netherlands: Martinus Nijhoff Publishers, 2007).

Maddaugh, Peter D. & John D. McCamus. *The Law of Restitution*, loose-leaf (Aurora, Ont.: Canada Law Book, 2004-).

Meehan, Eugene J. & John H. Currie. *Injunctions* (Scarborough, Ont.: Carswell, 1996).

Pitch, Harvin & Ronald Snyder. *Damages for Breach of Contract*, loose-leaf (Toronto: Carswell, 1989-).

Reinhart, Marshall, ed. *Goldsmith's Damages for Personal Injury and Death in Canada*, loose-leaf (Toronto: Carswell, 1989-).

Sharpe, Robert J. *Injunctions and Specific Performance*, loose-leaf (Aurora, Ont.: Canada Law Book, n.d.).

Soriano, Errol D. *Understanding Financial Analysis in Litigation* (Scarborough, Ont.: Thomson Carswell, 2004).

Waddams, S.M. *The Law of Damages*, 3d ed. (Toronto: Canada Law Book, 1997).

21) — Education Law

Texts and loose-leaf Services

Bowers, Grant & Rena Knox. *Sexual Misconduct in Education: Prevention, Reporting and Discipline* (Scarborough, Ont.: Carswell, 2006).

Bowlby, Brenda, Catherine Peters & Martha Mackinnon. *An Educator's Guide to Special Education Law* (Aurora, Ont.: Canada Law Book, 2001).

Brown, Anthony. *Legal Handbook for Educators*, 6th ed. (Toronto: Carswell, 2009).

.... & Marvin A. Zuker. *Education Law*, 4th ed. (Toronto: Thomson Carswell, 2007).

Delaney, Jerome G. *Legal Dimensions of Education: Implications for Teachers and School Administrators* (Calgary: Detselig Enterprises, 2007).

Doctor, Eleanor. *Legal Handbook for Alberta Educators* (Markham, Ont.: LexisNexis, 2006).

Faraday, Fay, Victoria Réaume & Sheilagh Turkington. *Education Labour and Employment Law in Ontario*, 2d ed., loose-leaf (Aurora, Ont.: Canada Law Book, n.d.).

Glasbeek, Sandra. *Occupational Health and Safety in Ontario Education*, loose-leaf (Scarborough, Ont,: Carswell, n.d.).

.... *OH&S for Ontario School Staff: A Principal's Guide* (Scarborough, Ont.: Carswell, 2007).

Jacobson, Robyn & Alan Rycroft. *Managing Conflict in Schools: A Practical Guide* (Scarborough: Carswell, 2007).

MacKay, A. Wayne. & Greg M. Dickinson. *Beyond The "Careful Parent": Tort Liability in Education* (Toronto: Emond Montgomery, 1998).

.... & Lyle (Chip) Sutherland. *Teachers and the Law*, 2d ed. (Toronto: Emond Montgomery, 2006).

Roher, Eric M., & Simon A. Wormwell. *An Educator's Guide to the Role of the Principal*, 2d ed. (Aurora, Ont.: Canada Law Book, 2008).

Sarna, Lazar & Noah Sarna. *The Law of Schools and Universities* (Markham, Ont.: LexisNexis, 2007).

Trepanier, Jennifer. *Student Discipline: A Guide to the Education Amendment Act, 2007*, 2d ed. (Scarborough, Ont.: Carswell, 2008).

Annotated Statutes

Annotated Ontario Education Act, loose-leaf (Scarborough, Ont.: Carswell, published annually).

Topical Journals/Newsletters

Canadian Legal Education Annual Review
Education & Law Journal

Risk Management in Canadian Education

22) — Environmental Law

Texts and loose-leaf Services

Benidickson, Jamie. *Environmental Law*, 3d ed. (Toronto: Irwin Law, 2009).

Berger, Stanley D. *The Prosecution and Defence of Environmental Offences*, loose-leaf (Aurora, Ont.: Canada Law Book, n.d.).

Boyd, David R., *Unnatural Law: Rethinking Canadian Environmental Law and Policy* (Vancouver: UBC Press, 2003).

Carter-Whitney, Maureen. *Environmental Regulation in Canada* (Markham, Ont.: LexisNexis Canada, 2008).

Coburn, Frederick F. & Garth Manning, *Toxic Real Estate Manual*, loose-leaf (Aurora, Ont.: Canada Law Book, 1994-).

Cotton, Roger & Alastair R. Lucas., *Canadian Environmental Law*, 2d ed., loose-leaf (Toronto: Butterworths, 1992-).

Doelle, Meinhard. *From Hot Air to Action? Climate Change, Compliance and the Future of International Environmental Law* (Scarborough, Ont.: Carswell, 2005).

Estrin, David. *Business Guide to Environmental Law*, loose-leaf (Toronto: Carswell, 1992-).

Gamble, Ian. *Taxation of Canadian Mining*, loose-leaf (Toronto: Carswell, 2004-).

Hughes, Elaine L., Alastair R. Lucas & William A. Tilleman. *Environmental Law and Policy*, 3d ed. (Toronto: Emond Montgomery, 2003).

Lucas, Alistair & Roger Cotton. *Halsbury's Laws of Canada: Environment* (Markham, Ont.: LexisNexis Canada, 2007).

McConnell, Dr. Moira & Erika C. Gerlock. *Environmental Spills: Emergency Reporting, Clean-Up and Liability (Alberta)* (Scarborough, Ont.: Carswell, 1995).

.... *Environmental Spills: Emergency Reporting, Clean-Up and Liability (British Columbia)* (Scarborough, Ont.: Carswell, 1995).

.... *Environmental Spills: Emergency Reporting, Clean-Up and Liability (Ontario)* (Scarborough, Ont.: Carswell, 1995).

Menzies, Robert, Dorothy Chunn & Susan Boyd, eds. *Toxic Criminology: Environment, Law and the State of Canada* (Halifax, N.S.: Fernwood, 2002).

Walton, Janice H. *Blakes Canadian Endangered Species Law*, loose-leaf (Scarborough, Ont.: Carswell, 2007-).

Annotated Statutes

Cameron, Duncan J, Daniel C. Blasioli & Michel Arès. *Annotated Guide to the Canadian Environmental Protection Act*, loose-leaf (Aurora, Ont.: Canada Law Book, 2005-).

Castrilli, Joseph. *Annotated Guide to the Canadian Environmental Protection Act*, loose-leaf (Aurora, Ont.: Canada Law Book, n.d.).

Doelle, Meinhard. *Canadian Environmental Protection Act and Commentary*, 2008 ed. (Markham, Ont.: LexisNexis Butterworths, 2008).

Hobby, Beverly *et al. Canadian Environmental Assessment Act: An Annotated Guide*, loose-leaf (Aurora, Ont.: Canada Law Book, 1997-).

Saxe, Dianne. *Ontario Environmental Protection Act Annotated*, loose-leaf (Aurora, Ont.: Canada Law Book, 1990-).

Topical Law Reports

Canadian Environmental Law Reports

Topical Journals and Newsletters

The CELA Newsletter
Environmental Law Alert
Environment Policy & Law Intervenor
Journal of Environmental Law and Practice
Newsletter of the Canadian Environmental Law Association

23) — Estates, Trusts, and Wills

Texts and loose-leaf Services

Allen, William P.G. & Thomas F.W. Allen. *Estate Planning Handbook*, 3d ed. (Toronto: -Carswell, 1999).

Armstrong, Anne E.P. *Estate Administration: A Solicitor's Reference Manual* (Scarborough, Ont.: Carswell, 1998).

Berryman, Jeffrey B. *et al. The Law of Trusts: A Contextual Approach*, 2d ed. (Toronto: Emond Montgomery, 2008).

Bollefer, Stuart F. & David Malach. *The Business in Transition: Making the Succession Plan Work* (Markham, Ont.: LexisNexis, 2008).

Brown, Catherine & Cindy L. Radu. *Taxation and Estate Planning*, loose-leaf (Toronto: Carswell, 1996-).

Butler, Alison Scott. *Tax Planned Will Precedents*, 4th ed., loose-leaf (Toronto: Thomson Carswell, 2007-).

CCH Canadian. *Canadian Estate Administration Guide*, loose-leaf (Don Mills, Ont.: CCH Canadian, 1994-).

Claxton, John. *Studies on the Quebec Law of Trusts* (Scarborough, Ont.: Carswell, 2005).

Doyle, Kelly R. *Asset Protection* (Markham, Ont.: LexisNexis Butterworths, 2005).

Ellis, Mark Vincent. *Professional Fiduciary Duties* (Scarborough, Ont.: Carswell, 1995).

Feeney, Thomas G. & Jim Mackenzie. *Feeney's Canadian Law of Wills*, 4th ed., loose-leaf (Toronto: Butterworths, 2000).

Gibbs, Karen M. *et al. The Practical Guide to Ontario Estate Administration*, 5th ed. (Toronto: Thomson Carswell, 2006).

Gillese, Eileen E. & Martha Milczynski. *The Law of Trusts*, 2d ed. (Toronto: Irwin Law, 2005).

Harvey, Cameron. *The Law of Dependants' Relief in Canada* (Scarborough, Ont.: Carswell, 1999).

Histrop, Lindsay Ann & Donna C. Cappon. *Estate Planning Precedents: A Solicitor's Manual*, loose-leaf (Toronto: Carswell, 1989-).

Howlett, David. *Estate Matters in Atlantic Canada* (Scarborough, Ont.: Carswell, 1999).

Hull, Ian. *Challenging the Validity of Wills* (Toronto: Carswell, 1996).

Hull, Rodney & Maurice C. Cullity. *MacDonnell, Sheard & Hull: Probate Practice*, 4th ed. (Toronto: Carswell, 1996).

Jenkins, Jennifer J. & H. Mark Scott. *Compensation and Duties of Estate Trustees, Guardians and Attorneys*, loose-leaf (Aurora, Ont.: Canada Law Book, 2006-).

Kessler, James & Fiona Hunter. *Drafting Trusts and Will Trusts in Canada*, 2d ed. (Markham, Ont.: LexisNexis Canada, 2007).

Louis, David. *Implementing Estate Freezes*, 2d ed. (North York, Ont.: CCH Canadian, 2006).

MacGregor, Mary L. *Preparation of Wills and Powers of Attorney: First Interview to Final Report*, 3d ed. (Aurora, Ont.: Canada Law Book, 2003).

MacKenzie, James. *Feeney's Canadian Law of Wills*, 4th ed., loose-leaf (Markham, Ont.: LexisNexis, n.d.).

MacKenzie, Jim. *Halsbury's Laws of Canada: Wills and Estates* (Markham, Ont.: LexisNexis Canada, 2007).

Morton, James C. & Risa M. Stone. *Essential Estate Administration in Ontario* (Toronto: CCH Canadian, 2002).

Ng, Michael. *Fiduciary Duties: Obligations of Loyalty and Faithfulness*, loose-leaf (Aurora, Ont.: Canada Law Book, 2003-).

O'Brien's Encyclopedia of Forms: Division V: Wills & Trusts, loose-leaf (Aurora, Ont.: Canada Law Book, 1989-).

Oosterhoff, A.H. *Oosterhoff on Trusts: Text, Commentary and Material*, 7th ed. (Toronto: Carswell, 2009).

.... *Oosterhoff on Wills and Succession: Text, Commentary and Cases*, 6th ed. (Toronto: Carswell, 2007).

Rintoul, Margaret E. *Ontario Estate Administration*, 5th ed. (Markham, Ont.: LexisNexis Butterworths, 2005).

.... *The Practitioner's Guide to Estate Practice in Ontario*, 4th ed. (Markham, Ont.: LexisNexis Canada, 2004).

Schnurr, Brian A. *Estate Litigation*, 2d ed., loose-leaf (Toronto: Carswell, 1994-).

Sokol, Stanley J. *Mistakes in Wills in Canada* (Scarborough, Ont.: Carswell, 1995).

Stephens, Glenn R., *Estate Planning with Life Insurance*, 3d ed. (Toronto: CCH Canadian, 2005).

Sweatman, M. Jasmine. *Guide to Powers of Attorney* (Aurora, Ont.: Canada Law Book, 2002).

Thériault, Carmen S., ed. *Widdifield on Executors and Trustees*, 6th ed., loose-leaf (Scarborough, Ont.: Carswell, 2002-).

Van Cauwenberghe, Christine. *Wealth Planning Strategies for Canadians* (Toronto: Thomson Carswell, 2006-).

Waters, Donovan W.M., ed. *Waters' Law of Trusts in Canada*, 3d ed. (Toronto: Thomson Carswell, 2005).

Annotated Statutes

Gordon, Robert. *The 2008 Annotated British Columbia Representation Agreement Act* (Scarborough, Ont.: Carswell, 2008).

Hoffstein, Maria Elena *et al. Ontario Estates Law and Commentary* (Markham, Ont.: LexisNexis, published annually).

Schnurr., Brian A. *The Annotated Ontario Estates Statutes*, 2d ed., loose-leaf (Toronto: Carswell, 2003-).

Topical Journals

Estates and Trusts Journal
Estates, Trusts & Pensions Journal
Estates & Trusts Quarterly

Topical Law Reports

Canadian Estate Planning and Administration Reporter
Estates and Trusts Reports
Reports of Family Law

24) — Evidence

Texts and loose-leaf Services

Anderson, Glenn R. *Expert Evidence*, 2d ed. (Markham, Ont.: Butterworths Canada, 2009).

Archibald, Todd L. & James C. Morton. *Discovery: Principles in Practice* (Toronto: CCH Canadian, 2004).

Atkinson, Paul. *Canadian Rules of Evidence* (Markham, Ont.: Lexis-Nexis, 2007).

Boilard, Jean-Guy. *Guide to Criminal Evidence*, loose-leaf (Scarborough, Ont.: Carswell, n.d.).

Brook, James. *A Lawyer's Guide to Probability and Statistics* (Toronto: Carswell, 1990).

Bryant, Alan W. *et al. The Law of Evidence in Canada*, 3d ed. (Toronto: LexisNexis, 2009).

Chayko, G.M. & E.D. Gulliver, eds. *Forensic Evidence in Canada*, 2d ed. (Aurora, Ont.: Canada Law Book, 1999).

Cochran, Doug, Mary Ann Kelly & Michael Gulcyz. *Rules of Evidence: A Practical Approach* (Toronto: Emond Montgomery, 2007).

Corbin, Ruth & A. Kelly Gill. *Survey Evidence and the Law Worldwide* (Markham, Ont.: LexisNexis, 2008).

Corbin, Ruth, Scott Joliffe & A. Kelly Gill. *Trial By Survey: Survey Evidence and the Law* (Scarborough, Ont.: Carswell, 2000).

Cudmore, Gordon. *Civil Evidence Handbook*, loose-leaf (Toronto: Carswell, 1987-).

Delisle, R.J. *Canadian Evidence Law in a Nutshell*, 3d ed. (Scarborough, Ont.: Carswell, 2009).

.........., Don Stuart & David Tanovich. *Evidence: Principles and Problems* (Scarborough, Ont.: Carswell, 2007).

Doherty, Michael P. *The Portable Guide to Evidence*, 3d ed. (Toronto: Carswell, 2009).

Finlay, Bryan and T.A. Cromwell. *Witness Preparation Manual*, 2d ed. (Aurora, Ont.: Canada Law Book, 1999).

Gahtan, Alan. *Electronic Evidence* (Scarborough, Ont.: Carswell, 1999).

Gibson, John. *Criminal Law Evidence: Practice and Procedure*, loose-leaf (Toronto: Carswell, 1988-).

Gold, Alan D. *Expert Evidence in Criminal Law: The Scientific Approach* (Toronto: Irwin Law, 2003).

Goldstein, Elliott. *Visual Evidence: A Practitioner's Manual*, loose-leaf (Toronto: Carswell, 1991-).

Gorsky, Morley R., S.J. Usprich & Gregory J. Brandt. *Evidence and Procedure in Canadian Labour Arbitration*, loose-leaf (Toronto: Carswell, 1991-).

Hageman, Cecilia, Derrill Prevett & Wayne Murray. *DNA Handbook*, 2d ed. (Markham, Ont.: LexisNexis, 2008).

Hill, S. Casey *et al. McWilliams' Canadian Criminal Evidence*, 4th ed., loose-leaf (Aurora, Ont.: Canada Law Book, 2003-).

Hubbard, Robert W., Susan Magotiaux, & Suzanne M. Duncan. *The Law of Privilege in Canada* (Toronto: Canada Law Book, 2005).

Jaffe, Frederick. *A Guide to Pathological Evidence for Lawyers and Police Officers*, 4th ed. (Toronto: Carswell, 1999).

Martin, Rene. *Admissibility of Statements*, 9th ed. (Aurora, Ont.: Canada Law Book, 1999).

Mewett, Alan. *Witnesses*, loose-leaf (Toronto: Carswell, 1991-).

Morton, James C. *Ontario Litigator's Pocket Guide to Evidence*, 4th ed. (Toronto: LexisNexis Butterworths, 2007).

Paciocco, David M. & Lee Stuesser. *The Law of Evidence*, 5th ed. (Toronto: Irwin Law, 2008).

Sankoff, Peter. The Portable Guide to Witnesses (Toronto: Carswell, 2006).

Sopinka, John, Sidney N. Lederman & Alan W. Bryant. *The Law of Evidence in Canada*, 2d ed. (Toronto: Butterworths, 1999).

Vogl, Robin & Nicholas Bala. *Testifying on Behalf of Children: A Handbook for Canadian Professionals* (Toronto: Thompson Educational Pub., 2001).

Annotated Statutes

Beach, David. *The Annotated Canadian Evidence Acts*, loose-leaf (Toronto: Carswell, 1991-).

25) — Family Law

Texts and loose-leaf Services

Bala, Nicholas *et al.*, eds., *Canadian Child Welfare Law*, 2d ed. (Toronto: Thompson Educational Publishing, 2004).

Benotto, Mary Lou and Williams & Partners, LLP. *Income Tax and Family Law Handbook*, loose-leaf (Markham, Ont.: LexisNexis, n.d.).

Bernstein, Marvin *et al. Child Protection Law in Canada*, loose-leaf (Toronto: Carswell, 1990-).

Birnbaum, Rachel, Barbara Jo Fidler & Katherine Kavassalis. *Child Custody Assessments: A Resource Guide for Legal and Mental Health Professionals* (Toronto: Thomson Carswell, 2007).

Boyd, Susan B. *Child Custody, Law, and Women's Work* (Don Mills, Ont.: Oxford University Press Canada, 2003).

Cochrane, Michael G. *Family Law in Ontario: A Practical Guide for Lawyers and Law Clerks*, loose-leaf (Aurora, Ont.: Canada Law Book, 1990-).

Christopher, T. Catherine. *Law of Domestic Conflict in Canada*, loose-leaf (Scarborough, Ont.: Carswell, 2002).

Freedman, Andrew *et al. Financial Principles of Family Law*, loose-leaf (Scarborough, Ont.: Carswell, n.d.).

Fiddler, Barbara Jo. *Challenging Issues in Child Custody Disputes: A Guide for Legal and Mental Health Professionals* (Scarborough, Ont.: Carswell, 2008).

Hainsworth, Terry W. *Child Support Guidelines Service*, loose-leaf (Aurora, Ont.: Canada Law Book, n.d.).

.... *Divorce Act Manual*, loose-leaf (Aurora, Ont.: Canada Law Book, n.d.).

.... *Ontario Family Law Act Manual*, 2d ed., loose-leaf (Aurora, Ont.: Canada Law Book, n.d.).

Harper, Mark. *International Trust and Divorce Litigation* (Bristol, U.K.: Jordans, 2007).

Holland, Winifred & Barbro Stalbecker-Pountney, eds., *Cohabitation: The Law in Canada*, loose-leaf (Toronto: Carswell, 1990-).

Landau, Barbara, Lorne Wolfson & Niki Landau. *Family Mediation and Collaborative Practice Handbook*, 5th ed. (Toronto: Butterworths, 2009).

Leonoff, Arthur & Robert J. Montague. *Guide to Custody and Access Assessments* (Scarborough, Ont.: Carswell, 1996).

Lewis, Catherine & Ellen Mole, *Ontario Family Law Quantum Service*, loose-leaf (Toronto: Butterworths, 1984-).

MacDonald, James *et al. Handling a Family Law Matter in Ontario*, loose-leaf (Scarborough, Ont.: Carswell, n.d.).

MacDonald, James C. & Lee K. Ferrier, *Canadian Divorce Law and Practice*, 2d ed. loose-leaf (Toronto: Carswell, 1986-).

MacDonald, James & Ann C. Wilton. *Child Support Guidelines Law and Practice*, 2d ed., loose-leaf (Scarborough, Ont.: Carswell, n.d.).

.... *Law and Practice Under the Family Law Act of Ontario*, Revised ed., loose-leaf (Toronto: Carswell, 1986-).

McLeod, James G. *Child Custody Law and Practice*, loose-leaf (Toronto: Carswell, 1992).

.... & Alfred A. Mamo. *Matrimonial Property Law in Canada*, loose-leaf (Toronto: Carswell, 1980-).

Nemet-Brown, Sheila, ed. *Matrimonial Property* (Markham, Ont.: Lexis-Nexis, 2007).

Noble, Cinnie. *Family Mediation: A Guide for Lawyers* (Aurora, Ont.: Canada Law Book, 1999).

O'Brien's Encyclopedia of Forms: Division VI: Ontario: Family Law (Aurora, Ont.: Canada Law Book, 1987-).

Ontario Annotated Family Law Service, loose-leaf (Toronto: Butterworths, 1978-).

Payne, Julien D. *Payne on Divorce*, 4th ed. (Toronto: Carswell, 1996).

.... & Marilyn A. Payne. *Canadian Family Law*, 3d ed. (Toronto: Irwin Law, 2008).

Rashkis, Morton & Mary Lou Benotto, *Income Tax and Family Law Handbook*, loose-leaf (Toronto: Butterworths, 1988-).

Shields, Richard, Judith Ryan & Victoria Smith. *Collaborative Family Law: Another Way to Resolve Family Disputes* (Scarborough, Ont.: Carswell, 2003).

Stark, Hugh & Kristie MacLise, *Domestic Contracts*, 2d ed., loose-leaf (Toronto: Carswell, 2004-).

Steinberg, David *et al. Ontario Family Law Practice* (Markham, Ont.: LexisNexis, published annually).

Wallace, Patricia H. & Debra Wallace. *Effective Advocacy in Family Law* (Markham, Ont.: LexisNexis Butterworths, 2004).

Wilson, Jeffrey. *Wilson on Children and the Law*, loose-leaf (Markham, Ont.: LexisNexis, n.d.).

Wilton, Ann, Judy Miyauchi, & Lynn Kirwin. *Enforcement of Family Law Orders and Agreements*, loose-leaf (Toronto: Carswell, 1989-).

Zuker, Marvin A., Randolph C. Hammond & Roderick C. Flynn. *Children's Law Handbook*, 2d ed. (Toronto: Thomson Carswell, 2009).

Annotated Statutes

Annotated Ontario Children's Law Reform Act (Toronto: Carswell, published annually).

Aston, David *et al. McLeod's Ontario Family Law Rules Annotated* (Scarborough, Ont.: Carswell, published annually).

MacDonald, James & Ann Wilton. *Annotated Divorce Act* (Toronto: Carswell, published annually).

.... *Annotated Ontario Family Law Act* (Toronto: Carswell, published annually).

Topical Journals/ Newsletters

Annual Review of Family Law
Canadian Family Law Quarterly
Canadian Journal of Family Law
Family Law Review
Money & Family Law

Topical Law Reports/Digests

Nemet-Brown, Sheila. *Canada Quantum Digest: Matrimonial Property* (Markham, Ont.: LexisNexis, published annually).

.... *Canada Quantum Digest: Spousal Support and Dependent's Relief* (Markham, Ont.: LexisNexis, published annually).

Ontario Family Law Reporter
Reports of Family Law
Weekly Digest of Family Law

26) — Fish, Forestry, and Wildlife

Texts and loose-leaf Services

Mancell, Garry E. & Brian D. Gilfillan. *Davis & Company's British Columbia Forestry Law: An Annotated Guide*, loose-leaf (Aurora, Ont.: Canada Law Book, n.d.).

Morin, Catherine. *Halsbury's Laws of Canada: Holidays, Hospitality, Hunting and Fishing* (Markham, Ont.: LexisNexis Canada, 2008).

27) — Health Law

Texts and loose-leaf Services

Bailey, Tracey M., Timothy Caulfield, & Nola M. Ries, eds. *Public Health Law and Policy in Canada*, 2d ed. (Markham, Ont.: LexisNexis, 2008).

Berger, Joseph. *The Independent Medical Examination in Psychiatry* (Aurora, Ont.: Canada Law Book, 2002).

Blake, Rod, Lori Stoltz & Jane Speakman. *Public Health Law and Practice in Ontario: Health Protection and Promotion Act* (Scarborough, Ont.: Carswell, 2008).

Bloom, Hy & Richard D. Schneider. *Mental Disorder and the Law: A Primer for Legal and Mental Health Professionals* (Toronto: Irwin Law, 2006).

Brecher, Jay *et al. Halsbury's Laws of Canada: Media and Postal Communications; Medicine and Health* (Markham, Ont.: LexisNexis, 2007).

Canadian Health Facilities Law Guide, loose-leaf (Don Mills, Ont.: CCH Canadian, 1983-).

Downie, Jocelyn & Elaine Gibson, eds. *Health Law at the Supreme Court of Canada* (Toronto: Irwin Law, 2007).

Downie, Jocelyn, Karen McEwen & William MacInnis. *Dental Law in Canada*, 2d ed. (Markham, Ont.: LexisNexis, 2010).

Downie, Jocelyn, Timothy Caulfield & Colleen M. Flood, eds. *Canadian Health Law and Policy*, 3d ed. (Toronto: LexisNexis Canada, 2007).

Dykeman, Mary Jane ed. *Canadian Health Law Practice Manual*, loose-leaf (Markham, Ont.: Butterworths, 2000-).

Gray, John E., Margaret A. Shone & Peter F. Liddle. *Canadian Mental Health Law and Policy* (Markham, Ont.: Butterworths, 2008).

Hiltz, D'Arcy & Anita Szigeti. *A Guide to Consent and Capacity Law in Ontario* (Markham, Ont: LexisNexis, published annually).

Kent, C. Adele. *Medical Ethics: The State of the Law* (Markham, Ont.: LexisNexis Butterworths, 2005).

Montrose, Laurel. *Medicare in Ontario: A Legal Reference Guide* (Markham, Ont.: LexisNexis, 2008).

Morris, John. *Canadian Nurses and the Law*, 2d ed. (Toronto: Butterworths, 1999).

Perun, Halyna, Michael Orr & Fannie Dimitriadis. *Guide to the Ontario Personal Health Information Protection Act* (Toronto: Irwin Law, 2005).

Picard, Ellen & Gerald B. Robertson. *Legal Liability of Doctors and Hospitals in Canada*, 4th ed. (Calgary: Carswell Legal Publications, 2007).

Rozovsky, Lorne. *Canadian Healthcare Forms and Policies* (Markham, Ont.: LexisNexis, 2007).

.... *The Canadian Law of Consent to Treatment*, 3d ed. (Toronto: Butterworths, 2003).

.... & Noela Inions. *Canadian Health Information: A Legal and Risk Management Guide*, 3d ed. (Toronto: Butterworths, 2002).

.... & Noela Inions. *Canadian Health Information: A Practical Legal and Risk Management Guide*, 3d ed. (Markham, Ont.: Butterworths, 2002).

Scott, Graham *et al., The Personal Health Information Protection Act: Implementing Best Privacy Practices*, 2005 ed. (Markham, Ont.: LexisNexis, 2005).

Sherman, David. *Taxes, Health and Disabilities* (Scarborough, Ont.: Carswell, 1995).

Sneiderman, Barney, John C. Irvine & Philip H. Osborne. *Canadian Medical Law: An Introduction for Physicians, Nurses and Other Health Care Professionals*, 3d ed. (Scarborough, Ont.: Carswell, 2003).

Annotated Statutes

Graham, Jeffrey et al. *Canadian Food and Drug Legislation and Commentary* (Markham, Ont.: LexisNexis, published biennially).

Schneider, Richard D. *Annotated Ontario Mental Health Statutes*, 4th ed. (Toronto: Irwin Law, 2007).

Topical Journals/Newsletters

Health Law Journal
Health Law News
Health Law in Canada
Journal of Women's Health and Law
Legal Medical Quarterly
McGill Journal of Law and Health
Telehealth Law

28) — Human Rights

Texts and loose-leaf Services

Bowland, Adelyn. *Disability and Human Rights in the Workplace* (Toronto: Thomson Carswell, 2004).

Bowlby, Brenda J., Daniel Michaluk & Jennifer Wootton Regan. *Educator's Guide to Human Rights*, 2d ed. (Aurora, Ont.: Canada Law Book, 2009).

Corbett, S.M. *Canadian Human Rights Law and Commentary* (Markham, Ont.: LexisNexis, 2007).

Cornish, Mary, Fay Faraday & Jo-Anne Pickel. *Enforcing Human Rights in Ontario* (Aurora, Ont.: Canada Law Book, 2009).

Grover, Sonja. *The Child's Right to Legal Standing* (Markham, Ont.: LexisNexis, 2008).

Howard-Hassmann, Rhoda E. & Claude E. Welch, Jr., eds. *Economic Rights in Canada and the United States* (Philadelphia: University of Pennyslvania Press, 2006).

Knight, Jamie & Laurie Jessome. *Canadian Human Rights Act: Quick Reference* (Toronto: Thomson Carswell, published annually).

Magnet, Joseph. *Modern Constitutionalism: Equality, Identity and Democracy* (Markham, Ont.: LexisNexis, 2004).

Ontario Human Rights Commission. *Human Rights at Work*, 3d ed. (Scarborough, Ont.: Carswell, 2008).

.... *Human Rights Policy in Ontario* (Scarborough, Ont.: Carswell, 2007).

Ray-Ellis, Soma. *Federal Equity Manual*, loose-leaf (Scarborough, Ont.: Carswell, 2002-).

.... *Halsbury's Laws Of Canada: Discrimination and Human Rights* (Markham Ont.: LexisNexis Canada, 2008).

Schabas, William & Stéphane Beaulac. *International Human Rights and Canadian Law: Legal Commitment, Implementation and the Charter*, 3d ed. (Toronto: Thomson Carswell, 2006).

Zinn, Russel W. *The Law of Human Rights in Canada: Practice and Procedure*, loose-leaf (Aurora, Ont.: Canada Law Book, n.d.).

Annotated Statutes

Bowland, Adelyn. *The Annotated Ontario Human Rights Code* (Scarborough, Ont.: Carswell, published annually).

Braha, W. Anita. *Annotated British Columbia Human Rights Code*, loose-leaf (Aurora, Ont.: Canada Law Book, n.d.).

Topical Law Reports

Canadian Rights Reporter

29) — Immigration and Refugee Law

Texts and loose-leaf Services

Allard, Lorraine *et al. Cross-Border Relocation Law* (Toronto: CCH Canadian, 2002).

Bart, Jacqueline & Austin T. Fragomen. *Canada/U.S. Relocation Manual: Immigration, Customs, Employment and Taxation*, loose-leaf (Scarborough, Ont.: Carswell, n.d.).

Canada, Immigration and Refugee Board, Immigration Division. *Detention Review Hearings* (Ottawa: Communications Directorate, Immigration and Refugee Board of Canada, 2006).

.... *Immigration Admissibility Hearings* (Ottawa: Communications Directorate, Immigration and Refugee Board of Canada, 2006).

Fournier-Ruggles, Lynn. *Canadian Immigration and Refugee Law for Legal Professionals* (Toronto: Emond Montgomery, 2009).

Galloway, Donald. *Immigration Law* (Concord, Ont.: Irwin Law, 1997).

Gaudet, Lynn & Camilla Jones. *Immigration Practitioner's Handbook* (Toronto: Thomson Carswell, published annually).

Jones, Martin & Sasha Baglay. *Refugee Law* (Toronto, Ont.: Irwin Law, 2007).

Kranc, Benjamin A. *North American Relocation Law*, loose-leaf (Aurora, Ont.: Canada Law Book, 2006-).

Lippert, Randy K. *Sanctuary, Sovereignty, Sacrifice: Canadian Sanctuary Incidents, Power, and Law* (Vancouver: UBC Press, 2005).

Pratt, Anna. *Securing Borders: Detention and Deportation in Canada* (Vancouver: UBC Press, 2005).

Schweitzer, Tony. *Canada-U.S. Work Permits: Issues for HR Professionals*, loose-leaf (Scarborough, Ont.: Carswell, n.d.).

Waldman, Lorne. *Canadian Immigration and Refugee Law Practice* (Toronto: Butterworths, published annually).

.... *The Definition of Convention Refugee* (Toronto: Butterworths, 2001).

.... *Halsbury's Laws of Canada: Immigration and Citizenship* (Markham, Ont.: LexisNexis, 2006).

.... *Immigration Law and Practice*, loose-leaf (Toronto: Butterworths, n.d.).

Zambelli, Pia. *Annotated Refugee Convention: Fifty Years of North American Jurisprudence* (Scarborough, Ont.: Carswell, 2004).

Annotated Statutes

Goslett, Henry M. & Barbara Jo Caruso. *The 2007 Annotated Citizenship Act* (Scarborough: Carswell, 2007).

Goslett, Henry M. & Barbara Jo Caruso. *The Annotated Immigration and Refugee Protection Act of Canada* (Toronto: Thomson Carswell, published annunally).

Waldman, Lorne. *Immigration and Refugee Protection Act and Commentary* (Markham, Ont.: Butterworths, published annually).

Zambelli, Pia. *Annotated Refugee Convention Act* (Scarborough, Ont.: Carswell, published annually).

Topical Journals

Canada's Immigration and Citizenship Bulletin
International Journal of Refugee Law
Refuge

Topical Law Reports

Immigration Appeal Cases
Immigration Law Reporter

30) — Insurance Law

Texts and loose-leaf Services

Boivin, Denis W. *Insurance Law* (Toronto: Irwin Law, 2004).

Borgmann, Fred, Jason Swales & Jillian Welch. *Canadian Insurance Taxation*, 3d ed. (Toronto, Ont.: LexisNexis, 2009).

Billingsley, Barbara. *General Principles of Canadian Insurance Law* (Markham, Ont.: LexisNexis Canada, 2008).

Brown, Craig. *Canadian Insurance Contracts Law in a Nutshell* (Toronto: Carswell, 1995).

Brown, Craig & Tom Donnelly. *Insurance Law in Canada*, 6th ed. (Toronto: Carswell, 2007).

Gosnell, Sean, Bruce Webster & John Seigel. *Business Interruption Insurance*, 2d ed. (Aurora, Ont.: Canada Law Book, 2006).

Grant, Anne. *Dispute Resolution in the Insurance Industry: A Practical Guide* (Aurora, Ont.: Canada Law Book, 2000).

Hayles, Richard. *Disability Insurance: Canadian Law and Business Practice* (Scarborough, Ont.: Carswell, 1998).

Hilliker, Gordon. *Liability Insurance in Canada*, 4th ed. (Toronto: Butterworths, 2006).

.... *Insurance Bad Faith*, 2d ed. (Toronto, Ont.: LexisNexis, 2009).

Holding, John. *Canadian Manual of International Air Carriage* (Toronto: Irwin Law, 2005).

Krempulec, Richard. *Property Damage Claims Under Commercial Insurance Policies*, loose-leaf (Aurora, Ont.: Canada Law Book, n.d).

Lacerte, Michel & Pierre G. Forcier. *Independent Medical Examinations for Insurance and Legal Reports* (Markham, Ont: LexisNexis, 2004).

Lichty, Mark G. & Marcus B. Snowden. *Annotated Commercial General Liability Policy*, loose-leaf (Aurora, Ont.: Canada Law Book, n.d.).

ManuLife Financial, Tax and Estate Planning Group. *Canadian Taxation of Life Insurance*, 5th ed. (Toronto, Ont.: Thomson Carswell, 2010).

Norwood, David & John Weir. *Norwood on Life Insurance Law in Canada*, 3d ed. (Toronto: Carswell, 2002).

Sanderson, Heather A., Robert Emblem & J. Lyle Woodley. *Commercial General Liability Insurance* (Toronto: Butterworths, 2000).

Shapiro, Robinson Sheppard. *Residential Insurance Policies Annotated*, loose-leaf (Scarborough, Ont.: Carswell, n.d.).

Strathy, George. *The Law and Practice of Marine Insurance in Canada* (Markham, Ont.: LexisNexis, 2003).

Winsor, Roderick S.W. *Good Faith in Canadian Insurance Law*, loose-leaf (Aurora, Ont.: Cartwright Group, 2007-).

Annotated Statutes

Bailey, Michael. *Alberta Insurance Law and Commentary* (Markham, Ont.: LexisNexis Canada, published annually).

Firestone, Stephen, ed. *Ontario Motor Vehicle Insurance Law and Commentary* (Markham, Ont.: LexisNexis Canada, published annually).

Gregory, Eleanor & George Gregory, *The Annotated British Columbia Insurance (Motor Vehicle) Act*, 2d ed., loose-leaf (Toronto: Carswell, 1990-).

Rubenstein, Gale & Daniel Gormley. *Insurance Companies Act: Legislation and Commentary*, loose-leaf (Markham, Ont.: LexisNexis, n.d.).

Teitelbaum, Michael. *Ontario Insurance Law and Commentary* (Markham, Ont.: LexisNexis, published annually).

Teolis, John W. & C. Dawn Jetten. *Insurance Act: Complete Text with Regulations, Guidelines and Analytical Comment* (Toronto: CCH Canadian, 1995).

Weir, John P. *Annotated Insurance Act of Ontario*, loose-leaf (Toronto: Carswell, 1986-).

Topical Law Reports

British Columbia Decisions, Insurance Law Cases
Canadian Cases on the Law of Insurance

Canadian Insurance Law Reporter
Financial Services Commission Of Ontario Arbitration Decisions
Insurance Case Law Digest
Insurance Law Digest

Topical Journals

Canadian Insurance Regulation Reporter
Canadian Insurance Law Review
Canadian Journal of Insurance Law

31) — Intellectual Property

Texts and loose-leaf Services

Barrigar, Robert H. *Canadian Patent Act Annotated*, 2d ed. (Aurora, Ont.: Canada Law Book, 1994).

Blanchard, Adrienne & Jane Steinberg. *Life Sciences Law in Canada*, loose-leaf (Scarborough, Ont.: Carswell, 2006-).

Burshtein, Sheldon. *The Corporate Counsel Guide to Intellectual Property Law* (Aurora, Ont.: Canada Law Book, 2000).

.... *Domain Names and Internet Trade-mark Issues: Canadian Law and Practice*, loose-leaf (Scarborough, Ont.: Carswell, 2005-).

Dimock, Ronald, ed. *Intellectual Property Disputes: Resolutions and Remedies*, loose-leaf (Scarborough, Ont.: Carswell, 2002-).

Duarte, Tony. *Canadian Film and Television Business and Legal Practice*, loose-leaf (Aurora, Ont.: Canada Law Book, n.d.).

Fecenko, Mark. *Biotechnology Law: Corporate-Commercial Practice* (Markham, Ont.: LexisNexis, 2002).

Geist, Michael, ed. *In the Public Interest: The Future of Canadian Copyright Law* (Toronto: Irwin Law, 2005).

Gill, A. Kelly & R. Scott Jolliffe. *Fox on Canadian Law of Trade-Marks and Unfair Competition*, 4th ed., loose-leaf (Toronto: Carswell, 2002-).

Gold, E. Richard & Bartha Maria Knoppers. *Biotechnology IP & Ethics* (Markham, Ont.: LexisNexis Canada, 2009).

Handa, Sunny. *Copyright Law in Canada* (Markham, Ont.: Butterworths, 2002).

Hughes, Roger *et al. Commercial Transactions: Intellectual Property*, loose-leaf (Markham, Ont.: LexisNexis, n.d.).

Hughes, Roger T., Dino P. Clarizio & Arjay Brecher. *Halsbury's Laws of Canada: Patents, Trade Secrets and Industrial Designs* (Markham, Ont.: LexisNexis Canada, 2007).

Hughes, Roger T. & Toni Polson Ashton. *Halsbury's Laws of Canada: Trade-Marks, Passing Off and Unfair Competition* (Markham, Ont.: Lexis-Nexis Canada, 2007).

Hughes, Roger, Dino P. Clarizio & Neal Armstrong. *Hughes and Woodley on Patents*, 2d ed., loose-leaf (Markham, Ont.: LexisNexis, n.d.).

Hughes, Roger T. *et al. Hughes on Trade Marks*, 2d ed., loose-leaf (Markham, Ont.: LexisNexis, 2005-).

Hughes, Roger *et. al. Hughes on Copyright and Industrial Design*, 2d ed., loose-leaf (Toronto: Butterworths, 2005-).

Judge, Elizabeth & Daniel Gervais. *Intellectual property: The Law in Canada* (Toronto: Thomson/Carswell, 2005).

Knopf, Howard, ed. *Security Interests in Intellectual Property* (Scarborough, Ont.: Carswell, 2002-).

Kratz, Martin P.J. *Canada's Intellectual Property Law in a Nutshell* (Toronto: Carswell, 1998).

.... *Obtaining Patents*, 2d ed. (Toronto: Carswell, 1999).

.... *Protecting Copyright and Industrial Design*, 2d ed. (Scarborough, Ont.: Carswell, 1999).

McKeown, John S. *Brand Management in Canadian Law*, 2d ed. (Toronto: Carswell, 2006).

.... *Fox on Canadian Law of Copyright and Industrial Designs*, 4th ed., loose-leaf (Scarborough, Ont.: Thomson/Carswell, 2003-).

O'Brien's Encyclopedia of Forms: Division X: Computers and Information Technology, 11th ed., loose-leaf (Aurora, Ont.: Canada Law Book, n.d.).

Odutola, Bayo & Sylvie-Emanuelle Bourbonnais. *Odutola on Canadian Trade-mark Practice*, loose-leaf (Scarborough, Ont.: Carswell, 2005-).

Richard, Hugues G. *et al. Canadian Copyright Act Annotated* (Toronto: Carswell, 1993-).

Sanderson, Paul. *Musicians and the Law in Canada*, 3d ed. (Scarborough, Ont.: Carswell, 2000).

Stikeman, Elliott. *Intellectual Property Law of Canada*, loose-leaf (Yonkers, N.Y.: Juris Publishing, 1999).

Vaver, D. *Copyright Law* (Toronto: Irwin Law, 2000).

Annotated Statutes

Barrigar, Robert H. *Canadian Patent Act Annotated*, 2d ed., loose-leaf (Aurora, Ont.: Canada Law Book, n.d.).

Canada Law Book. *Intellectual Property Statutes: Legislative History*, loose-leaf (Aurora, Ont.: Canada Law Book, n.d.).

Hughes, Richard. *Canadian Trade-Marks Act Annotated*, loose-leaf (Toronto: Carswell, 1984-).

Hughes, Richard & Laurent Carriere. *Canadian Copyright Act, Annotated*, loose-leaf (Scarborough, Ont.: Carswell, n.d.).

Hughes, Roger T. *Copyright Legislation and Commentary* (Markham, Ont.: LexisNexis Butterworths, published annually).

.... *Patent Legislation and Commentary* (Markham, Ont.: LexisNexis Butterworths, published annually).

.... *Trade-marks Act and Commentary* (Markham, Ont.: LexisNexis, published annually).

Sarna, Lazar & Hillel Neuer. *Annotated Copyright Act*, loose-leaf (Markham, Ont.: LexisNexis, n.d.).

Stratton, Bruce. *The Annotated Patent Act*, loose-leaf (Scarborough, Ont.: Carswell, 2009-).

Tamaro, Normand. *The Annotated Copyright Act* (Scarborough, Ont.: Carswell, published annually).

Topical Journals

Canadian Intellectual Property Review
Intellectual Property Journal

Topical Law Reports/Digests

Canadian Intellectual Property Reports
Canadian Patent Reporter
Digest of Canadian Intellectual Property Law
Fox's Patent Cases: Canada

32) — International Law

Texts and loose-leaf Services

Alebeek, Rosanne van. *The Immunity of States and Their Officials in International Criminal Law and International Human Rights Law* (Oxford: Oxford University Press, 2008).

Alvarez, José. *International Organizations as Law-Makers* (Oxford: Oxford University Press, 2005).

Amerasinghe, Chittharanjan Felix. *Jurisdiction of Specific International Tribunals* (Leiden: Martinus Nijhoff Publishers, 2009).

Armstrong, David, ed. *Routledge Handbook of International Law* (London: Routledge, 2009).

Aust, Anthony. *Handbook of International Law* (Cambridge, UK: Cambridge University Press, 2005).

Bhala, Raj. *Modern GATT Law: A Treatise on the General Agreement on Tariffs and Trade* (London: Sweet & Maxwell, 2005).

Biehler, Gernot. *Procedures in International Law* (Berlin: Springer, 2008).

Blair, Annice & Kathleen Ryan Elliott. *Canadian and International Law* (Toronto: Oxford University Press, 2004).

Botting, Gary. *Canadian Extradition Law Practice* (Markham, Ont.: LexisNexis Butterworths, published annually).

Bowett, D.W. *The Law of International Institutions*, 5th ed. (London: Sweet & Maxwell, 2001).

Boyle, Alan E. & Christine Chinkin. *The Making of International Law* (Oxford: Oxford University Press, 2007).

Brownlie, Ian. *Principles of Public International Law*, 7th ed. (Oxford: Oxford University Press, 2008).

Castel, J.G. *The Canadian Law and Practice of International Trade*, 2d ed. (Toronto: Emond Montgomery, 1997).

Currie, John H. *Public International Law*, 2d ed. (Toronto: Irwin Law, 2008).

Currie, John H., Craig Forcese, & Valerie Oosterveld. *International Law: Doctrine, Practice, and Theory* (Toronto: Irwin Law, 2007).

Dolzer, Rudolf & Christoph Schreuer. *Principles of International Investment Law* (Oxford: Oxford University Press, 2008).

Duncan, Garry & Elizabeth Peck. *Canadian Residents Abroad* (Scarborough, Ont.: Carswell, 2002).

El Zeidy, Mohamed M. *The Principle of Complementarity in International Criminal Law: Origin, Development, and Practice* (Leiden, Netherlands: Martinus Nijhoff Publishers, 2008).

Evans, Malcolm D. *International Law*, 2d ed. (Oxford: Oxford University Press, 2006).

Folsom, R.H. *NAFTA and Free Trade in the Americas in a Nutshell* (St. Paul, MN: Thomson/West, 2004).

Goldstone, Richard & Adam M. Smith. *International Judicial Institutions: The Architecture of International Justice at Home and Abroad* (London: Routledge, 2009).

Hall, William Edward. *A Treatise on International Law*, 8th ed. (Buffalo, N.Y.: W.S. Hein & Co., 2001).

Hillier, Tim. *Principles of Public International Law*, 2d ed. (London: Cavendish, 1999).

Hong, Seoung-Yong & Jon M. Van Dyke, eds. *Maritime Boundary Disputes, Settlement Processes, and the Law of the Sea* (Leiden, Netherlands: Martinus Nijhoff Publishers, 2009).

Jackson, John Howard. *The Jurisprudence of GATT and the WTO: Insights on Treaty Law and Economic Relations* (Cambridge: Cambridge University Press, 2000).

Janis, Mark W. *An Introduction to International Law*, 4th ed. (New York: Aspen Publishers, 2003).

Kindred, Hugh M. & Philip M. Saunders. *International Law: Chiefly as Interpreted and Applied in Canada*, 7th ed. (Toronto: Emond Montgomery, 2005).

Koul, Autar Krishan. *Guide to the WTO and GATT: Economics, Law and Politics* (The Hague: Kluwer Law International, 2005).

Krivel, Elaine & Thomas Beveridge. *A Practical Guide to Canadian Extradition* (Toronto: Carswell, 2002).

Malanczuk, Peter. *Akehurst's Modern Introduction to International Law*, 7th rev. ed. (London: Routledge, 1997).

Matsushita, Mitsuo, Thomas Schoenbaum & Petros Mavroidis. *The World Trade Organization: Law, Practice and Policy* (Oxford: Oxford University Press, 2003).

Mitchell, Andrew D. *Legal Principles in WTO Disputes* (Cambridge: Cambridge University Press, 2008).

Mo, John. *International Commercial Law*, 2d ed. (Sydney: Butterworths, 2000).

Muchlinski, Peter, Federico Ortino & Christoph Schreuer, eds. *The Oxford Handbook of International Investment Law* (Oxford: Oxford University Press, 2008).

Murphy, Sean D. *Principles of International Law* (St. Paul, MN: Thomson West, 2006).

Ryngaert, Cedric. *Jurisdiction in International Law* (Oxford: Oxford University Press, 2008).

Shaw, Malcolm Nathan. *International Law*, 6th ed. (Cambridge: Cambridge University Press, 2008).

Slomanson, William R. *Fundamental Perspectives on International Law*, 5th ed. (Belmont, CA: Thomson/Wadsworth, 2007).

Wallace, Rebecca M.M. *International Law*, 5th ed. (London: Sweet & Maxwell, 2005).

Winer, Anthony & Mary Ann E. Archer. *A Basic Course in Public International Law Research* (Lanham, Md.: University Press of America, 2005).

Annotated Acts

Prabhu, Mohan. *The Annotated Customs Act* (Toronto: Carswell, published annually).

Topical Journals

Canada

Canadian International Lawyer

Canadian Year Book of International Law
Journal of International Law & International Relations

United States

American University International Law Review
American Journal of International Law
Berkeley Journal of International Law
Boston College International and Comparative Law Review
Boston University International Law Journal
Brooklyn Journal of International Law
California Western International Law Journal
Cardozo Journal of International and Comparative Law
Case Western Reserve Journal of International Law
Chicago Journal of International Law
Connecticut Journal of International Law
Cornell International Law Journal
Denver Journal of International Law & Policy
Duke Journal of Comparative & International Law
Emory International Law Review
Florida Journal of International Law
Fordham International Law Journal
George Washington International Law Review
Georgia Journal of International and Comparative Law
Harvard International Law Journal
Hastings International and Comparative Law Review
Houston Journal of International Law
Indiana International and Comparative Law Review
Journal of International Law
Loyola of Los Angeles International and Comparative Law Review
Michigan Journal of International Law
New England International & Comparative Law Annual
New York University Journal of International Law & Politics
New York International Law Review
North Carolina Journal of International Law and Commercial Regulation
Northwestern Journal of International Law and Business
New York University Journal of International Law
Pace International Law Review
San Diego International Law Journal
Stanford Journal of International Law
Temple International and Comparative Law Journal
Texas International Law Journal

Touro International Law Review
Tulane Journal of International and Comparative Law
Tulsa Journal of International & Comparative Law
University of California, Davis Journal of International Law & Policy
UCLA Journal of International Law and Foreign Affairs
University of Pennsylvania Journal of International Economic Law
Virginia Journal of International Law
Willamette Journal of International Law and Dispute Resolution
Wisconsin International Law Journal
Yale Journal of International Law

Topical Law Reports

International Law Reports
International Law Reporter

33) — Labour and Employment Law

Texts and loose-leaf Services

a) — General

Cantin, Jean-Maurice. *Abuse of Authority in the Workplace: A Form of Harassment* (Scarborough, Ont.: Carswell, 2000).

Donais, Blaine. *Workplaces that Work: A Guide to Conflict Management in Union and Non-Union Work Environments* (Aurora, Ont.: Canada Law Book, 2006).

Gilbert, Douglas G., Brian W. Burkett & Moira K. McCaskill. *Canadian Labour and Employment Law for the U.S. Practitioner*, 2d ed. (Washington, D.C.: Bureau of National Affairs, 2006).

Keith, Norm & Ailsa Wiggins. *Alcohol and Drugs in the Canadian Workplace: An Employer's Guide to the Law, Prevention and Management of Substance Abuse* (Markham, Ont.: LexisNexis, 2008).

Knight, Jamie, Malcolm MacKillop & Kristin Taylor. *How to Conduct a Workplace Human Rights Investigation* (Scarborough, Ont.: Carswell, 2003).

Manning, Melanie. *Pregnancy, the Workplace and the Law* (Aurora, Ont.: Canada Law Book, 2003).

McArthur, Stephen *et al. Canadian Construction Labour and Employment Law*, loose-leaf (Markham, Ont.: LexisNexis, n.d.).

O'Brien's Encyclopedia of Forms: Division VII: Labour Relations and Employment, loose-leaf (Aurora: Canada Law Book, 1987-).

Rubin, Janice & Christine M. Thomlinson. *Human Resources Guide to Workplace Investigations* (Aurora, Ont.: Canada Law Book, 2006).

b) — Discrimination

Bowland, Adelyn. *Disability and Human Rights in the Workplace* (Toronto: Thomson Carswell, 2004).

Humphrey, Barbara G. *Human Resources Guide to the Duty to Accommodate* (Aurora, Ont.: Canada Law Book, 2002).

Macneill, Kevin D. *The Duty to Accommodate in Employment*, loose-leaf (Aurora, Ont.: Canada Law Book, 2003-).

c) — Employment Benefits and Pensions

Greenan. Jennifer. *The Handbook of Canadian Pension and Benefit Plans*, 12th ed. (Toronto: CCH Canadian, 2002).

Ian McSweeney & David S. McFarlane. *Pension Benefits Law in Ontario*, loose-leaf (Scarborough, Ont.: Carswell, 1996-).

Kaplan, Ari N. *Pension Law* (Toronto: Irwin Law, 2006).

Koskie, Raymond, ed. *Employee Benefits in Canada*, 3d ed. (Brookfield, Wis.: International Foundation of Employee Benefit Plans, 2001).

Sarra, Janis. *Employee and Pension Claims During Company Insolvency: A Comparative Study of 62 Jurisdictions* (Scarborough, Ont.: Carswell, 2008).

Seller, Susan Gail. *Ontario Pension Law Handbook*, 2d ed. (Aurora, Ont.: Canada Law Book, 2006).

d) — Employment Contracts

Steele, Gregory K. & Kenneth Wm. Thornicroft. *Employment Covenants and Confidential Information* (Markham, Ont.: Butterworths, 2002).

e) — Employment Equity

CCH Canadian. *Workplace Equity Guide*, loose-leaf (Don Mills, Ont.: CCH Canadian, 1999-).

Elliott, Cheryl J. *Ontario's Equity Laws: A Complete Guide to Pay and Employment Equity*, loose-leaf (Aurora, Ont.: Canada Law Book, 1992-).

LeGault, Anneli. *Fairness in the Workplace*, 3d ed. (Toronto: CCH Canadian, 2002).

Ray-Ellis, Soma. *Federal Equity Manual*, loose-leaf (Toronto: Carswell, 2002-).

f) — Employment Law

Aust, A. Edward, ed. *Executive Employment Law*, loose-leaf (Markham, Ont.: LexisNexis, n.d.).

Ball, Stacey Reginald. *Canadian Employment Law*, loose-leaf (Aurora, Ont.: Canada Law Book, 1996-).

Caron, Renée. *Employment in the Federal Public Service*, loose-leaf (Aurora, Ont.: Canada Law Book, 2001-).

CCH Canadian. *Canadian Employment Law Guide*, loose-leaf (CCH Canadian, 1989-).

Certosimo, Matthew L.O. *Federal Employment and Labour Law and Commentary* (Markham, Ont.: LexisNexis, published annually).

D'Andrea, James Anthony. *Employee Obligations in Canada* (Aurora, Ont.: Canada Law Book, 2003).

Echlin, Randall Scott & Christine M. Thomlinson. *For Better or For Worse: A Practical Guide to Canadian Employment Law*, 2d ed. (Aurora, Ont.: Aurora Professional Press, 2003).

England, Geoffery *Individual Employment Law*, 2d ed. (Toronto: Irwin Law, 2008).

.... & Roderick Wood. *Employment Law in Canada*, 4th ed., loose-leaf (Markham, Ont.: LexisNexis Butterworths, 2005-).

Flynn, Roderick C. *An Educator's Guide to Employment Law* (Aurora, Ont.: Canada Law Book, 2001).

Hadwen, Timothy. *Ontario Public Service Employment and Labour Law* (Toronto: Irwin Law, 2005).

Humber, Todd. *Canadian Employment Law Answers*, loose-leaf (Scarborough, Ont.: Carswell, 2008-).

Knight, James G., Lisa S. Goodfellow & Carman J. Overholt. *Employment Litigation Manual*, 2d ed., loose-leaf (Markham, Ont.: LexisNexis Canada, 2007-).

Knight, Jamie. *Managing Your Union-Free Workforce* (Toronto: Carswell, 2002).

Kuretzky, Barry & Jennifer MacKenzie. *Mediating Employment Disputes* (Aurora, Ont.: Canada Law Book, 2001).

Levitt, Howard A. *The Law of Dismissal in Canada*, 3d ed. (Aurora, Ont.: Canada Law Book, 2003).

McLarren, Philip H. *Employment in Alberta*, 2d ed., loose-leaf (Toronto: Butterworths, n.d.).

.... *Employment in Britsh Columbia*, 2d ed., loose-leaf (Toronto: Butterworths, n.d.).

.... *Employment in Ontario*, 2d ed., loose-leaf (Toronto: Butterworths, 2001-).

Rootham, Christopher. *Labour and Employment Law in the Federal Public Service* (Toronto: Irwin Law, 2007).

Saxe, Stewart. *Ontario Employment Law Handbook: An Employer's Guide*, 9th ed. (Markham, Ont.: LexisNexis, 2007).

Saxe, Stewart D. & Jean A. Brough. *Charities and Not-For-Profit Employment Law Handbook* (Markham, Ont.: Butterworths, 2002).

Sproat, John R. *Employment Law Manual: Wrongful Dismissal, Human Rights and Employment Standards*, loose-leaf (Toronto: Carswell, 1990-).
Steele, Gregory & Kenneth Thornicroft. *Employment Covenants and Confidential Information*, 2d ed. (Markham, Ont.: LexisNexis, 2009).
Turnbull, Ian J. *et al. Privacy in the Workplace: The Employment Perspective* (Toronto: CCH Canadian, 2004).
Wilson, Peter & Allison Taylor. *The Corporate Counsel Guide to Employment Law*, 3d ed. (Aurora, Ont.: Canada Law Book, 2010).

g) — Employment Standards

Certosimo, Matthew L.O. & Michael P. Fitzgibbon. *Understanding Ontario's Employment Standards Act, 2000* (Scarborough, Ont.: Carswell, 2002).
Leenheer, Chris E. & Lindsie M. Thomson. *A Practical Guide to Employment Standards in British Columbia* (Aurora, Ont.: Canada Law Book, 2004).
Ontario, Employment Practices Branch. *Employment Standards Act 2000: Policy and Interpretation Manual*, loose-leaf (Scarborough, Ont.: Carswell, 2001-).
Parry, R.M. *A Practical Guide to Employment Standards in Ontario*, 3d ed. (Aurora, Ont.: Aurora Professional Press, 2002).
Sproat, John R. *Employment Standards Act Handbook* (Toronto: Thomson Carswell, 2007).

h) — Labour Arbitration

Brandt, Gregory, Morley Gorsky & S.J. Usprich. *Evidence and Procedure in Canadian Labour Arbitration*, rev. ed., loose-leaf (Scarborough, Ont.: Carswell, 1991-).
Brown, Donald & David Beatty. *Canadian Labour Arbitration*, loose-leaf (Aurora, Ont.: Canada Law Book, 2006-).
Snyder, Ronald *et al.*, eds. *Palmer & Snyder: Collective Agreement Arbitration in Canada*, 4th ed. (Toronto: LexisNexis, 2008).
Weatherill, John. *A Practical Guide to Labour Arbitration Procedure*, 2d ed. (Aurora, Ont.: Canada Law Book, 1998).

i) — Labour Relations

Adell, B.L., Michel Grant & Allen Ponak. *Strikes in Essential Services* (Kingston, Ont.: IRC Press, 2001).
Andrew, Jeffrey. *Labour Relations Board Remedies in Canada*, loose-leaf (Aurora, Ont.: Canada Law Book, n.d.).
Carter, Donald *et al. Labour Law in Canada*, 5th ed. (Markham, Ont.: Butterworths, 2001).

CCH Canadian. *Canadian Master Labour Guide* (Don Mills, Ont.: CCH Canadian, published annually).

Certosimo, Matthew L.O. *Dismissals in the Unionized Workplace*, 2d ed. (Scarborough, Ont.: Carswell, 2004).

.... *When Can the Unionized Employee Sue?* (Scarborough, Ont.: Carswell, 1999).

Clarke, Graham J. *Clarke's Canada Industrial Relations Board*, new ed., loose-leaf (Aurora, Ont.: Canada Law Book, 1998-).

Gunderson, Morley, Allen Ponak & Daphne G. Taras, eds. *Union-Management Relations in Canada*, 5th ed. (Toronto: Pearson Addison-Wesley, 2005).

MacNeil, Michael, Michael Lynk & Peter Engelmann. *Trade Union Law in Canada*, loose-leaf (Aurora, Ont.: Canada Law Book, n.d.).

Rayner, Wesley B. *Canadian Collective Bargaining Law*, 2d ed. (Markham, Ont.: LexisNexis Canada, 2007).

Sack, Jeffrey & C. Michael Mitchell. *Ontario Labour Relations Board Law and Practice*, 3d ed., loose-leaf (Markham, Ont.: Butterworths, 1997-).

Sommer, Neal B. & Stewart D. Saxe. *Understanding the Labour Relations Act*, 2d ed. (Aurora, Ont.: Canada Law Book, 2001).

j) — Occupational Health & Safety

CCH Canadian. *Canadian Employment Safety and Health Guide* (Don Mills, Ont.: CCH Canadian, 1980-).

Edwards, Cheryl A. & Ryan Conlin. *Corporate and Organizational Liability for OH&S Under Bill C-45* (Scarborough, Ont.: Carswell, 2000).

Edwards, Cheryl A. & Ryan J. Conlin. *Employer Liability for Contractors Under the Ontario Occupational Health and Safety Act*, 2d ed. (Toronto: Thomson Carswell, 2007).

Edwards, Cheryl A., Ryan Conlin & Landon Young. *OH&S Due Dillegence in Ontario: A Practical Guide* (Scarborough, Ont.: Carswell, 2006).

Glasbeek, Sandra. *OH&S For Ontario School Staff: A Principal's Guide* (Markham, Ont.: LexisNexis Canada, 2007).

Humphrey, Charles E. & Cheryl A. Edwards. *The Employer's Health & Safety Manual, Ontario*, 2d ed., loose-leaf (Toronto: Thomson Carswell, 2005).

Keith, Norman. *Ontario Health and Safety Law: A Complete Guide to the Law and Procedures, with Digest of Cases*, loose-leaf (Aurora, Ont.: Canada Law Book, n.d.).

Keith, Norman & Elizabeth Rankin. *A Practical Guide to Occupational Health and Safety Compliance in Ontario*, 3d ed. (Aurora, Ont.: Canada Law Book, 2006).

Robertson, Dilys. *ABCs of OH&S: Ontario*, loose-leaf (Scarborough, Ont.: Carswell, 1993-).

.... *Accident Investigation in the Workplace* (Scarborough, Ont.: Carswell, 2004).

.... *Health and Safety Compliance in Canada by Topic* (Scarborough, Ont.: Carswell, 2004).

.... *Health and Safety Compliance Toolkit*, loose-leaf (Scarborough, Ont.: Carswell, 1999-).

.... *Ontario Occupational Health and Safety Act: Quick Reference* (Toronto, Ont.: Carswell, published annually).

Rock, Nora, *Occupational Health and Safety in Ontario* (Toronto: Emond Montgomery, 2008).

Roher, Eric M. *Violence in the Workplace*, 2d ed. (Toronto: Carswell, 2004).

Young, Landon P. & Ryan J. Conlin. *Managing OH&S Inspections and Search Warrants* (Toronto: Thomson Carswell, 2008).

k) — Sexual Harassment

Aggarwal, Arjun P. & Madhu M. Gupta. *Sexual Harassment: A Guide for Understanding and Prevention*, 2d ed. (Markham, Ont.: LexisNexis Butterworths, 2006).

Gupta, Neena. *Sexual Harassment: A Guide to Conducting Investigations* (Toronto: LexisNexis Butterworths, 2004).

l) — Workers' Compensation

Anstruther, Richard. *Employers' Guide to Ontario Workplace Safety and Insurance* (Toronto: Thomson Carswell, 2004).

Conlin, Ryan. *Employers' Guide to Ontario Workplace Safety and Insurance*, loose-leaf (Scarborough, Ont.: Carswell, n.d.).

Dee, Garth, Nick McCombie, & Gary Newhouse. *Butterworths Workers' Compensation in Ontario Service*, 2d ed., loose-leaf (Toronto: Butterworths, 1993-).

Gilbert, Douglas G. & L.A. Liversidge. *Workers' Compensation in Ontario: A Guide to the Workplace Safety and Insurance Act*, 3d ed. (Aurora, Ont.: Canada Law Book, 2001).

Knight, Jamie, Natasha Savoline & Cynthia Kontra. *Ontario Workplace Safety and Insurance Act: Quick Reference* (Toronto: Thomson Carswell, published annually).

Mah, Douglas R. *Workers' Compensation Practice in Alberta*, 2d ed., loose-leaf (Scarborough, Ont.: Carswell, 2005-).

Ontario, Workplace Safety & Insurance Board. *Employer Classification / Workplace Safety & Insurance Board*, loose-leaf (Toronto: Workplace Safety & Insurance Board, 2005-).

m) — Wrongful Dismissal

Harris, David. *Wrongful Dismissal*, loose-leaf (Agincourt, Ont.: Carswell, 1990-).

Mole, Ellen E. *Wrongful Dismissal Practice Manual*, 2d ed., loose-leaf (Markham, Ont.: LexisNexis, 2005-).

.... & Marion J. Stendon. *The Wrongful Dismissal Handbook*, 3d ed. (Markham, Ont.: LexisNexis Butterworths, 2004).

Sproat, John R. *Wrongful Dismissal Handbook*, 5th ed. (Toronto: Carswell, 2009).

Annotated Statutes

Annotated British Columbia Labour Relations Code, loose-leaf (Markham, Ont.: LexisNexis, n.d.).

Elliott, Cheryl J. *Ontario's Equity Laws: A Complete Guide to Pay and Employment Equity*, loose-leaf (Aurora, Ont.: Canada Law Book, 1992-).

Lavender, Stephen. *The Annotated Employment Insurance Act and Regulations*, loose-leaf (Scarborough, Ont.: Carswell, 1996-).

.... *The Annotated Employment Insurance Act* (Scarborough, Ont.: Carswell, published annually).

Randazzo, Daniel. *The Annotated Ontario Labour Relations Act* (Scarborough, Ont.: Carswell, published annually).

Snyder, Ronald M. *The Annotated Canada Labour Code* (Scarborough, Ont.: Carswell, published annually).

Topical Journals/Bulletins/Newsletters

Canada Labour Views Reports
Canadian Employer
Canadian Employment Law Today
Canadian HR Reporter White Paper
Canadian Human Rights Advocate
Canadian Human Rights Yearbook
Canadian Labour and Employment Law Journal
Canadian Labour Law Journal
Employment Bulletin: Legal Issues in the Workplace
Industrial Relations
Labour Arbitration Yearbook
Labour Alert
Labour Notes

Workplace Equity Guide — Newsletter

Topical Law Reports/Digests

British Columbia Decisions: Labour Arbitration
British Columbia Labour Relations Board Decisions
Canadian Cases on Employment Law
Canadian Cases on Pensions & Benefits
Canadian Employment Benefits and Pension Guide
Canadian Human Rights Reporter
Canadian Labour Arbitration Summaries
Canadian Labour Law Cases
Canadian Labour Law Reporter
Canada Labour Relations Board Reports
Canadian Occupational Health and Safety Cases
Employment and Labour Law Reporter
Focus on Canadian Employment and Equality Rights
Labour Arbitration Cases
Labour Arbitration Xpress
National Labour Review
Ontario Human Rights Commission Reports
Pension Review Board Reports
Public Service Staff Relations Board Decisions
Workers' Compensation Appeals Tribunal Reporter

34) — Landlord and Tenant Law

Texts and loose-leaf Services

Bentley, Christopher, John McNair & Mavis Butkus. *Williams & Rhodes' Canadian Law of Landlord and Tenant*, 6th ed., loose-leaf (Toronto: Carswell, 1988-).

Dickie, John & David Lyman. *Working with the Residential Tenancies Act*, 2d ed.(Toronto: Emond Montgomery, 2007).

Doumani, Robert & Carol A. Albert. *Ontario Residential Tenancies Law*, 2d ed., loose-leaf (Toronto: Carswell, 2007-).

Feldman, Richard. *Residential Tenancies*, 9th ed. (Aurora, Ont.: Canada Law Book, 2009).

Feldman, Richard A. *Residential Tenancies*, 8th ed. (Toronto: Thomson Carswell, 2007).

Ferguson, Jane L. & Rose H. McConnell. *Evictions: A Practical Guide to Residential Evictions in Ontario* (Toronto: CCH Canadian, 2001).

Haber, Harvey M. *Commercial Lease: A Practical Guide*, 4th ed. (Aurora, Ont.: Canada Law Book, 2004).

.... *Distress: A Commercial Landlord's Remedy* (Aurora, Ont.: Canada Law Book, 2001).

.........., ed. *Shopping Centre Leases: A Collection of Articles and Precedents*, 2d ed. (Aurora, Ont.: Canada Law Book, 2008).

.... *et al.*, eds. *Assignment, Subletting and Change of Control in a Commercial Lease: A Practical Guide* (Aurora, Ont.: Canada Law Book, 2002).

Fleming, Jack. *Ontario Landlord and Tenant Law Practice* (Toronto, Ont.: LexisNexis, published annually).

.... *Residential Tenancies in Ontario*, 2d ed. (Toronto, Ont.: LexisNexis, 2009).

Michaeloff, Dawn. *Insurance and Risk Management in Commercial Leasing* (Aurora, Ont.: Canada Law Book, 2009).

Olson, Richard. *Commercial Tenancy Handbook*, loose-leaf (Scarborough, Ont.: Carswell, n.d.).

Annotated Statutes

Butkus, Mavis. *The Annotated Ontario Landlord and Tenant Statutes* (Toronto: Carswell, published annually).

Wotherspoon, Allan. *Annotated British Columbia Residential Tenancy Act*, loose-leaf (Aurora, Ont.: Canada Law Book, n.d.).

35) — Legal Profession

Texts and loose-leaf Services

Dodek, Adam & Jeffrey Hoskins, eds. *Barristers and Solicitors in Practice*, loose-leaf (Markham, Ont.: LexisNexis, n.d.).

Grant, Stephen & Linda Rothstein. *Lawyers' Professional Liability*, 2d ed. (Markham, Ont.: LexisNexis, 1998).

Hardie, Robert. *Practical Guide to Successful Law Firm Management* (Markham, Ont.: LexisNexis, 2006).

MacKenzie, Gavin. *Lawyers and Ethics: Professional Responsibility and Discipline*, loose-leaf (Scarborough, Ont.: Carswell, n.d.).

Perell, Paul. *Conflicts of Interest in the Legal Profession* (Markham, Ont.: LexisNexis, 1995).

Sossin, Lorne Mitchell. *Halsbury's Laws of Canada: Legal Profession* (Markham, Ont.: LexisNexis Canada, 2007).

Wooley, Alice *et al. Lawyers' Ethics and Professional Regualtion* (Markham, Ont.: LexisNexis, 2008).

36) — Marine Law

Texts and loose-leaf Services

Anderson, David. *Modern Law of the Sea: Selected Essays* (Leiden, Netherlands: Martinus Nijhoff Publishers, 2008).

Basedow, Jürgen & Ulrich Magnus, eds. *Pollution of the Sea: Prevention and Compensation* (Berlin: Springer, 2007).

Brice, Geoffrey. *Brice on Maritime Law of Salvage*, 4th ed. (London: Sweet & Maxwell, 2003).

Calderbank, Bruce *et al. Canada's Offshore: Jurisdiction, Rights, and Management*, 3d ed. (Victoria, B.C.: Trafford, 2006).

Caminos, Hugo, ed. *Law of the Sea* (Burlington, VT: Ashgate, 2001).

Davies, Martin, ed. *Jurisdiction and Forum Selection in International Maritime Law: Essays in Honor of Robert Force* (The Hague: Kluwer Law International, 2005).

Fernandes, Rui M. *Shipping and Admiralty Law* (Scarborough, Ont.: Carswell, 1995).

Gavouneli, Maria. *Functional Jurisdiction in the Law of the Sea* (Leiden, Netherlands: Martinus Nijhoff, 2007).

Girvin, Stephen D. *Carriage of Goods by Sea* (New York: Oceana, 2007).

Gold, Edgar, Aldo Chircop & Hugh Kindred. *Maritime Law* (Toronto: Irwin Law, 2003).

Güner-Özbek, Meltem Deniz. *The Carriage of Dangerous Goods by Sea* (Berlin: Springer, 2008).

Hayashi, Moritaka. *New Directions in the Law of the Sea*, loose-leaf (New York: Oceana, 1995-).

Hendrikse, M.L., N.H. Margetson & N.J. Margetson, eds. *Aspects of Maritime Law: Claims Under Bills of Lading* (The Netherlands: Kluwer Law International, 2008).

Hong, Seoung-Yong & Jon M. Van Dyke, eds. *Maritime Boundary Disputes, Settlement Processes, and the Law of the Sea* (Leiden: Martinus Nijhoff Publishers, 2009).

Kwiatkowska, Barbara. *The Contribution of the World Court to the Development of the Law of the Sea* (The Netherlands: BookWorld Publications, 2002).

Marsden, Reginald G. *Marsden on Collisions at Sea*, 13th ed. (London: Sweet & Maxwell, 2003).

McDorman, Ted L. *Salt Water Neighbors: International Ocean Law Relations Between the United States and Canada* (Oxford: Oxford University Press, 2009).

Parameswaran, Benjamin. *The Liberalization of Maritime Transport Service: With Special Reference to the WTO/GATS Framework* (New York: Springer, 2004).

Rothwell, Donald R. & David L. VanderZwaag. *Towards Principled Oceans Governance: Australian and Canadian Approaches and Challenges* (London: Routledge, 2006).

Schoenbaum, Thomas J. *Admiralty and Maritime Law*, 4th ed. (St. Paul, MN: Thomson/West, 2004).

Tetley, William. *Marine Cargo Claims*, 4th ed. (Toronto: Carswell, 2008).

.... *Maritime Liens and Claims*, 2d ed. (Toronto: Carswell, 1998).

Todd, Paul. *Maritime Fraud* (London: LLP Professional Pub., 2003).

Wendel, Philipp. *State Responsibility for Interferences with the Freedom of Navigation in Public International Law* (New York: Springer, 2007).

Yang, Haijiang. *Jurisdiction of the Coastal State Over Foreign Merchant Ships in Internal Waters and the Territorial Sea* (Berlin: Springer, 2006).

Topical Journals

Lloyd's Maritime & Commercial Law Quarterly

Topical Law Reports

Lloyd's Law Reports

37) — Municipal and Planning Law

Texts and loose-leaf Services

Annibale, Quinto M. *Municipal Lands: Acquisition, Management and Disposal*, loose-leaf (Aurora, Ont.: Canada Law Book, 2005-).

Boghosian, David G. & J. Murray Davison. *The Law of Municipal Liability in Canada*, loose-leaf (Markham, Ont.: Butterworths, 1999-).

Buholzer, William A. *Halsbury's Laws of Canada: Planning and Zoning* (Markham, Ont.: LexisNexis Canada, 2008).

Chipman, John George. *A Law Unto Itself: How the Ontario Municipal Board has Developed and Applied Land Use Planning Policy* (Toronto: University of Toronto Press, 2002).

Coates, John & Stephen Waqué. *New Law of Expropriation*, loose-leaf (Toronto: Carswell, 1984-).

Dronshek, Edythe. *Municipal Business By-law Drafting Manual* (Markham, Ont.: LexisNexis, 2003).

Krushelnicki, Bruce Wayne. *A Practical Guide to the Ontario Municipal Board*, 2d ed. (Toronto: LexisNexis, 2007).

MacLean, M. Virginia & John R. Tomlinson. *A User's Guide to Municipal By-Laws*, 2d ed. (Markham, Ont.: LexisNexis, 2008).

MacLean, M. Virginia & Kelly G. Yerxa. *Ontario Municipal Act: A Comprehensive Guide* (Aurora, Ont.: Canada Law Book, n.d.).

Makuch, Stanley, Neil Craik & Signe B. Leisk. *Canadian Municipal and Planning Law*, 2d ed. (Toronto: Carswell, 2004).

Mascarin, John & Paul De Francesca. *Annotated Land Development Agreements*, loose-leaf (Scarborough, Ont.: Carswell, 2001-).

McGuinness, Kevin Patrick, Stephen Bauld, and Patrice Noé-Johnson. *Municipal Procurement Handbook*, 2d ed. (Markham, Ont.: Butterworths, 2009).

Noé-Johnson, Patrice & Allan C. Ross. *The Law of Municipal Finance* (Markham, Ont.: LexisNexis Butterworths, 2004).

O'Brien's Encyclopedia of Forms: Division IX: Municipal Corporations, 11th ed. (Aurora, Ont.: Canada Law Book, 1987-).

O'Connor, Michael Richard & George H. Rust-D'Eye. *Ontario's Municipal Conflict of Interest Act: A Handbook* (Union, Ont.: Municipal World, 2007).

O'Connor, Michael Richard, Peter-John Sidebottom & David G. White. *Conduct Handbook for Municipal Employees and Officials*, 2d ed. (Toronto: Butterworths, 2003).

Rogers, Ian. *Canadian Law of Planning and Zoning*, 2d ed., loose-leaf (Toronto: Carswell, 2005).

.... *The Law of Canadian Municipal Corporations*, 2d ed., loose-leaf (Toronto: Carswell, 1971-).

Russell, W.D. *Russell On Roads*, 2d ed. (Toronto: Carswell, 2008).

Rust-D'Eye, George H. & Ophir Bar-Moshe. *The Ontario Municipal Act: A User's Manual*, (Toronto: Thomson Carswell, 2008).

Watson, Shane M. *Municipal Emergency Management Procedures Handbook* (Markham, Ont.: Butterworths, 2002).

WeirFoulds LLP. *Ontario Planning Practice*, loose-leaf (Aurora, Ont.: Canada Law Book, 1989-).

Wood, Dennis. *Planning Act: A Sourcebook*, 6th ed. (Scarborough, Ont.: Carswell, 2007).

.... *Provincial Plans: A Sourcebook* (Scarborough, Ont.: Carswell, 2007).

Annotated Statutes

Auerback, Stephen & John Mascarin. *The Annotated Municipal Act*, 2d ed., loose-leaf (Toronto: Carswell, 2004-).

Johnson, Peter. *Annotated British Columbia Local Government Act and Community Charter*, loose-leaf (Aurora, Ont.: Canada Law Book, n.d.).

Mascarin, John & Christopher Williams. *Ontario Municipal Act and Commentary* (Markham, Ont.: LexisNexis, published annually).

McDannold, Guy & Colin Stewart. *British Columbia Municipal Law and Commentary* (Markham, Ont.: LexisNexis, published annually).

Wakefield, Kim. *Alberta Municipal Law and Commentary* (Markham, Ont.: LexisNexis, published annually).

Walker, Jack A. & Jerry Grad. *Ontario Property Tax Assessment Handbook*, 2d ed. (Aurora, Ont.: Canada Law Book, n.d.).

WeirFoulds LLP. *Ontario Planning Practice: Annotated Statutes and Regulations*, loose-leaf (Aurora, Ont.: Canada Law Book, 1989-).

Wood, Dennis H. *The Planning Act: A Sourcebook*, 6th ed. (Toronto: Carswell, 2008).

Topical Journals/Newsletters

Municipal Liability Risk Management
Municipal Monitor
Municipal World

Topical Law Reports/Digests

British Columbia Decisions, Municipal Law Cases
Digest of Municipal and Planning Law
Land Compensation Reports
Municipal and Planning Law Reports
Ontario Municipal Board Reports

38) — Personal Property and Personal Property Security Law

Texts and loose-leaf Services

Bennett, Frank. *Bennett on the PPSA (Ontario)*, 3d ed. (Markham, Ont.: LexisNexis Butterworths, 2006).

Benson, Marjorie L. & Marie-Ann Bowden. *Understanding Property: A Guide to Canada's Property Law*, 2d ed. (Toronto: Thomson Carswell, 2008).

CCH Canadian. *Canadian Commercial Law Guide*, loose-leaf (Don Mills, Ont.: CCH Canadian, 1980-).

Cuming, Ronald C.C., Catherine Walsh & Roderick Wood. *Personal Property Security Law* (Toronto: Irwin Law, 2005).

Fridman, Gerald Henry Louis. *The Sale of Goods in Canada*, 5th ed. (Toronto: Carswell, 2005).

Hatzikiriakos, Kiriakoula. *Secured Transactions in Intellectual Property: Software as Collateral* (Markham, Ont.: LexisNexis Butterworths, 2006).

Kershman, Stanley J. *Credit Solutions: Kershman on Advising Secured and Unsecured Creditors*, 2d ed. (Toronto: Thomson Carswell, 2007).

Leppmann, Karl F. *Security Documents: An Annotated Guide* (Aurora, Ont.: Canada Law Book, 1999).

MacDougall, Bruce. *Personal Property and Secured Transactions* (Markham, Ont.: LexisNexis Canada, 2008).

Manzer, Alison R. & Howard Ruda. *Asset Based Lending in Canada: Canadian Primer on Asset Based Financing* (Markham, Ont.: LexisNexis Canada, 2008).

McLaren, Richard. *British Columbia Personal Property Security Handbook* (Scarborough, Ont.: Carswell, published annually).

.... *Secured Transactions in Personal Property in Canada*, 2d ed., loose-leaf (Toronto: Carswell, 1989-).

Stikeman Elliott. *Ontario PPSA and Commentary* (Markham, Ont.: Butterworths, published annually).

Annotated Statutes

McLaren, Richard. *The Annotated Alberta Personal Property Security Act* (Scarborough, Ont.: Carswell, published annually).

.... *The Annotated Ontario Personal Property Security Act* (Scarborough, Ont.: Carswell, published annually).

Topical Law Reports

Personal Property Security Act Cases

39) — Professions and Occupations

Texts and loose-leaf Services

Campion, John and Diana Dimmer, *Professional Liability in Canada*, loose-leaf (Toronto: Carswell, 1994-).

Casey, James. *Regulation of Professions in Canada*, loose-leaf (Toronto: Carswell, 1994).

Ellis, Mark Vincent *et al. Professional Fiduciary Duties* (Scarborough, Ont.: Carswell, 1995).

40) — Real Property

Texts and loose-leaf Services

Atlas, Michael I. & Ian V. MacInnis. *Canadian Taxation of Real Estate*, 4th ed. (Toronto: CCH Canadian, 2009).

Bocska, Rosemary & Martin K.I. Rumack. *Legal Responsibilities of Real Estate Agents*, 2d ed. (Markham, Ont.: LexisNexis Canada, 2009).

Boiron, Pierre & Claude Boiron. *Commercial Real Estate Investing in Canada: The Complete Reference for Real Estate Investors and Professionals* (Mississauga, Ont.: J. Wiley & Sons Canada, 2008).

Cadesky, Micheal, ed. *Taxation of Real Estate in Canada*, loose-leaf (Toronto: Carswell, 1997-).

Carter, Craig *et al. Ontario Real Estate Law Guide*, loose-leaf (Don Mills, Ont.: CCH Canadian, 1975-).

Di Castri, J. Victor. *The Law of Vendor and Purchaser*, 3d ed., loose-leaf (Toronto: Carswell, 1988-).

.... *Registration of Title to Land*, loose-leaf (Toronto: Carswell, 1987-).

Donahue, D.J., P.D. Quinn & D.C. Grandilli. *Real Estate Practice in Ontario*, 6th ed. (Toronto: Butterworths, 2003).

Fleming, Jack. *Ontario Landlord and Tenant Law Practice* (Markham, Ont.: LexisNexis, published annually).

Gardiner, J. Robert. *The Condominium Act, 1998: A Practical Guide* (Aurora, Ont.: Canada Law Book, 2001).

Globe, Janet. *Title Searching in Ontario: A Procedural Guide*, 5th ed. (Toronto: Butterworths, 2003).

Gray, Wayne. *Marriott and Dunn: Practice in Mortgage Remedies in Ontario*, 5th ed., loose-leaf (Toronto: Carswell, n.d.).

Haber, Harvey. *The Commercial Lease: A Practical Guide* (Aurora, Ont.: Canada Law Book, 2004).

.... *Understanding the Commercial Agreement to Lease*, 2d ed. (Aurora, Ont.: Canada Law Book, 2006).

Lambden, David W. & Izaak de Rijcke. *Legal Aspects Of Surveying Water Boundaries* (Toronto: Carswell, 1996).

Lamont, Donald. *Lamont on Real Estate Conveyancing*, 2d ed., loose-leaf (Toronto: Carswell, 1991-).

Lipson, Barry. *The Art of the Real Estate Deal*, 2d ed. (Scarborough, Ont.: Carswell, 2006).

Loeb, Audrey. *Condominium Law and Administration*, 3d ed., loose-leaf (Toronto: Carswell, 2009).

.... *The Condominium Act: A User's Manual*, 2d ed. (Toronto: Carswell, 2005).

MacInnis, Ian V. *Canadian Real Estate Income Tax Guide*, loose-leaf (Don Mills, Ont.: CCH Canadian, n.d.).

MacIntosh, C.W. *Nova Scotia Real Property Practice Manual*, loose-leaf (Markham, Ont.: LexisNexis, n.d.).

Maguire, Robert J. & Rose H. McConnell. *British Columbia Real Estate Law Guide*, loose-leaf (Don Mills, Ont.: CCH Canadian, n.d.).

McCallum, Margaret & Alan M. Sinclair. *Introduction to Real Property Law*, 5th ed. (Markham, Ont.: LexisNexis, 2005).

McDermott, Jim, Kathleen Flynn & Edward G. Frackowrak, eds. *Canadian Commercial Real Estate Manual*, loose-leaf (Toronto: Carswell, 1990-).

McKenna, Bruce A. *Title Insurance: A Guide to Regulation, Coverage and Claims Process in Ontario* (Don Mills, Ont.: CCH Canadian, 1999).

Price, Francis. *Conducting a Foreclosure Action* (Scarborough, Ont.: Carswell, 1996).

O'Brien's Encyclopedia of Forms: Division III: Conveyancing and Mortgages, loose-leaf (Aurora, Ont.: Canada Law Book, 1987-).

O'Brien's Encyclopedia of Forms: Division IV: Leases, loose-leaf (Aurora, Ont.: Canada Law Book, 1987-).

Rice, Brenda L. *Ontario Residential Real Estate Practice Manual*, loose-leaf (Toronto: Butterworths Canada, 1991-).

Rumack, Martin & Rosemary Bocska. *Legal Responsibilities of Real Estate Agents* (Markham, Ont.: LexisNexis, 2006).

Sarna, Lazar & Asher Neudorfer. *The Law of Immovable Hypthecs in Quebec* (Markham, Ont.: LexisNexis, 2006).

Sinclair, Alan. *Introduction to Real Property Law*, 5th ed. (Toronto: Butterworths, 2005).

Traub, Walter, ed. *Falconbridge on Mortgages*, 5th ed. (Aurora, Ont.: Canada Law Book, 2003).

La Forest, Anne Warner. *Anger & Honsberger, Law of Real Property*, 3d ed. (Aurora, Ont.: Canada Law Book, 2006).

Ziff, Bruce. *Principles of Property Law*, 4th ed. (Toronto: Carswell, 2006).

Annotated Statutes

Sarna, Lazar and Philip Petraglia. *Annotated Real Estate Laws of Ontario*, loose-leaf (Markham, Ont.: LexisNexis, n.d.).

Topical Journals/Newsletters

British Columbia Real Estate Law Developments
National Real Property Review
Ontario Real Estate Law Developments

Topical Law Reports

Real Property Reports

41) — Securities Law

Texts and loose-leaf Services

Borden Ladner Gervais LLP. *Securities Law and Practice*, 3d ed., loose-leaf (Toronto: Carswell, 2003-).

Dolfato, Joanne. *Canadian Stock Exchanges Manual*, loose-leaf (Don Mills, Ont.: CCH Canadian, n.d.).

Ewasiuk, Rick, W. *Drafting Shareholders' Agreements: A Guide* (Toronto: Carswell, 1998).

Gillen, Mark. *Securities Regulation in Canada*, 3d ed. (Toronto: Carswell, 2007).

Groia, Joseph & Pamela Hardie. *Securities Litigation and Enforcement* (Toronto: Thomson Carswell, 2007).

Grottenthaler, Margaret & Philip J. Henderson. *The Law of Financial Derivatives in Canada*, loose-leaf (Scarborough, Ont.: Carswell, 1999-).

Hendrickson, Barbara. *Canadian Institutional Investment Rules* (Don Mills, Ont.: CCH Canadian, 2003).

Johnston, David L. & Kathleen Doyle Rockwell. *Canadian Securities Regulation*, 4th ed. (Markham, Ont.: LexisNexis, 2009).

Koehnen, Markus. *Oppression and Related Remedies* (Toronto: Thomson Carswell, 2004).

MacIntosh, Jeffrey G. & Christopher Nicholls. *Securities Law* (Toronto: Irwin Law, 2002).

MacLellan, Vaughn. *Halsbury's Laws of Canada: Securities* (Markham, Ont.: LexisNexis Canada, 2008).

Morritt, David S., Sonia L. Bjorkquist & Allan D. Coleman. *The Oppression Remedy*, loose-leaf (Aurora, Ont.: Canada Law Book, 2004-).

Sarna, Lazar. *Insider Trading: A Canadian Legal Manual*, loose-leaf (Markham, Ont.: LexisNexis, n.d.).

Sarna, Lazar & Philip Petraglia. *Corporate Securities Laws in Canada with a Guide to U.S. Laws*, loose-leaf (Markham, Ont.: LexisNexis, n.d.).

Toronto Stock Exchange Company Manual, loose-leaf (Don Mills, Ont.: CCH Canadian, n.d.).

Annotated Statutes

Annotated British Columbia Securities Legislation (Don Mills, Ont.: CCH Canadian, published annually).

Annotated Ontario Securities Legislation (Don Mills, Ont.: CCH Canadian, published annually).

British Columbia Securities Act and Rules Annotated (Scarborough, Ont.: Carswell, published annually).

Khimji, Mohamed. *Annotated Securities Transfer Act (Ontario)* (Markham, Ont.: LexisNexis, published biennially).

Ontario. *The Annotated Ontario Securities Act* (Toronto: Carswell, published annually).

Topical Journals/Newsletters

Canadian Securities Law News
Corporate Securities and Finance Law Report

Securities and Corporate Regulation Review
Canada-U.S. Business Law Review

Topical Law Reports

Business Law Reports
Canadian Securities Law Reporter
Canadian Cases on the Law of Securities
Ontario Securities Commission Bulletin

42) — Statutory Interpretation and Drafting

Texts and loose-leaf Services

Beaulac, Stéphane. *Handbook on Statutory Interpretation: General Methodology, Canadian Charter and International Law* (Markham, Ont.: Lexis-Nexis, 2008).

Beaupré, Remi. *Interpreting Bilingual Legislation*, 2d ed. (Toronto: Carswell, 1986).

Cote, Pierre-Andre. *The Interpretation of Legislation*, 3rd ed. (Scarborough, Ont.: Carswell, 2000).

Dick, Robert. *Legal Drafting in Plain Language* (Scarborough, Ont.: Carswell, 1995).

Graham, Randy N. *Statutory Interpretation: Theory and Practice* (Toronto: Emond Montgomery, 2001).

Gifford, D.J, Kenneth H. Gifford & Michael I. Jeffery. *How to Understand Statutes and By-Laws* (Toronto: Carswell, 1996).

Sullivan, Ruth. *Statutory Interpretation*, 2d ed. (Toronto: Irwin Law, 2007).

.... *Sullivan and Driedger on the Construction of Statutes*, 4th ed. (Markham, Ont.: Butterworths, 2002).

43) — Tax Law

Texts and loose-leaf Services

a) — General

Beriault, Yoko & Carol Mohammed. *The CCH Guide to Researching Canadian Tax* (Toronto: CCH Canadian, 2005).

Bourgard, Gordon & Robert McMechan. *Portable Tax Court Practice, Act and Rules* (Toronto: Thomson Carswell, published annually).

Chodikoff, David W. & James L. Horvath. *Advocacy and Taxation in Canada* (Toronto: Irwin Law, 2004).

Cook, Ted. *Canadian Tax Research: A Practical Guide*, 4th ed. (Toronto: Thomson/Carswell, 2005).

De Lisser, Maureen, Gena Katz, & Elise Rees. *Ernst & Young's Guide to Capital Gains* (Toronto: Canadian Institute of Chartered Accountants, 2008).

Duncan, Garry R. & Elizabeth Peck, *Canadians Resident Abroad*, 4th ed. (Toronto: Carswell, 2002).

Frostiak, Larry, John Poyser & Grace Chow. *Taxation of Trusts and Estates: A Practioner's Guide* (Scarborough, Ont.: Carswell, 2008).

Gamble, Ian. *Taxation of Canadian Mining*, loose-leaf (Scarborough, Ont.: Carswell, n.d.).

Hanson, Suzanne, ed. *Canada Tax Manual*, loose-leaf (Toronto: Carswell, 1971-).

.... *Death of a Taxpayer*, 9th ed. (North York, Ont.: CCH Canadian, 2009).

Innes, William. *Tax Evasion*, loose-leaf (Toronto: Carswell, 1995-).

Johnson, Howard. *The Acquisition Value Cycle* (Scarborough, Ont.: Carswell, 2009).

Li, Jinyan, Arthur Cockfield & J. Scott Wilkie. *International Taxation in Canada: Principles and Practices* (Markham, Ont.: LexisNexis Butterworths, 2006).

ManuLife Financial, Tax and Estate Planning Group. *Canadian Taxation Of Life Insurance*, 4th ed. (Toronto: Thomson Carswell, 2008).

McCarthy Tetrault LLP, ed. *Canada Tax Service*, loose-leaf (Toronto: Carswell, 1972-).

McKinnon, Chris W. *Practitioner's Guide to Ontario Corporate Tax* (Toronto: Carswell, published annually).

Merrick, Peter. *The Essential Individual Pension Plan Handbook* (Markham, Ont.: LexisNexis, 2007).

Morrisey, James, ed. *Ernst & Young's Guide to the Taxation of Canadian Charities* (Toronto: Canadian Institute of Chartered Accountants, 2006).

Munro, Gary & Kurt Oelschlagel. *Taxation of Farmers and Fisherman*, loose-leaf (Scarborough, Ont.: Carswell, 1990-).

Ng, Mei & Ryan Keey. *Practitioner's Guide to Ontario Corporate Tax* (Scarborough, Ont.: Carswell, published annually).

Shepherd, Catherine, ed. *National Trade and Tariff Service*, loose-leaf (Markham, Ont.: LexisNexis, n.d.).

Sherman, David. *Basic Tax and GST Guide for Lawyers* (Scarborough, Ont.: Carswell, published annually).

Thaw, Mitchell. *Taxation of Mutual Fund Trusts and Corporations in Canada*, loose-leaf (Scarborough, Ont.: Carswell, n.d.).

Tobias, Norman C. *Taxation of Corporations, Partnerships and Trusts*, 3d ed. (Scarborough, Ont.: Thomson Carswell, 2006).

Tunnicliffe, Ross D. *Offshore Trusts: Tax Rules & Trust Concepts* (Toronto: CCH Canadian, 2003).

Wruk, Brian D. *The Canadian in America: Real-Life Tax and Financial Insights into Moving and Living in the U.S.* (Toronto: ECW Press, 2007).

b) — Charities

Drache, Arthur. *Charities Taxation, Policy and Practice*, loose-leaf (Scarborough, Ont.: Carswell, n.d.).

Fraser Milner Casgrain LLP. *Charities, Non-Profits and Philanthropy Under the Income Tax Act* (Toronto: CCH Canadian, 2006).

c) — Goods and Services Tax

CCH Canadian. *Canadian Goods & Services Tax Reporter* (Don Mills, Ont.: CCH Canadian, 1989-).

D'Arcy, Steven K. *Non-residents, Cross-Border Transactions and the GST* (Toronto: CCH Canadian, 2005).

Jay, Brent. *GST and E-commerce: Planning and Risk Management* (Toronto: CCH Canadian, 2006).

Menon, Natasha. *A Practical Guide to the Goods and Services Tax*, 4th ed. (Toronto, Ont.: CCH Canada Limited, 2006).

Sherman, David M. *Basic Tax and GST Guide for Lawyers: The Essential Survival Guide to Income Tax and GST For Canadian Lawyers Who do not Specialize in Tax* (Toronto: Thomson, Carswell, 2003-).

.... *GST Memoranda, Bulletins, Policies and Info Sheets* (Toronto: Carswell, published annually).

d) — Income Tax

Beam, Robert E. *et al. Introduction to Federal Income Taxation in Canada: Fundamentals* (Toronto, Ont.: CCH Canadian, 2008).

Campbell, Colin. *Administration of Income Tax* (Toronto: Thomson Carswell, published annually).

Canada Income Tax Law and Policy, loose-leaf (Scarborough, Ont.: Carswell, n.d.).

Carlin, John L. & Robert R. Jason. *Section 85 Rollovers* (Toronto: CCH Canadian, 2001).

Duff, David *et al. Canadian Income Tax Law*, 3d ed. (Markham, Ont.: LexisNexis Butterworths, 2009).

Gorman, F. Barry. *Canadian Income Taxation: Policy and Practice*, 2d ed. (Scarborough, Ont.: Carswell, 2001).

Hogg, Peter, Joanne E. Magee & Jinyan Li. *Principles of Canadian Income Tax Law* (Toronto: Carswell, 2007).

Innes, William I., Patrick J. Boyle & Joel A. Nitikman. *The Essential GAAR Manual: Policies, Principles and Procedures* (Toronto: CCH Canadian, 2006).

Krishna, Vern. *Fundamentals of Canadian Income Tax*, 9th ed. (Toronto: Carswell, 2006).

.... *Halsbury's Laws of Canada: Income Tax (Corporate)* (Markham, Ont.: LexisNexis Canada, 2008).

.... *Halsbury's Laws of Canada: Income Tax (General)* (Markham, Ont.: LexisNexis Canada, 2008).

Rashkis, Morton & Mary Lou Benotto. *Income Tax and Family Law Handbook*, loose-leaf (Toronto: Butterworths, 1988-).

Schwartz, Alan M., ed. *GAAR Interpreted: The General Anti-Avoidance Rule*, loose-leaf (Toronto: Carswell, 2006-).

Tari, A. Christina. *Federal Income Tax Litigation in Canada*, loose-leaf (Markham: LexisNexis, n.d.).

Yelle, Andre. *Income Tax Reference*, loose-leaf (Toronto: Carswell, 1972-).

e) — Sales Tax

Spencer, Jonathan. *Practitioner's Guide to Retail Sales Tax* (Toronto, Ont.: Carswell, 2008).

f) — Taxation of Real Estate

Atlas, Michael I. & Ian V. MacInnis. *Canadian Taxation of Real Estate*, 4th ed. (Toronto: CCH Canadian, 2004).

Cadesky, Michael, ed. *Taxation of Real Estate in Canada*, loose-leaf (Scarborough, Ont.: Carswell, 1997-).

g) — Treaties

Fraser Milner Casgrain LLP. *Canada-U.S. Tax Treaty with Technical Explanations*, 2d ed. (Toronto: CCH Canadian, 2005).

Kerzner, David, ed. *The Tax Advisors' Guide to the Canada-U.S. Tax Treaty*, loose-leaf (Toronto: Thomson Carswell, 2008-).

Krishna, Vern. *Canada's Tax Treaties*, loose-leaf (Markham, Ont.: LexisNexis Canada, n.d.).

.... & Pamela Cross. *The Canada-UK Tax Treaty: Text and Commentary* (Markham, Ont.: LexisNexis Canada, 2005).

Annotated Statutes

Feldman, Giselle. *The Practitioner's Ontario Taxes Annotated* (Toronto: Carswell, published annually).

Income Tax Act: Department of Finance Technical Notes (Toronto: Carswell, published annually).

Pound, Richard, ed. *Stikeman Income Tax Act Annotated* (Toronto: Carswell, published annually).

Sherman, David M. *The Practitioner's Goods and Services Tax, Annotated* (Toronto: Carswell, 2008).

.... *The Practitioner's Income Tax Act* (Toronto: Carswell, published annually).

Sweeney, Terrance A. *Annotated Ontario Retail Sales Tax Act* (Markham, Ont.: LexisNexis Butterworths, published annually).

Topical Journals/Newsletters

Bottom Line
Canadian Current Tax
Canadian Real Estate Income Tax Guide
Canadian Tax Journal
Canadian Tax Objection And Appeal Procedures
Canadian Taxpayer
Insight Into Canadian Income Tax

Topical Law Reports

Canada Customs and Excise Reports
Canadian Tax Reporter
Canada Tax Appeal Board Cases
Canada Tax Cases
CCH, Dominion Tax Cases
Pound's Tax Case Notes
Trade and Tariff Reports

44) — Tort Law

Texts and loose-leaf Services

Berry, Leanne. *Remedies in Tort*, loose-leaf (Scarborough, Ont.: Carswell, n.d.).

Brown, Raymond. *Defamation Law: A Primer* (Toronto: Carswell, 2003).

.... *Law of Defamation*, 2d ed., loose-leaf (Toronto: Carswell, 1994-).

Cassels, Jamie & Craig E. Jones. *The Law of Large-Scale Claims: Product Liabilty, Mass Torts, and Complex Litigation in Canada* (Toronto: Irwin Law, 2005).

Downard, Peter A. *Libel* (Markham, Ont.: LexisNexis Butterworths, 2003).

Edgell, Dean F. *Product Liability Law in Canada* (Toronto: Butterworths, 2000).

Feldthusen, Bruce. *Economic Negligence: The Recovery of Pure Economic Loss*, 5th ed. (Toronto: Carswell, 2008).

Firestone, Stephen E., Bernard L. Gluckstein, & Lee Samis. *Personal Injury Practice Manual*, loose-leaf (Toronto: Butterworths, 1999-).

Fridman, G.H.L. *Sale of Goods in Canada*, 5th ed. (Toronto: Carswell, 2004).

.... *Introduction to the Canadian Law Of Torts* (Toronto: Carswell, 2003).

Grace, Elizabeth and Susan Vella. *Civil Liability for Sexual Abuse and Violence in Canada* (Markham: LexisNexis, 2000).

Kerr, Margaret Helen, JoAnn Kurtz & Laurence M. Olivo. *Canadian Tort Law in a Nutshell*, 3d ed. (Toronto: Thomson Carswell, 2009).

Klar, Lewis. *Remedies in Tort*, loose-leaf (Toronto: Carswell, 1987-).

.... *Tort Law*, 4th ed. (Toronto: Carswell, 2008).

Linden, Allen M. *Halsbury's Laws of Canada: Torts* (Markham, Ont.: LexisNexis Canada, 2007).

Linden, Allen M. & Bruce Feldthusen. *Halsbury's Laws Of Canada: Negligence* (Markham, Ont.: LexisNexis Canada, 2007).

McConchie, Roger, & David A. Potts. *Canadian Libel and Slander Actions* (Toronto: Irwin Law, 2004).

Oatley, Roger G. *Addressing the Jury: Achieving Fair Verdicts in Personal Injury Cases*, 2d ed. (Aurora, Ont.: Canada Law Book, 2006).

Oatley, Roger G. & John A. McLeish. *The Oatley-McLeish Guide to Personal Injury Practice in Motor Vehicle Cases* (Aurora, Ont.: Canada Law Book, 2002-).

Osborne, Philip H. *The Law of Torts*, 2d ed. (Toronto: Irwin Law, 2003).

Potts, David A. & Roger McConchie. *Canadian Libel and Slander Actions* (Toronto: Irwin Law, 2004).

Rodgers, Sandra, Rakhi Ruparelia & Louise Bélanger-Hardy, eds. *Critical Torts* (Markham, Ont.: LexisNexis, 2009).

Theall, Lawrence G. *et al. Product Liability: Canadian Law and Practice*, loose-leaf (Aurora, Ont.: Canada Law Book, 2001-).

Waddams, S.M. *Products Liability*, 4th ed. (Toronto: Carswell, 2002).

Annotated Statutes

Wagner, Eric J. *Annotated British Columbia Occupiers Liability Act*, (Aurora, Ont.: Canada Law Book, n.d.).

Topical Journals

The Canadian Class Action Review

Topical Law Reports

Canadian Cases on the Law of Torts

Index

Index